A Dictionary of
Literature in the English Language

from 1940 to 1970

A Dictionary of
Literature in the English Language

from 1940 to 1970

Complete with Alphabetical Title–Author Index and
a Geographical–Chronological Index to Authors

Compiled and Edited by
ROBIN MYERS

being a sequel to
A Dictionary of Literature in the English Language from Chaucer to 1940
2 vols., 1970

PERGAMON PRESS

OXFORD · NEW YORK · TORONTO · FRANKFURT
SYDNEY · PARIS

U.K.	Pergamon Press Ltd., Headington Hill Hall, Oxford OX3 0BW, England
U.S.A.	Pergamon Press Inc., Maxwell House, Fairview Park, Elmsford, New York 10523, U.S.A.
CANADA	Pergamon of Canada Ltd., 75 The East Mall, Toronto, Ontario, Canada
AUSTRALIA	Pergamon Press (Aust.) Pty. Ltd., 19a Boundary Street, Rushcutters Bay, N.S.W. 2011, Australia
FRANCE	Pergamon Press SARL, 24 rue des Ecoles, 75240 Paris, Cedex 05, France
FEDERAL REPUBLIC OF GERMANY	Pergamon Press GmbH, 6242 Kronberg/Taunus, Pferdstrasse 1, Federal Republic of Germany

First edition 1978

British Library Cataloguing in Publication Data

Myers, Robin
A dictionary of literature in the English
language from 1940 to 1970.
1. English literature—Bibliography
I. Title
016.82′08′00914   Z2013   77–30534

ISBN 0–08–018050–7

Filmset and Printed Offset Litho in Great Britain by
Cox & Wyman Ltd., London, Fakenham and Reading

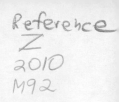

Reference
Z
2010
M92

Contents

Preface

SINCE every selection must follow some plan, that of literary authors cannot leave the question of literary merit quite out of account. However, the main task of the enumerative bibliographer is the listing of works without respect to their value as literature, a task which is left to the literary critic or scholar, and the place for such judgements is the guide or companion to literature. The present work is neither, nor yet a biographical dictionary. It is a short-title checklist with biographical notes on each author included. Certain dictionary features of my earlier *A Dictionary of Literature in the English Language from Chaucer to 1940* have been dropped. For instance, there are no longer entries on literary schools, while those on literary awards and on journals and magazines have been grouped together at the end, to form appendixes. My main aim has been to offer librarians, booksellers and others a finding tool for those authors currently in demand, whether meritorious or meretricious.

In my *Dictionary* I wrote: "The definition of literature is a wide one. It includes not only the great poets, dramatists and novelists, but also such writers as might be considered to form part of the literary history of their time, together with select examples of such semi-literary genres as the detective story and the romantic novel, too numerous and too ephemeral to be fully documented in a work of this nature. Certain non-literary writers, too, scientists, historians, economists, lawyers and statesmen, who have much influenced the thought of their day, or who have written excellently, have an undoubted place in literary history and are included in the dictionary. The user will find a selection of these peripheral literary figures who are often the very ones that the librarian finds most in demand."

I intend to select on exactly the same basis in the present work, which was conceived as a companion volume to the other, but I found that it was not at all the same thing for the contemporary scene. I now discovered that (although I had not realised it at the time) both selection and collection of material for that had been relatively easy.

With contemporary authors there were no authoritative works of reference to rely on, no clear path already beaten by others, to follow. For even if I had tried to apply the test of merit, who was to say that the now acclaimed *avant-garde* poet or the best-selling novelist would stand the test of time? Who, that those at present little regarded by us might not prove to be tomorrow's literary heirs? I have been much more selective with British and American authors than with those from Australasia and the Third World, where very much less is published. This was done partly to achieve some numerical balance, but chiefly because locally published work from those regions is so hard to find that any documentation of it must be useful to the searcher for it. I tried, as before, to give examples of every literary genre including such fresh ones as science fiction and concrete poetry. These last were a nightmare both to trace and to identify. For, was a polyhedron with words printed on it a book, a piece of ephemera or neither? I had to content myself with less than perfection in most cases, merely offering checklists that were as complete as possible in the circumstances.

I decided on another modification from my first work, that of limiting myself to authors for whom English was either the mother tongue or second language, and of excluding more or less all foreign authors who wrote in English as a foreign language. This more or less restricted my scope to Commonwealth or North American authors. Even so, such is the proliferation of modern publishing, I have listed some 1300 authors in a mere thirty-year period where in the previous 550 years I included 2600. The present work is a sequel, not a supplement, to the *Dictionary . . . Chaucer to 1940*. That first contained authors who began their published career in 1939 or before: this, authors who began publishing in 1940 or after (at the start of the period covered) and in 1969 or before, at the end. However, there were a handful of contemporary authors of stature who were excluded from *Chaucer to 1940* although they published one or two books in the later nineteen-thirties. Their omission seemed conspicuous beside the quantity of lesser writers of the forties, fifties and sixties who appear in the present work. Judgement seemed to dictate slight divergence from my own terms of reference in these cases, and I put them in.

As far as possible I followed the rules I drew up for the first work: "A distinction has been made," I then wrote, "where feasible, between an author's literary and non-literary or technical writings. The latter, if of sufficient importance, are generally mentioned in the biographical notes but without details of publication. I have attempted consistency to this principle, but each case has had to be individually considered in defining what is literary and what is not. Translations, editions, works in languages other than English, un-published plays and the like, are dealt with in the same way, namely placed in the biographical notes." In the modern era, writing for film, television and radio forms a large part of most authors' output, and these I treated as I did unpublished plays and contributions to anthologies and journals, listing them in the biographical notes.

In most respects the form of entry is as before: an author's full name, followed by pseudonym, or vice versa where that is better known, date of birth and, in rare cases, of death. In the indexes, the lists of awards and prizes and the page shoulder heads the name appears in its most known form (e.g. Main entry: Gunn, Thomson. Index entry: Gunn, Thom). The biographical note specifies type of writer as novelist, historian and so forth, nationality, place of birth sometimes, higher education if any, school if well enough known to make a point, war service if any, brief details of jobs held, literary or other honours, mention of works such as editions or translations which were not eligible for inclusion in the checklist. I give the marital status of women merely to avoid the confusion that a change of name might cause. I omit details of private life or critical assessment of work. The one I consider irrelevant, the other would have had to be so brief as to be useless, and out of place in an enumerative bibliography. Following the biographical note is a list of sources used in compilation to which users may go for fuller information. Single-author bibliographies are comparatively few for this period. None can be definitive where authors are still living and writing. Those listed are all separately published and have been inspected by me. After the list of sources, arranged alphabetically, separately published works in English are given, classified under novels, poetry, plays, works for children, *Other Works*. The sources are listed alphabetically, the works chronologically under each subsection.

In my earlier work I ill-advisedly wrote: "the main consideration [in choosing 1940 for the closing date] was that, after that date, adequate national bibliographies exist to which librarians and scholars can have easy access." I have lived to eat my words; those for Britain, America, New Zealand and Australia *were* adequate, but with developing countries it was far otherwise. Their national bibliographies were sparse and fallible in the main, late starters (rarely before the mid-1960s), and intermittent goers. Yet, despite reservations as to their accuracy or completeness, they had to be my mainstay for locally published work which it was essential to include. For, although those African writers, for instance, who have established themselves with British or American publishers may be the best, yet a list of locally published work filled out the picture amazingly.

Thus, although my results must be as scrappy as my sources, yet I hope that I have produced a new finding tool for material not previously listed in a single-volume British bibliography. I could have improved my work greatly by delaying publication indefinitely, but I decided to end in December 1973 with the vain hope of striking a balance between the meticulous study that never appears and the misleadingly slipshod one that is rushed out too soon.

June 1974   ROBIN MYERS

Postscript

Printing and production difficulties have regrettably caused a four-year delay between delivery of the typescript to the publisher and eventual appearance in print. Towards the end of 1977, therefore, when the typesetting was about to begin, the question arose whether to delay publication yet further in order to update and revise what must be retrospective as soon as published. Whilst it might have been a feasible matter to deal with the major British and American authors, these are precisely the ones whose bibliographies are easily accessible elsewhere. The real usefulness of this work will depend on the obscure entries, particularly those from Africa and India, where source material, as I have already pointed out, takes a great deal of searching for and of communication with libraries at the far corners of the earth. To have rooted all these out again, and to have looked for new sources published since 1973 would have been a lengthy and arduous business. Thus matters are left where they stood when the manuscript was first prepared for press in the autumn of 1974, and users are referred to the "Select handlist of general reference works consulted" for further data on authors published in the Western world.

February 1978   ROBIN MYERS

Acknowledgements

I AM indebted to many in libraries and publishing houses for help and advice. Without wishing to seem ungrateful to those who are not mentioned by name, I thank particularly the following who put their expertise at my disposal: Mr. Edward Blishen; Mr. Dan Davin; Dr. Andrew Fabinyi; Professor M. K. Joseph; Dr. E. F. C. Lludowyk; Professor Richard Ludwig; Professor J. E. Morpurgo; Mr. Andrew Salkey; Sardar Khushwant Singh; Mr. W. B. Stevenson; Mr. J. C. Trewin; Mr. Ian Willison; the staff of the Australian Reference Section of the National Library, Canberra. My thanks also go to the staffs of the following libraries which I used a good deal: Australia House; The India Office; The National Book League; New Zealand House; The Royal Commonwealth Institute; University College, London.

My special thanks go to Mr. Bernard Adams, at that time in charge of the British Council Home Library, who allowed me to use that library almost as if it were my personal collection.

Finally, thanks to Ms. Jenny Drummond who compiled the indexes, to Miss Nicolette Piggott who typed the whole work, and to Miss Jane With of the National Book League who checked most of it for me, and thus saved me from many errors.

Select handlist of general reference works consulted

Annals of Australian Literature. Oxford University Press. 1970.

Annual Catalogue of Australian Publications, 1936–60.

Australian National Bibliography, 1961 to date.

Authors' and Writers' Who's Who, 6th ed. London, Burke's Peerage. 1971.

Bibliographic Index: a cumulative bibliography of bibliographies, 1937. New York, H. W. Wilson. 1938 to date.

Bibliography of Indian Literature 1901–1953, vol. I, 1st ed. New Delhi, Sahitya Akademi. 1962.

Books in Print, 1973. New York, Bowker Company. 1973.

The Bookseller, export numbers spring and autumn. London, J. Whitaker & Sons.

British Books in Print: the reference catalogue of current literature, 1973. 2 vols. London, J. Whitaker and Sons. 1974.

British Museum General Catalogue. Supplements 1965–70 (cited as B.M. catalogue).

The British National Bibliography. London, the Council of the British National Bibliography. 1950 to date (cited as B.N.B.).

BURKE, W. J. and HOWE, W. D. *American Authors and Books 1640 to the Present Day*, rev. ed. London, Nicholas Vane. 1963.

Canadiana. Ottawa, Canada. 1951 to date.

Cassell's Encyclopaedia of Literature, ed. S. H. Steinberg, 2nd ed. 3 vols. London, Cassell. 1973.

The Concise Cambridge History of English Literature, 3rd ed. Cambridge University Press. 1970.

CONRON, BRANDON, KLINK, CARL F. and SYLVESTRE, GUY. *Canadian Writers: Écrivains Canadiens*. 1964.

Contemporary Dramatists. London, St. James's Press. 1973.

Contemporary Novelists. London, St. James's Press. 1972.

Contemporary Poets. London, St. James's Press. 1970.

Cumulative Book Index: World List of Books in the English Language. New York, The H. W. Wilson Company. 1940 to date (cited as C.B.I.).

Dictionary of International Biography, compiled by G. Handley–Taylor. 3 vols. London, 1963.

The Dictionary of National Biography. Supplement 1951–60. London, Oxford University Press. 1971 (cited as D.N.B.).

Encyclopaedia Canadiana. 10 vols. Ottawa, Grolier Canadian Company. 1963.

ENSER, A. G. S. *Filmed Books and Plays, 1928–74*, 2nd ed. André Deutsch. 1975.

ETHERIDGE, J. M. *Contemporary Authors*. 48 vols. to date. Detroit, Michigan, Gale Research Company. 1962 to date (cited as Gale).

Everyman's Dictionary of Literary Biography, English and American, with supplement of writers of the sixties, 4th ed. London, J. M. Dent. 1969.

Ghana National Bibliography 1965–71. Accra, Ghana Library Board. 1968–73.

Indian Dictionary of National Biography A–D. New Delhi, Sahitya Akademi. 1970 (cited as Indian D.N.B.).

Indian National Bibliography, 1958– , monthly, with annual cumulations; 1963– , also quarterly; cumulated indexes, 1958–62. Delhi, Central Reference Library.

JAHN, J. and DRESSLER, C. P. *A Bibliography of Neo-African Literature from Africa, America and the Caribbean*. Nendeln, Kraus-Thomson. 1971 (cited as Jahn and Dressler).

KLINCK, CARL F., editor. *Literary History of Canada: Canadian literature in English*. Toronto, University of Toronto Press. 1965.

KUNITZ, S. J. *Twentieth-Century Authors: a Biographical Dictionary of Modern Literature*; first supplement. New York, The H. W. Wilson Company. 1955 (cited as Kunitz).

Library of Congress Catalog (cited as L. of C.).

Literary and Library Prizes, 7th ed. New York, Bowker. 1970.

Longman Companion to Twentieth-Century Literature by A. C. Ward. London, Longman. 1970.

McCORMICK, E. H. *New Zealand Literature: a Survey*. London, Oxford University Press. 1959.

The Macmillan Dictionary of Canadian Biography, 3rd ed. London, Macmillan & Company. 1963.

MILLER, E. M. and MACARTNEY, F. T. *Australian Literature: a bibliography to 1950*. Angus and Robertson. 1956.

The National Bibliography of Indian Literature 1901–53. Vol. I. New Delhi, Sahitya Akademi. 1953.

The New Cambridge Bibliography of English Literature. Vol. IV, 1900–50. Ed. I. R. Willison. Cambridge University Press. 1972 (cited as N.C.B.E.L.).

New Zealand National Bibliography, 1947–65. National Library Centre, New Zealand. 1947 (cited as N.Z. national bibliography).

Nigerian Publications, 1950–74 (since 1972, *National Bibliography of Nigeria*), monthly, with three-monthly and annual cumulations.

The Oxford Companion to American Literature by James D. Hart. 4th ed. New York, Oxford University Press. 1965.

The Oxford Companion to Canadian History and Literature by Norah Story. London, Oxford University Press. 1967.

The Oxford Companion to English Literature, ed. Sir Paul Harvey. 4th ed. Oxford, Clarendon Press. 1967.

The Penguin Companion to Literature: Britain and the Commonwealth, ed. D. Daiches. London, Penguin. 1971.

SPILLER, ROBERT E. and others. *Literary History of the United States, Bibliography supplement II*. New York, Macmillan. 1972 (cited as Spiller).

TAYLOR, JOHN RUSSELL. *Anger and After: a Guide to the New British Drama*. London, Methuen. 1962.

Ulrich's International Periodicals Directory, 14th ed. 2 vols. New York, Bowker. 1971–2.

Who's Who. London, A. & C. Black. 1973.

Who's Who: a Biographical Dictionary of International Bookmen, 2nd ed. New York, Bowker. 1971.

Who's Who in America, 37th ed. Chicago, Ill., Marquis. 1972.

Who's Who in New Zealand. Sydney and London, Reed. 1st ed. 1932; 10th ed. 1971.

Who's Who in the Theatre, ed. John Parker. Pitman. 1st ed. 1912; 15th ed. 1972.

Who's Who of Indian Writers. New Delhi, Sahitya Akademi. 1961.

Who was Who, 1961–70. London, A. & C. Black. 1972.

Who was Who in America, 1897–1968. 4 vols. Chicago, Ill., Marquis. 1943–68.

ZELL, H. and SILVER, H. *A Reader's Guide to African Literature*. London, Heinemann. 1972 (cited as Zell and Silver).

Volumes in the following series:

Penguin African Writers.

Penguin Modern Poets.

Writers and Critics. Edinburgh, Oliver & Boyd.

Writers and their Work. London, Longman for the British Council and the National Book League.

Symbols and abbreviations

* First published in.

† Pseudonym or pen name.

[ ] Square brackets are used where the date, although established, does not appear on the title-page.

n.d. No date.

pr. ptd. Privately printed.

Anger and after: John Russell Taylor, Anger and After, Methuen. 1962.

B.M. catalogue: British Museum General Catalogue.

B.N.B.: British National Bibliography. 1950–.

Contemporary dramatists: St. James's Press. 1973.

Contemporary novelists: St. James's Press. 1972.

Contemporary poets: St. James's Press. 1970.

C.B.I.: Cumulative Book Index, The H. W. Wilson Company. 1940–.

Gale: J. M. Etheridge, Contemporary Authors, 48 vols., Gale Research Company. 1962–.

Jahn and Dressler: J. Jahn and C. P. Dressler, A Bibliography of Neo-African Literature, Kraus-Thomson. 1971.

Jain: Shushil Kumar Jain, Indian Literature in English, a bibliography, Ontario, Canada, University of Windsor. 1972.

Kunitz: S. J. Kunitz, Twentieth-Century Authors ... First Supplement, The H. W. Wilson Company. 1955.

L. of C.: Library of Congress Catalog.

N.C.B.E.L.: New Cambridge Bibliography of English Literature, vol. IV. 1972.

N.Z. national bibliography: New Zealand National Bibliography. 1947–65.

Patten: Margaret D. Patten, Ghanaian Imaginative Writing in English 1950–69; an annotated bibliography, Department of Library Studies, University of Lagos. 1971.

Spiller: Robert E. Spiller, Literary History of the United States, Supplement II, Macmillan. 1972.

Ulrich: Ulrich's International Periodicals Directory, 14th ed., Bowker. 1971–2.

Zell and Silver: H. Zell and H. Silver, A Reader's Guide to African Literature, Heinemann. 1972.

A

AARON, DANIEL (1912–)
American historian; educated at Michigan and Harvard universities; instructor at Harvard (1936–9); at Smith College, Northampton, Mass. (1939–); currently Professor there; visiting Professor at universities in Finland, Iceland, etc.; a contributor to *Hudson Review, Kenyon Review, New Republic*, etc.; his edited work is not listed below.

Bibliography
C.B.I.
Gale.

Works
Men of good hope: a story of American progressives. 1951.
The United States: the history of the republic (with others). 1957.
The American republic. 2 vols. (with others). 1959.
Writers on the left. 1961.
Unwritten war: American writers and the Civil War. 1973.

ABBAS, AHMAD KHWAJA
Indian novelist.

Bibliography
Indian D.N.B.
Indian national bibliography 1958–67.

Novels
Tomorrow is ours. 1943.
Defeat for death: a story without names. 1944.
Not all lies. 1945.
Blood and stones. 1947.
Inquilab. 1955.
One thousand nights on a bed of stones and other stories. 1957.

Play
Invitation to immortality. 1944.

ABLEMAN, PAUL (1927–)
English novelist and playwright; educated at King's College, London; served in the army.

Bibliography
B.N.B.
Contemporary novelists.

Novels
I hear voices. 1958.
As near as I can get. 1962.
Vac. 1968.
The twilight of the Vilp. 1969.

Plays
Green Julia (staged 1965). 1966.
Tests (playlets). 1966.
Blue comedy: madly in love: Hank's night (staged 1968). 1968.

Other Works
Bits: some prose poems. 1969.
The mouth and oral sex. 1969.

ABRAHAMS, PETER (1919–)
South African novelist; editor of the *West Indian Economist*; Jamaican radio commentator; settled in Jamaica; a contributor to the *Observer, New York Herald Tribune*, etc.; editor, with Nadine Gordimer, of *South African writing today*, Penguin (1967).

Bibliography
Authors' and writers' who's who. 1971.
B.N.B.
Contemporary novelists.
Jahn and Dressler.

Novels
Dark testament (stories). 1942.
Song of the city. 1945.
Mine boy. 1946.
The path of thunder. 1948.
Wild conquest. 1949.
A wreath for Udomo. 1956.
A night of their own. 1965.
This island now. 1967.

Other Works
Return to Goli. 1953.
Tell freedom: memoirs of Africa. 1953.
Jamaican island mosaic. 1956.
Jamaica. 1957.

ABRUQUAH, JOSEPH WILFRED
Ghanaian novelist.

Bibliography
B.N.B.
Jahn and Dressler.
Patten.
Zell and Silver.

Novels
The catechist. 1965.
The torrent. 1968.

ABSE, DANNIE (1923–)
Welsh-Jewish poet; born in Cardiff; educated University of South Wales, King's College, London, and Westminster Hospital Medical School; L.R.C.P.; served in the R.A.F. in the Second World War; his edited work and unpublished plays are not listed below.

Bibliography
B.N.B.
Contemporary novelists.
Contemporary poets.
Gale.

Novels
Ash on a young man's sleeve. 1954.
Some corner of an English field. 1956.
O. Jones, O. Jones. 1970.

Poetry
After every green thing. 1949.
Walking under water. 1952.
Tenants of the house, poems, 1951–56. 1957.
Poems, Golders Green. 1962.
A small desperation. 1968.
Selected poems. 1970.
Funland and other poems. 1973.

Plays
Fire in Heaven. 1956.
The eccentric. 1961.
Three Questor plays (The house of cowards, Gone, and In the cage) (produced 1960). 1967.

Other Work
Medicine on trial. 1967.

ACHEBE, CHINUA (1930–)
Nigerian novelist; educated at Ibadan University; Nigerian Broadcasting Corporation (1958–66); Senior Research Fellow, Nigeria University, Nsukka (1967–); Director, Heinemann Educational Books, Nigeria (1970–); editor of *Okike*, Nigerian journal of new writing; recipient of various literary awards.

Bibliography
B.N.B.
Contemporary novelists.
Gale.
Jahn and Dressler.
A. Ravenscroft. Chinua Achebe. 1973.
Who's who. 1973.
Zell and Silver.

Novels
Things fall apart. 1958.
No longer at ease. 1961.
The sacrificial egg and other stories. 1962.
Arrow of God. 1964.
A man of the people. 1966.
Girls at war (stories). 1972.
The insider (joint author). 1972.

Poetry
Beware soul-brother and other poems. 1971.

For Children
Chike and the river. 1966.
How the leopard got his claws. 1972.

ACORN, MILTON (1923–)
Canadian poet; editor of *Moment* magazine, Montreal; a contributor to *Tamarack Review*, *Canadian Forum*, *Fiddlehead*, etc.

Bibliography
Canadiana.
C.B.I.
Contemporary poets.

Poetry
In love and anger (pr. ptd.). 1957.
The brain's the target. 1960.
Against a league of liars. 1960.
Jawbreakers. 1962.
Selected poems. 1969.

ADCOCK, FLEUR (*Mrs.* ALISTAIR CAMPBELL) (1934–)
New Zealand poet; now lives in London; educated

at Victoria University, Wellington; university posts at Otago University (1959–61); Assistant Librarian, Foreign and Commonwealth Office Library, London (1963–   ); recipient of several awards; represented in numerous anthologies; a contributor to *Landfall*, the *Listener*, etc.

Bibliography
B.N.B.
Contemporary poets.
Gale.
N.Z. national bibliography.

Poetry
The eye of the hurricane. 1964.
Tigers. 1967.
High tide in the garden. 1971.

AIDOO, CHRISTINA AMA ATA
(1942–   )
Ghanaian poet, playwright and short-story writer; educated at the Wesley Girls' High School and the University of Ghana; travelled in the United States, England and East Africa (1967–9); Research Fellow in contemporary Ghanaian drama, University of Ghana; her poetry has been widely published in *Black Orpheus, Okyeame, New African*, etc.

Bibliography
B.N.B.
C.B.I.
Jahn and Dressler.
Zell and Silver.

Short Story
No sweetness here. 1970.

Plays
The dilemma of a ghost. 1965.
Anowa. 1969.

ALBEE, EDWARD FRANKLIN
(1928–   )
American playwright; educated at Valley Forge Military Academy and Trinity College, Hartford, Connecticut; wrote for music programmes on a radio station, among other jobs; since 1958 has been a full-time writer; recipient of many literary awards; his adaptations are not listed below.

Bibliography
C.B.I.
Gale.

Spiller.
Who's who. 1973.

Plays
Fam and Yam. 1960.
The zoo story (produced 1959). 1960.
The sandbox. 1960.
The death of Bessie Smith (produced 1959, with The sandbox). 1960.
The American dream. 1961.
Who's afraid of Virginia Woolf? (filmed 1965). 1962.
Ballad of the Sad Café (adapted from Carson McCullers's novel). 1965.
The substitute speaker. 1965.
Tiny Alice. 1965.
Malcolm. 1966.
A delicate balance (Pulitzer Prize 1967). 1966.
Everything in the garden. 1968.
Quotations from Chairman Mao Tse-tung. 1968.
Box. 1968.
All over. 1971.

ALDEN, JOHN RICHARD (1903–   )
American historian; educated at the University of Michigan; Professor of History, Duke University (1955–63); Professor of History, Dale University (1963–   ); his edited work is not listed below.

Bibliography
Authors' and writers' who's who. 1971.
C.B.I.

Works
John Stuart and the southern colonial frontier 1754–75. 1944.
General Gage in America. 1948.
General Charles Lee: traitor or patriot? 1951.
The American Revolution 1775–83. 1954.
The South in the Revolution 1763–89. 1957.
A history of the United States (with Alice Magenis). 1960.
First South. 1960.
The rise of the American Republic. 1963.
Pioneer America. 1966.
A history of the American Revolution. 1969.

ALDISS, BRIAN WILSON (1923–   )
English science fiction writer and critic; born in Norfolk; educated at Framlingham College; served in the army (1943–7) in the Second World War; bookseller (1947–56); literary editor, *Oxford Mail* (1958–69); president, British Science Fiction

Association (1960–4), etc.; a contributor to various science fiction magazines; editor of *SF Horizons* (1964–) and of *Penguin Science Fiction*; recipient of several science fiction awards.

Bibliography
Authors' and writers' who's who. 1971.
B.N.B.
Contemporary novelists.
Gale.
Who's who. 1973.

Novels
The Brightfount diaries. 1955.
Space, time and Nathaniel (stories). 1957.
Non-stop. 1958.
No time like tomorrow (stories). 1959.
Vanguard from Alpha. 1959.
Canopy of time (stories). 1959.
Bow down to Nul. 1960.
Galaxies like grains of sand. 1960.
The male response. 1961.
The interpreter. 1961.
Equator. 1961.
The primal urge. 1961.
Hothouse. 1962.
The airs of earth (stories). 1963.
The dark light years. 1964.
Greybeard. 1964.
Starswarm (stories). 1964.
Earthworks. 1965.
The saliva tree and other strange growths (stories). 1966.
An age (new edition as Cryptozoic, 1973). 1967.
Report on probability A. 1968.
Intangibles Inc. and other stories. 1969.
A Brian Aldiss Omnibus. 1969.
Barefoot in the head. 1969.
The hand-reared boy. 1970.
Neanderthal planet (stories). 1970.
The moment of eclipse (stories). 1970.
A soldier erect; or Further adventures of a hand-reared boy. 1971.
Frankenstein unbound. 1973.

Other Works
Cities and stones; a traveller's Jugoslavia. 1966.
Farewell, fantastic Venus! 1968.
The shape of further things. 1970.
The billion year spree: a history of science fiction. 1973.

ALDRIDGE, HAROLD EDWARD JAMES (1918–)
Australian journalist and writer; on the staff of the *Melbourne Herald, Sun, Daily Sketch*, and *Australian Newspaper Service* (1937–45); war correspondent in Finland, Norway, Middle East, Greece and the U.S.S.R.

Bibliography
Australian national bibliography.
B.N.B.
Contemporary novelists.
Who's who. 1973.

Novels
Signed with their honour. 1942.
The sea eagle (John Llewelyn Rhys Prize 1945). 1944.
Of many men. 1946.
The diplomat. 1950.
The hunter. 1951.
Heroes of the empty view. 1954.
I wish he would not die. 1958.
Gold and sand (stories). 1960.
The last exile. 1961.
The statesman's game. 1966.
My brother Tom (American title, My brother Tom, a love story). 1966.

Other Works
Underwater fishing for the inexperienced Englishman. 1962.
Living Egypt (with Paul Strand). 1969.
Cairo: the biography of a city. 1970.

ALDRIDGE, JOHN WATSON (1922–)
American writer and novelist; educated at University of California, Berkeley; served in the U.S. Army (1943–5) during the Second World War; held many academic posts; Professor of English, Ann Arbor (1963–); a contributor to *Nation, New Republic, Saturday Review*, etc.; his edited work is not listed below.

Bibliography
C.B.I.
Contemporary poets.
Gale.

Novel
The party at Cranton. 1960.

Other Works
After the lost generation (literary criticism). 1951.
In search of heresy (literary criticism). 1956.
Time to murder and time to create; the contemporary novel in crisis. 1966.

Hermeneutic of Erasmus. 1967.
In the country of the young. 1970.
Devil in the fire: retrospective essays in American
   literature and culture. 1972.

ALEXANDER, COLIN JAMES
(†SIMON JAY) (1920–)

New Zealand novelist; born in England; educated
at Otago University; practised as a radiologist in
New Zealand hospitals (1950–); served in the
New Zealand Army (1945–7) during the Second
World War.

Bibliography
C.B.I.
Gale.
N.Z. national bibliography.

Novels (as †Simon Jay)
Death of a skin diver. 1964.
Sleepers can kill. 1968.

ALI, AHMED (1910–)

Pakistani novelist; educated at Ailigarh and Lucknow universities; Lecturer and Professor at various
universities (1932–48); B.B.C. representative and
director, New Delhi (1941–4); Pakistan Foreign
Service (1950–60); managing director of Lomen
Fabrics, Karachi (1971–); editor of *Indian Writing*
(1939–41) and *Tomorrow*, Bombay (1941–2); his
works in Urdu are not listed below; his plays, *Hand
of twilight* (1931) and *Break the chains* (1932), were
not published.

Bibliography
B.N.B.
Contemporary novelists.
Gale.
Jain.

Novels
Twilight in Delhi. 1940.
Ocean of night. 1964.

Poetry
Flaming earth: selected poems from Indonesia.
   1949.
Purple gold mountain. 1960.
Bulbul and the rose. 1962.
Ghalib: selected poems. 1969.

Other Works
Mr. Eliot's penny-world of dreams. 1941.
Muslim China. 1949.
Problems of style and technique in Ghalib. 1969.

ALLEGRO, JOHN MARCO (1923–)

English biblical and Hebrew scholar; educated at
Manchester University; served in the Royal Navy
in the Second World War (1941–6); British
member of the international team editing the Dead
Sea Scrolls in Jordan (1953–); Lecturer in semitic
philology, etc. (1954–); secretary and trustee of
the Dead Sea Scrolls Fund; his television films
include *The Dead Sea Scrolls* (1957) and *Search in the
Kidron* (1963); a contributor on semitic philology
to learned journals.

Bibliography
B.N.B.
Gale.
Who's who. 1973.

Works
The Dead Sea Scrolls (revised edition 1964). 1956.
The people of the Dead Sea Scrolls. 1958.
The treasure of the copper scroll (revised edition
   1964). 1960.
The Shapiro affair. 1964.
Search in the desert. 1965.
Discoveries in the Judaean desert no. 5. Qumran
   Cave 4 (with Arnold A. Anderson). 1968.
The sacred mushroom and the cross. 1970.
The end of a road. 1970.
The chosen people. 1971.

ALLEN, RALPH (1913–66)

Canadian journalist and novelist; educated in
Ontario and Saskatchewan; a reporter on the Winnipeg *Tribune* and later the Toronto *Globe* (1938);
war correspondent during the Second World War;
on the staff, later managing editor, of *MacLean's
Magazine*; editor of Toronto *Star* (1964).

Bibliography
Canadiana.
C.B.I.

Novels
Home made banners. 1946.
The chartered libertine. 1954.
Peace River country. 1958.
Ask the name of the lion. 1962.
The high white forest. 1964.

Other Works
Ordeal by fire: 1915–45. 1961.
The man from Oxbow. 1967.

ALLEY, REWI (1897–)
New Zealand poet; served in the New Zealand
Expeditionary Force during the First World War
(1917–18); has worked and lived in China
(1926–); has contributed to many periodicals; is
represented in various anthologies; his translated
work is not listed below.

Bibliography
Contemporary poets.
A. P. V. Millet. Rewi Alley: a preliminary check-
list. Hamilton. 1972.
N.Z. national bibliography.

Poetry (all published in Christchurch, New Zealand)
Gung Ho. 1948.
Leaves from a Sandan notebook. 1950.
This is China today. 1951.
Fragments of living Peking and other poems. 1955.
Beyond the withered oak ten thousand saplings
grow. 1962.
Who is the enemy? 1964.
The mistake. 1965.
Not a dog: an ancient Thai ballad. 1966.
What is sin? 1967.
Twenty-five poems of protest. 1968.
Upsurge and the Pacific: poems. 1969.
73 man to be: poems. 1970.
Poems for Aotearoa. 1972.

Other Works (select)
Yo Banfa. 1952.
The people have strength. 1954.
Man against flood. 1956.
Spring in Vietnam. 1956.
Buffalo boys of Vietnam. 1956.
Journey to Outer Mongolia. 1957.
Human China: a diary with poems. 1957.
Peking opera. 1957.
Stories out of China. 1958.
Sandan: an adventure in creative education. 1959.
Towards a people's Japan. 1960.
"China's hinterland" in the leap forward. 1961.
Land and folk in Kiangsi. 1962.
Amongst the hills of Yunan. 1963.
In the spirit of Hunghu. 1966.
Fruition. 1967.
Oceana: an outline for study. 1969.
Chinese children. 1972.
The rebels (stories of children). 1973.

ALLOTT, KENNETH (1912–)
English poet and literary critic; educated Durham

and Oxford; Bradley Professor of Modern English
Literature, University of Liverpool (1947–);
contributed to *New Verse* during the 1930s; his
edited work includes *The Pelican Book of English
Prose* (1956), a complete edition of *Matthew
Arnold's poetry* (1965) and *Selections from Robert
Browning* (1967).

Bibliography
B.M. catalogue.
N.C.B.E.L.

Poetry
Poems. 1938.
The ventriloquist's doll. 1943.

Critical Works
Jules Verne. 1940.
The art of Graham Greene (with Miriam Farnis).
1951.
Matthew Arnold. 1955.

Novel
The rhubarb tree (with Stephen Tait). 1937.

Play
A room with a view (with Stephen Tait). 1951.

ALLSOP, KENNETH (1920–73)
English writer, journalist and television commentator; served in the R.A.F. (1940–4); journalist
since 1945; on the staff of *Picture Post* (1950–5);
Evening Standard (1955–7); *Daily Mail* (1957–64),
etc.; interviewer on B.B.C.'s *Twenty-four Hours*
programme (1960–73); Research Fellow, Merton
College, Oxford (1968); Rector, Edinburgh University (1968–73).

Bibliography
Gale.
Who's who. 1973.

Works
Adventure lit their star (novel) (John Llewelyn
Rhys Prize 1950). 1949.
The sun himself must die (short stories). 1949.
The daybreak edition. 1951.
Silver flame. 1951.
The last voyages of the Mayflower. 1955.
The angry decade (criticism). 1958.
A question of obscenity. 1960.
The bootleggers. 1961.
Scan (collected journalism). 1965.
Hard travellin'. 1967.

Countryside and conservation. 1970.
Fit to live in: the future of Britain's countryside. 1970.

ALPERS, ANTONY FRANCIS GEORGE (1919–)

New Zealand journalist and critic; educated at Christ's College; wrote for the *Press, New Zealand Listener* and *Auckland Star*; editor of *Education* (1959–61); Assistant Professor of English, Queen's University, Kingston, Ontario (1966–).

Bibliography
B.N.B.
Gale.
N.Z. national bibliography.

Works
Katherine Mansfield. 1953.
Dolphins: the myth and the mammal. 1961.
Maori myths and tribal legends. 1965.
Legends of the South Sea. 1970.

ALUKO, TIMOTHY MOFOLORUNSO (1918–)

Nigerian novelist; educated at the universities of Ibadan, London and Newcastle; engineer in Nigerian Government employ (1943–66); Senior Research Fellow in Engineering, Lagos University (1966–); O.B.E. (1963).

Bibliography
B.N.B.
Contemporary novelists.
Jahn and Dressler.
Zell and Silver.

Novels
One man, one wife. 1959.
One man, one matchet. 1964.
Kinsman and foreman. 1966.
Chief the honourable minister. 1970.
His worshipful majesty. 1972.

ALVAREZ, ALFRED (1929–)

English literary critic and poet; educated Corpus Christi College, Oxford; Research Fellow and Tutor in English, Corpus Christi (1952–5); Visiting Lecturer, Princeton University (1955–8); Visiting Professor, Brandeis University, Waltham, Mass. (1960–1), and at State University, New York at Buffalo (1966); freelance writer; editor of *Penguin New Poetry, Under Pressure, The Writer in Society*, etc.; editor of the *Journal of Education*

(1957); poetry editor and critic for the *Observer*; *New Statesman* drama critic (1958–60).

Bibliography
B.N.B.
Contemporary poets.
Gale.
Who's who. 1973.

Poetry
Lost. 1968.
Penguin modern poets no. 18 (with R. Fuller and A. Thwaite). 1970.
Apparition. 1972.

Critical Works
The shaping spirit (published in the United States as Stewards of excellence). 1958.
The school of Donne. 1961.
Under pressure. 1965.
Beyond all this fiddle: essays 1955–67. 1968.
The savage god. 1971.

AMADI, ELECHI EMMANUEL (1934–)

Nigerian novelist; educated at the University of Ibadan; served in the Nigerian Army (1963–6); and again during the Civil War (1968); Government Officer, Port Harcourt (1968–); joint author of two hymn books; his work in Ikwerre and unpublished plays are not listed below.

Bibliography
B.M. catalogue.
Gale.
Jahn and Dressler.
Nigerian national bibliography.
Zell and Silver.

Novels
The concubine. 1966.
The great ponds. 1969.

Other Work
Sunset in Biafra. 1973.

AMIS, KINGSLEY (†ROBERT MARKHAM) (1922–)

English novelist and critic; educated at the City of London School and St. John's College, Oxford; served in the Second World War (1942–5); Lecturer in English, University College of Swansea (1949–61); Fellow of Peterhouse, Cambridge (1961–3); a contributor to the *Spectator, Listener*, etc.

Bibliography
Authors' and writers' who's who. 1971.
B.N.B.
Contemporary novelists.
Gale.
Who's who. 1973.

Novels
Lucky Jim (Somerset Maugham Award 1955;
    filmed 1957). 1954.
That uncertain feeling (filmed as Only two can
    play, 1962). 1955.
I like it here. 1958.
Take a girl like you (filmed 1971). 1960.
My enemy's enemy (short stories). 1962.
One fat Englishman. 1963.
The Egyptologists (with Robert Conquest). 1965.
The anti-death league. 1966.
Colonel Sun (†Robert Markham). 1968.
I want it now. 1968.
The green man. 1969.
Girl, 20. 1971.
The Riverside Villas murder. 1973.

Poetry
Bright November. 1947.
A frame of mind. 1953.
Poems. 1954.
A case of samples: poems 1946–1956. 1956.
The Evans country. 1962.
Penguin modern poets no. 2 (with D. Moraes and
    P. Porter). 1962.
A look round the estate. 1967.

Other Works
Socialism and the intellectual. 1957.
New maps of Hell, a survey of science fiction.
    1960.
The James Bond dossier. 1965.
Lucky Jim's politics. 1968.
What became of Jane Austen? 1970.

AMMONS, ARCHIE R. (1926–)
American poet; educated at the University of
California, Berkeley; served in the U.S. Naval
Reserve (1944–6); poetry editor of *Nation* (1963); a
contributor to the *Hudson Review*, *Poetry*, etc.;
Associate Professor of English, Cornell University
(1969–); represented in various anthologies.

Bibliography
C.B.I.
Contemporary poets.
Gale.

Poetry
Ommateum *with* Doxology: poems. 1955.
Expressions of sea level. 1964.
Corson's inlet. 1965.
Tape for the turn of the year. 1965.
Northfield poems. 1966.
Selected poems. 1968.
Briefings. 1971.
Collected poems 1951–1971. 1972.
Uplands: new poems. n.d.

ANDERSON, ETHEL LOUISA
(1883–1958)
English-born Australian writer; wife of
Brigadier-General A. T. Anderson.

Bibliography
Annals of Australian literature.
C.B.I.
Miller and Macartney, Australian literature, a
    bibliography. 1956.

Works
Squatter's luck and other poems. 1942.
Adventures in Appleshire. 1944.
Timeless garden. 1945.
Sunday at Yarralumla (poems). 1947.
Indian tales. 1948.
At Parramatta (stories). 1956.
The song of Hagar (poetry). 1957.
The little ghosts (stories). 1959.

ANDERSON, PATRICK JOHN.
McALISTER (1915–)
English poet; born in Surrey; educated at Sherborne, Worcester College, Oxford, and Columbia
University, New York; travelled (1939–52); Assistant Professor, McGill University (1948–50); Lecturer, Malay University (1950–2); currently head
of English, Trent Park College of Education, Bar-
net.

Bibliography
B.N.B.
Contemporary poets.

Poetry
Poems (juvenilia, pr. ptd.). 1929.
On this side nothing (juvenilia, pr. ptd.). 1932.
A tent for April. 1945.
The white centre. 1946.
The colour as naked. 1953.

Autobiography
Snake wine. 1955.
Search me. 1957.
The character ball. 1963.

Other Works
First steps in Greece. 1958.
Finding out about the Athenians. 1961.
Dolphin days: a writer's notebook of Mediter-
    ranean pleasures. 1963.
The smile of Apollo: a literary companion to Greek
    travel. 1964.
Over the Alps. 1969.
Foxed!, or Life in the country. 1972.

†ANDERSON, POUL WILLIAM (WINSTON P. SANDERS) (1926–)
American science fiction writer; educated at the
University of Minnesota; full-time writer
(1948–); recipient of literary awards; a selection
of his works only is listed below.

Bibliography
B.N.B.
C.B.I.
Gale.

Novels
Vault of the ages. 1952.
The broken sword. 1954.
Brain wave. 1955.
The star ways. 1957.
Earthman's burden (with G. R. Dickson). 1957.
Virgin planet. 1959.
Perish by the sword. 1959.
The enemy stars. 1959.
Murder in black letter. 1960.
The golden slave. 1960.
The high crusade. 1960.
Rogue sword. 1960.
Guardians of time. 1960.
Twilight world. 1961.
Three hearts and three lions. 1961.
Orbit unlimited. 1961.
After doomsday. 1963.
Is there life on other worlds? 1963.
Trader to the stars. 1964.
Time and stars. 1964.
The star fox. 1965.
The corridors of time. 1965.
Flandry of Terra. 1965.
Shield. 1965.
Agent of the Terran empire. 1965.
The trouble twisters. 1966.

The fox, the dog and the griffin. 1966.
Ensign Flandry. 1966.
Planet of no return. 1967.
The infinite voyage. 1969.
The makeshift rocket. 1969.
Satan's world. 1969.
Seven conquests. 1969.
Beyond the beyond. 1970.
Let the spacemen beware. 1970.
War of the two worlds. 1970.
Tau zero. 1971.
Operation chaos. 1971.
Byworlder. 1971.
The day the sun stood still. 1972.
Dancer from Atlantis. 1972.
Un-man and other novellas. 1972.
The horn of time. 1973.
People of the wind. 1973.
The Queen of Air and Darkness. 1973.
War of the wingmen. 1973.
Hrolf Kraki's saga. 1973.

ANDERSON, ROBERT WOODRUFF (1917–)
American playwright; born in New York; served
in the U.S. Navy during the Second World War
(1942–6); taught playwriting (1946–50); wrote and
adapted plays for radio and television; film scripts
include *Until they sail* (1957), *The nun's story* (1959);
his unpublished plays *Eden rose* (1948) and *Hove
revisited* (1952) are not listed below.

Bibliography
C.B.I.
Contemporary dramatists.
Gale.
Who's who. 1973.

Novel
After. 1973.

Plays
Tea and sympathy (filmed 1956). 1953.
All summer long (adaptation of a novel, A wreath
    and a curse, by Donald Wetzel). 1954.
Silent night, lonely night. 1959.
The days between. 1965.
You know I can't hear you when the water's run-
    ning (4 short plays). 1967.
I never sang for my father (filmed 1970). 1968.
Solitaire/double solitaire. 1971.

ANGELES, CARLOS A. (1921–)
Filipino poet; educated at the University of the

Philippines; Chief of International News Service Bureau (1948–58); Public Relations Manager, Pan Am Airways, Manila (1959–); recipient of various honours and awards; represented in Filipino anthologies; a contributor to journals.

Bibliography
C.B.I.
Contemporary poets.

Poetry
A stun of jewels. 1963.

ANGLESEY, 7th Marquess of (GEORGE CHARLES HENRY VICTOR PAGET) (1922–)

Welsh military historian and biographer; educated at Eton; served in the Royal Horse Guards (1941–6) in the Second World War; past president of the National Museum of Wales; member of the Historical Buildings Council for Wales; Member of the Royal Fine Arts Commission; Director of the Welsh National Opera Company; Honorary Fellow of the Cambrian Society, etc.; a contributor to the *Sunday Times, Punch, Journal of Army History, T.L.S.,* etc.

Bibliography
Authors' and writers' who's who. 1971.
B.N.B.
Gale.
Who's who. 1973.

Works
The Capel letters 1814–1817 (editor). 1955.
One-leg; the life and letters of the 1st Marquess of Anglesey, K.G., 1768–1854. 1961.
Sergeant Pearman's memoirs (editor). 1968.
Little Hodge (editor). 1971.
History of the British Cavalry 1815–1914. 1973.

ANNAN, NOËL GILROY (Baron ANNAN) (1916–)

English scholar; educated at Stowe School and King's College, Cambridge; served in the Second World War (1939–45); Fellow of King's College, Cambridge (1944–56); Provost of King's (1956–66); Provost of University College, London (1966–); member of many academic advisory committees, etc.; awarded many honorary degrees; a contributor to *Victorian Studies* and other journals.

Bibliography
B.N.B.
Who's who. 1973.

Works
Leslie Stephen: his thought and character in relation to his time. 1951.
The intellectual aristocracy (in Studies in social history, a tribute to G. M. Trevelyan). 1956.
The curious strength of positivism in English political thought. 1959.
Kipling's place in the history of ideas (in Kipling's mind and art). 1964.
Roxburgh of Stowe. 1965.

ANSEN, ALAN (1922–)

American poet; educated at Harvard University; secretary to W. H. Auden (1949–53).

Bibliography
C.B.I.
Contemporary poets.
Gale.

Poetry
The old religion. 1959.
Disorderly houses. 1961.
Field report (pr. ptd.). 1963.
Believe and tremble (pr. ptd.). 1963.
Day by day (pr. ptd.). 1966.

ANTHONY, MICHAEL (1932–)

Trinidad novelist; emigrated to England; worked in factories before joining Reuter's (1964) as a subeditor; a contributor to the *Trinidad Guardian*.

Bibliography
Authors' and writers' who's who. 1971.
B.N.B.
Contemporary novelists.
Gale.
Jahn and Dressler.

Novels
The games were coming. 1963.
The year in San Fernando. 1965.
Green days by the river. 1967.

ARDEN, JOHN (1930–)

English playwright, educated at Sedbergh and Cambridge; practised as an architect before becoming a dramatist; those of his radio and television plays that have not been published are not listed below.

Bibliography
C.B.I.
Gale.
Glenda Leeming. John Arden. 1974.
Who's who. 1973.

Plays

Serjeant Musgrave's dance (produced 1959). 1960.
The business of good government (produced as A
    Christmas play, 1960). 1963.
The workhouse donkey (produced 1963). 1964.
Ironhand (an adaptation of Goethe's Goetz von
    Berlichingen, produced 1963). 1965.
Three plays (The waters of Babylon, produced
    1957; Live like pigs, produced 1958; The happy
    haven, produced 1960). 1965.
Armstrong's last goodnight (produced 1964).
    1965.
Left-handed liberty (produced 1965). 1965.
Soldier, soldier and other plays (Soldier, soldier,
    produced 1960). 1967.
The royal pardon (with Margaret D'Arcy). 1967.
The hero rises up. 1969.
The party. 1970.
The true history of Squire Jonathan and his unfor-
    tunate treasurer, and The bagman or The
    impromptu of Muswell Hill. 1971.

ARLEN, MICHAEL J. (1930–   )

English novelist; son of Michael Arlen; educated at
St. Paul's School and Harvard; emigrated to the
U.S.A. (1940); journalist (1952–70); currently staff
writer, *New Yorker*.

Bibliography
C.B.I.

Novels
Living-room war. 1969.
Exiles. 1970.
American verdict. 1973.

ARLOTT, LESLIE THOMAS JOHN
(1914–   )

English writer on cricket and topography; clerk in
a mental hospital (1930–4); police detective
(1934–45); B.B.C. producer (1951–3); Labour candidate (1955 and 1959); a regular contributor to the
Guardian and *Hampshire County Magazine*; his
edited works are not listed below.

Bibliography
B.N.B.
Gale.
Who's who. 1973.

Poetry
Of period and place. 1944.

Clausentum. 1946.
Death on the road. 1953.

Other Works
Landmarks (with G. R. Hamilton). 1943.
Gone to the cricket. 1948.
Come to the test match. 1949.
Concerning cricket. 1949.
How to watch cricket. 1949.
Gone with the cricketers. 1950.
Maurice Tate. 1951.
Cricket: a reader and guide. 1951.
Days at the cricket. 1951.
Concerning soccer. 1952.
The echoing green. 1952.
Test match diary. 1953.
The picture of cricket. 1955.
Australian test journal 1954–5. 1955.
English cheeses of the south and west. 1956.
Alletson's innings. 1957.
Rothman's jubilee history of cricket. 1965.
Lord's and the M.C.C. (with H. S. Altham).
    1967.
Vintage summer. 1967.
Pageantry of sport (with Arthur Daly). 1968.
D'Oliveira. 1968.
Fred Trueman: portrait of a fast bowler. 1971.
Island camera. 1973.

ARMAH, AYI KWEI (1938–   )

Ghanaian novelist; educated at Achimota, Harvard
and Legon; represented in *Messages: poems from
Ghana* (Heinemann African Writers series) (1971);
scriptwriter for Ghana Television; editor of *Jeune
Afrique*, Paris (1967–8); lives in New York; a contributor to *Atlantic Monthly, New African, Drum
Magazine*, etc.

Bibliography
B.N.B.
C.B.I.
Contemporary poets.
Jahn and Dressler.
Zell and Silver.

Novels
The beautyful ones are not yet born. 1969.
Fragments. 1970.
Why are we so blest? 1971.

Other Work
Africa's golden road. 1965.

ARNOTT, PETER DOUGLAS (1931–)
English classical and dramatic scholar; born in
Ipswich; educated at the University of Wales, and
Exeter College, Oxford; Professor of Classics at
University of Iowa (1958–); Professor of Drama,
Tufts University, Medford, Mass.; originator of
Peter Arnott Marionette Theater; a contributor to
the *Classical Journal, Classical Philology, Educational
Theatrical Journal*, etc.; his translations from clas-
sical drama are not listed below.

Bibliography
Authors' and writers' who's who. 1971.
B.N.B.
Gale.

Works
Two classical comedies. 1958.
An introduction to the Greek theatre. 1959.
Greek scenic conventions of the fifth century B.C.
 1962.
Plays without people: puppetry and serious drama.
 1964.
An introduction to the Greek world. 1967.
The theatre of Japan. 1969.
An introduction to the Roman world. 1970.
Byzantines and their world. 1973.

ASARE, BEDIAKOI
Ghanaian novelist and journalist; assistant editor of
the *Ghanaian Times*; publicity officer of the Ghana
T.U.C. and editor of the *Worker* and *Ghana Labour*;
started the *Nationalist* in Dar-es-Salaam (1963).

Bibliography
B.N.B.
Jahn and Dressler.
Zell and Silver.

Novels
Don't leave me, Mercy. 1966.
A husband for Esi Ellua. 1967.
Rebel. 1969.

ASHBERY, JOHN LAWRENCE
(1927–)
American poet; educated at Harvard and Columbia universities; publisher's copywriter
(1955–61); art critic of the *New York Herald Tribune*
in Paris (1960–); recipient of several literary

awards; has published several plays in journals; his
edited work is not listed below.

Bibliography
C.B.I.
Contemporary poets.
Gale.
L. of C.

Poetry
Turandot and other poems. 1953.
Some trees. 1956.
The poems. 1960.
The tennis court oath. 1962.
Rivers and mountains. 1966.
Selected poems. 1967.
A nest of ninnies (with James Schuyler). 1969.
Fragment: poem. 1969.
The double dream of spring. 1970.
Three poems. 1972.

**ASHTON-WARNER, SYLVIA CON-
STANCE (*Mrs*. HENDERSON)** (1908–)
New Zealand novelist; taught, with her husband,
in country schools; now Professor of Education,
Colorado, U.S.A.; a contributor of poetry and
articles on education to various periodicals.

Bibliography
B.N.B.
Contemporary novelists.

Novels
Spinster. 1958.
Incense to idols. 1960.
Teacher. 1963.
Bell call. 1964.
Greenstone. 1966.
Three. 1971.

Other Works
Myself. 1968.
Spearpoint: "teacher" in America. 1972.

ASIMOV, ISAAC (†PAUL FRENCH)
(1920–)
American biochemist and science fiction and mystery writer; educated at Columbia University;
served in the U.S. Army during the Second World
War; instructor, rising to Associate Professor of
Biochemistry, Boston University School of
Medicine (1949–); his edited work is not listed
below.

Bibliography
Isaac Asimov. The best of Isaac Asimov. Sidgwick
    and Jackson. 1973. pp. 332–6 is a bibliography of
    Asimov's science fiction.
C.B.I.
Contemporary novelists.
Gale.
Marjorie M. Miller. Isaac Asimov, a checklist ...
    1939–1972. 1972.

Novels and Short Stories
Pebble in the sky. 1950.
I, robot. 1950.
The stars, like dust. 1951.
Foundation. 1951.
Foundation and empire. 1952.
Currents of space. 1952.
Second foundation. 1953.
The caves of steel. 1954.
The Martian way and other stories. 1955.
The end of eternity. 1955.
The naked sun. 1957.
Earth is room enough (stories). 1957.
The death dealers. 1958.
Nine tomorrows: tales of the near future. 1959.
Triangle. 1961.
The rest of the robots. 1964.
Fantastic voyage. 1966.
Through a glass clearly (stories). 1967.
Asimov's mysteries. 1968.
A whiff of death. 1968.
Nightfall and other stories. 1970.
The gods themselves. 1972.
Space ranger. 1973.

As †Paul French
David Starr, space ranger. 1952.
Lucky Starr and the pirates of the asteroids. 1953.
Lucky Starr and the oceans of Venus. 1954.
Lucky Starr and the big sun of Mercury. 1956.
Lucky Starr and the moons of Jupiter. 1957.
Lucky Starr and the rings of Saturn. 1958.

Other Works
Biochemistry and human metabolism (with
    William C. Boyd and Burnham S. Walker).
    1952.
The chemicals of life: enzymes, vitamins, hor-
    mones. 1954.
Races and people (with William C. Boyd). 1955.
Inside the atom. 1956.
Chemistry and human health (with Burnham S.
    Walker and Mary K. Nicholas). 1956.
Building blocks of the universe. 1957.

The world of carbon. 1958.
The world of nitrogen. 1958.
Words of science and the story behind them. 1959.
Realm of numbers. 1959.
The clock we live on. 1959.
Breakthroughs in science. 1960.
The double planet. 1960.
The wellsprings of life. 1960.
The kingdom of the sun. 1960.
The intelligent man's guide to science. 1960.
Satellites in outer space. 1960.
Realm of measure. 1960.
The river of life (alternative title, The blood-
    stream). 1961.
Words from the myths. 1961.
Realm of algebra. 1961.
Marvels of science. 1962.
Words on the map. 1962.
Words in Genesis. 1962.
The search for the elements. 1962.
Life and energy. 1962.
Fact and fancy. 1962.
The human body: its structure and operation.
    1963.
The kite that won the revolution. 1963.
The genetic code. 1963.
View from a height. 1963.
A short history of biology. 1964.
Quick and easy maths. 1964.
The human brain. 1964.
Planets for man (with Stephen Dole). 1964.
Adding a dimension. 1964.
Asimov's biographical encyclopaedia of science
    and technology. 1964.
A short history of chemistry. 1964.
The Greeks: a great adventure. 1965.
Of time and space and other things. 1965.
The new intelligent man's guide to science.
    1965.
An easy introduction to the slide rule. 1965.
The neutrino: ghost particle of an atom. 1966.
The Roman republic. 1966.
Understanding physics. 1966.
Genetic effects of radiation (with T. Dobzhansky).
    1966.
The noble gases. 1966.
The universe. 1966.
The moon. 1966.
Is anyone there? (essays). 1966.
To the ends of the universe. 1967.
The Egyptians. 1967.
Mars. 1967.
From earth to Heaven; 17 essays on science. 1967.
Environments out there. 1967.

Science, numbers and I (essays). 1968.
The Near East: 1000 years of history. 1968.
Asimov's guide to the Bible. 2 vols. 1968–9.
The dark ages. 1968.
Galaxies. 1968.
Stars. 1968.
Words from history. 1968.
Photosynthesis. 1969.
20th-century discovery. 1969.
Opus 100. 1969.
ABCs of space. 1969.
Great ideas of science. 1969.
The solar system and back. 1970.
Asimov's guide to Shakespeare. 2 vols. 1970.
Constantinople. 1970.
ABCs of the ocean. 1970.
Lights. 1970.
Stars in their courses. 1971.
What makes the sun shine? 1971.
Isaac Asimov's treasury of humor. 1971.
The sensuous dirty old man (as Dr. Asimov). 1971.

ASTLEY, THEA BEATRICE MAY
(*Mrs.* **EDMUND GREGSON**) (1925–   )
Australian novelist; born in Brisbane; educated
University of Queensland, Brisbane; taught English (1944–67); Senior Tutor, Macquarie University (1968–   ); a contributor to periodicals and
anthologies; editor of *Coast to Coast 1969–70*
(1971).

Bibliography
Australian national bibliography.
Contemporary novelists.

Novels
Girl with a monkey. 1959.
A descant for gossips. 1960.
The well-dressed explorer. 1962.
The slow natives. 1965.
A boat load of home folk. 1968.

ATHILL, DIANA (1917–   )
English novelist; born in London; educated at
Lady Margaret Hall, Oxford; research worker in
the B.B.C. (1941–6); editor for Allan Wingate,
publishers (1946–51); director of André Deutsch,
publishers (1952–   ); a contributor to *London
Magazine, Harper's Bazaar*, etc.; has translated *The
Sultans of Christine de Rivoyre* (1968).

Bibliography
B.N.B.
Gale.

Novels and Short Stories
An unavoidable delay and other stories. 1962.
Don't look at me like that. 1967.

Autobiography
Instead of a letter. 1962.

ATWOOD, MARGARET ELEANOR
(1939–   )
Canadian poet and novelist; born in Ottawa; educated at Toronto and Harvard universities;
travelled widely; Lecturer in English, University
of British Columbia (1964–5); Instructor in English, Sir George William University, Montreal
(1967–8); recipient of several poetry awards; a contributor to *Tamarack Review, Canadian Forum,
Queen's Quarterly, New Yorker*, etc.; represented in
several anthologies including *New Voices in the
Commonwealth* (1968).

Bibliography
Canadiana.
C.B.I.
Contemporary poets.

Poetry
Double Persephone. 1961.
The circle game (Governor General's Award
   1967). 1966.
The animals in that country. 1968.
The journals of Susanna Moodie. 1970.
Procedures for underground. 1970.

Novels
The edible woman. 1969.
Surfacing. 1973.

AUCHINCLOSS, LOUIS STANTON
(†**ANDREW LEE**) (1917–   )
American novelist and writer; born in New York;
educated at Yale University; called to the New
York bar (1941); served in the U.S. Navy in the
Second World War (1941–5); author of several
plays; a contributor to the *New Yorker, Good
Housekeeping, Atlantic Monthly*, etc.; his edited
works are not listed below.

Bibliography
C.B.I.
Contemporary novelists.
Gale.
Who's who. 1973.

Novels
The indifferent children (as †Andrew Lee). 1947.
The injustice collectors. 1950.
Sybil. 1952.
A law for the lion. 1953.
The Romantic egoists. 1954.
The great world and Timothy Colt. 1956.
Venus in Sparta. 1958.
Pursuit of the prodigal. 1959.
The house of five talents. 1960.
Portrait in brownstone. 1962.
Powers of attorney (stories). 1963.
The rector of Justin. 1964.
The embezzler. 1966.
Tales of Manhattan. 1967.
A world of profit. 1968.
Second chance: tales of two generations. 1972.
I come as a thief. 1973.

Other Works
Edith Wharton. 1961.
Reflections of a Jacobite. 1962.
Ellen Glasgow. 1964.
Pioneers and caretakers: a study of nine American
    women novelists. 1965.
Motiveless malignity. 1968.
Henry Adams. 1971.
Richelieu. 1972.

AUCHTERLOUNIE, DOROTHY
(*Mrs.* **H. M. GREEN**) (1915–   )
English-born Australian poet; educated in England
and at Sydney University; news editor, Australian
Broadcasting Commission (1942–4); Principal of a
girls' college (1957–60); Senior Lecturer in English,
Canberra University (1964–   ); represented in
numerous anthologies; a contributor to *Meanjin,
Quadrant*, etc.

Bibliography
Annals of Australian literature.
Australian national bibliography.
Contemporary poets.

Poetry
Kaleidoscope. 1940.
The dolphin. 1967.

Literary Criticism
Fourteen minutes (with H. M. Green). 1950.

AUDLEY, ERNEST HENRY
New Zealand novelist.

Bibliography
C.B.I.
N.Z. national bibliography.

Novels
Myself when young. 1948.
Sometime – never (story). 1951.
Islands float at eleven. 1952.
No boots for Mr. Moehau. 1963.
A new gate for Mattie Dulivich. 1965.

AVISON, MARGARET (1918–   )
Canadian poet; educated at the University of
Toronto; a contributor to many anthologies and
periodicals.

Bibliography
Canadiana.
C.B.I.
Contemporary poets.
Gale.

Poetry
Winter sun (Governor General's Award 1961).
    1960.
The dumbfounding. 1966.

Other Work
The research compendium. 1964.

AWOONOR, KOFI
(AWOONOR-WILLIAMS, GEORGE)
(1935–   )
Ghanaian poet; educated at Achimota Secondary
School and the University of Ghana, Legon;
Research Fellow and Lecturer in African Literature
(1963–7); higher studies in London (1967–8) and
California; Chairman of the Department of Comparative Literature, State University of New York
(1967–8); has travelled widely; editor of *Okyeame*
and associate editor of *Transition* (1967–8); represented in numerous anthologies.

Bibliography
B.N.B.

C.B.I.
Jahn and Dressler.
Zell and Silver.

Poetry
This Africa. 1963.
Rediscovery and other poems. 1964.
Night of my blood. 1971.

Other Works
The breast of the earth: a study of the cultures and literature of Africa. 1971.
This earth, my brother. 1971.

AYCKBOURN, ALAN
(†ALLEN, RONALD) (1939–)
English playwright; educated at Haileybury and Imperial Service College, Herts.; actor and stage manager in repertory companies; B.B.C. Northern Region drama producer, Leeds (1964–70); artistic director, Scarborough Theatre Trust (1970–); unpublished plays include *Mr. Whatnot* (1963), *The story so far* (1970) and *Absurd person singular* (1973).

Bibliography
B.N.B.
Contemporary dramatists.
Gale.

Plays
Relatively speaking (staged as Meet my father, 1965). 1968.
Mixed doubles (with others). 1970.
How the other half loves. 1973.
Time and time again. 1973.

AYLMER, *Sir* FELIX
(*Sir* FELIX E. AYLMER-JONES)
(1889–1977)
English actor; educated at Exeter College, Oxford;

first London stage appearance (1911); served in the First World War (1914–18); President of Equity (1949–69); has played many leading roles on stage and in films, too numerous to specify; frequent broadcaster.

Bibliography
B.N.B.
Who's who. 1973.

Works
Dickens incognito. 1959.
The Drood case. 1964.

AYRTON, MICHAEL (1921–)
English painter, sculptor, illustrator and writer; educated in London, Vienna and Paris; art critic of the *Spectator* (1944–6); held exhibitions almost annually (1942–); décor for numerous theatrical productions including *Macbeth* (Gielgud) (1942), and Covent Garden's Purcell's *Fairy Queen* (1946 and 1951); documentary films of the drawings of Leonardo da Vinci (1953) and Greek sculpture (1960); has travelled widely.

Bibliography
B.N.B.
Gale.
Who's who. 1973.
Word and image I and II; two exhibitions N.B.L. 1971.

Works
British drawings. 1946.
Hogarth's drawings. 1948.
Tittivulus. 1953.
Degas. 1953.
Golden sections. 1957.
The testament of Daedalus. 1962.
Drawings and sculpture. 1962.
Virgil (with D. R. Dudley and others). 1964.
The maze maker. 1967.
Berlioz, a singular obsession. 1970.
Giovanni Pisano. 1970.
The rudiments of paradise. 1971.

B

BAGLEY, DESMOND (1923–)
English novelist; born at Kendal, Westmorland; freelance journalist; full-time novelist since 1963; has travelled widely.

Bibliography
Authors' and writers' who's who. 1971.
B.N.B.
Gale.

Novels
The golden keel. 1963.
High citadel. 1965.
Wyatt's hurricane. 1966.
Landslide. 1967.
The Vivero letter. 1968.
The spoilers. 1969.
Running blind. 1970.
The freedom trap (filmed as The mackintosh man, 1973). 1971.
The tightrope men. 1973.

BAIG, Mrs. TARA ALI (1916–)
Indian novelist and writer; born in Mussoorie and educated in Darjeeling, Switzerland, U.S.A. and Dacca University; a well-known social worker; President, Indian Council for Child Welfare; writes regularly for Indian and foreign journals.

Bibliography
C.B.I.
Indian national bibliography 1958–67.
National bibliography of Indian literature 1901–53.

Works
Women of India. 1956.
Directory of social services. 1964.
Moon in Rahu (novel). 1967.
Children's stories and "Zoleikha and the enchanted jungle". n.d.

BAIRD, ALEXANDER JOHN (1926–)
English poet and novelist; born in Liverpool; edu-

cated at Emmanuel College, Cambridge; Lecturer, University of Hiroshima, Japan (1959–62), and British Council (1963–5); Lecturer in Education, University of London Institute of Education (1965–); a contributor to the *London Magazine, Encounter, English Language Teaching, Listener, T.L.S.*

Bibliography
Authors' and writers' who's who. 1971.
B.N.B.
Contemporary poets.
Gale.

Novels
The mickey-hunters. 1957.
The unique sensations. 1959.

Poetry
Poems. 1963.

BAKER, CARLOS HEARD (1909–)
American novelist and scholar; educated at Harvard and Princeton universities; works in Department of English, Princeton (1937–); Professor (1951) and Woodrow Wilson Professor of English (1954–); awarded Litt.D., Dartmouth College (1957); his editions of English Romantic poets, etc., are not listed below.

Bibliography
C.B.I.
Gale.

Novels
A friend in power. 1958.
The land of Rumbelow. 1963.

Poetry
A year and a day. 1963.

Other Works
Shelley's major poetry: the fabric of a vision. 1948.
Hemingway: the writer as artist. 1952.
Ernest Hemingway: a life story. 1969.
The Gay Head conspiracy. 1973.

BAKER, ELLIOTT (1922–)
American novelist; educated at Indiana University; served in the U.S. Army during the Second World War; dramatised his novel *The penny wars* (produced 1969).

Bibliography
C.B.I.
Contemporary novelists.

Novels
A fine madness. 1964.
The penny wars. 1969.
Pocock and Pitt. 1971.

BAKER, RUSSELL WAYNE (1925–)
American journalist, essayist and humorist; educated as a lawyer at Princeton University; served with the U.S. Navy during the Second World War (1943–5); *Baltimore Sun* (1947–54); *New York Times* (1954–62); *Observer* (1962–).

Bibliography
C.B.I.

Works
An American in Washington. 1961.
No cause for panic. 1964.
All things considered. 1965.
Our next president. 1968.
Poor Russell's almanac. 1972.

BALDWIN, JAMES ARTHUR (1924–)
American Negro writer and novelist; born in New York; lived in Paris (1948–56); member of the Advisory Board for Racial Equality and many other bodies; active in Civil Rights movement in the United States; D.Litt., University of British Columbia (1963); a contributor to the *New Yorker, Harper's, Nation, Esquire*, etc.

Bibliography
B.N.B.
C.B.I.
Gale.
Who's who. 1973.

Novels
Go tell it on the mountain. 1953.
Giovanni's room. 1956.
Another country. 1962.
Going to meet the man (stories). 1965.
Tell me how long the train's been gone. 1968.
If Beal Street could talk. 1974.

Plays
The amen corner (produced 1955). 1955.
Blues for Mr. Charlie. 1964.
One day, when I was lost. 1972.
The woman at the well. 1972.

Essays
Notes of a native son. 1955.
Nobody knows my name (English title, No name in the street, 1972). 1961.
The fire next time. 1963.
Nothing personal (with Richard Avedon). 1964.
A rap on race (with Margaret Mead). 1971.

Other Work
One day, when I was lost (screenplay of Malcolm X's autobiography). 1972.

BALDWIN, MICHAEL (†MICHAEL JESSE) (1930–)
English poet and novelist; born at Gravesend; educated at St. Edmund Hall, Oxford; schoolmaster (1955–9); lecturer, College of Education (1959–); a contributor to the *Listener, T.L.S., Encounter*, etc.; edited *Poems by children* (1962) and *Billy the Kid* (1963).

Bibliography
Authors' and writers' who's who. 1971.
B.N.B.
Gale.

Novels and Short Stories
A world of men. 1962.
Miraclejack (also a film script). 1963.
A mouthful of gold. 1964.
Sebastian, and other voices (short stories). 1966.
The Great Cham. 1967.
Underneath and other situations (short stories). 1968.
There's a war on. 1970.

Poetry
The silent mirror [1953].
Voyage from spring. 1957.
Death on a live wire (with On stepping from a sixth storey window). 1962.
How Chas Egget lost his way in a creation myth. 1967.
Hob and other poems. 1972.

Educational Writing
Poetry without tears. 1959.
Poetry for children. 1962.

Autobiography
Grandad with snails. 1960.
In step with a goat. 1963.

BALLANTYNE, DAVID WATT
(1924–)
New Zealand novelist and journalist; born in Auckland; served in the New Zealand Army during the Second World War (1942–3); on the staff of the *Auckland Star* (1943–54), London *Evening News* (1955–63); editor of *Finding Out* (1964); feature writer, *Auckland Star* (1965–); recipient of various literary awards; a contributor to journals; many of his unpublished plays have been produced on British and New Zealand television.

Bibliography
B.N.B.
Contemporary novelists.
N.Z. national bibliography.

Novels
The Cunninghams. 1948.
The lost pioneer. 1963.
And the glory (stories). 1963.
A friend of the family. 1966.
Sydney Bridge upside down. 1968.

BALLARD, JAMES GRAHAM (1930–)
English science fiction writer; born in Shanghai; educated at King's College, Cambridge; served in the R.A.F.; a contributor to *Encounter, Ambit,* etc.

Bibliography
B.N.B.
Contemporary novelists.
Gale.

Novels
The wind from nowhere. 1962.
The drowned world. 1962.
The drought. 1965.
The crystal world. 1966.
The atrocity exhibition. 1970.
Crash. 1973.

Short Stories
The voices of time. 1962.
Billenium. 1962.
The 4-dimensional nightmare. 1963.

Passport to eternity. 1963.
The terminal beach. 1964.
The disaster area. 1967.
The day of forever. 1968.
The overloaded man. 1968.
Vermilion sands. 1971.

BALLIETT, WHITNEY (1926–)
American jazz musicologist and essayist; educated at Cornell University; on staff of *New Yorker* (1951–), of *Saturday Review, Atlantic Monthly* (1957–); contributor and performer on television.

Bibliography
C.B.I.

Writing on Jazz
The sound of surprise. 1959.
Dinosaurs in the morning. 1962.
Such sweet thunder. 1966.
Super-drummer: a profile of Buddy Rich. 1968.
Ecstasy at the Onion. 1971.

BANKS, LYNNE REID
(*Mrs.* CHAIM STEPHENSON) (1929–)
English–Israeli novelist; educated at the Royal Academy of Dramatic Art; acted in repertory (1949–53); wrote and worked for television (1954–61); taught in kibbutz schools in Israel (1962–71); her plays have been produced on radio and television; only her published plays are listed below.

Bibliography
B.N.B.
Contemporary novelists.

Novels
The L-shaped room (filmed 1962). 1960.
An end to running (American title, The house of hope). 1962.
Children at the gate. 1968.
The backward shadow. 1970.
One more river. 1972.
The kibbutz. 1972.

Plays
It never rains (televised and staged 1954). 1954.
The killer dies twice. 1956.
All in a row. 1956.
Already it is tomorrow (televised 1962). 1962.

BARKER, AUDREY LILIAN (1918–)
English novelist; worked with the Amalgamated Press (1936), the Cresset Press (1947–9) and the B.B.C. (1949–); the recipient of various literary awards.

Bibliography
B.N.B.
Contemporary novelists.
Gale.
Who's who. 1973.

Novels
Innocents (short stories) (Somerset Maugham Award 1947). 1947.
Apology for a hero. 1950.
Novelette and other stories. 1951.
The joy-ride and after (stories). 1963.
Lost upon the roundabouts (short stories). 1964.
A case examined. 1965.
The middling chapters in the life of Ellie Toms. 1967.
John Brown's body. 1969.
Femina real (stories). 1971.

BARLOW, JAMES HENRY STANLEY (†JAMES FORDEN) (1921–)
English novelist; born in Birmingham; educated in Leamington Spa, Newcastle and N. Wales; served in the R.A.F. during the Second World War (1940–1) and invalided out; worked for Birmingham Water Corporation (1946–60); full-time writer since 1960; a contributor to *Punch*, the *Sunday Times*, etc.

Bibliography
Authors' and writers' who's who. 1971.
B.N.B.
Gale.
Who's who. 1973.

Novels
The protagonists. 1956.
One half of the world. 1957.
The man with good intentions. 1958.
The patriots. 1960.
Term of trial (filmed 1962). 1961.
The hour of maximum danger. 1962.
This side of the sky. 1964.
One man in the world. 1966.
The love chase (as †James Forden). 1968.
The burden of proof (filmed as Villain, 1971). 1968.

Liner. 1970.
Both your houses. 1971.
All in good faith. 1971.

Autobiography
Goodbye, England. 1969.

BARNES, PETER (1931–)
English playwright; film critic of *Films and Filming* (1954); recipient of several awards; his unpublished plays include *Sclerosis* (1965), *Ring of spies* (1965), *The professionals* (1960).

Bibliography
B.N.B.
Contemporary dramatists.
Plays
The ruling class (staged 1968, filmed 1972). 1969.
Leonardo's last supper, and Noonday demons (staged 1969). 1970.
Lulu (adaptation of plays by Frank Wedekind, staged 1970). 1971.

BARON, JOSEPH ALEXANDER (né ALEC BERNSTEIN) (1917–)
English–Jewish novelist; served in the army during the Second World War (1939–45); a journalist (1945–8); freelance writer (1948–); television and film scriptwriter.

Bibliography
Authors' and writers' who's who. 1971.
B.N.B.
Gale.

Novels
From the city, from the plough. 1948.
The wine of Etna (alternative title, There is no home). 1950.
Rosie Hogarth. 1951.
Human kind (filmed as The Victors, 1963). 1953.
The golden princess. 1954.
Queen of the East. 1956.
Seeing life. 1958.
The lowlife (filmed). 1963.
Strip Jack naked. 1966.
King Dido. 1969.
The in-between time. 1971.

BARRY, CLIVE (1922–)
Australian novelist; born in Sydney; served in the Second World War; education officer in Africa; U.N. representative in the Congo (1961–).

Bibliography
Australian national bibliography.
B.N.B.
Contemporary novelists.

Novels
The spear grinner. 1963.
The crumb borne. 1965.
Fly Jamskoni. 1969.

BARSTOW, STANLEY (1928–)

English novelist; born in Yorkshire; engineering draughtsman (1944–62); full-time writer (1962–); has adapted several of his novels for radio; a contributor to television series *Z Cars*; a contributor to the *Yorkshire Post, Argosy*, etc.; editor of *Through the Green Woods* (1968).

Bibliography
Authors' and writers' who's who. 1971.
B.N.B.
Contemporary novelists.
Gale.
Who's who. 1973.

Novels
A kind of loving (filmed 1962 and dramatised 1970). 1960.
The desperadoes (short stories). 1961.
Ask me tomorrow (dramatised 1966). 1962.
Joby. 1964.
The watchers on the shore. 1966.
A raging calm. 1968.
A season with Eros (stories). 1971.

Play (with Alfred Bradley)
Stringer's last stand. 1972.

BARTH, JOHN SIMMONS (1930–)

American novelist; educated at Johns Hopkins University; Instructor in English, then Associate Professor, Pennsylvania State University (1953–65); Professor of English, New York State University, Buffalo (1966–); a contributor to *Kenyon Review, Hopkins Review, Esquire*, etc.

Bibliography
Authors' and writers' who's who. 1971.
C.B.I.
Contemporary novelists.
Gale.

Novels
The floating opera. 1956.

The end of the road (filmed 1969). 1958.
The sot-weed factor. 1960.
Giles goat-boy. 1966.
Lost in the funhouse; fiction for print, tape, live voice (stories). 1968.

BARTHELME, DONALD (1931–)

American novelist; served in the U.S. Army in Korea and Japan; newspaper reporter and museum director; editor, *Location*, an art and literary review; full-time writer; Guggenheim Fellow (1966).

Bibliography
C.B.I.
Contemporary novelists.
Gale.

Novels
Come back, Dr. Caligari (stories). 1964.
Snow white (*New Yorker* 1967). 1967.
Unspeakable practices, unnatural acts (stories). 1968.
City life (stories). 1971.
Sadness (stories). 1973.

BATES, RONALD GORDON NUDELL (1924–)

Canadian poet and writer; educated at Toronto University; English Lecturer at the University of Western Ontario; spent 3 years in Sweden; represented in several anthologies; a contributor to *Tamarack Review, Canadian Forum*, etc.

Bibliography
Canadiana.
C.B.I.
Contemporary poets.

Poetry
The wandering world. 1959.
The unimaginable circus, theatre and zoo (pr. ptd.). 1965.
Changes. 1968.

BAWDEN, NINA MARY (*née* MABEY, now *Mrs*. KARIS) (1925–)

English novelist; educated at Somerville College, Oxford; Town and Country Planning Association (1945–7); a contributor to *Evening Standard* and *London Mystery*.

Bibliography
Authors' and writers' who's who. 1971.
B.N.B.

Contemporary novelists.
Gale.

Novels
Eyes of green (American title, Who calls the tune?).
    1953.
The odd flamingo. 1954.
Change here for Babylon. 1955.
Solitary child. 1956.
Devil by the sea. 1957.
Just like a lady (American title, Glass slippers
    always pinch). 1960.
In honour bound. 1961.
Tortoise by candlelight. 1963.
Under the skin. 1964.
A little love, a little learning. 1966.
A woman of my age. 1967.
The grain of truth. 1969.
The birds in the trees. 1970.
Anna apparent. 1972.

For Children
The secret passage (American title, The house of
    secrets. 1964). 1963.
On the run (American title, Three on the run.
    1965). 1964.
The white horse gang. 1966.
The witch's daughter. 1966.
A handful of thieves. 1967.
The runaway summer. 1969.
Squib. 1971.
Carrie's war. 1972.

BAXTER, JAMES KEIR (1926–72)
New Zealand poet; educated at Otago and Victoria
universities; worked as a labourer and journalist;
editor of *Numbers* (1954–60); worked for the New
Zealand States Literary Fund; contributed to *Landfall, New Zealand Listener, Numbers*, etc.; represented in numerous anthologies.

Bibliography
B.M. catalogue.
Contemporary poets.
N.Z. national bibliography.

Poetry
Beyond the palisade. 1944.
Blow, wind of fruitfulness. 1948.
Poems unpleasant (with Anton Vogt and Louis
    Johnson). 1952.
The fallen house. 1953.
In fires of no return. 1958.
Howrah Bridge and other poems. 1962.

Pig Island letters. 1966.
Autumn testament. 1972.
Four God songs. 1972.
Letter to Peter Olds. 1972.
Runes. 1973.
Stonegut sugarworks. 1973.

Other Works
The fire and the anvil. 1955.
The iron breadboard. 1957.
The man on the horse. 1968.
Aspects of poetry in New Zealand. 1968.
Jerusalem daybook. 1972.
Six faces of love. 1972.

BAXTER, JOHN (†MARTIN LORAN)
(1939–)
Australian science fiction writer and cinema critic;
born and educated in Sydney; a contributor to
Science Fantasy, etc.; editor of *Film Digest*; government officer (1957–67); on the staff of the Commonwealth Film Unit (1967–70); awarded several
prizes for films; a contributor to *Bulletin, Nation*,
etc.; represented in various anthologies of short
stories.

Bibliography
Australian national bibliography.
B.N.B.
Gale.

Novels
The god-killers (American title, The off-
    worlders). 1966.
Adam's woman (from the film). 1970.

Other Works
Hollywood in the thirties. 1969.
Science fiction in the cinema. 1970.
The Australian cinema. 1970.
The gangster film. 1970.
The cinema of Josef von Sternberg. 1970.
The cinema of John Ford. 1970.

**BAYBARS, TANER
(†TIMOTHY BAYLISS)** (1936–)
Cypriot poet; born in Nicosia; came to England to
study; British Council officer (1956–); represented in numerous anthologies; his work in
Turkish is not listed below; has translated the
poetry of Nazim Hikmet (1967).

Bibliography
B.N.B.
Contemporary poets.

Novel
A trap for the burglar. 1965.

Poetry
To catch a falling man. 1963.

Autobiography
Plucked in a far-off land. 1970.

BAYLISS, JOHN CLIFFORD (†JOHN CLIFFORD) (1915–)

English poet; born in Gloucestershire; educated at St. Catherine's College, Cambridge; served in the R.A.F. in the Second World War; Colonial Service (1946–9); worked in publishing (1949–); his edited work is not listed below.

Bibliography
B.N.B.
Contemporary poets.
Gale.

Poetry
Indications. 1943.
The white knight. 1944.
Call wind to witness. 1945.
A romantic miscellany (with Derek Stanford). 1946.

Other Work (as †John Clifford)
Atlantis adventure. 1958.

BEAVER, BRUCE VICTOR (1928–)

Australian poet; born in Sydney; lived many years in New Zealand; now works in Sydney; recipient of several literary awards; represented in numerous anthologies.

Bibliography
Australian national bibliography.
B.M. catalogue.
Contemporary poets.

Novel
You can't come back. 1966.

Poetry
Under the bridge. 1961.
Sea wall and shoreline. 1964.
The hot men. 1965.
The hot spring. 1965.
The hot summer. 1965.
Open at random. 1967.
Letters to live poets. 1969.
Bruce Beaver reads from his own work. 1972.

BECK, WARREN

American novelist, short-story writer and scholar; educated at Columbia University; Instructor, now Professor of English at Lawrence College, Wisconsin (1926–); awarded various academic grants and awards; stories included in anthologies; a contributor to various journals and magazines.

Bibliography
C.B.I.
Contemporary novelists.
Gale.

Novels
Final score. 1944.
Pause under the sky. 1947.
Into thin air. 1951.

Short Stories
The blue sash. 1941.
The first fish. 1947.
The far whistle. 1951.
The rest is silence. 1963.

Other Works
Huck Finn at Phelps Farm. 1958.
Man in motion: Faulkner's trilogy. 1961.
Joyce's *Dubliners*: substance, vision and art. 1969.

BECKER, STEPHEN DAVID (†STEVE DODGE) (1927–)

American novelist and translator; educated at Harvard University; served in the U.S. Marines; has written screenplays; a contributor to numerous magazines and journals; his translations are not listed below.

Bibliography
C.B.I.
Contemporary novelists.
Gale.

Novels
The season of the stranger. 1951.
Shanghai incident. 1955.
Juice. 1959.
A covenant with death (filmed 1966). 1965.
The outcasts. 1967.
When the war is over. 1969.

Other Works
Comic art in America. 1959.
Marshall Field III: a biography. 1964.

BEDFORD, SYBILLE (1911–)
English novelist of German parentage; born in
Charlottenburg, Germany; a contributor to *Hori-
zon*, *Encounter*, *Vogue*, *Spectator*, etc.

Bibliography
Authors' and writers' who's who. 1971.
B.N.B.
Contemporary novelists.
Gale.

Novels
A legacy. 1956.
A favourite of the gods. 1963.
A compass of error. 1968.

Other Works
The sudden view: a Mexican journey. 1953.
The best we can do: an account of the trial of John
    Bodkin Adams. 1958.
A visit to don Ottavio. 1960.
The faces of justice; a traveller's report. 1961.
Aldous Huxley: a biography. Vol. I 1894–1939.
    1973.

BEER, PATRICIA (*Mrs.* PARSONS)
(1924–)
English poet; born in Devon; educated at St.
Hugh's College, Oxford; Lecturer in English,
University of Padua (1946–8) and British Institute,
Rome (1948); Senior Lecturer, Goldsmith's Col-
lege (1962–8); a contributor to the *Sunday Times*,
Listener, *New Statesman*, *Time and Tide*, etc.

Bibliography
Authors' and writers' who's who. 1971.
B.N.B.
Contemporary poets.
Gale.

Poetry
Loss of the Magyars. 1959.
The survivors. 1963.
Just like the resurrection. 1967.
The estuary. 1971.

Autobiography
Mrs. Beer's house. 1968.

BEHAN, BRENDAN (1923–64)
Irish playwright; educated by the French Sisters of
Charity in Dublin; joined the I.R.A. (1937); sentenced by a Liverpool court to 3 years in Borstal
(1939); sentenced by a military court in Dublin to
14 years (1942), of which he served 6.

Bibliography
Anger and after.
B.M. catalogue.
Gale.

Plays
The quare fellow (filmed 1962). 1956.
The hostage. 1958.

Other Works
Borstal boy (autobiography). 1958.
Brendan Behan's island; an Irish sketchbook. 1962.
Hold your hour and have another. 1963.
Brendan Behan's New York. 1964.
Confession of an Irish rebel. 1965.
The scarperer. 1966.
Richard Cork's leg. 1973.

BELL, DANIEL (1919–)
American sociologist; educated at Columbia University; managing editor, *New Leader*, New York
(1941–4); labour editor, *Fortune Magazine*
(1948–58); Professor of Sociology, Columbia
University (1959–); recipient of several awards;
a contributor to social science journals; his edited
work is not listed below.

Bibliography
C.B.I.
Gale.

Works
Marxist socialism in America. 1952.
The end of ideology. 1960.
The reforming of general education. 1966.
Toward the year 2000. 1969.
Confrontation: the student rebellion and the uni-
    versities (with Irving Kristol). 1969.
Coming of post-industrial society. 1973.

BELL, MARTIN (†TITUS OATES)
(1918–)
English poet; born in Southampton; educated at
University College, Southampton; member of the
Communist Party (1933–9); served in the Second
World War (1939–46); taught (1946–67); Gregory
Poetry Fellow, Leeds University (1966);
founder-member of *The Group* and *Writers' Work-
shop* (see p. 345 *Workshop*); opera critic of *Queen*
(1966); a contributor to the *Listener*, *New Statesman*,
Observer, *Guardian*.

Bibliography
B.N.B.
Contemporary poets.

Poetry
Collected poems 1938–67. 1967.
Letters from Cyprus (poetry and prose). 1970.

Other Works
Recent American fiction: a lecture. 1963.
The future of the moon. 1970.

BELL, WILLIAM (1924–48)
Ulster poet; born in Belfast; educated at Merton
College, Oxford; served in the Second World War
(1944–6); awarded the Carnegie medal for bravery
for rescuing a boy trapped on the cliffs near
Arbroath; killed climbing the Matterhorn without
guides; edited two volumes of *Poetry from Oxford in
Wartime* (1945 and 1947).

Bibliography
B.M. catalogue.

Poetry
Elegies. 1945.
Mountains beneath the horizon (edited by John
 Heath-Stubbs). 1950.

BELLOW, SAUL (1915–)
American novelist and playwright; educated at
Chicago University; editorial department, *Ency-
clopaedia Britannica* (1943–6); served in the Second
World War (1944–5); Associate Professor, Uni-
versity of Minnesota (1954–); a contributor to
the *New Yorker*, *New Republic*, *Nation*, *Saturday
Review*, etc.; some of his plays are published in
Collections of Modern Dramatists; edited *Great Jewish
Short Stories* (1963).

Bibliography
C.B.I.
Contemporary novelists.
Gale.
Spiller.
Who's who. 1973.

Novels
Dangling man. 1944.
The victim. 1947.
The adventures of Augie March. 1953.
Seize the day (short stories) and a play (The
 wrecker). 1956.
Henderson the rain king. 1959.
Herzog. 1964.
Mosby's memoirs and other stories. 1968.
Mr. Sammler's planet. 1970.

Play
The last analysis. 1967.

BENEDICTUS, DAVID (1938–)
English novelist; educated at Eton and Balliol College, Oxford; B.B.C. (1963–70); Assistant Director, Royal Shakespeare Company (1970–1); unpublished plays include *Fourth of June* (staged 1964)
and *What a way to run a revolution* (staged 1971);
television plays are *On the margin* series (1966) and
A day out (1972).

Bibliography
B.N.B.
Contemporary novelists.

Novels
The fourth of June. 1963.
You're a big boy now. 1963.
This animal is mischievous. 1965.
Hump; or, bone by bone alive. 1967.
The guru and the golf club. 1969.
The world of windows. 1971.

BENEDIKT, MICHAEL (1935–)
American poet; educated at New York and Columbia universities; editor for Horizon Books
(1959–62); freelance writer and editor (1962–);
edited *Modern French Theater* (1965), etc.; contributed translations to *Medieval Age* (1963); a contributor of poems and plays to *Poetry*, *Art and
Literature*, etc.; represented in various anthologies.

Bibliography
C.D.I.
Contemporary poets.
Gale.

Poetry
Changes: 21 poems. 1961.
The body. 1968.
Sky. 1970.
Mole notes. 1971.

BENNETT, ALAN (1934–)
English playwright and actor; educated at Exeter
College, Oxford; recipient of several awards.

Bibliography
B.N.B.
Contemporary dramatists.

Plays
Beyond the fringe (with others, staged 1960). 1962.
Forty years on (staged 1968). 1969.
Getting on (staged 1971). 1972.
Habeas corpus (staged 1972). 1973.

BENNETT, JOSEPHINE WATERS
(1899–)
American scholar; educated at the Ohio State University; held various academic posts; Professor of English, Hunter College, New York (1955–); awarded various academic honours; a contributor to learned journals; her edited works are not listed below.

Bibliography
C.B.I.
Gale.

Works
The evolution of The faerie queene. 1942.
The rediscovery of Sir John Mandeville. 1954.
Measure for measure as royal entertainment. 1966.
Theme of Spenser's Fowre hymns. 1970.

BENTLEY, ERIC (1916–)
English theatre critic, historian and playwright; educated at Oxford and Yale; taught history and directed plays at Black Mountain College (1942–4); Professor of Dramatic Literature, Columbia University (1954–); recipient of various awards; has translated much of Brecht; his edited work and translations are not listed below; a contributor to *Harper's*, *Kenyon Review*, etc.

Bibliography
C.B.I.
Gale.
N.C.B.E.L.

Works
A century of hero-worship (English title, The cult of the superman. 1947). 1944.
The playwright as thinker (English title, The modern theatre. 1948). 1946.
Bernard Shaw (alternative title, Bernard Shaw 1856–1950. 1957). 1947.
In search of the theatre. 1953.
The dramatic event. 1954.
What is theatre? 1956.
The life of the drama. 1964.
The theatre of commitment. 1967.
The theatre of the modern stage. 1968.

A time to die, and A time to live: 2 short plays. 1970.
Theatre of war. 1972.
Are you now or have you ever been? 1972.
The recantation of Galileo Galilei. 1972.

BERESFORD-HOWE, CONSTANCE ELIZABETH (1922–)
Canadian novelist; born in Montreal; educated at McGill and Brown universities; Assistant Professor at McGill University; has contributed short stories to *Saturday Night*, *McLean's*, etc.

Bibliography
Canadiana.
C.B.I.

Novels
The unreasoning heart. 1946.
Of this day's journey. 1947.
The invisible gate. 1949.
My lady greensleeves. 1955.

BERGER, JOHN (1926–)
English writer and novelist; educated at the Central and Chelsea schools of art; worked as a painter and art teacher.

Bibliography
B.N.B.
Contemporary novelists.

Novels
A painter of our time. 1958.
The foot of Clive. 1962.
Corker's freedom. 1964.
G (Booker Prize 1972; James Tait Black Prize 1973). 1972.

Other Works
Permanent red. 1960.
Selected essays and articles: the look of things. 1962.
A fortunate man. 1967.
Art and revolution. 1969.

BERGER, THOMAS LOUIS (1924–)
American novelist; educated at Cincinnati and Columbia universities; served in the U.S. Army during the Second World War; Librarian, Rand School of Social Science (1948–51); Associate Editor, *Popular Science Monthly* (1952–5); a contributor to *Saturday Evening Post*, etc.; his play *Other people* produced (1970).

Bibliography
C.B.I.
Contemporary novelists.
Gale.

Novels
Crazy in Berlin. 1958.
Reinhart in love. 1962.
Little big man (filmed). 1964.
Killing time. 1967.
Vital parts. 1970.

BERGONZI, BERNARD (1929–)
English scholar and literary critic; educated at
Wadham College, Oxford; Lecturer in English,
Manchester University (1959–66); Senior Lec-
turer, Warwick University (1966–); a con-
tributor to the *T.L.S.*, *Observer*, *New Society*, etc.

Bibliography
Authors' and writers' who's who. 1971.
B.N.B.
Gale.

Works
Godolphin and other poems. 1952.
Descartes and the animals. 1954.
The early H. G. Wells. 1961.
Anthony Powell (with P. Bloomfield and
  L. P. Hartley). 1962.
Heroes' twilight. 1965.
An English sequence (poems). 1966.
Innovations: essays on art and ideas. 1968.
T. S. Eliot: Four quartets, a casebook. 1969.
The situation of the novel. 1970.
The twentieth century (vol. 7 of the History of
  literature, Barrie and Jenkins). 1970.
T. S. Eliot. 1972.
Turn of a century. 1973.

BERLIN, *Sir* **ISAIAH** (1909–)
English philosopher; educated at St. Paul's School
and Corpus Christi College, Oxford; wartime diplomat (1941–6); Fellow of All Souls, Oxford
(1932–66); Chichele Professor of Social and Political Science (1957–67); President of Wolfson College, Oxford (1966–); President of the Aristotelian Society (1963–4); a member of many
learned academies; Governor of the University of
Jerusalem; awarded many academic honours;
C.B.E. (1946); broadcaster.

Bibliography
Authors' and writers' who's who. 1971.

B.N.B.
Gale.
Who's who. 1973.

Works
Karl Marx, his life and environment. 1939.
Translation of "First Love" by I. S. Turgenev.
  1950.
The hedgehog and the fox. Essay on Tolstoy's
  view of history. 1953.
Historical inevitability. 1954.
The age of enlightenment. 1956.
Life and opinions of Moses Hess. 1958.
Chaim Weizmann. 1958.
Two concepts of liberty. 1959.
John Stuart Mill and the ends of life. 1962.
Mr. Churchill in 1940. 1964.
Four essays on liberty. 1969.
Essays on J. L. Austin. 1973.

BERNARD, OLIVER (1925–)
English poet and translator; educated at Goldsmith's College, London. His edited work and
translations are not listed below.

Bibliography
B.N.B.
Contemporary poets.
Gale.

Poetry
Country matters. 1960.

BERRYMAN, JOHN (1914–)
American poet; educated at Columbia University
and Clare College, Cambridge; various academic
posts (1939–55); now Professor of Humanities,
Minnesota University; recipient of several literary
awards; a contributor to *Five Young American Poets*
(1940); *Southern Review, Kenyon Review, Nation*,
etc.; editor of Nash's *Unfortunate Traveller* (1960),
etc.

Bibliography
C.B.I.
Contemporary poets.
Gale.
L. of C.

Novel
Recovery. 1973.

Poetry
Poems. 1942.

The dispossessed. 1948.
Homage to Mistress Bradstreet and other poems.
  1956.
His thought made pockets and the plane buckt.
  1958.
77 dream songs (Pulitzer Prize 1965). 1964.
Berryman's sonnets. 1967.
Short poems. 1967.
His toy, his dream, his rest; 308 dream songs. 1968.
Dream songs. 1969.
Love and fame. 1970.
Selected poems 1938–68. 1972.
Delusions. 1972.

Biography
Stephen Crane. 1950.

BERTON, PIERRE FRANCIS DE MARIGNY (1920–)

Canadian journalist and writer; born in Yukon; educated at British Columbia University; journalist with the Vancouver *News*, *Herald*, *Sun*, *MacLean's Magazine*, Toronto *Star*, etc. (1942–); editor-in-chief of *MacLean's* (1963–); a contributor to *Reader's Digest*, *MacLean's*, *Toronto Quarterly*, radio, television, etc.; scriptwriter and narrator of the film *City of Gold*.

Bibliography
Authors' and writers' who's who. 1971.
Canadiana.
C.B.I.
Gale.

Works
The Royal family. 1954.
Stampede for gold. 1955.
The mysterious north. 1956.
Klondike fever. 1958.
Just add water and stir. 1959.
Adventures of a columnist. 1960.
The new city; a prejudicial view of Toronto. 1961.
The secret world of Og (for children). 1961.
Fast, fast, fast, relief. 1962.
The big sell. 1963.
The comfortable pew. 1965.
My war with the twentieth century. 1965.
The centennial food guide. 1966.
Remember yesterday. 1967.
Voices of the sixties. 1967.
The cool, crazy, committed world of the sixties.
  1967.
The making of the nation. 1967.
The smug minority. 1968.

BESTER, ALFRED (1913–)

American science fiction writer; educated at the University of Pennsylvania; full-time writer; has written many television scripts; a regular contributor to *Holiday*, *Venture*, *Vogue*, etc.

Bibliography
C.B.I.
Gale.

Novels
Who he? 1953.
The demolished man. 1953.
The rat race. 1955.
Tiger, Tiger! (Original title, The stars my destination. 1946.) 1956.
Starburst. 1958.
The dark side of the earth. 1964.

BEVAN, JACK (1920–)

English poet; born in Blackpool; educated at Cambridge University; served in the army in the Second World War (1940–6); Head of English Drama, Nonington College, Kent (1953–61); Senior Lecturer, Liverpool College of Art (1961–); a contributor to the *T.L.S.*, *English*, *New Opinion*, etc.; translated the poetry of Salvatore Quasimodo (1965).

Bibliography
B.N.B.
Gale.

Poetry
Dragon's teeth. 1957.
Brief candles. 1961.
My sad pharaohs. 1968.

BHAGAT, O. P. (1929–)

Indian poet and journalist; born in Dera Ismail Khan; educated at the Agra and Punjab universities; writes poems, sketches, short stories and children's stories for various Indian papers.

Bibliography
C.B.I.
Indian national bibliography 1958–67.
National bibliography of Indian literature 1901–53.

Poems
Another planet. 1967.
King-makers. 1968.

BHASKARAN, M. P. (1921–)
Indian poet; educated at Madras and Leeds universities; taught English in Madras (1949–63); Professor of English, Bangalore (1963–); translated the complete poetry of Asan from Mayalami; a contributor to *Illustrated Weekly of India*, *Thought*, New Delhi, etc.; represented in Indo-Anglian anthologies.

Bibliography
Contemporary poets.
Indian dictionary of national biography.

Poetry
The dancer and the ring. 1962.

BHATIA, PREM (1911–)
Indian writer and journalist; born and educated in Lahore; one-time editor of the *Tribune* (Punjab); High Commissioner in Kenya and Singapore.

Bibliography
C.B.I.
Indian D.N.B.
Indian national bibliography 1958–67.
National bibliography of Indian literature 1901–53.

Works
All my yesterdays. 1973.
Indian ordeal in Africa. n.d.

BHATTACHARYA, BHABINI (1906–)
Indian novelist; educated at Patna and London universities; press attaché, Indian Embassy, Washington D.C. (1949–50); consultant, Ministry of Education, Delhi (1961–7); currently Visiting Professor, University of Hawaii, Honolulu; recipient of various awards, his translations from Tagore are not listed below.

Bibliography
B.N.B.
Contemporary novelists.
Gale.
Indian national bibliography 1964–72.

Novels
So many hungers. 1947.
Music for mohini. 1952.
He who rides a tiger. 1954.
A goddess named gold. 1960.
Shadow from Ladakh. 1966.
Steel hawk and other stories. 1968.

Other Works
Some memorable yesterdays. 1940.
Indian cavalcade. 1944.
Gandhi the writer. 1969.

BILLING, JOHN GRAHAM (1936–)
New Zealand novelist and writer on Antarctic exploration.

Bibliography
C.B.I.
N.Z. national bibliography.

Novels
Forbush and the penguins (filmed). 1965.
The alpha trip. 1969.
Status. 1971.

Other Works
Antarctic regions. 1964.
South: man and nature in Antarctica: a New Zealand view. 1964.
New Zealand, the sunlit land. 1966.

BINGHAM, CHARLOTTE
(*Mrs.* BRADY) (1942–)
English writer; daughter of Madeleine and John Bingham (qq.v.); educated at the Sorbonne.

Bibliography
Authors' and writers' who's who. 1971.
B.N.B.

Novels
Coronet among the weeds. 1963.
Lucinda. 1965.
Coronet among the grass. 1972.

BINGHAM, JOHN MICHAEL WARD
(*7th Baron* CLANMORRIS) (1908–)
English detective novelist; educated at Cheltenham College and in France and Germany; journalist (1931–9); served in the army during the Second World War (1939–40); Control Commission in Germany during the 1940s; Ministry of Defence (1950–).

Bibliography
B.N.B.
Gale.
Who's who. 1973.

Novels
My name is Michael Sibley. 1952.

Five roundabouts to heaven (American title, The tender poison). 1953.
The third skin. 1954.
The Paton Street case (American title, Inspector Morgan's dilemma). 1955.
Marion (American title, Murder off the record). 1957.
Murder plan six. 1958.
Night's black agent. 1961.
A case of libel. 1963.
A fragment of fear (filmed 1969). 1965.
The double agent. 1966.
I love, I kill. 1969.
Vulture in the sun. 1971.

BINGHAM, MADELEINE (†JULIA MANNERING) (1912–)

English writer; wife of John Bingham (Baron Clanmorris) and mother of Charlotte Bingham (qq.v.); contributes to *Harper's*, *Vanity Fair*, *Punch*, etc.

Bibliography
C.B.I.
Gale.

Prose Works
The passionate poet (as †Julia Mannering). 1951.
Look to the rose (as †Julia Mannering). 1953.
Cheapest in the end. 1963.
Your wedding guide. 1967.
Something's burning: a bad cook's guide. 1968.
Teach your own child. 1968.
A career for your daughter. 1969.
Mary, Queen of Scots. 1970.
Scotland under Mary Stuart. 1971.
Sheridan: the track of a comet. 1972.

BIRLEY, JULIA (*née* DAVIES) (1928–)

English novelist; educated at Lady Margaret Hall, Oxford; taught classics (1950–4); a contributor to various periodicals.

Bibliography
B.N.B.
Gale.

Novels
The children on the shore. 1958.
The time of the cuckoo. 1960.
When you were there. 1963.
A serpent's egg. 1966.

BISHOP, ELIZABETH (1911–)

American poet; educated at Vassar College; lives in Brazil and the U.S.; consultant in poetry to the Library of Congress (1949–50), and in American letters (1958–); recipient of various literary awards; has travelled widely; represented in various anthologies; a contributor to the *New York Review of Books*, *Kenyon Review*, etc.; translated *Diary of Helena Morley* (1957).

Bibliography
C.B.I.
Contemporary poets.
Gale.
L. of C.

Poetry
North and south. 1946.
"Poems—north and south"—and a cold spring (Pulitzer Prize 1956). 1956.
Questions of travel. 1965.
Selected poems. 1967.
Ballad of the burglar of Babylon. 1968.
Complete poems. 1969.

Other Work
Brazil. 1967.

BISSELL, CLAUDE THOMAS (1916–)

Canadian critic and editor; educated at Toronto and Cornell universities; served in the Second World War (1941–6); Assistant Professor of English, University College, Toronto; Vice-President of Toronto University (1952–6); President of Carleton College, Ottawa (1956–8); President of Toronto University (1958–); a contributor of literary and educational articles to various academic journals.

Bibliography
Canadiana.
C.B.I.

Edited Works
University college: a portrait. 1953.
Our living tradition. 1957.
Canada's crisis in higher education. 1958.
The strength of the university: selected addresses. 1968.

BLACK, DAVID MACLEOD (1941–)

Scottish poet; born in South Africa; educated at Edinburgh University; lives in Brighton; represented in *The Faber Book of Modern Scottish Poetry* (1966), etc.

Bibliography
Contemporary poets.
Gale.

Poetry
Rocklestrakes. 1961.
Theory of diet. 1967.
With decorum. 1967.
A dozen short poems. 1968.
Penguin modern poets no. 11 (with Peter Red-
grove and D. M. Thomas). 1968.
The educators. 1969.

BLACK, HERMINA
Indian novelist.

Bibliography
C.B.I.
Indian national bibliography 1958–67.
National bibliography of Indian literature
1901–53.

Novels
Desert hearts. 1963.
The lordship of love. 1964.
Break with the past. 1964.
Distant star. 1964.
The house of fountains. 1965.
Yesterday's folly. 1965.
My old love came. 1965.
Gold moon of Africa. n.d.

BLACKBURN, PAUL (1926–71)
American poet and translator; educated at New
York, Wisconsin and Toulouse universities; served
in the U.S. Army; travelled in Spain (1953–7);
poetry editor of *Nation* (1962–71); translated *El Cid*
and other Spanish and Provençal poetry.

Bibliography
C.B.I.
Gale.

Poetry
The dissolving fabric. 1955.
Brooklyn–Manhattan transit. 1960.
The nets. 1961.
Sing-song. 1966.
The cities. 1967.
In, on, or about the premises. 1968.
Early selected Xmas: collected poems 1947–1961.
1972.

BLACKBURN, THOMAS (1916–)
English poet; educated at Durham University;
Gregory Poetry Fellow, Leeds University
(1956–8); Senior Lecturer in English, College of St.
Mark and St. John, Chelsea; edited an anthology of
post-war poetry, *45–60* (1960); a contributor to the
New Statesman, London Magazine, Listener, etc.; his
edited work is not listed below.

Bibliography
Authors' and writers' who's who. 1971.
B.N.B.
Contemporary poets.

Poetry
The outer darkness. 1951.
The holy stone. 1954.
In the fire. 1956.
The next word. 1958.
A smell of burning. 1961.
The price of an eye. 1961.
A breathing space. 1964.
Gift of tongues. 1967.

Criticism
Robert Browning. 1967.

Autobiography
A clip of steel. 1969.

Libretto
The Judas tree. 1965.

**BLAKE, ROBERT NORMAN
WILLIAM** (*Baron* **BLAKE**) (1916–)
English historian and biographer; educated at
Magdalen College, Oxford; served in the army in
the Second World War (1939–45); Fellow and
Tutor, Christ Church, Oxford (1946–69); Senior
Proctor (1959–60); Provost of The Queen's Col-
lege, Oxford (1968–); created a life peer (1971).
Edited the private papers of Douglas Haig 1914–19
(1952).

Bibliography
Authors' and writers' who's who. 1971.
B.N.B.
Gale.
Who's who. 1973.

Works
The unknown Prime Minister (Life of Andrew
Bonar Law). 1955.

31

Disraeli. 1966.
Disraeli and Gladstone (Leslie Stephen lecture. 1969). 1969.
The Conservative Party from Peel to Churchill. 1970.

BLASER, ROBIN (†AVALON) (1925–)
American poet; born in Denver, Colorado; educated at the University of California, Berkeley; has travelled extensively; Lecturer in Poetry, Simon Fraser University, British Columbia; represented in various anthologies; a contributor to little magazines; has translated the work of Gérard de Nerval (1965).

Bibliography
C.B.I.
Contemporary poets.

Poetry
The moth poem. 1964.
Cups. 1968.

BLECHMAN, BURT (1932–)
American novelist; educated at the University of Vermont; works as a full-time writer.

Bibliography
C.B.I.
Contemporary novelists.
Gale.

Novels
How much? 1961.
The war of Camp Omongo. 1963.
Stations. 1964.
The octopus papers. 1965.
Maybe. 1967.

BLISH, JAMES BENJAMIN (1921–)
American science fiction writer; educated at Rutgers and Columbia universities; served in the U.S. Army during the Second World War (1942–4); journalist in New York and Washington (1947); a contributor to numerous periodicals.

Bibliography
C.B.I.
Gale.

Novels
Jack of eagles. 1951.
There shall be no darkness (with Witches three). 1952.

The warriors of the day. 1953.
Earthman, come home. 1955.
They shall have stars. 1956.
The seedling stars. 1956.
Fallen star. 1957.
The frozen year. 1957.
The triumph of time. 1958.
A case of conscience. 1958.
Vor. 1958.
A clash of cymbals (stories). 1959.
The duplicated man (with Robert Lowndes). 1959.
Galactic cluster. 1960.
The star dwellers. 1961.
Titan's daughter. 1961.
The night shapes. 1962.
Life for the stars. 1962.
Doctor Mirabilis. 1964.
The issue at hand. 1964.
Mission to the heart stars. 1965.
Best science fiction stories of James Blish. 1965.
Star trek. 1967.
Welcome to Mars! 1967.
A torrent of faces (with Norman L. Knight). 1968.
The vanished jet. 1968.
Black Easter, or Faust Aleph-null. 1968.
We all died naked (in Three for tomorrow). 1969.
Anywhen. 1970.
Spock must die: a star trek novel. 1970.
And all the stars a stage. 1971.
Day after Judgement. 1971.
Midsummer century. 1972.

BLOOM, HAROLD (1930–)
American scholar; educated at Cornell and Yale universities; Yale University Instructor to Professor of English (1955–65), Professor (1965–); his edited works are not listed below.

Bibliography
C.B.I.
Gale.

Works
Shelley's mythmaking. 1959.
The visionary company. 1961.
Blake's apocalypse. 1963.
Yeats. 1970.
Ringers in the tower: studies in the Romantic tradition. 1971.
The anxiety of influence: a theory of poetry. 1973.

BLOOMFIELD, ANTHONY (†JOHN WESTGATE) (1922–)
English novelist; born in London; served in the

R.A.F. in the Second World War; B.B.C. Duty Officer (1955–); a contributor to *Writing Today, Books and Bookmen*, etc.; author of television scripts; his television plays as †John Westgate have not been published.

Bibliography
Authors' and writers' who's who. 1971.
B.N.B.
Gale.

Novels
Russian roulette. 1955.
The delinquents. 1958.
The tempter. 1961.
Throw. 1965.
Life for a life. 1971.

BLUM, JOHN MORTON (1921–)

American historian; educated at Harvard University; served in the U.S. Navy (1943–6); Massachusetts Institute of Technology, Associate Professor (1948–57); Professor of History, Yale University (1957–); Pitt Professor of American History, Cambridge (1963–4); member of many learned associations; his edited work is not listed below.

Bibliography
C.B.I.
Gale.

Works
Joe Tumulty and the Wilson era. 1951.
The Republican Roosevelt. 1954.
Woodrow Wilson and the politics of morality. 1956.
From the Morgenthau diaries: vol. I: Years of crisis. 1959; vol. II: Years of urgency. 1965; vol. III: Years of war. 1967.
Promise of America: an historical enquiry. 1965.
Roosevelt and Morgenthau. 1970.

BLY, ROBERT E. (1926–)

American poet; educated at Harvard and State University of Iowa; served in the U.S. Navy (1944–6); publisher and editor (1958–) and translator; has translated several volumes of verse from the Spanish, Swedish and German.

Bibliography
C.B.I.
Contemporary poets.
Gale.
L. of C.

Poetry
The lion's tail and eyes (with W. Duffy and J. Wright). 1962.
Silence in the snowy fields. 1962.
The sea and the honeycomb. 1966.
The light around the body. 1967.
Shadows–mothers. 1970.
Forty poems touching on recent American history. 1970.
Teeth–mother naked at last. 1971.
Neruda and Vallejo: selected poems. 1971.
Jumping out of bed. 1972.
Sleeping joining hands. 1973.
The old man rubbing his eyes (with Franz Richter). 1973.

Other Work
McGrath. 1972.

BOLD, ALAN NORMAN (1943–)

English poet and journalist; worked on the editorial staff of the *T.L.S.* (1966–7); edited the *Penguin modern poets no. 15* (1969) and the *Penguin book of Socialist verse* (1970).

Bibliography
B.N.B.
Contemporary poets.

Poetry
Society inebrius. 1965.
To find the new. 1967.
A perpetual motion machine. 1969.
The state of the nation. 1969.
A pint of bitter. 1971.
He will be greatly missed. 1971.

BOLT, ROBERT OXTON (1924–)

English playwright; educated at Manchester Grammar School and Manchester University; served in the Second World War; taught (1950–8); has written for radio, television and cinema; wrote the script for the film *Lawrence of Arabia*.

Bibliography
B.N.B.
Gale.
Who's who, 1973.

Plays
The flowering cherry (staged 1957). 1958.
A man for all seasons (televised 1957, staged 1960). 1961.
The tiger and the horse (staged 1960). 1961.

Gentle Jack (staged 1963). 1964.
The thwarting of Baron Bolligrew (for children).
   1967.
Vivat! Vivat Regina! 1971.

BOND, EDWARD (1934–)
English playwright; National Serviceman; member of the Royal Court Theatre Writers' group; recipient of various awards; wrote the film script *Blow Up* (1967).

Bibliography
B.N.B.
Contemporary dramatists.
Gale.

Plays
Saved (staged 1965). 1966.
Narrow road to the deep North. 1968.
Early morning. 1968.
Passion (in Plays and players). 1971.
The Pope's wedding and other plays (includes Mr.
   Dog, The king with the golden eyes, Sharpville
   sequence, Black mass). 1971.
Lear (staged 1971). 1972.
The sea. 1973.

BOND, RUSKIN (1934–)
Indian novelist; a full-time writer (1956–); a contributor to *Reader's Digest, Illustrated Weekly of India, Christian Science Monitor*, etc.; editor of *Imprint*, Bombay.

Bibliography
B.N.B.
Gale.
Indian national bibliography 1958–67.

Novels
The room on the roof (John Llewelyn Rhys Prize
   1957). 1957.
The neighbour's wife and other stories. 1967.
Panther's moon. 1969.
The last tiger. 1970.
Angry river (for children). 1972.
Love is a sad song. 1973.
Man-eater of Manjari and other stories. 1973.

BONHAM-CARTER, HELEN VIOLET
(*Baroness* ASQUITH) (1887–1969)
Daughter of Earl of Oxford and Asquith; among much public work she was President of the Women's Liberal Federation and President of the Royal Institute of International Affairs (1964–9);

Romanes Lecturer, Oxford (1963); D.B.E. (1953); Hon. LL.D., Sussex University (1963); life peeress as Baroness Asquith of Farnbury (1964); writer of radio and television scripts; a contributor to many periodicals.

Bibliography
B.N.B.
Gale.
Who's who. 1969.

Work
Winston Churchill as I knew him. 1965.

BONHAM-CARTER, VICTOR (1913–)
English writer; born at Bearsted, Kent; educated at Winchester and Magdalene College, Cambridge; served in the Second World War (1939–45); farmed for some years; freelance writer; secretary of the Royal Literary Fund; planning officer, Society of Authors; partner of the Exmoor Press; awarded several military medals and the Belgian Order of Leopold, etc.; a contributor to the *Countryman, Country Life, Spectator, T.L.S.*, etc.; author of many radio scripts; his edited work includes *Surgeon in the Crimea*.

Bibliography
Authors' and writers' who's who. 1971.
B.N.B.
Gale.
Who's who. 1973.

Works
The English village (with W. B. Curry). 1952.
Dartington Hall (with W. B. Curry). 1958.
Farming the land. 1959.
In a liberal tradition. 1960.
Exploring parish churches. 1961.
Soldier true (American title, Strategy of victory).
   1963.
The survival of the English countryside. 1971.

BOORSTIN, DANIEL JOSEPH
(†PROFESSOR X) (1914–)
American historian; born in Atlanta; educated at Harvard, Oxford and Yale universities; called to the Bar, Inner Temple (1937), and Massachusetts (1942); academic and legal posts in America, Rome, India, etc. (1939–60); first Professor of American History, Sorbonne, Paris (1961–2); Pitt Professor of American History, Cambridge (1964–5); recipient of various literary awards; editor of the *History of American civilization*, 25

vols., and formerly editor of American history for the *Encyclopaedia Britannica*.

Bibliography
C.B.I.
Gale.

Works
The mysterious science of the law. 1941.
The lost world of Thomas Jefferson. 1948.
The genius of American politics. 1952.
The Americans: the colonial experience. 1958.
America and the image of Europe. 1959.
The image: what happened to the American dream? 1961.
The Americans: the national experience. 1965.
Landmark history of the American people. 1968.
Decline of radicalism: reflections of America today. 1969.
Sociology of the absurd (by †Professor X). 1970.
American civilization. 1972.
The Americans: the democratic experience. 1973.

BOOTH, PHILIP E. (1923–   )
American poet; educated at Dartmouth College and Columbia University; served in the U.S. Air Force (1944–5); after several academic posts (1949–61) Associate Professor of English, Syracuse University, N.Y.; recipient of several literary awards; a contributor to journals; his edited work is not listed below.

Bibliography
C.B.I.
Contemporary poets.
Gale.
L. of C.

Poetry
Letter from a distant land. 1957.
The islanders. 1961.
Weathers and edges. 1966.
Margins. 1970.

BOOTH, WAYNE C. (1921–   )
American critic; educated at Chicago University; served in the U.S. Army during the Second World War (1944–6); held various academic posts, mostly in the University of Chicago, being currently Professor of English and Dean of the college there; a contributor to learned and professional journals; edited *Knowledge most worth having* (1967).

Bibliography
C.B.I.
Gale.

Works
The rhetoric of fiction. 1961.
Don't try to reason with me: essays and ironies for a credulous age. 1970.
Modern dogma and the rhetoric of assent. 1974.

BOOTHROYD, JOHN BASIL (1910–   )
English humorous writer; served with the R.A.F. Police in the Second World War (1941–5); a contributor to *Punch* continuously since 1938; *Punch* staff (1952–   ); member of the *Punch* Table (1955); broadcaster and journalist.

Bibliography
Authors' and writers' who's who. 1971.
B.N.B.
Who's who. 1973.

Works
Home Guard goings-on. 1941.
Adastral bodies. 1942.
Are sergeants human? 1945.
Are officers necessary? 1946.
Lost, a double-fronted shop. 1947.
The house about a man. 1959.
Motor if you must. 1960.
To my embarrassment. 1961.
The whole thing's laughable. 1964.
A word in public. 1965.
You can't be serious. 1966.
Let's stay married. 1967.
Stay married abroad. 1968.
Boothroyd at bay (radio talks). 1970.
Philip: an informal biography (an approved biography of H.R.H. the Duke of Edinburgh). 1971.

BOTTRALL, MARGARET FLORENCE (*née* **SAUMEREZ SMITH**) (1909–   )
English literary scholar and biographer; educated at Lady Margaret Hall, Oxford; worked for the British Council in Sweden and Italy (1942–50); lecturer for Department of Education, Cambridge University (1954–   ); Senior Lecturer (1967–   ); has translated Dante for the B.B.C.; Basic English versions of *Pinocchio* and *Midshipman Easy* (with R. Bottrall); a contributor to *Criterion, T.L.S., The Times, Critical Quarterly*, etc.; edited the *Zephyr book of English verse* (1950) and *The way*

to blessedness, a modernised text of Thomas Traherne, *Christian ethicks* (1963).

Bibliography
B.N.B.

Works
The divine image. 1950.
George Herbert. 1954.
Isaak Walton. 1955.
Every man a phoenix. 1958.
Personal records. 1961.
William Blake: songs of innocence and experience: a casebook. 1970.

BOURJAILY, VANCE NYE (1922–)

American novelist; educated at Bowdoin College; served in the American Field Service during the Second World War (1942–4); co-founder and editor of *Discovery* (1951–3); U.S. State Department in South America, etc.; a contributor to the *New Yorker* and other journals.

Bibliography
C.B.I.
Contemporary novelists.
Gale.

Novels
The end of my life. 1947.
The hound of earth. 1953.
The violated. 1958.
Confessions of a spent youth. 1960.
The man who knows Kennedy. 1967.
Brill among the ruins. 1971.

Other Works
The girl in the abstract bed (cartoons). 1954.
The unnatural enemy (on hunting). 1963.

BOWEN, JOHN GRIFFITH (†JUSTIN BLAKE) (1924–)

English novelist and playwright; born in Calcutta; educated at Pembroke College, Oxford, and Ohio State University; assistant editor of the *Sketch* (1953–6); worked in advertising; copywriter (1956–60); script consultant, Associated Television (1960–7); contributes reviews to *Punch*, the *Sunday Times*, *T.L.S.*, etc.

Bibliography
B.N.B.
Contemporary novelists.
Gale.
Who's who. 1973.

Novels
The truth will not help us. 1956.
After the rain. 1958.
The centre of the green. 1959.
Storyboard. 1960.
The birdcage. 1962.
A world elsewhere. 1965.

Plays
The essay prize (Television plays: with others). 1962.
I love you, Mrs. Patterson (produced 1965). 1964.
After the rain (from the novel). 1967.
Little boxes (in Methuen modern plays). 1968.
The fall and redemption of man. 1968.
The disorderly women (in Methuen modern plays). 1969.
The Corsican brothers. 1970.
The waiting room. 1971.
Robin Redbreast. 1972.

For Children
Pegasus. 1957.
The mermaid and the boy. 1958.
Garry Halliday and the disappearing diamond (as †Justin Blake with Jeremy Bullmore). 1960.
Garry Halliday and the ray of death (as †Justin Blake with Jeremy Bullmore). 1961.
Garry Halliday and the kidnapped five (as †Justin Blake with Jeremy Bullmore). 1962.
Garry Halliday and the sands of time (as †Justin Blake with Jeremy Bullmore). 1963.
Garry Halliday and the flying foxes (as †Justin Blake with Jeremy Bullmore). 1964.

BOWEN, ROBERT O. (1920–)

American novelist and writer; educated at the universities of Alabama and North Wales; served in the U.S. Navy (1937–45); worked in many jobs; Associate Professor of English, Alaska Methodist University (1962–); co-editor of the *Alaska Literary Directory* (1964); head of North Employment Agency, Anchorage (1970–); a contributor to *Holiday, Contact, Saturday Review*, etc.; his edited work is not listed below.

Bibliography
C.B.I.
Contemporary novelists.
Gale.

Novels
The weight of the cross. 1951.
Bamboo. 1953.

Sidestreet. 1954.
Marlow the master and other stories. 1963.

Other Works
The truth about Communism. 1962.
The college style manual. 1963.
The Alaskan dictionary. 1965.

BOWERING, GEORGE
(†THE PANAVISION KID) (1935–   )
Canadian poet; educated at the universities of British Columbia and Western Ontario; Assistant Professor, University of Calgary (1963–6); editor of the Montreal poetry magazine *Imago*; a contributor to *Atlantic Monthly, Tamarack Review, London Magazine*, etc.

Bibliography
Canadiana.
C.B.I.
Contemporary poets.
Gale.

Poetry
Sticks and stones. 1963.
Points on the grid. 1964.
The man in yellow boots. 1965.
The silver wire. 1966.
Baseball. 1967.
Rocky Mountain foot. 1968.
Imago. 1968.
Two police poems. 1968.
Solitary walk (with others). 1968.
How I hear howl 1969
The gangs of Kosmos. 1970.
Vibrations. 1970.
Al Purdy. 1970.
George Vancouver: a discovery poem. 1970.
Genève. 1971.
Touch. 1972.

Novels
Mirror on the floor. 1967.
The story so far. 1972.

BOWERS, EDGAR (1924–   )
American poet; educated at University of N. Carolina and Stanford; served in the U.S. Army (1943–6); taught at Duke University, Durham, N. Carolina (1952–5); Harpur College, Birmingham, New York (1955–8); Professor of English, University of California (1958–   ); represented in various anthologies; contributes to *Poetry, Listener, New Statesman*, etc.

Bibliography
C.B.I.
Contemporary poets.
Gale.

Poetry
The form of loss. 1956.
Five American poets (with others). 1963.
The astronomers. 1965.
Living together: new and selected poems. 1973.

BOWLES, JANE SYDNEY (*née* AUER)
(1917–   )
American novelist; educated in the U.S.A. and Switzerland; now lives in Morocco.

Bibliography
C.B.I.
Contemporary novelists.
Gale.

Novels
Two serious ladies. 1943.
Plain pleasures (stories). 1966.
The collected works of Jane Bowles. 1966.

Play
In the summer-house. 1954.

BOWLES, PAUL FREDERICK (1911–   )
American novelist and composer; studied music with Aaron Copland; his musical works include film scores, chamber music and score for the *Glass Menagerie*; music critic of the *New York Herald Tribune*; a contributor of travel articles for *Holiday*; now lives in Morocco; his translations from the French, Italian and Arabic are not listed below.

Bibliography
C.B.I.
Contemporary novelists.
Gale.

Novels and Short Stories
The sheltering sky. 1949.
The delicate prey (stories). 1950.
Let it come down. 1952.
The spider's house. 1955.
The hours after noon (stories). 1959.
Up above the world. 1966.
A hundred camels in the courtyard (stories). 1967.
Time of friendship (stories). 1967.
Pages from Cold Point and other stories. 1968.

Poetry
Scores. 1968.
The thicket of spring and selected poems. 1972.

Travel
Yallah. 1957.
Their heads are green and their hands are blue.
  1963.

BOYARS, ARTHUR (1925–)
English poet; educated at Wadham College,
Oxford; edited *Mandrake* (1946–57); edited *International Literature Annual*; reviewer and broadcaster; translator of A. Boucourechliev, *Schumann*
(1959).

Bibliography
B.N.B.
Contemporary poets.

Poetry
Poems. 1944.
Poems. 1953.

BOYD, ROBIN (1919–)
Australian writer; born in Melbourne; educated as
an architect at the Royal Melbourne Institute of
Technology; served in the Australian Army during
the Second World War (1941–5); practised as an
architect (1946–62); Lecturer on Design and
Architectural History, Melbourne University
(1948–56); Professor of Architecture, Massachusetts Institute of Technology (1956–7); a contributor to architectural journals.

Bibliography
C.B.I.
Gale.

Works
Victorian modern. 1947.
Australia's home. 1952.
The Australian ugliness. 1960.
The walls around us. 1962.
Kenzo tange. 1962.
The puzzle of architecture. 1965.
Artificial Australia (lectures). 1967.
New directions in Japanese architecture. 1968.
Living in Australia. 1970.
The great Australian dream. 1972.

BOYLE, ANDREW PHILIP MORE
(1922–)
Scottish writer; born in Dundee; educated at Aber-

deen and the Sorbonne; served in the R.A.F.
(1942–7) during the Second World War; B.B.C.
news editor of the *World at One*.

Bibliography
Authors' and writers' who's who. 1971.
B.N.B.
Gale.

Works
No passing glory (official biography of Leonard
  Cheshire, V.C.). 1955.
Heroes of our time (with Lord Shackleton and
  others). 1962.
Trenchard, man of vision. 1962.
The future of Catholic Christianity (with Michael
  de la Bedoyère). 1966.
The God I want (with Anthony Burgess and
  others). 1967.
Montagu Norman. 1967.
Only the wind will listen (biography of Lord
  Reith). 1972.

BRADBURY, MALCOLM STANLEY
(1932–)
English novelist; born in Sheffield; educated at the
universities of Leicester, London, Indiana and
Manchester; Lecturer at the universities of Hull
(1959–61), Birmingham (1961–5), and East Anglia
(1965–70); Professor of American Studies, University of East Anglia (1970–); a contributor to
the *London Magazine, Punch, Listener, Spectator,
Encounter, T.L.S.*, etc.; has edited E. M. Forster's
essays (1966), etc.

Bibliography
Authors' and writers' who's who. 1971.
B.N.B.
Contemporary novelists.
Gale.

Novels
Eating people is wrong. 1959.
Stepping westward. 1965.

Other Works
Phogey, or how to class people in a classless society. 1960.
All dressed up and nowhere to go. 1962.
Evelyn Waugh. 1964.
Two poets (with Alan Rodway). 1966.
What is a novel? 1969.
E. M. Forster's A passage to India; a casebook.
  1970.

Humorous prose. 1971.
Possibilities: essays on the state of the novel. 1972.

BRADBURY, RAY DOUGLAS
(†LEONARD SPAULDING) (1920–)
American novelist; after school did various jobs, mostly connected with writing and the theatre; full-time writer since 1943; recipient of various literary awards; has written numerous film scripts and stage and radio plays; is represented in countless anthologies; a contributor to the *New Yorker*, *Harper's*, *Saturday Evening Post*, etc.

Bibliography
C.B.I.
Contemporary novelists.
Gale.
Who's who. 1973.

Novels
The Martian chronicles. 1950.
The silver locusts. 1951.
Fahrenheit 451 (filmed 1966). 1953.
Something wicked this way comes. 1962.
The Halloween tree. 1972.

Short Stories
Dark carnival. 1947.
The illustrated man. 1951.
The golden apples of the sun. 1953.
The October country. 1955.
Dandelion wine. 1957.
A medicine for melancholy (English title, The day it rained forever). 1959.
The machineries of joy. 1964.
The vintage Bradbury. 1965.
The autumn people. 1965.
Twice twenty-two (contains Medicine for melancholy and Golden apples). 1966.
Tomorrow midnight. 1966.
I sing the body electric. 1969.
The small assassin. 1973.

For Children
Switch on the night. 1956.
R is for rocket. 1962.
S is for space. 1966.

Plays
The anthem sprinters. 1963.
The day it rained for ever, and The pedestrian. 1966.
The wonderful ice-cream suit (and other plays). 1972.

Poetry
When elephants last in the dooryard bloomed. 1972.

BRADDON, RUSSELL READING
(1921–)
Australian novelist and writer; educated at Sydney University; served for 8 years in the Second World War, being a Japanese prisoner of war for 4 years; a contributor to many journals; lives in London.

Bibliography
Annals of Australian literature.
B.N.B.
Gale.

Novels
Those in peril. 1953.
Out of the storm. 1955.
Gabriel comes to 24. 1957.
The proud American boy. 1960.
The year of the angry rabbit (filmed as Night of the Lepus, 1972). 1964.
Commital chamber. 1966.
The inseparables. 1968.
When the enemy is tired. 1968.
Will you walk a little faster? 1969.
Prelude and fugue for lovers. 1971.
The progress of Private Lilliworth. 1971.
End play. 1972.

Other Works
The Piddingtons. 1950.
The naked island (autobiography). 1952.
Cheshire, V.C. (American title, New wings for a warrior). 1954.
Nancy Wake (American title, The white mouse). 1956.
End of a hate (autobiography). 1958.
Joan Sutherland. 1962.
Roy Thomson of Fleet Street. 1965.
The siege. 1969.
Suez: splitting of a nation. 1973.
One hundred days of Darien. 1973.

BRADFORD, ERNLE DUSGATE
SELBY (1922–)
English writer; educated at Uppingham; editor of the *Antique Dealer and Collectors' Guide* (1947–50); advisory editor (1957–); served in the Royal Naval Volunteer Reserve during the Second World War; a contributor to the *Tatler*, *Country Life*, etc.

Bibliography
Authors' and writers' who's who. 5th ed. 1963.
B.N.B.

Works
Contemporary jewellery and silver design. 1950.
Four centuries of European jewellery. 1953.
The journeying moon. 1959.
English Victorian jewellery. 1959.
The mighty *Hood*. 1959.
The wind off the island. 1960.
Southward the caravels. 1961.
The great siege. 1961.
The touchstone (novel). 1962.
Antique collecting. 1963.
The companion guide to the Greek islands (American title, The Greek islands: a travel guide). 1963.
Dictionary of antiques. 1963.
Ulysses found. 1963.
The America's cup. 1964.
Three centuries of sailing. 1964.
Drake (American title, The wind commands me). 1965.
Wall of England: the Channel's 2000 years of history (American title, Wall of empire). 1966.
The great betrayal: Constantinople, 1204. 1967.
The sultan's admiral: the life of Barbarossa. 1969.
Antique furniture. 1970.
Mediterranean: portrait of a sea. 1971.
Gibraltar: the history of a fortress. 1971.
Cleopatra. 1971.
Christopher Columbus. 1973.

BRAGG, MELVYN (1939–)
English novelist; educated at Wadham College, Oxford; B.B.C. producer (1961–7); novelist and broadcaster (1967–); wrote film scripts for *Isadora* (1969) (with Clive Exton), *Music lovers* (1970), *Jesus Christ Superstar* (1973); a contributor to the *Listener* and *New Review*.

Bibliography
B.N.B.
Contemporary novelists.
Gale.
Who's who. 1973.

Novels
For want of a nail. 1965.
The second inheritance. 1966.
Without a city wall (John Llewelyn Rhys Prize 1969). 1968.
The hired man. 1970.
A place for England. 1971.

The nerve. 1972.
Josh Lawton. 1973.

BRAINE, JOHN GERARD (1922–)
English novelist; born in Bradford, Yorks.; served in the Royal Navy (1942–3); after doing various jobs, trained as a librarian (1950); full-time writer since 1957; a contributor to *Books and Bookmen, Encounter, New Statesman*, the *Sunday Times*, etc.

Bibliography
Authors' and writers' who's who. 1971.
B.N.B.
Contemporary novelists.
Gale.
Who's who. 1973.

Novels
Room at the top (filmed 1958). 1957.
The vodi. 1959.
Life at the top (filmed 1965). 1962.
The jealous god. 1964.
The crying game. 1968.
Stay with me till morning. 1970.
The queen of a distant country. 1972.

BRAITHWAITE, EDWARD (1930–)
Caribbean poet; born in Barbados; Lecturer in History at the University of the West Indies, Jamaica; joint editor of *Savacou*, the journal of the Caribbean Artists' Movement.

Bibliography
B.N.B.

Poetry
Rights of passage. 1967.
Masks. 1968.
Islands. 1969.
The arrivants. 1973.

Other Works
The folk culture of the slaves in Jamaica. 1970.
Development of Creole society in Jamaica 1770–1820. 1971.

BRAITHWAITE, EUSTACE ADOLPH (1912–)
Caribbean novelist; born in Georgetown, British Guiana; educated at New York University and Caius College, Cambridge; served in the Second World War (1939–45); taught in London schools (1950–7); consultant to the G.L.C. on Negro affairs; Guyanan representative to the U.N.

(1967–8); Guyanan Ambassador to Venezuela (1968–9).

Bibliography
B.N.B.
Contemporary novelists.
Who's who. 1973.

Novels
To sir, with love (filmed 1966). 1959.
Choice of straws. 1965.

Other Works
Paid servant (autobiography). 1962.
A kind of homecoming (autobiography). 1962.
Reluctant neighbours. 1972.

BRATHWAITE, ERROL FREEMAN
(1924–)
New Zealand novelist; served in the New Zealand Forces (1942–58); copywriter (1959–66); now manager of an advertising agency; has written several plays for radio.

Bibliography
B.N.B.
Contemporary novelists.
N.Z. national bibliography.

Novels
Fear in the night. 1959.
An affair of men. 1961.
Long way home. 1964.
The flying fish. 1964.
The needle's eye. 1965.
The evil day. 1967.

Other Works
The companion guide to the North Island of New Zealand. 1970.
The companion guide to the South Island of New Zealand. 1971.
Morning flight. 1971.

BRAUTIGAN, RICHARD (1933–)
American novelist.

Bibliography
C.B.I.
Contemporary novelists.
Contemporary poets.
Gale.

Novels
In watermelon sugar. 1964.

A confederate general from Big Sur. 1965.
Trout fishing in America. 1969.
The abortion: an historical romance. 1971.
Revenge of the lawn (stories). 1971.

Poetry
The return of the rivers. 1957.
The Galilee hitch-hiker. 1958.
The octopus frontier. 1960.
The pill versus the Spring Hill mine disaster (poems 1957–1968). 1968.
Rommel drives on deep into Egypt. 1970.

BRETTELL, NOEL HARRY (1908–)
Rhodesian poet; born in England; educated at Birmingham University; headmaster, Farm School, Rhodesia (1933–59); a contributor to *New South African Writing*, etc.; represented in *Commonwealth poems of today* and other anthologies.

Bibliography
B.N.B.
Contemporary poets.

Poetry
Bronze frieze: poems mostly Rhodesian. 1950.

BREW, KWESI
Ghanaian poet, civil servant and diplomat; educated at the University of Ghana; took part in several films; currently Ambassador in Senegal; represented in *Okyeame, Sergeant, Poetry for Africa* (1968) and other literary periodicals and anthologies.

Bibliography
B.N.B.
Contemporary poets.
Ghana national bibliography.
Jahn and Dressler.
Zell and Silver.

Poetry
The shadows of laughter. 1968.

BREWSTER, ELIZABETH WINIFRED
(1922–)
Canadian poet and librarian; educated at the universities of New Brunswick and Indiana; cataloguer, reference librarian, etc., in university libraries in Canada and U.S.A. (1953–70); Assistant Visiting Professor, Dept. of English, Alberta University (1970–); a contributor to *Alphabet, Canadian Forum, Queen's Quarterly*, etc.

Bibliography
Authors' and writers' who's who. 1971.
Canadiana.
C.B.I.
Contemporary poets.
Gale.

Poetry
East coast. 1951.
Lilloet. 1954.
Roads and other poems. 1957.
Passage of summer. 1969.

BRICKHILL, PAUL CHESTER JEROME (1916–)

Australian writer and journalist; educated at Sydney University; journalist, Sydney (1935–40); served in the R.A.F. during the Second World War (1940–5); foreign correspondent (1945–7); full-time writer (1949–).

Bibliography
B.N.B.
Gale.
Who's who. 1973.

Works
Escape to danger (with Conrad Norton). 1946.
The great escape (filmed 1963). 1951.
The dam busters (filmed 1954). 1951.
Escape or die. 1952.
Reach for the sky (filmed 1956). 1954.
The deadline. 1962.

BRIDSON, DOUGLAS GEOFFREY (1910–)

English poet and B.B.C. scriptwriter; educated in Lancashire; worked in business there (1926–33); full-time writer and critic (1933–5); B.B.C. (1935–70); for many years responsible for B.B.C. Third Programme poetry; a contributor to the *Criterion, Poetry Quarterly*, etc.; has travelled widely; has made countless adaptations for radio serials.

Bibliography
B.N.B.

Poetry
The Christmas child. 1950.

Play
Aaron's field (for radio). 1943.

Other Works
Prospero and Ariel: the rise and fall of radio. 1971.
The Filibuster: study of the political ideas of Wyndham Lewis. 1972.

BRIGGS, *Professor* ASA (1921–)

English historian; born in Keighley, Yorks.; educated at Sidney Sussex College, Cambridge; served in the Intelligence Corps during the Second World War (1942–5); his academic posts include Fellow of Worcester College, Oxford (1945–55), Professor of Modern History, Leeds University (1955–61), Professor of History, Sussex University (1961–) and Vice-Chancellor (1961–7); his honorary posts include chairman of the standing committee on local history, president of the Workers' Educational Association, member of the University Grants Committee (1959–67), etc.; awarded academic honours; a contributor to the *New Society, Listener, New Statesman and Nation, Economist*, etc.

Bibliography
Authors' and writers' who's who. 1971.
B.N.B.
Gale.
Who's who. 1973.

Works
Patterns of peacemaking (with D. Thomson and E. Meyer). 1945.
1851. 1951.
History of Birmingham (1865–1938). 1952.
Victorian people. 1954.
Friends of the people. 1956.
Where we came in. 1957.
The age of improvement. 1959.
Chartist studies (editor). 1959.
Essays in Labour history; in memory of G. D. H. Cole. (Co-editor with John Saville.) 1960.
They saw it happen, 1897–1940. 1961.
A study of the work of Seebohm Rowntree, 1871–1954. 1961.
The birth of broadcasting (vol. I, The history of broadcasting in the U.K.). 1961.
Selected writings and designs of William Morris. 1963.
Victorian cities. 1963.
The golden age of wireless (vol. II, The history of broadcasting in the U.K.). 1965.
William Cobbett. 1967.
How they lived, 1700–1815. 1969.

The war of words (vol. III, The history of broadcasting in the U.K.). 1970.
The nineteenth century: contradictions of progress
(with others). 1970.

BRINNIN, JOHN MALCOLM (1916–)
American poet; educated at Michigan University
and Harvard; after several academic posts, Associate Professor of English, University of Connecticut (1951–62); his edited works are not listed
below.

Bibliography
C.B.I.
Contemporary poets.
Gale.
L. of C.

Poetry
The garden is political. 1942.
Lincoln lyrics. 1942.
No arch, no triumph. 1945.
The sorrows of cold stone. 1951.
Arthur, the dolphin who didn't see Venice. 1961.
Selected poems. 1963.
Skin-diving in the Virgins. 1971.

Other Works
Dylan Thomas in America. 1955.
The third rose; Gertrude Stein and her world. 1959.
William Carlos Williams. 1963.
Sway of the grand saloon: a social history of the
North Atlantic. 1971.

BRISSENDEN, ROBERT FRANCIS
(1928–)
Australian scholar; educated at the universities of
Sydney and Leeds; after various university posts,
Reader in English, Canberra (1969–); regular
reviewer, *Sydney Morning Herald*; Associate Editor,
Meanjin Quarterly (1959–64); his edited work is not
listed below.

Bibliography
B.N.B.
Gale.

Works
Samuel Richardson. 1958.
Patrick White. 1966.
Winter matins and other poems. 1971.

BROCK, EDWIN (1927–)
English poet; born in London; served in the Royal

Navy; journalist (1947–51); Metropolitan Policeman (1951–9); worked for Benson's advertising
agency (1964–); poetry editor of *Ambit*; represented in various anthologies.

Bibliography
B.N.B.
Contemporary poets.

Novel
The little white god. 1962.

Poetry
An attempt at exorcism. 1959.
A family affair. 1960.
With love from Judas. 1963.
Penguin modern poets no. 8 (with F. Hill and
Stevie Smith). 1966.
Fred's primer. 1969.
A cold day at the zoo. 1970.
The portraits and the poses. 1973.

BRODEUR, PAUL ADRIAN Jr.
(1931–)
American novelist; educated at Harvard University; served with the U.S. Army (1953–6); on
the staff of the *New Yorker* (1958–); Lecturer at
the Columbia School of Journalism.

Bibliography
C.B.I.
Contemporary novelists.
Gale.

Novels
The sick fox. 1963.
The stunt man. 1970.
Downstream (stories). 1972.

Other Work
Asbestos and enzymes. 1972.

BROOKE, BERNARD JOCELYN
(1909–)
English novelist and writer; educated at Worcester
College, Oxford; worked in the book trade and his
father's wine business (1928–34); served in the
Royal Army Medical Corps in the Second World
War and after (1940–8); B.B.C. Talks Producer
(1949); full-time writer since 1949; a contributor to
*The Times, T.L.S., Punch, New Statesman, Time
and Tide, Spectator*, etc.; editor of *Denton Welch's
Journals* (1952) and *Denton Welch: a Selection* (1963).

Bibliography
B.N.B.
Gale.

Novels
The wonderful summer. 1949.
The scapegoat. 1950.
The image of a drawn sword. 1951.
The passing of a hero. 1953.
Conventional weapons (American title, The passing of Greene). 1961.

Autobiography
The military orchid. 1948.
A mine of serpents. 1949.
The dog at Clambercrown; an excursion. 1955.

Other Works
December spring (poems). 1946.
The wild orchids of Britain. 1950.
Goose cathedral. 1950.
Ronald Firbank. 1951.
Elizabeth Bowen. 1952.
Aldous Huxley. 1954.
The crisis in Bulgaria; or, Ibsen to the rescue. 1956.
Ronald Firbank and John Betjeman. 1963.
The birth of a legend. 1964.

BROOKE-ROSE, CHRISTINE
(Mrs. PETERKIEWICZ) (1926–   )
English novelist; born in Geneva; educated in Brussels and Somerville College, Oxford; Ph.D., University College, London; a contributor to the *London Magazine, Observer, Spectator, Sunday Times, T.L.S.*, etc.; the author of several radio plays; her translated works are not listed below.

Bibliography
Authors' and writers' who's who. 1971.
B.N.B.
Contemporary novelists.
Gale.

Novels
The languages of love. 1957.
The sycamore tree. 1958.
The dear deceit. 1960.
The middlemen. 1961.
Out. 1964.
Such (James Tait Black Prize 1967). 1966.
Between. 1968.
Go when you see the green man walking (stories). 1970.

Criticism
A grammar of metaphor. 1958.
A ZBC of Ezra Pound. 1971.

BROOKS, GWENDOLYN
(Mrs. HENRY BLAKELEY) (1917–   )
American poet; spent her childhood in Chicago; taught in schools; recipient of several awards; Poet Laureate of Illinois; represented in numerous anthologies.

Bibliography
C.B.I.
Contemporary poets.

Novel
Maud Martha. 1953.

Poetry
A street of Bronzeville. 1945.
Annie Allen (Pulitzer Poetry Prize 1950). 1949.
Bronzeville boys and girls. 1956.
Selected poems. 1963.
In the Mecca. 1968.
Riot, a poem. 1970.
Family pictures. 1970.
To Gwen with love. 1971.

Other Works
The bean eaters (for children). 1960.
A portion of that field (with others). 1967.
Report from part one: an autobiography. 1972.

BROOKS, JEREMY (CLIVE MEIKLE)
(1926–   )
English novelist; educated at Magdalen College, Oxford, and Camberwell School of Art; served in the Royal Navy (1944–7); stage manager, designer and book and drama critic (1951–61); literary manager of the Royal Shakespeare Company (1962–   ); a contributor to the *Observer, Guardian, Sunday Times, Daily Telegraph*, etc.

Bibliography
Authors' and writers' who's who. 1971.
B.N.B.
Contemporary novelists.
Gale.

Novels
The water carnival. 1957.
Jampot Smith. 1960.
Henry's war. 1962.
I'll fight you. 1963.

Smith, as hero. 1965.
Hat, 1971.

Children's Book
The magic perambulator. 1965.

Dramatic Adaptation of Gorky Plays
The government inspector (with O. Marsh). 1968.
Enemies (with Kitty Hunter Blair). 1972.

BROOKS, JOHN (1920–)
American novelist and essayist; educated at Princeton; editor *Time* magazine (1945–7); staff contributor to the *New Yorker* (1949–).

Bibliography
C.B.I.

Novels
The big wheel. 1949.
A pride of lions. 1954.
The man who broke things. 1958.

Other Works
The seven fat years: chronicle of Wall Street. 1958.
The fate of the Edsel and other businesses. 1963.
The great leap. 1966.
Business adventure. 1969.
Once in Golconda. 1969.
The go-go years. 1973.

BROPHY, BRIGID ANTONIA
(*Mrs.* LEVEY) (1929–)
English novelist; daughter of the novelist John Brophy; educated at St. Hugh's College, Oxford; a contributor to the *Listener, New York Times, Sunday Times,* etc.

Bibliography
Authors' and writers' who's who. 1971.
B.N.B.
Contemporary novelists.
Gale.
Who's who. 1973.

Novels
The crown princess and other stories. 1953.
Hackenfeller's ape. 1953.
The king of a rainy country. 1956.
Flesh. 1962.
The finishing touch. 1963.
The snow ball. 1964.
In transit. 1969.
The adventures of God in search of the black girl. 1973.

Plays
The waste disposal unit (radio play). 1968.
The burglar. 1968.

Other Works
Black ship to Hell. 1962.
Mozart the dramatist. 1964.
Don't never forget. 1966.
Fifty works of English literature we could do without (with Michael Levey and Charles Osborne). 1967.
Religious education in state schools. 1967.
Black and white, a portrait of Aubrey Beardsley. 1968.
Prancing novelist (a study of Ronald Firbank). 1973.

BROSSARD, CHANDLER
(†DANIEL HARPER) (1922–)
American novelist; self-educated, left school at 11; newspaperman (1940–67); Associate Professor, Old Westbury College, New York (1968–70); Visiting Professor, Center for Contemporary Culture, Birmingham, Alabama (1970); editor of *The scene before you: a new approach to American culture* (1955); his unpublished plays are not listed below.

Bibliography
C.B.I.
Contemporary novelists.

Novels
Who walk in darkness. 1952.
The bold saboteurs. 1953.
The wrong turn (as †Daniel Harper). 1954.
All passion spent. 1954.
The double view. 1960.
Wake up, we're almost there. 1971.

Other Works
The insane world of Adolf Hitler. 1967.
The Spanish scene. 1968.

BROUGHTON, JAMES (1913–)
American poet; educated at Stanford University; Lecturer at San Francisco State College; a contributor to *Poetry*; represented in numerous anthologies; author of several plays and film scripts.

Bibliography
C.B.I.
Contemporary poets.

Poetry
Songs for children. 1947.
The playground. 1949.
The ballad of mad Jenny. 1949.
Musical chairs. 1950.
Almanac of amorists. 1954.
Time and false unicorn. 1957.
The water circle. 1965.
Tidings. 1966.
Look in, look out. 1968.
High Kukus. 1968.
All about it. 1969.
Whistling in the labyrinth. 1969.

Other Work
The right playmate. 1964.

BROWER, BROCK HENDRICKSON
(1931–)
American novelist and journalist; born in New Jersey; educated at Merton College, Oxford; served in the U.S. Army (1957–8); assistant editor of *Esquire* (1960); Lecturer in Creative Writing, Princeton University (1968–); columnist for *Life* (1969–); a contributor to *Holiday, Playboy, New York Times Magazine*, etc.

Bibliography
C.B.I.
Gale.

Novels
Debris. 1967.
The late-great creature. 1972.
Remains. n.d.

Other Works
Other loyalties: a politics of personality. 1968.
The inch-worm war, and the butterfly peace. 1970.

BROWN, HARRY PETER M'NAB, Jr.
(1917–)
American novelist; educated at Harvard; newspaperman attached to the U.S. Army during the Second World War (1942); recipient of several literary and film-makers' awards; author of numerous film scripts.

Bibliography
C.B.I.

Novels
It's a cinch, Private Finch. 1943.
A walk in the sun (filmed 1945). 1944.

Artie Greengroin. 1945.
The stars in their courses (filmed as El Dorado, 1967). 1960.
Sun gods. 1970.
The wild hunt. 1973.

Play
A sound of hunting. 1946.

Poetry
The poem of Bunker Hill. 1941.
The violent. 1943.
Poems 1941–44. 1945.
The beast in his hunger. 1949.
The end of a decade. 1971.

Other Work
Suez and Sinai. 1971.

BROWNJOHN, ALAN CHARLES
(†JOHN BERRINGTON) (1931–)
English poet; educated at Merton College, Oxford; Senior Lecturer at Battersea College of Education; a contributor to the *London Magazine, New Statesman, Observer, Encounter* and *Ambit*; edited *New Poems*, Hutchinson (1970).

Bibliography
B.N.B.
Contemporary poets.
Gale.

Book
To clear the river (as †John Berrington). 1964.

Poetry
Travelling alone. 1954.
The railings. 1961.
The lion's mouth. 1967.
Sandgrains on a tray. 1969.
First I say this: a collection of poems. 1969.
Penguin modern poets no. 14 (with M. Hamburger and C. Tomlinson). 1969.
Brownjohn's beasts: poems for children. 1970.

Miscellany
Synopsis. 1970.

BRUTUS, DENNIS VINCENT (1924–)
South African poet of mixed descent; educated at Fort Hare University College; taught in African high schools for 14 years; dismissed (1962) and turned to reading law at Witwatersrand University; involved in anti-apartheid campaign and

arrested (1963); released and moved to Swaziland, but recaptured, and sentenced to 18 months' hard labour; freed 1965 and came to England (1966); a contributor to *Transition, Black Orpheus, Morning Star, Africa Today*, etc.; represented in *African Writing Today* and other anthologies.

Bibliography
B.N.B.
Contemporary poets.
Zell and Silver.

Poetry
Sirens, knuckles, boots. 1963.
Letters to Martha. 1968.

BUCHWALD, ARTHUR (1925–)
American journalist and humorous writer; educated at University of South Carolina; served in the U.S. Marines during the Second World War (1942–5); journalist in Paris (1948–62); now publishes an "Art Buchwald" column for the *Herald Tribune* from Washington D.C.; awarded the French *Grand prix de la humor* (1959).

Bibliography
C.B.I.
Gale.

Works
Art Buchwald's Paris. 1953.
The brave coward. 1955.
I chose caviar. 1957.
More caviar. 1958.
A gift from the boys (filmed 1959). 1958.
Don't forget to write. 1960.
How much is that in dollars? 1961.
Is it safe to drink the water? 1962.
I chose Capitol punishment. 1963.
Then I told the president: the secret papers of A. B. 1965.
Son of the great society. 1966.
Have I ever lied to you? 1968.
Establishment is alive and well in Washington. 1969.
Counting sheep: the log and complete play of sheep on the runway. 1970.
Getting high in government circles. 1971.
I never danced at the White House. 1973.

BUCKLER, ERNEST (1908–)
Canadian novelist and short-story writer; born in Nova Scotia; educated at Dalhousie and Toronto universities; worked as an insurance actuary in

Toronto (1931–6); has since devoted his time to farming and writing; a contributor of short stories and articles to *Esquire, MacLean's*, C.B.C. Radio.

Bibliography
Authors' and writers' who's who. 1971.
Canadiana.
C.B.I.
Contemporary novelists.
Gale.

Novels
The mountain and the valley. 1952.
The cruellest month. 1962.

Other Works
Ox bells and fireflies: a memoir. 1968.
Window on the sea (with Hans Weber). 1972.

BUCKLEY, VINCENT THOMAS (1925–)
Australian poet and critic; born in Victoria; educated at Melbourne and Cambridge universities; served in the Australian Air Force during the Second World War; a civil servant; Professor of English at Melbourne University (1967–); recipient of numerous awards for poetry; represented in anthologies.

Bibliography
Australian national bibliography.
B.N.B.
Contemporary poets.

Poetry
The world is flesh. 1954.
Masters in Israel. 1959.
Arcady and other places. 1966.

Other Works
Essays in poetry. 1957.
Poetry and morality. 1959.
Poetry and the sacred. 1968.

BUCKLEY, WILLIAM FRANK, Jr. (1925–)
American journalist; educated privately in England and at Mexico and Yale universities; served in the U.S. Army (1944–6); a contributor to *Esquire, Harper's, Atlantic*, etc.; founding editor of the New York *National Review* (1955–); his edited work is not listed below.

Bibliography
C.B.I.
Gale.

Works
God and men at Yale. 1951.
McCarthy and his enemies (with L. Brent Bozell). 1959.
Ocean racing (with others). 1959.
Up from liberalism. 1959.
The intellectuals (with others). 1960.
The committee and its critics (with others). 1962.
Rumbles left and right. 1963.
What is Conservatism? (with others). 1964.
The unmaking of a mayor. 1966.
Jeweler's eye: a book of irresistible political reflections. 1968.
Governor listeth: a book of inspiring political revelations. 1970.
Cruising speed: a documentary. 1971.
Inveighing we will go. 1972.

BUECHNER, CARL FREDERICK

(1926–   )
American novelist; educated at Princeton University; served in the U.S. Army (1944–6); taught English; ordained Presbyterian minister (1958); recipient of several literary awards.

Bibliography
C.B.I.
Contemporary novelists.
Gale.

Novels
A long day's dying. 1950.
The season's difference. 1953.
The return of Ansel Gibbs. 1958.
The final beast. 1965.
The entrance to Porlock. 1970.
Lion country. 1971.

Other Works
The magnificent defeat (meditations). 1967.
The hungering dark (meditations). 1969.
The alphabet of grace (autobiography). 1970.

BUKOWSKI, CHARLES (1920–   )

German-born American poet; studied journalism and art; travelled through the U.S.A.; turned from writing short stories to poetry at the age of 35; a contributor to various periodicals.

Bibliography
C.B.I.
Contemporary poets.
Gale.

Poetry
Flower, fist and bestial wall. 1959.
Longshot poems for broke players. 1961.
Run with the hunted. 1962.
It catches my heart in its hands . . . new and selected poems 1955–63. 1963.
Cold dogs in the courtyard. 1965.
Crucifix in a deathhand. 1965.
A terror and agony way. 1968.
Poems written before jumping out of an 8-story window. 1968.
Penguin modern poets no. 13 (with P. Lamantia and H. Norse). 1969.
Post office. 1971.
Mocking bird wish me luck. 1972.
Notes of a dirty old man. 1973.
South of no north. 1973.
Fire station. 1973.
Days run away like wild horses over the hills. 1973.
Burning in water, drowning in fire. 1974.

Other Works
Confession of a man insane enough to live with beasts. 1965.
All the assholes in the world and mine. 1966.
Erections, ejaculations, exhibitions and other tales of ordinary madness. 1972.

BULLINS, ED (1935–   )

Black American playwright; born in Philadelphia; educated at San Francisco State College; served in the U.S. Navy; playwright in residence (1967–71), and Associate Director (1967–   ) of New Lafayette Theatre, Harlem, New York; editor of *Black Theatre* (1969–   ); recipient of various grants and awards; only his separately published or collected editions of plays are listed below; unpublished plays include *Street Sounds* (1970).

Bibliography
C.B.I.
Contemporary dramatists.
Gale.

Story
The hungered one: early writings. 1971.

Poetry
To raise the dead and foretell the future. 1971.

Plays

How do you do: a nonsense drama. 1965.

Five plays (Goin' a buffalo, In the wine time, The electronic nigger, A son come home, Clara's ole man) (English title, The electronic nigger and other plays 1970). 1969.

The duplex: a black love fable in four movements (staged 1970). 1971.

Four dynamite plays (It bees dat way, Death list, The pig pen, Night of the beast). 1972.

Reluctant rapist. 1973.

The theme is blackness: The corner, and other plays. 1973.

BULLOCK, *Sir* ALAN LOUIS CHARLES (1914–)

English scholar and writer; educated at Wadham College, Oxford; B.B.C. diplomatic correspondent (1940–5); Fellow of Modern History, New College, Oxford (1945–52); Master, St. Catherine's College, Oxford (1960–); Vice-Chancellor, Oxford University (1969–73); awarded numerous academic honours; general editor, with F. W. Deakin, of *The Oxford History of Modern Europe*.

Bibliography

Authors' and writers' who's who. 1971.

B.N.B.

Gale.

Who's who. 1973.

Works

Hitler: a study in tyranny. 1952.

The Liberal tradition. 1956.

The life and times of Ernest Bevin; vol. I, 1960; vol. II, 1967.

The twentieth century: a Promethean age. 1971.

BULLOCK, MICHAEL HALE (†MICHAEL HALE) (1918–)

English poet and translator; educated at Stowe School and Hornsey College of Art; freelance writer and translator (1945–67); writer in residence, University of British Columbia (1968); McGuffey Visiting Professor of English, Ohio University (1969); Assistant Professor, University of British Columbia (1970); a contributor to *Encounter, London Magazine*, etc.; his translations, which number more than 100, are not listed below.

Bibliography

Authors' and writers' who's who. 1971.

B.N.B.

Contemporary poets.

Gale.

Poetry (as †Michael Hale)

Transmutations. 1938.

Sunday is a day of incest. 1960.

World without beginning, amen. 1963.

Zwei Stimmen in meinem Mund (Two voices in my mouth; poems in English with German translation). 1967.

Sixteen stories as they happened. 1969.

A savage darkness. 1969.

BULMER, HENRY KENNETH (†ERNEST CORLEY, †PHILIP KENT, †KARL MARAS, †KENNETH JOHNS) (1921–)

English science fiction writer; left school at 15; served in the army (1941–6) during the Second World War; representative for a firm of paper merchants (1947–54); full-time writer since that date.

Bibliography

B.N.B.

Contemporary novelists.

Gale.

Novels

Encounter in space. 1952.

Space treason (with A. V. Clarke). 1952.

Cybernetic controller (with A. V. Clarke). 1952.

Mission to the stars (as †Philip Kent). 1953.

Vassals of Venus (as †Philip Kent). 1953.

Space salvage. 1953.

The stars are ours. 1953.

Galactic intrigue. 1953.

Empire of chaos. 1953.

Slaves of the spectrum (as †Philip Kent). 1954.

Home is the Martian (as †Philip Kent). 1954.

Zhorani (as †Karl Maras). 1954.

Peril from space (as †Karl Maras). 1954.

World aflame. 1954.

Challenge. 1954.

City under the sea. 1957.

The secret of Zi. 1958.

The changeling worlds. 1959.

The gods are coming (English title, Of earth foretold, 1961). 1960.

White-out (as †Ernest Corley). 1960.

The true book about space travel (with John Newman as †Kenneth Johns). 1960.

Earth's long shadow (American title, No man's world, 1962). 1961.

Beyond the silver sky. 1961.

The fatal fire. 1962.
The wind of liberty. 1962.
Defiance. 1963.
The wizard of starship Poseidon. 1963.
The million year hunt. 1964.
Demon's world. 1964.
Land beyond the map. 1965.
Behold the stars. 1966.
The doomsday men. 1968.
The patient dark. 1969.
The fatal fire. 1969.
The ulcer culture. 1969.
Quench the burning stars. 1970.
Star trove. 1970.
Swords of the barbarians. 1970.
Hunters of Jungadai. 1971.
On the symb-rocket circuit. 1972.
The roller-coaster works. 1972.
The pretenders. 1972.

BURFORD, WILLIAM SKELLY
(1927–)
American poet; educated at Amherst College and
Johns Hopkins University; served in the U.S.
Army (1945); Assistant Professor of English, University of Texas (1958–); recipient of several
literary and academic awards; a contributor to
Poetry, Saturday Review, Texas Quarterly, etc.; his
edited and translated work is not listed below.

Bibliography
C.B.I.
Contemporary poets.
Gale.
L. of C.

Poetry
Man now. 1954.
A world. 1962.
A beginning. 1966.

BURGESS, ANTHONY (†JOSEPH KELL, †JOHN BURGESS WILSON)
(1917–)
English novelist; born in Manchester; educated at
the Xavian College and Manchester University;
served in the army (1940–6) in the Second World
War; Birmingham University Extra-Mural Lecturer (1946–8); taught (1950–4); education officer,
Malaya and Borneo (1954–9); a contributor to the
Observer, Spectator, Listener, Encounter, T.L.S., etc.;
edited *A Shorter Finnegan's Wake* (1967), and other
works not listed below.

Bibliography
Authors' and writers' who's who. 1971.
B.N.B.
Contemporary novelists.
Carol M. Dix. Anthony Burgess. 1973.
Gale.
Who's who. 1973.

Novels
Time for a tiger. 1956.
The enemy in the blanket. 1958.
Beds in the east. 1959.
The right to an answer. 1960.
The doctor is sick. 1960.
The worm and the ring. 1961.
Devil of a state. 1961.
One hand clapping (as †Joseph Kell). 1961.
A clockwork orange (filmed 1971). 1962.
The wanting seed. 1962.
Honey for the bears. 1963.
Inside Mr. Enderby (as †Joseph Kell). 1963.
Nothing like the sun. 1964.
Malayan trilogy (Time for a tiger, The enemy in
    the blanket, Beds in the east) (American title,
    The long day wanes). 1964.
The eve of Saint Venus. 1964.
Tremor of intent. 1966.
A vision of battlements. 1966.
Enderby outside. 1968.

Other Works
English literature – a survey for students (†John
    Burgess Wilson). 1958.
The novel today (revised edition, The novel now,
    1972). 1963.
Language made plain. 1964.
Here comes everybody – an introduction to James
    Joyce. 1964.
The novel now. 1967.
Urgent copy (literary studies). 1968.
Shakespeare. 1970.
Joysprick: an introduction to the language of James
    Joyce. 1972.

BURMEISTER, JON (1932–)
South African novelist; attorney and Notary
Public until he became a full-time writer; lives in
London.

Bibliography
Authors' and writers' who's who. 1971.
B.N.B.
Gale.

Novels
The edge of the coast. 1968.
A hot and copper sky. 1969.
The darkling plain. 1970.
The unloved ones. 1972.
Running scared. 1972.
Someone else's war. 1973.

BURNS, JAMES MACGREGOR
(1918–)
American historian; born in Boston; educated at
Williams College and Harvard; served in the U.S.
Army during the Second World War (1943–5);
Professor of Political Science, Williams College
(1947–); Democratic candidate for Congress
(1958); recipient of several literary awards; a contributor to learned journals.

Bibliography
C.B.I.
Gale.

Works
Congress on trial. 1949.
Government by the people (with Jack Peltason).
 1950.
Roosevelt: the lion and the fox. 1956.
John Kennedy: a political profile. 1960.
The deadlock of democracy. 1963.
Presidential government: the crucible of leader-
ship. 1966.
Roosevelt: the soldier of freedom. 1970.
Uncommon sense. 1972.

BURNS, JIM (1936–)
English poet; born in Lancashire; served in the
army (1954–7); published the little magazine
Move (1964–8); a contributor to *Jazz Sound*, the
Guardian, etc.

Bibliography
B.N.B.
Contemporary poets.

Poetry
Some poems. 1965.
Some more poems. 1965.
My sad story and other poems. 1967.
The store of things. 1969.
Types (poems and stories). 1970.

Prose
Cells (prose pieces). 1967.

BURROUGHS, WILLIAM SEWARD
(†WILLIAM LEE) (1914–)
American novelist; educated at Harvard and
Vienna universities; served in the U.S. Army
during the Second World War (1942); now a full-
time writer.

Bibliography
C.B.I.
Contemporary novelists.
Gale.

Novels
Junkie (as †William Lee). 1953.
The naked lunch. 1959.
The soft machine. 1961.
The ticket that exploded. 1962.
Dead fingers talk. 1963.
Nova express. 1964.
Exterminator. 1967.
Speed. 1970.
The wild boys. 1971.
The algebra of need. 1973.

Play
The last words of Dutch Schultz (film script). 1970.

Poetry
Minutes to go. 1960.
Time (pr. ptd.). 1965.
The third mind. 1970.

Other Works
The Yage letters. 1963.
APO – 33: a metabolic regulator. 1968.
Job: interviews with William Burroughs (with
 D. Odier). 1970.

BUTLER, FREDERICK GUY (1918–)
South African poet, born in Cape Province; edu-
cated at Rhodes University, Grahamstown, and
Brasenose College, Oxford; served in the Second
World War; Professor of English, Rhodes Uni-
versity; joint editor (with Ruth Hamett) of *New
Coin*; represented in various anthologies; editor of
A book of South African verse (1956) and *When boys
were men* (1969).

Bibliography
B.N.B.
Contemporary poets.

51

Poetry
Stranger to Europe. 1952.
South of the Zambezi. 1966.
On first seeing Florence. 1968.

Plays
The dove returns. 1956.
The dam. 1963.
Cape charade. 1968.

Literary Criticism
An aspect of tragedy. 1953.

BUTLER, GWENDOLINE
(*née* **WILLIAMS**) (1922–)
English detective novelist; born in London; educated at Haberdasher's Aske's Hatcham School and Lady Margaret Hall, Oxford.

Bibliography
Authors' and writers' who's who. 1971.
B.N.B.
Gale.

Novels
Receipt for murder. 1956.
Dead in a row. 1957.
The dull dead. 1958.
The murdering kind. 1958.
The interloper. 1959.
Death lives next door (American title, Dine and be dead). 1960.

Make me a murderer. 1961.
Coffin in Oxford. 1962.
Coffin for baby. 1963.
Coffin waiting. 1964.
Coffin in Malta. 1964.
A nameless coffin. 1966.
Coffin following. 1968.
Coffin's dark number. 1969.
Coffin from the past. 1970.
A coffin for Pandora. 1973.

BYATT, ANTONIA SUSAN
(*née* **DRABBLE**) (1936–)
English novelist; sister of the novelist Margaret Drabble (q.v.); educated at Newnham College, Cambridge; lecturer in English, University of London (1964–).

Bibliography
B.N.B.
Contemporary novelists.
Gale.

Novels
Shadow of a sun. 1964.
The game: a novel. 1967.

Other Works
Degrees of freedom, the novels of Iris Murdoch. 1965.
Wordsworth and Coleridge in their time. 1970.

C

CAGE, JOHN (1912–)
American composer and poet; recipient of several musical awards.

Bibliography
C.B.I.

Works
Virgil Thomson: his life and music (with K. O. Hoover). 1958.
Silence. 1961.
A year from Monday: new lectures and writings. 1967.
Ed.: Notations (with Alison Knowles). 1969.

CALDER, ANGUS (1942–)
Scottish historian; educated at King's College,

Cambridge; lecturer at the University of Nairobi; a contributor to the *New Statesman, Tribune*, etc.

Bibliography
B.N.B.
Gale.

Works
The people's war: Britain 1939–45 (John Llewelyn Rhys Prize 1970). 1969.
Scott. 1969.

CALDER, NIGEL DAVID RITCHIE
(1931–)
Scottish writer on science; educated at Sidney Sussex College, Cambridge; research physicist, Mullard Ltd. (1954–6); wrote for *New Scientist*

(1956–), editor (1962–6); a contributor to the *New Statesman*; edited *The world in 1984* (1965) and *Unless peace comes* (1968).

Bibliography
Authors' and writers' who's who. 1971.
B.N.B.

Works
What we read and why. 1954.
Robots. 1957.
Electricity grows up. 1958.
Radio astronomy. 1958.
The environment game. 1967.
Violent universe. 1969.
Technopolis. 1969.
Living tomorrow. 1970.
The mind of man. 1970.
Restless earth. 1972.
Life game. 1973.

CALISHER, HORTENSE (Mrs. CURTIS HARNACK) (1911–)

American novelist; educated at Barnard College; held various lecturing posts including Visiting Professor in Literature, Brandeis University (1963–4); Guggenheim Fellow twice, etc.; a contributor to the *New Yorker, Harper's Bazaar*, etc.; represented in various collections of short stories.

Bibliography
C.B.I.
Contemporary novelists.
Gale.

Novels
False entry. 1961.
Textures of life. 1963.
Journal from Ellipsia. 1965.
The railway police, and The last trolley ride (novellas). 1966.
The New Yorkers. 1969.
Queenie. 1971.
Herself. 1972.
Standard dreaming. 1972.

Short Stories
In the absence of angels. 1951.
Tale for the mirror. 1962.
Extreme magic. 1964.

CALLOW, PHILIP KENNETH (1924–)

English novelist; born in Birmingham; worked as apprentice toolmaker, telephonist and civil servant; settled in Cornwall to become full-time writer; a contributor to the *New Statesman, Listener, Spectator*, etc.

Bibliography
B.N.B.
Contemporary novelists.
Gale.

Novels
The Hosanna man. 1956.
Common people. 1958.
Native ground (short stories). 1960.
Clipped wings. 1964.
Going to the moon. 1968.
The bliss body. 1969.
Yours. 1972.

Poetry
Turning point. 1964.
The real life. 1964.
Bare wires. 1972.

Other Work
In my own land. 1966.

CAMERON, Professor JAMES MUNRO (1910–)

Scottish philosophical scholar; educated at Balliol College, Oxford; Lecturer in Philosophy at Leicester, Southampton and Leeds universities; Professor of Philosophy, University of Leeds (1960–7); Master of Rutherford College and Professor of Philosophy, University of Kent (1967–); a contributor to many periodicals.

Bibliography
B.N.B.
Gale.
Who's who. 1973.

Works
Scrutiny of Marxism. 1948.
Max Picard, the flight from God (translation with Marianne Kuschnitzky). 1951.
John Henry Newman. 1956.
Poetry and dialectic (inaugural lecture, University of Leeds). 1961.
The night battle. 1962.
Images of authority. 1966.

CAMERON, JAMES WALTER (1911–)

Scottish journalist and writer on travel and contemporary affairs; educated mostly in France; travelled widely as foreign correspondent; produced numerous television films; initiated the travel series, *Cameron Country*, B.B.C.2; recipient of various awards for journalism.

Bibliography
Authors' and writers' who's who. 1971.

B.N.B.
Who's who. 1973.

Works
Touch of the sun. 1950.
Mandarin red, a journey behind the bamboo curtain. 1955.
"1914". 1959.
The African revolution. 1961.
"1916", year of decision. 1962.
Witness (in Viet Nam). 1966.
Point of departure. 1967.
What a way to run a tribe, selected articles 1948–67. 1968.

CAMPBELL, ALISTAIR TE ARIKI
(1925–)
New Zealand poet; born in Cook Islands and went to New Zealand (1933) after his parents died; educated at Victoria University of Wellington; Department of Education, Wellington (1955–); has written radio plays; a contributor to *Landfall, New Zealand Listener*, etc.

Bibliography
B.M. catalogue.
Contemporary poets.
Gale.
N.Z. national bibliography.

Poetry
Mine eyes dazzle. 1950.
Sanctuary of spirits. 1963.
Wild honey. 1964.
Blue rain. 1967.
Drinking horn. 1970.
Kapiti: selected poems 1947–71. 1972.

Other Works
The happy summer (for children). 1961.
Maori legends. 1969.
Walk the black path. 1971.

CAMPBELL, DAVID (1915–)
Australian poet; educated at Jesus College, Cambridge; served in the Australian Air Force during the Second World War; now farms in New South Wales; a contributor to the Sydney *Bulletin*; represented in numerous anthologies.

Bibliography
Australian national bibliography.
B.N.B.
Contemporary poets.

Poetry
Speak with the sun. 1949.

The miracle of Mullion Hill. 1956.
Poems. 1962.
Selected poems 1942–1968. 1968.
The branch of Dodona and other poems. 1970.

Short Story
Evening under lamplight. 1959.

CAMPBELL, PATRICK
(*3rd Baron* GLENAVY) (1913–)
Irish humorous writer and columnist; educated at Rossall School and Pembroke College, Oxford: served in the Irish Marines during the Second World War (1941–4); columnist, *Irish Times* (1944–7); *Sunday Dispatch* (1947–59); assistant editor, *Lilliput* magazine (1947–53); writer for television and screen.

Bibliography
B.N.B.
Who's who. 1973.

Works
A long drink of cold water. 1950.
A short trot with a cultured mind. 1952.
Life in thin slices. 1954.
Patrick Campbell's omnibus. 1956.
Come here till I tell you. 1960.
Constantly in pursuit. 1962.
How to become a scratch golfer. 1963.
Brewing up in the basement. 1963.
Rough husbandry. 1965.
My life and easy times. 1967.
A bunch of new roses. 1967.
The coarse of events. 1968.
The high speed gasworks. 1970.
Fat Tuesday tails. 1972.
Thirty five years on the job. 1973.

CAMPTON, DAVID (1924–)
English playwright, born in Leicester; served in the Second World War (1942–6); worked for the Leicester Education Authority and East Midland Gas Board until 1956 when he turned to full-time writing for stage, radio and television; only his published plays are listed below.

Bibliography
B.N.B.
Contemporary dramatists.
Gale.

Plays
Change partners (staged 1952). 1951.
Going home (staged 1950). 1951.

Honeymoon express. 1951.
Sunshine on the righteous (staged 1953). 1952.
The laboratory (staged 1954). 1955.
Doctor Alexander. 1956.
Cuckoo song. 1956.
Little brother, little sister (staged 1966). 1960.
Soldier from the wars returning. 1960.
Mutatis mutandis (staged 1972). 1960.
Four minute warning (includes Little brother, little sister, Mutatis mutandis, Soldier from the wars returning). 1960.
The lunatic view (includes A smell of burning, Then ..., Memento mori, Getting and spending). 1960.
Funeral dance (staged 1960). 1962.
On stage: seventeen sketches and one monologue. 1964.
Little brother, little sister (with Out of the flying pan). 1966.
The cactus garden (staged 1955). 1967.
Two leaves and a stalk. 1967.
Getting and spending. 1967.
Incident (staged 1962). 1967.
More sketches. 1967.
Ladies' night (includes The manipulator, Silence on the battlefield, Incident, Two leaves and a stalk). 1967.
The manipulator (broadcast and staged 1964). 1967.
Passport to Florence. 1967.
Roses round the door (with The cactus garden, Passport to Florence). 1967.
Silence on the battlefield (staged 1961). 1967.
Then .... 1967.
Laughter and fear: 9 one-act plays. 1969.
On stage again: 14 sketches and 2 monologues. 1969.
Where have all the ghosts gone? 1969.
Resting place. 1970.
Angel unwilling (broadcast 1967, staged 1972). 1972.
The life and death of almost everybody (staged 1970). 1972.
Jonah (staged 1971). 1972.
The cage birds (staged 1971). 1972.
Us and them (staged 1972). 1972.
Come back tomorrow. 1972.
In committee. 1972.
Usher (adapted from Poe: House of Usher, staged 1962). 1973.
Frankenstein (adaptation of Mary Shelley's novel). 1973.
Split down the middle (broadcast 1965, staged 1966). 1973.

Now and then (staged 1970). 1973.
Camilla (adapted from Sheridan le Fanu, staged 1972). 1973.

CANAWAY, WILLIAM HAMILTON
(1925–)
English novelist; educated at the University of Wales; served in the army (1943–6); Technical College Lecturer (1949–62); his plays include *You did it, you feel sorry* (1971).

Bibliography
Authors' and writers' who's who. 1971.
B.N.B.

Novels
A creel of willow. 1957.
The ring-givers. 1958.
A Snowdon stream. The Gwyfrai, and how to fish it. 1958.
The seal. 1959.
Sammy going south (filmed 1962). 1961.
Find the boy. 1961.
The hunter and horns. 1962.
My feet upon a rock. 1963.
Crows in a green tree. 1965.
The grey seas of Jutland. 1966.
The mules of Borgo San Marco. 1967.
A moral obligation. 1969.
Genno. 1971.
A declaration of independence. 1971.

†CANNAN, DENIS
(DENIS PULLEIN THOMPSON)
(1919–)
English playwright; educated at Eton; served in the army during the Second World War (1939–45); radio plays include *Headlong Hall* (1950) and *The Greeting* (1964), film scripts include *The Beggar's Opera* (1953), *A Boy Ten Feet Tall* (1965) and *High Wind in Jamaica* (1965); unpublished plays include *Ghosts* (from Ibsen) (1969).

Bibliography
Anger and after.
B.N.B.
Contemporary dramatists.

Plays
Captain Carvallo (staged 1950). 1951.
Colombe (adaptation of Anouilh, staged 1951). 1952.
Misery me: a comedy of woe (staged 1955). 1956.
You and your wife (staged 1955). 1956.

Who's your father? (staged 1958). 1959.
The power and the glory (based on the novel by Graham Greene). 1959.
U.S. (with others, staged 1966). 1968.

CAPOTE, TRUMAN (1924–)

American novelist and painter on glass; worked in the art department of the *New Yorker*; reader of film scripts for a film company; a contributor to the *New Yorker, Atlantic Monthly, Harper's,* etc.

Bibliography
Authors' and writers' who's who. 1971.
C.B.I.
Contemporary novelists.
Gale.
Who's who. 1973.

Novels
Other voices, other rooms. 1948.
The tree of night (stories). 1949.
The grass harp (dramatised 1953). 1951.
Breakfast at Tiffany's (short stories, filmed 1961). 1958.
The thanksgiving visitor. 1968.
The house of flowers (with Harold Arlen). 1968.

Other Works
Local color (travel essays). 1950.
The muses are heard (essay). 1956.
Observations. 1959.
Selected writings. 1963.
In cold blood (filmed 1968). 1966.
Trilogy: an experiment in multi media (with others). 1969.

CAREW, JAN RYNVELD (1925–)

Guyanan novelist, poet and painter; educated at universities in America, Prague and the Sorbonne; customs officer in government service (1940–4); writer and editor, B.B.C. overseas service (1954–7); Senior Fellow in the Council of Humanities, Princeton, New Jersey (1969–); his poetry is represented in various anthologies; his plays have been produced on radio and television in England and Canada.

Bibliography
B.N.B.
Contemporary novelists.

Novels
Black Midas. 1958.
The wild coast. 1958.

The last barbarian. 1961.
Moscow is not my Mecca (American title, Green winter). 1964.

For Children
The third gift. 1972.

CARR, EMILY (1871–1945)

Canadian poet; born in British Columbia; educated at schools of art in San Francisco and London; taught art in Vancouver; studied in Paris (1910); back in Canada she supported herself by dog-breeding and pottery, etc.

Bibliography
Canadiana.
C.B.I.

Works
Klee Wyck (sketches). 1942.
The book of small (memoirs). 1942.
House of all sorts (memoirs). 1944.
Emily Carr: her paintings and sketches (edited by Ira Dilworth). 1945.
Growing pains (autobiography). 1946.
The heart of a peacock (edited by Ira Dilworth). 1953.

CARROLL, PAUL (1927–)

American poet; born in Chicago; educated at the University of Chicago; served in the U.S. Navy (1945–64); editor, Big Table Books, Follett Publishing Co. (1966–); Visiting Professor of English, Illinois University, Chicago (1968–); represented in numerous anthologies; his edited work is not listed below.

Bibliography
C.B.I.
Contemporary poets.
Gale.

Poetry
Odes: poems 1952–1968. 1968.
The Luke poems. 1971.
Odes and Li Po. n.d.

Criticism
The poem in its skin. 1968.

CARRUTH, HAYDEN (1921–)

American poet; educated at University of Chicago; associate editor, etc., Chicago University Press (1950–3); recipient of many literary awards; rep-

resented in many anthologies; a contributor to
Poetry, Hudson Review, Kenyon Review, etc.

Bibliography
C.B.I.
Contemporary poets.

Poetry
The crow and the heart. 1959.
Journey to a known place. 1961.
Norfolk poems. 1962.
North winter. 1964.
Nothing for tigers. Poems, 1959–1964. 1965.
Contra mortem. 1967.
The Clay Hill anthology: poems. 1970.
From snow, rock and chaos. 1973.

Other Works
Appendix A. 1963.
After the stranger: imaginary dialogues with Cam.
   1967.
For you. 1970.
The voice that is great within us. 1970.

CARTER, ANGELA (1940–)
English novelist; educated at Bristol University
after a spell as a reporter; on winning the Somerset
Maugham Award she travelled in Japan; a con-
tributor to the B.B.C., *New Society, Vogue, Nation,
Queen,* etc.

Bibliography
B.N.B.

Novels
Shadow dance (paperback title, Honey buzzard,
   1968). 1966.
The magic toyshop (John Llewelyn Rhys Prize
   1968). 1967.
Several perceptions (Somerset Maugham Award
   1969). 1968.
Heroes and villains. 1969.
Miss Z., the dark young lady (for children). 1970.
Love. 1971.
The infernal desire machines of Dr. Hoffman.
   1972.

CARTER, MARTIN DAVID (1927–)
Guyanan poet; active in progressive politics in
Georgetown; Minister of Information in the
Government of Guyana.

Bibliography
B.N.B.
Jahn and Dressler.

Poetry
The hill of fire glows red. 1951.
The kind eagle. 1952.
The hidden man. 1952.
Poems of resistance. 1954.

Other Work
An introduction to mass communications; problems in press and broadcasting. 1971.

CASSILL, RONALD VERLIN (†OWEN AHERNE, †JESSE WEBSTER) (1919–)
American novelist; educated at Iowa State University; served in the U.S. Army during the Second World War (1942–6); freelance writer and
teacher of writing (1960–); recipient of several
literary awards; a contributor to numerous
magazines.

Bibliography
C.B.I.
Contemporary novelists.
Gale.

Novels
Eagle on the coin. 1950.
Dormitory women. 1953.
The left bank of desire. 1954.
A taste of sin. 1955.
The hungering shame. 1956.
The wound of love. 1956.
Naked morning. 1957.
Lustful summer. 1958.
Nurses' quarters. 1958.
The wife next door. 1959.
Clem Anderson. 1961.
My sister's keeper. 1961.
Night school. 1961.
Pretty Leslie. 1963.
The president. 1964.
La vie passionée of Rodney Blackthorne. 1968.
Doctor Cobb's game. 1970.

Short Stories
Fifteen short stories (with others). 1957.
The father and other stories. 1965.
The happy marriage and other stories. 1966.

Other Works
Writing fiction. 1962.
In an iron time (essays). 1967.
Intro # two. 1970.

CATO, NANCY FOTHERINGHAM
(*Mrs.* de BRACTON NORMAN)
(1917–)
Australian poet and historical novelist; educated at Adelaide University; journalist and art critic (1935–48); freelance writer (1948–); has travelled widely in Europe and Australia.

Bibliography
Australian national bibliography.
B.N.B.
Contemporary poets.
Gale.
Miller and Macartney.

Historical Novels
All the rivers run. 1958.
Time flows softly. 1959.
Green grows the vine. 1960.
But still the stream. 1962.
The sea ants (stories). 1962.
North-west by south. 1965.

Poetry
The darkened window. 1950.
The dancing bough. 1957.

CATTON, BRUCE (1899–)
American historian and journalist; educated at Oberlin College; reporter on Boston and Cleveland newspapers (1920–6); Washington correspondent, Newspaper Enterprise Association (1926–41); director of information (1942–6); senior editor, *American Heritage* magazine (1954–); awarded various academic and literary honours and prizes; his edited work is not listed below.

Bibliography
C.B.I.
Gale.

Works
The army of the Potomac, 3 vols.:
   War lords of Washington (The army of the Potomac vol. I). 1948.
   Mr. Lincoln's army (The army of the Potomac vol. II). 1951.
   Glory road (The army of the Potomac vol. III). 1952.
A stillness at Appomattox. 1953.
U. S. Grant and the American military tradition. 1954.
Banners at Shenandoah. 1955.
This hallowed ground. 1956.

America goes to war. 1958.
Grant moves south. 1960.
American heritage picture history of the Civil War. 1960.
The coming fury (vol. I of the Centennial history of the American civil war). 1961.
Two roads to Sumter (with William Bruce Catton). 1963.
The terrible swift sword (vol. II of the Centennial history of the American civil war). 1963.
Never call retreat (vol. III of the Centennial history of the American civil war). 1965.
Grant takes command. 1969.
Prefaces to history. 1970.
Waiting for the morning train: an American boyhood. 1972.

CAUSLEY, CHARLES STANLEY
(1917–)
English poet; born in Cornwall; served in the Second World War (1940–6); Literary Editor of B.B.C. magazines (1953–6); a contributor to the *Observer, Sunday Times, Listener, New Statesman, T.L.S.*, etc.; his edited work is not listed below.

Bibliography
Authors' and writers' who's who. 1971.
B.N.B.
Contemporary poets.
R. N. Currey. Poets of the 1939–1945 war. 1960.
Gale.
Who's who. 1973.

Poetry
Farewell, Aggie Weston. 1951.
Survivor's leave. 1953.
Union Street. 1957.
Johnny Alleluia. 1961.
Penguin modern poets no. 3 (with G. Barker, M. Bell). 1962.
Underneath the water. 1968.
Figure of 8. 1969.
Figgie Hobbin. 1970.

Poetry for Children
Dawn and dusk. 1962.
Rising early. 1964.
The tale of the trinosaur. 1973.

Short Story
Hands to dance. 1951.

CAUTE, JOHN DAVID (1936–)
English novelist and writer; educated at Wel-

lington and Wadham College, Oxford; Fellow of All Souls (1959–65); Reader in Social and Political Theory, Brunel University (1969–70); unpublished plays are *Songs of an autumn rifle* (1961) and *Fall out* (1972).

Bibliography
B.N.B.
Contemporary novelists.
Gale.
Who's who. 1973.

Novels
At fever pitch (John Llewelyn Rhys Prize 1960). 1959.
Comrade Jacob. 1961.
The decline of the West. 1966.
The occupation. 1971.
The confrontation: a trilogy (The demonstration, a play, The occupation, a novel, and The illusion, an essay on politics, the theatre and the novel). 1971.

Play
The demonstration (staged 1969). 1970.

Other Works
The Left in Europe since 1789. 1961.
Communism and the French intellectuals 1914–1960. 1964.
Fanon. 1970.
The illusion (with The demonstration and The occupation). 1972.
The fellow-travellers. 1972.

CHADWICK, JOHN (1920–)
English classical scholar; educated at St. Paul's School and Corpus Christi College, Cambridge; served in the Royal Navy in the Second World War (1940–5); editorial assistant on the Oxford Latin Dictionary, Clarendon Press (1946–52); Lecturer at Cambridge (1952–69); Fellow of Downing College (1960–) and Reader in Classics, Cambridge (1969–); awarded several academic honours; a contributor to learned journals; edited, with E. L. Bennett and M. Ventris, *The Knossos tablets* (1956).

Bibliography
B.N.B.
Gale.
Who's who. 1973.

Works
The medical works of Hippocrates (joint translation with W. N. Mann). 1950.

Documents in Mycenaean Greek (jointly with M. Ventris). 1956.
The decipherment of Linear B. 1958.
The pre-history of the Greek language. 1963.

CHADWICK, *Professor* WILLIAM OWEN (1916–)
English historian; brother of John Chadwick (q.v.); educated at Tonbridge School and St. John's College, Cambridge; Master of Selwyn College, Cambridge (1956–); Regius Professor of Modern History (1968–); Vice-Chancellor, Cambridge University (1969–71); D.D., St. Andrews University, Hon. D.Litt., Kent University, etc.; a contributor to *The Times, Listener, Observer, English Historical Review, Journal of Ecclesiastical History,* etc.

Bibliography
Authors' and writers' who's who. 1971.
B.N.B.
Gale.
Who's who. 1973.

Works
John Cassian. 1950.
The founding of Cuddesdon. 1954.
Studies in early British history. 1954.
From Bossuet to Newman. 1957.
Western asceticism. 1958.
Creighton on Luther. 1959.
Mackenzie's grave. 1959.
The mind of the Oxford movement. 1960.
Victorian miniature. 1960.
The history of the church. 1962.
From uniformity to unity 1662–1962 (with G. F. Nuttall). 1962.
Westcott and the University. 1963.
The Reformation. 1964.
The Victorian church. 1966.
Freedom and the historian. 1969.

CHAMPKIN, PETER (1918–)
English poet; born in Hong Kong; educated at King's School, Canterbury, and St. Catherine's College, Cambridge; prisoner of war in Germany (1940–5); British Council officer (1947–50); G.C.E. administrator, University of London (1951).

Bibliography
B.N.B.
Gale.

Poetry
In another room. 1959.
The enmity of noon. 1960.
Poems of our time. 1962.
For the employed. 1966.

CHAPLIN, SIDNEY (1916–)

English novelist; born in Durham, the son of a miner; worked in the mines (1931–50); wrote for the *Coal Magazine* (1950–6), *Coal News* (1961–), etc.; member of the B.B.C. North Regional Advisory Council; public relations officer, National Coal Board (1956–64); a contributor to the *Guardian*, *Sunday Times*, etc.

Bibliography
Authors' and writers' who's who. 1971.
B.N.B.
Contemporary novelists.
Gale.

Novels
The leaping lad (short stories). 1947.
My fate cries out. 1949.
The thin seam (stories). 1950.
The big room. 1960.
The day of the sardine. 1961.
The watchers and the watched. 1962.
Sam in the morning. 1965.
Us Northerners (stories). 1970.
The mines of alabaster. 1971.

Other Works
Lakes to Tyneside. 1951.
Close the coalhouse day (play, with Alan Plater and Alex Glasgow). 1969.
The smell of Sunday dinner. 1971.

†CHARLES, GERDA (GERTRUDE LIPSON)

English-Jewish novelist; born in Liverpool; contributor to the *New Statesman*, *Jewish Chronicle*, *Daily Telegraph*, etc.; editor of *Modern Jewish stories* (1963).

Bibliography
Authors' and writers' who's who. 1971.
B.N.B.
Contemporary novelists.
Gale.

Novels
The true voice. 1959.
The crossing point. 1960.

A slanting light (James Tait Black Prize 1964). 1963.
A logical girl. 1967.
Destiny waltz. 1971.

CHARYN, JEROME (1937–)

American novelist; born in New York; educated at Columbia University; recreation leader, later teacher of English; a contributor of short stories to *Commentary* and *Mademoiselle*.

Bibliography
C.B.I.
Gale.

Novels
Once upon a droshky. 1964.
On the darkening green. 1965.
Going to Jerusalem. 1967.
The man who grew younger and other stories. 1967.
American scrapbook. 1969.
Eisenhower, my Eisenhower. 1971.
The tar baby: memorial number for Anatole Waxman-Weissman. 1973.

CHAUDHURI, NIRAD C. (1897–)

Indian writer and journalist; born in Kishorganj, District Mymensing; educated at Calcutta University; a contributor to *The Times*, *Encounter*, *New English Review*, *Atlantic Review*, *Pacific Affairs* as well as to all important Indian periodicals.

Bibliography
C.B.I.
Indian national bibliography 1958–67.
National bibliography of Indian literature 1901–53.

Works
The autobiography of an unknown Indian. 1951.
A passage to England. 1959.
The continent of Circe (Duff Cooper Memorial Prize 1967). 1966.
The intellectual in India. 1967.
To live or not to live. n.d.

Books for Children
Angry river. 1972.
The blue umbrella. 1973.
Once upon a monsoon time. 1973.
The world of trees. 1973.

CHAYEFSKY, PADDY (1923–)
American playwright; born in New York; educated at City College of New York and Fordham University; served in the U.S. Army during the Second World War (1943–5); television scriptwriter (1952–); president of Carnegie Productions Inc., etc. (1957–); recipient of various awards for his film *Marty* (1955); other films include *The Americanization of Emily* (1964); has also written other unpublished plays.

Bibliography
C.B.I.
Contemporary dramatists.
Gale.

Plays for Television
Television plays. 1955.
Bachelor party (filmed 1957). 1955.
Middle of the night. 1957.
The goddess (filmed 1958). 1958.
The tenth man. 1959.
Gideon (produced 1961). 1962.
The passion of Josef D. 1964.
Marty, a play (filmed 1955). 1964.
The latent homosexual: a play. 1967.
Marty, and Printer's measure. 1968.

CHEEVER, JOHN (1912–)
American novelist and short-story writer; served in the Second World War; television scriptwriter; taught at Barnard College, New York; a contributor to the *New Yorker, Collier's, New Republic*, etc.; a recipient of various literary awards.

Bibliography
C.B.I.
Gale.
Who's who. 1973.

Novels and Short Stories
The way some people live (stories). 1943.
The enormous radio and other stories. 1953.
The Wapshot chronicle. 1957.
The housebreaker of Shady Hill, and other stories. 1958.
Some people, places and things that will not appear in my next novel (stories). 1961.
The Wapshot scandal. 1964.
The brigadier and the golf widow. 1964.
Bullet Park. 1969.
The world of apples (stories). 1973.

CHITRE, DILIP (1938–)
Indian short-story writer, novelist, critic, cultural and political commentator; born in Baroda; educated in Baroda and Bombay; also writes in Marathi; editor and translator of *An anthology of Marathi poetry* (1968).

Bibliography
C.B.I.
Indian national bibliography 1958–67.
National bibliography of Indian literature 1901–53.

Works
The roots of obscenity (ed. A. B. Shah). 1967.
Orpheus (stories). 1968.

CHOMSKY, AVRAM NOAM (1928–)
American writer on linguistics; born in Philadelphia; educated at the University of Pennsylvania; Assistant, later Professor of Linguistics, etc., Massachusetts Institute of Technology (1955–); a member of various American learned societies; a contributor to learned journals.

Bibliography
C.B.I.
Gale.

Works
Syntactic structures. 1957.
Current issues in linguistic theory. 1964.
Aspects of the theory of syntax. 1965.
Cartesian linguistics. 1966.
Topics in the theory of generative grammar. 1966.
Language and mind. 1968.
The sound pattern of English (with Morris Halle). 1968.
American power and the new Mandarins. 1969.
Aspects of the theory of syntax. 1969.
At war with Asia. 1970.
Problems of freedom and knowledge (the Russell lectures). 1971.
Studies on semantics in generative grammar. 1972.

†CHRISTOPHER, JOHN
(CHRISTOPHER SAMUEL YOUD,
†HILARY FORD,
†WILLIAM GODFREY,
†PETER GRAAF,
†PETER NICHOLS,
†ANTHONY RYE) (1922–)
English novelist; served in the army in the Second

World War; has been a professional novelist since 1958; lives in Guernsey.

Bibliography
B.N.B.

Novels as †John Christopher
The twenty-second century. 1954.
The year of the comet. 1955.
The death of grass (American title, No blade of grass) (filmed 1972). 1956.
The caves of night. 1958.
A scent of white poppies. 1959.
The long voyage (American title, The white voyage). 1960.
The world in winter (American title, The white winter). 1962.
Cloud on silver (American title, Sweeney's island). 1964.
The possessors. 1965.
A wrinkle in the sun (American title, The ragged edge). 1965.
The little people. 1967.
The white mountains (for children). 1967.
The city of gold and lead (for children). 1967.
Pendulum. 1968.
Pool of fire. 1968.
The lotus caves (for adolescents). 1969.
The guardians (for children). 1970.
The prince in waiting (for children). 1970.
The sword of the spirits (for children). 1972.

Novels as †Hilary Ford
Felix walking. 1958.
Felix running. 1959.
Bella on the roof. 1965.

Novels as †William Godfrey
Malleson at Melbourne. 1956.
The friendly game. 1957.

Novels as †Peter Graaf
Dust and the curious boy (American title, Give the devil his due). 1957.
Daughter fair. 1958.
The sapphire conference. 1959.
The gull's kiss. 1962.

Novel as †Peter Nichols
Patchwork as death. 1965.

Novels as †Samuel Youd
Babel itself. 1951.
The brave conquerors. 1952.
Crown and anchor. 1953.

A palace of strangers. 1954.
Holly ash (American title, The opportunist). 1955.
Giant's arrow. 1956.
The choice. 1961.
The message of love. 1961.
The summers at Accorn. 1963.
The burning bird. 1964.

Poetry as †Anthony Rye
The inn of the birds. 1947.
To a modern hero. 1957.
Poems from Selbourne. 1962.

CIARDI, JOHN ANTHONY (1916–)

American poet; educated at the University of Michigan; served in the U.S. Air Force (1942–5); after various academic posts, became poetry editor of the *Saturday Review* (1956–); recipient of various literary awards and honours; translated Dante's *Inferno* and *Paradiso*; his edited work is not listed below.

Bibliography
C.B.I.
Contemporary poets.
Gale.
L. of C.
William White. John Ciardi: a bibliography. 1959.

Poetry
Homeward to America. 1940.
Other skies. 1947.
Live another day. 1949.
From time to time. 1951.
As if: poems new and selected. 1955.
I marry you: a sheaf of love poems. 1958.
Thirty-nine poems. 1959.
In the stoneworks. 1961.
In fact. 1962.
Person to person. 1964.
You know who. 1964.
The king who saved himself from being saved. 1965.
The strangest everything. 1966.
An alphabestiary. 1967.
The achievement of John Ciardi; a comprehensive selection (critical introduction by Miller Williams). 1969.
Lives of X. 1971.

For Children
The reason for the pelican. 1959.
Scrappy, the pup. 1960.
The man who sang the sillies. 1961.
I met a man. 1961.
You read to me, I'll read to you. 1962.

The wish tree. 1962.
John J. Plenty and the Fiddler Dan. 1963.
The monster den; or, Look what happened at my
house—and to it. 1966.
Someone who could win a polar bear. 1970.

Other Works
How does a poem mean? 1959.
Dialogue with an audience. 1963.
A manner of speaking. 1972.

CICELLIS, CATHERINE MATHILDA (Mrs. PALEOLOGOS) (1926–)
Greek novelist; born in France; translator for
U.N.R.R.A. (1945–7); Greek Broadcasting Insti-
tute, Athens (1953–5); lives in England; works as a
freelance translator; a contributor to *Harper's
Bazaar, London Magazine,* etc.

Bibliography
B.N.B.
Contemporary novelists.
Gale.

Novels and Short Stories
The easy way (stories). 1950.
No name in the street. 1952.
Death of a town (stories). 1954.
Ten seconds from now. 1956.
The way to Colonos (novellas). 1960.

CLARK, CHARLES MANNING HOPE (1915–)
Australian historian; born in Sydney; educated at
the University of Melbourne and Balliol College,
Oxford; after various university posts, Professor
of History, Canberra University (1960–); a contributor of short stories to *Sydney Bulletin* and
Quadrant; his edited works, which include *Select
documents in Australia,* 2 vols., with L. Pryor
(1950–5), are not listed below.

Bibliography
Australian national bibliography.
B.N.B.
Gale.

Works
Sources of Australian history. 1957.
Meeting Soviet man. 1960.
A history of Australia, vols. I–III, 1962–74.
A short history of Australia. 1964.
Disquiet and other stories. 1969.

CLARK, ELEANOR (1913–)
American novelist; wife of the poet Robert Penn
Warren; worked in the U.S. Office of Strategic
Services, Washington (1943–5), and in publishing
(1945–52); recipient of several literary awards; a
contributor to various periodicals; her translated
work is not listed below; translated Roman Sender,
The dark wedding (1943).

Bibliography
C.B.I.
Contemporary novelists.
Gale.

Novels
The bitter box. 1946.
Baldur's gate. 1970.

Other Works
Rome and a villa. 1952.
Song of Roland (for children). 1960.
The oysters of Locmariaquer. 1964.

CLARK, JOHN PEPPER (1935–)
Nigerian poet and playwright; educated at Ibadan
and Princeton universities; founder and editor of
the literary magazine, the *Horn*; on the staff of the
Daily Express, Lagos; Lecturer in African Litera-
ture, University of Lagos; represented in *Seven
African Writers* (1964), *West African Verse* (1967) and
New Voices of the Commonwealth (1968).

Bibliography
B.N.B.
Contemporary poets.
Jahn and Dressler.

Poetry
Poems (Ibadan). 1962.
A reed in the tide. 1965.
Casualties: poems 1966–68. 1970.

Plays
Song of a goat. 1962.
3 plays (Song of a goat, The masquerade, The raft).
1964.
Ozidi. 1966.

Other Work
America, their America. 1964.

CLARK, LEONARD (1905–)
English poet and writer; born in Guernsey; spent
his childhood in Gloucestershire; taught (1921–36);

H.M. Inspector of Schools (1936–70); his edited work is not listed below.

Bibliography
Authors' and writers' who's who. 1971.
B.N.B.
Contemporary poets.
Gale.
Who's who. 1973.

Poetry
Poems. 1925.
Passage to the Pole. 1944.
Rhandanim. 1945.
The mirror. 1948.
XII poems. 1948.
English morning. 1953.
Selected poems 1940–57. 1958.
Daybreak (for children). 1963.
The year round. 1965.
Fields and territories. 1967.
Flutes and cymbals (for children). 1968.
Good company (for children). 1968.
Near and far (for children). 1969.
Here and there. 1969.
The tale of Prince Igor. 1970.
Walking with trees. 1970.
The four seasons. 1970.
Sweet as hawthorn (for children). 1970.
Singing in the streets. 1970.
All along down along. 1971.
Poems for Christmas. 1972.
Secret as toads. 1972.
The broad Atlantic: poems for the young. 1972.

Autobiography
Green wood, a Gloucestershire childhood. 1962.
A fool in the forest. 1965.
Grateful Caliban. 1967.

Other Works
Alfred Williams: his life and work. 1945.
The rivers ran east. 1954.
The marching wind. 1955.
Sark discovered. 1956.
Andrew Young (with R. S. Thomas). 1957.
Yucatan adventure. 1959.
Walter de la Mare. 1960.
When they were children (biographies). 1964.
Who killed the bears? 1964.
Andrew Young. 1964.
The Robert Andrew books. 1965–6.
The year round (stories). 1965.
Prospect of Highgate and Hampstead. 1967.

CLARK, WALTER VAN TILBURG
(1909–)
American novelist; educated at the universities of Nevada and Vermont; teacher of English and creative writing at various universities; recipient of O. Henry Award; a contributor to the *New York Herald Tribune, Holiday, Saturday Review*, etc.

Bibliography
C.B.I.
Contemporary novelists.
Gale.

Novels
The ox-bow incident (filmed). 1940.
The city of trembling leaves (American title, Tim Hazard). 1945.
The track of the cat (filmed). 1949.
The watchful gods and other stories. 1950.

CLARKE, ARTHUR CHARLES
(1917–)
English science fiction writer; educated at King's College, London; civil servant (1936–44); served in the R.A.F. during the Second World War (1941–6); assistant editor, *Science Abstracts* (1949–50); full-time writer since 1951; much concerned in astronomical and astronautical societies; a contributor to numerous journals including the *New York Times, Harper's, Vogue, Horizon*, etc.

Bibliography
B.N.B.
Contemporary novelists.
Gale.

Novels
The sands of Mars. 1951.
Islands in the sky. 1952.
Childhood's end. 1953.
Against the fall of night. 1953.
Expedition to earth. 1953.
Prelude to space. 1953.
Earthlight. 1955.
Reach for tomorrow. 1956.
The city and the stars. 1956.
The deep range. 1957.
Tales from the White Hart. 1957.
Across the sea of stars (collection). 1959.
The other side of the sky. 1961.
A fall of moondust. 1961.
From the oceans, from the stars (collection). 1962.
Tales of ten worlds. 1962.
Dolphin Island. 1962.

Glide path. 1963.
Prelude to Mars (collection). 1965.
An Arthur C. Clarke omnibus. 1965.
Time probe. 1967.
2001; a space odyssey (with Stanley Kubrick; filmed 1968). 1968.
The lion of Comarre. 1968.
A second Arthur C. Clarke omnibus. 1969.
The wind from the sun. 1972.

Other Works
Interplanetary flight. 1950.
The exploration of space. 1951.
The young traveller in space (American title, Going into space). 1953.
The exploration of the moon. 1954.
The coast of coral. 1956.
The reefs of Taprobane. 1957.
The making of a moon. 1957.
Voice across the sea. 1958.
Boy beneath the sea (with Mike Wilson, for children). 1958.
The challenge of space. 1959.
The first five fathoms (with Mike Wilson, for children). 1960.
The challenge of the sea (for children). 1960.
Indian Ocean adventure (with Mike Wilson, for children). 1961.
Profiles of the future. 1962.
The treasure of the Great Reef. 1964.
Indian Ocean treasure (with Mike Wilson, for children). 1964.
Man and space. 1964.
Voices from the sky. 1965.
Coming of the space age. 1967.
The nine billion names of God. 1967.
Report on Planet Three. 1972.

CLARKE, AUSTIN CHESTERFIELD
(1934–   )
Caribbean novelist; born in Barbados; educated at the University of Toronto; producer, Canadian Broadcasting Corporation, Toronto (1963–   ); Visiting Professor of Afro-American Literature, Yale University (1968–   ).

Bibliography
B.N.B.
C.B.I.
Contemporary novelists.
Gale.

Novels
The survivors of the crossing. 1964.

Flight to Africa. 1964.
Amongst thistles and thorns. 1965.
The meeting point. 1967.
When he was free he used to wear silks (stories). 1971.
The impuritans. 1972.

Other Work
Black literature, twentieth century. 1968.

CLEARY, JON STEPHEN
(1917–   )
Australian novelist and screen writer; did a variety of jobs (1932–40); served in the Australian Army during the Second World War (1940–5); journalist and freelance writer (1945–51); since then a full-time writer; has travelled widely.

Bibliography
Authors' and writers' who's who. 1971.
B.N.B.
Gale.
Who's who. 1973.

Novels
These small glories (stories). 1946.
You can't see round corners. 1947.
The long shadow. 1949.
Just let me be. 1950.
The sundowners. 1952.
The climate of courage. 1953.
Justin Bayard. 1955.
The green helmet. 1957.
The back of sunset. 1959.
North from Thursday. 1960.
The Ten country of marriage. 1962.
Forest of the night. 1963.
A flight of chariots. 1964.
The fall of an eagle. 1964.
The pulse of danger. 1966.
The high commissioner. 1967.
The long pursuit. 1967.
Season of doubt. 1968.
Remember Jack Hoxie. 1969.
Helga's web. 1970.
Mask of the Andes. 1971.
Man's estate. 1972.
Ransom. 1973.

CLEAVER, ELDRIDGE (1935–   )
American Negro writer; educated at junior college and in California state prisons where he spent some years at different times, convicted of assault, attempted murder, the possession of drugs, etc.;

minister of information for the Black Panther Movement (1967); guest lecturer, University of Berkeley (1968) and at numerous other U.S. universities; previously a Black Muslim; a regular contributor to *Ramparts*; has lived in Cuba and Africa.

Bibliography
C.B.I.
Gale.

Works
Soul on ice. 1968.
Eldridge Cleaver: post-prison writings and speeches (ed. Robert Scheer). 1969.
Eldridge Cleaver's black papers. 1969.

CLEMO, REGINALD JOHN (†JACK CLEMO) (1916–)

English poet and writer; born in Cornwall; a contributor to the *London Magazine* and west-country journals, etc.; increasing deafness and the loss of his sight (1955) precludes employment; he is represented in numerous anthologies.

Bibliography
Authors' and writers' who's who. 1971.
B.N.B.
Contemporary poets.
Gale.

Poetry
The wintry priesthood (Cheltenham Poetry Prize 1951). 1951.
The clay verge. 1951.
The map of clay. 1961.
Cactus on Carmel. 1967.
The echoing tip. 1971.

Other Works
Wilding graft (novel). 1948.
Confession of a rebel (autobiography). 1949.
The invading gospel (theology). 1958.

CLEWES, HOWARD CHARLES VIVIAN (1912–)

English novelist; educated at Merchant Taylor's School; worked in advertising agencies (1931–7); served in the Second World War (1939–45); press officer, Milan (1945–7); full-time writer (1948–); scriptwriter of many films including *The Long Memory*, *Mutiny on the Bounty*, *Up from the Beach*, etc.

Bibliography
Authors' and writers' who's who. 1971.
B.N.B.
Gale.
Who's who. 1973.

Novels
Sailor come home. 1939.
Dead ground. 1945.
The unforgiven (American title, Thus am I slayn). 1948.
The mask of wisdom. 1948.
Green grow the rushes. 1949.
The long memory. 1951.
An epitaph for love. 1952.
The way the wind blows. 1954.
Man on a horse. 1964.
The libertines. 1964.

Plays
Quay south. 1947.
Image in the sun. 1955.

Other Works
Stendhal. 1950.

CLEWES, WINSTON DAVID ARMSTRONG (1906–)

English novelist, brother of Howard Clewes (q.v.); worked as a business executive, writing novels in his spare time.

Bibliography
B.N.B.

Novels
The violent friends. 1944.
Sweet river in the morning. 1946.
Journey into spring. 1948.
Men at work. 1951.
Peacocks on the lawn. 1952.
The merry month. 1954.
The tilting town. 1957.
Clementine. 1958.

CLOUTS, SYDNEY (1926–)

South African poet; born in Cape Town; educated at Cape Town University; Research Fellow at Rhodes University, Grahamstown (1969–); a contributor to *Contrast*, *Transatlantic Review*, *Listener*, etc.

Bibliography
Contemporary poets.

Poetry
One life. 1966.

CLURMAN, HAROLD (1901–)
American historian and dramatic critic; educated at
Columbia University and the Sorbonne; worked
in the theatre (1924–); Hollywood film director
(1941–5); director of many stage productions
including *Orpheus descending* (1957), *Incident at
Vichy* (1964) and *Tiger at the gates* (1960); recipient
of many awards and honours; a contributor to the
New York Times, *Observer*, etc.; drama critic of
Nation (1953–); his editions of plays are not listed
below.

Bibliography
C.B.I.
Gale.

Works
The fervent years. 1945.
Lies like truth. 1958.
The naked image. 1966.
On directing. 1972.
Ideas on theater. 1973.

COBBING, BOB (1920–)
English concrete poet; born in Middlesex; taught
for some years; was a bookshop manager, publisher of *Writers' Forum*; represented in numerous
anthologies.

Bibliography
B.N.B.
Contemporary poets.

Poetry
Massacre of the innocents. 1963.
Sound poems; an A.B.C. in sound. 1965.
Typestract 1. 1965.
Eyearun. 1966.
Chamber music. 1967.
Kurrirrurriri. 1967.
Six sound poems (S O). 1968.
Octo. 1969.
Whisper piece. 1969.
Typestract 2. 1969.
Why Shiva has ten arms. 1969.
Pamphlet 2—Whississippi. 1969.
12 days (of Xmas). 1970.
Etcetera; a new collection of found and sound
   poems. 1970.
St. Silvester plus, or minus six. 1970.

COBURN, *Professor* **KATHLEEN** (1905–)
English Coleridge scholar; educated at the universities of Toronto and Oxford; Professor of
English, University of Toronto (1953–); a contributor to the *Review of English Studies, University
of Toronto Quarterly*, etc.

Bibliography
Authors' and writers' who's who. 1971.
B.N.B.
Gale.
Who's who. 1973.

Works edited by Professor Coburn
The philosophical lectures of S. T. Coleridge.
   1949.
Coleridge, S. T. Inquiring spirit. 1951.
The letters of Sara Hutchinson, 1800–1835. 1954.
The notebooks of S. T. Coleridge, vol. i, Part I,
   1794–1804. 1957.
The notebooks of S. T. Coleridge, vol. ii, Part II,
   1804–1808. 1961.
Coleridge: a collection of critical essays. 1968.
The notebooks of S. T. Coleridge, vol. iii, Part III,
   1808–1819. 1969.
The collected Coleridge, 1961–69 (General editor).

COGHILL, *Professor* **NEVILL HENRY
KENDAL AYLMER** (1899–)
English literary scholar, producer and writer; educated at Haileybury and Exeter College, Oxford;
served in the First World War (1917–18); Tutor and
Fellow, Exeter College (1925–57); Merton Professor of English Literature, Oxford (1957–66); his
productions include *A Midsummer Night's Dream*,
Haymarket (1945), *Pilgrim's Progress*, Covent Garden (1951), etc.; governor of the Stratford Memorial Theatre (1956), etc.; has broadcast on Chaucer,
Langland, etc.

Bibliography
B.N.B.
Gale.
Who's who. 1973.

Works
The pardon of Piers Plowman (Gollancz Memorial
   Lecture, British Academy). 1945.
The mask of hope. 1948.
Visions from Piers Plowman. 1949.
The poet Chaucer. 1949.
The Canterbury tales translated into modern
   English. 1951.

Geoffrey Chaucer. 1956.
Shakespeare's professional skills. 1964.
Langland: Piers Plowman. 1964.
Troilus and Criseyde (in modern English). 1971.
A choice of Chaucer. 1972.

COGSWELL, FREDERICK WILLIAM (†FRED COGSWELL) (1917–)

Canadian poet and writer; born in New Brunswick; served in the Canadian Army in the Second World War (1940–5); educated at the universities of New Brunswick and Edinburgh; Professor of English at New Brunswick (1952–); editor of the little magazine *Fiddlehead*; compiled the anthology *Five New Brunswick Poets* (1962); translated *One Hundred Poems of Modern Quebec* (1970); a contributor to the *Dalhousie Review*, *Queen's*, *Canadian Forum*, etc.

Bibliography
Authors' and writers' who's who. 1971.
B.N.B.
Canadiana.
C.B.I.
Contemporary poets.
Gale.

Poetry
The stunted strong. 1954.
The haloed tree. 1955.
The testament of Cresseid (adaptation). 1957.
Descent from Eden. 1959.
Lost dimension. 1960.
The enchanted land. 1967.
Star people. 1968.
The immortal plowman. 1969.

Other Work
Arts in New Brunswick. 1967.

COHEN, JOHN MICHAEL (1903–)

English critic and translator; educated at St. Paul's School and Queen's College, Cambridge; after a short period in publishing he worked in the family manufacturing business (1925–40); wartime schoolmaster (1940–6); freelance writer, editor and translator since 1946; many works, not listed below, are translations and editions.

Bibliography
Authors' and writers' who's who. 1971.
B.N.B.
Gale.
Who's who. 1973.

Works
Robert Browning. 1952.
Life of Ludwig Mond. 1956.
Poetry of this age. 1959.
Robert Graves. 1960.
Penguin dictionary of quotations (with M. J. Cohen). 1960.
English translators and translations. 1962.
The baroque lyric. 1963.
Writers in the new Cuba. 1967.
En tiempos difíciles (a study of the new Cuban poetry). 1971.
Penguin dictionary of modern quotations (with M. J. Cohen). 1972.

COHEN, LEONARD NORMAN (1934–)

Canadian-Jewish poet and novelist; born in Montreal; educated at McGill and Columbia universities; lives mostly in Greece; recipient of various literary awards.

Bibliography
Canadiana.
C.B.I.
Contemporary novelists.

Novels
The favourite game. 1963.
Beautiful losers. 1966.

Poetry
Let us compare mythologies. 1955.
Spice-box of earth. 1961.
Flowers for Hitler. 1964.
Parasites of heaven. 1966.
Selected poems 1956–68. 1969.
Songs of Leonard Cohen. 1969.
The energy of slaves. 1972.

COLE, BARRY (1936–)

English poet and novelist; born at Woking; Northern Arts Fellow in literature, Durham and Newcastle universities (1970–2); a contributor to the *New Statesman*, *T.L.S.*, *Spectator*.

Bibliography
Authors' and writers' who's who. 1971.
B.N.B.
Contemporary poets.
Gale.

Novels
A run across the island. 1968.

Joseph's winter patronage. 1969.
The search for Rita. 1970.

Poetry
Blood ties. 1967.
Moonsearch. 1968.
Ulysses in the town of coloured glass. 1968.
The visitors. 1970.
Vanessa in the city. 1971.

COLE, JOHN REECE (1916–)
New Zealand novelist; born and educated in Palmerston North; served in the New Zealand Forces during the Second World War (1941–4); held various library posts, including chief librarian, Alexander Turnbull Library, and Unesco Library Adviser to Indonesia (1948–); a contributor to journals and literary magazines; represented in anthologies of short stories.

Bibliography
B.N.B.
N.Z. national bibliography.
Who's who in New Zealand, 10th edition. 1971.

Novels
It was so late, and other stories. 1949.
Pompallier, the house and the mission. 1957.

COLLYMORE, FRANK APPLETON (1893–)
Caribbean poet; born in Barbados; travelled widely; taught (1910–58); a contributor to *Bim*, *Kyk-over-al*, *Tamarack Review*; represented in several anthologies.

Bibliography
C.B.I.
Contemporary poets.
Jahn and Dressler.

Poetry (all published in Barbados)
Thirty poems. 1944.
Beneath the Casuarinas. 1945.
Flotsam. 1948.
Collected poems. 1959.
Rhymed ruminations on the fauna of Barbados. 1969.

Other Work
Notes for a glossary of words and phrases of Barbadian dialect. 1953.

COMBS, ELISHA TRAMMELL, Jr.
(1924–)
American poet; educated at Chicago, Washington, California and Harvard universities; served in the U.S. Army as a meteorologist (1943–6); oil-chemist (1948–51); owner-manager of Tram Books (1952–); trustee and co-founder of Virgin Island Museum (1955–6); has travelled widely; educated as a meteorologist and engineer, he is also a bibliographer; a contributor to *Bim*.

Bibliography
C.B.I.
Contemporary poets.
Gale.

Poetry
Pilgrim's terrace: poems american west indian. 1957.
Artists boys cats: lovers judges priests/ceremonies in mind. 1959.
But never mind: poems, etc., 1946–1950. 1961.
Saint Thomas: poems. 1965.

COMFORT, ALEXANDER (1920–)
English poet, novelist and medical biologist; educated at Highgate School, Trinity College, Cambridge, and the London Hospital, M.R.C.S.; L.R.C.P.; M.B.; D.C.II.; Ph.D., etc.; conscientious objector in Second World War; distinguished medical career; currently director of the Medical Research Council on Ageing (1965–); his specialist medical works are not listed below.

Bibliography
Authors' and writers' who's who. 1971.
B.N.B.
Contemporary poets.
Gale.
N.C.B.E.L.
Who's who. 1973.

Novels
The silver river. 1938.
No such liberty. 1941.
The almond tree. 1942.
The powerhouse. 1944.
On this side nothing. 1948.
A giant's strength. 1952.
Come out to play. 1961.

Poetry
Three new poets (with Roy McFadden and Ian Seraillier). 1942.

69

France and other poems. 1942.
Wreath for the living. 1942.
Elegies. 1944.
The song of Lazarus. 1945.
The signal to engage. 1946.
And all but he departed. 1951.
Haste to the wedding. 1962.

Plays
Into Egypt. 1942.
Cities of the plain. 1943.
Gengulphus. 1948.

Other Works
Art and social responsibility. 1947.
Letters from an outpost (short stories). 1947.
The novel and our time. 1948.
Barbaris and sexual freedom. 1948.
The pattern of the future (radio talks). 1950.
Authority and delinquency in the modern state. 1950.
Darwin and the naked lady. 1961.
Are you sitting comfortably? (political songs). 1962.
Sex and society. 1963.
Ageing: the biology of senescence. 1964.
The process of ageing. 1965.
Nature and human nature. 1966.
The anxiety makers (a study of medical moralism). 1967.

CONNELL, EVAN SHELBY, Jr.
(1924–)
American novelist; educated at Stanford and Columbia universities; served in the U.S. Army in the Second World War (1943–5); editor of *Contact Magazine* (1960–); his edited work is not listed below.

Bibliography
C.B.I.
Contemporary novelists.
Gale.

Novels and Short Stories
The anatomy lesson (stories). 1957.
Mrs. Bridge. 1958.
The patriot. 1960.
Notes from a bottle found on the beach at Carmel. 1963.
At the crossroads (stories). 1965.
The diary of a rapist. 1966.
Mr. Bridge. 1969.

Poetry
Points for a compass rose. 1973.

CONNOR, TONY
(†JOHN ANTHONY) (1930–)
English poet, born in Lancashire; educated at University of Manchester; worked as a textile designer (1944–60); served in the army (1948–50); Lecturer in Liberal Studies, Bolton, Lancs. (1961–4); Professor of Literature, Wesleyan University, Middletown, Conn.; has written numerous film scripts for television.

Bibliography
B.N.B.
Gale.

Poetry
With love somehow (with Austin Clarke and Charles Tomlinson). 1962.
Lodgers. 1965.
Kon in the springtime. 1968.
The memoirs of Uncle Harry. 1970.
In the happy valley. 1971.
Seven last poems. 1974.

Play
Billy's wonderful kettle. 1974.

CONQUEST, GEORGE ROBERT ACWORTH (†J. E. M. ARDEN) (1917–)
English writer; born at Malvern, Worcs.; educated at Winchester and Magdalene College, Cambridge; served (1939–46) in the Second World War; Foreign Office, Bulgaria and U.K. delegation to U.N.O. (1946–56); Research Fellow, London School of Economics (1956–8); edited *New Lines*, several volumes of Soviet studies, and *Spectrum*, a science fiction anthology (1961–), not listed below.

Bibliography
Authors' and writers' who's who. 1971.
B.N.B.
Contemporary poets.
Gale.
Who's who. 1973.

Novels
A world of difference. 1955.
The Egyptologists (with Kingsley Amis). 1965.

Poetry
Poems. 1955.

Between Mars and Venus. 1962.
Arias from a love opera. 1969.

Other Works
Where do the Marxists go from here?
  (†J. E. M. Arden). 1958.
Common sense about Russia. 1960.
The Soviet deportation of nationalities. 1960.
Power and policy in the U.S.S.R. 1961.
The last empire. 1962.
Courage of genius; the Pasternak affair. 1962.
The future of Communism today. 1963.
The Soviet succession problems. 1963.
Russian Marxism today. 1964.
Russia after Khrushchev. 1965.
Industrial workers in U.S.S.R. 1967.
Politics of ideas in U.S.S.R. 1967.
Soviet nationalities policy in practice. 1967.
Agricultural workers in the U.S.S.R. 1968.
Justice – the legal system in U.S.S.R. 1968.
The great terror: Stalin's purge of the thirties. 1968.
Religion in the U.S.S.R. 1968.
Soviet political system. 1968.
Soviet police system. 1968.
Where Marx went wrong. 1970.
Lenin. 1972.

CONRAN, ANTHONY (1931–)
Welsh poet, born in India; Research Fellow and
Tutor, University College of North Wales
(1957–); editor of the *Penguin book of Welsh verse*
(1967); a contributor to scholarly journals; represented in various anthologies.

Bibliography
B.N.B.
Contemporary poets.

Poetry (mostly privately printed)
Formal poems. 1960.
Metamorphoses. 1961.
Stele. 1965.
Collected poems, vol. I, 1951–58. 1966.
Collected poems, vol. II, 1959–61. 1966.
Collected poems, vol. III, 1962–66. 1967.
Collected poems, vol. IV, 1967. 1968.
Claim, claim, claim. 1969.

Pamphlets, privately printed (1963–7)
The mountain, opus 2. 1963.
Icons, opus 6. 1963.
Asymptotes. 1963.
A string of blethers, opus 8. 1963.
Guernica. 1966.

Sequence of the blue flower. n.d.
From the marriage of Garard and Linda. n.d.

CONRON, BRANDON
Canadian biographer and literary critic; Professor
of English at the University of Western Ontario.

Bibliography
Canadiana.
C.B.I.

Works
The literary works of Matthew Prior. 1959.
Canadian writers; écrivains canadiens (with Guy
  Sylvestre and Carl F. Klinck). 1964.
Mosley Callaghan. 1966.

COOK, KENNETH BERNARD (1929–)
Australian journalist, novelist, film director and
scriptwriter, radio interviewer and commentator.

Bibliography
Australian national bibliography.
B.N.B.

Novels
Wake in fright. 1961.
Chain of darkness. 1962.
Stormalong. 1963.
Blood red roses. 1963.
The wine of God's anger. 1969.
Money menagerie. 1970.
Piper in the market place. 1971.
Airborne invasion. 1971.
Tuna. 1972.
Wanted dead. 1972.

†COOK, ROBIN (ROBERT WILLIAM ARTHUR COOK) (1931–)
English novelist; born in London; educated at
Eton; a contributor to the *Sunday Telegraph*.

Bibliography
Authors' and writers' who's who. 1971.
B.N.B.

Novels
The crust on its uppers. 1962.
Bombe surprise. 1963.
The legacy of the stiff upper lip. 1966.
Private parts and public places. 1967.
A state of Denmark. 1970.
The tenants of Dirt Street. 1971.

COOKE, ALFRED ALISTAIR (1908–)
English-born journalist; educated at Blackpool Grammar School, Jesus College, Cambridge, and Yale; founded the Cambridge University Mummers (1928); B.B.C. film critic (1934–7); B.B.C. commentator on American affairs (1938–); correspondent of the *Guardian* (1945–); resident in the United States since 1938; edited *Garbo and the night watchmen* (1937, revised edition 1971), *USA v. Alger Hiss* (1950) and *The vintage Mencken* (1955).

Bibliography
B.N.B.
Who's who. 1973.

Works
Letters from America. 1951.
Generation on trial. 1951.
Christmas Eve. 1952.
Douglas Fairbanks: the making of a star. 1954.
A commencement address. 1954.
The ordeal of the South. 1956.
The election of 1955. 1956.
Around the world in fifty years. 1966.
Talk about America. 1968.

COOPER, *Lady* **DIANA**
(*Viscountess* **NORWICH,** *née Lady* **DIANA MANNERS)** (1901–)
English actress and writer; daughter of the Duke of Rutland; wife of Duff Cooper, Viscount Norwich; a nurse at Guy's Hospital during the First World War (1914–18); the leading actress in Max Reinhardt, *The Miracle*, for more than 12 years.

Bibliography
B.N.B.
Who's who. 1973.

Works
The rainbow comes and goes (memoirs). 1958.
The light of common day (memoirs). 1959.
Trumpets from the steep (memoirs). 1960.

COOPER, GILES (1918–71)
English playwright; born in Dublin; educated at Lancing College and Grenoble; served (1939–46) in the Second World War; began his career as an actor; wrote for radio and television as well as for the stage; author of *Everything in the garden* (staged 1962).

Bibliography
Anger and after.
B.N.B.

Novel
The other man (based on his television play). 1964.

Plays
Six plays for radio. 1966.

†**COOPER, WILLIAM (HARRY SUMMERFIELD HOFF)** (1910–)
English novelist; educated at Christ's College, Cambridge; taught (1933–40); served in the Second World War (1940–5); Civil Service Commission (1945–58); consultant to the Atomic Energy Authority (1958–) and to the Electricity Generating Board (1960–).

Bibliography
Authors' and writers' who's who. 1971.
B.N.B.
Gale.
Who's who. 1973.

Novels
Scenes from provincial life. 1950.
The struggles of Albert Woods. 1952.
The ever-interesting topic. 1953.
Disquiet and peace. 1956.
Young people. 1958.
Scenes from married life. 1961.
Memoirs of a new man. 1966.
You want the right frame of reference. 1971.
Love on the coast. 1972.

Play
Prince Genji. 1960.

Other Work
C. P. Snow. 1959.

COOVER, ROBERT (1932–)
American novelist; born in Iowa; educated at South Illinois, Indiana and Chicago universities; U.S. Navy (1953–7); recipient of several awards; a contributor to *Evergreen Review, Iowa Review*, etc.; his play *The Kid* published in *Tri-Quarterly* (1970) and *Love scene* in *New American 12* (1971).

Bibliography
C.B.I.
Contemporary novelists.

Novels
The origin of the Brunists. 1966.
The Universal Baseball Association Inc., J. Henry Waugh, Prop. 1968.

Pricksongs and descants (stories). 1969.
A theological position. 1972.

COPE, JACK (1913–   )

South African novelist; born in Natal; founding editor of *Contrast* (1960); co-editor of the *Penguin book of South African verse* (1968); co-translator of the poems of Ingrid Jonker (1968); represented in several anthologies.

Bibliography
B.N.B.
C.B.I.
Contemporary novelists.
Contemporary poets.

Novels
The fair house. 1955.
The golden oriole. 1958.
The road to Ysterberg. 1959.
The tame ox (stories). 1960.
Albino. 1963.
The man who doubted (stories). 1967.
The dawn comes twice. 1969.
The rainmaker. 1971.
The student of Zend. 1972.
Alley cat, and other stories. 1973.

Poetry
Lyrics and diatribes. 1948.
Marie: a satire. 1949.

Other Work
Comrade Bill (biography). 1943.

CORDELL, ALEXANDER (GRABER GEORGE ALEXANDER) (1914–   )

English novelist; born in Ceylon where his father was in the army; a civil engineer in Wales (1936–   ); served in the army in the Second World War (1939–45); began writing (1950); a contributor to various magazines; has travelled widely.

Bibliography
B.N.B.
Gale.

Novels
A thought of honour (in paperback as The enemy within). 1954.
Rape of the fair country. 1959.
Hosts of Rebecca. 1960.
Robe of honour. 1961.
Race of the tiger. 1963.

The sinews of love. 1965.
The bright Cantonese. 1967.
Song of the earth. 1969.
The white cockade (for children). 1970.
Witches' sabbath (for children). 1970.
Traitor within. 1971.
The healing blade. 1971.
Fire people. 1972.

CORNISH, JOHN BUCKLEY (1914–   )

Canadian novelist; born in Vancouver; educated at the University of British Columbia.

Bibliography
Authors' and writers' who's who. 1971.
Canadiana.
C.B.I.

Novels
The provincials. 1951.
Olga. 1959.
Sherborne Street. 1968.
A world turned turtle. 1970.

CORNISH, SAMUEL JAMES (1935–   )

American poet; after various jobs, became consultant on teaching techniques; editor of poetry magazine *Mimeo*; a contributor to *Ann Arbor Review, Poetry Review, Journal of Black Poetry*, etc.; represented in several anthologies.

Bibliography
C.B.I.
Contemporary poets.

Poetry
In this corner. 1961.
People under the window. 1962.
Generations. 1964.
Angles. 1965.
Winters. 1968.

For Children
Your hand in mine. 1970.
Grandmother's pictures. n.d.

CORRINGTON, JOHN WILLIAM (1932–   )

American poet; educated at Rice University and the University of Sussex; Instructor in English, Louisiana State University (1960–   ); a contributor to the *Kenyon Review, T.L.S.* and many others.

Bibliography
C.B.I.

Contemporary poets.
Gale.
L. of C.

Novels and Short Stories
And wait for the night. 1964.
The upper hand. 1967.
The lonesome traveler, and other stories. 1968.
Bombardier. 1970.

Poetry
Where we are. 1962.
The anatomy of love. 1964.
Lines to the south. 1965.

Other Work
Southern writing in the sixties (with Miller Williams). 2 vols. 1966–7.

CORSO, NUNZIO GREGORY (1930–)
American poet; worked at various jobs (1950–9); travelled widely before devoting himself to writing full-time; his play *The hung-up age* produced at Harvard (1955); his edited work is not listed below.

Bibliography
C.B.I.
Contemporary poets.
Gale.
L. of C.

Novel
The American express. 1961.

Poetry
Vestal lady on Brattle. 1955.
Gasoline. 1958.
Happy birthday of death. 1960.
Long live man. 1962.
Elegiac feelings American. 1970.

Other Work
Pardon me, sir, but is my eye hurting your elbow (with others). 1968.

COSTAIN, THOMAS BERTRAM
(1885–)
Canadian novelist and journalist; born in Ontario; journalist in Canada, United States (1908–36); advisory editor, Doubleday publishers (1939–46); editor of several anthologies of short stories; has devoted his time to writing full-time since 1946; general editor of *The white and the gold*, Canadian history series (1954–).

Bibliography
Canadiana.
C.B.I.
Gale.

Novels
For my great folly. 1942.
Ride with me. 1944.
The black rose. 1945.
The moneyman. 1947.
High towers. 1949.
Son of a hundred kings. 1950.
The silver chalice. 1952.
The Tontine. 2 vols. 1955.
Below the salt. 1957.
The darkness and the dawn. 1959.
The conquering family. 1971.

Other Works
Joshua: leader of a united people (with Rogers McVeagh). 1943.
The conquerors. 1949.
The magnificent century. 1951.
The three Edwards. 1958.
The chord of steel. 1960.
The last Plantagenets. 1962.

For Children
The Mississippi bubble. 1955.
William the Conqueror. 1959.
Read with me. 1965.

COTTERELL, GEOFFREY (1919–)
English novelist; educated at Bishop's Stortford College; served (1939–46) in the Second World War.

Bibliography
B.N.B.
Gale.
Who's who. 1973.

Novels
Then a soldier. 1944.
This is the way. 1947.
Randle in springtime. 1949.
Strait and narrow. 1950.
Westward the sun. 1952.
The strange enchantment. 1956.
Tea at Shadow Creek. 1958.
Tiara Tahiti (filmed 1962). 1960.
Go, said the bird. 1966.
Bowers of innocence. 1970.

Other Work
Amsterdam: life of a city. 1972.

COTTON, JOHN (1925–)
English poet; born in London; educated at London University; served in the Royal Navy in the Second World War; co-founder and editor of *Priapus* (1962); editor of *The Private Library* (1969); represented in many journals; a contributor to the *Observer, Encounter, Poetry Review,* etc.

Bibliography
B.N.B.
Contemporary poets.

Poetry
14 poems. 1967.
Outside the gates of Eden. 1969.
Old movies. 1971.

COTTRELL, LEONARD (1913–)
English writer and radio producer; educated at St. Edward's Grammar School, Birmingham; B.B.C. sound and television producer (1942–59); freelance writer since 1960; his edited works are not listed below.

Bibliography
Authors' and writers' who's who. 1971.
B.N.B.
Gale.
Who's who. 1973.

Works
All men are neighbours. 1947.
Madame Tussaud. 1951.
The lost Pharaohs: the romance of Egyptian archaeology. 1951.
The bull of Minos. 1953.
One man's journey. 1955.
Life under the Pharaohs. 1955.
Seeing Roman Britain (American title, Guide to Roman Britain). 1956.
The mountains of Pharaoh. 1956.
Lost cities. 1957.
The anvil of civilization. 1958.
The great invasion. 1958.
Wonders of antiquity. 1959.
Wonders of the world. 1959.
The concise encyclopaedia of archaeology. 1960.
Land of the Pharaohs. 1960.
Enemy of Rome (American title, Hannibal, enemy of Rome). 1960.

Land of the two rivers. 1962.
The tiger of Ch'in; how China became a nation. 1962.
Lost worlds. 1962.
The lion gate. 1963.
The secrets of Tutankhamen (American title, The secrets of the tomb. 1969). 1965.
The land of Shinar. 1965.
Quest for Sumer. 1965.
Crete, island of mystery. 1965.
The queens of the Pharaohs. 1966.
Great leaders of Greece and Rome. 1966.
Digs and digger. 1966.
Lady of the two lands: five queens of ancient Egypt. 1967.
The warrior Pharaohs. 1968.
Up in a balloon. 1970.
Reading the past. 1971.
The mystery of Minoan civilization. 1971.
Lost civilizations. 1973.
In search of the Pharaohs. 1973.

COUSINS, NORMAN (1912–)
American essayist, journalist and editor; educated at Columbia University; book critic, later managing editor, *Current History* (1935–60); editor, *Saturday Review of Literature* (1942–); editor, *World Magazine* (1971–); member and president of national educational boards, etc.; recipient of many academic honours; his edited work is not listed below.

Bibliography
C.B.I.
Gale.
Who's who. 1973.

Works
The good inheritance: the democratic chance. 1942.
Modern man is obsolete. 1945.
Talks with Nehru (with Jawaharlal Nehru). 1951.
Who speaks for man? 1953.
May Loveman, 1881–1955: a eulogy (pamphlet). 1956.
The rejection of nothingness. 1959.
Dr. Schweitzer of Lamberene. 1960.
The last defence in a nuclear age. 1960.
In place of folly. 1961.
Can cultures co-exist? 1963.
Present tense. 1966.
The improbable triumvirate: Kennedy, Khrushchev, Pope John. 1972.

COXE, LOUIS OSBORNE (1918–)
American poet; educated at Princeton University; served (1942–6) in the U.S. Naval Reserve during the Second World War; Professor of English, Bowdoin; a contributor to *Poetry*, *Sewanee Review*, *New Yorker*, etc.

Bibliography
C.B.I.
Contemporary poets.
Gale.

Poetry
The seafaring and other poems. 1947.
The second man and other poems. 1955.
The wilderness and other poems. 1958.
The middle passage. 1960.
Billy Budd (with R. Chapman). 1962.
Nikal Seyn, and Decoration day: a poem and a play. 1966.

Other Works
Edward Arlington Robinson. 1962.
The last hero. 1965.

COWAN, PETER WALKINSHAW (1914–)
Australian novelist; born in Perth, W. Australia; educated at the University of Western Australia; worked in various jobs (1930–9); served in the Royal Australian Air Force during the Second World War (1940–5); Senior Tutor in English, University of Western Australia (1964–); a contributor to *Meanjin Quarterly*; represented in various anthologies of short stories; his edited work is not listed below.

Bibliography
B.N.B.
Contemporary novelists.
Gale.

Novels
Drift (stories). 1944.
The unploughed land (stories). 1958.
Summer. 1964.
The empty street (stories). 1965.
Seed. 1966.
The tins, and other stories. 1973.

COWASJEE, SAROS (1931–)
Indian critic; born in Secunderabad; educated in Agra and Leeds; teaches English at the University of Saskatchewan, Regina Campus; managing editor of *Wascana Review* (1966–70).

Bibliography
C.B.I.
Indian national bibliography 1958–67.
National bibliography of Indian literature 1901–53.

Works
Sean O'Casey: the man behind the plays. 1963.
O'Casey. 1966.
Stories and sketches. 1970.
Goodbye to Elsa. 1973.

COWLEY, CASSIA JOY (*Mrs.* **SUMMERS**) (1936–)
New Zealand novelist; pharmacist's apprentice (1953–6); farmer's wife (1956–67); full-time writer (1967–); a contributor to New Zealand periodicals and radio.

Bibliography
Gale.
N.Z. national bibliography.

Novels
Nest in a falling tree (filmed as The nightdigger, 1971). 1967.
Man of straw. 1970.
Of men and angels. n.d.

For Children
The duck in the gun. 1969.

CRANSTON, *Professor* **MAURICE WILLIAM** (1920–)
English writer and scholar; educated at Birkbeck College, London University, and St. Catherine's College, Oxford; Lecturer at the London School of Economics (1950–69); Professor of Political Science, L.S.E. (1969–); Visiting Professor, Harvard University (1965–6), etc.; literary adviser to Methuen publishers (1959–69); awarded various honorary degrees and literary awards; B.B.C. broadcaster on literary topics; a contributor to the *Listener*, *Encounter*, *Sunday Times*, *Guardian*, etc.; translated Rousseau's *Social contract* (1967).

Bibliography
Authors' and writers' who's who. 1971.
B.N.B.
Gale.
Who's who. 1973.

Works
Freedom. 1953.

Human rights today. 1954.
John Locke: a biography. 1957.
The essence of democracy. 1958.
John Stuart Mill. 1958.
Locke. 1961.
Jean-Paul Sartre. 1962.
What are human rights? 1963.
Western political philosophers (ed.). 1964.
A glossary of political terms. 1966.
Political dialogues. 1968.
La quintessence de Sartre. 1969.
The theatre of politics. 1972.

CREELEY, ROBERT WHITE (1922–)

American poet and novelist; educated at Harvard and the University of New Mexico; after several posts as instructor in English, Professor of English at New York State University (1967–); recipient of several awards for poetry, including a Guggenheim Poetry Fellowship; a contributor to *Nation*, *Poetry*, *Evergreen Review*, etc.; his edited work is not listed below.

Bibliography
C.B.I.
Contemporary poets.
Gale.

Novels
The gold diggers (stories). 1954.
The island. 1963.

Poetry
Le fou. 1952.
The immoral proposition. 1953.
The kind of act of. 1953.
All that is lovely in men. 1955.
If you. 1956.
The whip. 1957.
A form of women. 1959.
For love, poems 1950–1960. 1962.
Poems: 1950–1965. 1966.
Words. 1967.
Pieces. 1969.
The charm: early and uncollected poems. 1969.
The finger: poems 1966–1969. 1970.
St. Martin's. 1971.
A daybook. 1972.
Listen (with Bobby Lester). 1972.

Other Work
Quick graph: collected notes and essays. 1970.

CREGAN, DAVID APPLETON QUARTUS (1931–)

English playwright; educated Leys School, Cambridge, and Clare College, Cambridge; taught (1958–67); *Guardian* critic; worked with the Royal Court Theatre Studio (1964, 1968), etc.; television plays include *That time of life* (1972).

Bibliography
Authors' and writers' who's who. 1971.
B.N.B.
Contemporary dramatists.

Novel
Ronald Rossiter. 1959.

Plays
Three men for Colverton (staged 1966). 1967.
Transcending, and The dancers (staged 1966). 1967.
The houses by the green (staged 1968). 1969.
Miniatures (staged 1965). 1970.
How we held the square: a play for children (staged 1971). 1972.
Land of palms and other plays. 1973.

CRONIN, ANTHONY (1926–)

Irish poet and critic; associate editor of the Dublin *Bell*; literary editor of *Time and Tide*; represented in various anthologies.

Bibliography
B.N.B.
Contemporary poets.

Novel
The life of Riley. 1964.

Poetry
Poems. 1957.

Criticism
A question of modernity. 1966.

CROSS, BEVERLY (1931–)

English playwright; educated at Balliol College, Oxford; Shakespeare Memorial Theatre (1954–6); his unpublished plays include *Boeing-Boeing* (1962); his television plays include *Catherine Howard* (1969).

Bibliography
B.N.B.
Who's who. 1973.

Plays and Libretti
Mars in capricorn. 1955.
The nightwalkers (television play). 1956.
One more river. 1959.
Plays for children. 1960.
Singing dolphin, and Three cavaliers. 1960.
Half a sixpence. 1967.
Jorrocks. 1968.
Rising of the moon. 1970.

CROSS, IAN (1925–)
New Zealand novelist; Associate Nieman Fellow of Journalism, Harvard University, Cambridge, Mass. (1954–5); Robert Burns Fellow, Otago University (1959–).

Bibliography
B.N.B.
Contemporary novelists.
N.Z. national bibliography.

Novels
The god boy. 1957.
The backward sex. 1960.
After Anzac Day. 1961.

CROSSLEY-HOLLAND, KEVIN JOHN WILLIAM (1941–)
English poet and children's writer; educated at Bryanston and St. Edmund Hall, Oxford; editor for Macmillan publishers (1962–); Gregory Poetry Fellow, Leeds University (1969–); translated the *Battle of Maldon* (1965), *Beowulf* (1968), and *Storm and other Old English poems* (1970); edited *Winter tales for children* (1968) and *Rushing to Paradise: an introductory selection of the poems of W. B. Yeats* (1968); represented in several anthologies; a contributor to the *Poetry Review, Spectator, Listener, Encounter*, etc.

Bibliography
B.N.B.
Contemporary poets.

Poetry
On approval. 1961.
My son. 1966.
Alderney; the nunnery. 1968.
Norfolk poems. 1970.

For Children
Havelock the Dane. 1964.
King Horn. 1965.

The green children. 1966.
The callow pit coffer. 1968.
Wordhoard. 1969.
The pedlar of Swaffham. 1971.
The sea stranger. 1973.

CROZIER, ERIC JOHN (1914–)
English writer and theatrical producer; educated at University College School and the Royal Academy of Dramatic Art; B.B.C. television producer (1936–9); producer for the Old Vic, Sadler's Wells Opera, Glyndebourne, etc. (1937–47); producer and librettist of Benjamin Britten's operas (1945–51).

Bibliography
Authors' and writers' who's who. 1971.
B.N.B.
Who's who. 1973.

Works
Christmas in the market place. 1945.
Albert Herring, a comic opera in three acts (with Benjamin Britten). 1947.
Saint Nicolas, a cantata (with Benjamin Britten). 1948.
Let's make an opera, an entertainment for children (with Benjamin Britten). 1949.
The life and legends of Saint Nicolas. 1949.
Billy Budd, an opera in four acts (with Benjamin Britten and E. M. Forster). 1951.
Noah gives thanks, a play. 1953.
Rab the rhymer, a play with songs. 1954.
Ruth, a lyrical opera (with Lennox Berkeley). 1956.
The story of Let's make an opera. 1962.
The Mastersingers of Nuremberg. 1963.
The Magic Flute. 1963.

CRUMP, BARRY JOHN (1935–)
New Zealand novelist; born in Auckland; worked at seventy jobs after leaving school; full-time writer (1961–); a contributor of short stories, etc., to New Zealand and Australian periodicals.

Bibliography
Gale.
N.Z. national bibliography.

Novels
A good keen man. 1960.
Hang on a minute, mate. 1961.

One of us. 1962.
There and back. 1963.
Gulf. 1964.
Nothing in particular. 1965.
Scrapwaggon. 1965.
The odd spot of bother. 1967.
Warm beer and other stories. 1970.
A good keen girl. 1970.
Bastards I have met. 1971.
No reference intended. 1972.
Fred. 1972.

CUNNINGHAM, JAMES VINCENT
(1911–   )
American poet; educated at Stanford University;
served as a mathematics teacher in the U.S. forces
during the Second World War; university teacher
(1937–   ); Professor of English, Brandeis University (1953–   ); Guggenheim Poetry Fellowship
(1959–60 and 1966–7); editor of *The problem of style*
(1966).

Bibliography
C.B.I.
Contemporary poets.
Gale.

Poetry
The helmsman. 1941.
The judge's fury. 1947.
Doctor Drink. 1950.
Woe or wonder: the emotional effect of Shake-
spearean tragedy. 1951.
The exclusions of a rhyme. 1960.
To what strangers what welcome. 1964.
The journal of John Carden, together with, The
quest of the opal, and The problem of form.
1964.
Collected poems and epigrams of J.V.C. 1971.

Other Works
Tradition and poetic structure. 1960.
The resurgent neighbourhood. 1965.
The Renaissance in England. 1966.
Urban leadership in the sixties. 1970.

D

DAHL, ROALD (1916–   )
Welsh-born Danish children's writer; educated at
Repton; Shell Oil Co. of East Africa (1933–7);
served in the R.A.F. during the Second World War
(1939–45); a freelance writer since then; a contributor to the *New Yorker*, *Atlantic Monthly*,
Harper's, etc.; wrote several film scripts, including
You only live twice, and a play, *The honeys* (1955);
represented in *Penguin modern stories* (1972).

Bibliography
B.N.B.
Contemporary novelists.
Gale.

Short Stories
Over to you. 1946.
Sometime never, a fable for supermen (novel).
1948.
Someone like you. 1953.
Kiss kiss. 1960.

Twenty-nine kisses from R.D. (stories from
Someone like you, and Kiss kiss). 1969.
Selected stories. 1970.

For Children
The gremlins. 1943.
James and the giant peach. 1961.
Charlie and the chocolate factory (filmed as Willie,
Wonka and . . ., 1971). 1964.
The magic finger. 1968.
The fantastic Mr. Fox. 1970.
Charlie and the great glass elevator. 1973.

DALAL, *Mrs.* NERGIS (1920–   )
Indian novelist; born in Panchgani, Maharashtra.

Bibliography
C.B.I.
Indian national bibliography 1958–67.
National bibliography of Indian literature
1901–53.

Works
Minari (novel). n.d.
The sisters (novel). n.d.
Never a dull moment (essays). n.d.
The birthday present (children's book). n.d.

DALLAS, RUTH (1919–)
New Zealand poet and children's writer; lives in Dunedin, New Zealand; recipient of literary awards; represented in numerous anthologies; a contributor to *Landfall, Meanjin*, etc.

Bibliography
B.M. catalogue.
Contemporary poets.
N.Z. national bibliography.

Poetry
Country road and other poems 1947–52. 1953.
The turning wheel. 1961.
Day book; poems of a year. 1966.
Shadow show. 1968.

For Children
The children in the bush. 1969.
Ragamuffin scarecrow. 1969.
A dog called Wig. 1970.
The wild boy in the bush. 1971.
The big flood in the bush. 1972.

DALY, ELIZABETH (1878–1967)
American mystery novelist; educated at Bryn Mawr College and Columbia University.

Bibliography
C.B.I.
Gale.

Novels
Deadly nightshade. 1940.
Unexpected night. 1940.
The street has changed. 1941.
Murders in volume 2. 1941.
The house without the door. 1942.
Evidence of things seen. 1943.
Nothing can rescue me. 1943.
Arrow pointing nowhere. 1944.
The book of the dead. 1944.
Any shape or form. 1945.
Somewhere in the house. 1946.
The wrong way down. 1946.
Night walk. 1947.
Book of the lion. 1948.
And dangerous to know. 1949.
Death and letters. 1950.

The book of crime. 1951.
An Elizabeth Daly mystery omnibus. 1960.

DANIEL, GLYN EDMUND (†DILWYN REES) (1914–)
Welsh archaeologist; educated at University College, Cardiff, and St. John's College, Cambridge; Fellow of St. John's College (1938–); served in the R.A.F. in the Second World War (1940–5); University Lecturer in Archaeology (1945–).

Bibliography
Authors' and writers' who's who. 1971.
B.N.B.
Who's who. 1973.

Archaeological Works
The three ages. 1942.
A hundred years of archaeology. 1950.
The prehistoric chamber tombs of England and Wales. 1950.
A picture book of ancient British art (with S. Piggott). 1951.
Lascaux and Carnac. 1955.
Myth or legend (ed.). 1955.
Barclodiad y Gawres (with T. G. E. Powell). 1956.
The megalith builders of western Europe. 1958.
The prehistoric chamber tombs of France. 1960.
The idea of prehistory. 1961.
The hungry archaeologist in France. 1963.
New Grange and the bend of the Boyne (with the late S. P. O'Riordain). 1964.
Prehistoric and early Wales (ed. with I. Ll. Foster). 1964.
Man discovers his past. 1966.
The origins and growth of archaeology. 1967.
The western Mediterranean (with S. D. Evans). 1967.
The first civilisations. 1968.
Archaeology and the history of art. 1970.
Megaliths in history. 1973.

Detective Novels
The Cambridge murders (†Dilwyn Rees). 1945.
Welcome death. 1954.

Other Works
The pen of my aunt (satirical prose). 1961.
Oxford chicken pie (cookery). 1965.

DANIELLS, ROY (1902–)
Canadian scholar and poet born in England; educated in the universities of British Columbia and Toronto; Professor of English in the universities of

British Columbia and Manitoba; a contributor to scholarly journals in Canada and the United States; represented in the *Oxford book of Canadian verse* and other anthologies.

Bibliography
Authors' and writers' who's who. 1971.
Canadiana.
C.B.I.
Contemporary poets.

Poetry
Deeper into the forest. 1948.
The chequered shade. 1963.

Other Works
Milton, mannerism and Baroque. 1963.
Alexander McKenzie and the North West. 1969.

DARUWALLA, KEKI N. (1937–)
Indian poet and short-story writer; born in Lahore; educated at the Punjab University.

Bibliography
C.B.I.
Indian national bibliography 1958–67.
National bibliography of Indian literature 1901–53.

Works
Under Orion. 1970.
Apparition in April. 1971.

DAS, DEB KUMAR (1935–)
Indian poet; born in Calcutta; educated at St. Xavier's College, Calcutta, and Queen's College, Cambridge; has travelled widely in Europe, America and the East; worked for British industry in India; instructor in a black ghetto in the United States (1967–); has contributed to the *Illustrated Weekly of India*, etc.; represented in numerous anthologies; translated *Two Upanishads* (1969).

Bibliography
Contemporary poets.
Indian D.N.B.
Indian national bibliography 1958–67.

Poetry (all published in Calcutta)
The night before us. 1958.
Through a glass darkly. 1964.
The eyes of autumn. 1968.
The four labyrinths. 1969.

Philosophy
Freedom and reality, 6 parts (pr. ptd.). 1968.

DAS, *Mrs.* KAMALA (†MADHAUIKUTTY) (1934–)
Indian short-story writer and poet; born in Malabar; privately educated; recipient of several awards; a contributor to Indian journals; represented in various anthologies; also writes in Malayalam.

Bibliography
Contemporary poets.
Indian national bibliography 1958–67.

Poetry
Summer in Calcutta. 1965.
The descendants. 1967.
The old playhouse. 1973.

DATHORNE, OSCAR RONALD (1934–)
Caribbean novelist; born in Guyana; educated Queen's College, Georgetown, and London and Sheffield universities; has travelled widely; Professor of English, Njala University College, Sierra Leone (1968–); a contributor to the *T.L.S.*, *London Magazine, Journal of Commonwealth Literature, Black Orpheus*, etc.; represented in several anthologies including *Commonwealth Poets of Today* (1967), etc.; his edited work is not listed below.

Bibliography
B.N.B.
Contemporary novelists.
Jahn and Dressler.

Novels
Dumplings in the soup. 1963.
The scholar man. 1964.

DAVIDSON, LIONEL (1922–)
English novelist; born in Hull; served in the Royal Navy in the Second World War; magazine writer and editor (1946–59).

Bibliography
B.N.B.
Gale.

Novels
The night of Wenceslas (filmed as Hot enough for June, 1963). 1960.

The rose of Tibet. 1962.
The Menorah men. 1966.
A long way to Shiloh. 1966.
Making good again. 1968.
Smith's gazelle. 1971.

DAVIE, DONALD ALFRED (1922–)

English poet and literary critic; born in Yorkshire; educated St. Catherine's College, Cambridge; served (1941–6) in the Second World War; university lecturer (1950–64); Professor of English, University of Essex (1964–8); Pro-vice-chancellor (1965–8); Professor of English, Stanford University, California (1968–); has edited several anthologies.

Bibliography
B.N.B.
Contemporary poets.
Gale.
Who's who. 1973.

Poetry
Brides of reason. 1955.
A winter talent. 1957.
The forests of Lithuania. 1959.
A sequence for Francis Parkman. 1961.
New and selected poems. 1961.
Events and wisdoms, 1957–63. 1964.
Essex poems. 1969.
Poems. 1969.
Six epistles to Eva Hesse. 1970.
Collected poems 1950–70. 1971.

Criticism
Purity of diction in English verse. 1952.
Articulate energy. 1955.
The heyday of Sir Walter Scott. 1961.
The language of literature and the language of science. 1963.
Ezra Pound; poet and sculptor. 1965.
Russian literature and modern English fiction. 1965.
The survival of poetry: a contemporary survey (with others). 1970.
Thomas Hardy and British poetry. 1973.

DAVIES, ROBERTSON (†SAMUEL MARCHBANKS) (1913–)

Canadian novelist, critic and writer; born in Thamesville, Ontario; educated at Queen's University, Kingston, and Balliol College, Oxford; joined the Old Vic before returning to Canada (1940); Master of Masey College, Toronto Uni-

versity; Vice-president, *Kingston Whig-Standard*; editor of *Shakespeare's boy actors* (1964).

Bibliography
Authors' and writers' who's who. 1971.
B.N.B.
Canadiana.
Contemporary novelists.

Novels
Tempest tost. 1951.
Leaven of malice. 1955.
A mixture of frailties. 1958.
Fifth business. 1970.
The manticore. 1972.

Plays
Eros at the breakfast table and other plays. 1949.
Fortune my foe. 1949.
At my heart's core. 1950.
A masque of Aesop. 1952.
A jig for the gypsy. 1955.
A masque of Mr. Punch. 1963.

Other Works
Shakespeare for young players. 1942.
The diary and table-talk of Samuel Marchbanks. 1947.
Renown at Stratford: a record of the Shakespeare Festival in Canada, 1953 (with Tyrone Guthrie). 1953.
Twice the trumpets have sounded: a record of the Shakespeare Festival in Canada, 1954 (with Tyrone Guthrie). 1954.
Thrice the brinded cat hath mewed: a record to the Shakespeare Festival in Canada, 1955. 1955.
A voice from the attic. 1960.
The personal art; reading to good purpose. 1961.
Samuel Marchbanks' almanack. 1967.
Stephen Leacock: feast of Stephen. 1970.

DAVIN, DANIEL MARCUS (1913–)

New Zealand novelist; educated at Otago University and Balliol College, Oxford; served in the army during the Second World War (1939–45); Clarendon Press (1946–); Deputy Secretary to the Delegates (1970–); Fellow of Balliol College (1965–); his edited work is not listed below.

Bibliography
B.N.B.
Contemporary novelists.
Gale.
N.Z. national bibliography.

Novels
Cliffs of fall. 1945.
For the rest of our lives. 1947.
The gorse blooms pale (stories). 1947.
Roads from home. 1949.
The sullen bell. 1956.
No remittance. 1959.
Not here, not now. 1970.
Brides of price. 1972.

Other Works
Introduction to English literature (with John Mulgan). 1947.
Crete. 1953.
Writing in New Zealand; the New Zealand novel (with W. K. Davin). 1956.
Katherine Mansfield in her letters. 1959.

DAVISON, PETER (1928–)
American poet; educated at Harvard and St. John's College, Cambridge; with Harcourt Brace publishers (1950–5); served in the U.S. Army (1953–5); Atlantic Monthly Press (1956–); a contributor to numerous magazines and journals including *Encounter, Kenyon Review, Poetry*, Chicago; editor of *Critics and apologists of the English theatre* (1972), etc.

Bibliography
C.B.I.
Contemporary poets.
Gale.

Poetry
The breaking of the day and other poems. 1964.
City and the island. 1966.
Pretending to be asleep. 1970.
Dark hours. 1971.

Other Works
Songs of the British music hall. 1970.
Half remembered: a personal history. 1973.

DAWES, NEVILLE AUGUSTUS
(1926–)
Caribbean novelist; born in Nigeria; educated at Jamaica College, Kingston, Jamaica, and Oriel College, Oxford; taught English in Kingston (1953–5); Lecturer in English, Ghana University (1956–); Visiting Professor, Guiana University (1963–4); a contributor to the B.B.C., *Focus*, Jamaica, *Bim*, Barbados.

Bibliography
Authors' and writers' who's who. 1971.
B.N.B.
Gale.
Jahn and Dressler.

Novel
The last enchantment. 1960.

DAWSON, JENNIFER
English novelist; educated at the Mary Datchelor School and St. Anne's College, Oxford; worked at the Clarendon Press; a social worker in a mental hospital; represented in *Penguin Short Stories 10* (1972).

Bibliography
B.N.B.
Contemporary novelists.

Novels
The ha-ha (James Tait Black Prize 1962). 1961.
Fowler's snare. 1963.
The cold country. 1966.

DE GRAFT, JOHN COLIMAN
Ghanaian playwright; currently with Unesco in Kenya; his poetry is included in *Messages: poems from Ghana* (Heinemann African Writers series), 1971.

Bibliography
B.N.B.
Jahn and Dressler.
Zell and Silver.

Plays
Sons and daughters. 1963.
The Tongo hamlet. 1965.

Other Works
Through a film darkly. 1970.
Visitor from the past. n.d.

DEHN, PAUL (1912–)
English poet and writer; born in Manchester; educated at Shrewsbury School and Brasenose College, Oxford; served in Second World War (1939–45); film critic of various London newspapers (1936–63); his film scripts include *Goldfinger, The spy who came in from the cold, The night of the generals*; adapted *The relapse* for musical production; wrote the libretti for several operas, etc.; president of the Critics' Circle (1956).

Bibliography
Authors' and writers' who's who. 1971.
B.N.B.
Contemporary poets.
Gale.
Who's who. 1973.

Poetry
The day's alarm. 1949.
Romantic landscape. 1952.
Quake, quake, quake. 1960.
The fern on the rock (collected poems). 1965.

Other Works
For love and money (a miscellany). 1956.
Cat's cradle (words by Paul Dehn, photographs by R. Spillman and J. Ramsay). 1959.
Cat's whiskers (words by Paul Dehn, photographs by R. Spillman and J. Ramsay). 1961.

DEIGHTON, LEN (1929–)

English novelist; born in London; educated at the Royal College of Art; worked in a variety of jobs from teaching to cooking; editor of *London Dossier* (1967).

Bibliography
B.N.B.
Contemporary novelists.
Gale.

Novels
The Ipcress file (filmed 1964). 1962.
Horse under water (filmed 1966). 1963.
Funeral in Berlin. 1964.
Billion dollar brain (filmed 1967). 1966.
An expensive place to die. 1967.
Only when I larf (filmed 1969). 1968.
Bomber. 1970.
Declarations of war (stories). 1971.
Close up. 1972.

Other Works
Action cookbook (American title, Cookstrip cookbook). 1965.
Où est le garlic?, or Len Deighton's French cookbook. 1965.
Len Deighton's continental dossier (with Victor and Margaret Pettitt). 1967.
The assassination of President Kennedy (with others). 1967.

DELANEY, SHELAGH (1939–)

English playwright; born at Salford, Lancs.; worked as a salesgirl, usherette, etc., before becoming a director of Granada Television; wrote the film script, *Charlie Bubbles* (1968) and a television play *Did your nanny come from Bergen?* (1970).

Bibliography
B.N.B.
Who's who. 1973.

Plays
A taste of honey (staged 1958, filmed 1961). 1959.
The lion in love (staged 1960). 1961.

Short Story
Sweetly sings the donkey. 1963.

DELDERFIELD, RONALD FREDERICK (1912–72)

English novelist and playwright; *Exmouth Chronicle* (1929–39); served in the R.A.F. during the Second World War (1940–5); his unpublished plays include *Spinster of South Street* (1945), *Worm's eye view* (1945), *The Mayerling affair* (1957).

Bibliography
B.N.B.
Who's who. 1973.

Novels
All over the town (filmed 1948). 1947.
Seven men of Gascony. 1949.
Farewell the tranquil mind. 1950.
The adventures of Ben Gunn (for children – also a television series). 1956.
The dreaming suburb. 1958.
The avenue goes to war. 1958.
There was a fair maid dwelling (American title, Diana). 1960.
The unjust skies. 1960.
Stop at the winner (filmed as On the fiddle, 1961). 1961.
The spring madness of Mr. Sermon. 1963.
Too few for drums. 1964.
The avenue story (contains The dreaming suburb and The avenue goes to war). 1964.
A horseman riding by: 3 vols. (contains The long summer, Post of honour and The green gauntlet). 1966.
Cheap day return. 1967.
The green gauntlet. 1968.
Come home, Charlie, and face them. 1969.
God is an Englishman. 1970.
Theirs was the kingdom. 1971.
Give us this day. 1973.

Plays
Sailor beware. 1950.
The bride wore an opal ring. 1952.
Made to measure. 1952.
Miaow! Miaow! 1952.
The old lady of Cheadle. 1952.
Waggonload o' monkeys. 1952.
Absent lover. 1953.
Golden rain. 1953.
Spark in Judaea. 1953.
Smoke in the alley. 1953.
The testimonial. 1953.
And then there were none. 1954.
Home is the hunted. 1954.
Musical switch. 1954.
The orchard walls (filmed as Now and forever, 1955). 1954.
Ten till five. 1954.
Where there's a will (filmed 1955). 1954.
Wild mink. 1962.
Once aboard the lugger. 1962.
My dearest angel. 1963.

Other Works
Nobody shouted author (reminiscences). 1951.
Bird's eye view (autobiography). 1956.
Napoleon in love. 1959.
The march of the twenty-six. 1962.
The gold millstones (biography). 1964.
Under an English sky (travel). 1964.
The retreat from Moscow. 1967.
For my own amusement (essays). 1968.
Imperial sunset: the fall of Napoleon 1813–14. 1969.
Overture for beginners (autobiography). 1970.

DELIUS, ANTHONY RONALD ST. MARTIN (1916–)
South African poet and writer; educated at Rhodes University; served in the Second World War (1940–5); co-founder, editor and political correspondent, *Saturday Post*, Port Elizabeth (1947–50); *Cape Times* (1951–); a contributor to the *New Yorker, Washington Post, Encounter, Guardian*, etc.

Bibliography
Contemporary poets.
Gale.

Poetry
The unknown border. 1954.
The last division. 1959.
A corner of the world. 1962.

Other Works
Young traveller in South Africa. 1947.
The long way round (travel). 1956.
The fall (play). 1960.
Upsurge in Africa. 1960.
The day Natal took off (satire). 1963.

DE MAUNY, ERIK (1920–)
English-born, New Zealand journalist and writer; educated at Victoria University of Wellington and London University; served in 2nd New Zealand Expeditionary Force during the Second World War (1940–5); B.B.C. correspondent (1958–); foreign correspondent in Paris, where he now lives (1966–); a contributor to the *Penguin New Writing, London Magazine, Encounter, T.L.S.*, etc.; his translations and edited work are not listed below.

Bibliography
B.N.B.
Gale.
N.Z. bibliography.

Novel
The huntsman in his career. 1949.

Other Works
Colette, a biographical study. 1958.
Russian prospect: notes of a Moscow correspondent. 1969.

DEMETILLO, RICARDO D. (1920–)
Filipino poet; educated at Silliman University, Dumaquiti City, and Iowa University; Assistant Professor, University of the Philippines (1959–); recipient of several awards; represented in several anthologies; a contributor to *Poetry*, Chicago, *Botteghe Oscure*, Rome, etc.

Bibliography
C.B.I.
Contemporary poets.

Poetry
No certain weather. 1956.
La via; a spiritual journey. 1958.
Daedalus and other poems. 1961.
Barter in Panay. 1961.
Masks and signature. 1968.

DEMPSTER, RONALD TOMBERAI
Liberian poet; represented in *Poems from Black Africa*, edited by Langston Hughes (1966).

Bibliography
B.N.B.
Jahn and Dressler.
Zell and Silver.

Poetry
The mystic reformation of Gondolia. 1953.
To Monrovia old and new. 1958.
A song out of midnight. 1959.

DENBY, EDWIN ORR (1903–)

American poet, dancer and choreographer; born in China; educated at Harvard and in Austria; travelled widely; dancer (1920–); dance critic of *Modern Music* (1938–42); *New York Herald Tribune* (1942–5); freelance essayist and critic (1946–); recipient of various awards; represented in numerous anthologies.

Bibliography
C.B.I.
Contemporary poets.

Poetry
In public, in private. 1948.
Mediterranean cities. 1956.

Other Works
Second hurricane (libretto of Aaron Copland's opera). 1937.
Ballet. 1945.
Looking at the dance (criticism). 1949.
Dancers, buildings, and people in the street (essays). 1965.
Mrs. W's last sandwich. 1972.
A scream in a cave. 1973.

DENNIS, NIGEL FORBES (1912–)

English novelist, playwright and literary critic; son of an army officer; educated in Rhodesia and Germany; book reviewer on papers in New York and London (1937–); lives in Malta.

Bibliography
B.M. catalogue.
Contemporary dramatists.
Gale.
Who's who. 1973.

Novels
Boys and girls come out to play. 1949.
Cards of identity. 1955.
A house in order. 1966.

Plays
Two plays and a preface (Cards of identity, based on the novel, staged 1956, and The making of Moo, staged 1958). 1958.
August for the people. 1962.

Other Works
Dramatic essays. 1962.
Jonathan Swift; a short character (biography). 1965.
Exotics (poems). 1970.
Essay on Malta. 1972.

DENT, ALAN HOLMES (1905–)

Scottish critic; born in Ayrshire; educated at Glasgow University; served in the Second World War; drama critic of the *Manchester Guardian* (1935–43); film critic of the *Sunday Telegraph* and *Illustrated London News*; frequent broadcaster since 1942; president of the Critics' Circle (1962); text editor of Laurence Olivier's films of *Henry V, Hamlet* and *Richard III*; edited the correspondence of Bernard Shaw and Mrs. Patrick Campbell (1952); a contributor to *Time and Tide*, etc.

Bibliography
Authors' and writers' who's who. 1971.
B.N.B.
Gale.
Who's who. 1973.

Works
Preludes and studies. 1942.
Nocturnes and rhapsodies. 1950.
My dear America .... 1954.
Mrs. Patrick Campbell: a biography. 1961.
Burns in his time. 1966.
My Covent Garden. 1970.
Vivien Leigh: a biography. 1970.
The world of Shakespeare's plants (World of Shakespeare, vol. I). 1971.
Animals and monsters (World of Shakespeare, vol. II). 1971.
Sports and pastimes (World of Shakespeare, vol. III). 1972.

DESAI, *Mrs.* ANITA (1937–)

Indian novelist; educated at Delhi University; a contributor to *Writers' Workshop*, Calcutta, *Envoy*, etc.

Bibliography
Contemporary novelists.
National bibliography of Indian literature 1901–53.

Novels
Cry, the peacock. 1963.
Voices in the city. 1965.
Bye-bye, blackbird. 1971.

DESANI, G. V. (1909–)
East African–Indian writer; born in Nairobi;
Fulbright-Hays Exchange Lecturer to U.S.A.
(1968); Professor of Philosophy, University of
Texas (1969).

Bibliography
C.B.I.
Indian national bibliography 1958–67.
National bibliography of Indian literature
   1901–53.

Works
All about H. Hatterr. 1948.
Hali. 1950.

DESHPANDE, *Mrs.* **GAURI**
(*née* **KARUE**) (1942–)
Indian poet; born and educated in Poona; also
translates from Marathi; a contributor to *Opinion,
Quest*, Bombay, etc.

Bibliography
C.B.I.
Contemporary poets.
Indian national bibliography 1958–67.
National bibliography of Indian literature
   1901–53.

Poems
Between births. 1967.
Lost love. n.d.
Beyond the slaughterhouse. n.d.

DE VRIES, PETER (1910–)
American novelist and journalist; educated at
Northwestern University, Illinois; freelance writer
(1931–8); editor, *Poetry*, Chicago (1938–44); on the
staff of the *New Yorker* (1944–).

Bibliography
Authors' and writers' who's who. 1971.
B.N.B.
C.B.I.
Contemporary novelists.
Gale.
Who's who. 1973.

Novels
But who wakes the burglar? 1940.
The handsome heart. 1943.
Angels can't do better. 1944.
No, but I saw the movie (stories). 1952.
The tunnel of love. 1954.
Comfort me with apples. 1956.
The mackerel plaza. 1958.
The tents of wickedness. 1959.
Through the fields of clover. 1961.
The blood of the lamb. 1962.
Reuben, Reuben. 1964.
Let me count the ways. 1965.
The vale of laughter. 1967.
The cat's pyjamas and witch's milk. 1968.
Mrs. Wallop. 1970.
Into your tent I'll creep. 1971.
Without a stitch in time. 1972.
Forever panting. 1973.

Play
The tunnel of love (from the story). 1957.

DICKEY, JAMES LAFAYETTE
(1923–)
American poet; educated at Vanderbilt University;
served in the U.S. Army during the Second World
War and Korean War; member of the English
faculty at Rice University (1952–4) and of the University of Florida (1955–6); poet-in-residence,
Reed College, Portland, Oregon (1963–4);
awarded various poetry prizes and fellowships; a
contributor to various journals; anthologised in
Contemporary American Poets, Penguin (1962), etc.

Bibliography
C.B.I.
Contemporary poets.
Gale.
Eileen Glancy, James Dickey, the critic as poet: an
   annotated bibliography. 1971.

Novel
Deliverance (filmed 1972). 1970.

Poetry
Into the stone and other poems. 1960.
Drowning with others. 1962.
Interpreter's house. 1963.
Helmets. 1964.
Two poems of the air. 1964.
Buckdancer's choice. 1965.
Poems 1957–1967. 1967.

The eye-beaters, blood, victory, madness, buck-
head and Mary. 1970.
Move under Saturn. 1971.

Criticism
The suspect in poetry. 1964.
Babel to Byzantium. 1968.
The self or agent. 1970.
Self-interviews. 1970.

DICKINSON, PATRIC THOMAS
(1914–)
English poet and writer; born in India; educated at
St. Catherine's College, Cambridge; B.B.C. producer (1942–8); freelance broadcaster and critic
(1948–); contributor to the *Sunday Times,
T.L.S., Listener, Observer*, etc.; his edited work and
translations of the classics are not listed below.

Bibliography
Authors' and writers' who's who. 1971.
B.N.B.
Contemporary poets.
Gale.
N.C.B.E.L.
Who's who. 1973.

Poetry
The seven days of Jericho. 1944.
Theseus and the minotaur. 1946.
Stone in the midst. 1948.
The sailing race. 1952.
The scale of things. 1955.
The world I see. 1960.
This cold universe. 1964.
Selected poems. 1968.
More than time. 1970.
A wintering tree. 1973.
The iron lion. 1973.

Other Works
A round of golf courses. 1951.
A durable fire (verse play). 1962.
The good minute (autobiography). 1965.

DIDION, JOAN (*Mrs.* J. G. DUNNE)
(1934–)
American novelist and journalist; educated at University of California, Berkeley; associate editor of
Vogue (1956–); recipient of fiction awards; a contributor to *Mademoiselle*, etc.

Bibliography
C.B.I.
Gale.

Novels
Run river. 1963.
Slouching towards Bethlehem. 1968.
Play it as it lays (filmed 1972). 1970.

DIPOKO, MBELLA SONNE (1936–)
Cameroonian novelist; educated in Cameroon and
Nigeria; a clerk with the Development Corporation, Tiko; Nigerian Broadcasting Corporation news reporter, Lagos; settled in Paris
(1960) to study law at the Sorbonne and to write;
on the staff of *Présence Africaine*; his poems have
been published in various journals and anthologies;
his play *Overseas* produced by the B.B.C.

Bibliography
B.N.B.
Jahn and Dressler.
Zell and Silver.

Novels
A few nights and days. 1966.
Because of women. 1968.
Black and white in love. 1972.

DI PRIMA, DIANE (*Mrs.* MARLOWE)
(1934–)
American poet and novelist; worked as printer,
publisher and editor (1960–); freelance editor
and writer; her plays have been staged in New
York but not published.

Bibliography
C.B.I.
Contemporary poets.
Gale.

Novels
Dinners and nightmares (short stories). 1961.
The calculus of variation. 1966.
Spring and autumn annals. 1966.
Memoirs of a beatnik. 1969.

Poetry
This kind of bird flies backward. 1959.
The new handbook of heaven. 1963.
Poems for Freddie. 1966.
Some Haiku. 1966.
Earth song: poems 1957–1959. 1968.
Kerhonson journal. 1971.
Revolutionary letters (poems). 1971.
Monuments: a book of monologues. 1974.

DISCH, THOMAS
(†DOBBIN THORPE,
†THOM DEMIJOHN) (1940–)
American writer of science fiction; educated at
New York University; after working at various
jobs, including copywriting, became a full-time
writer (1964–); a contributor to *Playboy*, etc.

Bibliography
C.B.I.
Gale.

Novels
Mankind under the leash. 1966.
102 H-bombs, and other stories. 1966.
The genocides. 1967.
Echo 'round his bones. 1967.
Black Alice (with John Sladek, as †Thom Demi-
    john). 1968.
Camp concentration. 1968.
Under compulsion. 1968.
Fun with your new head (stories). 1968.
The ruins of earth. 1971.
"334". 1972.
Bad moon rising. 1973.

DOBSON, ROSEMARY
(*Mrs.* BOLTON) (1920–)
Australian poet; born in Sydney; educated at Sydney University and at art school; London editor for
the publishers Angus and Robertson; lives in
London; represented in numerous anthologies.

Bibliography
Australian national bibliography.
B.N.B.
Contemporary poets.

Poetry
In a convex mirror. 1944.
The ship of ice. 1948.
Child with a cockatoo. 1954.
Selected poems. 1963.
Cock crow. 1965.
Three poems on water-springs (pr. ptd.). 1973.

Other Work
Focus on Ray Crooke. 1971.

DONLEAVY, JAMES PATRICK
(1926–)
Irish–American novelist and playwright; educated
New York and Trinity College, Dublin; served
with the U.S. Navy; contributes to *Atlantic* and
New Yorker.

Bibliography
Anger and after.
Authors' and writers' who's who. 1971.
B.N.B.
Contemporary dramatists.
Gale.
Who's who. 1973.

Novels
The ginger man. 1958.
A singular man. 1963.
Meet my maker the mad molecule (stories and
    sketches). 1964.
The saddest summer of Samuel S. 1966.
The beastly beatitudes of Balthazar B. 1968.
The onion eaters. 1971.
A fairy tale of New York. 1973.

Plays
The ginger man (from the novel, English title,
    What they did in Dublin with the ginger man,
    staged 1959 and 1963). 1961.
Fairy tales of New York (staged 1960). 1961.
A singular man (from the novel, staged 1964).
    1965.
The plays of J. P. Donleavy. 1972.

DORN, EDWARD (1929–)
American poet; educated at the University of
Illinois; Visiting Professor, University of Essex
(1965–8); Visiting Poet, University of Kansas
(1968–); represented in various anthologies.

Bibliography
C.B.I.
Contemporary poets.

Poetry
Idaho out. 1961.
The newly fallen. 1961.
Hands up, Jones! 1964.
Geography. 1966.
The North Atlantic turbine. 1967.
Gunslinger Part I. 1968.
Gunslinger Part II. 1969.
24 love songs. 1969.
Songs: set two: a short count. 1970.
By the sound. 1971.
The circle. 1971.

Other Works
Rites of passage. 1965.
The shoshoneans. 1967.
Some business recently transacted in the white
    world. 1971.

89

DOUGLAS, KEITH (1920–44)

English poet; educated at Christ's Hospital and Oxford; served in the Second World War and was killed in Normandy.

Bibliography
B.M. catalogue.
B.N.B.
C.B.I.
R. N. Currey. Poets of the 1939–1945 war. 1960.
N.C.B.E.L.

Poetry
Selected poems (with J. Hall and N. Nicolson). 1943.
From Alamein to Zem-Zem. 1946.
Collected poems (ed. J. Waller and G. S. Fraser). 1951.
Selected poems (with an introduction by Ted Hughes). 1964.

DOUGLAS, WILLIAM ORVILLE

(1898–)
American lawyer and historian; educated at Columbia University; admitted to the New York bar (1926); associate justice, Washington Supreme Court (1939–); served in the U.S. Army during the First World War (1918); member of many learned bodies and mountaineering societies; his legal casebooks on commercial law and bankruptcy are not listed below; a contributor to law journals.

Bibliography
C.B.I.
Gale.

Works
Democracy and finance. 1940.
Being an American. 1948.
Of men and mountains. 1950.
Strange lands and friendly people. 1951.
Beyond the high Himalayas. 1952.
North from Malaya. 1953.
An almanac of liberty. 1954.
We the judges. 1956.
Russian journey. 1956.
Exploring the Himalayas. 1958.
The right of the people. 1958.
West of the Indus. 1958.
Douglas of the Supreme Court: a selection of his opinions. 1959.
My wilderness: the Pacific west. 1960.
America challenged. 1960.

A living bill of rights. 1961.
Muir of the mountains. 1961.
My wilderness: east of Katahdin. 1961.
Democracy's manifesto. 1962.
The anatomy of liberty. 1963.
Mr. Lincoln and the negroes. 1963.
Freedom of the mind. 1964.
A wilderness Bill of Rights. 1965.
Towards a global federalism. 1968.
Points of rebellion. 1970.
International dissent. 1970.
Holocaust or hemispheric co-op. 1971.
The 300 year war: a chronicle of ecological disease. 1972.

DOWLING, BASIL CAIRNS (1910–)

New Zealand poet; born in Canterbury, New Zealand; educated at Canterbury University College, Christchurch, Dunedin and Cambridge; travelled widely; Librarian, Otago University (1947–52); taught at Downside, Surrey (1952–4); Head of English, Raine's Grammar School, London (1965–); represented in various anthologies.

Bibliography
B.N.B.
Contemporary poets.
N.Z. national bibliography.

Poetry
A day's journey. 1941.
Signs and wonders. 1944.
Canterbury and other poems. 1949.
Hatherley; recollective lyrics. 1968.
A little gallery of characters (pr. ptd.). 1971.
Bedlam (pr. ptd.). 1972.

DOYLE, CHARLES DESMOND

(1928–)
English-born New Zealand poet; educated at Auckland University; Associate Professor of English, University of Victoria, British Columbia; recipient of various fellowships and awards; represented in numerous anthologies; editor of *Recent Poetry in New Zealand* (1965).

Bibliography
B.N.B.
Contemporary poets.
Gale.
N.Z. national bibliography.

Poetry
A splinter of glass; poems 1951–56. 1956.

Distances; poems 1956–61. 1963.
A message for Herod. 1965.
A sense of place. 1965.
Earth meditations: I to V. 1971.

Other Work
R. A. K. Mason. 1972.

DRABBLE, MARGARET (*Mrs.* SWIFT)
(1939–)
English novelist; educated at the Mount School,
York, and Girton College, Cambridge; a contributor to *Punch, Vogue*, etc.; she also wrote a film
script, *A touch of love* (1969) and a play, *Bird of
paradise* (produced 1969).

Bibliography
Authors' and writers' who's who. 1971.
B.N.B.
Gale.
Who's who. 1973.

Novels
A summer bird-cage. 1963.
The Garrick year. 1964.
The millstone (John Llewelyn Rhys Prize 1966,
　　filmed as A touch of love, 1969). 1966.
Jerusalem the golden (James Tait Black Prize
　　1968). 1967.
The waterfall. 1969.
The needle's eye. 1972.

Other Work
Wordsworth. 1966.

DRAYTON, GEOFFREY (1924–)
Caribbean novelist and poet; born in Barbados;
educated at Cambridge; taught in Canada
(1948–52); freelance journalist in London and
Madrid (1952–4); on the staff of *Petroleum Times*,
then its editor (1954–65); consultant in petroleum,
Economist Intelligence Unit (1966–); lives in
London; a contributor to numerous magazines and
periodicals; represented in various anthologies of
West Indian writing.

Bibliography
B.N.B.
C.B.I.

Novels
Christopher. 1959.
Zohana. 1961.

Poetry
Three meridians. 1951.

DRIVER, CHARLES JONATHAN
(1939–)
South African novelist and poet; educated at Cape
Town University and Trinity College, Oxford;
taught in England (1964–); represented in several
anthologies; a contributor to the *London Magazine*,
etc.

Bibliography
B.N.B.
Contemporary poets.
Gale.

Novels
Elegy for a revolutionary. 1969.
Send war in our time, O Lord. 1970.
Death of fathers. 1971.
Messiah of the last days. n.d.

DRURY, ALLEN STUART (1918–)
American novelist; educated at Stanford University; served in the U.S. Army during the Second
World War (1942–3); journalist; political correspondent, *Reader's Digest* (1959–); recipient of
awards for journalism and fiction.

Bibliography
C.B.I.
Contemporary novelists.

Novels
Advise and consent (Pulitzer Prize 1960). 1959.
A shade of difference. 1962.
That summer. 1965.
Capable of honor. 1966.
Preserve and protect. 1968.
The throne of Saturn. 1971.

Other Works
A Senate journal, 1943–45. 1963.
Three kids in a cart; a visit to Ike and other diver-
　　sions. 1965.
A very strange society: a journey to the heart of
　　South Africa. 1967.
Courage and hesitation: notes and photographs of
　　the Nixon administration. 1971.

DUBERMAN, MARTIN B. (1930–)
American historian and playwright; educated at
Harvard; Instructor, then Associate Professor at
Yale (1957–62) and Princeton (1962–); recipient

of several awards; edited *The antislavery vanguard* (1965); unpublished plays include *Groups* (1968) and *The colonial dudes* (1969).

Bibliography
C.B.I.
Contemporary dramatists.
Gale.

Plays
In White America (staged 1963). 1964.
Metaphors (staged 1968). 1968.
The memory bank (with The recorder, and The electric map). 1970.
Guttman ordinary scale. 1972.

Other Works
Charles Francis Adams 1807–1886. 1961.
James Russell Lowell. 1966.
The uncompleted post (essays). 1969.
Black Mountain College. 1971.
Black Mountain: an exploration in community. 1972.

DUFFY, MAUREEN (1933–)

English novelist and dramatist; educated at King's College, London; taught for 5 years; her unpublished plays include *Lay-off* (produced 1961), *The silk room* (produced 1966).

Bibliography
Authors' and writers' who's who. 1971.
B.N.B.
Contemporary dramatists.
Gale.

Novels
That's how it was. 1962.
The simple eye. 1964.
The microcosm. 1966.
The paradox players. 1967.
Wounds. 1969.
Love child. 1971.
I want to go to Moscow. 1972.

Play
Rites (staged 1969). 1969.

Poetry
Lyrics for the dog hour. 1968.
The Venus touch. 1971.

Other Work
The erotic world of faery. 1972.

DUGAN, ALAN (1923–)

American poet; served in the U.S. Air Force during the Second World War; recipient of many poetry prizes; a frequent contributor to poetry magazines.

Bibliography
C.B.I.

Poetry
Poems (Pulitzer Prize 1962). 1961.
Poems 2. 1963.
Poems 3. 1967.
Collected poems. 1969.

DUGAN, JAMES MICHAEL (1929–)

American writer; educated at Pennsylvania State University; served in the U.S. Air Force during the Second World War (1942–5); president of the U.S. committee for oceanography research; president of the Academy of Underwater Arts and Sciences, etc.; wrote the scripts of various films, including *The silent world*; his edited work is not listed below.

Bibliography
C.B.I.
Gale.

Works
The great iron ship. 1953.
Man under the sea. 1956.
Undersea explorer, the story of Captain Cousteau. 1957.
Ploesti (with Carroll Stewart). 1962.
American Viking. 1963.
The living sea (with Jacques Cousteau). 1963.
The great mutiny. 1965.
World beneath the sea. 1967.

DUGGAN, MAURICE (1922–)

New Zealand novelist; born in Auckland; educated at Auckland University; has worked in advertising (1961–); recipient of various literary awards; represented in *New Authors: short story I* (1965).

Bibliography
B.M. catalogue.
Contemporary novelists.
N.Z. national bibliography.

Short Stories
Immanuel's land: stories. 1956.
Summer in the gravel pit; stories. 1965.
O'Leary's orchard. 1970.

For Children
Falter Tom and the water boy. 1957.

DUNCAN, ROBERT (*né* **EDWARD HOWARD DUNCAN**) (1919–   )
American poet; educated at University of California, Berkeley; recipient of many literary awards; included in various anthologies.

Bibliography
C.B.I.
Gale.

Poetry
Heavenly city, earthly city. 1947.
Medieval scenes. 1950.
Poems 1948–49. 1950.
Song of the borderguard. 1951.
The artist's view. 1952.
Caesar's gate. 1956.
Letters. 1958.
Faust foutu. 1959.
Selected poems. 1959.
The opening of the field. 1960.
Roots and branches. 1964.
Wine. 1964.
The years as catches, first poems 1939–46. 1966.
Bending the bow. 1968.
The first decade: selected poems 1940–50. 1968.
Derivations: selected poems 1950–60. 1969.

Essay
As testimony: the poem and the scene. 1958.

DUNCAN, RONALD (1914–   )
English poet and playwright; educated in Switzerland and Cambridge; travelled widely; lived with Gandhi in India; founder of the English Stage Company, Royal Court Theatre; has written several libretti for Benjamin Britten operas, television plays, etc.; his translations and edited works are not listed below.

Bibliography
B.N.B.
Contemporary poets.
Gale.

Poetry
Postcards to Pulcinella. 1940.
The mongrel. 1947.
Judas. 1960.
The solitudes. 1960.
Selected poems. 1960.

Unpopular poems. 1969.
Man. Part I of a poem. 1970. Part II. 1972.

Plays
The dull ass's hoof (3 verse plays). 1940.
This way to the tomb (verse play). 1946.
Stratton. 1950.
Our lady's tumbler. 1951.
The rape of Lucretia (libretto for Benjamin Britten). 1953.
Don Juan. 1954.
The death of Satan. 1955.
Abélard and Héloïse. 1961.
The catalyst. 1962.
O–B–A–F–G. 1964.

Other Works
Journal of a husbandman. 1944.
Home made home. 1947.
Jan's journal. 1949.
Tobacco cultivation in England. 1951.
The Blue Fox. 1951.
Jan at the Blue Fox. 1952.
The last Adam (novel). 1952.
Where I live (about Devonshire). 1953.
Saint Spiv. 1961.
All men are islands (autobiography). 1964.
Devon and Cornwall. 1967.
How to make enemies (autobiography). 1968.
The perfect mistress (stories). 1969.

DUNN, NELL (*Mrs.* **JEREMY SANDFORD**) (1936–   )
English novelist; born in London; educated at a convent school; lives in Somerset.

Bibliography
B.N.B.

Novels
Up the junction (John Llewelyn Rhys Prize 1964) (cinema and television film 1963). 1963.
Poor cow (filmed 1967). 1967.
Freddy gets married (for children). 1968.
The incurable. 1971.
I want (with Adrian Henri). 1972.
Tear his head off his shoulders. 1974.

Other Work
Talking to women. 1965.

DUODO, CAMERON
Ghanaian novelist; his short stories published in *Okyeame*, etc.

Bibliography
Ghana national bibliography. 1967–70.
Jahn and Dressler.
Patten.

Novel
The gab boys. 1967.

DURGNAT, RAYMOND ERIC
(†O. O. GREEN) (1932–)
English writer; born in London; currently Senior
Lecturer, St. Martin's School of Art (1964–).

Bibliography
Authors' and writers' who's who. 1971.
B.N.B.
Gale.

Works
Nouvelle vague—the first decade. 1963.
Greta Garbo (with John Kobal). 1965.
Eros in the cinema. 1966.
Luis Buñuel. 1967.
The Marx brothers. 1967.
Films and feelings. 1967.
Franju. 1968.
The crazy mirror. 1969.
A mirror for England. 1970.
Sexual alienation in the cinema. 1972.
The strange case of Alfred Hitchcock or, The plain
  man's Hitchcock. 1973.

DURRELL, GERALD MALCOLM
(1925–)
English zoologist and writer; brother of the novelist Lawrence Durrell; born in India; educated on
the Continent; has led animal-collecting expeditions in Cameroons, British Guiana, the Argentine
and Paraguay, etc.; founder and honorary director
of the Jersey Zoological Park (1958–); a contributor to the *Listener, Harper's Magazine,
Observer*, etc.

Bibliography
Authors' and writers' who's who. 1971.
B.N.B.
Gale.
Who's who. 1973.

Works
The overloaded ark. 1953.
Three singles to adventure. 1954.
The Bafut beagles. 1954.
The new Noah. 1955.

The drunken forest. 1956.
My family and other animals. 1956.
Encounters with animals. 1958.
A zoo in my luggage. 1960.
The whispering land. 1961.
Island zoo. 1961.
Look at zoos. 1961.
My favourite animal stories. 1962.
Menagerie manor. 1964.
Two in the bush (televised 1962). 1966.
Rosy is my relative. 1968.
The donkey rustlers. 1968.
Birds, beasts and relatives. 1969.
Fillets of plaice. 1971.
Catch me a colobus (televised 1966). 1972.
Beasts in my belfry. 1972.
Gerald. 1973.

DUTTON, GEOFFREY PIERS (1922–)
Australian poet, critic and novelist; served in the
Australian Air Force during the Second World
War; educated at Oxford after the war; Lecturer at
Adelaide University (1955–62); founder and co-
editor of *Australian Letters*; a regular broadcaster;
his edited work is not listed below.

Bibliography
Australian national bibliography.
B.N.B.
Contemporary novelists.
Contemporary poets.

Novels
The mortal and the marble. 1950.
Seal Bay (with Dean Hay). 1966.
Andy. 1968.
Tamara. 1969.

Poetry
Nightflight and sunrise. 1945.
Antipodes in shoes. 1955.
Flowers and fury. 1963.
On my island (for children). 1967.
Poems soft and loud. 1968.
Findings and keepings. 1970.
New poems to 1972. 1972.
Swimming free. 1972.

Other Works
A long way south (travel). 1953.
Africa in black and white (travel). 1958.
Founder of a city: the life of William White. 1960.
Patrick White. 1961.
Walt Whitman. 1961.

Paintings of S. T. Gill. 1962.
Russell Drysdale. 1962.
Tisi and the Yabby (for children). 1965.
The hero as murderer: the life of John Edward
     Eyre. 1967.
Tisi and the pageant (for children). 1968.
Australia's last explorer: Ernest Giles. 1970.
From federation to war, 1901–1914. 1972.

DYER, CHARLES RAYMOND (1928–   )

English playwright and novelist; R.A.F. (1944–7);
writes for stage, cinema and television;
actor–director as Raymond Dyer. Only his published plays are listed below.

Bibliography
Contemporary dramatists.
Who's who. 1973.

Novels
Rattle of a simple man (from the play; filmed
     1964). 1964.
Staircase or, Charlie always told Harry almost
     everything (from the play; filmed 1969). 1969.
The rising of our Herbert. 1972.

Plays
Wanted—one body! (staged 1958; filmed 1964).
     1961.

Time, murderer, please (staged with Poison in jest!
     1956). 1962.
Rattle of a simple man (staged 1962). 1963.
Staircase (staged 1966). 1966.
Mother Adam (staged 1970). 1970.
The loneliness trilogy. 1972.

†DYLAN, BOB (ROBERT ZIMMERMAN) (1941–   )

American folk-singer, composer and poet; educated at the University of Minnesota; made tours
of Europe; has performed at many music festivals
and at concert halls in New York, Chicago and
London; his recordings include *Bob Dylan* (1962),
The times they are changin' (1964), *Bob Dylan's greatest hits* (1967); scores include the *Bob Dylan songbook*
(1963), *Songs for voice and guitar* (n.d.); represented
in *Poets of today*, International publishers (1964).

Bibliography
C.B.I.
Contemporary poets.

Poetry
Tarantula. 1966.
Bob Dylan self portrait. n.d.
New morning. n.d.

E

EASMON, RAYMOND SARIF

Sierra Leonean playwright and short-story writer;
practises as a doctor in Freetown; his plays *Mate and
Checkmate* and *Dilys, dear Dilys* were produced on
the Nigerian Television Service.

Bibliography
B.N.B.
Jahn and Dressler.

Novel
The burnt-out marriage. 1967.

Plays
Dear parent and ogre. 1964.
The new patriots. 1966.

EDEL, JOSEPH LEON (1907–   )

American scholar; educated at McGill University,
Toronto, and Paris; miscellaneous writer and journalist (1934–43); served in the U.S. Army (1943–7)
during the Second World War; currently Henry
James Professor of English, New York (1966–   )
and Citizens' Professor of English, Hawaii
(1970–   ); recipient of many academic and literary
awards; edited the *Complete Plays of Henry James*
(1949), etc.

Bibliography
C.B.I.
Who's who. 1973.

Works
Willa Cather (with E. K. Brown). 1953.

The untried years. 1953.
The psychological novel. 1955.
The conquest of London. 1962.
The life of Henry James (Pulitzer Prize for Biography for the first three volumes 1963). 1963.
The middle years. 1963.
The treacherous years. 1969.
The master. 1972.

EDELMAN, MAURICE (1911–75)

English novelist, writer and politician; educated at Cardiff High School and Trinity College, Cambridge; industrial research in the aircraft industry (1932–41); journalist and war correspondent; major diplomatic and political appointments (1949–67); Labour M.P. (1945–75); recipient of various honours; television plays include *The trial of Admiral Byng* (1958).

Bibliography
B.N.B.
Who's who. 1973.

Novels
A trial of love. 1951.
Who goes home. 1953.
A dream of treason. 1953.
The happy ones. 1957.
A call on Kuprin. 1959.
The minister. 1961.
The fratricides. 1963.
The Prime Minister's daughter. 1964.
Shark Island. 1967.
All on a summer's night. 1969.
Disraeli in love. 1972.

Other Works
France: the birth of the Fourth Republic. 1945.
David Ben Gurion. 1964.
The mirror: a political history. 1966.

EGBERT, DONALD DREW (1902–73)

American art historian; educated at Princeton University; taught at Princeton (1929–73); Professor of the History of Architecture (1968–73); colour photographer, holding one-man shows at Princeton University Library (1957) and elsewhere; member of many learned bodies; a contributor to art, history and architecture journals.

Bibliography
C.B.I.
Gale.

Works
The Tickhill psalter and related manuscripts (pamphlet). 1940.
Princeton portraits. 1947.
Socialism and American life (with S. Persons). 2 vols. 1952.
Socialism and American art. 1952.
Social radicalism and the arts: Western Europe since the French Revolution. 1970.

EGBUNA, OBI BENEDICT (1938–)

Nigerian novelist and playwright; unpublished plays for stage are *Theatre of power* (1969) and *The agony* (1970) and for radio, *Divinity* (1965).

Bibliography
B.N.B.
Contemporary dramatists.
Jahn and Dressler.
Zell and Silver.

Novels
Wind versus polygamy (broadcast and stage versions 1966). 1964.
The gods are not to blame. 1970.
Daughter of the sun and other stories (radio version 1970). 1970.
Emperor of the sea and other stories. 1973.

Play
The ant hill. 1965.

Other Work
Destroy this temple; the voice of black power in Britain. 1971.

EISELEY, LOREN COREY (1907–)

American anthropologist and poet; educated at the universities of Nebraska and Pennsylvania; university posts since 1937; Provost of Pennsylvania University (1959–61); Professor of Anthropology (1961–), etc.; awarded numerous honours; a contributor to many scientific and general journals including *Science, Harper's, Atlantic, New York Herald Tribune, New York Times*.

Bibliography
C.B.I.
Gale.

Works
The immense journey. 1957.
Darwin's century. 1958.
Firmament of time. 1960.

Social control in a free society, with others. 1960.
The mind as nature. 1962.
Francis Bacon and the modern dilemma. 1963.
The unexpected universe. 1969.
The invisible pyramid. 1970.
The night country. 1971.
The shape of likelihood: relevance and the university (with others). 1972.
Notes of an alchemist. 1972.
The man who saw through time. 1973.
The innocent assassins. 1973.

EKWENSI, CYPRIAN (1921–)
Nigerian novelist; educated in Ghana and London; Lecturer in Pharmaceutics, Lagos (1949–56); Nigerian Broadcasting Company (1956–61); Federal Ministry of Information (1961–6); Director of Information Services, Enugu (1966–).

Bibliography
B.N.B.
Contemporary novelists.
Gale.
Jahn and Dressler.
Zell and Silver.

Novels
People of the city. 1954.
The passport of Mallam Ilia. 1960.
Jagua Nana. 1961.
Yaba roundabout murder. 1962.
An African night's entertainment: a tale of vengeance. 1962.
Burning grass: a story of the Fulani of Northern Nigeria. 1962.
Beautiful feathers. 1963.
The rainmaker and other stories. 1965.
Iska. 1966.
Lokotown and other stories. 1966.
People of the world. 1969.

For Children
When love whispers. 1947.
Ikolo the wrestler. 1947.
The leopard's claw. 1950.
The drummer boy. 1960.
Great elephant bird. 1965.
Trouble in Form Six. 1966.
The boa suitor. 1966.
Juju rock. 1966.

ELDER, LONNE, III (1931–)
Black American playwright; born in Georgia;

American Broadcasting Company Television Writing Fellowship (1965–6), etc.; served in the U.S. Army; worked as a doctor, waiter and professional gambler; playwright and producer in stage and film companies (1967–71); recipient of numerous awards; television series are *Camera* (1963), *The terrible vest* (1964), *NYPD* (1968) and *McCloud* (1970–1); film scripts are *Sounder* (1972) and *Melinda* (1972).

Bibliography
C.B.I.
Contemporary dramatists.

Plays
Ceremonies in dank old men. 1969.
Charades in East 4th Street (staged 1967. *Black Drama Anthology). 1971.

ELLIOTT, GEORGE PAUL (1918–)
American novelist; educated at University of California, Berkeley; after various academic posts became Professor of English, Syracuse University (1963–); recipient of various literary awards and grants; a contributor to *Hudson Review, Poetry*, etc.; edited *15 Modern American Poets* (1956) and *Types of Prose Fiction* (1964).

Bibliography
C.B.I.
Contemporary novelists.
Gale.

Novels
Perktilden village. 1958.
Among the dangs (stories). 1961.
David Knudsen. 1962.
In the world. 1965.
An hour of last things and other stories. 1968.
Never from nothing. 1971.
Muriel. 1972.

Poetry
Fevers and chills. 1961.
From the Berkeley hills. 1969.
Syracuse poems. 1970.

Other Works
A piece of lettuce (essays). 1964.
Dorothea Large: catalogue of an exhibition. 1966.
Conversions (essays). 1971.

†ELLIS, ROYSTON (CHRISTOPHER ROYSTON, GEORGE ELLIS)
(1941–)
English poet; born in Middlesex; journalist, lecturer and radio and television personality; contributor to *Beat, Honey, News of the World, Sunday Pictorial*, etc.

Bibliography
Authors' and writers' who's who. 1971.
B.N.B.
Gale.

Novels
Myself for fame. 1964.
Hell has its heroes. 1965.
The flesh merchants. 1966.
The rush at the end. 1967.

Poetry
Jiving to Gyp. 1959.
Rave. 1960.
The rainbow walking-stick. 1961.
A seaman's suitcase. 1963.
Selected poems. 1965.
The cherry boy. 1968.

Biography
Driftin' with Cliff Richard (with Jet Harris). 1959.
The big beat scene. 1961.
The Shadows by themselves. 1961.
The rebel (life of James Dean). 1962.

ELLISON, RALPH WALDO (1914–)
American novelist; served in the U.S. Merchant Marine during the Second World War; among other university posts was Visiting Professor of Writing, Rutgers University, New Brunswick (1962–4); Visiting Fellow of American studies, Yale University (1964–); recipient of several literary awards; a contributor to the *Quarterly Review of Literature, Partisan Review*, etc.; represented in various volumes of short stories.

Bibliography
C.B.I.
Contemporary novelists.
Gale.

Novels and Short Stories
Invisible man. 1952.

Essay
Shadow and act. 1964.

ELLMANN, RICHARD (1918–)
American critic and scholar; educated at Yale University and Trinity College, Dublin; served in the U.S. Navy during the Second World War (1943–5); Assistant Professor, Harvard (1947–51); Professor of English, Northwestern University, Evanston (1951–); recipient of several literary awards; his edited work is not listed below.

Bibliography
C.B.I.
Gale.

Works
Yeats: the man and the masks. 1948.
The identity of Yeats. 1954.
James Joyce. 1959.
The modern tradition. 1965.
Eminent domain. 1967.
Ulysses on the Liffey. 1972.
Golden codgers: essays in literary biography. 1973.

ELMSLIE, KENWARD (1929–)
American poet; born in New York; educated at Harvard; has travelled widely; worked in the Karamu inter-racial theatre, Cleveland; represented in *Young American Poets* (1968) and other anthologies; has translated an *Anthology of medieval lyrics* (1962) and *Leopardi* (1966).

Bibliography
C.B.I.
Contemporary poets.
Gale.

Poetry
Pavilions. 1961.
Power plant poems. 1967.
The champ. 1968.
Album. 1969.
Circus nerves. 1969.
Motor disturbance. 1971.

Other Works
Miss Julie (libretto). 1965.
The baby book. 1966.
The sweet bye and bye (libretto). 1966.
Lizzie Borden (libretto). 1967.
The 1967 gamebook calendar. 1967.
Yellow drum (musical based on Truman Capote, The grass harp). 1968.
The orchid stories. 1973.

ELTON, *Professor* GEOFFREY RUDOLPH (*né* EHRENBURG)

(1921–)
English constitutional historian; educated in Prague and London University (external degree); taught at Rydal School (1940–4); served in the army (1944–6) in the Second World War; Cambridge University Reader and Lecturer, etc. (1949–67); Fellow of Clare College, Cambridge (1954–); Professor of Constitutional History (1967–); LL.D. (1960); a contributor to *English Historical Review, History Journal, T.L.S., Listener,* etc.

Bibliography
Authors' and writers' who's who. 1971.
B.N.B.
Gale.
Who's who. 1973.

Works
The Tudor revolution in government. 1953.
England under the Tudors. 1955.
New Cambridge Modern History, vol. 2 (ed.). 1958.
Star Chamber stories. 1958.
The Tudor constitution. 1960.
Henry VIII: an essay in revision. 1962.
Renaissance and Reformation (ideas and institutions in western civilization). 1963.
Guide to research facilities in history in the universities of Great Britain and Ireland (with G. K. Clark). 1963.
Reformation Europe. 1963.
The practice of history. 1967.
The future of the past. 1968.
The sources of history: England 1200–1640. 1969.
Modern historians on British history 1485–1945: a critical bibliography 1945–1969. 1970.
Political history: principles and practice. 1970.
Policy and police: the enforcement of the Reformation in the age of Thomas Cromwell. 1972.

ELY, DAVID (1927–)

American novelist; educated at universities of North Carolina, Harvard and Oxford; served in the U.S. Navy (1945–6); journalist (1949–56); lives in Italy; contributor of stories to *Cosmopolitan, Saturday Evening Post, Playboy,* etc.

Bibliography
C.B.I.
Contemporary novelists.

Novels
Trot. 1963.
Seconds (filmed 1965). 1963.
The tour. 1967.
Poor devils. 1970.

Other Work
Time out. 1968.

ENGLAND, BARRY (1932–)

English novelist and playwright; educated at Downside School; served in the army (1950–2); actor, playwright and novelist (1961–); author of numerous television plays; his stage plays are *End of conflict* (1961), *The big contract* (1963), *The damn givers* (1964).

Bibliography
Authors' and writers' who's who. 1971.
B.N.B.
Gale.

Novel
Figures in a landscape (filmed 1969). 1968.

Play
Conduct unbecoming (staged 1969). 1971.

ENRIGHT, DENNIS JOSEPH (1920–)

English poet, novelist and literary critic; educated Downing College, Cambridge; university lecturer (1947–57); Professor of English, University of Singapore (1960–70); joint editor of *Encounter* (1970–); edited *English critical texts* (1962) and translated a volume of Japanese poetry (1957).

Bibliography
B.N.B.
Contemporary poets.
Gale.
Who's who. 1973.

Novels
Academic year. 1955.
Heaven knows where. 1957.
Insufficient poppy. 1960.
Figures of speech. 1965.

Poetry
The laughing hyena. 1953.
Bread rather than blossoms. 1956.
Some men are brothers. 1960.
Addictions. 1962.
The old Adam. 1965.

Unlawful assembly. 1968.
Selected poems. 1969.
The happier life. 1972.

Critical Works
The apothecary's shop. 1957.
Conspirators and poets. 1966.
Shakespeare and the students. 1970.

Travel
The world of dew: aspects of living Japan. 1955.
Memoirs of a mendicant professor. 1969.

ERIKSON, ERIK HOMBURGER
(1902–)
American philosopher and psychologist; born in
Germany of Danish parents; moved to America
(1933); educated at Vienna Psychoanalytic Institute
and Harvard Psychological Clinic; practising psy-
choanalyst (1933–); Professor of Human
Development and Lecturer on Psychology
(1960–); Professor Emeritus (1970); recipient of
various academic honours and literary awards; a
contributor to numerous professional and general
journals; a contributor to numerous works on psychology.

Bibliography
C.B.I.
Gale.

Works
Observations on the Yurok: childhood and world
image. 1943.
Childhood and society. 1950.
Young man Luther: a study in psychoanalysis and
history. 1958.
Identity and the life cycle. 1959.
Youth: change and challenge. 1963.
Insight and responsibility. 1964.
Identity: young and crisis. 1968.
Gandhi's truth on the origins of non-violence.
1969.
In search of common ground (with H. P. Newton).
1973.

ERSKINE-LINDOP, AUDREY
BEATRICE NOËL
(Mrs. DUDLEY GORDON LESLIE)
English novelist and playwright; worked in reper-
tory at Worthing and later became a scriptwriter in
England and Hollywood; a Freeman of the City
of London (1954); *Beware of angels* (with Dudley
Gordon Leslie) produced (1955), *Let's talk turkey*
produced (1959).

Bibliography
Authors' and writers' who's who. 1971.
B.N.B.
Who's who. 1973.

Novels
In me my enemy. 1948.
Soldiers' daughters never cry. 1949.
The tall headlines. 1950.
Out of the whirlwind. 1951.
The singer, not the song (filmed 1961). 1953.
Details of Jeremy Stretton. 1955.
The Judas figures. 1956.
I thank a fool. 1958.
The way to the lantern. 1961.
Nicola. 1964.
I start counting. 1966.
Sight unseen. 1969.

ESPEY, JOHN JENKINS (1913–)
American novelist and writer; born in Shanghai;
educated at Oxford; taught English at the University of California, Berkeley, becoming Professor (1956); a contributor to *Harper's*, *New
Yorker*, *Arizona Quarterly*, etc.

Bibliography
C.B.I.
Contemporary novelists.
Gale.

Novels
The anniversaries. 1963.
An observer. 1965.

Other Works
Minor heresies. 1945.
Tales out of school. 1947.
The other city. 1950.
Ezra Pound's "Mauberley"; a study in com-
position. 1955.

ESSLIN, MARTIN J. (1918–)
British, Viennese born, drama critic; educated at
Vienna University; B.B.C. (1940–); Head of
Radio Drama (1963–); Visiting Professor of
Drama, Florida State University (1969–); edited
Beckett (essays) (1965), *New Theatre of Europe*, and
The genius of the German theatre (1968).

Bibliography
B.N.B.
Who's who. 1973.

Works
Brecht: a choice of evils, a critical study of the man, his work and opinions. 1959.
The theatre of the absurd. 1962.
Harold Pinter. 1967.
Berthold Brecht. 1969.
Reflections, essays on modern theatre (English title, Brief chronicles). 1969.
The peopled wound; the work of Harold Pinter. 1970.

EVANS, BERGEN (1904–   )

American linguist and television personality; educated at Miami, Harvard and Oxford universities; Professor of English at Northwestern University, Evanston (1945–   ); master of ceremonies on radio and television shows (1949–   ); a contributor to *Atlantic Monthly*, *Harper's*, *Scribners*, etc.

Bibliography
C.B.I.
Gale.

Works
The psychiatry of Robert Burton. 1944.
The natural history of nonsense. 1946.
The spoor of spooks. 1954.
A dictionary of contemporary American usage (with Cornelia Evans). 1957.
Comfortable words. 1962.
Word-a-day. Vocabulary builder. 1963.
Dictionary of mythology. 1970.

EVANS, PAUL (1945   )

Welsh poet of the Underground; born in Cardiff; educated at University of Sussex.

Bibliography
B.N.B.
Contemporary poets.

Poetry
Love heat. 1969.
February. 1969.

EXTON, CLIVE JACK MONTAGUE (1930–   )

English playwright; educated at Christ's Hospital and the Central School of Speech and Drama; acted in repertory (1951–9); film scripts include *Night must fall* (1963), *Isadora* (1969) (with Melvyn Bragg), and *Nightmare Park* (1973); television plays include *No fixed abode* (1959), *The land of my dreams* (1964), *Conversation piece* (1970) and *The Rainbirds* (1971).

Bibliography
Anger and after.
B.N.B.

Plays
No fixed abode (in Six Granada plays, televised 1959). 1960.
Have you any dirty washing, Mother dear? (in Plays of the year, 37). 1970.

EZEKIEL, NISSIM (1924–   )

Indian poet; born in Bombay; educated at Bombay University; lived in London (1948–52); Professor of English, Mithbai College of Arts, Bombay (1961–   ); Visiting Professor, Leeds (1964) and Chicago (1967); a contributor to *Encounter*, *Spectator*, *Poetry Quarterly*, etc.; represented in various anthologies; his edited work is not listed below.

Bibliography
Contemporary poets.
C.B.I.
National bibliography of Indian literature 1901–53.

Poetry
A time to change. 1952.
Sixty poems. 1953.
The third. 1958.
The unfinished man. 1960.
The exact name. 1965.

Plays
Three plays. 1969.

F

FAIRBANK, JOHN KING (1907–)
American historian of China; educated at Harvard, Balliol College, Oxford, and Pekin College of Chinese Studies; among other wartime posts, special assistant to the American Ambassador, Chungking; Professor of History, Harvard (1946–); Director of Far Eastern Operations, United States Information Service (1945–6); a contributor to professional journals of articles on Chinese civilisation, etc.

Bibliography
C.B.I.
Gale.

Works
The United States and China. 1948.
The next step in Asia (co-author). 1949.
Modern China: a bibliographical guide (with K. C. Liu). 1950.
A documentary history of Chinese Communism 1921–1950 (with Conrad Brandt and Benjamin Schwartz). 1952.
Ch'ing documents: an introductory syllabus. 1952.
Trade and diplomacy on the China coast, 1842–1854. 2 vols. 1954.
China's response to the West (with S. Y. Teng), 2 vols. 1954.
Japanese studies of Modern China (with Mataka Banno). 1955.
Chinese thought and institutions. 1957.
A history of East Asian civilization: vol. I: East Asia, the great tradition (with J. K. Fairbank). 1960; vol. II: East Asia, the modern transformation (with J. K. Fairbank). 1965.
Ch'ing administration: three studies (with Teng Tsu-yu). 1960.
New thinking about China. 1967.
China: people's middle kingdom and the United States of America. 1967.
Chinese world order. 1968.
United States and China. 1972.

FANE, JULIAN (1927–)
English novelist; educated at Harrow.

Bibliography
Authors' and writers' who's who. 1971.
B.N.B.
Gale.

Novels
Morning. 1956.
A letter. 1960.
Memoir in the middle of a journey. 1971.
Gabriel Young. 1973.

FARRELL, JAMES GORDON (1935–)
English novelist; has lived much abroad and travelled widely in Mexico, Morocco, the Canadian Arctic and India where he went to research for his latest novel; he is the recipient of major literary awards.

Bibliography
B.N.B.

Novels
A man from elsewhere. 1963.
The lung. 1964.
A girl in the head. 1967.
Troubles. 1970.
The siege of Krishnapur (Booker Prize 1973). 1973.

FEDDEN, HENRY ROBIN ROMILLY (1908–)
English writer; educated at Clifton and Magdalene College, Cambridge; Director-general of the National Trust; contributor to *T.L.S.* and *Cornhill*; co-editor, with Lawrence Durrell and Bernard Spencer, of *Personal landscape, an anthology of exile* (1942–5).

Bibliography
Authors' and writers' who's who. 1971.
B.N.B.
Contemporary poets.
Gale.
Who's who. 1973.

Novel
As the unicorn. 1933.

Poetry
The white country. 1968.

Other Works
Suicide; a social and historical study. 1938.
The land of Egypt. 1939.
Syria. 1946.

Crusader castles. 1950.
Alpine ski tour. 1956.
Skiing in the Alps. 1958.
English travellers in the Near East. 1958.
The enchanted mountains. 1962.
Chantemesle. 1964.
The continuing purpose; a history of the National
    Trust. 1968.
Anglesey Abbey. 1968.
Churchill at Chartwell. 1969.

FEIFFER, JULES (1929–)
American cartoonist and playwright; born in New
York; educated at the Pratt Institute, New York;
cartoonist in the U.S. Army Signal Corps
(1951–3); cartoonist since 1946; Faculty Member,
Yale Drama School (1973–4); recipient of various
drama and cartoon awards; unpublished plays
include *God bless* (1968) and *Feiffer's people* (1968).

Bibliography
C.B.I.
Contemporary dramatists.
Gale.

Novel
Harry, the rat with women. 1963.

Plays
Little murders (staged 1966, filmed 1972). 1968.
The White House murder case (staged 1970). 1970.
Carnal knowledge: a screenplay. 1971.

Other Works
Sick, sick, sick. 1958.
Passionella and other stories. 1959.
The explainers (also a play). 1960.
Boy, girl, boy, girl. 1961.
Hold me! 1963.
Feiffer's album. 1963.
The unexpurgated memoirs of Bernard Mergen-
    deiler. 1965.
The Penguin Feiffer. 1966.
Feiffer on civil rights. 1966.
Feiffer's marriage manual. 1967.
Pictures at a prosecution: drawings and text from
    the Chicago conspiracy trial. 1971.

FELDMAN, IRVING MORDECAI
(1928–)
American poet; educated at Columbia University;
taught in Puerto Rico University (1957–8); Associate Professor of English, Kenyon College, Gam-
bier, Ohio (1958–64); Associate Professor of Eng-

lish, State University of New York (1964–); a
contributor to the *New Yorker, Atlantic Monthly,
Harper's Bazaar*, etc.

Bibliography
C.B.I.
Contemporary poets.
Gale.

Poetry
Works and days. 1961.
The Pripet marshes. 1965.
Magic papers and other poems. 1970.
Lost originals. 1972.

FERLINGHETTI, LAWRENCE
(1919–)
American poet; educated at the universities of
North Carolina, Columbia and the Sorbonne;
served in the U.S. Navy during the Second World
War (1941–5); founded City Lights, the first
American paperback shop, and the paperback
series Pocket Books (1953); editor of *City Lights
Journal*; translated Jacques Prévert (1958) and
others.

Bibliography
C.B.I.
Contemporary poets.
Gale.

Novel
Her. 1960.

Plays
Unfair arguments with existence (contains Three
    thousand red ants, Allegation, Victims of
    amnesia, Motherlode, Customs collector in
    baggy pants). 1963.

Poetry
Coney Island of the mind. 1958.
Starting from San Francisco (with L.P. record of
    the poet's reading of his work). 1961.
Routines. 1964.
An eye on the world. 1967.
Pictures of the gone world. 1967.
The secret meaning of new things. 1969.
Tyrannus Nix? 1969.
Back roads to far places. 1971.
Love is no stone on the thorn. 1972.

Other Works
Howl of the censor. 1961.

One thousand fearful words with Fidel Castro. 1961.

Mexican night (travel journal). 1970.

FERMOR, PATRICK MICHAEL LEIGH (1915–)

English novelist and writer; born in London; educated at King's School, Canterbury; served in the Second World War (1939–45); O.B.E. (1943); D.S.O. (1944); deputy director, British Institute, Athens (1945–6); travelled in the Caribbean and Central America; a contributor to *Encounter*, the *New Statesman*, *Sunday Times*, etc.; recipient of several literary awards; translated George Psychoundakis, *The Cretan runner* (1966) and *Roumeli* (1966).

Bibliography
Authors' and writers' who's who. 1971.
B.N.B.
Who's who. 1973.

Novel
The violins of St. Jacques. 1953.

Travel and Other Work
The traveller's tree. 1950.
A time to keep silence. 1953.
Mani. 1958.

FERRIS, PAUL FREDERICK (1929–)

Welsh novelist and author; born in Swansea; served in the R.A.F. (1947–9); editorial staff of the *South Wales Evening Post* (1949–52); of *Woman's Own* (1953); of *Observer* (1953–4); freelance writer (1953–); a contributor to *Observer*, radio and television, etc.

Bibliography
Authors' and writers' who's who. 1971.
B.N.B.
Gale.
Who's who. 1973.

Novels
A changed man. 1958.
Then we fall. 1960.
A family affair. 1963.
The destroyer. 1965.
The dam. 1967.

Other Works
The city. 1960.
The Church of England. 1962.

The doctors. 1965.
The nameless; abortion in Britain today. 1966.
Men and money; financial Europe today. 1968.
The house of Northcliffe. 1971.

FIEDLER, *Professor* LESLIE AARON (1917–)

American novelist and scholar; educated at the universities of New York, Wisconsin and Harvard; served as Japanese interpreter in the U.S. Navy (1942–6) during the Second World War; taught English and creative writing in American, Greek and Italian universities (1948–); recipient of several literary and academic awards; *Kenyon Review* Fellow in literary criticism (1956–7); a contributor to *Poetry*, Chicago, *New Republic*, *Saturday Review*, etc.

Bibliography
C.B.I.
Contemporary novelists.
Gale.

Novels
An end to innocence. 1955.
Pull down vanity! (stories). 1962.
The second stone; a love story. 1963.
Back to China. 1965.
The last Jew in America. 1966.

Other Works
Love and death in the American novel. 1960.
No! in thunder. 1960.
The continuing debate (with Jacob Vinocut). 1964.
Waiting for the end. 1964.
The return of the vanishing American. 1968.
Nude croquet. 1969.
Being busted. 1970.
Collected essays. 1971.
Cross the border—close the gap. 1972.
The stranger in Shakespeare. 1972.
To the gentiles. 1972.
Unfinished business. 1972.

FIELD, EDWARD (1924–)

American poet; served in the U.S. Army (1942–6) during the Second World War; scriptwriter of documentary films; edited *Eskimo songs and stories*.

Bibliography
C.B.I.
Gale.

Poetry
Stand up, friend, with me. 1962.
Variety photoplays (poems). 1967.

FIELDING, ALAN GABRIEL BARNSLEY (1916–)
English poet and novelist; a descendant of Henry Fielding; educated at St. Edward's School, Oxford, Trinity College, Dublin, and St. George's Hospital, London; served in the R.A.M.C. (1943–6) during the Second World War; medical officer, Maidstone (1954–64); Professor of English, Washington State University (1967–).

Bibliography
B.M. catalogue.
B.N.B.
Who's who. 1973.

Novels
Brotherly love. 1954.
In the time of Greenbloom. 1956.
Eight days. 1958.
Through streets broad and narrow. 1960.
The birthday king. 1962.
Gentlemen in their season. 1966.

Poetry
The frog prince and other poems. 1952.
Twenty-eight poems. 1955.

FIGES, EVA
German-born English writer and translator from the German; educated at Queen Mary College, University of London.

Bibliography
Authors' and writers' who's who. 1971.
B.N.B.

Novels
Equinox. 1966.
Musicians of Bremen. 1967.
Winter journey. 1967.
Konek landing. 1969.
B. 1972.
Days. 1973.

Other Work
Patriarchal attitudes: women in society. 1970.

FIGUEROA, *Professor* JOHN JOSEPH MARIA (1920–)
Caribbean poet and writer; born in Kingston, Jamaica; educated at London University; taught and lectured at universities in the United States; has travelled widely; broadcaster; Professor of Education, University of the West Indies, Jamaica; a contributor to *Bim*, *Caribbean Quarterly*, etc.; editor of *Caribbean Voices* (1966); represented in *Caribbean Verse* (1967).

Bibliography
C.B.I.
Contemporary poets.

Poetry
Blue mountain peak. 1944.
Love leaps here. 1962.

Other Work
Society, schools, and progress in the West Indies. 1967.

FINKEL, DONALD (1929–)
American poet; born in New York; educated at Columbia University; Instructor, University of Iowa (1957–8), etc.; Poet in residence, Washington University (1960–); a contributor to *Poetry*, Chicago, *New Yorker*, etc.

Bibliography
C.B.I.
Contemporary poets.
Gale.

Poetry
Poets of to-day VI (includes Clothing's new emperor). 1959.
Simeon. 1964.
A joyful noise. 1966.
Answer back. 1968.
The garbage wars. 1970.
Adequate earth. 1972.

FINLAY, IAN HAMILTON (1925–)
Scottish poet; born in the Bahamas; left school at 13; an exhibition of his concrete poetry in stone, glass, wood, etc., was held in London (1968).

Bibliography
B.N.B.
Contemporary poets.

Poetry
The dancers inherit the party. 1960.
Glasgow beasts, and a bird. 1961.
Concertina. 1962.

Rapel. 1963.
Telegrams from my windmill. 1964.
Standing poems nos. 1, 2 and 3. 1963 and 1965.
Ocean strip series 2. 1965.
Earthship (paper sculpture poem). 1965.
Cytherea. 1965.
Ocean strip series 3. 1965.
Autumn poem. Edinburgh. 1966.
6 small pears for Eugen Gomringer. 1966.
6 small songs in 3's. 1966.
Tea-leaves and fishes. 1966.
Ocean strip series 4. 1966.
4 sails. 1966.
Headlines cavelines. 1967.
Stonechats. 1967.
Ocean strip series 5. 1967.
Canal game. 1967.
3/3's. 1967.
The collected coaltown of Callange Tri-Kai. 1968.
Air letters. 1968.
The blue and the brown poems. 1968.
Waves. 1969.
Rhymes for lemons. 1970.
Lanes. 1970.

Play (translated into German)
Und alles blieb wie es war. 1966.

Short Story
The sea-bed. 1958.

Miscellaneous
Canal strips 3 and 4. 1964.

FINNIGAN, JOAN (*Mrs*. GRANT MACKENZIE) (1925–)

Canadian poet; born in Ottawa; educated at Queen's University; a contributor to magazines; represented in various anthologies.

Bibliography
Canadiana.
C.B.I.
Contemporary poets.
Gale.

Poetry
Through the glass, darkly. 1957.
A dream of lilies. 1965.
Entrance to the greenhouse. 1969.
It was warm and sunny when we set out. 1970.

FISHER, ROY (1930–)

English poet; born in Birmingham; educated at Birmingham University; pianist with jazz groups (1946–); taught (1953–63); head of English, Bordesley College of Education, Birmingham; represented in various anthologies.

Bibliography
B.N.B.
Contemporary poets.

Poetry
City. 1960.
Ten interiors with various figures. 1966.
The memorial fountain. 1967.
Collected poems: the ghost of a paper bag. 1969.

Other Works
Then hallucinations: city II. 1962.
The ship's orchestra. 1966.
Titles. 1969.

FITZGIBBON, ROBERT LOUIS CONSTANTINE (1919–)

Irish-American novelist and writer; born in Lenox, Mass.; educated at Wellington College, Munich University, the Sorbonne and Exeter College, Oxford; served in the British and U.S. Armies during the Second World War (1939–45); taught in Bermuda (1946–7); full-time writer since 1947; lives in Dorset; his translations from the French, German and Italian are not listed below; edited *Selected letters of Dylan Thomas* (1966); a contributor to many periodicals.

Bibliography
Authors' and writers' who's who. 1971.
B.N.B.
Gale.
Who's who. 1973.

Novels
The Arabian bird. 1948.
The iron hoop. 1949.
Cousin Emily. 1952.
The holiday. 1953.
The fair game (American title, Love and war). 1956.
Paradise lost and more (short stories and a play). 1959.
Watcher in Florence (pr. ptd.). 1959.
When the kissing had to stop. 1960.
Going to the river. 1963.
High heroic. 1969.

Other Works
Miss Finnigan's fault. 1953.
Norman Douglas; a pictorial record. 1953.
The little tour (with Giles Playfair). 1954.
The shirt of Nessus. 1956.
The blitz. 1957.
Random thoughts of a Fascist hyena. 1963.
The life of Dylan Thomas. 1965.
Through the minefield (autobiography). 1967.
Denazification. 1969.
Out of the lion's paw. 1969.
Red hand; the Ulster colony. 1972.

FLANDERS, MICHAEL HENRY
(1922–76)
English actor and writer; born in London; educated at Westminster School and Christ Church,
Oxford; served in the Navy in the Second World
War (1940–3); contracted polio (1943) and became
confined to a wheelchair; broadcast regularly
(1948–76); wrote the lyrics of many reviews
(1948–76) including *Penny plain* (1951) and *Airs on a
shoestring* (1953); two-man revues with Donald
Swann, *At the drop of a hat* (1956) and *At the drop of
another hat* (1961); translated Stravinsky's *The
soldier's tale* and other opera libretti.

Bibliography
Authors' and writers' who's who. 1971.
B.N.B.
Gale.
Who's who. 1973.

Works
Creatures great and small. 1964.
Captain Noah and his floating zoo. 1971.

FLEMING, IAN LANCASTER (1908–64)
English novelist; brother of Peter Fleming; educated at Eton, Sandhurst, and Munich and Geneva
universities; Reuters (1929–33); merchant banking
(1933–5); stockbroker (1935–9); personal assistant
to director of Naval Intelligence during the Second
World War (1939–45); foreign manager Kemsley,
later Thomson, newspapers (1945–59); publisher
of the *Book Collector* (1959–64); many of his novels
have been filmed; a contributor to *Horizon*, *Sunday
Times*, *Spectator*, etc.

Bibliography
B.N.B.
Gale.
Who's who. 1964.

Novels
Casino Royale (filmed 1966). 1953.
Live and let die (filmed 1974). 1954.
Moonraker (paperback title, Too hot to handle).
    1955.
Diamonds are forever (filmed 1971). 1956.
From Russia with love (filmed 1963). 1957.
Dr. No (filmed 1962). 1958.
Goldfinger (filmed 1963). 1959.
For your eyes only; five secret occasions of James
    Bond. 1960.
Gilt-edged Bonds (omnibus volume). 1961.
Thunderball (filmed 1964). 1961.
The spy who loved me. 1962.
On Her Majesty's secret service (filmed 1969).
    1963.
You only live twice (filmed 1966). 1964.
The man with the golden gun (filmed 1974). 1965.
Octopussy, and The living daylights. 1966.

For Children
Chitty-chitty-bang-bang, the magical car (filmed
    1968). 1964.

Other Works
The diamond smugglers. 1957.
Thrilling cities. 1963.

**FLETCHER, GEOFFREY
SCOWCROFT** (1923–)
English author and artist; educated at University
College, London, and British School, Rome;
author of television features on little-known
London; his London drawings and articles featured
in the *Daily Telegraph* (1958–).

Bibliography
B.N.B.
Who's who. 1973.

Works
Town's eye view. 1960.
The London nobody knows (filmed 1968). 1962.
Popular art in England. 1962.
City sights. 1963.
Pearly kingdom. 1965.
London overlooked. 1965.
Down among the meths men. 1966.
London's river. 1966.
Elements of sketching. 1966.
London pavement pounders. 1967.
Sketch it in colour. 1967.
Geoffrey Fletcher's London. 1968.
London after dark. 1969.

Changing London (*Daily Telegraph*). 1969.
Pocket guide to Dickens' London. 1969.
The London Dickens knew. 1970.

FOOT, MICHAEL MACKINTOSH
(1913–)
English politician and journalist; educated at
Wadham College, Oxford; Labour M.P.
(1945–); assistant editor, later editor, *Tribune*
(1937–60); political columnist and book critic,
Evening Standard (1964–); Honorary Fellow,
Wadham College, Oxford (1969–).

Bibliography
Authors' and writers' who's who. 1971.
B.N.B.
Who's who. 1973.

Works
Armistice 1918–39. 1940.
Trial of Mussolini. 1943.
Brendan and Beverley. 1944.
Who are the patriots? (with D. W. T. Bruce). 1949.
Still at large. 1950.
Full speed ahead. 1950.
Guilty men (with Mervyn Jones). 1957.
The pen and the sword. 1957.
Parliament in danger. 1959.
Aneurin Bevan: vol. I, 1897–1945. 1962.
Harold Wilson, a pictorial biography. 1964.

FOOTE, SHELBY (1916–)
American novelist; educated at University of
North Carolina; served in the U.S. Army during
the Second World War; awarded Guggenheim
Fellowship (1958–60); full-time writer.

Bibliography
C.B.I.
Contemporary novelists.
Gale.

Novels
Tournament. 1949.
Follow me down. 1950.
Love in a dry season. 1951.
Shiloh. 1952.
Jordan country (also a play). 1953.

Other Works
The civil war, 3 vols. 1958–73.

FORD, JESSE HILL, Jr. (1928–)
American novelist; educated at Vanderbilt and

Florida universities; served in the U.S. Navy
(1951–2); director of public service, Tennessee
Medical Association; then American Medical
Association, Chicago (1955–7); full-time writer
(1957–); wrote several television plays.

Bibliography
C.B.I.
Contemporary novelists.
Gale.

Novels
Mountains of Gilead. 1961.
The liberation of Lord Byron-Jones (filmed 1969).
   1965.
Fishes, birds and sons of men (stories). 1967.
The feast of Saint Barnabas. 1969.

Play
The conversion of Buster Drumwright. 1964.

FORD, ROBERT ARTHUR
DOUGLAS (1915–)
Canadian poet; born in Ottawa; educated at the
universities of Western Ontario and Cornell; on
the staff of the Canadian Department of External
Affairs; Ambassador to Russia; his translated
works, including a translation of Pasternak, which
won the Governor General's Award (q.v.), are not
listed below.

Bibliography
Canadiana.
C.B.I.

Poetry
A window on the north (Governor General's
   Award 1957). 1956.

Other Work
The solitary city. 1949.

FORSYTH, JAMES LAW (1913–)
Scottish playwright; educated at Glasgow School
of Art; served in the Scots Guards (1940–6) during
the Second World War; G.P.O. film unit
(1937–40); dramatist-in-residence, Old Vic
(1946–8); Distinguished Professor in residence,
Florida State University (1964) and other visiting
academic posts; founding member of the Theatres
Advisory Council; unpublished plays include *Trog*
(1949), *The pier* (1957), *Defiant island* (1962); radio
plays include *The bronze horse* (1948), *Pig* (1953),
The English boy (1969); television plays include

Kicky with a tuft (1959), *Old Mickmack* (1961); film scripts include *Francis of Assisi* (1961).

Bibliography
B.N.B.
Contemporary dramatists.

Plays
Emmanuel; a nativity play (broadcast 1950, staged 1960). 1952.
Three plays (The other heart, Héloïse, Adelaide). 1956.
The road to Emmaus; a play for Eastertide. 1958.
Brand (adapted from Ibsen, broadcast 1949, staged 1969). 1960.
Dear Wormwood (adapted from C. S. Lewis, The Screwtape letters, staged 1965). 1961.
Cyrano de Bergerac (adapted from Rostand, staged 1963). 1968.

FOWLES, JOHN (1926–)

English novelist; educated at Bedford School and New College, Oxford; taught in France and Greece; head of English at a London college; now a full-time writer.

Bibliography
Authors' and writers' who's who. 1971.
B.N.B.
Contemporary novelists.
Gale.

Novels
The collector (filmed 1961). 1963.
The magus (filmed 1969). 1966.
The French lieutenant's woman. 1969.
Double feature. 1972.

Other Work
The aristos: a self-portrait in ideas. 1965.

FRAME, JANET (JANET PATERSON FRAME CLUTHA) (1924–)

New Zealand novelist and short-story writer; educated at Otago University and Dunedin Teachers' Training College; was ill in hospital for 8 years, then travelled in Europe before returning to New Zealand, where she settled down to writing full-time.

Bibliography
B.N.B.
Contemporary novelists.

Gale.
N.Z. national bibliography.

Novels
The lagoon and other stories. 1952.
Owls do cry. 1957.
Faces in the water. 1962.
The edge of the alphabet. 1962.
Scented gardens for the blind. 1963.
The reservoir; snowman, snowman; fantasies and fables. 1963.
The adaptable man. 1965.
A state of siege. 1966.
The rainbirds (American title, Yellow flowers in the antipodean room). 1968.
Intensive care. 1970.

Poetry
The pocket mirror. 1967.

For Children
Mona Minim and the smell of the sun. 1969.

FRANCE, RUTH (†PAUL HENDERSON) (1913–68)

New Zealand poet and novelist.

Bibliography
C.B.I.
N.Z. national bibliography.

Novels (as Ruth France)
Travellers (story). 1955.
The race. 1958.
Hamilton. 1960.
Ice cold river. 1961.

Poetry
Object lesson. 1949.
Stream and the discovery. 1949.
Deserted house. 1950.
Rock garden. 1951.
Unwilling pilgrim (as †Paul Henderson). 1955.

Other Work
The shining year. 1964.

FRANKLIN, JOHN HOPE (1915–)

American historian; educated at Fisk and Harvard universities; Professor of History, Howard University, Washington (1947–56), and of Brooklyn College (1956–); Visiting Professor at numerous universities in America, and outside; Pitt Professor of History, Cambridge (1962–3); member of various academic boards; recipient of several academic honours; his edited work is not listed below.

Bibliography
C.B.I.
Gale.

Works
Free negro in North Carolina 1790–1860. 1943.
From slavery to freedom. 1947.
Militant south 1800–1861. 1956.
Reconstruction after the Civil War. 1961.
The emancipation proclamation. 1963.
Illustrated history of black Americans. 1970.

FRASER, Lady ANTONIA (*née* PAKENHAM) (1932–)

English historical writer; daughter of the Earl and Countess of Longford (q.v.); educated at the Dragon School, Oxford, St. Mary's Convent, Ascot, and Lady Margaret Hall, Oxford; has lectured, broadcast and appeared on television; translated Christian Dior's Autobiography (1957).

Bibliography
B.N.B.
Who's who. 1973.

Works
King Arthur and the knights of the round table. 1954.
Robin Hood (as Antonia Pakenham). 1957.
Dolls. 1963.
A history of toys. 1966.
Mary Queen of Scots (James Tait Black Prize 1969). 1969.

FRASER, GEORGE MACDONALD (1925–)

Scottish novelist and journalist; born in Carlisle; served in the army (1943–7) in the Second World War; journalist (1947–69); deputy editor, *Glasgow Herald* (1964–9); a contributor to the *Economist*, *Book World*, etc.

Bibliography
Authors' and writers' who's who. 1971.
B.N.B.

Novels
Flashman. 1969.
Royal Flash. 1970.
The general danced at dawn (stories). 1970.
Flash for freedom. 1971.

Other Work
The steel bonnets: the story of the Anglo-Scottish Border reivers. 1971.

FRAYN, MICHAEL (1933–)

English journalist and novelist; educated at Kingston Grammar School and Emmanuel College, Cambridge; served in the army (1952–4); *Guardian* columnist (1957–63), *Observer* columnist (1963–8); author of several television plays; his play *The Sandboy* produced (1971).

Bibliography
Authors' and writers' who's who. 1971.
B.N.B.
Contemporary novelists.
Gale.
Who's who. 1973.

Novels
The tin men (Somerset Maugham Award 1966). 1965.
The Russian interpreter (Hawthornden Prize 1967). 1966.
Towards the end of the morning. 1967.
A very private life. 1968.
Sweet dreams. 1972.

Play
The two of us. 1970.

Collections of Columns
The day of the dog. 1962.
The book of Fub. 1963.
On the outskirts. 1964.
A bay in Gear Street. 1967.

FREEMAN, GILLIAN (*Mrs.* EDWARD THORPE, †ELIOT GEORGE) (1929–)

English novelist; educated at Reading University; taught; worked as a copywriter, and as literary secretary to Louis Golding (1951–5) when she married; a contributor to various journals; her film scripts are *The leather boys* (1961), *Cold day in the park* (1968) and *I want what I want* (1970).

Bibliography
B.N.B.
Contemporary novelists.

Novels
The liberty man. 1955.
Fall of innocence. 1956.
Jack would be a gentleman. 1959.

The leather boys (as †Eliot George). 1961.
The campaign. 1963.
The leader. 1965.
The alabaster egg. 1970.

Other Works
The story of Albert Einstein (for children). 1960.
The undergrowth of literature. 1967.

FRIEDMAN, BRUCE JAY (1930–)
American novelist and playwright; in publishing
(1953–66); a frequent contributor to *Esquire*,
Harper's, *New York Times*, etc.

Bibliography
C.B.I.

Novels
Stern. 1962.
Far from the city of class and other stories. 1963.
A mother's kisses. 1964.
Black angels (stories). 1966.
The dick. 1970.

Plays
Scuba duba. 1968.
Steambath. 1971.

FRIEL, BRIAN (1929–)
Irish playwright; educated in Derry and Belfast;
taught (1950–60); full-time writer (1960–); his
plays have been produced in New York and Dublin.

Bibliography
B.N.B.
Gale.
Who's who. 1973.

Short Stories
The saucer of larks. 1962.
The gold in the sea. 1966.

Plays
Philadelphia, here I come. 1965.
The loves of Cass McGuire. 1967.
Lovers (includes Winners, and Losers). 1968.
The Mundy scheme. 1969.
Crystal and fox. 1970.
The gentle island. 1971.

FRISBY, TERENCE (1932–)
English playwright; educated at the Central School
of Dramatic Art; worked at various jobs such as

factory hand and waiter; professional actor
(1957–); resident director, New Theatre, Brom-
ley (1963–4); television plays include *Guilty* (1964),
Don't forget the basics (1967).

Bibliography
B.N.B.
Contemporary dramatists.

Plays
The subtopians. 1964.
There's a girl in my soup (staged 1966, filmed
    1970). 1968.
The bandwagon (staged 1969). 1973.

FROST, DAVID PARADINE (1939–)
English author, producer and columnist; born in
Suffolk; educated at Gonville and Caius College,
Cambridge; his television series include *That was
the week that was* (1962–3), *Not so much a programme,
more a way of life* (1964–5), *The Frost programme*
(1966–8); the recipient of several television awards.

Bibliography
B.N.B.
Who's who. 1973.

Works
That was the week that was. 1963.
How to live under Labour or at least have as much
    chance as anybody else. 1964.
To England with love (with A. Jay: English title,
    The English). 1967.
The Presidential debate, 1968. 1968.
The Americans. 1971.

FRYE, *Professor* **HERMAN NORTHRUP**
(1912–)
Canadian scholar and literary critic; educated at
Victoria College, Toronto, and Merton College,
Oxford; English Lecturer, Victoria College,
Toronto (1941–); Professor of English and Prin-
cipal (1959–); Visiting Professor in many
American universities; editor-in-chief of the *Cana-
dian Forum*; contributor of Letters in Canada in the
University of Toronto Quarterly (1956–60); a con-
tributor to learned journals in Canada, the United
States and England; his edited works are not listed
below.

Bibliography
Canadiana.
C.B.I.
Gale.

Works

Fearful symmetry, a study of William Blake. 1947.
Anatomy of criticism. 1957.
Culture and the national will (an address). 1957.
By liberal things (an address). 1960.
T. S. Eliot. 1963.
The well-tempered critic. 1963.
Fables of identity, studies on poetic mythology. 1963.
Design for living. 1963.
The educated imagination (an address). 1964.
The return of Eden; five essays on Milton's epics. 1965.
A natural perspective; the development of Shakespearian comedy and romance. 1965.
The modern century. 1968.
The morality of scholarship (with others). 1968.
Fools of time: studies in Shakespearian tragedy. 1968.
A study of English Romanticism. 1969.
Stubborn structure: essays on criticism and society. 1970.
The critical path. 1971.

FUGARD, ATHOL (1932–)

South African playwright; born in Cape Province; educated at Cape Town University; seaman, journalist, stage manager; devoted himself to writing, directing and acting (1959–); co-founder of the Space Experimental Theatre, Cape Town (1972–); two of his plays are unpublished, as is his television play *Mille miglia* (1968).

Bibliography
B.N.B.
Contemporary dramatists.

Plays
The blood knot (staged 1960). 1963.
Hello and goodbye (staged 1965). 1966.
The occupation (in 10 one-act plays, Heinemann). 1968.
People are living there (staged 1968). 1969.
Boesman and Lena (staged 1969). 1969.
Three plays (The blood knot, Hello and goodbye, Boesman and Lena). 1972.

FUKUDA, TSUTOMU (1905–)

Japanese poet and translator; educated at Osaka Foreign Language College; Kansei Gakuin University; a Fulbright Scholar to the U.S. (1963) and Europe (1964); taught (1927–49); Professor of English, Kobe University (1959–69); Professor of English, Tezukayama women's junior college

(1969–); his poetry in English is not separately published; his translations of Japanese novels are not listed below.

Bibliography
C.B.I.
Contemporary poets.

Works
A study of Charles Lamb's essays of Elia. 1964.
Literary and linguistic travels in America and Europe. 1968.

FULLER, EDMUND
(†AMICUS CURIAC) (1914–)

American writer, novelist and scholar; taught English at Columbia University; his numerous edited works are not listed below.

Bibliography
C.B.I.
Contemporary novelists.

Novels
A star pointed north. 1946.
Brothers divided. 1951.
The corridor. 1963.
Flight. 1970.

Other Works
A pageant of the theatre. 1941.
John Milton. 1944.
George Bernard Shaw; critic of western morals. 1950.
Vermont: a history of the green mountain state. 1952.
Tinkers and giants; the story of the Yankee inventors. 1955.
Man in modern fiction. 1958.
Books with men behind them. 1962.
Successful calamity: a writer's follies on a Vermont farm. 1966.
Commentary on Charles Williams' "All-Hallows Eve". 1967.
God in the White House (with D. E. Green). 1968.
Prudence Crandall: an incident of racism in 19th century Connecticut. 1971.
An introduction to the Gray (with O. B. Davis). 1972.

FULLER, JOHN (1937–)

English poet; son of Roy Fuller; born in Kent; educated at St. Paul's School and New College, Oxford; Fellow of Magdalen College, Oxford

(1966–); contributor to the *T.L.S.*, *Listener*, *New Statesman*, etc.; represented in numerous anthologies; editor of *Oxford poetry* (1960), etc.; edited the works of John Gay.

Bibliography
B.N.B.
Contemporary poets.
Gale.

Poetry
Fairground music. 1961.
Final epitaph. 1965.
The tree that walked. 1967.
The art of love. 1968.
All the golden gifts. 1968.
The wreck. 1970.
Cannibals and missionaries. 1972.

Other Works
Herod, do your worst (libretto). 1968.
A reader's guide to W. H. Auden. 1969.

FYZEE, ASAF A. A. (1899–)
Indian lawyer, diplomat and writer; born in

Matheran; educated at the Bombay University, St. John's College, Cambridge, and the Middle Temple; Indian Ambassador to Egypt (1949–51); Vice-Chancellor, University of Jammu and Kashmir (1957–60); Visiting Professor, McGill University, Montreal, Canada (1957–8); Commonwealth (Professorial) Fellow, St. John's College, Cambridge (1962–3); Visiting Professor, Islamic Law, University of California at Los Angeles (1966); awarded Padma Bhushan by the Government of India (1962).

Bibliography
B.N.B.
C.B.I.
Indian national bibliography 1958–67.
National bibliography of Indian literature 1901–53.

Works
Outlines of Muhammadan Law. 1949.
A modern approach to Islam. 1963.
Cases in the Muhammadan Law of India and Pakistan. 1965.

G

GADDIS, WILLIAM (1922–)
American novelist; educated at Harvard; freelance writer for films, magazines, etc.; a contributor to *Writers in revolt* (1963).

Bibliography
C.B.I.
Contemporary novelists.
Gale.

Novel
The recognitions. 1955.

GAINHAM, SARAH RACHEL
(*Mrs.* KENNETH AMES) (1922–)
English novelist; travelled widely in Eastern Europe; Central Europe correspondent of the *Spectator* (1956–66); a contributor to *Encounter*, *Atlantic Monthly*, B.B.C., etc.

Bibliography
B.N.B.
Who's who. 1973.

Novels
Time right deadly. 1956.
Cold dark night. 1957.
The mythmaker. 1957.
Stone roses. 1959.
Silent hostage. 1960.
Night falls on the city. 1967.
A place in the country. 1968.
Takeover bid. 1970.
Private worlds: a trilogy with Night falls on the city, and A place in the country. 1971.
    Maculan's daughter. 1973.

GALLANT, MAVIS (1922–)
Canadian short-story writer; lives in Paris; a contributor to the *New Yorker*, *Harper's Bazaar*, *Glamour*, etc.

Bibliography
Authors' and writers' who's who. 1971.
Canadiana.
C.B.I.

Novels
Green water, green sky. 1959.
A fairly good time. 1970.

Short Stories
The other Paris. 1956.
My heart is broken (English title, An unmarried man's summer. 1965). 1964.

Other Work
The affair of Gabrielle Russier (with Raymond Jean). 1973.

GANN, ERNEST KELLOG (1910–)
American novelist and screen writer; educated at Yale University; served in the U.S. Army (1942–6) in the Second World War.

Bibliography
C.B.I.
Gale.

Novels
Island in the sky (filmed 1953). 1944.
Blaze of noon (filmed 1947) (English title, Blaze at noon). 1946.
Benjamin Lawless. 1948.
Fiddler's Green (filmed as The raging tide, 1951). 1950.
The high and the mighty (filmed 1954). 1952.
Soldier of fortune (filmed 1955). 1953.
Twilight for the gods (filmed 1957). 1956.
The trouble with lazy Ethel. 1958.
Fate is the hunter (filmed 1964). 1961.
Of good and evil. 1963.
In the company of eagles. 1966.
Song of the sirens. 1968.
The antagonists. 1971.

GARDNER, ISABELLA STEWART (*Mrs.* **A. TATE**) (1915–)
American poet and editor of *Poetry*; Associate Editor of *Poetry*, Chicago (1952–6); has travelled widely; represented in numerous anthologies.

Bibliography
C.B.I.
Contemporary poets.
Gale.

Poetry
Birthdays from the ocean. 1955.
Un altra infanzia (selected poetry translated from the Italian). 1959.
The looking glass. 1961.
West of childhood: poems 1950–1965. 1965.

GARDNER, JOHN (1926–)
English novelist; educated at St. John's College, Cambridge; full-time writer (1967–).

Bibliography
B.N.B.
C.B.I.

Novels
The liquidator (filmed 1965). 1964.
Spin the bottle; autobiography of an alcoholic. 1964.
Understrike. 1965.
Amber nine. 1966.
Madrigal. 1967.
Complete state of death (filmed as The stone killer, 1973). 1969.
The airline pirates. 1970.
Traitor's exit. 1970.
Air apparent. 1971.
Every night's a bullfight (alternative title, Every night's a festival). 1971.
The censor. 1972.
The stone killers. 1973.
The corner man. 1974.

GARDNER, JOHN CHAMPLIN (1933–)
American novelist and Middle English scholar; his translations from Middle English are not listed below; edited (with Berners Dunlap) *The forms of fiction* (1967).

Bibliography
C.B.I.

Novels
The wreckage of Agathon. 1970.
Grendel. 1971.
The sunlight dialogues. 1972.
The nickel mountain. 1973.
Jason and Medeia. 1973.

GARDNER, JOHN WILLIAM (1912–)
American psychologist and writer; educated at Stanford and California universities; served in the U.S. Marines (1943–6) during the Second World

War; taught psychology (1936–); President, Carnegie Foundation; member of various government and consultative bodies; director of various companies including Shell Oil; recipient of many honorary degrees and other awards.

Bibliography
C.B.I.
Who's who. 1973.

Works
Excellence. 1961.
Self renewal. 1964.
No easy victories. 1968.
One year later. 1969.
Recovery of confidence. 1970.
In common cause. 1972.

GARGI, BALWANT (1916–)

Indian theatre critic; born near Bhatinda; educated at Lahore; taught Indian drama at the University of Washington (1964–6); won Sahitya Akademi Award (1962).

Bibliography
C.B.I.
Indian national bibliography 1958–67.
National bibliography of Indian literature 1901–53.

Works
Theatre in India. n.d.
Folk theatre of India. 1967.

GARLAND, PATRICK

English playwright, short-story writer and actor; educated at St. Edmund Hall, Oxford; worked as an actor, director of television, film and stage.

Bibliography
Authors' and writers' who's who. 1971.
B.N.B.

Plays
Light blue, dark blue. 1959.
Brief lives (adaptation of John Aubrey's Brief lives). 1967.

GARNER, HUGH (1913–)

Anglo-Canadian novelist; born in Yorkshire; educated in Toronto; a professional writer since 1949; fought in Spain in the International Brigade (1937); served in the army in the Second World War (1940–5); a contributor to many magazines; writes plays for English, Canadian and Australian television.

Bibliography
Authors' and writers' who's who. 1971.
Canadiana.
C.B.I.
Contemporary novelists.

Novels
Storm below. 1949.
Waste no tears. 1950.
Cabbage town. 1950.
Present reckoning. 1951.
The silence on the shore. 1962.
The sin sniper. 1970.
A nice place to visit. 1970.

Short Stories
The yellow sweater and other stories. 1952.
Hugh Garner's best stories (Governor General's Award 1964). 1963.
Men and women. 1966.
Violation of the virgins. 1971.

Other Work
Author! Author! (essays). 1964.

GARRETT, GEORGE PALMER (1929–)

American poet and novelist; educated at Princeton University; Assistant Professor at various universities; served in the U.S. Army (1952–5); awarded various grants and fellowships; poetry editor of the *Transatlantic Review*; a contributor to various journals; his edited work is not listed below; his film scripts include *The young lovers* (1964) and *The playground* (1965).

Bibliography
C.B.I.
Contemporary novelists.
Contemporary poets.
Gale.

Novels
The finished man. 1959.
Which ones are the enemy? 1961.
Do, Lord, remember me. 1964.
Death of the fox. 1971.

Stories
King of the mountain. 1958.
In the briar patch. 1961.

Cold ground was my bed last night. 1964.
A wreath for Garibaldi. 1969.

Poetry
The reverend ghost. 1957.
The sleeping gypsy. 1958.
Abraham's knife. 1961.
For a bitter season (new and selected poems). 1967.

Play for Children
Sir Slob and the princess. 1962.

GARRIGUE, JEAN (1914–   )
American poet; educated at Chicago and Iowa universities; member of the English department of various universities (1942–   ); awarded various grants and fellowships in poetry, creative writing, etc.; a contributor to *Kenyon Review*, *Poetry*, *New Republic*, *New York Herald Tribune*, etc.

Bibliography
C.B.I.
Contemporary poets.
Gale.

Novel
The animal hotel. 1966.

Poetry
The ego and the centaur. 1947.
The monument rose. 1953.
A water walk by Villa d'Este. 1959.
Country without maps. 1964.
New and selected poems. 1967.
Chartres and prose poems. 1971.

Other Work
Marianne Moore. 1965.

GASCOIGNE, ARTHUR BAMBER (1935–   )
English drama critic and novelist; educated at Eton and Magdalene College, Cambridge; drama critic, the *Spectator* (1961–3), the *Observer* (1963–4); Chairman, *University Challenge* (1962–   ).

Bibliography
Authors' and writers' who's who. 1971.
B.N.B.

Novels
Murgatreud's empire. 1972.
The heyday. 1973.

Other Works
Twentieth century drama. 1967.
World theatre. 1968.
The great Moghuls. 1971.

GASKELL, JANE (*Mrs*. **GERALD LYNCH**) (1941–   )
English novelist; *Daily Express* feature writer.

Bibliography
B.N.B.
Gale.

Novels
Strange evil. 1957.
King's daughter. 1958.
Attic summer. 1962.
The serpent. 1963.
The narrow shiny grin. 1964.
Atlan. 1965.
The fabulous heroine. 1965.
All neat in black stockings (filmed 1968). 1966.
The city. 1966.
A sweet, sweet summer (Somerset Maugham Award 1970). 1969.

GASKIN, CATHERINE (*Mrs*. **CORNBERG**) (1929–   )
Irish-born novelist; educated and brought up in Australia; lived in London (1948–55) and New York (1955–67).

Bibliography
B.N.B.
Who's who. 1973.

Novels
This other Eden. 1946.
With every year. 1947.
Dust in sunlight. 1950.
All else is folly. 1951.
Daughter of the house. 1952.
Sara Dane. 1955.
Blake's Reach. 1958.
Corporation wife. 1960.
I know my love. 1962.
The Tilsit inheritance. 1963.
The file on Devlin. 1965.
Edge of glass. 1967.
Fiona. 1970.
A falcon for a queen. 1972.
Property of a gentleman. 1974.

GASS, WILLIAM HOWARD (1924–   )
American novelist; educated at Kenyon College,

Ohio Wesleyan University and Cornell University; served in the U.S. Navy (1943–6) during the Second World War; Instructor, then Assistant Professor, then Associate Professor, then Professor of Philosophy, Purdue University, Lafayette, Indiana (1950–9); Professor of Philosophy, Washington University (1969–); recipient of several awards.

Bibliography
C.B.I.
Contemporary novelists.

Novels
Omensetter's luck. 1966.
In the heart of the heart of the country and other stories. 1968.
Willie Masters' lonesome wife. 1971.

Other Work
Fiction and the figures of life. 1971.

GELBER, JACK (1932–)
American playwright; born in Chicago; educated at University of Illinois; writer in residence, City College of New York (1965–6); Guggenheim fellowship for creative writing on the theatre (1963–4, 1966–7).

Bibliography
C.B.I.
Contemporary dramatists.
Gale.

Novel
On ice. 1964.

Plays
The connection. 1960.
The apple. 1961.
Square in the eye (original title, Let's face it). 1966.
Sleep: a play. 1972.

GHISELIN, BREWSTER (1906–)
American poet and writer; educated at universities of California and Utah; after various university posts, Professor of English, University of Utah (1950–).

Bibliography
C.B.I.
Contemporary poets.
Gale.

Poetry
Against the circle. 1946.
The nets. 1955.
Country of the Minotaur. 1969.

Other Work
The creative process; a symposium. 1952.

GHOSE, ZULIFIKAR (1935–)
Pakistani novelist and poet; educated at University of Keele; cricket correspondent of the *Observer* (1960–5); taught in London (1963–9); emigrated to the U.S. (1969); Lecturer in English at the University of Texas, Austin; represented in numerous anthologies; a contributor to the *New York Times*, etc.

Bibliography
B.N.B.
Contemporary novelists.
Contemporary poets.
Indian national bibliography 1958–67.

Novels and Short Stories
Statement against corpses (stories) (with B. S. Johnson). 1964.
The contradictions. 1966.
The murder of Aziz Khan. 1967.
The incredible Brazilian, book I. 1969.

Poetry
The loss of India. 1964.
Jets from orange. 1967.
The violent west. 1972.

Autobiography
Confessions of a native-alien. 1965.

GIBSON, WILLIAM (1914–)
American playwright; born in New York; educated at the College of the City of New York; full-time writer and piano teacher.

Bibliography
C.B.I.
Contemporary dramatists.
Gale.

Novel
The cobweb. 1954.

Poetry
Winter crook. 1948.
Mass for the dead. 1960.

Plays

I lay in Zion. 1947.

The miracle worker (for television; filmed 1962). 1957.

The seesaw log. 1959.

Dinny and the witches (with The miracle worker). 1960.

Two for the seesaw (filmed 1962). 1960.

Golden boy, the book of a musical (with Clifford Odets). 1965.

A cry of players. 1969.

American primitive (original title, John and Abigail). 1972.

GILBERT, FLORENCE RUTH
(*Mrs.* JOHN B. MACKAY) (1917–)

New Zealand poet; physiotherapist at the Otago School of Physiotherapy before her marriage; represented in several anthologies; a contributor to poetry magazines in England, Canada, India and New Zealand.

Bibliography

B.N.B.

Contemporary poets.

Poetry

Lazarus and other poems. 1949.

The sunlit hour. 1955.

GILBERT, MARTIN JOHN (1936–)

English historian; educated at Magdalen College, Oxford; research assistant to Randolph Churchill (1962–7); official biographer of Winston Churchill (1968–); Fellow of Merton College, Oxford (1962–); a contributor to learned journals and reviews; editor of *Plough my own furrow; the life of Lord Allen of Hurtwood* (1965), *Servant of India; a study of Imperial rule 1905–1910* (1966), *A century of conflict; essays presented to A. J. P. Taylor* (1966), *Churchill* (1968), and *Lloyd George* (1969).

Bibliography

B.N.B.

Who's who. 1973.

Works

The appeasers (with Richard Gott). 1963.

Britain and Germany between the wars. 1964.

The European powers 1900–1945. 1965.

The roots of appeasement. 1966.

Recent history atlas, 1870 to the present day. 1966.

Winston Churchill (for young people). 1966.

British history atlas. 1968.

American history atlas. 1968.

Jewish history atlas. 1969.

Winston Churchill. 1969.

The Second World War. 1970.

First world war atlas. 1971.

Winston S. Churchill, vol. III 1914–1916. 1971.

Russian history atlas. 1972.

The coming of war 1939. 1973.

GILBERT, MICHAEL FRANCIS
(1912–)

English novelist and playwright; educated at Blundell's School and University College, London; served in the army during the Second World War (1939–45); solicitor (1947–); legal adviser to the government of Bahrain (1960); member of the Arts Council Committee on Public Lending Rights (1966); founder member of the Crime Writers' Association; writes for radio and television.

Bibliography

B.N.B.

Gale.

Who's who. 1973.

Novels

Close quarters. 1947.

They never looked inside (American title, He didn't mind danger). 1948.

The doors open. 1949.

Smallbone deceased. 1950.

Death has deep roots (filmed as Guilty? 1956). 1951.

Death in captivity (American title, The danger within; filmed as The danger within, 1958). 1952.

Fear to tread. 1953.

Sky high (American title, The country house burglar). 1955.

Be shot for sixpence. 1956.

The claimant. 1957.

Blood and judgement. 1959.

Crack in the teacup. 1966.

After the fine weather. 1967.

The dust and the heat. 1967.

Games without rules. 1968.

The Etruscan net. 1969.

Stay of execution and other legal stories. 1971.

The body of a girl. 1972.

Plays

A clean play. 1960.

The bargain. 1961.

After the fine weather. 1963.

Windfall. 1963.
The shot in question. 1963.

GILL, M. LAKSHMI
(*Mrs.* **U. G. GODFREY)** (1943–)
Indian poet; born in the Philippines; educated in
Washington and University of British Columbia;
Instructor of English, British Columbia (1965–7);
lives in Kingston, Ontario; has contributed to
Canadian reviews.

Bibliography
Contemporary poets.
Indian national bibliography 1958–67.

Poetry
Rape of the spirit. 1962.
During rain, I plant chrysanthemums. 1966.
Confrontations. 1969.

GILLIATT, PENELOPE
(*née* **CONNER)** (1932–)
English novelist and journalist; educated at
Queens' College and Bennington College; feature
editor of *Vogue*; film critic and later drama critic of
the *Observer* (1961–); a contributor to the *New
Statesman, Encounter, Guardian,* etc.; film script of
Sunday, bloody Sunday (1971).

Bibliography
B.N.B.
Contemporary novelists.
Gale.

Novels
One by one. 1965.
A state of change. 1967.
What's it like out, and other stories. 1968.

Other Work
A house in the country. 1973.

GILMAN, RICHARD (1925–)
American critic; educated at University of Wisconsin; served in the Second World War (1943–6);
freelance writer (1950–4); editor (1954–70); Professor of Drama, Yale (1970–).

Bibliography
C.B.I.

Works
The confusion of realms. 1970.
Common and uncommon marks. 1971.

GILROY, FRANK DANIEL (1925–)
American playwright; educated at Yale University
Drama School; served in the army (1943–6) during
the Second World War; recipient of several awards;
writes plays for film and television.

Bibliography
C.B.I.
Contemporary dramatists.

Novel
Private. 1970.

Plays
Who'll save the plowboy? (staged 1962). 1962.
The subject was roses (staged 1964) (Pulitzer Prize
   1965). 1962.
That summer—that fall, and Far rockaway. 1967.
The only game in town (staged 1968). 1968.
A matter of pride (adaptation from John Langdon).
   1970.
From noon till three. 1973.

GINSBERG, ALLEN (1926–)
American poet; of Russian parentage; educated at
Columbia University; worked as night porter,
literary agent, film actor, etc. (1945–);
Guggenheim Fellow (1965–6); a contributor to
*Evergreen Review, Playboy, Atlantic, Journal for the
Protection of All Beings,* etc.; a contributor to *The
New American Poet 1945–60,* ed. D. M. Allen
(1961), etc.

Bibliography
C.B.I.
Contemporary poets.
Gale.

Selected Poetry
Howl, and other poems. 1955.
Kaddish poems 1958–1960. 1961.
Empty mirror. 1961.
Reality sandwiches (poems 1953–1960). 1963.
The age letters (with William Burroughs). 1964.
Kraj Majales. 1965.
Wichita-Vortex sutra. 1966.
T.V. baby poems. 1967.
Planet news: new poems 1961–7. 1968.
Airplane dreams: compositions from journals.
   1968.
Ankov Wat. 1969.
Fall of America. 1972.
Bikby canyon ocean path word breeze. 1972.
Gates of wraths: rhymed poems 1948–1953. 1972.

Other Works
Indian journals. 1970.
Interview with Allen Young. 1973.

GIOVANNI, NIKKI (1943–)

Black American poet; born in Knoxville, Tennessee; educated at Columbia University; Assistant Professor of English, Rutgers University, New Brunswick (1969–); editor of the anthology *Night comes softly* (1970).

Bibliography
C.B.I.
Gale.

Poetry
Black feeling, black talk. 1968.
Black judgement (with Black feeling, black talk). 1968.
Re: creation. 1970.
Spin a soft black song: poems for children. 1971.
My house. 1972.
Ego-tripping, and other poems for young readers. 1973.

Other Work
Gemini: extended autobiographical statement on my twenty-five years of being a black poet. 1971.

GLANVILLE, BRIAN LESTER

(1931–)
Anglo-Jewish novelist and sports writer; educated at Charterhouse; *Sunday Times* football correspondent (1958–); English correspondent of the *Corriere dello sport*, Rome (1954); freelance journalist in Rome and Florence (1952–5); a contributor to the *Sunday Times*, etc.

Bibliography
Authors' and writers' who's who. 1971.
B.N.B.
Contemporary novelists.
Who's who. 1973.

Novels and Short Stories
The reluctant dictator. 1952.
Henry sows the wind. 1954.
Along the Arno. 1956.
The bankrupts. 1958.
After Rome, Africa. 1959.
A bad streak (short stories). 1961.
Diamond. 1962.
The director's wife and other stories. 1963.

The rise of Gerry Logan. 1963.
Goalkeepers are crazy (short stories). 1964.
The king of Hackney Marshes and other stories. 1965.
A second home. 1965.
A Roman marriage. 1966.
The artist type. 1967.
The Olympian. 1969.
A betting man (stories). 1969.
A cry of crickets. 1970.
The financiers. 1972.

Non-fiction
Cliff Bastin remembers (with Cliff Bastin). 1950.
Arsenal Football Club. 1952.
Soccer nemesis. 1955.
World Cup (with Jerry Weinstein). 1958.
Soccer round the globe. 1959.
People in sport. 1967.
Soccer; a panorama. 1969.
Puffin book of football. 1970.
Know about football. 1971.
Goalkeepers are different (for children). 1971.
The thing he loves. 1973.

GLASKIN, GERALD MARCUS (†NEVILLE JACKSON) (1923–)

Australian novelist; served in the Second World War (1941–6); sales statistician at Ford's; a partner of Lyall and Evatt, Singapore.

Bibliography
Authors' and writers' who's who. 1971.
B.N.B.

Novels
A world of our own. 1955.
A minor portrait (alternative title, The mistress). 1957.
A change of mind. 1959.
A lion in the sun. 1960.
The beach of passionate love. 1961.
The land that sleeps. 1961.
A waltz through the hills. 1961.
A small selection of short stories (alternative title, Sometimes it wasn't so nice). 1962.
Flight to landfall. 1963.
O love, O loneliness. 1964.
No end to the way (as †Neville Jackson). 1965.
The man who didn't count. 1965.
The road to nowhere. 1967.

Play
Turn on the heat. 1967.

Memoir
A bird in my hands. 1967.

GLAZER, NATHAN (1923–)
American sociologist; educated at Pennsylvania and Columbia universities; editor, *Commentary Magazine* (1945–53); consulting editor, Random House, publishers.

Bibliography
C.B.I.
Gale.

Works
The lonely crowd (with David Riesman and Reuel Denney). 1950.
Faces in the crowd (with David Riesman). 1952.
American Judaism. 1957.
The social basis of American Communism. 1961.
Beyond the melting pot (with Daniel Moynihan). 1963.
Remembering the answers: essays on the American student revolt. 1970.

GLÜCK, LOUISE ELISABETH (1943–)
American poet; educated at Columbia University; recipient of Academy of America Poet's Prize (1966), etc.; a contributor to *Poetry*, *Chicago*, *Nation*, *New Yorker*, etc.; represented in *Young American Poets*, Follett (1968) and *Young American Writers* (1969).

Bibliography
C.B.I.
Contemporary poets.

Poetry
Firstborn. 1968.

GLYN, Sir ANTHONY (GEOFFREY LEO SIMON DAVISON), Bt. (1922–)
English novelist; educated at Eton; served in the Guards (1941–5); a contributor to the *Evening Standard, Spectator*, etc.; lives in France.

Bibliography
Authors' and writers' who's who. 1971.
B.N.B.
Who's who. 1973.

Novels
Romanza. 1953.
The jungle of Eden. 1954.

The ram in the thicket. 1957.
I can take it all. 1959.
Kick turn. 1963.
The terminal. 1965.
The dragon variation. 1969.

Other Works
Elinor Glyn, a biography. 1955.
The Seine. 1966.
The blood of a Britishman. 1970.

GLYN, CAROLINE (1947–)
English novelist and poet; daughter of Anthony Glyn (q.v.); studied art in Paris where she lives; a contributor to *Cornhill* and other journals; teenage correspondent for the colour supplement of the *Observer*.

Bibliography
B.N.B.
Gale.

Novels
Love and joy in the Mabillon. 1965.
The unicorn girl. 1966.
Heights and depths. 1968.
The tree. 1969.
The tower and the rising tide. 1971.

Poetry
Dream saga. 1962.
Don't knock the corners off. 1963.

GOLD, HERBERT (1924–)
American novelist; educated at the universities of the Sorbonne and Columbia; served in the U.S. Army (1943–6) during the Second World War; recipient of various literary and academic awards; a contributor to *Botteghe Oscure, Harper's Bazaar, New Yorker, Atlantic*, etc.; his edited work is not listed below.

Bibliography
C.B.I.
Contemporary novelists.
Gale.

Novels
Birth of a hero. 1951.
The prospect before us. 1954.
The man who was not with it. 1956.
The optimist. 1959.
Love and like. 1960.
Therefore be bold. 1960.

Salt. 1963.
The fathers: a novel in the form of a memoir. 1967.
The great American jackpot. 1969.
The magic will; stories and essays of a decade. 1971.

Other Works
The age of happy problems. 1962.
Biafra goodbye. 1970.
My last 2000 years. 1972.

GOLDING, WILLIAM GERALD
(1911–)

English novelist; born in Cornwall; educated at Brasenose College, Oxford; served in the Royal Navy in the Second World War (1940–5); taught; acted and produced (1934–40, 1945–54); Writer-in-residence, Hollins College, Virginia (1961–2); C.B.E. (1966); Hon. D.Litt., Sussex (1970).

Bibliography
B.N.B.
Gale.
Clive Pemberton, William Golding, Writers and their work. 1969.
Who's who. 1973.

Novels
Lord of the flies (filmed 1963). 1954.
The inheritors. 1955.
Pincher Martin. 1956.
Free fall. 1959.
The spire. 1964.
The pyramid. 1967.
The scorpion god: two short novels. 1971.

Play
Brass butterfly. 1958.

Essay
The hot gates. 1965.

GOLDMAN, WILLIAM (†HARRY LONGBAUGH) (1931–)

American novelist and dramatist; educated at Columbia University; served in the U.S. Army (1952–4); his unpublished plays are not listed below.

Bibliography
C.B.I.
Contemporary novelists.

Novels
The temple of gold. 1957.

Your turn to curtsy, my turn to bow. 1958.
Soldier in the rain (filmed 1965). 1960.
Boys and girls together. 1964.
No way to treat a lady (as †Harry Longbaugh; filmed 1968). 1964.
The thing of it is .... 1967.
Father's day. 1971.
The princess bride. 1973.

Screenplays
Harper. 1966.
Butch Cassidy and the Sundance Kid. 1969.

Other Work
The season: a candid look at Broadway. 1969.

GOMBRICH, *Professor* ERNST HANS JOSEF (1909–)

Art historian; originally Austrian; educated in Vienna; B.B.C. Monitoring Service in the Second World War (1939–45); Fellow and Reader, Warburg Institute, London University (1946–59); Director of the Institute (1959–); Professor of Art History, University College, London (1956–9); Slade Professor of Fine Art, Oxford (1950–3), Cambridge (1961–3), etc.; member of many foreign academies; recipient of many academic honours; a contributor to many learned journals; his early work in German is not listed below.

Bibliography
B.N.B.
Gale.
Who's who. 1973.

Works in English
Caricature, 1940 (with E. Kris). 1940.
The story of art. 1950.
Art and illusion (The A. W. Mellon Lectures in the Fine Arts, 1956). 1960.
Meditations on a hobby horse. 1963.
Norm and form. 1966.
Aby Warburg, an intellectual biography. 1970.
Myth and reality in German wartime broadcasts. 1970.
Symbolic images. 1972.
Art, perception and reality. 1973.

GOODMAN, PAUL (1911–)

American novelist; educated at Chicago University; taught in various schools and universities; practised as a lay psychotherapist at the New York Institute for Gestalt Therapy; television and film editor; a contributor to *Harper's, Poetry, Playboy* and numerous other periodicals; his edited works and unpublished plays are not listed below.

Bibliography
C.B.I.
Contemporary novelists.
Gale.

Novels
The grand piano or, The almanac of alienation. 1942.
The facts of life (stories). 1945.
State of nature. 1946.
The break-up of our camp, and other stories. 1950.
The dead of spring. 1950.
Parents' day. 1952.
The empire city (collected novels). 1959.
Our visit to Niagara (stories). 1960.
Making do. 1963.
Adam and his works: collected stories. 1968.
Homespun of oatmeal gray. 1970.

Plays
Three plays. 1965.
Jonah. 1966.

Poetry
Stop-light. 1941.
Pieces of three. 1942.
Red jacket (pr. ptd.). 1956.
The lordly Hudson: collected poems. 1962.
Hawkweed. 1967.
North Percy. 1968.

Other Works
Art and social nature. 1946.
Communitas: means of livelihood and ways of life. 1947.
Kafka's prayer. 1947.
Gestalt therapy. 1951.
The structure of literature. 1954.
Censorship and pornography on the stage. 1959.
Growing up absurd; problems of youth in the organised system. 1960.
The community of scholars. 1962.
Utopian essays and practical proposals. 1962.
Drawing the line. 1962.
The society I live in is mine. 1963.
Compulsory miseducation. 1964.
People or personnel; decentralizing and the mixed system. 1965.
Five years (partly autobiography). 1967.
Like a conquered province. 1967.

Open look. 1969.
New reformation. 1970.
American constitution. 1970.
The American colonial experience (with F. O. Gatell). 1970.
Tragedy and comedy. 1970.
Speaking and language. 1972.

GOPAL, *Dr.* **SARVEPALLI** (1923–)
Indian historian; born in Madras; educated at Mill Hill School and at the universities of Madras and Oxford; Director, Historical Division of the External Affairs Ministry (1954–66); Reader, South Asian History, Oxford University (1966–71); currently Professor of History at Nehru University, New Delhi (1972–); editor of Nehru's works and speeches; a contributor to historical journals.

Bibliography
B.N.B.
C.B.I.
Indian national bibliography 1958–67.
National bibliography of Indian literature 1901–53.
Who's who. 1973.

Works
The permanent settlement in Bengal and its results. 1949.
The Viceroyalty of Lord Ripon (biography). 1953.
The Viceroyalty of Lord Irwin (biography). 1957.
British policy in India. 1965.
Modern India. 1967.

GORDIMER, NADINE
(*Mrs.* **R. H. CASSIRER**) (1923–)
South African novelist; educated at the Convent School, Witwatersrand; Ford Foundation Visiting Fellow to the United States (1961); a contributor to the *New Yorker, Atlantic's, Kenyon Review, Encounter, London Magazine, Observer*, etc.; edited *South African Writing Today* (1967); recipient of several literary awards.

Bibliography
Authors' and writers' who's who. 1971.
B.N.B.
Contemporary novelists.
Gale.
R. J. Nell, Nadine Gordimer ... a bibliography of her works. 1964.
Who's who. 1973.

Novels and Short Stories
Face to face: short stories. 1949.
The soft voice of the serpent (stories). 1953.
The lying days. 1953.
Six feet of the country (stories). 1956.
A world of strangers. 1958.
Friday's footprint (stories). 1960.
Occasion for loving. 1963.
Not for publication (stories). 1965.
The late bourgeois world. 1966.
A guest of honour (James Tait Black Prize 1972). 1971.
Livingstone's companions (stories). 1972.

†GORDON, RICHARD
(*Dr.* **GORDON OSTLERE**) (1921–)
English novelist; educated at Selwyn College, Cambridge, and St. Bartholomew's Hospital; senior resident anaesthetist, St. Bartholomew's (1945–8); assistant editor, *British Medical Journal* (1949–51); ship's surgeon (1950–1); Nuffield Department of Anaesthetics, Oxford (1951–2); full-time writer since 1952; a contributor to *Punch*; his textbooks on anaesthetics are not listed below.

Bibliography
Authors' and writers' who's who. 1971.
B.N.B.
Who's who. 1973.

Novels
Doctor in the house (filmed 1954, staged 1956, radio series 1968, TV series 1969). 1952.
Doctor at sea (filmed 1955, staged 1961). 1953.
The captain's table (filmed 1959). 1954.
Doctor at large (filmed 1957, radio series 1969). 1955.
Doctor in love (filmed 1960, staged 1966). 1957.
Doctor and son (filmed as Doctor in distress, 1963). 1959.
Doctor in clover (filmed 1966). 1960.
Doctor on toast (filmed as Doctor in trouble, 1970). 1961.
Doctor in the swim. 1962.
Nuts in May. 1964.
The summer of Sir Lancelot. 1965.
Love and Sir Lancelot. 1966.
The facemaker. 1967.
Surgeon at arms. 1968.
The facts of life. 1969.
Doctor on the boil (with Mary Ostlere). 1970.
The medical witness. 1971.
Doctor on the brain. 1972.
Doctor in the nude. 1973.

Other Work
A baby in the house: a guide to practical parenthood (with Mary Ostlere). 1966.

GOTLIEB, PHYLLIS FAY
(*née* **BLOOM**) (1926–)
Canadian-Jewish poet and science fiction writer; born in Toronto; educated at the University of Toronto; a contributor to *Tamarack Review, Canadian Forum*, etc.

Bibliography
Authors' and writers' who's who. 1971.
Canadiana.
C.B.I.
Gale.

Novels
Sunburst. 1964.
Why should I have all the grief? 1969.

Poetry
Within the zodiac. 1964.
Ordinary moving. 1969.

GOTTFRIED, MARTIN (1933–)
American theatrical critic; educated at Columbia University; served in the U.S. Army (1957–9); drama and music critic (1960–); a contributor to national magazines.

Bibliography
C.B.I.
Gale.

Works
A theater divided. 1968.
Opening nights. 1969.

GOVEIA, ELSA VESTA (1925–)
Guyanan historian; educated in Guyana and London University; taught history at the University of the West Indies, Kingston, Jamaica (1950–); her edited works are not listed below.

Bibliography
C.B.I.
Gale.

Works
Historiography of the British West Indies. 1956.
Slave society in the British Leeward Islands at the end of the eighteenth century. 1965.

GOVER, JOHN ROBERT (1929–)
American novelist; educated at Pittsburgh University; worked as a reporter in Pennsylvania and Maryland (1961–); now a full-time writer.

Bibliography
C.B.I.
Contemporary novelists.
Gale.

Novels
One hundred dollar misunderstanding. 1962.
The maniac responsible. 1963.
Here goes Kitten. 1964.
Poorboy at the party. 1967.
J. C. saves. 1968.

GOWERS, *Sir* ERNEST ARTHUR
(1880–1966)
English civil servant; educated at Rugby and Clare College, Cambridge; entered the Civil Service (1903); Private Secretary to the Under-Secretary of State, India Office (1907–11); Permanent Under-Secretary for Mines (1920–7); chairman of many committees, including the Commission on Capital Punishment (1949–53); awarded many honours.

Bibliography
B.N.B.
Who's who. 1966.

Works
Plain words; a guide to the use of English. 1948.
ABC of plain words (revised as The complete plain words, 1954). 1951.
A life for a life: the problems of capital punishment. 1956.
H. W. Fowler. 1957.
Fowler's modern English usage (editor). 1965.

GOYEN, WILLIAM (1915–)
American novelist; educated at Rice University; instructor in literature, New School for Social Research, New York (1955–60); served in the U.S. Navy during the Second World War (1940–5); critic and reviewer for the *New York Times*; awarded several grants and fellowships in creative writing; also writes plays for stage and television.

Bibliography
C.B.I.
Contemporary novelists.
Gale.

Novels
The house of breath. 1950.
Ghost and flesh (stories). 1952.
In a farther country. 1955.
The faces of blood kindred (stories). 1960.
The fair sister (English title, Savator, my fair sister). 1963.
The collected stories of William Goyen. 1972.

Other Work
A book of Jesus. 1973.

GRAHAM, WILLIAM SYDNEY
(1918–)
Scottish poet; served his apprenticeship as a structural engineer; studied literature and philosophy at Edinburgh; lectured in the U.S.A.; lives in Cornwall; represented in numerous anthologies; a contributor to the *Listener, New Statesman*, etc.

Bibliography
B.N.B.
Contemporary poets.

Poetry
Cage without grievance. 1942.
The seven journeys. 1943.
Second poems. 1945.
The white threshold. 1949.
Nightfishing. 1955.
Malcolm's mooney land. 1970.
Penguin modern poets no. 17 (with David Gascoyne and Kathleen Raine). 1970.

GRAU, SHIRLEY ANN (*Mrs.* KERN FEIBLEMAN) (1929–)
American novelist; educated at Tulane University; a contributor to the *New Yorker, Atlantic's, Saturday Evening Post*, etc.

Bibliography
C.B.I.
Contemporary novelists.
Gale.

Novels
The black prince and other stories. 1955.
The hard blue sky. 1958.
The house on Coliseum Street. 1961.
The keepers of the house (Pulitzer Prize 1965). 1964.
The condor passes. 1972.

†GRAY, SIMON (†JAMES HOLLIDAY, †HAMISH READE) (SIMON DAVIDSON) (1936–)

English novelist and playwright; educated at Westminster School, and Dalhousie and Cambridge universities; freelance writer, living in France and Spain (1960–3); lecturer, Queen Mary College, London University (1965–); unpublished plays for television include *Death of a teddy bear, A way with the ladies, Spoiled, Pig in a poke.*

Bibliography
B.N.B.
Contemporary novelists.
Gale.

Novels
Colmain. 1962.
Simple people. 1964.
Little Portia. 1966.
A comeback for Starke (as †Hamish Reade). 1968.

Plays
Wisechild (staged 1967). 1968.
Sleeping dog (televised 1967). 1968.
Dutch uncle (staged 1969). 1969.
Spoiled (staged). 1971.
Butley (staged). 1971.
The idiot (adapted from Dostoievsky). 1971.

GREEN, PETER MORRIS (†DENIS DELANEY) (1924–)

English classical scholar and writer; educated at Charterhouse and Trinity College, Cambridge; served in the Royal Air Force (1943–7); editor of the *Cambridge Review* (1950–1); Director of Studies in Classics, Selwyn College, Cambridge (1951–2); Fiction editor, *Daily Telegraph* (1953–63); Consulting editor, Hodder and Stoughton, publishers (1960–3), television critic, the *Listener* (1961–3), etc.; member of various selection committees for literary prizes; Visiting Professor of Classics, University of Texas (1971–2); emigrated to Greece to write full time (1963); a contributor to *T.L.S., American Horizon,* etc.; translator of many works from the French and Italian, not listed below, and *Juvenal, the sixteen satires* (1967).

Bibliography
Authors' and writers' who's who. 1971.
B.N.B.
Contemporary novelists.
Gale.
Who's who. 1973.

Novels
Achilles his armour. 1955.
Cat in gloves (as †Denis Delaney). 1956.
The sword of pleasure. 1957.
Habeas corpus and other satires (stories). 1962.
The laughter of Aphrodite. 1965.

Other Works
The expanding eye (travel). 1953.
Kenneth Grahame, 1859–1932: a study of his life, work and times. 1959.
Sir Thomas Browne. 1959.
Essays in antiquity. 1960.
John Skelton. 1961.
Look at the Romans (for children). 1963.
Armada from Athens: the failure of the Sicilian expedition, 415–413 B.C. 1970.
Alexander the Great: a biography. 1970.
The year of Salamis, 480–479 B.C. 1970.
The shadow of the Parthenon. 1972.

GREENWOOD, GORDON (1913–)

Australian historian of Australia; educated at Sydney and London universities; currently Professor of History, University of Queensland, Brisbane (1949–); editor, *Australian Journal of Politics and History*; a contributor to learned journals; his edited works are not listed below.

Bibliography
Annals of Australian literature.
Australian national bibliography.
Gale.

Works
Early American–Australian relations. 1944.
The future of Australian federalism. 1946.
Australia: a social and political history. 1955.
The modern world: vol. I: from early European expansion to the outbreak of World War II. 1965.

GREER, GERMAINE (1939–)

Writer on women's liberation; born in Australia; educated at Melbourne and Sydney universities and at Newnham College, Cambridge; Lecturer at Warwick University (1967–).

Bibliography
B.N.B.
C.B.I.

Work
The female eunuch. 1970.

GRIFFITHS, REGINALD (1912–)
Rhodesian novelist and poet; born in Bulawayo; studied photography at the Polytechnic of London; served in the R.A.F. during the Second World War; works as a photographer; represented in various anthologies.

Bibliography
B.N.B.
Contemporary poets.

Novels
The grey about the flame. 1947.
Children of pride. 1959.
This day's madness. 1960.
Man of the river. 1968.

Poetry
Tugela and other poems. 1948.

GRIFFITHS, TREVOR (1935–)
English playwright; educated at St. Bede's College, Manchester, and Manchester University; served in the Manchester Regiment (1955–7); taught and lectured for 8 years; B.B.C. Education Officer (1965–72); unpublished plays include *The wages of thin* (1969), *Apricots* (1971), *The party* (1973); unpublished radio play is *Jake's brigade* (1971).

Bibliography
B.N.B.
Contemporary dramatists.

Plays
Lay by (with others, staged 1971). 1972.
Sam, Sam (in Plays and Players). 1972.
Occupations, and The big house (Occupations staged 1970, The big house broadcast 1969). 1972.

GRIMBLE, *Sir* **ARTHUR FRANCIS** (1888–1956)
English civil servant; born in Hong Kong; educated at Chigwell School and Cambridge; Colonial Service (1914–48); Governor and Commander in Chief, Windward Islands (1942–8); gave several series of B.B.C. talks.

Bibliography
B.N.B.
Who was who, 1951–60. 1961.

Autobiographical Works
A pattern of islands (filmed as South Pacific, 1956). 1952.
Return to the islands. 1957.

GROSSMAN, ALFRED (1927–)
American novelist; educated at Harvard; served in the U.S. Navy (1945–6); editor of the Free Europe Committee, New York (1954–61).

Bibliography
C.B.I.
Contemporary novelists.
Gale.

Novels
Acrobat admits. 1959.
Many slippery errors. 1964.
Marie beginning. 1964.
The do-gooders. 1968.

GUEST, BARBARA (Mrs. TRUMBULL HIGGINS) (1920–)
American poet; educated at the University of California, Berkeley; travels widely; editorial associate, *Art News* (1951–4); represented in several anthologies.

Bibliography
C.B.I.
Contemporary poets.
Gale.

Poetry
Poems: The location of things: Archaics: The open skies. 1962.
The blue stairs. 1968.
Moscow mansions. 1973.

Other Work
Goodnough (with B. H. Friedman). 1962.

GUEST, HARRY (HENRY BAYLY GUEST)
Welsh poet; born in Glamorgan; educated Malvern College, Trinity Hall, Cambridge, and the Sorbonne; head of modern languages, Lancing College, Sussex (1961–6); lecturer in English literature, Yokohama University, Japan (1966–); represented in various anthologies; his translations are not listed below.

Bibliography
B.N.B.
Contemporary poets.

127

Poetry
Private view. 1962.
A different darkness. 1964.
Arrangements. 1968.
The cutting room. 1969.

GUNN, THOMPSON WILLIAM
(1929–)
English poet, educated at Trinity College, Cambridge, and Stanford University; lecturer, then Associate Professor of English, University of California, Berkeley (1958–66); served in the army (1948–50); contributes to *Encounter, New Statesman, Poetry*, etc.

Bibliography
Authors' and writers' who's who. 1971.
B.N.B.
Contemporary poets.
Gale.
Who's who. 1973.

Poetry
Poems. 1953.
Fighting terms. 1954.
The sense of movement (Somerset Maugham Award 1959). 1957.
My sad captains. 1961.
A geography. 1966.
Positives (with Anders Gunn). 1966.
Touch. 1967.
Poems 1950–66. 1969.
Moly. 1971.

GUTHRIE, ALFRED BERTRAM, Jr.
(1901–)
American novelist; educated at Washington Uni-

versity, Seattle; journalist (1929–47); academic posts (1945–) include Professor of Creative Writing, Kentucky University, Lexington (1947–52); recipient of various literary awards.

Bibliography
C.B.I.
Contemporary novelists.

Novels·
Murders at Moon Dance. 1943.
The big sky. 1947.
The way west (Pulitzer Prize 1950; filmed 1966). 1949.
These thousand hills (filmed 1958). 1956.
The big it and other stories. 1960.
The blue hen's chick—a life in context. 1965.
Arfive. 1971.

GUTTERIDGE, BERNARD (1916–)
English novelist and poet; served in the army in the Second World War; represented in *Poetry of war* (1965); contributed to *Penguin new writing* and *Horizon*.

Bibliography
B.N.B.
Contemporary poets.

Novel
The agency game. 1954.

Poetry
Traveller's eye. 1947.

H

HAILEY, ARTHUR (1920–)
English-born Canadian novelist and television playwright; served in the R.A.F. in the Second World War; went to Canada (1947); full-time writer (1956–); the author of many film scripts.

Bibliography
Authors' and writers' who's who. 1971.
Canadiana.

C.B.I.
Contemporary novelists.
Gale.

Novels
Runway zero flight (from the television play, with John Castle, Flight into danger). 1959.
The final diagnosis (filmed as The young doctors, 1961). 1959.

In high places. 1962.
Hotel (filmed 1967). 1965.
Airport (filmed 1970). 1968.
Wheels. 1972.

Other Work
Close-up on writing for television. 1960.

HALBERSTAM, DAVID (1934–)
American journalist; educated at Harvard; worked
on *West Point Daily Times* (1955–6), *Nashville Ten-
nessean* (1956–60); correspondent in Vietnam,
Warsaw, etc.; editor, *Harper's Magazine* (1967–71);
recipient of various awards.

Bibliography
C.B.I.

Works
The noblest Roman. 1961.
The making of a quagmire. 1965.
One very hot day. 1968.
The unfinished odyssey of Robert Kennedy. 1969.
Ho (Ho Chi Minh). 1971.
The best and the brightest. 1972.

HALE, JOHN (1926–)
English novelist and playwright; educated at army
schools in Egypt, Ceylon and Malta, and at the
Royal Naval College, Greenwich; served in the
Fleet Air Arm (1941–51); worked in a variety of
capacities in repertory companies; founder and
artistic director of Lincoln Theatre (1955–8); Artistic Director, Bristol Old Vic (1959–61); freelance
director and writer (1964–); unpublished plays
include *It's all in the mind* (1968), *Here is the news*
(1970), *Decibels* (1971); television plays include *The
noise stopped* (1966), *Anywhere but England* (1972),
etc.

Bibliography
B.N.B.
Contemporary dramatists.

Novels
Kiss'd the girls and made them cry. 1963.
The grudge fight. 1964.
A fool after the feast. 1966.
The paradise men. 1969.
Mary Queen of Scots (the book of the film). 1972.
The fort. 1973.

Plays
The black swan winter (staged as Smile boys, that's

the style, 1968; published in Plays of the year 37).
1970.
Spithead (staged 1969; published in Plays of the
year 38). 1971.
The lion's cub (televised 1971; published in
Elizabeth R.). 1971.

HALL, DONALD ANDREW, Jr.
(1928–)
American poet; educated at Harvard and Oxford
universities; poetry editor of *Paris Review*
(1953–60); Associate Professor, University of
Michigan, Ann Arbor (1957–); recipient of several awards; his edited work is not listed below.

Bibliography
B.N.B.
C.B.I.
Contemporary poets.
Gale.

Poetry
Exiles and marriages. 1955.
The dark houses. 1958.
Alligator bride: poems new and selected. 1969.
Yellow room: love poems. 1971.

Other Works
Andrew the lion farmer. 1959.
String too short to be saved (autobiography). 1961.
Modern stylists: writers on the art of writing. 1968.
Marianne Moore: the cage and the animal. 1970.
Writing well (with D. L. Emblem). n.d.

HALL, JAMES BYRON (1918–)
American novelist; educated at the State University of Iowa and other universities; after various
academic posts, Professor of English, University
of California (1965–); founder-editor of the
Oregon Summer Academy of Contemporary
Arts; served in the U.S. Army (1941–6) during the
Second World War; represented in various
anthologies of poetry and short stories; a contributor to *Esquire, Harper's Bazaar*, etc.; co-
founder of the *Northwest Review* (1957–); his
edited works are not listed below.

Bibliography
C.B.I.
Contemporary novelists.
Contemporary poets.
Gale.

Novels
Not by the door. 1954.
TNT for two. 1956.
15×3 (stories with R. V. Cassill and Herbert Gold).
  1957.
Racers to the sun. 1960.
Us he devours (stories). 1964.
Mayo sergeant. 1967.

Other Works
The short story (with Joseph Langland). 1956.
Modern culture and arts. 1967.

HALL, JOHN CLIVE (1920–)

English poet; born in London; educated at Oriel
College, Oxford; worked in publishing until 1955;
on the staff of *Encounter* (1955); edited the poems of
Edwin Muir (1960) and Keith Douglas (1966).

Bibliography
B.N.B.
Contemporary poets.

Poetry
Selected poems (with Keith Douglas and Norman
  Nicholson). 1943.
The summer dance. 1951.
The burning love. 1956.

Criticism
Edwin Muir. 1956.
Rousseau. 1971.

HALL, RODNEY (1935–)

English-born Australian poet; educated in Brisbane; freelance scriptwriter and radio actor, Brisbane Radio (1957–67); co-editor of *New impulses in
Australian poetry* (1968); poetry editor of *Australian*
(1967–); represented in various anthologies; a
contributor to Australian newspapers and journals.

Bibliography
Annals of Australian literature.
Australian national bibliography.
Contemporary poets.

Poetry
Penniless till doomsday. 1961.
Forty beads on a hangman's rope. 1967.
Eyewitness. 1967.
The law of Karma. 1968.
The autobiography of a Gorgon. 1968.
Heaven, in a way. 1970.
Rodney Hall reads "Romulus & Remus". 1971.

The ship on the coin: a fable of the bourgeoisie.
  1972.

Criticism
Focus on Andrew Sibley. 1968.

HALL, WILLIS (1929–)
(*see also* KEITH WATERHOUSE)

English playwright; born in Leeds; has written
over 100 radio and television scripts and numerous
film scripts, often in collaboration with Keith
Waterhouse, including *Whistle down the wind, A
kind of loving, Billy Liar, Man in the middle*; his
adaptations and radio plays are not listed below; his
unpublished plays include *Children's day* (1969) and
Who's who (1971).

Bibliography
B.N.B.
Contemporary dramatists.
Who's who in the theatre. 1967.
Who's who. 1973.

Plays
Final at Furnell. 1956.
The long and the short and the tall (staged 1959,
  with The dumb waiter and A resounding tinkle
  by N. F. Simpson). 1959.
Poet and pheasant (with Lewis Jones). 1959.
A glimpse of the sea (staged 1959). 1960.
Play of the royal astrologers (staged 1958). 1960.
The days beginning. An Easter play. 1964.
Come laughing home (produced in Bristol as They
  called the bastard Stephen). 1965.
The gentle knight (staged 1964). 1966.

Plays with Keith Waterhouse
Billy Liar. 1960.
Celebration. 1961.
England, our England. 1962.
All things bright and beautiful (staged 1962). 1963.
Squat Betty, and The sponge room (two plays).
  1963.
Say who you are (staged 1965). 1965.

Other Works
They found the world (with Idrisyn Oliver Evans).
  1960.
The royal astrologers (for children). 1960.
Writers' theatre (with Keith Waterhouse). 1967.
The A to Z of soccer. 1970.
The A to Z of television. 1971.

HALLIWELL, DAVID WILLIAM
(1936–   )
English playwright, actor and director; educated at
Huddersfield College of Art and R.A.D.A.;
Visiting Fellow, Reading University (1969–70);
his unpublished plays include *An armour and a feast*
(1971), *Bleats from a Brighouse pleasure ground* (1972)
and *Janitress thrilled by prehensile penis* (1972).

Bibliography
Authors' and writers' who's who. 1971.
B.N.B.
Contemporary dramatists.

Plays
Little Malcolm and his struggle against the
    eunuchs. 1967.
K. D. Dufford hears K. D. Dufford ask K. D.
    Dufford how K. D. Dufford'll make K. D. Duf-
    ford. 1970.
A who's who of Flapland and other plays. 1971.

HAMBLETON, RONALD (1917–   )
English-born Canadian poet and novelist; emigrated to Canada (1924); educated in Vancouver;
lives in Toronto, where he writes radio
documentaries; compiled *Unit of five* (1944), a
poetry anthology; editor, with Lister Sinclair and
Allan Anderson, of *Reading* (1946); a contributor to
Canadian Forum, Partisan Review, etc.

Bibliography
Canadiana.
C.B.I.
Contemporary poets.

Novels
Every man is an island. 1959.
There goes McGill. 1962.

Poetry
Object and event. 1953.

Biography
Mazo de la Roche of Jalna. 1966.

**HAMBURGER, MICHAEL PETER
LEOPOLD** (1924–   )
English (German born) poet and scholar of Ger-
man literature; educated Westminster School and
Christ Church, Oxford; served (1943–7) in the
Second World War; lecturer in German studies
(1952–66); his translations of German poets are not
listed below.

Bibliography
B.N.B.
Contemporary poets.
Gale.
Who's who. 1973.

Poetry
Flowering cactus. 1950.
Poems 1950–1951. 1952.
The dual site. 1958.
Weather and season. 1963.
Feeding the chickadees. 1968.
Penguin modern poets no. 14 (with A. Brownjohn
    and C. Tomlinson). 1969.
Travelling. 1970.
Nineteen poems. 1972.
New and selected poems. 1973.

Critical Works
Reason and energy. 1957.
In flashlight. 1965.
From prophecy to exorcism. 1965.
The truth about poetry. 1970.
Hugo von Hofmannsthal. 1971.

HAMILTON, IAN (1938–   )
Scottish poet; born in King's Lynn; educated at
Keble College, Oxford; poetry and fiction editor,
T.L.S. (1965); founder of the *Review*; has edited
poetry of the war (1964), the work of Alun Lewis
(1965), etc.; contributor to the *Observer, New
Statesman, Listener*, etc.

Bibliography
Authors' and writers' who's who. 1971.
B.N.B.
Contemporary poets.

Poetry
Pretending not to sleep. 1964.
The visit. 1970.

Other Works
The modern poet; essays from the Review. 1969.
The thrill machine (science fiction). 1972.
A poetry chronicle: essays and reviews. 1973.

HAMPTON, CHRISTOPHER JAMES
(1946–   )
English playwright; educated Lancing College and
New College, Oxford; resident dramatist, Royal
Court Theatre (1968–70); his translations are not
listed below.

Bibliography
Authors' and writers' who's who. 1971.
B.M. catalogue.
B.N.B.
Contemporary dramatists.
Gale.
Who's who. 1973.

Plays
When did you last see my mother? (staged 1966). 1967.
Total eclipse (staged 1968). 1969.
The philanthropist (staged 1970). 1970.
Savages. 1973.

HAMPTON, CHRISTOPHER MARTIN (1929–)

English poet, travel writer and pianist; born in London; educated at Ardingly College and The Guildhall School of Music; has taught English to foreign students in Italy and London (1954–); a contributor to the *Observer, New Statesman, Listener, London Magazine*, etc., in which his poetry has been published.

Bibliography
Authors' and writers' who's who. 1971.
B.N.B.

Works
Island of the southern sun. 1962.
The Etruscan survival. 1969.

HANDLIN, OSCAR (1915–)

American historian; educated at Harvard University; taught there, becoming Professor of History (1939–); director of the Center for the study of liberty in America (1958–9); first Winthrop Professor of History (1962–5); director of Center for the study of American history (1965–); Chairman, U.S. Board of foreign scholarship (1962–); recipient of many awards; his edited work which includes 18 volumes of the *Library of American biography* is not listed below; a contributor to many periodicals.

Bibliography
C.B.I.
Gale.
Who's who. 1973.

Works
Boston's immigrants. 1941.

Commonwealth (with his wife Mary Handlin). 1947.
Danger in discords: the origin of anti-Semitism in the U.S.A. 1948.
The uprooted (Pulitzer Prize 1952). 1951.
American people in the twentieth century. 1954.
Adventure in freedom, 300 years of Jewish life in America. 1954.
Chance or destiny. 1955.
Race and nationality in American life. 1957.
Al Smith and his America. 1958.
Newcomers: Negroes and Puerto Ricans in a changing metropolis. 1959.
John Dewey's challenge to education. 1959.
Immigration as a factor in American history. 1959.
The dimensions of liberty (with Mary Handlin). 1961.
The Americans: a new history of the people of the United States. 1963.
Fire-bell in the night: the crisis in civil rights. 1964.
A continuing task. 1965.
History of the United States, vol. I. 1967.
The American as an instrument of republican culture. 1970.
Facing life (with Mary Handlin). Statue of liberty. 1971. 1971.
A pictorial history of immigration. 1972.

HANLEY, GERALD ANTHONY (*né* HANLY)

Irish novelist; born in County Wicklow; served in the Royal Irish Fusiliers.

Bibliography
Authors' and writers' who's who. 1971.
B.N.B.
Contemporary novelists.
Gale.
Who's who. 1973.

Novels
Monsoon victory. 1946.
The consul at sunset. 1951.
The year of the lion. 1953.
Drinkers of darkness. 1955.
Without love. 1957.
The journey homeward. 1961.
Gilligan's last elephant (filmed as The last safari, 1968). 1962.
See you in Yasukuni. 1969.

Other Work
Warriors and strangers. 1971.

HANLEY, WILLIAM (1931–)
American playwright; born in Ohio; educated at
Cornell University and the American Academy of
Dramatic Art; served in the U.S. Army (1952–4);
has written a radio play, *A country without rain*
(1970), a film script *The gypsy moths* (1969) and an
unpublished play *Conversations in the dark* (1963).

Bibliography
C.B.I.
Contemporary dramatists.

Novels
Blue dreams. 1971.
Mixed feelings. 1972.

Plays
Mrs. Dally has a lover and other plays (includes
   Whisper into my good ear and Today is Inde-
   pendence Day). 1963.
Slow dance on the killing ground. 1964.
Flesh and blood (televised 1968). 1968.

HANSBERRY, LORRAINE (1930–65)
Black American playwright.

Bibliography
C.B.I.

Plays
A raisin in the sun (filmed 1968). 1959.
The sign in Sidney Brunstein's window. 1965.
The movement: documentary of a struggle for
   equality (American title, A matter of colour.
   1965). 1964.
To be young, gifted, black: a portrait in her own
   words (edited by W. R. Nemiroff). 1971.
Les blancs: the last collected plays of L. H. 1972.

†**HAN SUYIN (***Mrs.* **ELIZABETH
COMBER,** *née* **K. CHOW)** (1917–)
Anglo-Chinese novelist; born in Peking; educated
at the universities of Peking, Brussels and London;
lived in China during the Sino-Japanese War
(1938–42); qualified as a doctor in London (1948);
returned to Asia (1952).

Bibliography
B.N.B.
Gale.
Who's who. 1973.

Autobiography
Destination Chungking. 1942.

A many splendoured thing. 1952.
The crippled tree. 1965.
A mortal flower. 1966.

Other Works
And the rain my drink. 1956.
The mountain is young. 1958.
Cast but one shadow, and Winter love. 1962.
The four faces. 1963.
China in the year 2001. 1967.
The morning deluge: Mao Tse-tung and the
   Chinese revolution 1893–1954. 1972.

HARDY, RONALD HAROLD (1919–)
English novelist; certified public accountant
(1950–60); has written plays for radio and television.

Bibliography
B.N.B.
Gale.

Novels
The place of jackals. 1954.
A name like Herod. 1955.
Kampong. 1957.
The men from the bush. 1959.
A winter's tale. 1959.
Act of destruction (James Tait Black Prize 1963).
   1962.
The savages. 1968.
The face of Jalanath. 1973.

HARE, DAVID (1947–)
English playwright; director of the Portable
Theatre, London and Brighton (1968–71), literary
manager, Royal Court Theatre (1969–70), and
Resident Dramatist (1970–1); Director of *Shoot*
(1971–); unpublished plays include *What happened to Blake?* (1970), *Deathshead* (1971).

Bibliography
B.N.B.
Contemporary dramatists.

Plays
How Brophy made good (staged 1969, published
   in *Gambit*). 1970.
Slag (staged 1970). 1971.
Lay by (with others, staged 1971). 1972.
The great exhibition. 1972.

HARLING, ROBERT

English editor, designer and novelist; editor of *House and Garden* (1957–); design consultant to the *T.L.S.* and *Sunday Times*; editor of *Historic houses* (1969).

Bibliography
B.N.B.

Novels
The paper palace. 1951.
The dark saviour. 1952.
The enormous shadow. 1958.
The endless colonnade. 1958.
The hollow Sunday. 1967.

Other Works
The steep Atlantic stream (autobiography). 1946.
Notes on the wood engravings of Eric Ravilious. 1946.
Edward Bawden. 1950.
Amateur sailor (autobiography). 1952.
Modern interior. 1964.
Dictionary of design and decoration. 1973.

HARRIS, MARK (†HENRY H. WIGGEN) (1922–)

American novelist; educated at the universities of Minnesota and Denver; served in the U.S. Army during the Second World War; Associate Professor of English at San Francisco State College, among other academic posts; recipient of literary awards; a contributor to *Life, Harper's Bazaar, New York Times,* etc.; a contributor, under many pseudonyms, including †Henry H. Wiggen, to *Negro Digest* and *Ebony* (1946–51).

Bibliography
C.B.I.
Contemporary novelists.
Gale.

Novels
Trumpet to the world. 1946.
City of discontent. 1952.
The southpaw. 1953.
Bang the drum slowly (adapted for television). 1956.
A ticket for a steamstitch. 1957.
Something about a soldier (adapted for stage 1962). 1957.
Wake up, stupid. 1959.
The goy. 1970.
Killing everybody. 1973.

Play
Friedman and son. 1963.

Other Works
Mark the glove boy; the last days of Richard Nixon (autobiography). 1964.
Twenty-one twice; a journal (autobiography). 1966.
Public television: a program for action (with others). 1967.

HARRIS, MAX (1921–)

Australian poet and editor; born in Adelaide; educated at the University of Adelaide; co-founder of the publishing house of Reid and Harris; editor of *Angry Penguins* (1941–6); co-editor and founder of *Australian Letters*; represented in the *Penguin Book of Australian Verse* (1958), etc.; his edited work is not listed below.

Bibliography
Australian national bibliography.
Contemporary poets.

Novel
The vegetative eye. 1943.

Poetry
Gifts of blood. 1940.
Dramas from the sky. 1942.
The coorang and other poems. 1955.
Selected verse, window at night. 1968.

Other Work
The land that waited (with Alison Forbes). 1967.

HARRIS, THEODORE WILSON (1921–)

Caribbean novelist; born in New Amsterdam, Guyana; .educated at Queen's College, Georgetown, Guyana; Senior Surveyor, Government of British Guiana (1955–8); writer-in-residence, universities of the West Indies and Toronto (1970); Visiting Lecturer, New York State University, Buffalo (1970).

Bibliography
Authors' and writers' who's who. 1971.
B.N.B.
Contemporary novelists.
Jahn and Dressler.
Who's who. 1973.

Novels
Eternity to season. 1954.
Palace of the peacock. 1960.
The far journey of Oudin. 1961.
The whole armour. 1962.
The secret ladder. 1963.
Heartland. 1964.
The eye of the scarecrow. 1965.
The waiting room. 1967.
Tumatumari. 1968.
Ascent to Omai. 1970.
The sleepers of Roraima (stories). 1970.
The age of the rainmakers (stories). 1971.
Black Marsden. 1972.

Other Works
Tradition and the West Indian novel. 1965.
Tradition, the writer and society. 1967.

HARROWER, ELIZABETH (1928–   )
Australian novelist; born in Sydney; the Australian
representative of the publishing firm of Macmillan
(1961–7); represented in anthologies of Australian
short stories.

Bibliography
Australian national bibliography.
B.N.B.
Contemporary novelists.

Novels
Down in the city. 1957.
The long prospect. 1958.
The catherine wheel. 1960.
The watch-tower. 1966.

HARTMAN, GEOFFREY H. (1929–   )
American scholar; born in Germany; emigrated to
America (1946); educated at Queen's College, Yale
and University of Dijon; member of faculty, later
Professor of English and Comparative Literature,
Yale (1955–   ); Visiting Professor in Chicago,
Jerusalem, Zurich, etc.; edited *Hopkins: a collection
of critical essays* (1966).

Bibliography
C.B.I.

Works
The unmediated vision: an interpretation of
  Wordsworth, Hopkins, Rilke and Valéry. 1954.
André Malraux. 1960.
Wordsworth's poetry 1787–1814. 1964.

Beyond formalism: literary essays 1958–1970.
  1970.

HART-SMITH, WILLIAM (1911–   )
English-born, Australian poet; educated in England and New Zealand; Tutor in adult education,
Canterbury University, Christchurch (1948–55);
advertising copywriter (1955–65); radio technician
since that date; represented in numerous anthologies.

Bibliography
B.M. catalogue.
Contemporary poets.
Gale.

Poetry
Columbus goes west. 1943.
Harvest. 1945.
The unceasing ground. 1946.
Christopher Columbus: a sequence. 1948.
On the level. 1950.
Poems of discovery. 1959.
The talking clothes. 1966.

HARWOOD, LEE (1939–   )
English poet; born in Leicester; educated Queen
Mary College, London University; did various
jobs (1961–   ); represented in several anthologies.

Bibliography
B.N.B.
Contemporary poets.
Gale.

Poetry
Title illegible. 1965.
Darazt. 1965.
The man with blue eyes. New York. 1966.
Landscapes. 1968.
The white room. 1969.
The beautiful atlas. Brighton. 1969.
The sinking colony. 1972.

HASSAN, IHAB HABIB (1925–   )
Egyptian-born American critic; educated at the
universities of Cairo and Pennsylvania; currently
Professor of English, Wesleyan University,
Middletown, Conn. (1962–   ); Director, College
of Letters (1964–   ); a contributor to *Saturday
Review, Nation, Modern Fiction Studies*, etc.

Bibliography
C.B.I.
Gale.

Works

Radical innocence: studies in the contemporary American novel. 1961.

Literature of silence: Henry Miller and Samuel Beckett. 1967.

Dismemberment of Orpheus: towards a post-modern literature. 1971.

Contemporary American literature. 1973.

HAWKES, JOHN CLENDENNIN BURNE, Jr. (1925–)

American playwright and novelist; educated at Harvard University; served in the American Field Service during the Second World War (1944–5); after various academic posts, Associate Professor of English, Brown University, Providence (1958–); recipient of several literary awards; a contributor to *Wake, Harvard Advocate, Sewanee Review*, etc.; his edited work is not listed below.

Bibliography

C.B.I.

Contemporary dramatists.

Contemporary novelists.

Gale.

Novels

The cannibal. 1949.

The beetle leg. 1951.

The goose on the grave, and The owl: two short novels. 1954.

The lime twig. 1961.

Second skin. 1964.

Lunar landscapes: stories and short novels 1949–1963. 1969.

The blood oranges. 1971.

Plays

The innocent party (4 short plays, The wax museum, The questions, The undertaker and The innocent party). 1967.

HAYDEN, ROBERT E. (1913–)

Black American poet; educated at the University of Michigan, Ann Arbor; currently Professor of English, Fisk University, Nashville (1946–); represented in *Poetry of the Negro* (1949) and other anthologies; editor of *Kaleidoscope: poems by Negro poets* (1967).

Bibliography

C.B.I.

Gale.

Poetry

Heartshape in the dust. 1940.

The lion and the archer. 1948.

A ballad of remembrance. 1962.

Selected poems. 1966.

Words in the mourning time. 1970.

Night blooming Cereus. 1972.

Other Works

Afro-American literature: an introduction (with others). 1971.

Why are you? n.d.

HAYDN, HIRAM COLLINS (1907–)

American novelist, editor and writer; educated at Columbia University; lecturer and Associate Professor of English at various universities (1928–44); since 1944 has worked in publishing; associated with Harcourt, Brace (1964–); General Editor of *Twentieth Century Library* series (1946–51), *Makers of American Tradition* (1953–5) and editor of numerous books not listed below.

Bibliography

C.B.I.

Contemporary novelists.

Gale.

Novels

By nature free. 1943.

Manhattan furlough. 1945.

The time is noon. 1948.

The hands of Esau. 1962.

Report from the red windmill. 1967.

Other Work

The counter-renaissance. 1950.

HAYES, JOSEPH (†JOSEPH H. ARNOLD) (1918–)

American playwright and novelist; educated at Indiana University; producer of plays on Broadway and full-time writer; recipient of various literary awards; only his published plays are listed below.

Bibliography

C.B.I.

Contemporary novelists.

Gale.

Novels

The desperate hours (also stage and screen versions). 1954.

Bon voyage (with Marrijane Hayes). 1957.
The hours after midnight. 1958.
Don't go away mad. 1962.
The third day. 1964.
Deep end. 1967.
Like any other fugitive. 1972.

Plays
The Thompsons (as †Joseph H. Arnold). 1943.
Sneak date (as †Joseph H. Arnold). 1943.
The bridegroom waits (with Marrijane Hayes).
   1943.
Where's Laurie? (as †Joseph H. Arnold). 1946.
Christmas at home. 1946.
A woman's privilege (with Marrijane Hayes).
   1947.
Too young, too old (with Marrijane Hayes). 1952.
Desperate hours (play based on the novel). 1955.
Calculated risk. 1962.

Plays for Amateurs (with Marrijane Hayes)
And came the spring. 1944.
Too many dates. 1944.
Come rain, or shine. 1944.
Ask for me tomorrow. 1946.
Change of heart. 1946.
Come over to our house. 1946.
Quiet summer. 1947.
Life of the party. 1949.
Curtain going up. 1950.
Turn back the clock. 1950.
Once in every family. 1951.
June wedding. 1951.
Penny. 1951.
Mister Peepers. 1952.
Head in the clouds. 1952.

HAZZARD, SHIRLEY
(*Mrs.* F. STEEGMULLER) (1931–)
Australian novelist; born in Sydney; worked for
U.N.O. in New York and Italy (1952–62); a con-
tributor to the *New Yorker*.

Bibliography
Annals of Australian literature.
Australian national bibliography.
C.B.I.
Gale.

Novels
Cliffs of fall (stories). 1963.
The evening of the holiday people. 1966.
People in glass houses. 1967.
Bay of noon. 1970.

Other Works
Defeat of an ideal: a study of the self destruction of
   the United Nations. 1973.

HEAD, BESSIE (1937–)
South African (now stateless) novelist; born in
Pietermaritzburg; taught in primary schools in
South Africa and Botswana for 4 years; journalist
in Johannesburg for 2 years; a contributor to *New
African, Transition*, etc.

Bibliography
B.N.B.
Contemporary novelists.
Gale.
Zell and Silver.

Novels
When rain clouds gather. 1968.
Maru. 1971.
A question of power. 1973.

HEANEY, SEAMUS (1939–)
Irish poet; born in County Derry; educated at
Queen's University, Belfast; lecturer there
(1966–); recipient of several awards; represented
in various anthologies.

Bibliography
B.N.B.
Contemporary poets.
Gale.

Poetry
Eleven poems. 1965.
Death of a naturalist (Somerset Maugham Award
   1968). 1966.
A Lough Neagh sequence. 1969.
Door into the dark. 1969.
Wintering out. 1972.

HEARNE, JOHN (†JOHN MORRIS)
(1926–)
Canadian-born Jamaican novelist; educated at
Jamaica College and Edinburgh University; a contributor to the *New Statesman, Atlantic Monthly,
Trinidad Guardian*, Radio Jamaica, B.B.C., etc.; his
play *The golden savage* produced (1965).

Bibliography
Authors' and writers' who's who. 1971.
B.N.B.
Contemporary novelists.
Jahn and Dressler.

Novels
Voices under the window (John Llewelyn Rhys
 Prize 1956). 1955.
Stranger at the gate. 1956.
The faces of love (American title, The eye of the
 storm, 1958). 1957.
The autumn equinox. 1959.
Land of the living. 1961.
Fever grass (as †John Morris with Morris Cargill).
 1969.
The candywine development (as †John Morris
 with Morris Cargill). 1970.

HEATH-STUBBS, JOHN FRANCIS ALEXANDER (1918–)

English poet; educated at The Queen's College,
Oxford; Gregory Poetry Fellow, Leeds University
(1952–5); Visiting Professor of English at Alexandria University (1955–8) and Michigan
(1959–60); Lecturer in English, College of St.
Mark and St. John, Chelsea (1953–73); has edited
several volumes of poetry and translated from the
Italian; contributor to many magazines.

Bibliography
Authors' and writers' who's who. 1971.
B.N.B.
Contemporary poets.
Gale.
N.C.B.E.L.
Who's who. 1973.

Poetry
Wounded Thammuz. 1942.
Beauty and the beast. 1944.
The divided ways. 1946.
The charity of the stars. 1948.
The swarming of the bees. 1950.
A charm against the toothache. 1954.
The triumph of the muse. 1958.
The blue-fly in his head. 1962.
Selected poems. 1964.
Satires and epigrams. 1968.

Play
Helen in Egypt. 1959.

Criticism
The darkling plain. 1950.
Charles Williams. 1955.
The pastoral. 1969.
The ode. 1969.
The verse satire. 1969.

HECHT, ANTHONY EVAN (1923–)

American poet; educated at Columbia University;
served in the U.S. Army during the Second World
War; taught at Kenyon College, Smith College,
etc.; Associate Professor of English, Bard College,
New York (1962–); awarded various fellowships; a contributor to the *Hudson Review, New
York Review of Books*, etc.; his poetry has been
included in various anthologies.

Bibliography
C.B.I.
Contemporary poets.
Gale.

Poetry
A summoning of stones. 1954.
The seven deadly sins. 1958.
The hard hours (Pulitzer Prize 1968). 1967.
Aesopic; 24 couplets to accompany the Thomas
 Bewick wood engravings of Select Fables. 1968.

HEJMADI, PADMA (†PADMA PERERA)

Indian short-story writer; born in Madras; educated at Madras, Delhi and Michigan, U.S.A.;
short stories published in the *New Yorker, Southern
Review, Saturday Evening Post* and non-fiction in
Horizon; fellowships to Yaddo and the MacDowell
Colony; citation from the University of Michigan
for outstanding contribution to international
understanding.

Bibliography
C.B.I.
Indian national bibliography 1958–67.
National bibliography of Indian literature
 1901–53.

Short Story
Coigns of vantage. n.d.

HELLER, JOSEPH (1923–)

American novelist; educated at Columbia and
Oxford universities; served in the U.S. Air Force
during the Second World War; taught English at
Pennsylvania State University (1950–2); advertising writer (1952–63).

Bibliography
C.B.I.
Contemporary novelists.
Gale.

Novels
Catch 22. 1961.
Something happened. 1966.

Plays
We bombed in New Haven. 1968.
Catch 22 (from the novel). 1971.

Other Work
Zionist idea. 1949.

HELWIG, DAVID (1938–)
Canadian novelist; born in Toronto; educated at
Toronto and Liverpool universities; Lecturer in
English, Queen's University, Kingston, Canada.

Bibliography
Authors' and writers' who's who. 1971.
Canadiana.
C.B.I.

Novels
Figures in a landscape (filmed 1969). 1968.
The streets of summer. 1969.
The sign of a gunman. 1969.
The day before tomorrow. 1971.
Fourteen stories high. 1971.

HENDERSON, DAVID (1942–)
Black American poet, actor and short-story writer;
educated at Hunter College, New York; editor of
the little magazine *Umbra*; member of the
Teachers' and Writers' Collaborative, Columbia
University; represented in *New Negro poets U.S.A.*
(1964) and other anthologies, a contributor to
Umbra, 7th Street Quarterly, etc.

Bibliography
C.B.I.
Contemporary poets.
Gale.

Poetry
Felix of the silent forest. 1967.
De Mayor of Harlem. 1970.

HENRI, ADRIAN MAURICE (1932–)
English poet; born in Cheshire; educated at King's
College, Newcastle; lecturer at Liverpool College
of Art (1964–8); full-time member of *Liverpool
scene* pop poetry and music group (1969–); his
play *I wonder* was produced at the Institute of Contemporary Arts (1968); represented in *Liverpool
scene* (1967), etc.

Bibliography
B.N.B.
Contemporary poets.
Gale.

Novel
I want. 1972.

Poetry
The Mersey sound (Penguin modern poets no. 10,
with R. McGough and B. Patten). 1967.
Tonight at noon. 1968.
City. 1969.
America. 1972.
Environments and happenings. 1973.

Other Work
Autobiography. 1971.

HENSHAW, JAMES ENE (1924–)
Nigerian playwright; educated at King's College,
Onitsha, and the National University of Ireland,
Dublin; also writes in Efik.

Bibliography
B.N.B.
Contemporary dramatists.
Jahn and Dressler.
Zell and Silver.

Plays
This is our chance (also includes The jewels of the
crown, and A man of character). 1957.
Children of the goddess and other plays (also
includes Companions for a chief, and Magic in
the blood). 1964.
Medicine for love: a comedy. 1964.
Dinner for promotion. 1967.

HERLIHY, JAMES LEO (1927–)
American playwright and novelist; educated at
Black Mountain College; served in the U.S. Navy
for 2 years; actor (1962–); has worked as a professional actor and taught playwriting; his unpublished plays include *Terrible Jim Fitch* and
Crazy October; a contributor to *Esquire, Eve, Paris
Review*, etc.; his unpublished plays are not listed
below.

Bibliography
C.B.I.
Contemporary dramatists.
Contemporary novelists.
Gale.

Novels
The sleep of Baby Filbertson and other stories. 1959.
All fall down (filmed 1962). 1960.
Midnight cowboy (filmed). 1965.
A story that ends with a scream and eight others. 1968.
The season of the witch. 1971.

Plays
Blue denim (with William Noble; filmed as Blue jeans, 1959). 1958.
Stop, you're killing me. 1970.

HERSEY, JOHN RICHARD (1914–)
American novelist and journalist; born in China; educated at Yale University; correspondent for *Time* (1937–44) in various parts of the world; Editor of *Life* (1944–5); Master of Pierson College, Yale University (1965–); member of various educational bodies; Fellow of Berkeley College, Yale (1950–65); a contributor to the *New Yorker, Life, Atlantic Monthly*, etc.

Bibliography
C.B.I.
Contemporary novelists.
Gale.

Novels
A bell for Adano (filmed 1945; Pulitzer Prize 1945). 1944.
The wall. 1950.
The marmot drive. 1953.
A single pebble. 1956.
The war lover (filmed 1963). 1959.
The child buyer. 1960.
White lotus. 1965.
Too far to walk. 1966.
Under the eye of the storm. 1967.
The conspiracy. 1972.

Other Works
Men on Bataan. 1942.
Into the valley; a skirmish of the Marines. 1943.
Hiroshima (*New Yorker*). 1946.
Here to stay; studies on human tenacity. 1963.
The Algiers motel incident. 1968.
Robert Capa (with others). 1969.
Letter to the alumni. 1970.

HETHERINGTON, JOHN AIKMAN (1907–)
Australian writer and journalist; born in Mel-

bourne; journalist (1923–); war correspondent (1939–45); Editor-in-chief, *Adelaide News* (1945–9); *Melbourne Age* (1954–67); full-time writer (1967–); a contributor to journals.

Bibliography
Australian national bibliography.
C.B.I.

Works
Airborne invasion. 1943.
The winds are still. 1947.
Blamey. 1954.
Australians: nine profiles. 1960.
Forty-two faces. 1962.
Australian painters. 1963.
Witness to things past. 1964.
Uncommon men. 1965.
Pillars of the faith. 1966.
Melba. 1967.
Norman Lindsay. 1969.
The tour to the Hebrides. 1973.

HEWITT, JOHN HAROLD (1907–)
Irish poet; born in Belfast; educated at Queen's University, Belfast; deputy director, Belfast Museum and Art Gallery (1930–57); Art Director Herbert Gallery and Museum, Coventry (1957–); represented in numerous anthologies; his edited works are not listed below.

Bibliography
B.N.B.
Contemporary poets.

Poetry
Conacre. 1943.
No rebel word. 1948.
Tesserae. 1967.
Collected poems, 1932–67. 1968.
The day of the corncrake. 1969.

Other Work
Coventry; the tradition of change and continuity. 1966.

HEYWOOD, TERENCE
South African poet; born in Johannesburg; educated at Malvern College, Worcester College, Oxford, and Uppsala University; has lived in England since his teens; a contributor to numerous periodicals including the *New Statesman, English Horizon, Anglo-Swedish Review, Norseman*, etc.; represented in numerous anthologies.

Bibliography
B.N.B.
Contemporary poets.
Gale.

Poetry
How smoke gets into the air. 1951.
Architectonic. 1953.
Facing north; poems and pictures of the north (with Edward Lowbury). 1958.

Other Work
Background to Sweden. 1951.

HIGGINS, AIDAN (1927–)
Irish novelist; educated at Clongowes Wood College; copywriter in Dublin; factory hand, etc., in London; puppet-operator and scriptwriter in South Africa and Rhodesia; recipient of several awards.

Bibliography
B.N.B.
Contemporary novelists.
Gale.

Novels
Felo de se (stories). 1960.
Langrishe, go down (James Tait Black Prize 1967). 1966.
Balcony of Europe. 1972.

Other Work
Images of Africa. 1971.

HIGHAM, CHARLES (1931–)
English poet and film critic; born in London; emigrated to Australia (1954); book critic of the *Sydney Morning Herald* (1955–63); literary editor of *Bulletin* (1963–); a contributor to *John O'London's, New Statesman, London Magazine, Poetry Review*, etc.; translated Marc Chagall's poems (1953).

Bibliography
Australian national bibliography.
Authors' and writers' who's who. 1971.
B.N.B.
Contemporary poets.
Gale.

Poetry
A distant star. 1951.
Spring and earth. 1953.
The earthbound. 1959.

Noonday country. 1966.
The voyage to Brindisi. 1969.

Other Works
They came to Australia (with F. W. Cheshire). 1961.
Hollywood in the forties (with Joel Greenberg). 1969.
The celluloid muse; Hollywood directors speak (with Joel Greenberg). 1969.
The films of Orson Welles. 1970.
Hollywood cameramen; sources of light. 1970.
When the pictures talked and sang. 1971.
Life in the Old Stone Age. 1971.
Australians abroad (with F. W. Cheshire). n.d.

HIGHET, GILBERT ARTHUR (1906–)
Scottish classical scholar; educated at Glasgow University and Balliol College, Oxford; Fellow of St. John's College, Oxford (1932–8); Professor of Greek and Latin, Columbia University (1938–50); on leave for war service (1941–6); Professor of Latin Language and Literature, Columbia University (1950–); awarded various academic honours; a contributor to the *Classical Review, American Journal of Philology*, etc.; his translations are not listed below.

Bibliography
Authors' and writers' who's who. 1971.
B.N.B.
Gale.
Who's who. 1973.

Works
The classical tradition: Greek and Roman influences on western literature. 1949.
The art of teaching. 1950.
People, places and books. 1953.
Migration of ideas. 1954.
Juvenal the satirist. 1954.
Man's unconquerable mind (American title, The mind of man). 1954.
A clerk of Oxenford. 1954.
Poets in a landscape. 1957.
Talents and geniuses. 1957.
The powers of poetry. 1960.
The anatomy of satire. 1962.
Explorations. 1971.
The speeches in Virgil's Aeneid. 1972.

HIGHSMITH, MARY PATRICIA (†CLAIRE MORGAN) (1921–)
American novelist; educated at Barnard College;

recipient of several literary awards; lives in France.

Bibliography
B.N.B.
C.B.I.
Contemporary novelists.
Gale.

Novels
Strangers on a train (filmed 1951). 1950.
The price of salt (as †Claire Morgan). 1952.
The blunderer (filmed as Enough rope, 1966). 1954.
The talented Mr. Ripley (filmed as The purple noon, 1961). 1955.
Deep water. 1957.
A game for the living. 1958.
This sweet sickness. 1960.
The cry of the owl. 1962.
The two faces of January. 1964.
The glass cell. 1964.
The story-teller (English title, A suspension of mercy). 1965.
Those who walk away. 1967.
The tremor of forgery. 1969.
The snail-watcher and other stories (English title, Eleven). 1970.
Ripley underground. 1970.
A dog's ransom. 1972.

Other Works
Miranda the panda is on the veranda (for children). 1958.
Plotting and writing suspense fiction. 1966.

HILL, GEOFFREY (1932–)
English poet; educated at Keble College, Oxford; lecturer in English, University of Leeds; represented in numerous anthologies.

Bibliography
B.N.B.
Contemporary poets.

Poetry
Poems. 1952.
For the unfallen. 1959.
Preghiere. 1964.
Penguin modern poets no. 8 (with Edwin Brock and Stevie Smith). 1966.
King Log (Hawthornden Prize 1970). 1968.

HILL, SUSAN (1942–)
English novelist; educated at King's College,

London; literary critic of the *Coventry Evening Telegraph* for 5 years; contributes fiction reviews to various periodicals.

Bibliography
B.N.B.

Novels
The enclosure. 1961.
Do me a favour. 1963.
Gentlemen and ladies. 1969.
A change for the better. 1969.
The albatross (John Llewelyn Rhys Prize 1972). 1969.
I'm the king of the castle. 1970.
Strange meeting. 1971.
The custodian. 1972.
The bird of the night. 1972.
A bit of singing and dancing. 1973.
In the springtime of the year. 1973.

HILLIARD, NOEL HARVEY (1929–)
New Zealand novelist; educated at Victoria University of Wellington; journalist (1945–50); teacher in Wellington (1955–64); chief sub-editor, New Zealand *Listener* (1965–70); Robert Burns Fellow, Otago University (1971–); a contributor to New Zealand periodicals.

Bibliography
B.N.B.
Contemporary novelists.
Gale.
N.Z. national bibliography.

Novels and Short Stories
Maori girl. 1960.
A piece of land (stories). 1963.
Power of joy. 1966.
A night at Green River. 1969.

For Children
We live by a lake. 1972.

HIMES, CHESTER BOMAR (1909–)
American novelist; educated at Ohio State University; served 7 years for armed robbery (1928–35); while in prison started writing; various jobs before and during the Second World War; travelled abroad (1953); now lives in Spain; a contributor to many periodicals and magazines.

Bibliography
C.B.I.

Contemporary novelists.
Gale.

Novels
If he hollers let him go. 1945.
Lonely crusade. 1947.
Cast the first stone. 1953.
The third generation. 1954.
The primitive. 1955.
For love of Ima Belle. 1957.
The crazy kill. 1959.
The real cool killers. 1959.
All shot up. 1960.
The big gold dream. 1960.
Pink toes. 1961.
Cotton comes to Harlem (filmed 1969). 1965.
A rage in Harlem. 1965.
The heat's on (filmed as Come back Charleston blue, 1972). 1966.
Run, man, run. 1966.
Blind man with a pistol. 1969.

Other Work
The quality of hurt (autobiography). 1972.

†HINDE, THOMAS (*Sir* THOMAS WILLES CHITTY) (1926–   )
English novelist; born in Felixstowe; educated at Winchester and University College, Oxford; served in the Royal Navy (1944–7); Inland Revenue (1953–8); worked for Shell Petroleum (1958–60); freelance writer (1960–   ); Granada Arts Fellow, York University (1964–5); Visiting Lecturer, Illinois University (1965–7); Visiting Professor, Boston University (1969–70); a contributor to *The Times, Observer, Spectator*, etc.

Bibliography
Authors' and writers' who's who. 1971.
B.N.B.
Gale.
Who's who. 1973.

Novels
Mr. Nicholas. 1952.
Happy as Larry. 1957.
For the good of the company. 1961.
A place like home. 1962.
The cage. 1962.
Ninety double martinis. 1963.
The day the call came. 1964.
Games of chance. 1965.
The village. 1966.
High. 1968.

Bird. 1970.
Generally a virgin. 1972.

Other Work
Spain: a personal anthology. 1963.

HINE, WILLIAM DARYL (1936–   )
Canadian poet; born in Vancouver; educated at McGill and Chicago universities; settled in New York; has written many radio plays; a contributor to the *New Yorker*, etc.

Bibliography
Canadiana.
C.B.I.
Contemporary poets.
Gale.

Novel
The prince of darkness and co. 1961.

Poetry
Five poems. 1955.
Carnal and the crane. 1957.
The devil's picture book. 1960.
The wooden horse. 1965.
A still salt pool. 1967.
Minutes. 1968.

Other Work
Polish subtitles (travel). 1962.

HIRO, DILIP
Indian writer; a contributor to the *Observer* and *New Society*; edited a number of documentaries for the B.B.C. on race relations in Britain and America; settled in England.

Bibliography
B.N.B.
C.B.I.
Indian national bibliography 1958–67.
National bibliography of Indian literature 1901–53.

Works
A triangular view (novel). 1969.
The Indian family in Britain. 1969.
Black British, white British (socio-historical study of race relations). 1971.
To anchor a cloud (historical play). n.d.

HOBSBAUM, PHILIP DENNIS

(1932–)

English poet; born in London; educated at Downing College, Cambridge, The Royal Academy of Music and The Guildhall School of Music; Ph.D., Sheffield (1962); part-time lecturer and teacher (1955–9); lecturer, Queen's University, Belfast (1963–6); lecturer, Glasgow University (1966–); his edited work is not listed below; has contributed to the *Listener, Spectator, T.L.S., Encounter, Poetry Review*, etc.

Bibliography
Authors' and writers' who's who. 1971.
Contemporary poets.
Gale.

Poetry
The place's fault. 1963.
In retreat. 1966.
Snapshots. 1967.
Coming out fighting. 1969.
Women and animals. 1972.

Criticism
A theory of communication. 1970.

HOBSON, HAROLD (1904–)

English theatre critic; educated at Oriel College, Oxford; drama critic, later literary editor, of the *Christian Science Monitor* (1932–); literary editor, later drama editor, of the *Sunday Times* (1942–); television critic of the *Listener* (1947–51).

Bibliography
B.N.B.
Who's who. 1973.

Works
The first three years of the war. 1942.
The devil in Woodford Wells. 1946.
Theatre. 2 vols. 1948–50.
Theatre II. 1950.
Verdict at midnight. 1952.
The theatre now. 1953.
The French theatre of today (ed.). 1953.
The international theatre annual, 1956, 1957, 1958, 1959, 1960.
Ralph Richardson. 1958.

HOBSON, LAURA (*née* ZAMETKIN)

(1900–)

American novelist; educated at Cornell University; advertising copywriter (–1934); pro-

motion writer for *Time, Life* and *Fortune* magazines (1934–62); editorial consultant for the *Saturday Review* (1960–); a contributor to numerous magazines.

Bibliography
C.B.I.
Contemporary novelists.
Gale.

Novels
A dog of his own (for children). 1941.
The trespassers. 1943.
Gentleman's agreement (filmed 1947). 1947.
The other father. 1950.
The celebrity. 1951.
First papers. 1964.

Other Works (for Children)
I'm going to have a baby. 1967.
Tenth month. 1971.

HODDER-WILLIAMS, JOHN CHRISTOPHER GLAZEBROOK (†JAMES BROGAN) (1927–)

English writer of science fiction and song-writer; educated at Eton; served in the army (1944–8); tried to set up a long-distance bus service in Africa; directed an all-African dance band; has written musicals; his television plays include *The higher they fly* and *The ship that couldn't stop*.

Bibliography
B.N.B.
Gale.

Novels
Chain reaction. 1959.
Final approach. 1960.
Turbulence. 1961.
The higher they fly (also television play). 1963.
The main experiment. 1964.
The egg-shaped thing. 1967.
Fistful of digits. 1968.
98.4. 1969.
Panic o'clock. 1973.

Other Work
The Cummings report (as †James Brogan). 1958.

HODGE, MERLE (1944–)

Caribbean novelist; born in Trinidad; educated at University College, London; has travelled widely in Europe and Africa; Lecturer in French at the University of the West Indies, Jamaica.

Bibliography
B.N.B.

Novel
Crick, crack, monkey. 1970.

HOFFMAN, *Professor* **DANIEL GERARD** (1923–   )
American writer; educated at Columbia University; served in the U.S. Air Force (1943–6) during the Second World War; after a varied academic career is now Professor of English, Pennsylvania University, Philadelphia (1966–   ); the recipient of various literary and academic awards.

Bibliography
C.B.I.
Contemporary poets.
Gale.

Poetry
An armada of thirty whales. 1954.
A little geste and other poems. 1960.
The city of satisfactions. 1963.
Striking the stones: poems. 1968.

Other Works
Paul Bunyan, the last of the frontier demigods. 1952.
The poetry of Stephen Crane. 1957.
Form and fable in American fiction. 1961.
American poetry and poetics. 1962.
Barbarous knowledge (myths in the poetry of W. B. Yeats, Robert Graves and Edwin Muir). 1967.
Broken laws. 1970.
Poe Poe Poe Poe Poe Poe Poe. 1972.

HOFFMAN, FREDERICK JOHN
(1909–   )
American scholar; educated at Stanford, Minnesota and Ohio State universities; taught at Ohio State University (1942–7); Fulbright Professor in France and Italy (1953–4); Distinguished Professor of English, University of Wisconsin (1965–   ); editor of the *Publications of the Modern Language Association* (1954–   ); his edited work is not listed below.

Bibliography
C.B.I.
Gale.

Works
Freudianism and the literary mind. 1945.
The little magazine: a history and a bibliography. 1946.
The modern novel in America. 1951.
The twenties: American writing in the postwar decade. 1955.
Gertrude Stein. 1961.
William Faulkner. 1961.
Conrad Aiken. 1962.
Samuel Beckett: the language of self. 1962.
The mortal no: death and the modern imagination. 1963.
The art of southern fiction. 1967.
Imagination's new beginning: theology and modern literature. 1967.
The achievement of Randall Darrell. 1970.

HOGGART, *Professor* **RICHARD** (1918–   )
English literary scholar and educationalist; educated at Leeds University; served in the army (1940–6) in the Second World War; Assistant Director General, Unesco (1970–   ); Professor of English, Birmingham University (1962–   ); Director, Centre for Contemporary Cultural Studies (1964–   ); member of many advisory councils, etc.; a contributor to *Essays in Criticism, Observer, Listener, Guardian, T.L.S., Sunday Times,* etc.; his edited work and contributions to collections are not listed below; B.B.C. Reith Lecturer (1971).

Bibliography
Authors' and writers' who's who. 1971.
B.N.B.
Gale.
Who's who. 1973.

Works
Auden. 1951.
The uses of literacy. 1957.
Teaching literature. 1963.
Your Sunday paper. 1967.
Speaking to each other: vol. I, About society. 1970.
Speaking to each other: vol. II, About literature. 1970.
Only connect (the Reith Lectures for 1971). 1972.

HOLBROOK, DAVID KENNETH
(1923–   )
English critic and poet; born in Norwich; educated

at Downing College, Cambridge; served in the Second World War (1942–5); Tutor, Workers' Educational Association, East Anglia (1951–4); Tutor, Bassingbourn Village College, Cambridgeshire (1954–61); Fellow of King's College, Cambridge (1961–5); a contributor to the *Guardian, Spectator, Listener, New Statesman*, etc.; edited work includes the anthologies *Iron, honey, gold* (1961), *People and diamonds*, short stories (1962), *Thieves and angels*, plays (1963), and *Plucking the rushes* (Chinese verse in translation) (1968).

Bibliography
Authors' and writers' who's who. 1971.
B.N.B.
Contemporary novelists.
Contemporary poets.
Gale.

Novels
Lights in the sky country (short stories). 1962.
Flesh wounds. 1964.

Poetry
Imaginings. 1961.
Against the cruel frost. 1963.
Penguin modern poets no. 4 (with C. Middleton and D. Wevill). 1963.
Object relations. 1967.
Old world, new world. 1969.
Are the apple buds loaded? (for children). n.d.
Something to sing about. n.d.

Criticism and Other Works
Children's games. 1957.
English for maturity. 1961.
Llareggub revisited. 1962.
English for the rejected. 1964.
Books at bedtime. 1964.
The quest for love. 1964.
The secret places. 1965.
I've got to use words. 1966.
Children's writing. 1966.
The flowers shake themselves free. 1966.
The quarry (children's opera). 1966.
The exploring word. 1967.
Human hope and the death instinct. 1971.
The masks of hate. 1971.
Sex and dehumanisation. 1972.
Pseudo-revolution. 1972.
The case against pornography. 1972.
English in Australia now. 1973.

HOLLANDER, JOHN (1929–)
American poet and writer; educated at Columbia and Indiana universities; after lecturing posts at Harvard, Yale, etc., currently Professor of English, Hunter College, New York (1966–); recipient of several poetry awards; a contributor to the *New Yorker, Kenyon Review, Esquire*, etc.; his edited work is not listed below.

Bibliography
C.B.I.
Contemporary poets.
Gale.

Poetry
A crackling of thorns. 1958.
Movie-going and other poems. 1962.
A book of various owls. 1963.
Visions from the ramble. 1965.
City and country matters. 1965.
The quest of the gole. 1966.
Types of shape. 1969.
Dark museum. 1971.
Night mirror. 1971.

Other Works
Modern poetry: essays in criticism. 1968.
Images of voice: music and sound in romantic poetry. 1970.
The untuning of the sky. 1970.
The immense parade or supererogation day, and what happened to it. 1972.

HOLLO, ANSELM (†BERGEI BIELGEI, †ANTON HOFMAN) (1934–)
Finnish poet; born in Helsinki; educated at Helsinki and Tübingen universities; journalist for the Finnish Press in Germany (1950–5) and for the European Service, B.B.C. (1958–66); Visiting Lecturer in Poetry, Iowa University (1968); his work in Finnish, translations and edited works are not listed below; represented in numerous anthologies; contributor to various journals; author of numerous radio scripts for Finnish and German services of the B.B.C., some as †Anton Hofman.

Bibliography
B.N.B.
Contemporary poets.
Gale.

Poetry
Loverman. 1961.

Texts and Finnpoems. 1961.
We just wanted to tell you. 1963.
And what else is new? 1963.
History. 1964.
And it is a song. 1965.
Faces and forms. 1965.
Here we go. 1965.
The claim. 1966.
The going-on poem. 1966.
Isadora. 1967.
Poem/Runoja (bilingual edition). 1967.
The coherences. 1968.
The man in the tree-top hat. 1968.
Tumbleweed. 1968.
Haiku (with John Esam and Tom Raworth). 1968.
Maya. 1970.

Other Work
The minicab war (with Gregory Corso and Tom
    Raworth). 1966.

HOLLOWAY, JOHN (1919–)
English poet and critic; educated at New College,
Oxford; served in the Second World War
(1935–45); Fellow of All Souls College, Oxford
(1946–60); Byron Professor of English at Athens
(1961–3); Fellow of Queen's College, Cambridge
(1954–); Reader in Modern English, Cambridge
(1966–); his edited works and his contributions
to anthologies are not listed below.

Bibliography
Authors' and writers' who's who. 1971.
B.N.B.
Gale.
Who's who. 1973.

Poetry
Poems. 1954.
The minute. 1956.
The fugue. 1960.
The landfallers. 1962.
Wood and windfall. 1965.
New poems. 1970.

Criticism
Language and intelligence. 1951.
The Victorian sage. 1953.
Skelton (lecture). 1958.
Story of the night; Shakespeare's major tragedies.
    1961.
Widening horizons in English poetry. 1965.
Blake's lyric poetry. 1968.
Language and intelligence. 1971.

Essays
The charted mirror. 1960.
Colours of clarity. 1964.
The lion hunt. 1964.

Autobiography
A London childhood. 1966.

HOLMES, JOHN CLELLON (1926–)
American novelist; educated at Columbia University; served in the U.S. Navy (1944–5); full-
time writer; a contributor of poetry to little
magazines, and of articles to *Holiday*, *New York
Times Magazine*, *Playboy*, etc.

Bibliography
C.B.I.
Contemporary novelists.
Gale.

Novels
Go. 1952.
The horn. 1958.
Get home free. 1964.

Other Work
Nothing more to declare (essays and memoirs).
    1967.

**HOLROYD, MICHAEL DE COURCY
FRASER** (1935–)
English literary critic; educated at Eton; a con-
tributor to *The Times*, *Sunday Times*, *Punch*, etc.;
edited *The best of Hugh Kingsmill* (1970) and *Lytton
Strachey by himself* (1971).

Bibliography
Authors' and writers' who's who. 1971.
B.N.B.
Who's who. 1973.

Works
Hugh Kingsmill. 1964.
Lytton Strachey; the unknown years. 1967.
Lytton Strachey; the years of achievement. 1968.
A dog's life. 1969.
Unreceived opinions (novel). 1973.

**HOLZAPFEL, RUDI (RUDOLF
PATRICK HOLZAPFEL, †ROOAN
HURKEY, †R. PATRICK WARD)**
(1938–)
French-born poet and novelist; educated in

America and at Trinity College, Dublin; one-time member of the I.R.A. and El Fatah, etc.; teaches bibliography at Bradford Technical College (1968–); a contributor to the *Irish Times*, *Modern Language Review*, etc.

Bibliography
B.N.B.
Gale.

Poetry
Cast a cold eye (with Brendan Kennelly). 1959.
The rain, the moon (with Brendan Kennelly). 1961.
The dark about our loves (with Brendan Kennelly) (pr. ptd.). 1962.
Poems, green townlands (with Brendan Kennelly). 1963.
Why Hitler is in Heaven. 1964.
Soledades (pr. ptd.). 1964.
Nollaig (with Oliver Snoddy) (pr. ptd.). 1965.
Translations from the English (pr. ptd.). 1965.
The rebel bloom (pr. ptd.). 1967.
For lovers of Ireland (pr. ptd.). 1967.

Political Pamphlets
The Jews must go. 1966.
Who needs Yankee money? 1966.

Other Works
Romances (as †Rooan Hurkey). 1960.
The leprechaun (as †R. Patrick Ward) (pr. ptd.). 1963.
Transubstantiations (pr. ptd.). 1963.
Nessaycitos (essays). 1965.

HOME, WILLIAM DOUGLAS (1912–)

Scottish playwright; educated at Eton, New College, Oxford, and R.A.D.A.; served in the army during the Second World War (1940–4); stood for Parliament three times; unpublished plays include *Passing by* (1940), *Ambassador extraordinary* (1948), *The grouse moor image* (1968), *Lloyd George knew my father* (1972); television plays include *Up a green tree* (1962), *The editor regrets* (1970).

Bibliography
B.N.B.
Contemporary dramatists.
N.C.B.E.L.

Poetry
Home truths. 1939.

Plays
Now Barabbas . . . (staged 1947, filmed 1949). 1947.
The Chiltern Hundreds (staged 1947, staged in New York as Yes, m'Lord, filmed 1949). 1949.
Master of Arts (staged 1949). 1950.
The thistle and the rose (staged 1949, published in Plays of the Year 4). 1951.
The bad samaritan (staged 1952). 1954.
The manor of Northstead (staged 1954). 1956.
The reluctant débutante (staged 1955, filmed 1959). 1956.
The iron duchess (staged 1957). 1958.
The plays of William Douglas Home (Now Barabbas ..., The Chiltern Hundreds, The thistle and the rose, The bad samaritan, The reluctant débutante). 1958.
Aunt Edwina (staged 1959). 1960.
The bad soldier Smith (staged 1961). 1962.
The reluctant peer. 1964.
A friend indeed (staged 1965). 1966.
The secretary bird (staged 1968). 1968.
The bishop and the actress (televised 1968). 1969.
The Jockey Club stakes (staged 1970). 1973.

Other Work
Half-term report: an autobiography. 1954.

HOOD, HUGH JOHN BLAGDON (1928–)

Canadian short-story writer; born in Toronto; educated at the University of Toronto; Fellow (1951–5); Professor of English, Hartford, Conn. (1955–61); Professor of English, Montreal University (1961–); a contributor to *Kenyon Review*, *Canadian Forum*, *Tamarack Review*, etc.

Bibliography
Authors' and writers' who's who. 1971.
Canadiana.
C.B.I.
Contemporary novelists.

Novels and Short Stories
Flying a red kite (stories). 1962.
White figure, white ground. 1964.
Around the mountain; scenes of Montreal life (stories). 1967.
The camera always lies. 1967.
Strength down centre. 1970.
A game of touch. 1970.
The fruit man, the meat man, and the manager (stories). 1971.
You can't get there from here. 1972.

HOPE, ALEC DERWENT (1907–)
Australian poet; born in New South Wales; educated at Sydney and Oxford universities; taught English (1933–); Professor of English, Canberra University College (1950–60); Professor of English, Australian National University, Canberra (1960–8); represented in numerous anthologies.

Bibliography
Australian national bibliography.
B.N.B.
Contemporary poets.
Gale.

Poetry
The wandering islands. 1955.
Poems. 1960.
Selected poems. 1963.
Collected poems, 1930–1965. 1966.

Other Works
Australian literature 1950–52. 1964.
The cave and the spring. 1965.

HOPKINS, JOHN RICHARD (1931–)
English playwright; educated at St. Catherine's College, Cambridge; television writer, producer and studio manager (1962–4); full-time writer (1964–); recipient of screenwriters' awards; his film scripts include *Thunderball* (1965), *Virgin Soldiers* (1970); his numerous television plays, some published in selections of plays, with others, include *Dancers in mourning* (1959), *Z cars* (55 episodes in the series), *Walk in the dark* (1972).

Bibliography
B.N.B.
Contemporary dramatists.

Poetry
Talking to a stranger; four television plays (with Anytime you're ready I'll sparkle, No skill or special knowledge is required, Gladly my cross-eyed bear, The innocent must suffer, televised 1966). 1967.
This story of yours (staged 1968). 1969.
Find your way home (staged 1970). 1970.

HORNE, DONALD (1921–)
Australian writer; born in Sydney; educated at Sydney University; editor of the *Sydney Observer* (1958–61); of *Bulletin* (1961–2 and 1967–); of

Quadrant (1963–6); a contributor to various magazines.

Bibliography
Australian national bibliography.
B.N.B.

Works
The lucky country. 1964.
The permit. 1965.
Southern exposure. 1967.
The education of young Donald. 1967.
God is an Englishman. 1969.
But what if there are no pelicans? (novel). 1971.
The next Australia. 1971.
The Australian people: biography of a nation. 1973.

HOROVITZ, FRANCES MARGARET (*née* HOOKER) (1938–)
English poet; educated at Bristol University and R.A.D.A.; teaches in a girls' school; regular B.B.C. poetry reader; a contributor to various journals; represented in *Children of Albion*, Penguin (1969).

Bibliography
B.N.B.
Contemporary poets.

Poetry
Poems. 1967.
The high tower. 1970.

HOROVITZ, ISRAEL (1939–)
American playwright; educated at Harvard, R.A.D.A. London, and the City University of New York; stage manager in New York (1961–7); Professor of Playwriting, New York University (1967–9); Professor of English, City College of New York (1968–); contributor to *Village voice* (1971–); recipient of numerous awards; film scripts include *The strawberry statement* (1969) and *UD blues* (with Jules Feiffer) (1972); only his plays, published separately or in collected editions of his own work, are listed below.

Bibliography
C.B.I.
Contemporary dramatists.
Gale.

Novel
Cappella. 1973.

Poetry
Spider poem and other writings. 1973.

Plays
Morning. 1960.
First season (Line, The Indian wants the Bronx, It is called the sugar plum, Rats). 1968.
The Indian wants the Bronx (in "Showcase", ed. J. Lahr). 1970.
Leader, and Play for trees (televised 1969). 1970.
Acrobats (staged 1968, filmed 1972). 1971.
The honest to God Schnozzola (staged 1969). 1971.
Clair–obscur. 1972.
Play for germs (televised as UD blues, 1972), and Shooting gallery. 1973.

HOROVITZ, MICHAEL (1935–)
British poet; born in Frankfurt of Jewish parents; educated in London and at Brasenose College, Oxford; editor and publisher of *New Departure* (1959–); conducts poetry seminars in art colleges; edited *Children of Albion, poetry of the underground in Britain* (1969).

Bibliography
B.N.B.
Contemporary poets.

Poetry
Nude lines for Barking. 1965.
Poetry for the people. 1966.
Bank holiday. 1967.
Wolverhampton wanderer. 1969.

Other Work
Alan Davie. 1963.

HOSAIN, ATTIA (1913–)
Indian novelist; born and educated in Lucknow; a contributor to the Indian periodicals *Statesman* and *Pioneer*; also in *Lilliput* and *Atlantic Monthly*; settled in England.

Bibliography
B.N.B.
C.B.I.
Indian national bibliography 1958–67.
National bibliography of Indian literature 1901–53.

Novels
Phoenix fled (short stories). 1951.
Sunlight on a broken column. 1961.

HOUGH, *Professor* GRAHAM GOULDER
(1908–)
English scholar; educated at Liverpool University and Queen's College, Cambridge; Lecturer in English, Raffles College, Singapore (1930–41); served in the Second World War (1941–5); Professor of English, Malaya University (1946–50); Fellow of Christ's College, Cambridge (1950–); Praelector and Fellow of Darwin College, Cambridge (1964–); Professor of English, Cambridge (1966–); his edited works are not listed below.

Bibliography
B.N.B.
Contemporary poets.
Who's who. 1973.

Poetry
Legends and pastorals. 1961.

Criticism
The last Romantics. 1949.
The Romantic poets. 1953.
The dark sun. 1956.
Image and experience. 1960.
A preface to the Faery Queene. 1962.
The dream and the task. 1963.
An essay on criticism. 1966.
Style and stylistics. 1969.

HOUSEHOLD, GEOFFREY EDWARD WEST (1900–)
English novelist; educated at Clifton and Magdalen College, Oxford; practised at the Bar until he became a full-time writer.

Bibliography
Authors' and writers' who's who. 1971.
B.N.B.
Contemporary novelists.
N.C.B.E.L.
Who's who. 1973.

Novels and Short Stories
The third hour. 1937.
The salvation of Pisco (stories). 1938.
Rogue male. 1939.
Arabesque. 1948.
The high place. 1950.
A rough shoot. 1951.
A time to kill. 1952.
Tales of adventurers (stories). 1952.

Fellow passenger. 1955.
The brides of Solomon (stories). 1958.
Watcher in the shadows. 1960.
Thing to love. 1963.
Olura. 1965.
Sabres in the sand (stories). 1966.
The courtesy of death. 1967.
Dance of the dwarfs. 1968.
Doom's caravan. 1971.
The three sentinels. 1972.
The lives and times of Bernardo Brown. 1973.

For Children
The Spanish cave. 1940.
Xenophon's adventure. 1955.
Prisoner of the Indies. 1967.

Autobiography
Against the wind. 1958.

HOWARD, ELIZABETH JANE
(1923–   )
English novelist; actress at Stratford-on-Avon,
etc., B.B.C. (1939–46); publisher's editor; a contributor to *Encounter, Vogue, Daily Telegraph*, etc.

Bibliography
Authors' and writers' who's who. 1971.
B.N.B.
Contemporary novelists.
Gale.
Who's who. 1973.

Novels
The beautiful visit (John Llewelyn Rhys Prize
    1951). 1950.
We are for the dark (ghost stories). 1951.
The long view. 1956.
The sea change. 1959.
After Julius. 1965.
Something in disguise. 1969.
Odd girl out. 1972.

Biography
Portrait of Bettina (with Arthur Helps). 1957.

HOWARD, LEON (1903–   )
American critic and biographer; educated at the
universities of Chicago and Johns Hopkins and in
Finland; various academic posts (1927–50); Pro-
fessor of English, University of California, Los
Angeles (1950–71); Visiting Lecturer in London,
Copenhagen, Australia, etc.; a contributor to pro-
fessional journals.

Bibliography
C.B.I.

Works
The Connecticut wits. 1943.
Herman Melville: a biography. 1951.
Victorian knight-errant: a study of the early liter-
    ary career of James Russell Lowell. 1952.
Literature and the American tradition. 1960.
Herman Melville. 1961.
The mind of Jonathan Edwards. 1963.
Wright Morris. 1968.

HOWARD, RICHARD (1929–   )
American poet; educated at Columbia University
and the Sorbonne; worked as lexicographer and
translator; a contributor to *Poetry* magazine,
Chicago; his translated work is not listed below.

Bibliography
C.B.I.
Contemporary poets.

Poetry
Quantities. 1962.
The damages. 1967.
Untitled subjects: poems (Pulitzer Prize 1970).
    1969.
Findings: poems. 1971.

Other Works
Second growth: studies in American poetry since
    1950. 1967.
Alone with America; studies in the art of poetry in
    the United States since World War II. 1969.
Pre-eminent Victorians (dramatic monologue).
    1969.

HOWARTH, DONALD (1931–   )
English playwright; stage manager and actor
(1951–6); recipient of several awards; unpublished
plays include *Ogodivele for the gason* (1967), *The
appointment* (1970); television plays include *Scarborough* (1972) and *Stanley* (1972).

Bibliography
B.N.B.
Contemporary dramatists.

Plays
All good children (staged 1960 and 1964). 1965.
A lily in Little India (televised 1962, staged 1965).
    1966.

School play (in Playbill one). 1969.
Three months gone (staged 1970). 1970.

HOWE, HELEN (*Mrs.* **A. G. ALLEN**) (1905–)

American writer and actress; educated at Radcliffe College; recitals of monologues written by herself (1946–).

Bibliography
C.B.I.
Gale.

Novels
The whole heart. 1943.
We happy few. 1946.
The circle of the day. 1950.
The success. 1956.
The fires of autumn. 1959.

Biography
The gentle Americans. 1965.

HOWE, IRVING (1920–)

American literary critic and scholar; born in New York; educated at the City College of New York and Brooklyn College; served in the U.S. Army during the Second World War (1943–5); Professor of English, Brandeis University (1953–61), Stanford University (1961–3), Hunter College, New York (1963–); recipient of several awards; a contributor to *Commentary*, *New Republic*, *New York Review of Books*, etc.; his edited work is not listed below; editor of *Dissent* (1953–).

Bibliography
C.B.I.
Gale.

Works
U. A. W. and Walter Reuther (with B. J. Widick). 1949.
Sherwood Anderson. 1951.
William Faulkner, a critical study. 1952.
Politics and the novel. 1957.
American Communist party, a critical history (with Lewis Coser). 1958.
A world more attractive; a view of modern literature and politics. 1963.
Steady work: essays in the politics of democratic radicalism, 1956–66. 1966.

Thomas Hardy. 1967.
The decline of the new: essays. 1970.
Beyond the new Left. 1972.
The critical point: on literature and culture. 1973.

HOWES, BARBARA (*Mrs.* **W. J. SMITH**) (1914–)

American poet; born in New York; educated at Bennington College; recipient of various awards; editor of the literary magazine *Chimera* (1943–7); full-time writer.

Bibliography
C.B.I.
Contemporary poets.
Gale.

Poetry
The undersea farmer. 1948.
In the cold country. 1954.
Light and dark. 1959.
Looking up at leaves: poems. 1966.
The blue garden. 1972.

HOYLE, *Professor Sir* FRED (1915–)

English astrophysicist and novelist; born in Yorkshire; educated at Emmanuel College, Cambridge; Professor of Astronomy and Experimental Philosophy, Cambridge (1958–); Professor of Astronomy, Royal Institution (1969–), etc.; F.R.S. (1957); his writings on astronomy include *The nature of the universe* (1950), *Of men and galaxies* (1965) and *Man in the universe* (1966); his scientific works are not listed below.

Bibliography
B.N.B.
Contemporary novelists.
Gale.
Who's who. 1973.

Novels
The black cloud. 1957.
Ossian's ride. 1959.
A for Andromeda (televised). 1962.
Fifth planet (with G. Hoyle). 1963.
Andromeda breakthrough (televised). 1964.
October 1st is too late (with G. Hoyle). 1966.
Elements 79 (stories). 1967.
Rockets of Ursa Major. 1969.
Seven steps to the sun (with G. Hoyle). 1970.
The molecule men (with G. Hoyle). 1971.

Play
Rockets in Ursa Major. 1962.

HUGHES, SPIKE PATRICK CAIRNS
(1908–)
English musicologist; educated at the Perse
School, Cambridge, and Vienna, Berlin and Florence; music and radio critic, *Daily Herald*
(1933–44); producer, B.B.C. German service; a
contributor to *The Times, Punch, Tatler, Opera,
High Fidelity*, etc.

Bibliography
Authors' and writers' who's who. 1971.
B.N.B.

Works
Opening bars (autobiography). 1946.
Second movement (autobiography). 1952.
The art of coarse cricket. 1954.
Great opera houses. 1956.
Out of season. 1956.
Famous Mozart operas. 1957.
The art of coarse travel. 1957.
Famous Puccini operas. 1959.
The Toscanini legacy. 1959.
Glyndebourne. 1965.
Gateway guide to eating in France. 1966.
The art of coarse gardening. 1968.
Gateway guide to eating in Italy. 1968.
Famous Verdi operas. 1968.
The art of coarse bridge. 1970.
How to survive abroad. 1971.
The art of coarse entertaining. 1972.

HUGHES, TED (1930–)
English poet; born in Yorkshire; educated at Pembroke College, Cambridge; husband of the poet
Sylvia Plath (q.v.); visited America; holder of several poetry awards; has edited a volume of American poets (1963), the poetry of Keith Douglas
(1964) and of Emily Dickinson (1968); a contributor to the *London Magazine, Encounter,
Observer, Vogue, T.L.S.*, etc.; edited the anthology
Here today (1963).

Bibliography
B.N.B.
Contemporary poets.
Keith Sagar. Ted Hughes. 1973.
Who's who. 1973.

Poetry
The hawk in the rain (Somerset Maugham Award
 1960). 1957.
Lupercal (Hawthornden Prize 1961). 1960.
The burning of the brother. 1966.
Scapegoats and rabies. 1966.
Recklings. 1967.
Poetry in the making. 1968.
A crow hymn. 1970.
Crow, from the life and songs of crow. 1970.
The martyrdom of Bishop Farrar. 1970.

Plays
Seneca's Oedipus (adapted). 1969.
The coming of the kings. 1970.
Shakespeare's poem. 1971.

Poetry for Children
Meet my folks! 1961.
The earth-owl and other moon people. 1963.
Nessie, the mannerless monster. 1964.
Five autumn songs for children's voices. 1970.

Children's Stories
How the whale became. 1963.
The iron man. 1968.

Other Work
Wodwo. 1967.

HUGO, RICHARD FRANKLIN
(1923–)
American poet; born in Seattle; educated at Seattle
University; Associate Professor of English, Mon-
tana University, Missoula (1964–); represented
in *Poetry* (1968) and other anthologies.

Bibliography
C.B.I.
Contemporary poets.

Poetry
A run of jacks. 1961.
Five poets of the Pacific North West (with others).
 1964.
Death of the Kapowsin Tavern. 1965.
Good luck in cracked Italian. 1969.
The lady in Kicking Horse Reservoir. 1973.

HUMPHREY, WILLIAM (1924–)
American novelist; born in Texas; educated at the
University of Texas, Austin; lives in Virginia.

Bibliography
C.B.I.
Contemporary novelists.

Novels and Short Stories
The last husband and other stories. 1953.
Home from the hill. 1958.
The Ordways. 1965.
A time and a place; stories. 1968.
Proud flesh. 1973.

Other Work
The spawning run: a fable. 1970.

HUMPHREYS, EMYR OWEN (1919–)
Welsh novelist; born in Wales; educated at the
University College of North Wales; taught; radio
and television drama producer until 1962; Lecturer
in Drama, University College of Bangor, North
Wales (1965–); also writes in Welsh.

Bibliography
Authors' and writers' who's who. 1971.
B.N.B.
Contemporary novelists.
Gale.
Brynmor Jones. A bibliography of Anglo-Welsh
literature 1900–1965. 1970.
Who's who. 1973.

Novels
The little kingdom. 1946.
The voice of a stranger. 1949.
A change of heart. 1951.
Hear and forgive (Somerset Maugham Award
1953). 1952.
A man's estate. 1955.
The Italian wife. 1957.
A toy epic (Hawthornden Prize 1959). 1958.
The gift. 1963.
Outside the house of Baal. 1965.
Natives (stories). 1968.
National winner. 1971.

Poetry
Ancestor worship. 1970.

Plays
Roman dream. 1968.
An apple tree and a pig (music by Alun Hod-
dinott). 1969.
Dinas (with W. S. Jones). 1970.

**HUNTER, EVAN (†ED McBAIN,
†HUNT COLLINS, †RICHARD
MARSTEN)** (1926–)
American novelist and author; educated at Hunter
College; served in the U.S. Navy (1944–6) in the
Second World War; author of film script of *Stran-
gers when we meet.*

Bibliography
Authors' and writers' who's who. 1971.
C.B.I.
Contemporary novelists.
Gale.

Novels as Evan Hunter
Find the feathered serpent. 1952.
The blackboard jungle (filmed 1954). 1954.
Second ending. 1956.
Strangers when we meet (filmed as Col, 1959).
1958.
A matter of conviction (filmed 1960). 1959.
The remarkable Harry (for children). 1960.
The last spin and other stories. 1960.
The wonderful button (for children). 1961.
Mothers and daughters (for children). 1961.
Happy New Year, Herbie, and other stories. 1963.
Buddwing (filmed 1967). 1964.
The paper dragon. 1966.
A horse's head. 1967.
Last summer (filmed 1969). 1968.
Sons. 1969.
Nobody knew they were there. 1971.
The beheading and other stories. 1971.
Every little crook and nanny (filmed 1972). 1972.
Come winter. 1973.

Novels as †Ed McBain
Cop hater. 1958.
Killer's payoff. 1958.
Lady killer. 1958.
The mugger. 1959.
The pusher. 1959.
The April Robin murders (with Craig Rice). 1959.
Killer's wedge. 1959.
87th Precinct (Cop hater, The mugger, The
pusher). 1959.
'Til death. 1959.
King's ransom. 1959.
The conman. 1960.
Killer's choice. 1960.
Give the boys a great big hand. 1960.
The heckler. 1960.
See them die. 1960.
Lady, lady, I did it. 1961.

Like love. 1962.
The empty hours (3 novelettes). 1962.
Ten plus one. 1963.
Ax. 1964.
Doll. 1965.
He who hesitates. 1965.
The sentries. 1965.
Eighty million eyes. 1966.
Fuzz. 1968.
Shotgun. 1969.
Jigsaw. 1970.
Runaway black. 1970.
Hail, hail, the gang's all here. 1971.
Sadie when she died. 1972.
Let's hear it for the deaf man. 1973.

Novels as †Hunt Collins
Cut me in. 1954.
Tomorrow's world. 1956.

Novels as †Richard Marsten
Rocket to Luna. 1953.
Danger; dinosaurs. 1953.
The spiked heel. 1956.
Vanishing ladies. 1957.

Play as Evan Hunter
Easter man (a play and six stories). 1972.

HUNTER, JIM (1939–)
English novelist and literary critic; educated at
Gonville and Caius College, Cambridge, and
Indiana University; taught English at Bradford
Grammar School (1962–6); senior English master,
Bristol Grammar School (1966–); his edited
work includes *Modern Short Stories* (1964), *Modern
Poets*, 4 vols. (1967–8), the *Metaphysical Poets*
(1965), *Gerard Manley Hopkins* (1966); a con
tributor to the *Guardian*, *Time and Tide*, *Evening
News*, *Spectator*, etc.; edited *The human animal*
(1973), etc.

Bibliography
Authors' and writers' who's who. 1971.
B.N.B.
Contemporary novelists.
Gale.

Novels
The sun in the morning. 1961.
Sally Gray. 1963.
Earth and stone (American title, A place of stone).
  1963.

The flame. 1966.
Walking in the painted sunshine. 1970.
Kinship. 1973.

HUTCHINSON, ALFRED (1924–)
South African novelist and playwright of mixed
blood; born in Eastern Transvaal; educated at Fort
Hare and Sussex universities; arrested on a treason
charge for his disagreement with apartheid;
escaped and, after many difficulties, reached
Ghana; came to England (1960); writer for radio;
represented in numerous anthologies of writing
from Africa.

Bibliography
B.N.B.
Zell and Silver.

Novel
Road to Ghana. 1960.

Play
The rain-killers. 1964.

HUTCHISON, MARGARET
Canadian regional novelist of British Columbia.

Bibliography
Canadiana.
C.B.I.

Novel
Tamarac. 1957.

HUTCHISON, WILLIAM BRUCE
(1901–)
Canadian writer and journalist; born in Ontario;
worked in journalism (1920–); joined the Press
Gallery, Ottawa (1925); associate editor, Winnipeg
Free Press (1944); editor of the Victoria *Daily Times*
(1950); editor of the Vancouver *Sun*.

Bibliography
Canadiana.
C.B.I.
Who's who. 1973.

Works
The unknown country (English title, Unknown
  dominion). 1942.
The hollow men (novel). 1944.

The Fraser. 1950.
The incredible Canadian; a candid portrait of Mackenzie King. 1952.
Canada's lonely neighbour. 1954.

The struggle for the border. 1955.
Canada; tomorrow's giant. 1957.
Mr. Prime Minister: 1867–1964. 1964.
Western windows. 1967.

I

IGGULDEN, JOHN MANNERS
(1917–)
Australian novelist; national gliding champion and director of the Australian National Gliding School (1960–4); partner in family engineering firms (1959); full-time writer (1959–).

Bibliography
Annals of Australian literature.
Australian national bibliography.
B.N.B.
Gale.

Novels
Breakthrough. 1960.
The storms of summer. 1960.
The clouded sky. 1964.
Dark stranger. 1966.

IGNATOW, DAVID (1914–)
American poet, freelance writer and editor; editor of the *Beloit Poetry Journal* (1949–59); poetry editor of *Nation* (1962–3); represented in numerous anthologies; a contributor to *Nation*, *New York Times*, *Poetry*, etc.

Bibliography
C.B.I.
Contemporary poets.
Gale.

Poetry
Poems. 1948.
Gentle weight lifter. 1955.
Say pardon. 1961.
Figures of the human. 1964.
Rescue the dead. 1968.
Earth hard: selected poems. 1968.
Poems 1934–1969. 1970.

Other Work
The note-books of David Ignatow (ed. J. Mills). 1973.

INGE, WILLIAM MOTTER (1913–73)
American playwright; educated at Kansas and Yale universities; taught (1937–49); art critic, *Star Times*, St. Louis (1943–6); recipient of several awards.

Bibliography
C.B.I.
Contemporary dramatists.
Gale.

Novels
Good luck, Miss Wyckoff. 1971.
My son is a splendid driver. 1972.

Plays
Come back, little Sheba (staged 1950, filmed 1952). 1950.
Picnic: a summer romance (staged 1953, filmed 1955; Pulitzer Prize 1953). 1953.
Bus stop (staged 1955, filmed 1956). 1955.
The dark at the top of the stairs (staged as Farther off from Heaven, 1947, filmed 1960). 1958.
Four plays (Come back, little Sheba, Picnic, Bus stop, The dark at the top of the stairs). 1958.
Loss of roses (staged 1959, filmed 1963). 1960.
Splendor in the grass: a screen play. 1961.
Summer brave and eleven short plays. 1962.
Natural affection (staged 1962). 1963.
Where's Daddy? (staged as Family things, etc., 1965). 1966.
Two short plays: The call, and A murder. 1968.

ISRAEL, CHARLES EDWARD (1920–)
American-born Jewish novelist; son of a rabbi;

educated at North Carolina and Cincinnati universities and Hebrew Union College; served in the U.S. Marines (1943–5); U.N.R.R.A. (1946–50); radio and television scriptwriter in Hollywood (1950–3); moved to Toronto and worked for Canadian radio and films (1953–   ); a director of Association of Canadian Radio and Television Artists (1965–6).

Bibliography
Authors' and writers' who's who. 1971.
C.B.I.
Contemporary novelists.
Gale.

Novels
How many angels. 1956.
The mark. 1958.
Rizpah. 1960.
Who was then the gentleman? 1963.
Shadows on the wall. 1965.
The hostages. 1966.

Play
The labyrinth. 1969.

Other Works
The true north (with T. C. Farley). 1957.
Five ships west: the story of Magellan. 1966.

J

JABAVU, NONI (*Mrs.* **MICHAEL CROSFIELD)**
South African writer; born in Cape Province; educated at the Lovedale Missionary Institute, The Mount School, York, and Royal Academy of Music; broadcaster and lecturer; a contributor to various anthologies of African writing.

Bibliography
B.N.B.
Jahn and Dressler.
Zell and Silver.

Works
Drawn in colour. 1960.
The ochre people: scenes from South African life. 1963.

JACKSON, ALAN (1938–   )
Scottish poet; born in Liverpool; educated at Edinburgh University; founder and director of the Kevin Press (1965); represented in various anthologies.

Bibliography
B.N.B.
Contemporary poets.

Poetry
Underwater wedding. 1961.
Sixpenny poems. 1962.

Well ye ken noo. 1963.
All fall down. 1965.
The worstest beast. 1967.
Penguin modern poets no. 12 (with J. Nuttall and W. Wantling). 1968.
The grim wayfarer. 1969.

JACKSON, SHIRLEY (*Mrs.* **S. E. HYMAN)** (1919–65)
American novelist; educated at Syracuse University; worked as a full-time writer; her short stories have appeared in magazines and anthologies; wrote for radio and television.

Bibliography
C.B.I.
Gale.

Novels
The road through the wall (published as The other side of the street, 1956). 1948.
The lottery. 1949.
Hangsaman. 1951.
Life among the savages. 1953.
The bird's nest. 1954.
The witchcraft of Salem village. 1956.
Raising demons. 1957.
The sundial. 1958.
The haunting of Hill House. 1959.
We have always lived in the castle. 1962.

The magic of Shirley Jackson (edited by Stanley Edgar Hyman). 1966.
Come along with me. 1968.

For Children
The bad children (play). 1959.
Nine magic wishes. 1963.
Famous Sally. 1966.

JACOB, PAUL (1940–)
Indian poet; educated in Delhi and Madras; on the staff of Krishna Menon's *Century* (1963–5); on the staff of *Enact*, Delhi (1966–); represented in *Modern Indian Poetry in English* (1969).

Bibliography
Contemporary poets.
Indian national bibliography 1958–67.

Poetry
Sonnets. 1968.
Altar sonnets. 1969.
Swedish exercises. 1973.

JACOBS, JANE (*née* DECKER) (1916–)
American historian and critic; educated in Canada; shorthand-typist and reporter in New York; associate director, *Architectural Forum* (1952–62); contributed to *The exploding metropolis* (1958).

Bibliography
C.B.I.
Gale.

Works
The death and life of great American cities. 1961.
The economy of cities. 1969.

JACOBSON, DAN (1929–)
South African novelist; born in Johannesburg; educated at Witwatersrand University; worked for the South African Jewish Board of Deputies; Visiting Professor, Syracuse University, New York (1965–6); recipient of several literary awards; a contributor to various magazines.

Bibliography
B.N.B.
Contemporary novelists.
Gale.
Myra Yudelman, Dan Jacobson: a bibliography. Johannesburg. 1967.

Novels
The trap. 1955.
A dance in the sun. 1956.
The price of diamonds. 1957.
A long way from London (John Llewelyn Rhys Prize 1959). 1958.
The Zulu and the Zeide. 1959.
Evidence of love. 1960.
Beggar my neighbour (stories). 1964.
The beginners. 1966.
Through the wilderness (stories). 1968.
The rape of Tamar. 1970.
A way of life and other stories. 1972.
Inklings: selected stories. 1972.
The wonder worker. 1973.

Other Works
No further west: California re-visited. 1959.
Time of arrival and other essays (Somerset Maugham Award 1964). 1963.

†JAMES, BRIAN (JOHN LAWRENCE TIERNEY) (1892–)
Australian novelist; educated at Sydney and Oxford universities; taught in New South Wales; served in the Second World War; a writer since 1942; a contributor to newspapers and periodicals; editor of *Australian Short Stories* (1963).

Bibliography
Australian national bibliography.
B.N.B.
Gale.

Novels as †Brian James
First furrow. 1944.
Cookabundy Bridge and other stories (serialised in *Sydney Bulletin*). 1946.
The advancement of Spencer Button. 1950.
The bunyip of Barney's elbow (stories). 1956.
Orchards. 1963.
Hopeton high. 1963.
The big burn (stories). 1965.

JAMES, ROBERT VIDAL RHODES (1933–)
English historian; born in India; educated at Sedbergh and Worcester College, Oxford; assistant clerk, later senior clerk, House of Commons (1955–64); Fellow of All Souls College, Oxford (1965–); visited the United States to study defence procedures (1965); lecturer on military history, Sandhurst (1965 and 1966); a contributor to *History Today*, *Spectator*, *New Statesman*, *Observer*,

etc.; edited "*Chips*": *the diaries of Sir Henry Channon* (1967), *The Czechoslovak crisis 1968* (1969), *Memoirs of a Conservative: J. C. C. Davidson's memoirs and papers 1910–1937* (1969).

Bibliography
B.N.B.
Gale.
Who's who. 1973.

Works
Lord Randolph Churchill. 1959.
An introduction to the House of Commons (John Llewelyn Rhys Prize 1962). 1961.
Rosebery. 1963.
Gallipoli. 1965.
Standardization and common production of weapons in Nato (Institute for Strategic Studies, Defence, Technology and the Western Alliance no. 3). 1967.
Churchill: a study in failure 1900–1939. 1970.
Winston Churchill: the wilderness years 1929–1939. 1970.
Britain's role in the United Nations. 1970.
The General Election of 1970. 1971.
The constitutional yearbook of 1970. 1971.
Staffing the United Nations secretariat. 1971.
Ambitions and realities: British politics 1964–70. 1972.

JANEWAY, ELIZABETH (*née* HALL) (1913–   )
American novelist; educated at Barnard College; lecturer, critic and novelist, judge of Pulitzer Prize in letters (1971); Hon. D.Litt. (Sampson College), 1972; a contributor to numerous magazines and literary journals; her edited work is not listed below.

Bibliography
C.B.I.
Gale.

Novels
The Walsh girls. 1943.
Daisy Kenyon. 1945.
The question of Gregory. 1949.
Leaving home. 1953.
The third choice. 1958.
Accident (English title, Accident on route 37). 1964.
Angry Kate. 1964.

Other Works
The Vikings (for children). 1951.
The early days of the automobile. 1956.
Ivanov VII (for children). 1967.
Man's world—woman's place. 1971.

JARRELL, RANDALL (1914–65)
American poet; educated at Vanderbilt University; served in the U.S. Air Force (1942–6) during the Second World War; among academic posts was Professor of English at Women's College of the University of North Carolina (1958–65); consultant in poetry at the Library of Congress (1956–8); awarded numerous literary prizes; poetry critic of the *Yale Review* (1955–7), etc.; a contributor to *New Republic*, *Nation*, etc.; his translations and edited works are not listed below.

Bibliography
C.B.I.
Gale.
Spiller: supplement 1959.

Novel
Pictures from an institution. 1954.

Poetry
Blood for a stranger. 1942.
Little friend, little friend. 1945.
Losses. 1948.
The seven-league crutches. 1951.
Selected poems. 1955.
Uncollected poems. 1958.
The woman at the Washington Zoo (poems and translations). 1960.
The lost world. 1965.
The complete poems. 1969.

Other Works
Poetry and the age. 1953.
A sad heart at the supermarket (essays and fables). 1962.
The gingerbread rabbit (for children). 1963.
The bat poet (for children). 1964.
The animal family (for children). 1965.
The third book of criticism. 1969.

JELLICOE, PATRICIA ANN (*Mrs.* ROGER MAYNE) (1927–   )
English playwright; actress, stage-manager and director at theatres in London and the provinces (1947–51); founded and ran the Cockpit Theatre Club to experiment with the open stage (1952–4); taught acting and directed plays at the Central

School of Speech and Drama (1954–6); has translated plays from Swedish and German; her unpublished plays include *You'll never guess* (produced 1973).

Bibliography
B.N.B.
Contemporary dramatists.
Who's who. 1973.

Plays
Rosmersholm (translation) (staged 1960). 1961.
The knack (staged 1961; filmed 1965). 1962.
The sport of my mad mother (staged 1958). 1964.
Shelley (staged 1965). 1966.
The giveaway (staged 1969). 1970.

Other Work
Some unconscious influences in the theatre. 1967.

JENKINS, JOHN ROBIN (1912–)
Scottish novelist; educated at Glasgow University; taught English in Afghanistan, Barcelona and Malaysia (1957–68).

Bibliography
Authors' and writers' who's who. 1971.
B.N.B.
Contemporary novelists.
Gale.
Who's who. 1973.

Novels
So gaily sings the lark. 1951.
Happy for the child. 1953.
The thistle and the Grail. 1954.
The cone gatherers. 1955.
Guests of war. 1956.
The missionaries. 1957.
The changeling. 1958.
Love is a fervent fire. 1959.
Some kind of grace. 1960.
Dust on the paw. 1961.
The tiger of gold. 1962.
A love of innocence. 1963.
The Sardana dancers. 1964.
A very Scotch affair. 1968.
The holy tree. 1969.
The expatriates. 1971.
A toast to the lord. 1972.

JENKINS, *Right Hon.* **ROY HARRIS** (1920–)
English politician; educated at Balliol College,

Oxford; served in the Second World War (1939–45); Minister of Aviation (1964–5); Home Secretary (1965–7); Chancellor of the Exchequer (1967–70); Deputy Leader of the Labour Party (1970–6); Fellow of Balliol College, Oxford; chairman and director of many committees and pressure groups; a contributor to the *Observer, Spectator, Encounter, New Statesman,* etc.; a contributor to *New Fabian Essays* (1952) and *Hugh Gaitskell, a memoir* (1964).

Bibliography
Authors' and writers' who's who. 1971.
B.N.B.
Gale.
Who's who. 1973.

Works
Purpose and policy (A volume of the Prime Minister's speeches (ed.)). 1947.
Mr. Attlee: an interim biography. 1948.
Post-war Italy (with others). 1950.
Pursuit of progress. 1953.
Mr. Balfour's poodle. 1954.
Sir Charles Dilke: a Victorian tragedy. 1958.
The Labour case. 1959.
Asquith. 1964.
Essays and speeches. 1967.
What happens now? 1972.
Afternoon on the Potomac? A British view of America's changing position in the world. 1972.

JENNINGS, ELIZABETH JOAN (1926–)
English poet; born in Boston, Lincs.; educated at St. Anne's College, Oxford; worked as an advertising copy-writer, librarian and publisher's reader; the only woman contributor to *New lines*; freelance writer since 1960; editor of *The Batsford book of children's verse* (1958) and *Christina Rossetti's verse* (1970); a contributor to the *London Magazine, New Statesman, Spectator, T.L.S., New Yorker,* etc.

Bibliography
Authors' and writers' who's who. 1971.
B.N.B.
Contemporary poets. 1970.
Who's who. 1973.

Poetry
Poems. 1953.
A way of looking (Somerset Maugham Award 1956). 1955.
A sense of the world. 1958.

Song for a birth or a death. 1961.
The sonnets of Michelangelo (translation). 1961.
Recoveries. 1964.
The mind has mountains. 1966.
The secret brother. 1966.
Collected poems 1967. 1967.
The animals' arrival. 1969.
Lucidities. 1970.

Other Works
Let's have some poetry. 1960.
Poetry today. 1961.
Every changing shape. 1961.
Frost. 1964.
Christianity and poetry. 1965.

JENNINGS, PAUL FRANCIS (1918–)
English humorous writer; educated at King Henry
VIII School, Coventry and Douai; served in the
army in the Second World War; started freelance
writing for *Punch* and the *Spectator* while still in the
army; scriptwriter, C.O.I. (1946–7); copywriter
for the advertising agency of Colman, Prentice and
Varley (1947–9); on staff of the *Observer* (1949–66).

Bibliography
Authors' and writers' who's who. 1971.
B.N.B.
Gale.
Who's who. 1973.

Works
Oddly enough. 1950.
Even oddlier. 1952.
Oddly bodlikins. 1953.
Next to oddliness. 1955.
Model oddlies. 1956.
Gladly oddly. 1958.
Idly oddly. 1959.
I said oddly, diddle I? 1961.
Oodles of oddlies. 1963.
Oddly ad lib. 1965.
I was joking, of course. 1968.
The living village. 1968.
Just a few lines; Guinness trains of thought. 1969.
It is an odd thing but . . . 1971.

For Children
The hopping basket. 1965.
The great jelly of London. 1967.

JHABVALA, *Mrs.* **RUTH PRAWER**
(1927–)
Indian novelist of Polish parentage; born in Col-

ogne, Germany; educated at London University;
her film scripts include *The Shakespeare Wallah*
(1965).

Bibliography
B.N.B.
C.B.I.
Contemporary novelists.
Indian national bibliography 1958–67.
National bibliography of Indian literature
    1901–53.
Who's who. 1973.

Novels
To whom she will. 1955.
The nature of passion. 1956.
Esmond in India. 1958.
The householder. 1960.
Get ready for battle. 1962.
A backward place. 1965.
A new dominion. 1972.

Short Stories
Like birds, like fishes. 1963.
A stronger climate. 1968.
An experience of India. 1971.

**JOHNSON, BRYAN STANLEY
WILLIAM** (1933–73)
English novelist; educated at King's College,
London; Gregory Award winner (1962); 1st Gregynog Arts Fellow, University of Wales (1970);
poetry editor, *Transatlantic Review* (1965–73);
director of films, television and stage plays; author
of several film scripts; a contributor to *Encounter,
Listener, New Society,* etc.; edited *All bull: the
national serviceman* (1973).

Bibliography
Authors' and writers' who's who. 1971.
B.N.B.
Gale.
Who's who. 1973.

Novels
Travelling people. 1963.
Alberto Angelo. 1964.
Trawl (Somerset Maugham Award 1967). 1966.
The unfortunates. 1969.
House mother normal. 1971.
Xtie Malry's own double entry. 1972.

Short Story
Statement against corpses (with Zulfikar Ghose).
   1964.

Poetry
Poems. 1963.
Poems two. 1972.

Other Work
Aren't you rather young to be writing your
   memoirs? 1973.

JOHNSON, *Very Reverend* **HEWLETT**
(1874–1966)
English theologian; educated at Victoria Uni-
versity, Wadham College, Oxford, and Prague and
Berlin universities; Dean of Manchester (1924–31);
Dean of Canterbury (1931–63); founder and editor
of the *Interpreter* (1905–24); known as the Red
Dean for his political affiliations.

Bibliography
B.N.B.
Who's who. 1966.

Works
The socialist sixth of the world. 1940.
Soviet strength: its source and challenge. 1942.
Christianity in the U.S.S.R. 1945.
Soviet success. 1947.
China's new creative age. 1953.
Eastern Europe in the socialist world. 1954.
Christians and Communism; 14 sermons. 1956.
The upsurge of China. 1961.

JOHNSON, LOUIS (1924–)
New Zealand poet; born in Wellington; founder of
the Capricorn Press; radio and television commentator; recipient of several literary awards; represented in numerous anthologies; a contributor to
Landfall, Sydney *Bulletin*, *London Magazine*, *Poetry*,
Chicago, etc.; founder and editor of the *New Zealand Yearbook*, vols. I–II (1951–64); founder and
editor of *Numbers* (1954–60).

Bibliography
B.M. catalogue.
Contemporary poets.

Poetry
Stanza and scene. 1945.
The sun among the ruins. 1951.
Roughshod among the lilies. 1952.

Poems unpleasant (with Anton Vogt and James K.
   Baxter). 1952.
Two poems. 1955.
The dark glass. 1955.
New worlds for old. 1957.
Bread and a pension. 1964.
Land like a lizard (New Guinea poems). 1970.

**JOHNSON, RONALD (†THEODORE
CHAMBERLAIN)** (1935–)
American poet; educated at Columbia University;
served in the U.S. Army (1954–6); did various jobs
(1956–62); itinerant poet in England and U.S.A.
(1962–).

Bibliography
C.B.I.
Gale.

Poetry
A line of poetry, a row of trees. 1964.

JOHNSTON, GEORGE BENSON
(1913–)
Canadian poet; educated at Toronto University;
served in the R.C.A.F. during the Second World
War (1940–5); Assistant Professor, Mount Ellison
University, New Brunswick (1946–9); Lecturer,
later Professor, Carleton College, Ontario
(1950–); contributed poems to the *Atlantic
Monthly*, *Tamarack Review*, *Queen's Quarterly*, etc.;
his edited work and translations of *Nostre sapos* etc.
are not listed below.

Bibliography
Canadiana.
C.B.I.
Contemporary poets.
Gale.

Poetry
The cruising auk. 1959.
Home free. 1966.
Basset hound. 1968.
Happy enough: poems 1935–1972. 1972.

Other Work
Spirit—paraclete in the gospel of John. 1970.

**JOHNSTON, GEORGE HENRY
(†SHANE MARTIN)** (1912–70)
Australian novelist.

Bibliography
Annals of Australian literature.
Australian national bibliography.

Novels
Death takes small bites. 1948.
Monsoon. 1950.
The Cyprian woman. 1955.
The sponge divers (with Charmian Clift). 1956.
The darkness outside. 1959.
Closer to the sun. 1960.
The far road. 1962.
My brother Jack. 1964.
The far face of the moon. 1965.
The Australians. 1966.
Clean straw for nothing. 1969.
A cartload of clay. 1971.

Other Works
Grey gladiator (also published as Lioness of the
    seas, 1941 and Action at sea, 1942). 1941.
Battle of the seaways, from the *Athenia* to the
    Bismarck. 1942.
Australia at war. 1942.
Toughest fighting in the world (English title, New
    Guinea Diary). 1943.
Pacific partner. 1944.
Skyscrapers in the mist. 1946.
Journey through tomorrow. 1947.
Moon at perigee. 1948.

JONES, DOUGLAS GORDON (1929–)
Canadian poet; born in Ontario; educated at
McGill and Queens universities; Lecturer in Eng
lish, University of Sherbrooke; represented in *Penguin book of Canadian verse* (1967) and other
anthologies of Canadian poetry.

Bibliography
Canadiana.
C.B.I.
Contemporary poets.

Poetry
Frost on the sun. 1957.
The sun is axeman. 1961.
Phrases from Orpheus. 1968.

Criticism
Butterfly on the rock. 1970.

JONES, JAMES (1921–)
American novelist; educated at the universities of
Hawaii and New York; served in the U.S. Army

(1939–44) in the Second World War; lives in Paris;
a contributor of short stories to various periodicals.

Bibliography
C.B.I.
Contemporary novelists.
Gale.

Novels
From here to eternity (filmed 1953). 1951.
Some came running (filmed 1958). 1958.
The pistol. 1959.
The thin red line. 1962.
Go to the widow-maker. 1967.
The ice-cream headache, and other stories. 1968.
Merry month of May. 1971.
A touch of danger. 1973.

JONES, LEROI (†IMAMU AMIRI BARAKA) (1934–)
Black American playwright, novelist and editor;
born in New Jersey; educated at Rutgers, Howard
and Columbia universities, etc.; founder and director of the Black Arts Repertory Theatre (1964);
served in the U.S. Air Force (1954–7); his com-
pilations and edited works are not listed below; a
contributor to *Evergreen Review*, *Poetry*, *Saturday
Review*, *Negro Digest*, etc.; only his separately published plays are listed below.

Bibliography
C.B.I.
Contemporary dramatists.
Gale.

Novels
The system of Dante's Hell. 1965.
Tales. 1967.

Poetry
April 13 (broadsheet). 1959.
Spring and so forth (broadsheet). 1960.
Preface to a twenty volume suicide note. 1961.
The disguise (broadsheet). 1961.
The dead lecturer. 1964.
Black art. 1966.
Black magic poetry 1961–1967. 1969.
It's nation time (as †I. A. Baraka). 1970.
Spirit reach. 1972.

Plays
Dutchman, and The slave. 1964.
Arm yourself and harm yourself. 1967.
The baptism, and The toilet. 1967.

Striptease. 1967.

Four black revolutionary plays (Experimental death unit one, A black mass, Great goodness of life, Madheart). 1969.

Jello (as †I. A. Baraka) (staged 1965). 1970.

Other Works
Cuba libre. 1961.
Blues people; negro music in White America. 1965.
Information (with others). 1965.
Home: social essays. 1966.
Black music. 1967.
In our terribleness (with Billy Abernathy). 1969.
A black value system. 1970.
Raise race rays raize (essays) (as †I. A. Baraka). 1971.
Kawaida studies: the new nationalism (as †I. A. Baraka). 1972.

JONES, MADISON PERCY, Jr.
(1925–)
American novelist; educated at Vanderbilt and Florida universities; served in the U.S. military police (1944–5); a farmer and horse trainer before becoming a university teacher of English; Professor, Auburn University (1968–); a contributor to *Perspective* and *Sewanee Review*.

Bibliography
C.B.I.
Contemporary novelists.
Gale.

Novels
The innocent. 1957.
Forest of the night. 1960.
A buried land. 1963.
An exile (paperback title, As I walk the line, 1970). 1967.
Cry of absence. 1971.

Other Work
History of the Tennessee state dental association. 1958.

JONES, MERVYN (1922–)
Welsh novelist; educated at New York University; assistant editor, later drama critic, *Tribune* (1955–67); *New Statesman* (1966–8); a contributor to the *Observer*, *New Statesman*, etc.

Bibliography
Authors' and writers' who's who. 1971.

B.N.B.
Who's who. 1973.

Novels
No time to be young. 1952.
The new town. 1953.
The last barricade. 1953.
Helen Blake. 1955.
On the last day. 1958.
A set of wives. 1965.
John and Mary. 1966.
A survivor. 1968.
Joseph. 1970.
Mr. Armitage isn't back yet. 1971.
Life on the dole. 1972.

Other Works
Guilty men (with Michael Foot). 1957.
Potbank. 1961.
Freed from fear. 1962.
Big two. 1962.
Two ears of corn. 1965.
Kingsley Martin. 1970.

JOSEPH, MICHAEL KENNEDY
(1914–)
English-born New Zealand poet and novelist; educated at Auckland University College and Merton College, Oxford; served in the army (1940–6) during the Second World War; Lecturer, later Associate Professor of English Literature, University of Auckland (1935–); a contributor to *Landfall*, *New Zealand Listener*, *Comment*, etc.

Bibliography
B.N.B.
Contemporary poets.
Gale.

Novels
I'll be no more a soldier. 1958.
A pound of saffron. 1962.
The hole in the zero. 1967.

Poetry
Imaginary islands (pr. ptd.). 1950.
The living countries. 1959.

Other Work
Byron the poet. 1964.

JOSHI, ARUN (1939–)
Indian novelist; educated in India and the U.S.A.; director of Shri Ram centre for industrial relations.

Bibliography
C.B.I.
Indian national bibliography 1958–67.
National bibliography of Indian literature
    1901–53.

Novels
The foreigner. 1968.
The strange case of Billy Biswas. 1971.
The apprentice. 1974.

Biography
Shri Ram (with Khushwant Singh). 1969.

JUSSAWALLA, ADIL JEHANGIR
(1940–   )
Indian poet; born and educated at Bombay and
Oxford universities; taught English to foreign students at a language school in London for more than
four years; a contributor to several British and
Indian journals and newspapers; a lecturer in English at St. Xavier's College, Bombay; editor of
Penguin's *New Writing in India* (1974).

Bibliography
C.B.I.
Indian national bibliography 1958–67.

National bibliography of Indian literature
1901–53.

Poetry
Land's End. 1962.

JUSTICE, DONALD RODNEY
(1925–   )
American poet and writer; educated at Miami and
Iowa and other universities; Assistant Professor of
English at various universities; Associate Professor, Iowa State University (1963–   ); recipient
of several awards; Ford Fellow in theatre (1964–5);
a contributor to *Poetry*, *New Yorker*, etc.; anthologised in *Twentieth Century American Poetry* (Conrad Aiken), etc.; his edited work is not listed below.

Bibliography
C.B.I.
Contemporary poets.
Gale.

Poetry
The summer anniversaries. 1960.
A local storm. 1963.
Night light. 1967.
Departures. 1973.

K

KARP, DAVID (1922–   )
American novelist; educated at City College, New
York; served in the U.S. Army during the Second
World War; freelance writer since 1950; writes for
radio and television; recipient of several literary
grants and awards; a contributor to *Argosy*, *Saturday Evening Post*, *Collier's*, etc.

Bibliography
C.B.I.
Contemporary novelists.
Gale.

Novels
One. 1953.
The day of the monkey. 1955.
All honorable men. 1956.
Leave me alone. 1957.

Enter, sleeping. 1960.
Vice president in charge of revolution (with
    Murray D. Lincoln). 1960.
The last believers. 1964.

KAUFMANN, WALTER ARNOLD
(1921–   )
American scholar; born in Germany; educated at
Harvard University; served in the U.S. Army
(1944–6) during the Second World War; Instructor, rising to Professor of Philosophy, Princeton
University (1947–   ); Visiting Professor in
Germany, Israel and American universities; a contributor to many encyclopaedias, etc.; his numerous edited works and translations are not listed
below; a contributor to numerous scholarly journals.

Bibliography
C.B.I.

Works
Nietzsche. 1950.
Existentialism from Dostoevsky to Sartre. 1956.
Critique of religion and philosophy. 1958.
From Shakespeare to existentialism (English title,
   The owl and the nightingale, 1960). 1959.
The faith of a heretic. 1961.
Cain and other poems. 1962.
Hegel: reinterpretation, texts and commentary.
   1965.
Tragedy and philosophy. 1969.
Without guilt and justice. 1973.

KAVANAGH, PATRICK JOSEPH GREGORY (P. J.) (1931–)

Irish poet; born in Worthing; educated in Lausanne and at Merton College, Oxford; lectured at the University of Indonesia, Java; a contributor to the *London Magazine, Encounter, New Statesman*, etc.

Bibliography
Authors' and writers' who's who. 1971.
B.N.B.
Contemporary poets.
N.C.B.E.L.

Novel
A song and dance. 1968.

Poetry
One and one. 1959.
On the way to the depot. 1967.
About time. 1970.
Such men are dangerous. 1971.
A happy man. 1972.
Collected poems. 1973.

Autobiography
The perfect stranger. 1966.

KAYIRA, LEGSON

Malawi novelist, born in a village in the bush; educated at mission schools before setting out on a 2500-mile walk across Africa to Khartoum in search of further education, which resulted in his studying at the universities of Washington and Cambridge.

Bibliography
B.N.B.

Jahn and Dressler.
Zell and Silver.

Novels
The looming shadow. 1968.
Jingala. 1969.
The civil servant. 1971.

Autobiography
I will try. 1965.

KAZIN, ALFRED (1915–)

American writer and editor; educated at Columbia University; academic posts include Professor of English, State University of New York, Stony Brook (1963–   ); literary editor of *New Republic* (1942–3); associate editor of *Fortune Magazine*; recipient of numerous academic and literary awards; a contributor to *Partisan Review, Atlantic Monthly*, etc.; his edited work is not listed below.

Bibliography
C.B.I.
Gale.

Works
On native grounds. 1942.
A walker in the city. 1951.
The inmost leaf. 1955.
Contemporaries. 1962.
Starting out in the thirties. 1965.
Open form: essay for our time. 1970.
Bright book of life: American novelists and story-
   tellers. 1973.

KEATING, HENRY REYMOND FITZWALTER (1926–)

English novelist; educated at Merchant Taylors' School and Trinity College, Dublin; journalist (1952–60); reviewer of crime fiction for *The Times* (1967–   ); edited *Blood on my mind* (1972).

Bibliography
Authors' and writers' who's who. 1971.
B.N.B.
Gale.
Who's who. 1973.

Novels
Death and the visiting fireman. 1959.
Zen there was murder. 1960.
A rush on the ultimate. 1961.
The dog it was that died. 1962.
Death of a fat god. 1963.

The perfect murder. 1964.
Is skin-deep, is fatal. 1965.
Inspector Ghote's good crusade. 1966.
Inspector Ghote caught in meshes. 1967.
Inspector Ghote hunts the peacock. 1968.
Inspector Ghote plays a joker. 1969.
Inspector Ghote breaks an egg. 1970.
Inspector Ghote goes by train. 1971.
Inspector Ghote trusts the heart. 1972.

KEELEY, EDMUND LEROY (1928–)

American novelist and translator; educated at
Princeton and Oxford universities; served in the
U.S. Navy (1945–6) during the Second World
War; lecturer and professor at Salonika University
(1953–4); Associate Professor of English, Princeton University (1954–); his edited work is not
listed below.

Bibliography
C.B.I.
Gale.

Novels
The libation. 1958.
The gold-hatted lover. 1961.
Voyage to a dark island. 1972.

KEESING, NANCY FLORENCE (Mrs. HERTZBERG) (1923–)

Australian poet; born in Sydney; clerk in the
Navy Department (1942–5); social hospital worker
(1947–51); freelance writer (1951–); a contributor to *Bulletin, Meanjin*, etc.; her edited works
are not listed below.

Bibliography
Australian national bibliography.
Contemporary poets.
Gale.

Poetry
Imminent summer. 1951.
Three men and Sydney. 1955.
Showground sketch and other poems. 1968.

For Children
By gravel and gum. 1963.

Other Work
The history of the Australian gold rushes, by those
   who were there. 1972.

KEMELMAN, HARRY (1908–)

American detective novelist; educated at Boston

Latin School, Boston University and Harvard;
taught in high schools and colleges (1935–41);
served in the U.S. Army transportation corps
(1942–6) during the Second World War; War
Assets Administration (1948–9); freelance writer
and private businessman (1949–63); Associate Professor of English, Franklin Technical Institute,
Boston (1963–); a contributor to *Bookman, Ellery
Queen Mystery Magazine*, etc.

Bibliography
C.B.I.
Gale.

Novels
Friday the rabbi slept late. 1964.
Saturday the rabbi went hungry. 1966.
Nine mile walk. 1967.
Sunday the rabbi stayed home. 1969.
Monday the rabbi took off. 1971.
Tuesday the rabbi saw red. 1974.

KENEALLY, THOMAS MICHAEL (1935–)

Australian novelist; studied for the priesthood and
then law; served in the Australian Forces; taught in
Sydney (1960–4); Lecturer in Drama, University
of New England, New South Wales (1968–70).

Bibliography
Annals of Australian literature.
Australian national bibliography.
B.N.B.
Contemporary novelists.

Novels
The place at Whitton. 1964.
The fear. 1965.
Bring larks and heroes. 1967.
Three cheers for the paraclete. 1968.
The survivor. 1969.
A dutiful daughter. 1971.
The chant of Jimmie Blacksmith. 1972.

KENNAN, GEORGE FROST (1904–)

American historian; educated at Princeton and
Berlin; State Department, Foreign Service
(1926–53); Professor of Historical Studies and,
later, Institute of Advanced Study, Princeton
(1956–); recipient of academic awards.

Bibliography
C.B.I.
Gale.

Works

American diplomacy 1900–1950. 1951.

Realities of American foreign policy. 1954.

Russia leaves the war (Soviet–American relations 1917–1920, vol. I; Pulitzer Prize 1957). 1956.

Russia, the atom, and the West. 1958.

The decision to intervene (Soviet–American relations 1917–1920, vol. II). 1958.

On dealing with the Communist world. 1964.

Memoirs: 1925–1950. 1967.

Democracy and the student Left. 1968.

From Prague after Munich: diplomatic papers 1938–9. 1968.

Memoirs: 1950–1963. 1972.

KENNEDY, JOSEPH
(†X. J. KENNEDY) (1929–   )

American poet; educated at Columbia and Paris universities; served in the U.S. Navy (1951–5); after various university posts, currently Assistant Professor of English, Tufts University, Medford, Mass. (1963–   ); recipient of several literary awards; poetry editor, *Paris Review* (1961–4); a contributor to *New York Times Book Review, New Yorker, Poetry*, etc.; represented in numerous anthologies.

Bibliography

C.B.I.

Contemporary poets.

Gale.

Poetry

Nude descending a staircase. 1961.

Growing into love. 1969.

Messages: a thematic anthologized poetry. 1973.

Other Works

An introduction to poetry. 1966.

Emily Dickinson on Southern California. 1973.

Mark Twain's frontier: primary source material for student research and writing (with others). 1973.

KENNELLY, BRENDAN (1936–   )

Irish poet; born in County Derry; educated at Trinity College, Dublin; Associate Professor, Pro-junior Dean and Fellow of Trinity College, Dublin; edited *The Penguin book of Irish verse* (1970).

Bibliography

B.N.B.

Contemporary poets.

Gale.

Poetry

Cast a cold eye (with Rudi Holzapfel). 1959.

The rain, the moon (with Rudi Holzapfel). 1961.

Dream of a black fox. 1968.

Selected poems. 1969.

A drinking cup; poems from the Irish. 1970.

KENNER, WILLIAM HUGH (1923–   )

Canadian critic; educated at Toronto and Yale universities; University of California, Santa Barbara (1950–   ); Professor of English (1958–   ); recipient of several academic honours; his edited work is not listed below.

Bibliography

C.B.I.

Gale.

Works

Paradox in Chesterton. 1947.

The poetry of Ezra Pound. 1951.

Wyndham Lewis, a critical guidebook. 1954.

Dublin's Joyce. 1956.

Gnomon (essays on contemporary literature). 1958.

The art of poetry. 1959.

The invisible poet: T. S. Eliot. 1959.

Samuel Beckett, a critical study. 1961.

Flaubert, Joyce and Beckett: the stoic comedians. 1962.

Studies in change: a book of the short story. 1965.

The counterfeiters. 1968.

The Pound era. 1971.

A readers' guide to Samuel Beckett. 1973.

Bucky: a guided tour of Buckmaster Fuller. 1973.

KENYON, FRANK WILSON (1912–   )

English novelist; born in Preston, Lancs.; educated in Lancashire and New Zealand.

Bibliography

Authors' and writers' who's who. 1971.

B.N.B.

Gale.

Historical Novels

The emperor's lady. 1952.

Royal merry-go-round. 1954.

Emma. 1955.

Marie Antoinette. 1956.

Legacy of hate. 1957.

Without regret. 1957.

Mary of Scotland. 1957.

Never a saint. 1958.

Shadow in the sun. 1959.
The golden years. 1960.
Mrs. Nelly (American title, Mistress Nell). 1961.
The seeds of time. 1961.
I, Eugenia (American title, That Spanish woman). 1962.
Glory and the dream. 1963.
The questing heart. 1964.
The shadow and the substance. 1965.
The absorbing fire. 1966.
Imperial courtesan. 1967.
The naked sword. 1968.
The duke's mistress. 1969.
The consuming flame. 1970.
My brother Napoleon. 1971.
Passionate rebel. 1972.

KENYON, *Professor* JOHN PHILIPPS (1927–)

English historian; educated at King Edward VII School, Sheffield, and Sheffield University; Fellow of Christ's College, Cambridge (1954–62); Professor of History, University of Hull (1962–); a contributor to the *English Historical Review, History today*, etc.; edited *The Stuart constitution: documents with commentary* (1965) and *The Complete Works of Halifax* (1969).

Bibliography
Authors' and writers' who's who. 1971.
B.N.B.
Gale.

Works
Robert Spencer, Earl of Sunderland. 1958.
The Stuarts. 1958.
The nobility in the revolution of 1688. 1964.
The popish plot. 1972.

KERMODE, *Professor* JOHN FRANK (1919–)

English literary scholar; educated at Liverpool University; served in the Royal Navy (1940–6) in the Second World War; lecturer at King's College, Newcastle (1947–9), and at Reading (1949–58); Northcliffe Professor of English, University College, London (1967–); a contributor to the *Review of English Studies, New Statesman*, etc.; edited the Arden edition of *The Tempest* (1954), etc.

Bibliography
Authors' and writers' who's who. 1971.
B.N.B.

Gale.
Who's who. 1973.

Works
Romantic image. 1957.
John Donne. 1957.
The living Milton. 1960.
Wallace Stevens. 1960.
Spenser the allegorist (Warton lecture). 1962.
Puzzles and epiphanies. 1962.
The final plays of William Shakespeare. 1962.
The sense of an ending. 1967.
Continuities. 1968.
Shakespeare, Spenser, Donne. 1971.
Modern essays. 1971.

KEROUAC, JACK (JEAN LOUIS LEBRIS DE KEROUAC) (1922–69)

American novelist and poet; served in the U.S. Navy and Merchant Marine; travelled in Mexico; coined the term "beat generation"; represented in several poetry anthologies.

Bibliography
C.B.I.
Contemporary poets.
Gale.

Novels
The town and the city. 1950.
On the road. 1957.
The Dharma bums. 1958.
The subterraneans. 1958.
Doctor Sax. 1959.
Maggie Cassidy. 1960.
Tristessa. 1960.
Big Sur. 1962.
Visions of Gerard. 1963.
Desolation angels. 1965.
Vanity of Duluoz: the adventurous education of a young man. 1968.
Pic, and The subterraneans. 1971.
Visions of Cody. 1972.

Poetry
Mexico city blues. 1959.
The scripture of the golden eternity. 1960.
Rimbaud. 1960.
Scattered poems. 1971.

Other Works
Lonesome traveler (autobiography). 1960.
Pull my daisy (film script). 1961.

Book of dreams. 1961.
Satori in Paris. 1961.

KERR, JEAN (*née* **COLLINS**) (1923–)
American playwright and novelist; educated at the Marywood College and the Catholic University of America; her unpublished plays include *Jenny kissed me* (with W. Kerr, 1948); a contributor to *Harper's, Saturday Evening Post*, etc.

Bibliography
C.B.I.
Gale.

Novels
Please don't eat the daisies. 1957.
The snake has all the lines. 1960.
Penny Candy. 1970.

Plays
King of hearts (with Eleanor Brooke, produced 1954). 1955.
Goldilocks (with W. Kerr, produced 1948). 1959.
Mary, Mary. 1963.

KESEY, KEN ELTON (1935–)
American novelist; educated at the universities of Oregon and Stanford; worked in a mental hospital; imprisoned for possessing drugs; president of Intrepid Trips, Inc.; author of film script *Intrepid traveller looks for a cool place*; recipient of several awards.

Bibliography
C.B.I.
Contemporary novelists.
Gale.

Novels
One flew over the cuckoo's nest (filmed). 1962.
Sometimes a great notion (filmed 1972). 1964.
Kesey's garage sale. 1973.

KEYES, SIDNEY (1922–43)
English poet; born in Kent; educated at Oxford; served in the Second World War; killed in Tunisia.

Bibliography
B.M. catalogue.
R. N. Currey. Poets of the 1939–1945 war. 1960.
N.C.B.E.L.

Poetry
The iron laurel (Hawthornden Prize 1943). 1942.

The cruel solstice (Hawthornden Prize 1943). 1944.
Collected poems (edited with a memoir by Michael Meyer). 1945.

Other Work
Minos of Crete (plays and stories edited by Michael Meyer). 1948.

KHOSLA, GOSPALDAS D. (1901–)
Born in Lahore and educated at Mussoorie, Cambridge, and Lincoln's Inn, London; joined Indian Civil Service (1926); Chief Justice, Punjab High Court (1959–61); Chairman of inquiry committee on film censorship, national academies, the national library, etc.

Bibliography
C.B.I.
Indian national bibliography 1958–67.
National bibliography of Indian literature 1901–53.

Novel
The last Mughal. n.d.

Short Stories
The horoscope cannot lie. 1962.
The price of a wife. n.d.
A way of loving. n.d.

Other Works
Our judicial system. 1948.
Stern reckoning (Partition of India). 1950.
Himalayan circuit. 1956.
The murder of the Mahatma and other cases from a judge's notebook. 1963.
Grim fairy tales and other facts and fancies. 1967.
A taste of India. n.d.
Indira Gandhi – a portrait. n.d.
Memories and opinions. n.d.

KIELY, BENEDICT (1919–)
Irish novelist; educated at the National University of Ireland; worked for various periodicals (1939–64); Writer-in-residence at Hollins College (1964–5), Oregon University (1965–); a regular contributor to the *New Yorker*.

Bibliography
C.B.I.
Contemporary novelists.
Gale.

Novels
Land without stars. 1946.
Call for a miracle. 1949.
The cards of the gambler. 1953.
Honey seems bitter. 1954.
There was an ancient house. 1955.
The captain with the whiskers. 1960.
A journey to the seven streams (stories). 1963.

Other Works
Counties of contention; study of Irish partition.
 1945.
Poor scholar; study of William Carleton. 1947.
Modern Irish fiction. 1950.

KIM, RICHARD E. (1932–)
American novelist, born in Korea; educated at
Johns Hopkins, Iowa State and Harvard universities; served in the Republic of Korea Army
(1950–4); Assistant Professor of English, University of Massachusetts (1964–   ).

Bibliography
C.B.I.
Contemporary novelists.
Gale.

Novels
The martyred. 1964.
The innocent. 1968.
Lost names. 1970.

KING, FRANCIS HENRY (†FRANK CAULDWELL) (1923–)
English novelist; born in Switzerland; educated at
Shrewsbury and Balliol College, Oxford; British
Council officer, mainly overseas (1949–64); a con-
tributor to *Cornhill, Encounter, London Magazine,
Listener,* etc.; recipient of literary awards; novel
reviewer, *Sunday Telegraph*; his edited work is not
listed below.

Bibliography
Authors' and writers' who's who. 1971.
B.N.B.
Contemporary novelists.
Contemporary poets.
Gale.
Who's who. 1973.

Novels
To the dark tower. 1946.
Never again. 1948.
An air that kills. 1948.

The dividing stream (Somerset Maugham Award
 1952). 1951.
The dark glasses. 1954.
The fire-walkers (as †Frank Cauldwell). 1956.
The widow. 1957.
The man on the rock. 1957.
The custom house. 1961.
The last of the pleasure gardens. 1965.
The waves behind the boat. 1967.
A domestic animal. 1969.
Flights. 1973.

Short Stories
So hurt and humiliated. 1959.
The Japanese umbrella. 1964.
The Brighton Belle. 1968.

Poetry
Rod of incantation. 1952.

Other Work
Japan (with Martin Hurlimann). 1970.

KINNELL, GALWAY (1927–)
American poet; educated at the universities of
Princeton and Rochester; has lived in France,
where he taught at Grenoble University, and Iran;
served in the U.S. Navy (1945–6); Guggenheim
Fellow (1962), etc.; represented in *Contemporary
American poetry* (Penguin, 1962); his translations
from the French are not listed below.

Bibliography
C.B.I.
Contemporary poets.
Gale.

Poetry
What a kingdom it was. 1960.
Flower herding on Mount Monadock. 1964.
Black light. 1966.
Body rags. 1968.
Book of nightmares. 1971.

KINSELLA, THOMAS (1928–)
Irish poet; born in Dublin; civil servant (1946–65);
writer-in-residence (1965–7), then Professor of
English (1967–70), Southern Illinois University,
Carbondale; since 1970, Professor of English,
Temple University, Philadelphia; his translations
and works in Irish are not listed below.

Bibliography
B.N.B.
Contemporary poets.
Gale.

Poetry
Poems. 1956.
Another September. 1958.
Moralities. 1960.
Poems and translations. 1961.
Downstream. 1962.
Wormwood. 1966.
Nightwalker. 1968.
Poems by T. Kinsella, Douglas Livingstone and
    Anne Sexton. 1968.
Nightmare and other poems. 1968.
Finistere. 1972.
Notes from the land of the dead. 1973.
Selected poems 1958–1968. 1973.
Vertical man. 1973.
The good fight. 1973.

**KIRKUP, *Sir* JAMES (†TERAHATA
JUN, †TSUYUKI SHIGERA,
†ANDREW JAMES)** (1923–)
English poet and travel writer; born in South
Shields; educated Durham University; first Gregory Poetry Fellow, Leeds University (1950–2);
Professor of English, Salamanca University
(1957–8), Tohoku University, Sendai, Japan
(1959–61), Nagoya University (1969–); his
translations and unpublished radio plays are not
listed below; edited anthologies *The shepherding
winds* (1969), *Songs and dreams* (1970).

Bibliography
B.N.B.
Contemporary poets.
Gale.
N.C.B.E.L.
Who's who. 1973.

Novels
The love of others. 1962.
Insect summer (for children). 1971.

Poetry
The cosmic shape (with Ross Nichols). 1946.
The drowned sailor. 1947.
The creation. 1948.
The submerged village. 1951.
A correct compassion. 1952.
A spring journey. 1954.
The descent into the cave. 1957.

The prodigal son. 1960.
Refusal to conform. 1963.
Paper windows. 1968.
Japan physical. 1969.
White shadows, black shadows: poems of peace
    and war. 1970.
Broad daylight. 1971.
The body servant: poems of exile. 1971.
A Bewick bestiary. 1971.

Plays
Upon this rock. 1955.
The triumph of harmony. 1955.
The true mystery of the Nativity. 1957.
The true mystery of the Passion (adaptation from
    the French). 1962.

Autobiography
The only child. 1957.
Sorrows, passions and alarms. 1959.

Travel
These horned islands; a journal of Japan. 1962.
Tropic temper; a memory of Malaya. 1963.
England, now. 1964.
Japan industrial, vols. I and II. 1964–5.
Tokyo. 1966.
Frankly speaking. 1966.
Japan, now. 1966.
Bangkok. 1968.
Filipinescas. 1968.
One man's Russia. 1968.
Streets of Asia. 1969.
Hong Kong and Macao. 1970.
Japan behind the fan. 1970.

KISSINGER, HENRY ALFRED
(1923–)
American Secretary of State (1973–6); born in
Germany; educated at Harvard University; held
various posts in the university; Director, Harvard
international seminar; Director, Harvard Defense
Studies Program (1958–71); consultant to various
government agencies; Nobel Peace Prize (1973); a
contributor to *Harper's Magazine, New York Times
Sunday Magazine*, etc.

Bibliography
C.B.I.
Who's who. 1973.

Works
A world restored: Castlereagh, Metternich and the
    restoration of peace. 1957.

Nuclear weapons and foreign policy. 1957.
The necessity for choice: prospects of American foreign policy. 1961.
The troubled partnership. 1965.
Problems of national strategy; a book of readings. 1965.
American foreign policy. 1969.

KIZER, CAROLYN (1925–)

American poet, translator and teacher; born in Washington; founder editor of *Poetry Northwest*, Seattle; poet-in-residence in Pakistan for the U.S. State Department; Director of the literary programme of the national endowment for the arts; represented in *Anthology of Modern Poetry*, Hutchinson (1963), etc.; a contributor to *Sewanee Review*, *New Yorker*, *Botteghe Oscure*, *Spectator*, etc.

Bibliography
C.B.I.
Contemporary poets.

Poetry
The ungrateful garden. 1961.
Knock upon silence. 1965.
Midnight was my cry. 1971.

KIZERMAN, RUDOLPH (1934–)

Caribbean novelist and playwright; born in Barbados; studied medicine in England; became an actor.

Bibliography
B.N.B.

Novel
Stand up in the world. 1968.

KLEIN, ABRAIIAM MOSES (1909–72)

Canadian-Jewish poet, novelist and Talmudic scholar; born in Montreal; educated at McGill and Montreal universities; called to the Bar (1933); retired from legal practice (1954); edited the *Canadian Zionist* (1936–7); contributed poetry to *Canadian Forum*, *Menorah Journal*, etc.

Bibliography
Canadiana.
C.B.I.
Contemporary poets.
Gale.

Novel
The second scroll. 1951.

Poetry
Hath not a Jew. 1940.
Poems. 1944.
The Hitleriad. 1944.
The rocking chair and other poems (Governor General's Award 1949). 1948.
Of Jewish music, ancient and modern (translation from Yiddish). 1952.

KLINCK, CARL FREDERICK (1908–)

Canadian scholar; born in Ontario; educated at the University of Western Ontario; head of English Department (1948–); his edited work includes *Essays by and about Dunlop* (1958), *Canadian Writers*, with Brandon Conron and Guy Sylvestre (1964), and the *Literary History of Canada* (1965).

Bibliography
Canadiana.
C.B.I.

Works
Wilfrid Campbell; a study in late provincial Victorianism. 1942.
Edwin J. Pratt; the man and his poetry. 1947.

KNEBEL, FLETCHER (1911–)

American novelist and journalist; educated at Miami University; served in the U.S. Navy during the Second World War; journalist (1934–71); recipient of several awards and academic honours.

Bibliography
C.B.I.
Contemporary novelists.

Novels
Seven days in May (filmed 1963) 1962.
Convention. 1964.
Night of Camp David. 1965.
The Zinzin road. 1966.
Vanished. 1968.
Trespass. 1969.
Exit nine. 1972.
Dark horse. 1972.

Other Work
No high ground (with Charles Bailey). 1960.

KNOWLES, JOHN (1926–)

American novelist; educated at Yale University; freelance writer (1952–6); associate editor, *Holiday* magazine (1956–60); recipient of several awards.

Bibliography
C.B.I.
Contemporary novelists.

Novels
A separate peace. 1959.
Morning in Antibes. 1962.
Indian summer. 1966.
Phineas: 6 stories. 1968.
The paragon. 1971.

Other Work
Double vision: American thoughts abroad. 1964.

KNOWLES, MICHAEL CLIVE DAVID
(1896–1974)
English priest and medieval historian of the
church; educated at Downside and Christ's Col-
lege, Cambridge; ordained priest (1922); Professor
of Medieval History, Cambridge (1947–54);
Regius Professor of Modern History (1954–63);
awarded various honorary degrees; editor of
Downside Review (1930–4); President of the Royal
Historical Society (1956–60); a contributor to
*English Historical Review, Journal of Ecclesiastical
History*, etc.

Bibliography
B.N.B.
Gale.
Who's who. 1973.

Works
Religious houses of medieval England (revised,
  with Neville Hadcock, 1953). 1940.
The monastic order of England. 1940.
Prospects of medieval studies: inaugural lecture.
  1947.
The religious orders of England, 3 vols. 1948–59.
The monastic orders of Lefranc. 1951.
The episcopal colleagues of Archbishop Becket.
  1951.
Monastic sites from the air (with J. K. St. Joseph).
  1952.
Charterhouse (with W. F. Grimes). 1954.
Cistercians and Cluniacs. 1955.
The historian and character. 1955.
Cardinal Gasquet as historian. 1957.
The historical context of the philosophical works
  of St. Thomas Aquinas. 1958.
Lord Macaulay 1800–1859. 1960.
The English mystical tradition. 1961.
Saints and scholars. 1962.
The evolution of medieval thought. 1962.

Great historical enterprises and problems in
  monastic history. 1963.
From Pachomius to Ignatius. 1966.
What is mysticism? 1967.
Christian monasticism. 1969.
Thomas Becket. 1970.
Grace, the life of the soul. 1970.
Heads of religious houses 940–1216 (with
  C. N. L. Brooke and V. London). 1972.

KOCH, KENNETH (1925–)
American poet and playwright; born in Cincinnati;
educated at Harvard and Columbia universities;
served in the U.S. Army (1943–6) during the Second World War; Director, Poetry Workshop
(1958–); currently Associate Professor of English and Comparative Literature (1966–); a contributor to *Art and Literature, Portfolio, Poetry, Evergreen Review*, etc.; represented in various
anthologies.

Bibliography
C.B.I.
Contemporary poets.
Gale.

Poetry
Poems. 1953.
Ko, or, A season on earth. 1959.
Permanently. 1960.
Guinevere, or, The death of the kangaroo. 1961.
Thank you and other poems. 1962.
Poems from 1952 and 1953. 1968.
When the sun tries to go on. 1969.
Sleeping with women. 1969.
The pleasures of peace and other poems. 1969.
Rose, where did you get that red? 1973.

Plays
Bertha and other plays. 1966.
A change of heart: films, plays, and other dramatic
  works. 1973.

KONADU, ASARE (1932–)
Ghanaian novelist; educated at the Abuawaka State
College, Ashanti; Ghana Information Service
(1951–) and reporter for government newspaper
and broadcasting services; studied journalism in
London and Strasbourg; Ghana News Agency;
full-time writer and researcher into local folk customs (1963–); started his own publishing firm,
Akowno Publications.

Bibliography
B.N.B.
Ghana national bibliography.

Novels
A woman in her prime. 1967.
Ordained by the oracle. 1969.

KOPIT, ARTHUR LEE (1937–)
American playwright; born in New York; educated at Harvard; lives in Paris; recipient of several
awards; only his published plays are listed below.

Bibliography
C.B.I.
Contemporary dramatists.

Plays
Oh Dad, poor Dad, Mama's hung you in the closet
    and I'm feelin' so sad (staged 1960). 1960.
The day the whores came out to play tennis and
    other plays (with Sing to me through open win-
    dows, Chamber music, The conquest of Ever-
    est, The hero, and The questioning of Nick).
    1965.
Indians (staged 1968). 1969.

KOPS, BERNARD (1926–)
English-Jewish poet and playwright; resident
dramatist, Bristol Old Vic (1959); lectured for
P.E.N. and the British Council; broadcast for the
B.B.C.; television plays include *I want to go home*
and *Stray cats and empty bottles*.

Bibliography
B.M. catalogue.
B.N.B.
Contemporary poets.
Gale.
Who's who. 1973.

Novels
Awake for mourning. 1958.
Motorbike. 1962.
Yes from No-man's-land. 1965.
The dissent of Dominick Shapiro. 1966.
By the waters of Whitechapel. 1969.
The passionate past of Gloria Gaye. 1972.

Poetry
Poems. 1955.
Poems and songs. 1958.
An anemone for Antigone. 1959.
Erica, I want to read you something. 1967.

For the record. 1971.
Settle down, Simon Katz. 1973.

Plays
David, it is getting dark (staged 1970). 1959.
The Hamlet of Stepney Green. 1959.
The dream of Peter Mann. 1960.
Enter Solly Gold. 1961.
Four plays (The Hamlet of Stepney Green, Enter
    Solly Gold, Home sweet honeycomb, The
    Lemmings). 1964.

Autobiography
The world is a wedding. 1963.

KORIYAMA, NAOSHI (1926–)
Japanese poet; educated at Okinawa Foreign Lan-
guage School and New York State College of
Teachers; Professor of English, Tokyo University
(1961–); a Chaucerian scholar; his work on
Chaucer is not separately published.

Bibliography
C.B.I.
Contemporary poets.

Poetry
Coral reefs. 1957.
Plum time in Japan and other poems. 1959.
Songs from Sagamihara. 1967.

KOSINSKI, JERZY NIKODEM
(†JOSEPH NOVAK) (1933–)
Polish-born American novelist and writer; edu-
cated at the universities of Lodz and Columbia;
Associate Professor, Polish Academy of Sciences,
Warsaw (1955–7); various American university
appointments (1968–); recipient of various
awards and prizes.

Bibliography
C.B.I.
Contemporary novelists.
Gale.

Novels
The painted bird. 1965.
Steps. 1968.
Being there. 1971.
The devil tree. 1973.

Other Works
The future is ours, comrade (as †Joseph Novak).
    1960.

No third path (as †Joseph Novak). 1962.
Notes of the author on The painted bird, 1965. 1965.
The art of the self; essays à propos "Steps". 1968.
The time of life; the time of art (essays, in Dutch). 1970.

KRAMM, JOSEPH (1907–)

American playwright and actor; born in Philadelphia; educated at the University of Pennsylvania; became an actor (1928–) and a journalist on the staff of the Philadelphia *Record* (1929–); served in the army during the Second World War (1943–5); only his published play is listed below.

Bibliography
C.B.I.

Play
The shrike (Pulitzer Prize 1952). 1952.

KREISEL, HENRY (1922–)

Austrian-born Canadian novelist and short-story writer; born in Vienna; educated there and at the University of Toronto; escaped to England (1938) and sent to Canada as an internee (1940); Head of the English Department, University of Alberta; a contributor to many Canadian journals; his edited work is not listed below.

Bibliography
Canadiana.
C.B.I.

Novels
The rich man. 1948.
The betrayal. 1964.

KRIEGER, MURRAY (1923–)

American critic; born in Newark; educated at Rutgers, Chicago and Ohio State universities; served in the U.S. Army (1942–6) during the Second World War; after various university posts, Professor of English, University of California (1967–); a contributor to critical and scholarly journals; his edited works and those to which he has contributed are not listed below.

Bibliography
C.B.I.
Gale.

Works
The new apologists for poetry. 1956.
The tragic vision. 1960.
A window to criticism: Shakespeare's sonnets and modern poetics. 1964.
The play and place of criticism. 1967.
The classic vision: the retreat from extremity in modern literature. 1971.

KRIGE, UYS (1910–)

South African, Afrikaaner novelist; born in Cape Province; educated at Stellenbosch University; lived in France and Spain (1931–6); was correspondent in Egypt and Abyssinia during the Second World War; p.o.w. in Italy (1941–3), when he escaped; returned to South Africa (1946); neither his edited works nor his more numerous works in Afrikaans are listed below.

Bibliography
Contemporary novelists.

Novels
The dream and the desert. 1953.
Orphan of the desert. 1967.

Other Work
The way out; Italian intermezzo. 1946.

KROETSCH, ROBERT (1927–)

Canadian novelist; born in Alberta; educated at Alberta and McGill universities; worked for a riverboat company (1948–50); served in the U.S. Air Force (1951–4); Assistant, later Associate Professor of English, New York State University (1961–); a contributor to *MacLean's Magazine, Canadian Forum*, etc.

Bibliography
Canadiana.
C.B.I.
Gale.

Novels
But we are exiles. 1966.
The words of my roaring. 1966.
Alberta. 1969.
The studhorse man. 1970.

Criticism
Creation (with others). 1971.

L

LA GUMA, ALEX (1923–)
South African poet, novelist and journalist; formerly a journalist in South Africa and a member of the Cape Town Council; charged with high treason with 156 South Africans; placed under house arrest (1963); represented in *Black Orpheus, African Poetry* (C.U.P.) and numerous anthologies of African poetry.

Bibliography
Contemporary novelists.
Contemporary poets.
Jahn and Dressler.
Zell and Silver.

Novels
A walk in the night (stories). 1962.
And a threefold cord. 1964.
The stone country. 1967.
In the fog of the season's end. 1972.

Poetry
New voices from South Africa (with others). 1963.

LAING, RONALD DAVID (1927–)
Scottish psychiatrist; educated at Glasgow University; Tavistock Clinic (1956–60); Tavistock Institute of Human Relations (1960–), etc.

Bibliography
B.N.B.
Who's who. 1973.

Works
The divided self. 1960.
The self and others. 1961.
Reason and violence (with D. G. Cooper). 1964.
Sanity, madness and the family (joint author, vol. I of Families of schizophrenics). 1965.
Interspersal perception (with others). 1966.
The politics of experience and The bird of paradise. 1967.
Knots. 1970.
The politics of the family. 1971.

LAL, P. (1929–)
Indian poet, translator and editor; educated at Calcutta University; Professor of English, Calcutta University (1967–); founder of Writers' Workshop, Calcutta; Editor, *Writers' Workshop Miscellany*; recipient of awards; a contributor to *Illustrated Weekly of India* and other Indian journals; represented in various anthologies; his large output of translations and edited work is not listed below.

Bibliography
Contemporary poets.
Gale.
Indian national bibliography 1958–67.

Poetry
The parrot's death and other poems. 1960.
Love is the first. 1963.
"Charge!" they said. 1966.
Draupadi and Jayadratha and other poems. 1967.
Yakshi from Didarganj and other poems. 1969.
Creations and transcreations. 1969.

Other Works
The art of the essay. 1950.
The concept of an Indian literature. 1967.

LAMANTIA, PHILIP (1927–)
American poet; born in San Francisco; assistant editor *View* magazine (1944); semi-nomad in the U.S.A., Mexico, Tangier, Paris, etc. (1952–68); a contributor to *View*, etc.; represented in various anthologies.

Bibliography
C.B.I.
Contemporary poets.

Poetry
Erotic poems. 1946.
Ekstasis. 1959.
Destroyed works. 1962.
Touch of the marvelous. 1966.
Selected poems 1943–1966. 1969.
The blood of the air. 1970.

LAMBERT, ERIC (†FRANK BRENNAND, †GEORGE KAY)
(1921–66)
English-born Australian novelist and writer; edu-

177

cated at the universities of Sydney and Oxford; served in the Australian Army (1940–6) during the Second World War; biologist (1946–9); professional cricketer, later coach in England; full-time writer (1949–66); author of various television plays and film scripts.

Bibliography
Annals of Australian literature.
B.N.B.
Gale.

Novels
The twenty thousand thieves. 1952.
The veterans. 1954.
The bright stars. 1954.
Watermen. 1956.
The dark backward. 1958.
Glory thrown in. 1959.
The rehabilitated man. 1960.
Ballarat. 1962.
The drip dry man. 1963.
Dolphin. 1963.
A short walk to the stars. 1964.
Kelly. 1964.
The tender conspiracy. 1965.

Other Works as †Frank Brennand
Sink the Bismarck. 1960.
Oscar Wilde. 1961.
North to Alaska. 1962.
Winston S. Churchill. 1965.

Other Work as †George Kay
The siege of Pinchgut. 1964.

LAMBERT, GAVIN (1924–)
English novelist; educated at Cheltenham and Magdalen College, Oxford; short-story writer (1947–50); editor of *Sight and sound* (1950–6); free-lance writer in Hollywood (1957–); film scripts include *Sons and lovers* (1960); a contributor to the *Observer, Sunday Times, New Statesman, Harper's Bazaar*, etc.

Bibliography
B.N.B.
Gale.

Novels
The slide area. 1960.
The Roman spring of Mrs. Stone (filmed 1961). 1961.
Inside Daisy Clover (filmed 1965). 1965.

Norman's letter. 1966.
A case for the angels. 1968.
Goodbye people. 1971.
On Cukor. 1972.

LAMMING, GEORGE (1927–)
Caribbean novelist and poet; born and educated in Barbados; taught in Trinidad and Venezuela; emigrated to England (1950); has travelled widely; B.B.C. West Indies Service (1951–); member of the Faculty of the University of West Indies, Jamaica (1968–); recipient of various literary awards; represented in various anthologies including *Caribbean voices* (1966), *Caribbean literature* (1966) and *Caribbean verse* (1967).

Bibliography
B.N.B.
Contemporary novelists.
Contemporary poets.
Jahn and Dressler.

Novels
In the castle of my skin (Somerset Maugham Award 1957). 1953.
The emigrants. 1954.
Of age and innocence. 1958.
Season of adventure. 1960.
Water with berries. 1971.
Natives of my person. 1972.

Other Work
The pleasures of exile. 1960.

LANNING, GEORGE WILLIAM, Jr. (1925–)
American novelist and short-story writer; educated at Kenyon College; assistant, later acting, editor, *Kenyon Review* (1960–5); lecturer in novel and short-story writing; *Kenyon Review* Fellow in fiction (1954–5); represented in several volumes of short stories; a contributor to *Kenyon Review, Sewanee Review*, etc.

Bibliography
C.B.I.
Gale.

Novel and Short Story
This happy rural seat. 1953.

Other Work
Technique in fiction (with Robie Macauley). 1964.

LARKIN, OLIVER ATERMAN
(1896–1970)
American art historian; educated at Harvard University; assistant at Harvard (1921–4); served in the U.S. Army during the First World War (1918–19); Smith College (1924–64), becoming Professor of Art; a contributor to *New York Times*, etc.

Bibliography
C.B.I.
Gale.

Works
Art and life in America (Pulitzer Prize 1950). 1949.
Samuel F. B. Morse and American democratic art. 1954.
Daumier: man of his time. 1966.

LARKIN, PHILIP ARTHUR (1922–)
English poet and novelist; educated St. John's College, Oxford; Librarian, University of Hull (1955–); Visiting Fellow of All Souls, Oxford (1970–1); awarded several academic honours; jazz feature writer, *Daily Telegraph* (1961–); edited the *Oxford book of twentieth century verse* (1963).

Bibliography
B.N.B.
Contemporary poets.
Gale.
Who's who. 1973.

Novels
Jill. 1946. Revised edition. 1964.
A girl in winter. 1947.

Poetry
The north ship. 1945.
The less deceived. 1955.
The Whitsun weddings. 1964.

Essay
All what jazz? 1970.

LARRABEE, ERIC (1922–)
American historian; educated at Harvard University; served in the U.S. Army during the Second World War; associate editor of *Harper's Magazine* (1946–58); editor of *Heritage*, New York (1958–61); managing editor, *Horizon Magazine* (1961–3); editorial consultant, Doubleday Inc. (1964–); a regular contributor to *Harper's*, etc.; his edited work is not listed below.

Bibliography
C.B.I.
Gale.

Work
The self-conscious society. 1960.

LASKI, MARGHANITA (*Mrs.* J. E. HOWARD) (1917–)
English novelist, author, journalist and broadcaster; educated at Somerville College, Oxford; a contributor to *The Times*, etc.; her edited works are not listed below.

Bibliography
Authors' and writers' who's who. 1971.
B.N.B.
Who's who. 1973.

Novels
Love on the supertax. 1944.
The patchwork book. 1946.
To bed with grand music (anonymous novel). 1946.
Little boy lost. 1949.
The village. 1952.
The Victorian chaise-longue. 1953.

Other Works
Tory heaven. 1948.
Mrs. Ewing, Mrs. Molesworth, Mrs. Hodgson Burnett. 1950.
The offshore island (play). 1959.
Ecstasy: a study of some secular and religious experiences. 1961.
Domestic life in Edwardian England. 1964.
The secular responsibility. 1967.
Jane Austen and her world. 1969.
George Eliot and her world. 1973.

LAUMER, JOHN KEITH (1925–)
American science fiction writer of Swedish parentage; educated at universities of Stockholm and Illinois; served in the U.S. Forces (1943–56); U.S. foreign service in Rangoon (1956–8); U.S. Air Force (1960–); a contributor to science fiction magazines and aero modelling magazines.

Bibliography
C.B.I.
Gale.

Novels
Worlds of the imperium. 1962.

A trace of memory. 1963.
Envoy to new worlds. 1963.
The great time machine hoax. 1964.
A plague of demons. 1965.
Galactic diplomat. 1965.
Embassy. 1965.
The other side of time. 1965.
Earthblood (with R. G. Brown). 1966.
Relief's war. 1966.
Catastrophe planet. 1966.
Axe and dragon. 1967.
Galactic odyssey. 1968.
The monitors. 1968.
Relief and the warlords. 1968.
Nine (stories). 1968.
The other sky. 1968.
The long twilight. 1969.
It's a mad, mad galaxy. 1969.
The day before forever. 1969.
Hierarchies. 1970.
World shuffler. 1970.
The time trap. 1970.
House in November. 1971.
Dinosaur beach. 1971.
Once there was a giant. 1971.
Relief's ransom. 1971.
The star treasure. 1971.
The infinite cage. 1972.
The wig show. 1972.
Night of delusions. 1972.
Assignment to nowhere. 1972.
The shape changer. 1972.
The glory game. 1973.

Other Work
How to design and build flying models. 1960.

**LAURENCE, JEAN MARGARET (*née*
WEMYS)** (1926–)
Canadian novelist; educated at the University of
Manitoba; spent two years in the Haud desert of
Somaliland with her husband; settled in England;
has contributed stories to the *Saturday Evening Post,
Queen's Quarterly*, etc.; edited *A tree for poverty*
(Somali poetry and prose) (1954).

Bibliography
Authors' and writers' who's who. 1971.
B.N.B.
Canadiana.
Contemporary novelists.
Gale.
Clara Thomas, Margaret Laurence, Toronto. 1969.

Novels
This side Jordan. 1960.
The tomorrow tamer and other stories. 1963.
The stone angel. 1964.
A jest of God (Governor General's Award 1967;
    filmed as Rachel, Rachel). 1966.
The fire dwellers. 1969.
A bird in the house (stories). 1970.
Jason's quest (for children). 1970.

Other Works
The prophet's camel bell (American title, New
    wind in a dry land). 1963.
Long drums and cannons; essays on African litera-
    ture. 1968.

LAURENTS, ARTHUR (1920–)
American playwright; educated at Cornell University; served in the U.S. Army during the Second World War (1941–5); radio, stage and screen
writer (1939–); recipient of various radio and
literary awards; film scripts include *The snake pit*
(1948), *Rope* (1948), *Anastasia* (1956); represented
in many anthologies of stage and radio plays.

Bibliography
C.B.I.
Contemporary dramatists.
Gale.

Novel
The way we were (filmed 1972). 1972.

Plays
Home of the brave (filmed 1949). 1946.
The bird cage. 1950.
The time of the cuckoo (staged 1952, filmed 1955).
    1953.
A clearing in the woods. 1957.
West Side story (musical by Leonard Bernstein,
    staged 1957, filmed 1959). 1958.
Gypsy (music by Jule Styne, filmed 1962). 1960.
Invitation to a march (staged 1960). 1961.
Anyone can whistle (libretto, musical staged 1964).
    1965.
Do I hear a waltz? (music by Richard Rodgers,
    staged 1965). 1966.

**LAVIN, MARY (*Mrs.* MICHAEL
MACDONALD SCOTT)** (1912–)
Irish-American short-story writer and novelist;
born in the United States and educated there and in
Ireland; her first husband, William Walsh, died
(1954) and she remarried; a full-time writer.

Bibliography
Authors' and writers' who's who. 1971.
B.N.B.
Contemporary novelists.
Gale.
Who's who. 1973.

Novels
The house in Clewe Street. 1945.
Mary O'Grady. 1950.
A likely story (for children). 1957.
The second best children in the world (for children). 1972.

Short Stories
Tales from Bective Bridge (James Tait Black Prize 1944). 1942.
The long ago. 1944.
The Becker wives. 1946.
At Sallygap. 1947.
A single lady. 1951.
Patriot son. 1956.
Selected stories. 1959.
The great wave. 1961.
Stories of Mary Lavin. 1964.
In the middle of the fields. 1967.
Happiness. 1969.
Collected stories. 1971.
A memory and other stories. 1972.

LAWLER, RAY (1921–)
Australian playwright; his unpublished plays are *The unshaven cheek* (1963) and *A breach in the wall* (1967).

Bibliography
Annals of Australian literature.
Australian national bibliography.

Plays
The summer of the seventeenth doll. 1957.
The Piccadilly bushman. 1961.

LAYTON, IRVING PETER (né LAZAROVITCH) (1912–)
Rumanian-Jewish-born Canadian poet; his family emigrated to Canada (1913); educated at McGill University; served in the Canadian artillery in the Second World War (1942–3); edited *Preview* (1945–51); lecturer at the Jewish Public Library, Quebec (1943–58); taught in Montreal (1945–60); Lecturer in English, Sir George Williams University (1949–); poet-in-residence (1965–); writer-in-residence, University of Guelph; Pro-

fessor of English Literature, York University; a contributor to *Canadian Forum, Tamarack Review, Encounter, Poetry*, etc.; his anthologies include *Canadian poems 1850–1952* with Dudek and Souster (1952), *Love where the nights are long* (1962); recipient of various awards.

Bibliography
Authors' and writers' who's who. 1971.
B.N.B.
Canadiana.
Contemporary poets.
Gale.

Poetry
Here and now. 1945.
Now is the place (includes short stories). 1948.
The black huntsmen. 1951.
Love the conqueror worm. 1952.
In the midst of my fever. 1954.
The long peashooter. 1954.
The cold green element. 1955.
The blue propellor. 1955.
Bull calf and other poems. 1956.
The improved binoculars. 1957.
A laughter in the mind. 1958.
A red carpet for the sun (collected poems) (Governor General's Award 1960). 1959.
The swinging flesh (includes short stories). 1961.
Balls for a one-armed juggler. 1963.
The laughing rooster. 1964.
Collected poems. 1965.
Periods of the moon. 1967.
The shattered plinths. 1968.
The whole bloody bird. 1969.
Nail polish. 1971.

LEARY, LEWIS GASTON (1906–)
American critic and scholar; educated at Vermont and Columbia universities; instructor at Beirut University, Lebanon (1928–31); Associate Professor, Miami University (1935–41); served in secret intelligence during the Second World War (1942–5); Professor of English, Columbia University (1951–); awarded LL.D., Vermont University (1963); his numerous edited works are not listed below.

Bibliography
C.B.I.
Gale.

Works
The rascal Freneau. 1941.

The literary career of Nathaniel Tucker, 1750–1807. 1951.
Articles on American literature, 1900–1950. 1954.
Mark Twain. 1960.
John Greenleaf Whittier. 1961.
Washington Irving. 1963.
Norman Douglas. 1968.
Southern excursions: essays on Mark Twain. 1971.
William Faulkner of Yoknapatawpha County. 1973.

LEARY, PARIS (1931–)

American poet and novelist; educated at St. Edmund's College, Oxford; Fulbright Fellow in English Literature, Leicester University (1964–); represented in several anthologies; his play, *A rushing of wings*, produced 1960; a contributor to the *New Yorker, Hudson Review*, etc.

Bibliography
C.B.I.
Contemporary poets.
Gale.

Novel
The innocent curate. 1963.

Poetry
Views of the Oxford colleges and other poems. 1960.

Other Work
Jack Sprat cookbook. 1965.

LEASOR, THOMAS JAMES (1923–)

English novelist and journalist; educated at Oriel College, Oxford; served in the army (1942–6) during the Second World War; on the staff of the *Daily Express* (1948–55); adviser on women's magazines to George Newnes, publishers (1955–); contributor to television and many popular magazines and newspapers.

Bibliography
B.N.B.
Gale.
Who's who. 1973.

Novels
Not such a bad day. 1946.
The strong delusion. 1951.
The Monday story. 1951.
N.T.R.—nothing to report. 1955.

Passport to oblivion (filmed as Where the spies are, 1965). 1964.
Spylight. 1965.
Passport to peril. 1966.
Passport in suspense. 1967.
Passport for a pilgrim. 1968.
They don't make them like that any more. 1969.
A week of love. 1969.
Never had a spanner on her. 1970.
Love-all. 1971.
Follow the drum. 1972.
Host of extras. 1973.
Mandarin gold. 1973.

Other Works
Author by profession. 1951.
The sergeant major. 1954.
Wheels of fortune. 1954.
The red fort. 1956.
The one that got away (with Kendal Bart). 1956.
The millionth chance. 1957.
War at the top. 1959.
Conspiracy of silence (with Peter Eton). 1959.
Plague and the fire. 1961.
Rudolf Hess: the uninvited envoy. 1962.
Singapore: the battle that changed the world. 1968.

†LE CARRÉ, JOHN (DAVID JOHN MOORE CORNWELL) (1931–)

English novelist; educated at Sherborne, Berne University and Lincoln College, Oxford; taught at Eton (1956–8); Foreign Office (1960–4); full-time writer since 1964; recipient of several literary awards.

Bibliography
Authors' and writers' who's who. 1971.
B.N.B.
Gale.
Who's who. 1973.

Novels
Call for the dead (filmed as The deadly affair, 1967). 1961.
A murder of quality. 1962.
The spy who came in from the cold (filmed 1964). 1963.
The looking-glass war (filmed 1969). 1965.
A small town in Germany. 1968.
The naïve and sentimental lover. 1971.

LEE, LAURIE (1914–)

English poet and author; born in Gloucestershire;

travelled in the Mediterranean (1935–9); documentary film scriptwriter (1940–3); Ministry of Information (1944–5).

Bibliography
Authors' and writers' who's who. 1971.
B.N.B.
Contemporary poets. 1970.
N.C.B.E.L.
Who's who. 1973.

Poetry
The sun my monument. 1944.
The bloom of candles. 1947.
My many-coated man. 1955.
Selected poems. 1960.
The first-born. 1964.

Autobiography
Cider with Rosie. 1959.
As I walked out one midsummer morning. 1969.

Other Works
Land at war. 1945.
We made a film in Cyprus (with Ralph Keene). 1947.
The voyage of Magellan (verse play for radio). 1948.
A rose for winter (travel in Spain). 1955.

LEE, NELLIE HARPER (1926–)
American novelist; educated at the universities of Alabama and Oxford; airline reservation clerk in the 1950s; since then has been a full-time writer; a contributor to *Vogue* and other journals.

Bibliography
C.B.I.
Gale.

Novel
To kill a mockingbird (Pulitzer Prize 1961, filmed 1962). 1960.

LEECH, CLIFFORD (1909–)
English scholar; educated at Queen Mary College, London; Lecturer at Swansea (1933–6) and Durham (1936–50); seconded to the British Council in the Middle East (1941–5); Professor of English, Durham University (1954–63); Professor of English at Toronto University (1963–); Fellow of the Royal Society of Canada (1969); a contributor to learned journals; general editor of the

Revels Plays (1958–); his other edited work including various *Festschriften* is not listed below.

Bibliography
Authors' and writers' who's who. 1971.
B.N.B.
Gale.
Who's who. 1973.

Works
Shakespeare's tragedies and other studies in seventeenth-century drama. 1950.
John Webster: a critical study. 1951.
A school of criticism (inaugural lecture). 1955.
John Ford and the drama of his time. 1957.
The John Fletcher plays. 1962.
Shakespeare: the chronicles. 1962.
O'Neill. 1963.
Webster: the Duchess of Malfi. 1963.
John Ford. 1964.
Twelfth Night and Shakespearean comedy. 1965.
Comedy in the grand style. 1966.
Tragedy (the critical idiom). 1969.
The dramatist's experience with other essays in literary theory. 1970.

LEEMING, OWEN ALFRED (1930–)
New Zealand poet and playwright; born in Christchurch, New Zealand; educated at the University of Canterbury; studied music in Paris; B.B.C. producer in London (1956–62); New Zealand television producer (1962–4); Unesco (1965–6); full-time writer (1967–); lives in France; represented in various anthologies; a contributor to the *London Magazine*, etc.; his plays have not been published.

Bibliography
Contemporary poets.
N.Z. national bibliography.

Poetry
Venus is setting. 1970.

LEJEUNE, CAROLINE ALICE (*Mrs*. E. ROFFE THOMPSON) (d. 1973)
English film critic, broadcaster and television scriptwriter; born in Manchester; educated at Manchester University; Hon. D.Litt., Durham; *Observer* film critic (1928–60); adapted for television Sherlock Holmes series, the *Three hostages*, etc., and wrote *Vicky's first ball* (play, with Anthony Lejeune).

Bibliography
Authors' and writers' who's who. 1971.
B.N.B.
Who's who. 1973.

Works
Chestnuts in her lap. 1947.
Three score and ten (completion of Angela Thir-
kell's posthumous novel). 1961.
Enjoy making a garden out of nothing. 1964.
Thank you for having me. 1964.

LENNON, JOHN (1940–)
English pop star and writer; born in Liverpool;
member of the Beatles group.

Bibliography
Authors' and writers' who's who. 1971.
B.N.B.

Works
In his own write. 1964.
A Spaniard in the works. 1965.
The Penguin John Lennon. 1966.

LEPAN, DOUGLAS VALENTINE
(1914–)
Canadian poet; born in Toronto; educated at
Toronto, Oxford and Harvard universities; served
in the artillery in the Second World War; after a
distinguished career in government service he was
appointed Professor of English, Queen's University (1959–64); Principal of University College,
Toronto (1964–).

Bibliography
Canadiana.
C.B.I.
Contemporary poets.

Poetry
The wounded prince and other poems. 1948.
The net and the sword (Governor General's Award
1954). 1953.

Novel
The deserter (Governor General's Award 1965).
1964.

LESSING, DORIS (*née* TAYLOR)
(1919–)
South African novelist; born in Persia; lived in
Southern Rhodesia (1924–49); only her separately
published plays are listed below.

Bibliography
Authors' and writers' who's who. 1971.
B.N.B.
Contemporary novelists.
Gale.
Michael Sharpe. Doris Lessing. 1973.
Who's who. 1973.

Novels
The grass is singing. 1950.
This was the old chief's country. 1951.
Children of violence (5 vols. Martha Quest, 1952,
A proper marriage, 1954, A ripple from the
storm, 1958, Landlocked, 1965, The four-gated
city, 1969). 1952–69.
Five short novels (Somerset Maugham Award
1954). 1953.
Retreat to innocence. 1956.
The habit of loving. 1957.
The golden notebook. 1962.
A man and two women (short stories). 1963.
African stories. 1964.
Winter in July (first published in African stories).
1966.
Briefing for a descent into hell. 1971.
The story of a non-marrying man. 1972.
The summer before the dark. 1973.

Poetry
Fourteen poems. 1959.

Play
Play with a tiger. 1962.

Other Works
Going home. 1957.
In pursuit of the English. 1960.
Particularly cats. 1966.

LEVERTOV, DENISE (*Mrs.*
GOODMAN) (1923–)
American English-born poet; educated and
worked in England until 1948; became a U.S. citizen (1956); Visiting Lecturer at Drew University
(1965–6) and Vassar College (1966–7), etc.; started
the writers' and artists' protests against the war in
Vietnam (1965); recipient of various literary and
academic awards; a contributor to various journals; represented in *Penguin contemporary American
poetry* and many other anthologies; her edited and
translated works are not listed below.

Bibliography
B.N.B.

Contemporary poets.
Gale.

Poetry
The double image. 1946.
Here and now. 1957.
Overland to the island. 1958.
With eyes at the back of our heads. 1959.
The Jacob's ladder. 1961.
O taste and see. 1964.
The sorrow dance. 1967.
Embroideries. 1969.
Relearning the alphabet. 1970.
To stay alive. 1971.
Footprint poems. 1972.
A poet in the world. 1973.

LEVEY, MICHAEL VINCENT (1927–)
English art historian; educated at Exeter College,
Oxford; served in the army (1945–8); Assistant
Keeper, then Deputy Keeper, then Keeper,
National Gallery (1951–); Slade Professor of
Fine Art, Cambridge (1963–4); a contributor to the
Burlington Magazine, etc.

Bibliography
Authors' and writers' who's who. 1971.
B.N.B.
Gale.
Who's who. 1973.

Works
Six great painters. 1956.
National Gallery catalogues: 18th century Italian
Schools. 1956.
Brief history of the National Gallery. 1957.
Talking of pictures. 1958.
The German school. 1959.
Painting in 18th century Venice. 1959.
A concise history from Giotto to Cézanne. 1962.
A room-to-room guide to the National Gallery.
1964.
Dürer. 1964.
The later Italian paintings in the collection of H.M.
the Queen. 1964.
Canaletto paintings in the collection of H.M. the
Queen. 1964.
Tiepolo's banquet of Cleopatra (Charlton Lecture
1962). 1966.
Rococo to revolution. 1966.
Bronzino (The Masters). 1967.
Early Renaissance (Hawthornden Prize 1968).
1967.

Fifty works of English literature we could do
without (co-author). 1967.
Holbein's Christina of Denmark, Duchess of
Milan. 1968.
A history of western art. 1968.
The seventeenth and eighteenth centuries. 1969.
Painting at Court (Wrightsman Lectures). 1971.
The seventeenth and eighteenth centuries' Italian
schools. 1971.
The life and death of Mozart. 1971.
The nude: themes and painters in the National
Gallery. 1972.
Art and architecture in 18th century France (with
others). 1972.

LEVI, PETER (†CHAD TIGAR).
(1931–)
English poet; after leaving school he became a
Jesuit; educated at Oxford; taught after coming
down; ordained priest; translator, with Robin
Milner-Gulland, of the poems of Yevtushenko
(1962); editor of the poems of Richard Selif (1963).

Bibliography
Authors' and writers' who's who. 1971.
B.N.B.
Contemporary poets.
Gale.

Poetry
The earthly paradise (pr. ptd.). 1958.
The gravel ponds. 1961.
Water, rock and sand. 1961.
Orpheus Head (pr. ptd.). 1962.
The sheerwaters. 1965.
Fresh water, sea water. 1966.
Ruined abbeys. 1968.
Pancakes for the Queen of Babylon. 1968.
Life is a platform. 1971.
Death is a pulpit. 1971.
Light garden of the angel king. 1973.

Other Work
Beaumont. 1961.

LEVINE, ALBERT NORMAN (1924–)
Canadian poet and novelist; born in Ottawa; educated at McGill University and King's College,
London; served in the Second World War; poet-
in-residence, University of New Brunswick
(1965–6); left Canada and settled in Cornwall;
edited *Canadian Winters Tale*; a contributor to the
*Sunday Times, Canadian Writing Today, Globe
Magazine*, etc.

Bibliography
Authors' and writers' who's who. 1971.
B.N.B.
Canadiana.
Contemporary novelists.

Novels and Short Stories
The angled road. 1953.
One way ticket (short stories). 1961.
From a seaside town. 1970.
I don't want to know anyone too well: 15 stories.
   1971.

Poetry
The tightrope walker. 1950.

LEVINE, PHILIP (†EDGAR POE)
(1928–   )
American poet; born in Detroit; educated at the
State University of Iowa; member of the English
faculty of Fresno State College, California
(1958–   ); recipient of several poetry awards; represented in various anthologies; a contributor to
New Yorker, Harper's, Poetry, etc.; edited with
H. Coulette *Character and crisis: a contemporary
reader* (1966).

Bibliography
C.B.I.
Contemporary poets.
Gale.

Poetry
On the edge. 1963.
Not this pig. 1968.
5 Detroits. 1970.
Thistles. 1970.
Pili's wall. 1971.
Red dust. 1971.
They feed the lion. 1972.

LEWIS, ALUN (1915–44)
Welsh poet; educated at the University of Wales;
served in the Second World War and died in
Arakan.

Bibliography
B.M. catalogue.
B.N.B.
R. N. Currey. Poets of the 1939–1945 war. 1960.

Poetry
Raiders' dawn. 1942.

Ha! ha! Among the trumpets (with foreword by
   Robert Graves). 1945.

Other Works
The last inspection (John Llewelyn Rhys Prize
   1944). 1942.
Letters from India (with a preface by A. L. Rowse).
   1946.
In the green tree (letters and stories with a preface
   by A. L. Rowse). 1949.

LIDDY, JAMES (†DANIEL REEVES, †BRIAN LYNCH, †LIAM O'CONNOR) (1934–   )
Irish poet and novelist; born in Kilkee, Ireland;
educated at University College, Dublin, and
King's Inns, Dublin; practises as a barrister.

Bibliography
B.N.B.
Contemporary poets.
Gale.

Novels
Tee-Hee-mutt. 1967.
Passion's slave. 1967.

Poetry
Esau, my kingdom for a drink. 1962.
In a blue smoke. 1964.
James Liddy '66. 1966.
Blue mountain. 1969.
A Munster song of love and war. 1971.

LIEBERMAN, LAURENCE JAMES
(1925–   )
American poet and editor; educated at Michigan
and California universities; Associate Professor of
English, College of the Virgin Islands (1966–   );
awarded various fellowships; a contributor to *New
Yorker, Atlantic Monthly, Poetry*, etc.; represented in
various anthologies; his edited works are not listed
below.

Bibliography
C.B.I.
Contemporary poets.
Gale.

Poetry
The unblinding. 1968.
The osprey suicides. 1973.

Other Work
Achievement of James Dickey. 1968.

LITVINOFF, EMANUEL (1915–)
British novelist; worked as a tailor, cabinet maker and furrier; served in the Second World War (1940–6); journalist and broadcaster after the war; edited *Jews in Eastern Europe*; Director of the Contemporary Jewish Library (1958–); wrote plays for television (1966–71); represented in several anthologies.

Bibliography
B.N.B.
Contemporary novelists.

Novels
The lost Europeans. 1959.
The man next door. 1968.
Journey through a small planet (stories). 1972.

Poetry
Conscripts: a symphonic declaration. 1941.
The untried soldier. 1942.
A gown for Cain. 1948.

LIVINGS, HENRY (1929–)
English playwright; born in Prestwich, Lancs.; served in the R.A.F. (1950–2); professional actor for many years, also writes for radio and television.

Bibliography
B.M. catalogue.
Contemporary dramatists.
Gale.

Plays
Stop it, whoever you are (staged 1961, published in New English Dramatists 5). 1962.
Nil carborundum (in New English Dramatists 6). 1963.
Kelly's eye, Big soft Nellie, and There's no room for you here for a start. 1964.
Eh? (staged 1964). 1965.
Good grief. 1968.
Honour and offer. 1969.
The little Mrs. Foster show (staged 1966). 1969.
Pongo plays 1–6. 1971.
This jockey drives late nights. 1972.

LIVINGSTONE, DOUGLAS JAMES
(1932–)
South African poet and bacteriologist; born in Kuala Lumpur; educated in Natal and at the Pas-

teur Institute, Salisbury, Rhodesia; bacteriologist (1958–); in charge of Marine Work, Natal (1964–); awarded several poetry prizes; a contributor to *London Magazine, Southern Review*, etc.; represented in numerous anthologies.

Bibliography
B.N.B.
Contemporary poets.
Gale.

Poetry
The skull in the mud. 1960.
Sjambok and other poems from Africa. 1964.
Poems (with Thomas Kinsella and Anne Sexton). 1968.
Eyes closed against the sun. 1970.

Poetic Drama
The sea my winding sheet. 1964.

LOCHEAD, DOUGLAS GRANT
(1922–)
Canadian poet; educated at McGill and Toronto universities; served in the Second World War; copywriter and journalist (1947–50); travelled in Europe; held various university teaching and library posts (1951–65); Professor of English and Special Lecturer in History of Printing, Toronto University (1965–); a contributor to *Canadian Forum, Queen's Quarterly, Dalhousie Review*, etc.; his edited works are not listed below.

Bibliography
Canadiana.
C.B.I.
Contemporary poets.

Poetry
The heart is fire. 1959.
Poems in Folios 1 and 2. 1959.
It is all around. 1960.
Shepherds before kings. 1963.
Poet talking. 1964.
A&B&C&: an alphabet. 1969.
Millwood Road poems. 1970.
The full furnace. 1970.

Other Work
The anatomy of theology. 1967.

LOEWINSOHN, RONALD WILLIAM
(1937–)
American poet; born in the Philippines; educated at

the University of California, Berkeley; taught at poetry workshops in San Francisco State College (1960–6) and Cambridge Center for Adult Education (1968–   ); Teaching Fellow, Harvard (1967–   ); recipient of various awards; lives in California; represented in *New American poetry*, Grove Press (1960), etc.; a contributor to *Poetry*, Chicago, *Lion*, Berkeley, etc.

Bibliography
C.B.I.
Contemporary poets.
Gale.

Poetry
Watermelons. 1959.
The world of the lie. 1963.
Against the silences to come. 1965.
L'autre. 1967.
Lying together, Turning the head and shifting the weight, The produce district and other places, Moving—a spring poem. 1967.
The sea, around us. 1968.
The step. 1968.
Meat air: poems 1957–1969. 1970.

LOGUE, CHRISTOPHER (1926–   )
English poet; born in Portsmouth; served in the army (1944–8); his unpublished plays include a version of *Antigone* (1961) and *The trial of Cob and Leach* (1959).

Bibliography
Authors' and writers' who's who. 1971.
B.N.B.
Contemporary poets.
Gale.
Who's who. 1973.

Poetry
Wand and quadrant. 1953.
First testament. 1955.
Weekdream sonnets. 1955.
Devil maggot and son. 1956.
The man who told his love: 20 poems based on Pablo Neruda, *Los Cantos d'Amore*. 1958.
A song for Kathleen. 1958.
Songs. 1959.
Patrocleia: book 16 of Homer's *Iliad* freely adapted into English. 1962.
The arrival of the poet in the city. 1964.
Logue's ABC. 1966.
The words of the establishment songs. 1966.

Pax, book 19 of Homer's *Iliad* freely adapted into English. 1967.
New numbers, 1969.
The girls. 1969.
Twelve cards. 1972.
The song of the dead soldier. n.d.

Plays
Songs from *The lily-white boys* (with Harry Cookson). 1960.
Friday (with Hugo Claus). 1971.

Other Works
Lust, a pornographic novel (as †Count Palmiro Vicarion). 1957.
True stories. 1966.

LO LIYONG, TABAN (1939–   )
Ugandan writer; educated at the National Teachers' College, Kampala, Harvard University, Knoxville College and the Writers' Workshop at Iowa University; returned to E. Africa (1968).

Bibliography
Jahn and Dressler.
Zell and Silver.

Works
Eating chiefs, two cultures from Lokure to Maikal. 1960.
The last word: cultural synthesism. 1969.
Fixions and other stories. 1969.
Franz Fahon's uneven ribs and poems more and more. 1971.

LONGFORD, ELIZABETH, *Countess of* **(ELIZABETH PAKENHAM)** (1906–   )
English historian and author; wife of Lord Longford and mother of Antonia Fraser (q.v.); educated at Lady Margaret Hall, Oxford; university extension lecturer (1929–35); member of the Paddington and St. Pancras rent tribunal (1947–54), etc.; trustee of the Victoria and Albert Museum, etc.; Hon. D.Litt., Sussex (1970); a contributor to *The Times*, *Sunday Times*, *Observer*, *Daily Express*, etc.

Bibliography
Authors' and writers' who's who. 1971.
B.N.B.
Gale.
Who's who. 1973.

Works
Points for parents (as E. Pakenham). 1956.
Catholic approaches (ed.) (as E. Pakenham). 1959.
Jameson's raid (as E. Pakenham). 1960.
The Pakenham party book (as E. Pakenham). 1964.
Victoria RI. 1964.
Wellington: vol. I, years of the sword. 1969.
Wellington: vol. II, the pillar of state. 1972.
Piety in Queen Victoria's reign. 1973.

LONGRIGG, ROGER (†ROSALIND ERSKINE, †IVOR DRUMMOND)
(1929–   )
Scottish novelist; born in Edinburgh; educated at Bryanston School and Magdalen College, Oxford; television commercial and advertising agency copywriter; a contributor to *The Times*, *Telegraph*, *Sunday Times*, *Queen*, *Harper's*, etc.

Bibliography
Authors' and writers' who's who. 1971.
B.N.B.
Gale.

Novels
High pitched buzz. 1956.
Switchboard. 1957.
Wrong number. 1959.
Daughters of Mulberry. 1961.
Passion flower hotel (as †Rosalind Erskine). 1962.
Passion flowers in Italy (as †Rosalind Erskine). 1963.
Passion flowers in business (as †Rosalind Erskine). 1965.
Paper boats. 1965.
Love among the bottles. 1967.
Sun on the water. 1969.
Man with the tiny head (as †Ivor Drummond). 1969.
Priests of the abomination (as †Ivor Drummond). 1970.
Desperate criminals. 1971.
Frog in the moonflower (as †Ivor Drummond). 1971.

Other Work
Artless gambler. 1965.

LOVELL, Sir ALFRED CHARLES BERNARD (1913–   )
English astronomer; educated at Bristol University; Assistant Lecturer in Physics, Manchester University (1936–9); Telecommunications Research (1939–45); Professor of Radioastro-nomy, Manchester University, and Director of Jodrell Bank Experimental Station (1951–   ); honorary member of many foreign and British scientific academies; awarded many honorary degrees; O.B.E. (1946); F.R.S. (1955); a contributor to many learned scientific journals.

Bibliography
Authors' and writers' who's who. 1971.
B.N.B.
Gale.
Who's who. 1973.

Works
Science and civilisation. 1939.
World power resources and social development. 1945.
Radio astronomy. 1952.
Meteor astronomy. 1954.
The exploration of space by radio (with Robert H. Brown). 1957.
The individual and the universe (B.B.C. Reith Lectures 1958). 1959.
The exploration of outer space (Gregynog Lectures 1961). 1962.
Discovering the universe (with Joyce Lovell). 1963.
Our present knowledge of the universe. 1967.
The explosion of science: the physical universe (ed. with T. Margerison). 1967.
The story of Jodrell Bank. 1968.

LOWELL, ROBERT TRAILL SPENCE, Jr. (1917–   )
American poet; educated at Harvard University and Kenyon College; a conscientious objector during the Second World War; awarded various literary honours and prizes; consultant in poetry, Library of Congress (1947–8); Lecturer, Harvard University (1963–4) and other academic posts; translated *Phaedra* (1961), etc.; a contributor to *Kenyon Review*, *Observer*, etc.; represented in the *Oxford book of American poetry* and many other anthologies; his edited works and his translation of Racine's *Phèdre* (1961) are not listed below.

Bibliography
C.B.I.
Contemporary poets.
Gale.
Spiller.

Poetry
Land of unlikeness. 1944.
Lord Weary's castle (Pulitzer Prize 1947). 1946.

Poems 1938–1949. 1950.
The mills of the Kavanaughs. 1951.
Life studies. 1959.
Imitations (versions of poems by Homer, Sappho, Villon, Rilke). 1962.
For the union dead. 1964.
Selected poems. 1965.
The achievement of Robert Lowell: a comprehensive selection of his poems, with a critical introduction by William J. Marty. 1966.
Near the ocean. 1967.
The voyage and other versions of poems by Baudelaire. 1968.
Notebook 1967–1968. 1969.

Plays
The old glory (3 plays). 1964.
Prometheus bound. 1969.

LOWRY, CLARENCE MALCOLM (1909–57)

English novelist; educated at Cambridge; went to sea and travelled through several countries, including Mexico; became a dipsomaniac; took his own life.

Bibliography
B.N.B.

Novels
Ultramarine. 1933.
Under the volcano (autobiographical). 1947.
Dark as the grave wherein my friend is laid. 1969.

Correspondence
The selected letters of Malcolm Lowry (edited by Harvey Breit and Margerie Lowry). 1967.

LOWRY, ROBERT JAMES (1919–)

American novelist and poet; served in the U.S. Army (1942–5) during the Second World War; worked in publishing, and journalist in editorial and design departments (1938–56); a contributor of short stories, etc., to popular magazines.

Bibliography
C.B.I.

Novels
Journey out: three stories. 1945.
Blaze beyond the town; the toy balloon; a Phistevus. 1945.
Casualty. 1946.

Find me in fire. 1948.
The wolf that fed us. 1949.
The big cage. 1949.
The violent wedding. 1953.
Happy New Year, Kamerades! 1954.
The last party. 1956.
What's left of April. 1956.
New York call girl. 1958.
That kind of woman. 1959.
The prince of pride starring. 1959.
Party of dreamers. 1962.

LUCIE-SMITH, JOHN EDWARD McKENZIE (1933–)

English poet; born in Kingston, Jamaica; educated at King's School, Canterbury, and Merton College, Oxford; worked in advertising, journalism and broadcasting; recipient of several literary awards; a contributor to *Encounter, The Times, Listener, New Statesman, London Magazine, Spectator*, etc.; his edited work is not listed below.

Bibliography
Authors' and writers' who's who. 1971.
B.N.B.
Contemporary poets.
Gale.
Who's who. 1973.

Poetry
A tropical childhood and other poems (John Llewelyn Rhys Prize 1962). 1961.
Confession and histories. 1964.
Penguin modern poets no. 6 (with J. Clemo and G. MacBeth). 1964.
Borrowed problems. 1967.
Towards silence. 1968.
More beasts for Guillaume Apollinaire. 1968.
Snow poem. 1968.
Egyptian ode. 1969.

Other Works
Raphael. 1962.
Rubens. 1962.
What is a painting? 1966.
Thinking about art. 1968.
Movements in art since 1945. 1969.
Art in Britain (with Patricia White). 1970.
Symbolist art. 1972.
Eroticism in Western art. 1972.

LUDWIG, JACK (1922–)

Canadian-Jewish novelist and short-story writer; born in Winnipeg; educated at Manitoba and

California universities; lecturer at various American colleges; Professor of English, New York State University (1961–); given several awards for fiction; his stories are published in anthologies including Desmond Pacey, *Book of Canadian short stories*; a contributor to many magazines; co-founder and editor of *The noble savage*.

Bibliography
Canadiana.
C.B.I.
Contemporary novelists.

Novels
Confusions. 1963.
Above ground. 1968.
Hockey's night in Moscow. 1974.

Other Work
Recent American novelists. 1962.

LUSHINGTON, CLAUDE (1925–)
Caribbean painter and poet; born in Trinidad; served in the R.A.F. during the Second World War; manager in public housing in Trinidad Government; read law in the Inner Temple (1955); lives in England; full-time writer; has written film scripts.

Bibliography
B.N.B.

Poetry
The mystic rose. 1969.

LYALL, GAVIN TUDOR (1932–)
English detective novelist; born in Birmingham; educated at King Edward's School, Birmingham, and Pembroke College, Cambridge; married the journalist Katharine Whitehorn (q.v.); R.A.F. pilot (1951–3); on staff of *Picture Post* (1956–7); B.B.C. television film director (1958); on staff of the *Sunday Times* (1959–63); freelance writer (1963–); a contributor to the *Sunday Times*, *Observer*, *Daily Telegraph*, etc.; editor of *The war in the air 1939–45* (1968).

Bibliography
Authors' and writers' who's who. 1971.
B.N.B.
Gale.

Novels
The wrong side of the sky. 1961.
The most dangerous game. 1963.
Midnight plus one. 1965.
Shooting script. 1966.
Venus with pistol. 1969.
Blame the dead. 1972.

Other Work
Your guide map to North West Scotland. 1973.

LYNES, JOSEPH RUSSELL, Jr.
(1910–)
American journalist and historian; educated at Yale University; clerk, Harper Bros., publisher (1932–6); Principal, Shipley School, Bryn Mawr (1937–44); *Harper's Magazine* (from 1947, managing editor) (1944–); a contributor to numerous magazines; has written introductions to many Harper and other books.

Bibliography
C.B.I.
Gale.

Works
Highbrow, lowbrow, middlebrow. 1949.
Snobs: a guide book to your friends, your enemies, your colleagues and yourself. 1950.
Guests, or How to survive hospitality. 1951.
The tastemakers. 1954.
A surfeit of honey. 1957.
Cadwallader: a diversion. 1959.
The domesticated Americans. 1963.
Confessions of a dilettante. 1966.
Art-makers of the nineteenth century. 1970.
Good old moderns: an intimate portrait of the Museum of Modern Art. 1973.

M

McAULEY, JAMES PHILLIP (1917–)
Australian poet and critic; born and educated in
Sydney; Lecturer in Government (1946–60); Professor of English, Tasmania University (1961–);
a contributor to many periodicals; editor of *Quadrant* (1956–).

Bibliography
Annals of Australian literature.
Australian national bibliography.
Contemporary poets.

Poetry
Under Aldebaran. 1946.
A vision of ceremony. 1957.
The six days of creation. 1963.
Selected poems. 1963.
Captain Quiros. 1964.
Surprises of the sun. 1969.
Collected poems 1936–1970. 1971.

Criticism
The end of modernity. 1959.
C. J. Brennan. 1963.
Edmund Spenser and George Eliot. 1963.
A primer of English versification. 1966.
Generations. 1969.
The personal element in Australian poetry. 1970.
Romanticism and utopianism. 1972.

MACAULEY, ROBIE MAYHEW
(1919–)
American novelist; born in Michigan; educated at
Kenyon College, University of Iowa; served in the
U.S. Army (1942–6) during the Second World
War; after several university posts (1946–66),
editor of the *Kenyon Review* (1959–66); fiction
editor of *Playboy* (1966–); recipient of several
awards and fellowships.

Bibliography
C.B.I.
Contemporary novelists.

Novels
The disguises of love. 1952.
The end of pity and other stories. 1957.

Other Works
Technique in fiction (with George Lanning). 1964.
America and its discontents (with L. Zift).
 1971.

MACBETH, GEORGE MANN (1932–)
Scottish poet; educated at New College, Oxford;
B.B.C. producer (1955–); editor of *The Poet's
Voice* (1958–65), *New Comment* (1959–64) and
Poetry Now (1965–); has edited several
anthologies for Penguin Books; a contributor to
*Ambit, Poetry Review, London Magazine, New
Statesman*, etc.

Bibliography
B.N.B.
Contemporary poets.
Who's who. 1973.

Poetry
A form of words. 1954.
The broken places. 1963.
A Doomsday book. 1965.
The screens. 1967.
The colour of blood. 1967.
The night of stones. 1968.
A death. 1969.
A war quartet. 1969.
The burning cone. 1970.
The Hiroshima dream. 1970.
Two poems. 1970.
The bamboo nightingale. 1970.
Mad Jack's gnomes, and Visitors to Shakespeare.
 1970.
Poems. 1970.
Poems 1958–69. 1971.
The Orlando poems. 1971.
Shrapnel. 1972.

Children's Books
Noah's journey. 1966.
Jonah and the Lord. 1969.
The dark wind. 1970.

Prose Poem
My Scotland. 1973.

MACCAIG, NORMAN ALEXANDER
(1910–)
Scottish poet; educated at Edinburgh University; has taught in Edinburgh (1933–); edited an anthology of Scottish poetry *Hono' red shade* (1959); contributes articles and poetry to many journals.

Bibliography
B.N.B.
Contemporary poets.
Gale.
N.C.B.E.L.

Poetry
Far cry. 1943.
The inward eye. 1946.
Riding lights. 1955.
The Sinai sort. 1957.
A common grace. 1960.
A round of applause. 1962.
Measures. 1965.
Surroundings. 1966.
Rings on a tree. 1968.
A man in my position. 1969.
Selected poems. 1971.
Penguin modern poets no. 21 (with I. Crichton Smith and N. MacCaig). 1972.

McCARTHY, MARY THERESE (*Mrs.* WEST) (1912–)
American novelist; educated at Vassar College; drama critic, *Partisan Review* (1937–48); Instructor in English, Bard College, Annandale (1945–56); lecturer and broadcaster (1952–65); recipient of various book awards; Guggenheim Fellow (1949–50, 1959–60); a contributor to the *New Yorker*, *Observer*, *Encounter*, etc.; her translated work is not listed below.

Bibliography
B.N.B.
Contemporary novelists.
Gale.
Goldman Shenli. Mary McCarthy: a bibliography, Harcourt Brace. 1968.
Who's who. 1973.

Novels
The company she keeps. 1942.
The oasis (English title, Source of embarrassment). 1949.
Cast a cold eye. 1950.
The groves of academe. 1952.

A charmed life. 1955.
On the contrary. 1961.
The group. 1963.

Other Works
Sights and spectacles 1937–56. 1956.
Venice observed. 1956.
Memories of a Catholic girlhood. 1957.
The stones of Florence. 1959.
Theatre chronicles 1937–62. 1963.
Vietnam. 1967.
Hanoi. 1968.
The writing on the wall and other literary essays. 1970.
Birds of America. 1971.
Medina. 1972.

McCOURT, EDWARD ALEXANDER
(1907–)
Irish-Canadian novelist; his family emigrated to Canada (1909); educated at Alberta and Oxford universities; taught at various Canadian colleges and universities; Professor of English at Saskatchewan University (1944–).

Bibliography
Canadiana.
C.B.I.

Novels
The flaming hour (for children). 1947.
Music at the close. 1947.
Home is the stranger. 1950.
The wooden sword. 1956.
Walk through the valley. 1958.
The Ettinger affair. 1963.
Fasting friar. 1963.

Other Works
Canadian West in fiction. 1949.
Buckskin brigadier (for children). 1955.
Revolt in the west. 1958.
The road across Canada. 1965.
Remember Butler: the story of Sir William Butler. 1968.
Saskatchewan; the traveller's Canada. 1968.
The Yukon and northwest territories. 1970.

McCULLERS, CARSON (*née* SMITH)
(1917–67)
American novelist; educated at Columbia and New York universities; awarded a Guggenheim Fellowship and others; a contributor to *Vogue*, *Harper's Bazaar*, etc.

Bibliography
B.N.B.
C.B.I.
Gale.

Novels
The heart is a lonely hunter. 1940.
Reflections in a golden eye. 1941.
The member of the wedding. 1946.
The ballad of the sad café and other stories. 1951.
Clock without hands. 1961.
Mortgaged heart: uncollected writings of Carson
    McCullers. 1971.

Poetry for Children
Sweet as a pickle and clean as a pig. 1964.

Play
The square root of wonderful. 1958.

MACDONALD, DWIGHT (1906–)
American historian and journalist; educated at Yale
University; on the staff of *Fortune Magazine*
(1929–36), *Partisan Review* (1938–43); editor and
publisher of *Politics* (1944–9); staff writer for *New
Yorker* (1951–); film critic, then political columnist of *Esquire* (1960–); Visiting Professor at
various American universities (1966–71); recipient
of Litt.D., Wesleyan University (1964); a contributor to *Encounter, Harper's, New Yorker*, etc.; his
edited works are not listed below.

Bibliography
C.B.I.
Gale.

Works
Henry Wallace, the man and the myth. 1948.
The root is man. 1953.
The Ford Foundation: the men and the millions.
    1956.
Responsibility of peoples. 1957.
Memoirs of a revolutionist (later published as Poli-
    tics past. 1970). 1957.
Masscult and midcult. 1961.
Our invisible poor (**New Yorker*). 1962.
Against the American grain. 1962.
Dwight Macdonald on movies. 1969.

MACDONALD, NANCY MAY (1921–)
Australian poet; educated at Sydney University;
editor of the publishing house of Angus and
Robertson (1943–); represented in numerous
anthologies.

Bibliography
Annals of Australian literature.
Australian national bibliography.
Contemporary poets.

Poetry
Pacific sea. 1947.
The lonely fire. 1954.
The lighthouse. 1959.
Selected poems. 1969.

McELDOWNEY, RICHARD DENNIS
(1926–)
New Zealand writer; unemployed until 1963;
clerical assistant, School of Physical Education,
Dunedin (1963–6); Librarian, Knox College
(1966–); a contributor to newspapers and journals.

Bibliography
N.Z. national bibliography.
Who's who in New Zealand. 1971.

Works
The world regained. 1957.
Donald Anderson: a memoir. 1966.

**MACEWAN, GWENDOLYN
MARGARET** (1941–)
Canadian poet and novelist; born in Toronto;
travelled in the Middle East; a contributor to *Canadian Forum, Tamarack Review, Alphabet*, etc.; represented in various anthologies including *Oxford
book of Canadian verse* (1965); and *Penguin book of
Canadian verse* (1967); her radio plays are *Tesla,
Terror and Erebus*, and *The world of Nesmah*.

Bibliography
Canadiana.
C.B.I.
Contemporary poets.

Novels
Julian the magician. 1963.
The twelve circles of the night. 1970.
Norman. 1972.

Poetry
Selah. 1961.
The drunken clock. 1961.
The rising fire. 1963.
A breakfast for barbarians. 1966.
The shadow maker. 1969.

McFADDEN, ROY (1921–)
Irish poet; born in Belfast; educated at Queen's University, Belfast; co-editor of *Rann*, an Ulster poetry quarterly (1948–53); practised as a lawyer; represented in numerous anthologies.

Bibliography
B.N.B.
Contemporary poets.

Poetry
Russian summer. 1941.
Three new poets (with Alex Comfort and Ian Seraillier). 1942.
Swords and ploughshares. 1943.
Flowers from a lady. 1945.
The heart's townland. 1947.
Elegy for the death of the *Princess Victoria*. 1952.
The garryowen. 1972.

McGAHERN, JOHN (1935–)
Irish novelist; educated at University College, Dublin; Research Fellow, Reading University (1968); Visiting Professor, Colgate University, New York (1969 and 1972); a contributor to *Listener, Encounter, Atlantic Monthly*, etc.; also writes for television; his play *Sinclair* produced (1972).

Bibliography
Authors' and writers' who's who. 1971.
B.N.B.
Contemporary novelists.
Gale.

Novels
The barracks. 1963.
The dark. 1965.
Nightlines (stories). 1970.

McGILL, RALPH EMERSON
(1898–1969)
American historian and writer; educated at Vanderbilt University; on the staff of the *Banner* (1922–8); *Atlanta Constitution*, sports editor, editor, publisher (1929–69); covered the Nüremberg trials and many other important events; recipient of many literary and academic awards; a contributor to *Harper's, Atlantic's, Saturday Evening Post* and numerous other journals.

Bibliography
C.B.I.
Gale.

Works
Israel revisited. 1950.
The fleas come with the dog. 1954.
A church, a school. 1959.
The South and the southerner. 1963.

McGOUGH, ROGER (1937–)
English poet; born in Liverpool; educated at Hull University; lecturer at Liverpool College of Art; member of *The Scaffold*, a humour, music and poetry group; represented in anthologies.

Bibliography
B.N.B.
Contemporary poets.

Poetry
The Mersey sound. Penguin modern poets no. 10 (with A. Henri and B. Patten). 1967.
Frinck, and "A day in the life of Monika". 1967.
Watchwords. 1969.
After the merrymaking. 1971.
Gig. 1973.

MACINNES, COLIN (1914–)
English writer; son of Angela Thirkell; born in London; grew up in Australia; served in the army in the Second World War; radio scriptwriter for some years.

Bibliography
B.N.B.
Who's who. 1973.

Works
To the victors the spoils. 1950.
June in her spring. 1952.
City of spades. 1957.
Absolute beginners. 1959.
Mr. Love and Mr. Justice. 1960.
England, half English. 1961.
Sidney Nolan. 1961.
All day Saturday. 1966.
Sweet Saturday night. 1967.
Westward to laughter. 1969.
Visions of London (City of spades, Absolute beginners, Mr. Love and Mr. Justice). 1969.
Three years to play. 1970.
Loving them both, or Study of bisexuality and bisexuals. 1973.

McINNES, HELEN CLARK (Mrs. G. HIGHET) (1907–)

Scottish novelist; educated at Glasgow University; married Gilbert Highet (q.v.); university librarian; took American nationality (1951); her translated work is not listed below.

Bibliography
Authors' and writers' who's who. 1971.
B.N.B.
Contemporary novelists.
Gale.
Who's who. 1973.

Novels
Above suspicion. 1941.
Assignment in Brittany. 1942.
The unconquerable. 1944.
Horizon. 1945.
Friends and lovers. 1947.
Rest and be thankful. 1949.
Neither five nor three. 1951.
I and my true love. 1953.
Pray for a brave heart. 1955.
North from Rome. 1958.
Decision at Delphi. 1961.
The Venetian affair. 1964.
The double image. 1966.
The Salzburg connection. 1969.
While still we live. 1971.
Message from Malaga. 1971.
Triple threat. 1973.
The snare of the hunter. 1974.

Play
Home is the hunter. 1964.

MACKAY, SHENA (Mrs. ROBIN BROWN) (1944–)

Scottish novelist; born in Edinburgh; educated at Kidbrooke Comprehensive School.

Bibliography
Authors' and writers' who's who. 1971.
B.N.B.

Novels
Dust falls on Eugene Schlumburger. 1964.
Toddler on the run. 1964.
Music upstairs. 1965.
Old crow. 1967.
An Advent calendar. 1971.

McKIE, RONALD CECIL HAMLYN (1909–)

Australian journalist and writer; born in Queensland; educated at Queensland University; war correspondent in Burma and Europe (1943–5); feature writer in Australia, Singapore and China (1937–60).

Bibliography
Annals of Australian literature.
Australian national bibliography.
C.B.I.
Gale.

Works
This was Singapore. 1942.
Proud echo (American title, The survivors). 1953.
With the Australians in Korea. 1954.
The heroes. 1960.
Malaysia in focus (American title, The emergence of Malaysia). 1963.
Bali. 1969.

MACKINNON, *Professor* DONALD MACKENZIE (1913–)

Scottish philosopher; educated in Edinburgh, at Winchester College, and New College, Oxford; Fellow and Tutor, Keble College, Oxford (1937–47), etc.; Regius Professor of Moral Philosophy, Aberdeen (1947–60); Professor of Divinity, Cambridge (1960–); a contributor to learned journals.

Bibliography
B.N.B.
Who's who. 1973.

Works
Christian faith and Communist faith (ed.). 1953.
The notion of a philosophy of history. 1954.
A study in ethical theory. 1957.
Objections to Christian belief (with others). 1965.
The resurrection (with Professor G. W. H. Lampe). 1966.
Borderlands of theology and other essays (edited G. W. Roberts and D. E. Smucker). 1968.
The stripping of the altars. 1969.
Making moral decisions (with others). 1969.
The problem of metaphysics. 1973.

MACLEAN, ALISTAIR (†IAN STUART) (1922–)

Scottish novelist; educated at Glasgow University; served in the Royal Navy (1941–6) in the Second World War; taught for nine years; an underwriting member of Lloyd's.

Bibliography
B.N.B.
Gale.
Who's who. 1973.

Novels
H.M.S. *Ulysses*. 1955.
The guns of Navarone (filmed 1959). 1957.
South by Java Head (filmed 1959). 1958.
The last frontier (American title, The secret ways) (filmed 1960). 1959.
Night without end. 1960.
Fear is the key (filmed 1972). 1961.
The golden rendezvous. 1962.
The Satan bug. 1962.
Ice station Zebra (filmed 1968). 1963.
When eight bells toll (filmed 1970). 1966.
Where eagles dare (filmed 1968). 1967.
Force 10 from Navarone. 1968.
Puppet on a chain (filmed 1970). 1969.
Bear Island. 1971.
Caravan to Vaccares (filmed 1974). 1971.
The way to dusty death. 1973.

Novels as †Ian Stuart
The dark crusader (American title, The black shrike). 1961.
Snow on the Ben. 1961.

For Children
All about Lawrence of Arabia. 1962.

Other Work
Captain Cook. 1972.

McLEAN, Sir FITZROY HEW (1911–)

Scottish writer; born in Cairo; educated at Eton and Cambridge; Foreign Service (1933–9); served in the Second World War (1939–45); British military mission to Yugoslav partisans (1943–5); Parliamentary Under-Secretary, War Office (1954–7); Conservative M.P. for Bute and N. Ayrshire (1959–); awarded many academic and public honours; a contributor to the *Sunday Times, Daily Telegraph*, etc.

Bibliography
B.N.B.
Contemporary novelists.
Who's who. 1973.

Works
Eastern approaches. 1949.
Disputed barricade. 1957.
A person from England. 1958.
Back to Bokhara. 1959.
Jugoslavia. 1969.
A concise history of Scotland. 1970.
The battle of Neretva. 1970.

MACLENNAN, JOHN HUGH (1907–)

Canadian novelist; born in Nova Scotia; educated at Dalhousie University, Oriel College, Oxford, and Princeton; teacher and writer in Montreal (1935–45); Professor of English Literature, McGill University (1951–); a contributor to *MacLean's Magazine, Holiday, Saturday Review*, etc.

Bibliography
B.N.B.
Canadiana.
Contemporary novelists.
Gale.
Who's who. 1973.

Novels
Barometer rising. 1941.
Two solitudes (Governor General's Award 1946). 1945.
The precipice (Governor General's Award 1949). 1948.
Each man's son. 1951.
The watch that ends the night (Governor General's Award 1960). 1959.
The return of the sphinx. 1967.

Essays and Other Works
Oxyrhynchus: an economic and social study. 1935.
Cross country. 1949.
Thirty and three. 1954.
The Scotchman's return and other essays. 1960.
Seven rivers of Canada. 1961.
Synaptic transmission. 1963.
The colour of Canada. 1968.

MACLOW, JACKSON (1922–)

American concrete poet; born in Chicago; educated at Chicago University and Brooklyn College, New York; teacher of English and music, editor and translator (1950–66); in publishing

(1957–66); instructor, American Language Institute, New York University (1966–); poetry editor *Win* (1966–); represented in *Chicago Review Quarterly* (1969), *An anthology of concrete poetry*, Something Else Press (1967), etc.; a contributor to *Win, Hudson Review, Nation, Now*, etc.; wrote the music for W. H. Auden, *The age of anxiety* (1964); his unpublished plays are not listed below.

Bibliography
C.B.I.
Contemporary dramatists.
Contemporary poets.

Poetry
The pronouns—a collection of 40 dances—for the dances—6 February–22 March 1964. 1964.
August light poems. 1967.
22 light poems. 1968.
23rd light poem/7th poem for Larry Eigner. 1969.
Stanzas for Iris Lezak. 1972.

Verse Plays
The marrying maiden: a play of changes. 1960.
The twin plays: Port-au-Prince and Adams County, Illinois. 1963.
Questions and answers ... a topical play. 1963.
Verdurous Sanguinaria. 1967.

McLUHAN, *Professor* HERBERT MARSHALL (1911–)

Canadian writer; born in Edmonton, Alberta; educated at the universities of Manitoba and Cambridge; held positions in American universities (1936–44); Professor of English, Toronto University (1948–); Director of Centre for Culture and Technology (1963–); F.R.S. (1964); editor of *Explorations* (1953–).

Bibliography
Canadiana.
C.B.I.
Gale.
Who's who. 1973.

Works
The mechanical bride; folklore of industrial man. 1951.
The Gutenberg galaxy; the making of typographic man. 1962.
Understanding media. 1964.
The medium is the message. 1967.
Verbi-voco-visual explorations. 1967.

War and peace in the global village (with Quentin Fiore). 1968.
Through the vanishing point (with Harley Parker). 1968.
Counterblast. 1969.
Interior landscape (with Eugene McNamara). 1969.
Culture is our business. 1970.
From cliché to archetype (with Wilfred Watson). 1970.
Exploration in communication (with E. Carpenter). 1970.
Take today; the executive as drop-out (with Barrington Nevitt). 1972.

MACNAB, ROY MARTIN (1923–)

South African poet; born in Durban; educated at Hilton College, Natal, and Jesus College, Oxford; served in the navy during the Second World War; South African diplomat in London and Paris (1955–67); Director, South African Foundation, London (1968–); a contributor to *Contrast, New Coin, Poetry Review*, etc.; represented in the *Oxford book of South African verse* and others; co-editor of *Oxford poetry* (1947), *South African poetry* (1948) and editor of *Poets in South Africa* (1958).

Bibliography
B.N.B.
Contemporary poets.

Poetry
Testament of a South African. 1947.
The man of grass and other poems. 1960.

Other Works
South and Central Africa. 1954.
Journey into yesterday. 1962.

McNALLY, TERENCE (1939–)

American poet; born in Florida; educated at Columbia University; film critic, the *Seventh Art* (1963–5); recipient of two Guggenheim Fellowships (1966 and 1969); *Botticelli* and *Last gasps* were televised; plays not separately published include *The roller coaster* (1960) and *And things that go bump in the night* (1962).

Bibliography
C.B.I.
Contemporary dramatists.

Plays
Apple pie (with Next, Tour, Botticelli). 1969.
Sweet Eros, Next, and other plays (with Botticelli,
  ¡Cuba si!, Witness). 1969.
Noon (with I. Horowitz). 1969.
Three plays: ¡Cuba si!, Bringing it all back home,
  Last gasps. 1970.
Where has Tommy Flowers gone? 1972.

MACPHERSON, JEAN JAY (1931–)
English-born Canadian poet; educated at Carleton
University, Ottawa, and University College,
London; Lecturer in English, Toronto University
(1953–); represented in numerous anthologies.

Bibliography
Canadiana.
C.B.I.
Contemporary poets.
Gale.

Poetry
Nineteen poems. 1952.
O earth return. 1964.
The boatman (Governor General's Award 1958).
  1957.

Other Work
Four ages of man: the classical myths. 1962.

McROBBIE, KENNETH ALAN
(1929–)
Anglo-Canadian poet; born in England; educated
at Liverpool and Toronto universities; Professor of
History, Manitoba University, Winnipeg; editor
of *Mosaic*; a contributor to *Canadian Forum, Poetry,
Chicago*, etc.; represented in several anthologies
including *Poetry 62*; translator of *Selected poems of
Ferenc Juhász* (1970).

Bibliography
Canadiana.
C.B.I.
Contemporary poets.

Poetry
Jupiter C: 4 poems of the missile age. 1958.
Eyes without a face. 1960.

MADHAVAN, A. (1933–)
Indian poet; born in South India; educated at Loyola College, Madras, and Trinity College, Cambridge; Indian Foreign Service (1956–); has

contributed to the *Illustrated Weekly of India*;
represented in *New Poems*, P.E.N. (1958).

Bibliography
Contemporary poets.
Indian national bibliography 1958–67.

Poetry
Poems. 1968.

MAGEE, BRYAN EDGAR (1930–)
English journalist and television presenter; edu-
cated at Christ's Hospital, Lycée Hoche and Keble
College, Oxford; radio and television critic and
commentator (1957–); a contributor to *The
Times, Observer, Spectator, New Society, Guardian,
Listener*, etc.

Bibliography
Authors' and writers' who's who. 1971.
B.N.B.
Gale.

Works
Crucifixion and other poems. 1951.
Go west, young man. 1958.
To live in danger. 1960.
The new radicalism. 1962.
The democratic revolution. 1964.
Towards 2000. 1965.
The television interviewer. 1966.
Aspects of Wagner. 1968.
One in twenty; a study in homosexuality. 1966.
Modern British philosophy. 1971.

MAGNUS-ALLCROFT, Sir PHILIP
MONTEFIORE (1906–)
English historian; educated at Westminster School
and Wadham College, Oxford; a civil servant
(1928–33); served in the army in the Second World
War (1939–45); trustee of the National Portrait
Gallery, etc.; a contributor to *The Times, Observer,
T.L.S.*, etc.

Bibliography
Authors' and writers' who's who. 1971.
B.N.B.
Gale.
Who's who. 1973.

Works
Life of Edmund Burke. 1939.
Selected studies. 1949.
Sir Walter Raleigh. 1952.

Gladstone—a biography. 1954.
Kitchener—portrait of an imperialist. 1958.
King Edward the Seventh. 1964.

MAILER, NORMAN (1923–)

American novelist; educated at Harvard University; served in the U.S. Army (1944–6) in the Second World War; editor of *Dissent* (1953–63); Democratic candidate, Mayoral Primaries, New York City (1969); a contributor to *New York Post, Discovery, Esquire*, etc.

Bibliography
Authors' and writers' who's who. 1971.
B.N.B.
Contemporary novelists.
Gale.
Spiller.
Who's who. 1973.

Novels
The naked and the dead (filmed 1958). 1948.
The deer park. 1955.
The man who studied yoga (in New Short Novels no. 2). 1956.
An American dream (filmed as See you in Hell, darling, 1966). 1964.
Why are we in Vietnam? 1967.
The short fiction of Norman Mailer. 1967.

Play
The deer park (from the novel). 1967.

Other Works
Barbary shore. 1951.
The white negro. 1957.
Advertisements for myself. 1959.
Deaths for the ladies and other disasters (poems). 1962.
The presidential papers. 1963.
Cannibals and christians. 1965.
The bull fight. 1967.
The armies of the night. 1968.
The idol and the octopus: political writings in the Kennedy and Johnson administrations. 1968.
Miami and the siege of Chicago. 1968.
Maidstone. 1971.
Of a fire on the moon. 1971.
Existential errands. 1972.
Prisoner of sex. 1972.
Marilyn. 1973.

MAIS, ROGER (1905–55)

Jamaican novelist, painter, poet and playwright;
became a journalist; came to London (1953); lived in France and England for some years; returned to Jamaica shortly before his death; a contributor to journals.

Bibliography
B.M. catalogue.
B.N.B.

Novels
The hills were joyful together. 1953.
Brother man (illustrated by the author). 1954.
Face and other stories. 1955.
Black lightning. 1955.

MALAMUD, BERNARD (1914–)

American novelist; educated at Columbia University; taught English in New York (1940–9); Instructor, later Associate Professor, Oregon State University (1949–61); recipient of various fiction awards, etc.; a contributor to *Harper's Bazaar, New Yorker, Commentary*, etc.

Bibliography
C.B.I.
Contemporary novelists.
Gale.
Who's who. 1973.

Novels and Short Stories
The natural. 1952.
The assistant. 1957.
The magic barrel (stories, one filmed 1970). 1958.
A new life. 1961.
Idiots first (stories). 1963.
The fixer (Pulitzer Prize 1967, filmed 1969). 1966.
Pictures of Fidelman. 1969.
The tenants. 1971.
Rembrandt's hat (stories). 1973.

MALANGA, GERARD (1943–)

American poet; born in New York; educated at Cincinnati University, Ohio; recipient of various poetry prizes; executive producer, Andy Warhol Films Inc. (1963–); represented in *Young American poets*, Folkett (1968), *New Yorker book of poems* (1969), etc.; a contributor to the *New Yorker, Sunday Herald-Tribune Magazine*, etc.

Bibliography
C.B.I.
Contemporary poets.

Poetry
3 poems for Benedetta Barzini. 1967.
Prelude to international velvet debutante. 1967.
The last Benedetta poems. 1969.
Poetry on film. n.d.

Other Works
Screen tests/a diary (with Andy Warhol). 1967.
Gerard Malanga: a poet's self-portrait. 1970.
Ten poems for ten poets. 1970.

MALGONKAR, MONOHAR DATTA TRAY (1913–)

Indian novelist; born in Bombay; educated at Bombay University; professional big-game hunter (1935–7); served in the Maratha Light Infantry (1942–52); has farmed in Jagabet since 1959; a frequent contributor of stories to *Illustrated Weekly of India*, etc.

Bibliography
C.B.I.
Contemporary novelists.
Indian national bibliography 1958–67.

Novels
Distant drum. 1960.
Combat of shadows. 1962.
The princes. 1963.
A bend in the Ganges. 1964.
The devil's wind; Nana Saheb's story. 1972.

Screenplay
Spy in amber. 1971.

Other Works
Kanhoiji Angray, Maratha admiral; an account of his life and battles with the English. 1959.
Puars of Dewas Senior. 1963.
The chatrapatis of Kolhapur. 1971.

MANCHESTER, WILLIAM (1922–)

American novelist and writer; educated at the universities of Massachusetts and Missouri; served in the U.S. Marines (1942–5); a journalist on the *Daily Oklahoman* (1945–6) and *Baltimore Sun* (1947–54); managing editor, Wesleyan University Press (1955–64); a contributor to *Harper's, Saturday Review, Nation*, etc.

Bibliography
C.B.I.
Gale.
Who's who. 1973.

Novels
The city of anger. 1953.
Shadow of the monsoon. 1956.
Beard the lion. 1958.
The long gainer. 1961.

Other Works
Disturber of the peace; the life of H. L. Mencken (U.K. title, The sage of Baltimore. 1952). 1951.
A Rockefeller family portrait. 1959.
Portrait of a president; John F. Kennedy in profile. 1962.
The death of a president (*Look*). 1967.
The arms of Krupp, 1587–1968. 1968.

MANDEL, ELIAS WOLF (1922–)

Canadian poet; born in Saskatchewan; educated at Saskatchewan and Toronto universities; Professor of English, University of Alberta; a contributor to *Tamarack Review, Canadian Forum, Alphabet, Queen's Quarterly, Fiddlehead*; represented in various anthologies including *Oxford book of Canadian verse* (1960); *Penguin book of Canadian verse* (1958); co-editor of *Poetry 62* (1961); edited *Five modern Canadian poets* (1970) and *English poems of the 20th century* (1970).

Bibliography
Canadiana.
C.B.I.
Contemporary poets.

Poetry
Trio. 1954.
Fuseli poems. 1960.
Black and secret man. 1964.
An idiot joy (Governor General's Award 1968). 1967.

Other Works
Criticism: the silent-speaking words. 1967.
Contexts of Canadian criticism. 1971.

MANIFOLD, JOHN STREETER (1915–)

Australian poet; born in Melbourne; educated at Jesus College, Cambridge; served in the Second World War (1940–6); freelance journalist and radio scriptwriter; editor of the *Australian song book*, Penguin (1964).

Bibliography
Annals of Australian literature.
Australian national bibliography.

Poetry
The death of Ned Kelly. 1941.
Trident (with David Martin and H. Nicholson). 1944.
Selected verse. 1946.
Nightmares and sunhorses. 1961.
Opus 8 poems, 1961–1969. 1971.

Other Works
The amorous flute: an unprofessional handbook for recorder players. 1948.
The music in English drama. 1956.
Who wrote the ballads? 1964.

MANKOWITZ, WOLF (1924–)
English novelist, playwright and writer on ceramics; educated at Cambridge; has written many film scripts; has directed many London productions.

Bibliography
B.N.B.
Contemporary novelists.
Gale.
Who's who. 1973.

Novels
Make me an offer (filmed 1954). 1952.
A kid for two farthings (filmed 1954). 1953.
Laugh till you cry. 1955.
My old man's a dustman. 1956.
Cockatrice. 1963.
The biggest pig in Barbados. 1965.

Short Stories
The Mendelman fire. 1957.
The blue Arabian nights. 1972.

Poetry
12 poems. 1971.

Plays
The bespoke overcoat (produced 1953). 1955.
Expresso Bongo (produced 1961 with Make me an offer and other stories). 1961.
Belle (musical). 1961.
Pickwick (musical). 1963.
Passion flower hotel (musical based on R. Longrigg's novel). 1965.

The Samson riddle. 1972.
Stand and deliver! (musical). 1972.

Other Works
Wedgwood. 1953.
The Portland vase. 1953.
The concise encyclopaedia of English pottery and porcelain (with R. G. Hopper). 1957.
ABC of show business. 1960.

For Children
Majollika and company. 1955.

MANNES, MARYA (1904–)
American writer; *Vogue* feature editor (1933–6); U.S. government service (1942–5); staff writer, the *Reporter* (1952–63); columnist, *MacCall's* (1965–); frequent radio and television broadcaster; recipient of many awards; a contributor to *New York Times, Harper's, New York Herald Tribune,* etc.

Bibliography
C.B.I.
Gale.

Works
Message from a stranger (novel). 1948.
More in anger (essays). 1958.
Subverse (poetry with Robert Osborn). 1959.
Who owns the air? 1960.
The New York I know (essays). 1961.
But will it sell? 1964.
Out of my time. 1971.
Uncoupling: the art of coming apart (with Norman Sheresky). 1972.

**MANNING, ROSEMARY JOY
(†MARY VOYLE)** (1911–)
English novelist; educated at Royal Holloway College, London; for some years was a secretary and later a teacher; now a full-time writer; a contributor to *Horizon, Cornhill,* etc.

Bibliography
Authors' and writers' who's who. 1971.
B.N.B.
Gale.

Novels
Remaining a stranger (as †Mary Voyle). 1953.
A change of direction (as †Mary Voyle). 1955.
Look, stranger (American title, The shape of innocence). 1960.

Shadowed starlight. 1961.
The Chinese garden. 1962.
Man on a tower. 1965.

Children's Books
Green smoke. 1957.
Dragon in danger. 1959.
The dragon's quest. 1961.
Arripay. 1963.
Heraldry (illustrated by Janet Price). 1966.
Boney was a warrior. 1966.

MANVELL, ARNOLD ROGER (1909–)
English biographer, broadcaster and writer on
cinema; educated at the universities of Leicester
and London; extramural lecturer, Bristol University (1938–40); M.O.I. (1940–5); director of the
British Film Academy (1947–59); consultant of the
Society of Film and Television Arts (1959); Visiting Fellow, Sussex University (1970); a contributor to the B.B.C., *Annual register*, etc.; edited
the *Penguin film review* (1947), the *Year's work in film*
(1949 and 1950), etc.; has written (with H. Fraen-
kel) several books on aspects of Germany before
and during the Second World War.

Bibliography
Authors' and writers' who's who. 1971.
B.N.B.
Gale.
Who's who. 1973.

Novels
The dreamers. 1958.
The passion. 1960.

Other Works
Film. 1944.
A survey of the cinema and its public. 1947.
Twenty years of British film (contributed). 1947.
Experiment in the film (ed. and contributed). 1949.
A seat at the cinema. 1951.
On the air (a study of broadcasting in sound and
vision). 1953.
The animated film (with pictures from the film
Animal farm). 1954.
The film and the public. 1955.
The living screen (a study of film and TV). 1961.
What is a film? 1965.
New cinema in Europe. 1966.
This age of communication. 1967.
New cinema in the U.S.A. 1968.
Ellen Terry. 1968.
New cinema in Britain. 1969.

Sarah Siddons. 1970.
Shakespeare and the film. 1971.
Films and the Second World War. 1973.

MARCUS, FRANK (1928–)
English playwright; born in Germany of German-
Jewish parents; educated in England; businessman
(1944–65); founder of the International Theatre
Group (1968); drama critic for the *London
Magazine, Sunday Telegraph, New York Times*, etc.;
recipient of various awards; unpublished plays
include *Minuet for stuffed birds* (1950), *Studies of the
nude* (1967), *Blank pages* (1969); television plays
include *Temporary typist* (1966) and *The glove puppet* (1969).

Bibliography
B.N.B.
Contemporary dramatists.
Who's who in the theatre. 1967.

Plays
Merry-go-round (adaptation of A. Schutzler, La
    Ronde). 1953.
The formation dancers (in Plays of the Year, 28).
    1964.
The killing of sister George (filmed 1968). 1965.
Mrs. Mouse, are you within? (staged 1968, in Plays
    of the Year, 35). 1969.
The window (televised 1966, staged 1970). 1970.
Notes on a love affair (staged 1972, in Plays of the
    Year, 42). 1973.

**MARKANDANDAYA, *Mrs.* KAMALA
PURNALYA** (1924–)
Indian novelist; educated at Madras University;
has worked as a journalist; married and settled in
England (1948).

Bibliography
C.B.I.
Contemporary novelists.
Indian national bibliography 1958–67.

Novels
Nectar in a sieve. 1954.
Some inner fury. 1955.
A silence of desire. 1960.
Possession. 1963.
A handful of rice. 1966.
The coffer dams. 1969.
The nowhere man. 1972.
Two virgins. 1973.

MARKFIELD, WALLACE ARTHUR (1926–)

American-Jewish novelist; born in New York; educated at Brooklyn College and New York University; film critic, *New Leader* (1954–5); has contributed stories to *Partisan Review* and *Commentary*.

Bibliography
B.N.B.
C.B.I.
Contemporary novelists.

Novels
To an early grave. 1964.
Teitlebaum's window. 1970.

MARKHAM, FELIX MAURICE HIPPESLEY (1908–)

English historian; educated at Eton and Balliol College, Oxford; Fellow of Hertford College, Oxford (1932–70); Senior Proctor (1946–7); a contributor to the *Spectator, Sunday Times, Sunday Telegraph, Cambridge Modern History*, vol. 9, etc.; edited the *Selected writings of Henri Saint-Simon* (1952).

Bibliography
Authors' and writers' who's who. 1971.
B.N.B.
Gale.

Works
Napoleon and the awakening of Europe. 1954.
Napoleon. 1963.
Oxford. 1967.

MARLYN, JOHN (1912–)

Hungarian-born Canadian novelist; educated at Carleton University, Ottawa; served in the Second World War (1942–5); taught creative writing at Carleton University; a contributor to *Queen's Quarterly*, Canadian radio, etc.

Bibliography
Canadiana.
C.B.I.
Gale.

Novel
Under the ribs of death. 1957.

MAROWITZ, CHARLES (1935–)

American drama critic and producer, now living and writing in England; London dramatic critic of the *New York Times*.

Bibliography
Authors' and writers' who's who. 1971.
B.N.B.

Works
Method as means. 1961.
Theatre at work (with S. Trussler). 1967.
The Marowitz Hamlet, and The tragical history of Doctor Faustus. 1970.

MASON, RICHARD (1919–)

English novelist; educated at Bryanston School.

Bibliography
B.N.B.
Gale.
Who's who. 1973.

Novels
The wind cannot read (John Llewelyn Rhys Prize 1948; filmed 1958). 1947.
The shadow and the peak (filmed as Passionate summer, 1958). 1949.
The world of Suzie Wong (filmed 1959). 1957.
The fever tree. 1962.

MASSEY, REGINALD

Indian poet; born in Lahore; educated at Punjab, Delhi and Lille universities; lived in England; represented in several anthologies; has contributed to *Illustrated Weekly of India, New Statesman, Tribune*, etc.

Bibliography
B.N.B.
Contemporary poets.
Gale.

Poetry
The splintered mirror. 1960.

Other Works
Indian dances; their history and growth (with Rina Singha). 1967.
The immigrants (with Jamila Massey). 1973.

MASSINGHAM, HAROLD WILLIAM (1932–)

English poet; educated at Manchester University;

taught (1955–   ); recipient of several awards; a contributor to the *Listener, London Magazine, T.L.S., Observer,* etc.; represented in various anthologies.

Bibliography
B.N.B.
Contemporary poets.

Poetry
Black bull guarding apples. 1965.
The magician. 1969.
Storm. 1970.
Frost gods. 1971.
Snow dream. 1971.

MASTERS, ANTHONY (†RICHARD TATE)

English novelist; journalist (1958–9); worked in publishing (1959–64); full-time writer (1964–   ).

Bibliography
B.N.B.
Gale.

Novels
A pocketful of rye. 1964.
The Seahorse (John Llewelyn Rhys Prize 1967). 1966.
A literary lion. 1968.
Conquering heroes. 1969.
The donor (as †Richard Tate). 1970.
The syndicate. 1971.
Leaning on the wind. 1971.
The dead travel fast (as †Richard Tate). 1971.

Other Works
Natural history of the vampire. 1972.
The summer that bled. 1972.
Dreams about H.M. the Queen and other members of the royal family. 1972.

MASTERS, JOHN (1914–   )

English novelist; educated at Wellington and Sandhurst; Gurkha Rifles (1934–48); now a full-time writer.

Bibliography
Authors' and writers' who's who. 1971.
B.N.B.
Contemporary novelists.
Who's who. 1973.

Novels
Nightrunners of Bengal. 1951.
The deceivers. 1952.
The lotus and the wind. 1953.
Bhowani Junction (filmed 1955). 1954.
Coromandel! 1955.
Far, far, the mountain peak. 1957.
Fandango rock. 1959.
The Venus of Konpara. 1960.
To the coral strand. 1962.
Trial at Monomoy. 1964.
The breaking strain. 1967.
The rock. 1969.
The Ravi Lancers. 1972.

Other Works
Bugles and a tiger (autobiography). 1956.
The road past Mandalay (autobiography). 1961.
Fourteen eighteen. 1965.
Casanova. 1969.
Pilgrim son (autobiography). 1971.

MATHEW, RAYMOND FRANK

(1929–   )
Australian poet and writer; born and educated in Sydney; taught for many years in schools and universities; full-time writer (1961–   ); awarded several literary prizes; a contributor to literary journals in England and Australia, his unpublished plays are not listed below.

Bibliography
B.N.B.
Contemporary dramatists.
Contemporary poets.
Gale.

Novels
A Bohemian affair (short stories). 1961.
The time of the peacock (stories, with Mena Abdullah). 1965.
The joys of possession. 1967.

Poetry
With cypress pine. 1951.
Song and verse. 1956.
South of the equator. 1961.

Plays
A spring song (staged 1958). 1961.
The life of the party (staged 1960). 1965.
We find the bunyip (in Three Australian plays – includes Khaki, Bush and Bigotry). 1969.

Other Works
Miles Franklin. 1963.
Charles Blackman's painting. 1965.

MATTHIESSEN, PETER (1927–)
American writer; educated at Yale University; captain of deep-sea fishing boat, Montauban, Long Island (1954–6); took part in expeditions to Alaska, New Guinea, etc.; founder and editor of *Paris Review*; recipient of literary awards.

Bibliography
C.B.I.
Contemporary novelists.
Gale.

Novels
Race rock. 1954.
Partisans. 1955.
Raditzer. 1961.
At play in the fields of the Lord. 1965.

Other Works
The cloud forest. 1961.
Under the mountain wall. 1962.
Wildlife in America. 1964.
The shorebirds of North America. 1966.
Oomingmak. 1967.
Sal si puedes: Cesar Chavez and the New American revolution. 1970.
Shark. 1971.
Blue meridian. 1971.
The tree where man was born (with Eliot Porter). 1972.
The wind birds. 1973.
Seal pool. 1973.

MAUDE, ANGUS EDMUND UPTON (1912–)
English politician and journalist; educated at Rugby and Oriel College, Oxford; financial journalist with *The Times* (1933–4), *Daily Mail* (1935–9); served in the R.A.M.C. in the Second World War (1939–45); editor of the *Sydney Morning Herald* (1958–61); Conservative M.P. (1950–).

Bibliography
B.N.B.
Who's who. 1973.

Works
The English middle classes (with Roy Lewis). 1949.

One nation (with Iain Macleod). 1951.
Professional people. 1952.
Change is our ally (with Enoch Powell). 1954.
Biography of a nation (with Enoch Powell). 1955.
Good learning. 1964.
South Asia. 1966.
The consuming society. 1967.
The common problem. 1969.

MAUGHAM, ROBERT CECIL ROMER (†ROBIN MAUGHAM) *(2nd Viscount)* (1916–)
English novelist; nephew of W. Somerset Maugham; educated at Eton and Trinity Hall, Cambridge; served in the Second World War (1939–44); called to the Bar, Lincoln's Inn (1945); the author of several film scripts; a contributor to *Chambers' Journal, Argosy*, etc.; has adapted several plays not listed below.

Bibliography
B.N.B.
Contemporary novelists.
Gale.
Who's who. 1973.

Novels
Come to dust. 1945.
The servant (dramatised and filmed 1963). 1948.
Line on Ginger (filmed as The intruder, 1959 and republished thus 1968). 1949.
The rough and the smooth (filmed 1959). 1951.
Behind the mirror. 1955.
The man with two shadows (filmed). 1958.
November reef (filmed). 1962.
The green shade. 1966.
The second window. 1968.
The link. 1969.
The wrong people. 1970.
The last encounter. 1972.

Plays
The lonesome road (with Philip King, staged 1959). 1960.
Mr. Lear (staged 1956). 1963.
The claimant. 1964.
Enemy! 1969.
The servant (staged 1958). n.d.

Other Works
Nomad. 1947.
Approach to Palestine. 1947.
North African notebook. 1948.
Journey to Siwa. 1950.

The slaves of Timbuktu. 1961.
The Joyita mystery. 1962.
Somerset and all the Maughams. 1966.
Escape from the shadows (autobiography). 1972.

MAXWELL, GAVIN (1914–70)
Scottish writer on natural history and journalist; educated at Stowe School and Hertford College, Oxford; served in the Scots Guards in the Second World War (1939–44); owner of Soay Shark Fisheries (1944–9); portrait painter (1949–51); writer since 1952; contributed to the *Observer, New Statesman, National Geographical*, etc.

Bibliography
B.N.B.
Gale.
Who's who. 1961–1970.

Works
Harpoon at a venture. 1952.
God protect me from my friends (American title, Bandit). 1956.
A reed shaken by the wind (American title, People of the reeds. 1957). 1957.
The ten pains of death. 1959.
Ring of bright water. 1960.
The otter's tale (for children). 1962.
The rocks remain. 1963.
The house of Elrig. 1965.
Lords of the Atlas; the rise and fall of the House of Glaoua, 1893–1956. 1966.
Seals of the world. 1967.
Raven seek thy brother. 1968.
The white island. 1972.

MAY, DERWENT JANUS (1930–)
English novelist and critic; born in Eastbourne; educated at Lincoln College, Oxford; a journalist on the staff of the Continental *Daily Mail*, Paris (1963–5); English lecturer, Djakarta (1955–8); lecturer in Polish universities (1952–); contributor to *Essays in criticism, T.L.S.,* etc.

Bibliography
B.N.B.
Gale.

Novels
The professionals. 1964.
Dear parson. 1969.

MAYFIELD, JULIAN (1928–)
Black American novelist; educated at Lincoln University; served in the U.S. Army (1946–7); chief writer and editor in the office of President Nkrumah (1962–6); editor of *African Review*, Ghana (1964–6); a contributor to *Nation, Commentary, New Republic*, etc.; wrote the film of *Uptight* (1968) and the play *417* (1954); edited the papers of the Accra Assembly (1963).

Bibliography
C.B.I.
Contemporary novelists.
Gale.

Novels
The hit. 1957.
The long night. 1958.
The grand parade. 1960.

MAYNE, RICHARD (1926–)
English historian and writer; educated at St. Paul's School and Trinity College, Cambridge; director, Documentation Centre (1963–6), etc.; a contributor to the *New Statesman, Spectator, Observer, Sunday Times*, etc.

Bibliography
B.N.B.

Works
The community of Europe. 1962.
The institutions of the European community. 1968.
The recovery of Europe. 1970.

MAYNE, WILLIAM (†JAMES DYNELY) (1928–)
English children's novelist; taught in Yorkshire; a full-time writer; his edited works are not listed below.

Bibliography
B.N.B.

Children's Novels
Follow the footprints. 1953.
The world upside down. 1954.
A swarm in May. 1955.
Choristers' cake. 1956.
The member for the marsh. 1956.
The blue boat. 1957.
A grass rope. 1957.
Underground alley. 1958.
The thumbstick. 1959.

The fishing party. 1960.
The rolling season. 1960.
Thirteen o'clock. 1960.
Cathedral Wednesday. 1960.
Summer visitors. 1960.
The glass ball. 1961.
The changeling. 1961.
The twelve dancers. 1962.
The last bus. 1962.
Plot night. 1963.
On the stepping stones. 1963.
The man from the North Pole. 1963.
Words and music. 1963.
A parcel of trees. 1963.
Whistling Rufus.1963.
Sand. 1964.
Water boatman. 1964.
A day without wind. 1964.
Big wheel and little wheel. 1965.
No more school. 1965.
Pig in the middle. 1965.
Old Zion. 1966.
Rooftops. 1966.
Earthfasts. 1966.
The battlefield. 1967.
Big egg. 1967.
Toffee join. 1968.
The yellow aeroplane. 1968.
House on Farmont. 1968.
Over the hills and far away. 1968.
The gobbling billy. 1969.
Ravensgill. 1970.
Game of dark. 1971.
Ghosts. 1971.
Royal Harry. 1971.
Skiffy. 1972.
The incline. 1972.
Robin's real engine. 1972.
The jersey shore. 1973.

MAZANI, ERIC C. F. NHANDO
(†E. C. MARS) (1948–)
Rhodesian poet; mathematics teacher (1967–9);
teaching at St. Alban's Mission, Sagambe,
Rhodesia; represented in anthologies of Rhodesian
poetry.

Bibliography
C.B.I.
Contemporary poets.

Poetry
My grandmother is my love. 1965.

For my mother (pr. ptd.). 1968.
A brown tender "God" (pr. ptd.). 1968.

MEDAWAR, *Sir* PETER BRIAN
(1915–)
English zoologist and medical scholar; educated at
Marlborough and Magdalen College, Oxford; Fel-
low of Magdalen (1938–47); Professor of Zoology,
Birmingham University (1947–51); Professor of
Zoology and Comparative Anatomy, University
College, London (1951–62); Director of the
National Institute for Medical Research (1962–71);
Reith Lecturer (1959); holder of many honorary
fellowships and other honours; Nobel Prize for
Medicine (1960); a contributor to many journals.

Bibliography
Authors' and writers' who's who. 1971.
B.N.B.
Who's who. 1973.

Works
An unsolved problem of biology. 1952.
The uniqueness of the individual. 1957.
The future of man (Reith Lectures 1959). 1960.
The art of the soluble. 1967.
Induction and intuition. 1969.
The hope of progress. 1972.

MEHROTRA, ARVIND KRISHNA
(1947–)
Indian poet; born in Lahore and educated at the
universities of Allahabad and Bombay; Visiting
Writer at the University of Iowa's International
Writing Programme (1971–3); teaches English at
the University of Allahabad.

Bibliography
C.B.I.
Indian national bibliography 1958–67.

Poems
Bharatmata. 1965.
Woodcuts on paper. 1967.
Pomes/poèmes/poemas. 1971.

MEHTA, VED PARKASH (1934–)
Pakistani writer; born in Lahore; blind from the
age of 3; educated at Balliol College, Oxford, and
Harvard University; lives in New York; on the
staff of the *New Yorker* (1961–); a frequent contributor to journals and newspapers.

Bibliography
C.B.I.
Gale.
Who's who. 1973.

Works
Face to face (an autobiography). 1957.
Walking the Indian streets. 1960.
Fly and the fly-bottle; encounters with English
   intellectuals. 1963.
The new theologian. 1966.
Delinquent chacha (novel). 1967.
Portrait of India. 1970.
John is easy to please. 1971.
Daddyji. 1972.

MELTZER, DAVID (1937–)

American poet; educated at University of California, Los Angeles; worked in the Discovery Bookshop, San Francisco (1959–); a contributor to
Yale Review, Renaissance, Beatitude, etc.; represented in various anthologies; editor of *Journal for
the protection of all beings* (with L. Ferlinghetti and
Michael Semina) (1960), *San Francisco poets* (1971)
and *Birth, an anthology* (1973).

Bibliography
C.B.I.
Contemporary poets.
Gale.

Novels
How many blocks in the pile? 1968.
Orf. 1968.
The martyr. 1968.
The agent. 1968.
The healer. 1969.
The brain-plant tetrology. 1970.
Star. 1970.

Poetry
Poems (with Donald Schenker). 1957.
Ragas. 1959.
The clown. 1959.
The process. 1965.
In hope I offer a fire wheel. 1965.
The dark continent. 1967.
Yesod. 1969.
Round the lunch box. 1969.
From Eden book. 1969.
Abuliafia song. 1969.
Greenspeech. 1970.
Luna. 1970.
Letters and numbers. 1970.

Isla vista notes. 1970.
Knots. 1971.
The eyes: the blood. 1973.
Tens: selected poems 1961–71. 1973.
Hero-Lil. 1973.

Essays
We all have something to say to each other (essay
   on Kenneth Patchen). 1962.
Introduction to the outsiders (essay on Beat
   poetry). 1962.
Bazascope mother (on Robert Alexander). 1964.
Journal of the birth. 1967.
The brain plant factory. 1969.
Bark: a polemic. 1973.

MENDELSSOHN, OSCAR ADOLF (†OSCAR MILSEN) (1896–)

Australian writer; educated at Melbourne University; consulting industrial research chemist
(1925–); served in the Australian Air Force during the Second World War (1941–4); member of
Australian government industrial mission to
Europe and U.S., etc.; composer (as †Oscar
Milsen) and conductor; radio and television personality; a contributor to journals and magazines.

Bibliography
C.B.I.
Gale.

Works
The earnest drinker's digest. 1950.
The earnest drinker. 1952.
Trinken. 1953.
Liars and letters anonymous. 1960.
Drinking with Pepys. 1963.
Glossary of alcoholic beverages and related terms.
   1966.
From cellar to kitchen. 1968.
Nicely thank you; a frolic with some synonyms.
   1971.

MENEN, SALVATOR AUBREY CLARENCE (1912–)

Anglo-Indian writer; born in London; educated at
University College, London; drama critic of the
Bookman (1934); Personalities Press Service
(1937–9); All-India Radio (1940–1); script editor of
Indian information films (1943–5); advertising
agency (1947–8); a contributor to *Vogue, Harper's,
New Yorker*, etc.

Bibliography
B.N.B.
Contemporary novelists.
Gale.

Novels
The prevalence of witches. 1947.
Stumbling stone. 1949.
The backward bride. 1950.
The Duke of Gallodoro. 1952.
The abode of love. 1957.
The fig tree. 1959.
She La; a satire. 1962.
A conspiracy of women. 1966.

Other Works
Dead man in the silver market. 1954.
Rama retold (adaptation of Valmiki poem, American title, The Ramayana). 1954.
Rome revealed (American title, Rome for ourselves). 1960.
Speaking the language like a native. 1963.
India (with R. Beny). 1969.
The space within the heart (autobiography). 1970.

MENON, K. P. S. (1898–)
Indian writer and historian; born in Kottayam, Kerula; educated at Kottayam, Madras and Oxford; entered the Indian Civil Service (1921) and held a variety of appointments in India and abroad, culminating as Foreign Secretary to the Government of India (1948–52) and Ambassador to the U.S.S.R. (1952–61); President of the Sangeet Natak Akademi; was awarded Padma Bhushan by the Government of India in 1957.

Bibliography
C.B.I.
Indian national bibliography 1958–67.
National bibliography of Indian literature 1901–53.

Works
Delhi–Chungking. 1947.
Russian panorama. 1962.
Flying troika. 1963.
Many worlds (autobiography). 1966.
The lamp and the lampstand. 1968.
China past and present. 1969.
Russia revisited. 1971.
Journey round the world. n.d.
Twilight in China. n.d.
Sri C. Sankaran Nair (biography). n.d.

MERCER, DAVID (1928–)
English playwright; born in Wakefield, Yorkshire; educated at King's College, Newcastle; taught (1956–61); television playwright (1961–); wrote the script of the film *Morgan* and others; his unpublished plays and television scripts are not listed below.

Bibliography
B.N.B.
Contemporary dramatists.
Gale.
Who's who. 1973.

Plays
The generations (a trilogy of television plays, Where the difference begins, A climate of fear, The birth of a private man). 1964.
Three TV comedies (A suitable case for treatment (filmed 1966), For tea on Sunday, And did those feet). 1966.
Ride a cock horse (staged 1965). 1966.
The parachute: with two more plays (Let's murder Vivaldi, In two minds). 1967.
Belcher's luck (staged 1966). 1967.
The governor's lady (broadcast 1960, staged 1965). 1968.
On the eve of publication and other plays (for television; includes The cellar and The almond tree). 1970.
After Haggerty (staged 1970). 1970.
Flint. 1970.

MEREDITH, WILLIAM MORRIS (1919–)
American poet; educated at Princeton University; academic posts include Associate Professor of English, Connecticut College, New London (1955–); a contributor to poetry magazines; opera critic, *Hudson Review* (1955–6); awarded various literary grants and prizes; translated Apollinaire's poems (1964).

Bibliography
C.B.I.
Contemporary poets.
Gale.

Poetry
Love letter from an impossible land. 1944.
Ships and other figures. 1948.
The open sea and other poems. 1958.
The wreck of the *Thresher* and other poems. 1964.
Earth walk: new and selected poems. 1970.

MERRILL, JAMES INGRAM (1926–)
American novelist, poet and playwright; educated at Amherst College; served in the U.S. Army during the Second World War (1944–5); his plays include *The immortal husband* (1956) and *The bait* (1960); recipient of several poetry awards; a contributor to *Poetry*, Chicago, etc.

Bibliography
C.B.I.
Contemporary poets.
Gale.

Novels
Short stories. 1954.
The seraglio. 1957.
The Diblos notebook. 1965.

Poetry
The black swan. 1946.
First poems. 1951.
The country of a thousand years of peace. 1959.
Selected poems. 1961.
Water Street. 1962.
Nights and days. 1966.
The thousand and second night. 1966.
Fire screen. 1969.
Braving the elements. 1972.

Plays
Immortal husband. 1950.
Bait. 1960.

MERWIN, WILLIAM STANLEY
(1927–)
American poet, playwright and translator; educated at Princeton University; lived in England (1951–4) translating and writing for the B.B.C.; wrote plays for the Poets' Theatre, Cambridge, Mass. (1956); awarded various literary fellowships and grants; now lives in France; a contributor to *Nation, Botteghe Oscure, Encounter, T.L.S., Kenyon Review* and many other journals; represented in numerous anthologies; his translated works and unpublished plays are not listed below.

Bibliography
C.B.I.
Contemporary poets.
Gale.

Poetry
A mask for Janus. 1952.

The dancing bears. 1954.
Green with beasts. 1956.
The drunk in the furnace. 1960.
The moving target. 1963.
The lice. 1967.
Animae. 1969.
Japanese figures. 1970.
Carrier of ladders. 1970.

Other Work
Miner's pale children: a book of prose. 1970.

MICHENER, JAMES ALBERT (1907–)
American novelist and writer; educated at Colorado State University; taught in various American universities; Professor at Colorado State College of Education (1936–41); associate editor, Macmillan, New York (1941–9); awarded various academic honours and literary prizes; edited a study of the art of Jack Levine (1970).

Bibliography
C.B.I.
Contemporary novelists.
Day, A. Grove; James Michener, Twayne. 1964.
Gale.
Who's who. 1973.

Novels and Short Stories
Tales of the South Pacific (stories, Pulitzer Prize 1948, filmed 1958). 1947.
The fires of spring. 1949.
Return to Paradise (stories, filmed 1953). 1951.
The bridges at Toko-ri (filmed 1954). 1953.
Sayonara (filmed 1957). 1954.
The bridge at Andau. 1957.
Hawaii (filmed as Master of the islands, 1970). 1959.
Caravans. 1963.
The source. 1965.
The drifters. 1971.

Other Works
The unit in the social studies (with Harold Long). 1940.
The voice of Asia. 1951.
The floating world: the story of Japanese prints. 1954.
Rascals in Paradise (with A. Day). 1957.
Selected writings. 1957.
Japanese prints. 1959.
Report of the county chairman. 1961.
Iberia: Spanish travels and reflections. 1968.
The modern Japanese print: an appreciation. 1968.

America versus Americans: the revolution in middle-class values. 1969.

Presidential lottery: the reckless gamble in our electoral system. 1969.

The quality of life. 1970.

Kent state. 1971.

MIDDLETON, JOHN CHRISTOPHER (1926–)

English poet and scholar of German; educated at Felsted School and Merton College, Oxford; lecturer in German at various universities; served (1944–8) in the Second World War; his edited work is not listed below.

Bibliography
Authors' and writers' who's who. 1971.
B.N.B.
Contemporary poets.
Gale.

Poetry
Poems. 1944.
Nocturne in Eden. 1945.
Torse 3; Poems 1949–1961. 1962.
Nonsequences/self poems. 1965.
Our flowers and nice bones. 1969.
The fossil fish. 1970.
Brief case history. 1972.

Libretto
The metropolitans (comic opera, music by Jan Vogt). 1964.

MIDDLETON, OSMAN EDWARD (1925–)

New Zealand short-story writer; born in Christchurch; educated at Auckland University and the Sorbonne; served in the New Zealand Air Force (1944–5); recipient of several literary fellowships.

Bibliography
Contemporary novelists.
N.Z. national bibliography.

Short Stories
Short stories. 1953.
The stone and other stories. 1959.
A walk on the beach. 1964.
The loners. 1972.

Poetry
Six poems. 1951.

For Children
From the river to the tide. 1964.

MIKES, GEORGE (1912–)

Hungarian-born comic writer and journalist; educated in Budapest; London correspondent of Budapest papers (1931–8); B.B.C. Hungarian monitoring service (1941–5); LL.D., Budapest; a contributor to *T.L.S., Sunday Times, Punch,* etc.

Bibliography
Authors' and writers' who's who. 1971.
B.N.B.
Gale.
Who's who. 1973.

Works
How to be an alien. 1946.
How to scrape skies. 1948.
Wisdom for others. 1950.
Milk and honey, Israel explored. 1950.
Down with everybody! 1951.
Shakespeare and myself. 1952.
Über Alles. 1953.
Eight humorists. 1954.
A leap through the curtain: the story of Nova Kovach and Istvan Rabovsky. 1955.
Little cabbages. 1955.
Italy for beginners. 1956.
The Hungarian revolution. 1957.
East is east. 1958.
A study in infamy. 1959.
How to be inimitable. 1960.
Tango. 1961.
Switzerland for beginners. 1962.
The best of Mikes. 1962.
Mortal passion (novel). 1963.
Prison (ed.). 1963.
How to unite nations. 1963.
Eureka! Rummaging in Greece. 1965.
The book of snobs (with J. R. Russell, 13th Duke of Bedford). 1965.
How to be affluent. 1966.
Not by sun alone. 1967.
Boomerang. 1968.
The prophet motive. 1969.
Humour in memoriam. 1970.
The land of the rising yen: Japan. 1970.
How to run a stately home (with the Duke of Bedford). 1971.
Any souvenirs? 1971.
The spy who died of boredom. 1973.

MILES, JOSEPHINE LOUISE (1911–   )
American poet and critic; born in Chicago; educated at the universities of California, Los Angeles
and Berkeley; member of staff of University of
California, Berkeley; Professor of English
(1952–   ); recipient of many awards; her edited
works are not listed below; represented in many
anthologies.

Bibliography
C.B.I.
Contemporary poets.
Gale.

Poetry
Lives at intersection. 1939.
Poems on several occasions. 1941.
Local measures. 1946.
Prefabrications. 1955.
Poems 1930–1960. 1960.
House and home. 1961.
Civil poems. 1966.
Kinds of affection. 1967.

Other Works
Wordsworth and the vocabulary of emotion. 1942.
Pathetic fallacy in the nineteenth century. 1942.
The vocabulary of poetry: three studies. 1946.
Major adjectives in English poetry: from Wyatt to
    Auden. 1946.
Continuity of poetic language: studies in English
    poetry from the 1540s to the 1940s. 1948–51.
Eras and modes in English poetry. 1957.
Renaissance, eighteenth century and modern lan-
    guage in English poetry. 1960.
Ralph Waldo Emerson. 1964.
The language of prose and poetry. 1966.

**MILLAR, KENNETH (†JOHN
MACDONALD, †JOHN ROSS
MACDONALD, †ROSS
MACDONALD)** (1915–   )
American detective novelist; educated at the University of Western Ontario; Department of English, University of Michigan (1941–4); freelance
writer (1946–   ); a contributor to magazines and
newspapers.

Bibliography
C.B.I.

Novels
The dark tunnel. 1944.
Trouble follows me. 1946.

Blue city. 1947.
The three roads. 1948.
The moving target. 1949.
The drowning pool. 1950.
The way some people die. 1951.
The ivory grin. 1952.
Meet me at the morgue (English title, Experience
    with evil). 1953.
Find a victim. 1954.
The name is Archer. 1955.
The barbarous coast. 1956.
The doomsters. 1958.
The Galton case. 1959.
The Ferguson affair. 1960.
The Wycherly woman. 1961.
The zebra-striped hearse. 1962.
The chill. 1964.
The far side of the dollar. 1965.
Black money. 1966.
Archer in Hollywood (contains, The moving
    target, The way some people die, The barbarous
    coast). 1967.
The instant enemy. 1968.
The goodbye look. 1969.
Archer at large (contains, The Galton case, The
    chill, Black money). 1970.
The underground man. 1971.
Sleeping beauty. 1973.

MILLAR, RONALD (1919–   )
English playwright; educated at Charterhouse and
King's College, Cambridge; served in the Navy in
the Second World War; film script writer in Hollywood (1947–9); film scripts include *The Miniver
story* (1950), *Betrayed* (1954); unpublished plays
include *Zero hour* (1944) and *Parent's day* (1972).

Bibliography
B.N.B.
Contemporary dramatists.

Plays
Frieda (staged 1946, filmed 1947). 1947.
Waiting for Gillian (adaptation of Nigel Balchin, A
    way through the world) (staged 1954). 1955.
The bride and the bachelor (staged 1956). 1958.
A ticklish business (staged as The big tickle, 1958).
    1959.
The more the merrier (staged 1960). 1960.
The bride comes back (staged 1960). 1961.
The affair, The new men, The masters: three plays
    based on the novels and with a preface by
    C. P. Snow. 1964.

Robert and Elizabeth (libretto of musical based on Rudolph Besier, The Barretts of Wimpole Street, staged 1964). 1967.

Number 10 (from the novel by William Clark, staged 1967). 1967.

They don't grow on trees (staged 1968). 1969.

Abélard and Héloïse (from Helen Waddell, Peter Abelard) (staged 1970). 1970.

MILLER, ARTHUR (1915–)

American playwright; educated at the University of Michigan; married, as his second wife, the film actress Marilyn Monroe; worked at various jobs, mostly connected with the stage or films; awarded various literary prizes and honours; a contributor to several volumes of plays (not listed below) and to the *New York Times, Nation, Life*, etc.; his unpublished radio, television and stage plays are not listed below.

Bibliography
C.B.I.
Contemporary dramatists.
Gale.
Spiller.
Who's who. 1973.

Novels
Focus. 1945.
The misfits (from the film script). 1961.
I don't need you any more (stories). 1967.

Plays
That they may win (produced 1943). 1945.
The man who had all the luck (produced 1944). 1945.
All my sons. 1947.
Death of a salesman (Pulitzer Prize 1949, filmed 1951). 1949.
Enemy of the people (adapted from Ibsen). 1951.
The crucible (filmed as Witches of Salem, 1957). 1953.
A memory of two Mondays. 1955.
A view from the bridge (filmed 1961). 1955.
Collected plays. 1958.
After the fall. 1964.
Incident at Vichy (produced 1964). 1965.
The price (produced 1967). 1968.
The creation of the world and other business. 1972.

Other Works
Situation normal (reportage on the army). 1944.
Jane's blanket (for children). 1963.
In Russia (with Inge Morath). 1969.

MILLER, PETER (1920–)

Canadian poet; a contributor to *Fiddlehead, Delta, Canadian Forum*, etc.; a translator of *Alain Grandbois; selected poems with translation* (1964).

Bibliography
Canadiana.
C.B.I.
Contemporary poets.

Poetry
Meditation at noon. 1958.
A shifting pattern. 1962.

MITCHELL, ADRIAN (1932–)

English poet and journalist; educated at Christ Church, Oxford; journalist on the *Oxford Mail, Evening Standard, Daily Mail, Sunday Times*; Granada Fellow in Arts, Lancaster University (1967–9); a contributor to the *Guardian, New Statesman, Sunday Times, Observer, London Magazine, Kenyon Review, T.L.S.*; edited *Oxford poetry*, with R. Selig (1955).

Bibliography
Authors' and writers' who's who. 1971.
B.N.B.
Contemporary poets.

Novels
If you see me comin'. 1962.
The bodyguard. 1970.
Wartime. 1973.

Poetry
Poems. Oxford. 1955.
Poems. 1964.
Out loud. 1968.
Ride the nightmare. 1971.

Play
Tyger: a celebration based on the life and work of William Blake. 1971.

MITCHELL, CHARLES JULIAN HUMPHREY (1935–)

English novelist; educated at Winchester and at Wadham and St. Anthony's colleges, Oxford; television plays include *Shadow in the sun, A question of degree*, and *The alien corn*.

Bibliography
B.N.B.

Contemporary novelists.
Gale.
Who's who. 1973.

Novels
Imaginary toys. 1961.
A disturbing influence. 1962.
As far as you can go. 1963.
The white father (John Llewelyn Rhys Prize 1965;
    Somerset Maugham Award 1966). 1964.
A circle of friends. 1966.
The undiscovered country. 1968.

Play
A heritage and its history (adapted from
    I. Compton-Burnett). 1965.

MITCHELL, JOSEPH BRADY (1915–)
American military historian; educated at the U.S.
Military Academy; U.S. Army (1937–54); his-
torian, American Battle Monuments Commission,
Washington (1950–61); curator, Fort Ward
Museum, Alexandria, Va. (1963–); a contributor
to journals and encyclopaedias; his edited work is
not listed below.

Bibliography
C.B.I.
Gale.

Works
Decisive battles of the Civil War. 1955.
Decisive battles of the American Revolution. 1962.
Twenty decisive battles of the world (revision of
    E. Creasey's work) 1964
Disciplines and bayonets: the armies and leaders of
    the revolution. 1967.
Badge of gallantry. 1968.
Military leaders of the Civil War. 1972.

MITCHELL, WILLIAM ORMOND
(1914–)
Canadian novelist; educated at Manitoba University; worked at many jobs; headmaster; recipient of various awards; his unpublished plays
include many for radio and stage.

Bibliography
Canadiana.
C.B.I.
Contemporary novelists.

Novels
Who has seen the wind? 1947.

The alien (serialised in *Maclean's Magazine*). 1954.
Jake and the kid. 1961.
The kite. 1962.
The vanishing point. 1972.

**MITCHELL, YVONNE (Mrs. DEREK
MONSEY)** (1925–)
English novelist and playwright; educated at St.
Paul's Girls' School; actress (1939–); played in
repertory, with the Bristol Old Vic (1945–6), Old
Vic (London) (1946–53), Royal Shakespeare
Company (1953–4), etc.; recipient of various
awards for acting, etc.; a contributor to numerous
journals.

Bibliography
B.N.B.
Contemporary novelists.
Gale.
Who's who. 1973.

Novels
The bedsitter. 1959.
Frame for Julian. 1960.
A year in time. 1964.
Cathy away (for children). 1964.
Cathy at home (for children). 1965.
The family. 1967.
Martha on Sunday. 1970.

Plays
The same sky (staged as Here choose I. 1951). 1953.
Actress. 1957.

**MITCHISON, SONJA LOIS (Mrs. J.
GODFREY)** (1928–)
English author; daughter of Naomi Mitchison;
educated at Lady Margaret Hall, Oxford; lecturer
in Government College, Karachi; *Guardian* reporter in London, Vietnam, Laos and Cambodia;
freelance journalist in Asia and Africa.

Bibliography
B.N.B.
Gale.

Works
Nigeria; newest nation. 1960.
The overseas Chinese. 1961.
Gillian Lo (novel). 1964.
China. 1966.
Cinema in the twentieth century. 1970.

MITTELHOLZER, EDGAR AUSTIN
(1909–65)
Caribbean novelist; born and educated in New Amsterdam, British Guiana; came to England (1948); for many years a full-time writer; took his own life.

Bibliography
B.N.B.
Gale.
Jahn and Dressler.
Who was who. 1961–70.

Novels
Corentyne thunder. 1941.
A morning at the office. 1950.
Shadows move among them. 1951.
Children of Kaywana. 1952.
The Weather in Middenshot. 1952.
The life and death of Sylvia. 1953.
The harrowing of Hubertus. 1954.
My bones and my flute. 1955.
Of trees and the sea. 1956.
A tale of three places. 1957.
The Weather family. 1958.
Kaywana blood. 1958.
A tinkling in the twilight. 1959.
Latticed echoes. 1960.
Eltonsbrody. 1960.
The mad Macmullochs. 1961.
Thunder returning. 1961.
The piling of clouds. 1961.
The wounded and the worried. 1962.
Uncle Paul. 1963.
The aloneness of Mrs. Chatham. 1965.
The Jilkington drama. 1965.

Autobiography
With a Carib eye. 1958.
A swarthy boy. 1963.

MODISANE, WILLIAM BLOKE
(1923–)
South African poet and writer; associated with *Drum* magazine before emigrating to England (late 1950s); full-time writer, actor and broadcaster; represented in *Modern poetry from Africa* (Penguin, 1963), etc.; a contributor to various journals.

Bibliography
B.N.B.
Contemporary poets.
Zell and Silver.

Autobiography
Blame me on history. 1963.

MOMADAY, NATACHEE SCOTT
(1934–)
American scholar and novelist; educated at the universities of New Mexico and Berkeley, California; currently Associate Professor of English at Berkeley (1969–); edited *The complete poems of Frederick Goddard Tuckerman* (1965), etc.; reviews books on Indian subjects for the *New York Times*.

Bibliography
B.N.B.
C.B.I.
Gale.

Novels
Owl in the cedar tree. 1965.
The journey of Tai-me. 1967.
House made of dawn (Pulitzer Prize 1969). 1968.
The way to rainy mountain. 1969.

Other Work
Colorado. 1973.

MONTAGUE, ELIZABETH (1917–)
English novelist; daughter of 9th Earl of Sandwich; trained as a nurse at St. Thomas's Hospital; Lecturer at Royal College of Nursing (1947–50); a contributor to *Encounter*, etc.

Bibliography
B.N.B.
Gale.

Novels
Waiting for Camilla. 1953.
The small corner. 1955.
This side of the truth. 1957.

MONTGOMERY, STUART (1940–)
Rhodesian-born poet; educated at University College, London; founder of the Fulcrum Press (1965) and the Association of Little Presses (1966); a contributor to *Ambit*, and other little magazines.

Bibliography
B.N.B.
Contemporary poets.

Poetry
Circe. 1969.

MOORE, BRIAN (1921–)
Canadian, Irish-born, novelist; born in Belfast; served in the Second World War; emigrated to Canada (1948); recipient of various literary awards; a contributor to the *Spectator, Atlantic Monthly*, etc.; co-author with Alfred Hitchcock of the film script of *Torn curtain* (1966).

Bibliography
Authors' and writers' who's who. 1971.
B.N.B.
Canadiana.
Contemporary novelists.
Gale.
Who's who. 1973.

Novels
The lonely passion of Judith Hearne (filmed 1964). 1955.
The feast of Lupercal. 1956.
The luck of Ginger Coffey (Governor General's Award 1961; filmed 1966). 1960.
An answer from limbo. 1962.
The emperor of ice-cream. 1965.
A woman of no identity. 1968.
I am Mary Dunne. 1968.
Fergus. 1970.
The revolution script. 1972.
Catholics. 1972.

Other Work
Canada. 1964.

MOORE, NICHOLAS (1918–)
English poet; son of the philosopher G. E. Moore; edited *Poetry London*; recipient of several prizes for poetry; a contributor to various poetry reviews; represented in several anthologies; his edited work is not listed below.

Bibliography
B.N.B.
Contemporary poets.

Poetry
Buzzing around with the bee. 1941.
The island and the cattle. 1941.
A wish in season. 1941.
The cabaret, the dancer, the gentleman. 1942.
The glass tower. 1944.
Three poems. 1944.
Recollections of the gala; selected poems 1943–1948. 1950.
Book for Priscilla. n.d.

Other Works
Henry Miller. 1943.
The tall bearded iris. 1956.

MOORE, PATRICK (1923–)
English writer on astronomy; served with the R.A.F. during the Second World War (1940–5); navigator, Bomber Command (1945–52); freelance writer since 1952; Director of Armagh planetarium (1965–8); Vice-President, British Astronomical Association (1970); Lorimer Gold Medallist (1962), etc.; television broadcaster on *The Sky at Night*; a selection only of his 59 books is given below.

Bibliography
Authors' and writers' who's who. 1971.
B.N.B.
Who's who. 1973.

Works
Guide to the moon. 1953.
Suns, myths and men. 1954.
True book about worlds around us. 1955.
True book about the earth. 1955.
Guide to Mars. 1956.
The planet Venus. 1956.
The amateur astronomer. 1957.
True book about earthquakes and volcanoes. 1957.
Isaac Newton. 1957.
True book about man. 1959.
Stars and space. 1960.
Moon flight atlas. 1969.
Atlas of the universe. 1970.
Guide to the planets. 1971.
Astronomy for Birr Castle. 1972.
Challenge of the stars (with D. A. Hardy). 1972.

MOOREHEAD, ALAN McRAE (1910–)
Australian journalist; educated at Melbourne University; correspondent for the *Daily Express* in the Second World War; retired from active journalism (1946); a contributor to the *New Yorker, Holiday*, etc.

Bibliography
Authors' and writers' who's who. 1971.
B.N.B.
Gale.
Who's who. 1973.

Works
Mediterranean front. 1941.

A year of battle. 1943.
The end in Africa. 1943.
African trilogy. 1944.
Eclipse. 1945.
Montgomery. 1946.
The rage of the vulture. 1948.
The villa Diana. 1951.
The traitors. 1952.
Rum jungle. 1953.
A summer night. 1954.
Gallipoli. 1956.
The Russian revolution. 1958.
No room in the ark. 1959.
The White Nile. 1960.
The Blue Nile. 1962.
Cooper's Creek. 1963.
The fatal impact. 1966.
Darwin and the *Beagle*. 1969.
A late education (autobiography). 1970.

MORAES, DOMINIC F. (1938–)

Indian poet and writer; son of Frank Moraes; educated at Jesus College, Oxford; lived in England 1954–72; scriptwriter for Granada Television; managing editor, *Asia Magazine*, Hong Kong (1972–); represented in numerous anthologies.

Bibliography
B.N.B.
Contemporary poets.
Gale.
Indian national bibliography 1958–67.
National bibliography of Indian literature 1901–53.
Who's who. 1973.

Poetry
A beginning (Hawthornden Prize 1958). 1957.
Poems. 1960.
Penguin modern poets no. 2 (with K. Amis and P. Porter). 1962.
The brass serpent (translations from the Hebrew). 1964.
John Nobody. 1965.
Poems 1955–1965. 1966.

Other Works
Green is the grass. 1951.
Gone away; an Indian journal. 1960.
My father's son (autobiography). 1968.

MORAN, *Lord* (CHARLES McMORAN WILSON) (1882–1977)

English physician; educated at London University; served as medical officer in the First World War (1914–18); Dean, St. Mary's Hospital (1920–45); President of the Royal College of Physicians (1941–50); examiner in medicine, Cambridge and Birmingham universities; served on many committees; a contributor to medical journals, chiefly on medical education.

Bibliography
Authors' and writers' who's who. 1971.
B.N.B.
Who's who. 1973.

Works
The anatomy of courage. 1945.
Winston Churchill, the struggle for survival. 1966.

MORENO, VIRGINIA (*née* REYES, †PILÈ (1925–)

Philippine poet and playwright; educated at the universities of the Philippines and Kansas; studied stage craft at the New York City Center; currently Assistant Professor, Department of the Humanities, University of the Philippines; awarded various literary and academic fellowships and prizes; her poetry has been published in various journals and anthologies; a contributor to many periodicals, sometimes as †Pilè; her unpublished plays are not listed below.

Bibliography
C.B.I.

Plays
Straw patriot. 1967.
Itim Asu and the onyx wolf. 1971.

Poetry
Batik maker and other poems. 1969.

MORGAN, EDWIN GEORGE (1920–)

Scottish poet; born in Glasgow; educated at Glasgow University; served in the R.A.M.C. in the Second World War (1940–5); Glasgow University Lecturer and Senior Lecturer in English (1947–); a contributor to the *Encyclopaedia Britannica*, to anthologies and journals; his translations are not listed below; translated *Beowulf* into modern English (1952).

Bibliography
B.N.B.
Contemporary poets.
Gale.

Poetry
The vision of Cathkin Braes. 1952.
The Cape of Good Hope. 1955.
Starryveldt. 1965.
Scotch mist. 1965.
Emergent poems. 1967.
The second life. 1968.
Gnomes. 1968.
Vowel folder. 1969.
Penguin modern poets no. 15 (with A. Bold and E.
   Braithwaite). 1969.

MORPURGO, *Professor* **JACK ERIC**
(1918–   )
English writer and scholar; educated at Christ's
Hospital, and William and Mary College, U.S.A.;
served in the army (1939–46) during the Second
World War; Penguin Books (1946–9); general
editor, Pelican Histories (1949–61); Assistant
Director, Nuffield Foundation (1950–4); Director
General, National Book League (1955–69); Professor of American Literature, University of Leeds
(1969–   ); recipient of various academic honours;
his edited work is not listed below.

Bibliography
B.N.B.
Gale.
Who's who. 1973.

Works
American excursion. 1949.
A history of the United States (with Russell B.
   Nye). 1955.
The road to Athens. 1963.
Venice (with Martin Hürlimann). 1964.
Barnes Wallis. 1972.

MORRIS, DESMOND JOHN (1928–   )
English zoologist; educated at Birmingham University and Magdalen College, Oxford; head of
Granada Television and Film Unit, London
Zoological Society (1956–9); Curator of mammals, London Zoological Society (1959–67);
Director of Institute of Contemporary Arts
(1967–8); Chairman of zoological television programmes (1956–68); full-time writer since 1968; a
contributor to many zoological journals; editor of
Private ethnology (1967).

Bibliography
B.N.B.
Who's who. 1973.

Works
International zoo yearbook. 1959–62.
Introducing curious creatures. 1961.
The biology of art. 1962.
Apes and monkeys (for children). 1964.
The mammals: a guide to the living species. 1965.
The big cats (for children). 1965.
Men and snakes (with Ramona Morris). 1965.
Men and apes (with Ramona Morris). 1966.
Men and pandas (with Ramona Morris). 1966.
Zoo time. 1966.
The naked ape. 1967.
The human zoo. 1969.
Patterns of reproductive behaviour. 1970.
Intimate behaviour. 1971.

MORRIS, JAMES HUMPHREY
(*now* **JAN)** (1926–   )
English journalist and writer; educated at Lancing
College and Christ Church, Oxford; editorial staff
of *The Times* (1951–6); special correspondent with
the Mount Everest expedition (1953); editorial
staff of the *Guardian* (1957–62).

Bibliography
B.N.B.
Gale.
Who's who. 1973.

Works
Coast to coast (American title, As I saw the
   U.S.A.). 1956.
Sultan in Oman. 1957.
The market of Seleukia (American title, Islam
   inflamed). 1957.
Coronation Everest. 1958.
South African winter. 1958.
The Hashemite kings. 1959.
Venice. 1960.
The upstairs donkey (for children). 1962.
The world bank (American title, The road to Hud-
   dersfield). 1963.
Cities. 1963.
The outrider: a liberal view of Britain. 1963.
The presence of Spain. 1964.
Oxford. 1965.
Barcelona. 1967.
Pax Britannica, the climax of an empire. 1968.
The great port. 1970.
Heaven's command. 1973.

MORRIS, WRIGHT MARION (1910–   )
American novelist; educated at Pomona College;

lecturer at Haverford College, etc.; awarded Guggenheim Fellowship, etc.; edited *Ceremony of lone tree* (1960).

Bibliography
C.B.I.
Contemporary novelists.
Gale.

Novels
My uncle Dudley. 1942.
The man who was there. 1945.
The inhabitants. 1946.
The home place. 1948.
The world in the attic. 1949.
Man and boy. 1951.
The works of love. 1952.
The deep sleep. 1953.
The huge season. 1954.
The field of vision. 1956.
Love among the cannibals. 1957.
What a way to go. 1962.
Cause for wonder. 1963.
One day. 1965.
In orbit. 1967.
God's country and my people. 1968.
Green grass, blue sky, white house (stories). 1970.
Fire sermon. 1971.
War games. 1971.
Love-affair—a Venetian journal. 1972.

Other Works
The territory ahead; critical interpretations of American literature. 1958.
A bill of rites, a bill of wrongs, a bill of goods (essays). 1967.

MORRISON, JOHN GORDON (1904–)
English-born Australian novelist and short-story writer; a contributor to *Meanjin, Overland*, etc.

Bibliography
Annals of Australian literature.
Australian national bibliography.

Novels and Short Stories
Sailors belong ships (stories). 1947.
The creeping city. 1949.
Port of call. 1950.
Black cargo (stories). 1955.
Twenty-three (stories). 1962.
Selected stories. 1972.

MORTIMER, JOHN CLIFFORD (†GEOFFREY LINCOLN) (1923–)
English playwright, novelist and barrister; educated Harrow and Oxford; called to the Bar (1948); has written reviews for the *Evening Standard, Observer*, and *New Statesman*; his unpublished plays for stage, screen and television are not listed below; his published plays have all been produced on the London stage.

Bibliography
B.N.B.
Contemporary novelists.
Gale.
Who's who. 1973.

Novels
Charade. 1948.
Rumming Park. 1949.
Answer yes or no (American title, Silver hook and Here in transworld. 1952). 1950.
Like men betrayed. 1953.
The narrowing stream. 1954.
Three winters. 1956.

Plays
The dock brief and other plays (The dock brief produced 1958, filmed 1962, also contains What shall we tell Caroline?, I spy). 1959.
The wrong side of the park. 1960.
Lunch hour and other plays (Lunch hour produced 1960, filmed 1963, also contains Collect your hand luggage, David and broccoli, Call me a liar). 1960.
Two stars for comfort (produced 1960). 1960.
A flea in her ear (translation from Feydeau, produced 1966, filmed 1967). 1965.
The judge (produced 1967). 1967.
Five plays. 1970.
Come as you are (produced 1970). 1971.
Voyage round my father (produced 1970). 1971.
The captain of Köpenick (adapted from Zuckmeyer; produced 1971). 1971.
Collaborators (produced 1973). 1973.

Travel
With love and lizards (with Penelope Mortimer). 1957.

Other Work
No moaning at the Bar (as †Geoffrey Lincoln). 1957.

MORTIMER, PENELOPE RUTH (*née* **FLETCHER**) (1918–)
Welsh novelist; wife of John Mortimer (q.v.); a contributor to the *New Yorker, Cornhill, Observer,* etc.

Bibliography
B.N.B.
Contemporary novelists.
Who's who. 1973.

Novels
A villa in summer. 1954.
The bright prison. 1956.
Daddy's gone a-hunting. 1958.
Saturday lunch with the Brownings (short stories). 1960.
The pumpkin eater (filmed 1963). 1962.
My friend says it's bulletproof. 1967.
The home. 1971.

Travel
With love and lizards (with John Mortimer). 1957.

MOSEL, TAD (1922–)
American playwright; educated at Amherst College, Massachusetts, and at Yale and Columbia universities; served in the U.S. Army (1943–6) during the Second World War; recipient of several drama awards; has written numerous television plays; only his separately published plays are listed below.

Bibliography
C.B.I.
Contemporary dramatists.

Plays
Jinxed (televised 1949). n.d.
Other people's houses: six television plays. 1956.
The five-dollar bill (televised 1957). 1958.
All the way home (adaptation of Death in the family, by James Agee, staged 1960; Pulitzer Prize 1961). 1961.
Impromptu (staged 1961). 1961.
That is where the town's going (televised 1962). 1962.

MOSS, HOWARD (1922–)
American poet; educated at Wisconsin and Columbia universities; Instructor at Vassar College (1945–6); Poetry Editor, *New Yorker* (1948–); a contributor to *New Yorker, Harper's Bazaar,*

Nation, etc.; represented in many anthologies; his published plays and edited works are not listed below.

Bibliography
C.B.I.
Contemporary poets.
Gale.

Poetry
The wound and the weather. 1943.
The toy fair. 1954.
A swimmer in the air. 1957.
A winter come, a summer gone, poems 1946–60. 1960.
Finding them lost. 1965.
Second nature. 1968.
Selected poems. 1971.

Other Works
The magic lantern of Marcel Proust. 1962.
Writing against time: critical essays and reviews. 1969.

MOTT, MICHAEL (†CHARLES ALSTON) (1930–)
English poet and novelist; born in London; educated in New York, at Stowe School and Oriel College, Oxford; after studying art and writing in Italy and the Middle East, edited trade and technical journals, worked in book publishing and taught in the United States and Canada; a contributor to the *Listener, London Magazine, Sunday Times,* etc.

Bibliography
Authors' and writers' who's who. 1971.
B.N.B.
Contemporary poets.
Gale.

Novels
The notebooks of Susan Berry. 1962.
Helmet and wasps. 1964.

Children's Books
Master Entrick. 1966.
The blind cross. 1969.

Poetry
The cost of living, 29 poems 1953–57. 1957.
Tales of idiots. 1961.
New exile. 1961.
A book of pictures. 1962.

MOWAT, FARLEY McGILL (1921–)

Canadian writer and novelist; born in Ontario, educated at Toronto University; served in the army (1940–6) in the Second World War; spent 2 years in the Arctic (1947–8); full-time writer since 1946; a contributor to various Canadian and American periodicals.

Bibliography
Authors' and writers' who's who. 1971.
Canadiana.
C.B.I.
Gale.

Novels
Ordeal by ice. 1960.
The serpent's coil. 1961.

For Children
Lost in the barrens. 1956.
The dog who wouldn't be. 1957.
The black joke. 1962.
Owls in the family. 1963.
Never cry wolf. 1963.
The boat who wouldn't float. 1969.

Other Works
People of the deer. 1952.
The grey seas. 1958.
Desperate people. 1959.
Westviking. 1965.
The curse of the Viking grave. 1966.
Canada North. 1967.
Polar passion. 1967.
The rock within the sea. 1968.

MOYNIHAN, DANIEL PATRICK (1927–)

American sociologist; educated at the Fletcher School of Law and Diplomacy; office of the Governor, Albany, New York (1955–9); a contributor to *Commentary, Journal of Criminal Law, Public Administration Review*, etc.

Bibliography
C.B.I.
Gale.

Works
Beyond the melting pot (with Nathan Glazer). 1963.
The negro family: a case for national action (known as the Moynihan report, published anonymously). 1966.

Maximum feasible misunderstanding. 1967.
Violent crime. 1970.
Towards a national urban policy. 1970.
On equality and educational opportunity (with F. R. Mostellar). 1972.
The politics of guaranteed income. 1973.
Coping: on the practice of government. 1973.

MPHAHLELE, EZEKIEL (1919–)

South African novelist; born in Pretoria; educated at Adam's College, Natal, and the universities of South Africa, Pretoria, and Denver, Colorado; fiction editor of *Drum* magazine (1955–7); after various academic posts, currently Associate Professor of English, University of Denver (1970–).

Bibliography
B.N.B.
C.B.I.
Contemporary novelists.
Zell and Silver.

Novels and Short Stories
Man must live and other stories. 1947.
The living and the dead and other stories. 1961.
The corner B and other stories. 1967.
The wanderers. 1972.

Other Works
Down Second Avenue (autobiography). 1959.
The African image (essays). 1962.
Voices in the wind and other essays. 1972.

MUDIE, IAN MAYELSTON (1911–)

Australian poet; among numerous other jobs, he worked as a journalist and a farmhand; edited *Poets at War* (1944), etc.; Lecturer in Creative Writing, University of Adelaide Adult Education Department (1959–66); recipient of several literary awards; represented in various anthologies of Australian verse.

Bibliography
Australian national bibliography.
Contemporary poets.

Poetry
Corroboree to the sun. 1940.
This is Australia. 1941.
Their seven stars unseen. 1943.
The Australian dream. 1943.
Poems 1934–1944. 1945.
The blue crane. 1959.

The north-bound ride. 1963.
Look, the kingfisher! 1970.

For Children
The Christmas kangaroo. 1946.
Rivers of Australia. 1966.
Australia today. 1970.

Other Works
Riverboats. 1961.
Wreck of the *Admella*. 1967.
The heroic journey of John McDouall Stuart. 1968.
Murray River sketch book. 1970.

MULIKITA, FWANYANGA MATALE
(1928–)
Zambian writer and politician; educated at Fort
Hare University College, and Stanford and Columbia universities; interpreter-clerk in the high
court (1950–2); teacher (1954–6); Welfare Officer
(1956–7); Headmaster (1960–4); Zambia's first
ambassador to the U.N. (1964–6); Education Secretary (1966–8); Foreign Affairs Secretary
(1968–); Cabinet Minister (1969–); only his
work in English is listed below.

Bibliography
B.N.B.
Jahn and Dressler.
Zell and Silver.

Works
Shaka Zulu (play). 1967.
A point of no return (stories). 1967.

MUNONYE, JOHN (1929–)
Nigerian novelist; born in Akokwa; educated at
Christ the King College, Onitsha, University College, Ibadan, and London University; worked in
the Ministry of Education, Nigeria (1954–); currently principal of the Alvan Ikoku College,
Owerri.

Bibliography
B.N.B.
Jahn and Dressler.
Zell and Silver.

Novels
The only son. 1966.
Obi. 1969.
The oil man of Obange. 1971.
A wreath for maidens. 1973.
A dancer of fortune. 1974.

MUNRO, ALICE (*née* LAIDLAW)
(1931–)
Canadian novelist; born in Ontario; educated at the
University of Western Ontario; full-time writer.

Bibliography
Canadiana.
C.B.I.
Gale.

Novels and Short Stories
Dance of the happy shades (stories, Governor Gen-
eral's Award 1969). 1968.
Lives of girls and women. 1971.

MURDOCH, JEAN IRIS (*Mrs.*
BAYLEY) (1919–)
Irish novelist; born in Dublin; educated at Somer-
ville College, Oxford; tutor in philosophy at St.
Anne's College, Oxford (1948–); contributor to
the *Listener*, etc.; contributed to *The Nature of
Metaphysics*, a symposium (1957).

Bibliography
B.N.B.
Contemporary dramatists.
Contemporary novelists.
Gale.
Who's who. 1973.

Novels
Under the net. 1954.
The flight from the enchanter. 1956.
The sandcastle. 1957.
The bell. 1958.
A severed head (dramatised 1963, filmed 1969).
    1961.
An unofficial rose. 1962.
The unicorn. 1963.
The Italian girl (dramatised 1967). 1964.
The red and the green. 1965.
The time of the angels. 1966.
The nice and the good. 1968.
Bruno's dream. 1969.
A fairly honourable defeat. 1970.
An accidental man. 1971.
The black prince. 1973.

Plays
A severed head (from the novel, with
    J. B. Priestley). 1964.
The Italian girl (from the novel, with James Saun-
    ders). 1968.

Other Works
Sartre; romantic rationalist. 1953.
The sovereignty of good. 1970.

MURPHY, RICHARD (1927–)
Irish poet; born in County Mayo; educated at King's School, Canterbury, Wellington and Magdalen College, Oxford; writer-in-residence, University of Virginia (1965); Visiting Fellow, Reading University (1968); O'Connor Professor of Literature, Colgate University (1971); recipient of several poetry awards; represented in various anthologies.

Bibliography
Authors' and writers' who's who. 1971.
B.N.B.
Contemporary poets.
Gale.

Poetry
The archaeology of love. 1955.
The last Galway hooker. 1961.

Sailing to an island. 1963.
Penguin modern poets no. 7 (with J. Silkin and N. Tarn). 1965.
The battle of Anghrin, and The god who eats the corn. 1968.

MURRAY, LESLIE ALLAN (1938–)
Australian poet; born in New South Wales; educated at New South Wales University, Sydney; scholarly and technical translator (1963–); represented in numerous anthologies; a contributor to the Australian radio, *Meanjin*, *Quadrant*, etc.

Bibliography
Annals of Australian literature.
Australian national bibliography.
Contemporary poets.
Gale.

Plays
The ilex tree (with G. Lehmann). 1965.
The weatherboard cathedral. 1969.
Poems against economics. 1972.

N

NAIPAUL, VIDIADHAR SURAJPRASAD (1932–)
Caribbean novelist; born in Trinidad; educated at University College, Oxford; a contributor to the *T.L.S.*, *New Statesman*, *Punch*, etc.; recipient of several literary awards.

Bibliography
Authors' and writers' who's who. 1971.
B.N.B.
Contemporary poets.
Gale.
Jahn and Dressler.
Who's who. 1973.

Novels
The mystic masseur (John Llewelyn Rhys Prize 1958). 1957.
The suffrage of Elvira. 1958.
Miguel Street (Somerset Maugham Award 1961). 1959.

A house for Mr. Biswas. 1961.
Mr. Stone and the knight's companion (Hawthornden Prize 1964). 1963.
The mimic men. 1967.
A flag on the island. 1967.
In a free state (Booker Prize 1971). 1971.
The chip-chip gatherers. 1973.

Other Works
The middle passage; impressions of five societies. 1962.
An area of darkness, an experience of India. 1964.
The loss of El Dorado: a history. 1969.
The overcrowded barracoon: selected articles 1958–1972. 1972.

NAMJOSHI, SINITI (1941–)
Indian poet; born in Bombay; educated at University of Poona; Indian Administrative Service; a contributor to *Poetry India*, etc.

Bibliography
Contemporary poets.
Indian national bibliography 1958–67.

Poetry
Poems. 1967.
Transcreations from Gorindagraj. 1968.

NANDY, PRITISH (1947–)
Indian poet and editor; educated in Calcutta; a contributor to journals in India and the U.S.A.; his edited and translated work is not listed below.

Bibliography
C.B.I.
Contemporary poets.
Indian national bibliography 1958–67.

Poetry
Of gods and olives. 1967.
I hand you in turn my Nebbuk wreath. 1968.
On either side of arrogance. 1968.
Rites for a plebeian statue; an experiment in verse drama. 1969.
From the outer bank of the Brahmaputra. 1969.
Masks to be interpreted in terms of messages. 1970.
Madness is the second stroke. 1971.
The poetry of Pritish Nandy. 1973.

NAUGHTON, BILL (1910–)
Irish playwright and novelist; Civil Defence driver during the Second World War; worked as a lorry driver, weaver, etc.; recipient of two screenwriters' awards; unpublished plays include *Annie and Fanny* (1967), *Lighthearted intercourse* (1971); radio plays include *Timothy* (1956) and *November day* (1963); television plays include *It's your move* (1967) and several series including the *Nathaniel Titlark* series (1957).

Bibliography
B.N.B.
Contemporary dramatists.

Novels
Rafe Granite. 1947.
One small boy. 1957.
Late night in Watling Street (radio play 1959) and other stories. 1959.
The goal keeper's revenge (stories). 1961.
Alfie (filmed 1965). 1961.
Alfie darling. 1971.

Plays
Alfie (broadcast as Alfie Elkins and his little life, 1962, staged 1963, filmed 1966). 1963.
All in good time (staged 1963). 1964.
Spring and port wine (broadcast as My flesh, my blood, 1957; staged in Birmingham, 1964 and in New York as Keep it in the family, 1967, filmed 1969). 1967.

Autobiography
A roof over your head. 1945.
Pony boy. 1966.

NAYAR, KULDIP (1923–)
Indian writer; born in Sialkot; educated at the North Western University, Evanston, U.S.A.; editor and general manager, *United News of India* (1964–7); a contributor to *The Times*, *Spectator* and *Washington Evening Star*; secretary general of All India Newspaper Editors' Conference; resident editor, the *Statesman*, New Delhi.

Bibliography
C.B.I.
Indian national bibliography 1958–67.
National bibliography of Indian literature 1901–53.

Works
Between the lines. n.d.
India critical years. n.d.
Distant neighbours. n.d.

NEMEROV, HOWARD (1920–)
American novelist; educated at Harvard University; served in the Air Force during the Second World War (1942–5); member of the faculty of English at colleges and universities (1946–), etc.; consultant in poetry, Library of Congress (1963–4); recipient of various literary awards; a contributor to many journals; edited *Poets on poetry* (1967).

Bibliography
C.B.I.
Contemporary novelists.
Contemporary poets.
Gale.

Novels
The melodramatists. 1949.
Feredigo, or the power of love. 1954.
The homecoming game. 1957.

A commodity of dreams and other stories. 1959.
Endor. 1962.
Stories, fables and other diversions. 1971.

Poetry
The image and the law. 1947.
Guide to the ruins. 1950.
The salt garden. 1955.
Mirrors and windows. 1958.
New and selected poems. 1960.
The next room of the dream (poems and verse plays). 1962.
Blue swallows. 1967.
The winter lightning: selected poems. 1968.
Gnomes and occasions: poems. 1972.

Other Works
Poetry and fiction (essays). 1963.
Journal of the fictive life. 1965.
Reflections on poetry and poetics. 1972.

NETTLEFORD, REX M.

English-born Jamaican social historian; born in Falmouth; educated at the universities of the West Indies and Oxford; after various academic posts in the West Indies, Director of Extra-Mural Studies, Jamaica (1971–   ); leader of cultural missions to the United States, England, Canada, etc.; founder and Artistic Director of Jamaican National Dance Theatre Company; a contributor to *The Times*, *Caribbean Quarterly*, etc.

Bibliography
B.N.B.
C.B.I.
Gale.

Works
The Rastafari in Jamaica (with M. G. Smith and F. R. Angier). 1960.
Our heritage (with John Hearne). 1963.
Jamaica labrish (with Louise Bennett). 1965.
Roots and rhythms; Jamaica's national dance theatre (with Maria La Yacona). 1969.
Mirror, mirror: identity, race and protest in Jamaica. 1970.

NEWBY, GEORGE ERIC (†JAMES PARKER) (1919–   )

English travel writer; educated at St. Paul's School; served in the army in the Second World War (1939–45); manager of Worth-Paquin (1945–56); with Secker and Warburg, publishers (1956–9);

dress buyer, John Lewis Partnership (1959–63); has travelled widely; travel editor of the *Observer*; a member of the Association of Cape Horners; a contributor to *The Times*, *Vogue*, *Flair*, *Holiday*, etc.

Bibliography
B.N.B.
Contemporary novelists.
Gale.
Who's who. 1973.

Works
The last grain race. 1956.
A short walk in the Hindu Kush. 1958.
Something wholesale. 1962.
Slowly down the Ganges. 1966.
Grain race: pictures of life before the mast in a windjammer. 1968.
The wonders of Britain (with Diana Petry). 1968.
The wonders of Ireland (with Diana Petry). 1969.
Something wholesale (epilogue). 1970.
Love and war in the Apennines. 1971.
The world of Evelyn Waugh. 1973.
Ganga. 1973.

NEWBY, PERCY HOWARD (1918–   )

English novelist; served in the Second World War (1939–45); lecturer at Fouad First University (1942–6); joined the B.B.C. (1949); currently Controller, B.B.C. Radio Three; recipient of several literary awards.

Bibliography
B.N.B.
Contemporary novelists.
G. S. Fraser. P. H. Newby. 1974.
Gale.
N.C.B.E.L.
Who's who. 1973.

Novels
A journey to the interior (Somerset Maugham Award 1948). 1945.
Agents and witnesses. 1947.
Mariner dances. 1948.
The snow pasture. 1949.
The young May moon. 1950.
A season in England. 1951.
A step to silence. 1952.
The retreat. 1953.
The picnic at Sakkara. 1955.
Revolution and roses. 1957.

Ten miles from anywhere (stories). 1958.
A guest and his going. 1959.
The Barbary light. 1962.
One of the founders. 1965.
Something to answer for (Booker Prize 1969). 1968.
A lot to ask. 1973.

For Children
The spirit of Jem. 1947.
The loot runners. 1951.

Other Works
Maria Edgeworth. 1950.
The novel, 1945–50. 1952.

NEWLOVE, JOHN HERBERT (1938–)
Canadian poet; born in Saskatchewan; represented in various anthologies; a contributor to *Tamarack Review*.

Bibliography
Canadiana.
C.B.I.
Contemporary poets.
Gale.

Poetry
Grave sirs (pr. ptd.). 1962.
Elephants, mothers and others. 1963.
The moving in alone. 1965.
Notebook pages. 1966.
What they say. 1967.
Black night widow. 1968.
The cave. 1971.

NGUGI, JAMES TIIIONG'O (1938–)
Kenyan novelist, son of a Kenyan peasant; educated at Makerere University College, and Leeds University; Lecturer in English, University College, Nairobi (1967–9); resigned in protest at the college's closure following a student strike; editor of *Zuka: a journal of East African creative writing*; on the staff of the North Western University, Evanston, Illinois (1970–1); a contributor of short stories to *Transition*, *New African*, etc.

Bibliography
B.N.B.
Contemporary novelists.
Jahn and Dressler.
Zell and Silver.

Novels
The river between. 1965.
A grain of wheat. 1967.
Homecoming. 1973.

Play
The black hermit (staged in Nairobi, 1962). 1968.

†**NIALL, IAN (JOHN McNEILIE)**
Scottish novelist and writer.

Bibliography
Authors' and writers' who's who. 1971.
B.N.B.

Novels
No resting place. 1948.
Tune on a melodeon. 1948.
Fox hollow. 1950.
The deluge. 1951.
The boy who saw tomorrow. 1952.
A tiger walks. 1960.
The harmless albatross. 1961.
Hey, Delaney. 1962.
Fishing for trouble (for children). 1968.
The owl hunters (for children). 1969.
The Galloway shepherd. 1970.
The village policeman. 1971.
The forester. 1972.

Other Works
Poacher's handbook. 1950.
Fresh words. 1951.
Pastures new. 1952.
The new poacher's handbook. 1960.
Trout from the hills. 1961.
The gamekeeper. 1965.
The way of the countryman. 1965.
Country blacksmith. 1966.
A Galloway childhood. 1967.
A fowler's world. 1968.
Wild life of field and hedgeside. 1970.
Wild life of moor and mountain. 1970.
The forester. 1972.
Around my house. 1973.

NICHOL, BARRIE PHILLIP
(bp nichol) (1944–)
Canadian concrete poet; born in Vancouver; educated at the University of British Columbia; co-editor of *grOnk*, Toronto; a contributor to *Quarry*, *Talon*; represented in various anthologies including *New Wave Canada* (1966), *Anthology of concrete*.

poetry (1967) and *Concrete poetry* (1969); such of his works (1965–71) as can be traced are listed below.

Bibliography
Canadiana.
C.B.I.
Contemporary poets.

Novels
Andy. 1969.
For Jesus lunatick. 1969.

Poetry
Cycles, etc. 1965.
Konfessions of an Elizabethan fan dancer. 1967.
bp (a three-part package of a book of trad poems *Journeying; the returns*, a record of sound poems *Borders*, a package of concrete poems objects *Letters home*). 1967.
Journeyings and returns. 1968.

Poem Units (pamphlets)
Scraptures; 2nd sequence. 1965.
Calendar. 1966.
Strange grey town. 1966.
Scraptures; 3rd sequence. 1966.
Scraptures; 4th sequence. 1966.
Fodder folder. 1966.
Portrait of David. 1966.
A vision in the U of T stacks. 1966.
A little pome for yur fingertips. 1966.
Langwedge. 1966.
Alphabit. 1966.
Stan's ikon. 1966.
The birth of O. 1966.
Chocolate poem. 1966.
Last poems with you in mind. 1967.
Scraptures; 10th sequence. 1967.
Scraptures; 11th sequence. 1967.
Ruth. 1967.
The year of the fog. 1967.
Ballads of the restless Ar. 1968.
Dada Lama. 1968.
A new calendar. 1969.
Complete works. 1969.
Pope Leo, el elope: a tragedy in four letters. 1969.
Lament. 1969.
Third fragment from a poem continually in the process of being written. 1969.
Still water. 1970.
The cosmic chef. 1970.
Nights on prose mountain. 1970.
The true eventual story of Billy the Kid. 1970.

NICHOLS, PETER (1927–   )

English playwright and actor; educated at Bristol Grammar School, Bristol Old Vic School, and at college of education; taught (–1960); television and film scriptwriter (1960–7); his unpublished plays, or those only published in anthologies, include *Hooded terror* (1963) and *Neither up nor down* (1972).

Bibliography
B.N.B.
Contemporary dramatists.

Plays
A day in the death of Joe Egg (staged 1967, filmed 1972). 1967.
The national health, or Nurse Morton's affair (staged 1969, filmed 1972). 1970.
Forget-me-not Lane. 1971.
Italia, Italia. 1973.

NICHOLSON, NORMAN CORNTHWAITE (1914–   )

English poet and writer; lecturer on modern poetry and religion; book-critic and broadcaster; editor of the *Pelican anthology of religious verse*.

Bibliography
Authors' and writers' who's who. 1971.
B.N.B.
Contemporary poets.
Gale.
N.C.B.E.L.
Who's who. 1973.

Novels
The fire of the Lord. 1945.
The green shore. 1947.

Poetry
Five rivers. 1944.
Rock face. 1948.
The pot geranium. 1954.
Selected poems. 1966.
A local habitation. 1972.

Verse Drama
The old man of the mountains (produced 1946). 1946.
Prophesy to the wind. 1949.
A match for the devil. 1955.
Birth by drowning. 1960.

Criticism
Man and literature. 1943.

H. G. Wells. 1948.
William Cowper. 1951.

Topography
Cumberland and Westmorland. 1949.
The lakers. 1955.
Provincial pleasures. 1959.
Portrait of the lakes. 1963.
Greater lakeland. 1969.

†NICOL, ABIOSEH (DAVIDSON SYLVESTER HECTOR WILLOUGHBY NICOL) (1924–)

Sierra Leonean novelist, poet, doctor and diplomat; born in Freetown; educated in Nigeria, Sierra Leone and at Christ's College, Cambridge; qualified as a pathologist; lectured in natural sciences and pathology in Cambridge, California, etc.; senior pathologist, Mayo Clinic, Rochester, Minnesota (1957–9); Vice-Chancellor, Fourah Bay College, Freetown (1966–8); ambassador to the U.N., etc. (1968–); recipient of awards and honorary degrees; his poetry has been published in numerous anthologies.

Bibliography
B.N.B.
Contemporary novelists.
G. J. Williams, A bibliography of Sierra Leone (1925–69). New York. 1970.
Zell and Silver.

Short Stories
The truly married woman and other stories. 1965.
Two African tales. 1965.

Other Works
Alienation: an essay. 1960.
Africa: a subjective view. 1964.
Africanus Horton: the dawn of nationalism in modern Africa (American title, Black nationalism in Africa. 1967). 1969.

NICOL, ERIC PATRICK (†JABEZ)

(1919–)
Canadian journalist and humorous writer; born in Ontario; educated at the universities of British Columbia and the Sorbonne; radio scriptwriter and freelance journalist (1950–).

Bibliography
Authors' and writers' who's who. 1971.
Canadiana.
C.B.I.

Humorous Works
Sense and nonsense. 1948.
The roving I. 1950.
Twice over lightly. 1953.
Shall we join the ladies? 1955.
Girdle me a globe. 1957.
In darkest domestica. 1959.
Uninhibited history of Canada (with Peter Whalley). 1961.
Say Uncle (with Peter Whalley). 1961.
A herd of yaks. 1962.
Russian anyone? (with Peter Whalley). 1963.
Space age, go home! 1964.
100 years of what? 1966.
A scar is born. 1968.
Don't move. 1970.

Other Work
Vancouver. 1970.

NICOLE, CHRISTOPHER ROBIN (†ANDREW YORK, †PETER GRANGE) (1930–)

Caribbean novelist; born and educated in Georgetown, British Guiana; worked in West Indian branches of the Royal Bank of Canada (1947–56); settled in Guernsey and devoted himself to full-time writing.

Bibliography
B.N.B.
Contemporary novelists.
Gale.

Novels
Off white. 1959.
Shadows in the jungle. 1961.
Ratoon. 1962.
Dark noon. 1963.
Amyot's cay. 1964.
Blood Amyot. 1964.
The Amyot crime. 1965.
White boy. 1966.
The self lovers. 1968.
The thunder and the shouting. 1969.
The longest pleasure. 1970.
The face of evil. 1970.

As †Andrew York
The eliminator. 1966.
The co-ordinator. 1967.
The predator. 1968.
The deviator. 1969.
The denominator. 1969.

The doom fishermen. 1969.
The infiltrator. 1971.
The expurgator. 1972.
Appointment in Kiltone (American title, Operation Neptune). 1972.
Operation destruct. 1974.

As †Peter Grange
King Creole. 1966.
The devil's emissary. 1969.
The tumult at the gate. 1970.

For Children
Manhunt for a general. 1970.
Where the cavern ends. 1971.

Other Works
West Indian cricket. 1957.
The West Indies, their people and history. 1965.

NKOSI, LEWIS (1936–)
South African essayist and literary critic; worked on the Zulu–English weekly, *Ilanga lase Natal* (1955); on the staff of *Drum* magazine (1956–60); studied at Harvard University on a fellowship (1960–1) and was not allowed re-entry into South Africa; a contributor to the *New Yorker, New Statesman, Africa Today, Black Orpheus*, etc.; now lives in London; his play *Malcolm* televised (1967) and staged (1972); radio plays are *The trial* (1967) and *We can't all be Martin Luther King* (1971).

Bibliography
B.N.B.
Contemporary dramatists.
Jahn and Dressler.
Zell and Silver.

Works
The rhythm of violence (play). 1964.
Home and exile (essays). 1965.

NKRUMAH, *Dr.* **KWAME** (1909–72)
First President of Ghana (1960–6); educated at Pennsylvania and London universities; taught (1931–4); after a distinguished and controversial political career, Prime Minister of Ghana (1957–60); recipient of many academic and other awards; deposed (1966) and fled the country.

Bibliography
B.N.B.

Ghana national bibliography.
Who's who. 1972.

Works
Towards colonial freedom. 1946.
What I mean by positive action. 1950.
Ghana: the autobiography of Kwame Nkrumah. 1957.
I speak of freedom. 1961.
Africa must unite. 1963.
Consciencism. 1964.
Neo-colonialism. 1965.
Challenge of the Congo. 1966.
Axioms of Kwame Nkrumah. 1967.
Dark days in Ghana. 1968.
Handbook of revolutionary warfare. 1968.
A guide to the armed phase of the African revolution. 1968.
The big lie. 1969.
The struggle continues. 1969.
Voice from Conakry. 1969.
The way out. 1969.
Two myths. 1969.
Class struggle in Africa. 1970.
Revolutionary path. 1973.

NORMAN, FRANK (1939–)
English playwright; son of a costermonger; jailed for burglary (1954–7); worked as a van-driver; served in the army; has written television plays and film scripts not listed below.

Bibliography
B.N.B.
Contemporary dramatists.
Gale.

Novels
The monkey pulled his hair. 1967.
Barney snip-artist. 1968.
Dodgem-greaser. 1971.
One of your own. 1973.

Play
Fings ain't wot they used t'be (musical, staged 1960). 1962.

Other Works
Bang to rights. 1958.
Stand on me. 1960.
The Guntz. 1962.
Soho day and night. 1966.
Norman's London. 1969.
Banana boy (autobiography). 1969.

Lock 'em up and count 'em (on penal reform). 1971.
Lives of Frank Norman (anthology). 1972.

Bibliography
Canadiana.
C.B.I.
Contemporary poets.
Gale.

NORSE, HAROLD
American poet; born in New York; educated at New York University; lived in Europe and North Africa (1953–); a contributor to *Evergreen Review*, etc.; represented in two anthologies; translated Belli, *Roman Sonnets* (1960).

Bibliography
C.B.I.
Contemporary poets.

Poetry
The undersea mountain. 1953.
The dancing beasts. 1962.
Karma circuit. 1967.
Penguin modern poets no. 13 (with C. Bukowski and P. Lamantia). 1969.

NORTON, MARY
English children's novelist; acted at the Old Vic until her marriage; lives in Portugal; started writing while in the U.S.A. during the Second World War; returned to England (1943).

Bibliography
B.N.B.
C.B.I.

Children's Novels
The magic bed-knob. 1945.
Bonfires and broomsticks. 1947.
The borrowers. 1952.
The borrowers afield. 1955.
Bed-knob and broomstick (reissue of The magic bed-knob, and Bonfires and broomsticks; filmed 1971). 1957.
The borrowers afloat. 1959.
The borrowers aloft. 1961.
The borrowers omnibus. 1966.

NOWLAN, ALDEN (1933–)
Canadian poet and journalist; born in Nova Scotia; journalist for New Brunswick newspapers (1952–); a contributor to the *New York Times*, *Canadian Forum*, *Tamarack Review*, *New York Herald Tribune*, etc.; represented in numerous anthologies.

Short Story
Miracle at Indian River. 1968.

Poetry
The rose and the puritan. 1958.
A darkness in the earth. 1959.
Wind in a rocky country. 1960.
Under the ice. 1961.
The things which are. 1962.
Bread, wine and salt (Governor General's Award 1968). 1967.
A black plastic button and a yellow rag. 1967.
The mysterious naked man. 1969.
Playing the Jesus game. 1970.
Between tears and laughter. 1971.

NUTTALL, JEFF (1933–)
English poet, musician and editor; born at Clitheroe, Lancs.; taught art; Lecturer in Fine Arts, Leeds College of Art.

Bibliography
B.N.B.
Contemporary poets.

Novels
The case of Isabel and the bleeding foetus. 1966.
Come back sweet prince. 1966.
Mr. Watkins got drunk and had to be carried home. 1968.
Oscar Christ and the immaculate conception. 1969.

Poetry
The limbless virtuoso. 1963.
Songs sacred and secular (pr. ptd.). 1964.
Poems I want to forget. 1965.
Journals. 1968.
Penguin modern poets no. 12 (with A. Jackson and W. Wantling). 1968.
Poems 1963–69. 1970.

Other Works
Bomb culture (social criticism). 1968.
Pig. 1969.

NUTTING, *Rt. Hon.* **HAROLD ANTHONY** (1920–)
English Conservative politician; educated at Eton and Trinity College, Cambridge; Parliamentary Under-secretary of State for Foreign Affairs (1951–4); Privy Councillor (1954); Foreign Secretary (1954–6).

Bibliography
B.N.B.
Gale.
Who's who. 1973.

Works
I saw for myself. 1958.
Disarmament. 1959.
Europe will not wait. 1960.
Lawrence of Arabia. 1961.
The Arabs. 1964.
Gordon, martyr and misfit. 1966.
No end of a lesson. 1967.
The scramble for Africa. 1970.
Nasser. 1972.

NWAPA, FLORA NWANZURUANA
Nigerian novelist; brought up in Oguta, E. Nigeria; educated in Lagos and at Edinburgh University; worked in school administration and taught.

Bibliography
B.N.B.
Jahn and Dressler.
Zell and Silver.

Novels
Efuru. 1966.
Idu. 1969.

NYE, RUSSELL BLAINE (1913–)
American historian; educated at the University of Wisconsin; university instructor, etc. (1936–); currently Distinguished Professor of English (Michigan State University); Pulitzer prizewinner; his edited work is not listed below.

Bibliography
C.B.I.
Gale.

Works
George Bancroft, Brahmin rebel. 1944.
Fettered freedom; civil liberties and the slavery controversy. 1949.
Midwestern progressive politics; a historical study of its origins and development 1870–1950. 1951.
A history of the United States (with J. E. Morpurgo). 1955.
William Lloyd Garrison and the humanitarian reformers. 1955.
Baker's dozen; thirteen unusual Americans. 1956.
The cultural life of the new nation, 1776–1830. 1960.
Structure reading and writing (with Wilma R. Ebbitt). 1961.
Michigan (for children). 1966.
This almost chosen people; essays in the history of American ideas. 1966.
The writing of American history. 1967.
The unembarrassed muse; the popular arts in America. 1970.

NZEKWU, ONUORA (1928–)
Nigerian novelist; born in Kafanchan, Northeastern Nigeria; trained as a teacher; taught for 9 years; editor of *Nigerian Magazine* (1962–); a Biafran partisan during the Civil War; has travelled in Europe and America.

Bibliography
B.N.B.
Jahn and Dressler.
Zell and Silver.

Novels
Wand of noble wood. 1961.
Blade among the boys. 1962.
Eze goes to school (with Michael Crowder). 1963.
Highlife for lizards. 1965.

O

OAKES, PHILIP (1928–)
English novelist and poet; born in Stafford; educated at the Royal School, Wolverhampton; film critic and columnist (1956–8); Granada Television scriptwriter (1959–61); a contributor to the *Sunday Times*; represented in various anthologies.

Bibliography
Authors' and writers' who's who. 1971.
B.N.B.
Contemporary poets.

Novels
Exactly what we want. 1962.
The God botherers. 1969.
Experiment at Proto. 1973.

Poetry
Unlucky Jonah, twenty poems. 1955.
In the affirmative. 1968.
Married/singular. 1973.

OAKLEY, BARRY K. (1931–)
Australian novelist; born in Melbourne; educated at Melbourne University; taught (1955–62); advertising copywriter (1964–5); writer, Australian Department of Trade and Industry (1966–); a contributor to *Meanjin*, *Quadrant*, etc.

Bibliography
Australian national bibliography.
C.B.I.

Novels
A wild ass of a man. 1967.
A salute to the great McCarthy. 1970.
Let's hear it from Prendergast: a novel. 1971.
How they caught Kevin Farrelly. 1973.

OATES, JOYCE CAROL (1938–)
American novelist, poet and short-story writer; educated at Syracuse and Wisconsin universities; instructor in English, Detroit University; a contributor to numerous magazines and periodicals; her edited work and unpublished plays are not listed below.

Bibliography
C.B.I.

Contemporary novelists.
Gale.

Novels
By the North Gate (stories). 1963.
With shuddering fall. 1964.
Upon the sweeping flood and other stories. 1966.
Garden of earthly delight. 1967.
Expensive people. 1968.
Them. 1969.
Marriages and infidelities. 1972.
Wheel of love (stories). 1972.
Wonderland. 1973.

Poetry
Anonymous sin. 1969.
Love and its derangement. 1970.

Other Work
The edge of impossibility; tragic forms in literature. 1972.

O'BRIEN, CONOR CRUISE (†DONAT O'CONNELL) (1917–)
Irish writer and diplomat; educated at Trinity College, Dublin; Department of External Affairs of Ireland (1944–); U.N. (1956–61); Vice-chancellor of Ghana University (1962–5); Professor of Humanities, New York University (1965–9); edited *The shaping of modern Ireland* (1959), *Power and consciousness* (1969) and *Edmund Burke; reflections on the revolution in France* (1969).

Bibliography
B.M. catalogue.
B.N.B.
Who's who. 1973.

Works
Maria Cross (as †Donat O'Connell). 1952.
Parnell and his party. 1957.
To Katanga and back. 1962.
Conflicting concepts of the United Nations. 1964.
Writers and politics. 1965.
The United Nations; sacred drama (illus. by Felix Topolski). 1967.
Murderous angels. 1968.
Conor Cruise O'Brien introduces Ireland. 1969.
Camus. 1970.

The Mourides of Senegal. 1971.
A concise history of Ireland. 1972.
The suspecting glance (with Maire Cruise O'Brien). 1972.
States of Ireland. 1972.

O'BRIEN, EDNA (*Mrs.* GEBLER) (1932–)

Irish novelist; author of several film and television scripts; a contributor to the *New Yorker*, etc.

Bibliography
B.N.B.
Gale.

Novels
The country girls. 1960.
The lonely girl (published as The girl with green eyes, and filmed 1964). 1962.
Girls in their married bliss. 1964.
August is a wicked month. 1964.
Casualties of peace. 1966.
The love object (short stories). 1968.
A pagan place (dramatised 1971). 1970.
Zee & Co. 1971.
Night. 1972.

O'CONNOR, EDWIN (1918–68)

American novelist; served in the Coast Guard during the Second World War; radio writer and producer.

Bibliography
C.B.I.

Novels
The oracle. 1951.
The last hurrah (filmed 1958). 1956.
The edge of sadness (Pulitzer Prize 1962). 1960.
I was dancing. 1964.
All in the family. 1966.
The best and last of Edwin O'Connor. 1970.

O'CONNOR, FLANNERY (1925–64)

American novelist; educated at the State University of Iowa; a full-time author; recipient of several literary awards and fellowships.

Bibliography
C.B.I.
Gale.
Spiller.

Novels
Wise blood. 1952.
A good man is hard to find (stories). 1955.
The violent bear it away. 1960.
Everything that rises must converge (stories). 1965.
Flannery O'Connor: the complete stories. 1971.

Other Work
Mystery and manners: occasional prose. 1969.

†O'CONNOR, PHILIP (MARIE CONSTANT BANCROFT) (1916–)

Anglo-French poet; born in Leighton Buzzard; educated in France and England; worked as a librarian for some years and in a telephone exchange; now devotes his time to writing full time including B.B.C. scriptwriting; contributor to the *Observer*, *T.L.S.*, *New Statesman*, etc.

Bibliography
B.N.B.
Contemporary poets.
Gale.

Poetry
Selected poems 1936–66. 1968.

Autobiography
The lower view. 1960.
Living in Croesor. 1962.
Journal (edited by John Berger). 1969.

Other Works
Memoirs of a public baby. 1958.
Steiner's tour. Paris. 1960.
Vagrancy. 1963.
London character. 1965.
Steiner's personality. 1965.
Walking good. 1971.

O'DONOVAN, JOAN MARY (*née* KNAPE) (1914–)

English novelist; educated at Furzedown Teacher Training College; adviser for girls' education, Oxfordshire.

Bibliography
Authors' and writers' who's who. 1971.
B.N.B.

Novels
Dangerous worlds (short stories). 1958.

The visited (American title, Singular passion). 1959.
Shadows on the wall (short stories). 1960.
The middle tree. 1961.
The niceties of life. 1964.
She, alas. 1965.

Other Works
Little Brown Jesus and others. 1970.
Background to "Little Brown Jesus": notes for teachers. 1970.

OGOT, GRACE OKINYI (1930–)
Kenyan novelist and short-story writer; trained as a nurse in Uganda and England; nursing sister and tutor at Maseno Hospital and Tutor in the Student Health Service, Makerere University College; subsequently scriptwriter and broadcaster for the Overseas Service, B.B.C., London, and Public Relations Officer, Air India, Nairobi; a contributor of short stories to *Transition*, *Black Orpheus*, etc.; represented in many anthologies of short stories.

Bibliography
B.N.B.
Jahn and Dressler.
Zell and Silver.

Novels
The promised land. 1966.
Land without thunder (stories). 1968.

O'HAGAN, HOWARD (1902–)
Canadian novelist; educated at McGill University; reporter on the *Montreal Star*, *Edmonton Journal* and *Sydney Sunday Times* (1925–7); publicity chief, Central Argentine Railway (1931–4); recipient of several literary awards; a contributor to *MacLean's*, *Argosy*, *Esquire*, etc.

Bibliography
C.B.I.
Contemporary novelists.
Gale.

Novels
Wilderness men. 1958.
Tay John. 1960.
The woman who got on at Jaspar Station and other stories. 1963.

O'HARA, FRANK (1926–)
American poet; educated at Harvard and Michigan universities; served in the U.S. Navy (1944–6); Assistant Curator, New York Museum of Modern Art (1955–); author of many one-act plays staged in New York and elsewhere, including *Change your bedding* (1952), *Awake in Spain* (1960), etc.

Bibliography
C.B.I.
Gale.

Poetry
A city winter and other poems. 1952.
Meditations in an emergency. 1956.
Second Avenue. 1960.
Odes. 1960.
Lunch poems. 1964.
Nakiari. 1966.
Selected poems. 1971.

Other Works
Jackson Pollock. 1959.
New Spanish painting culture. 1960.
Try! try! (with H. Machiz). 1960.
Robert Motherwell. 1966.

OKAI, JOHN
Ghanaian poet; lived and studied in Russia (1961–7) and at the universities of Ghana and London; lives in London; a contributor to *Atlantic*, *Outposts*, *Black Orpheus*, etc.

Bibliography
B.N.B.
Contemporary novelists.
Contemporary poets.
Jahn and Dressler.

Poetry
Flowerfall. 1969.

OKARA, GABRIEL MOMOTIMI GBAING-BAIN (1921–)
Nigerian poet and novelist; born in the Ijano country of the Niger Delta; became bookbinder; contributed regularly to *Black Orpheus*; Information Officer in Europe; included in *Poetry from Africa*, Pergamon (1969), and many other anthologies of African writing in English.

Bibliography
B.N.B.

Contemporary novelists.
Jahn and Dressler.
Zell and Silver.

Novel
The voice. 1964.

OKIGBO, CHRISTOPHER (1932–67)
Nigerian poet; born in Ojoto in Eastern Nigeria; educated at the University of Ibadan; a keen jazz clarinettist; taught at Fiditi Grammar School before becoming Librarian at Nsukka University; West African manager for the C.U.P.; killed in battle (1967).

Bibliography
B.N.B.
Jahn and Dressler.
Zell and Silver.

Poetry
Heavensgate. 1962.
Limits. 1964.
Labyrinths. 1971.

OLIVER, WILLIAM HOSKING
(1925–)
New Zealand poet; born in Wellington; educated at Victoria University and Oxford; Professor of History, Massey University of Manawater; currently Professor of History, Wellington, New Zealand; editor of *Comment*, Wellington; represented in various anthologies; a contributor to the *New Zealand Listener*, *Numbers*, *Landfall* and *Oxford Poetry*.

Bibliography
Contemporary poets.

Poetry
Fire without phoenix; poems 1946–54. 1957.

Other Works
Poetry in New Zealand. 1960.
The story of New Zealand. 1963.

OLSON, CHARLES JOHN (1910–)
American poet and writer; educated at Harvard University and Mountain College, Black Mountain; rector of Black Mountain; Guggenheim Fellow, etc.; a contributor to the *Evergreen Review*, *Poetry*, New York, etc.; represented in various anthologies.

Bibliography
C.B.I.
Contemporary poets.
Gale.

Poetry
To Corrado Cagli (pr. ptd.). 1947.
Y&X (pr. ptd.). 1948.
Letter for Melville (pr. ptd.). 1951.
This (pr. ptd.). 1952.
In cold hell, in thicket (pr. ptd.). 1953.
The Maximus poems 1–10 (pr. ptd.). 1953.
The Maximus poems 11–22 (pr. ptd.). 1956.
O'Ryan 246810 (pr. ptd.). 1958.
Projective verse. 1959.
The distances. 1961.
Maximus from Dogtown I. 1961.
Prophioception (pr. ptd.). 1965.
Charles Olson reading at Berkeley. 1966.
Selected writings. 1967.
Stocking cap. 1968.
Archaeologist of the morning. 1971.

Other Works
Call me Ishmael; a study of Melville. 1947.
Apollonius of Tyana (dance play) (pr. ptd.). 1951.
Mayan letters. 1953.
Human universe, and other essays. 1964.
A bibliography on America for Ed Dorn. 1964.
Casual mythology. 1969.
Letters of origin 1950–55. 1969.
Anecdotes of the late war (pr. ptd.). n.d.

OMOTOSO, KOLE (1943–)
Nigerian poet and novelist and modern Arabic scholar; born in Akure; educated at King's College, Lagos, Ibadan and Edinburgh universities; a contributor to newspapers and journals.

Bibliography
Jahn and Dressler.
Nigerian publications (1967–).

Novels
The edifice. 1971.
The combat. 1972.

ONDAATJE, PHILIP MICHAEL
(1943–)
Canadian poet; born in Colombo, Ceylon; educated at Dulwich College and the universities of Toronto and Queen's, Kingston, Ontario; Lecturer in English at the University of Western Ontario (1967–); recipient of various poetry

awards; a contributor to *Canadian Forum, Tamarack Review, Queen's Quarterly*, etc.; represented in several anthologies including *Commonwealth poets of today* (1967), *Penguin book of Canadian verse* (1967).

Bibliography
Canadiana.
C.B.I.
Contemporary poets.

Poetry
The dainty monsters. 1967.
The man with seven toes. 1969.
The left-handed poems; collected works of Billy the Kid. 1970.

Other Work
Leonard Cohen (criticism). 1969.

O'NEILL, WILLIAM L. (1935–)
American historian; educated at Michigan and Berkeley University; served in the U.S. Army (1960–6); Assistant Professor of History, University of Wisconsin (1966–); a contributor to learned journals; his edited work is not listed below.

Bibliography
C.B.I.
Gale.

Works
Divorce in the progressive era. 1967.
Everyone was brave: the rise and fall of feminism in America. 1969.
American society since 1945. 1969.
The woman movement: feminism in the United States and England. 1969.
Coming apart: an informal history of America in the 1960s. 1971.
Women at work. 1972.
Insights and parallels: problems and issues of American social history. 1973.

OPPENHEIM, JOEL LESTER (†AQUARIUS) (1930–)
American poet; educated at Cornell and Chicago universities; production manager of Arrow Typographic Service Inc. (1964–); a contributor to little magazines; has also written plays which have been produced but not published; represented in various anthologies.

Bibliography
C.B.I.
Contemporary poets.
Gale.

Poetry
The dancer. 1952.
The dutiful son. 1957.
The love bit. 1962.
Sirventes on a sad occurrence. 1967.
In time. 1969.

Play
The great American desert. n.d.

ORLOVITZ, GIL (1918–)
American novelist and poet; born in Philadelphia; Hollywood film scriptwriter and television film writer (1950s); his plays published in periodicals are not listed below.

Bibliography
C.B.I.
Contemporary novelists.
Contemporary poets.

Novels
The story of Erica Keith and other stories, poems and a play. 1957.
Milkbottle H. 1967.
Ice never F. 1970.

Poetry
Concerning man. 1947.
Keep to your belly. 1952.
The diary of Dr. Eric Zeno. 1953.
The diary of Alexander Patience. 1958.
The papers of Professor Bold. 1958.
Selected poems. 1960.
The art of the sonnet. 1961.
Couldn't say, might be love. 1969.

ORTON, JOE (ORTON, JOHN KINGSLEY) (1933–67)
English playwright; studied at the R.A.D.A. and became an actor; he was murdered by a companion who then took his own life.

Bibliography
B.M. catalogue.
B.N.B.

Plays
Entertaining Mr. Sloane (filmed 1969). 1964.

Crimes of passion. 1967.

Loot (in New English Dramatists, filmed 1972). 1967.

What the butler saw (in Methuen modern plays). 1969.

Funeral games, and The good and faithful servant. 1970.

OSBORNE, CHARLES (1927–)

Australian poet and writer; came to London (1953); assistant editor, *London Magazine* (1957–); literary editor, Arts Council; a contributor to the *New York Times*, *New Statesman*, *Spectator* and *Observer*; represented in several anthologies; edited *Australian stories of today*, Faber (1962), etc.; a contributor to *Fifty works of English literature we could do without* (1967).

Bibliography
B.M. catalogue.
B.N.B.
Contemporary poets.
Gale.

Works
Opera sixty six. 1966.
Swansong (poems, drawings by Sidney Nolan). 1968.
Kafka (criticism). 1967.
Complete operas of Verdi. 1969.
Ned Kelly (biography). 1970.
Australia, New Zealand and the South Pacific. 1970.
Letters of Guiseppe Verdi. 1971.

OSBORNE, JOHN JAMES (1929–)

English playwright and actor; left school at 16 and worked on trade journals; made his first stage appearance at the Lyceum, Sheffield (1948); produced his first play at the Theatre Royal (1949); founder-director of Woodfall Films (1958); wrote the film script for the film of *Tom Jones* (1964).

Bibliography
Gale.
Simon Trussler. John Osborne. 1969.
Who's who. 1971.

Plays
Look back in anger (produced 1956, filmed 1959). 1957.
The entertainer (produced 1957, filmed 1960). 1957.

Epitaph for George Dillon (with A. Creighton; produced 1957). 1958.
The world of Paul Slickey (produced 1959). 1959.
Subject for scandal and concern. 1961.
Luther (produced 1960). 1961.
Plays for England (The blood of the Bambergs, Under plain covers). 1963.
Inadmissible evidence (produced 1965, filmed 1968). 1965.
A patriot for me (produced 1965). 1966.
A bond honoured (produced 1966). 1966.
Coriolanus. 1967.
The hotel in Amsterdam, and Time present (produced 1968). 1968.
The right prospectus, and Very like a whale. 1970.
West of Suez (produced 1970). 1971.
The picture of Dorian Gray. 1973.

Other Works
A place calling itself Rome. 1972.
A sense of detachment (produced 1972). 1972.

O'SULLIVAN, VINCENT GERARD (1937–)

New Zealand poet; born in Auckland; educated at Auckland and Oxford universities; Senior Lecturer, Waikato University; represented in several anthologies; a contributor to *Landfall*, etc.

Bibliography
Contemporary poets.
N.Z. national bibliography.

Poetry
Our burning time. 1965.
Revenants. 1969.

OWEN, ALUN DAVIES (1924–)

Welsh playwright and actor (1942–58); wrote first for radio, also some 30 plays for television and cinema; recipient of several screen-writers' awards; TV plays not published separately include *Dare to be a Daniel* (1963) and *The water* (1967); only his published plays are listed below.

Bibliography
B.N.B.
Contemporary dramatists.
Gale.
Who's who. 1973.

Plays
The rough and ready lot (staged 1958). 1959.

Three TV plays (No trams to Lime Street, After the funeral, Lena, oh my Lena). 1961.
Progress to the park (staged 1958 in New English dramatists no. 5). 1961.
The rose affair (television play published in Anatomy of a television play). 1961.

A little winter love (staged 1963). 1965.
George's room. 1968.
Shelter (televised 1967, staged 1971). 1968.
Norma (staged 1969, published in We who are about to ...). 1970.

P

PACEY, *Professor* **WILLIAM CYRIL DESMOND** (1917–)
New Zealand-born Canadian scholar; educated at Victoria College, Toronto, and Trinity College, Cambridge; taught in Manitoba (1941–4); Head of English, University of New Brunswick (1944–); a contributor to the *T.L.S.*, *Canadian Forum*, *Queen's Quarterly*, etc.

Bibliography
Authors' and writers' who's who. 1971.
Canadiana.
C.B.I.
Gale.

Short Story
The picnic and other stories. 1958.

Poetry for Children
The cow with the musical moo. 1952.
Hippity Hobo and the bees. 1953.
The cat, the cow and the kangaroo. 1968.

Other Works
Frederick Philip Grove. 1945.
Creative writing in Canada. 1952.
Essays in Canadian criticism. 1969.
Ten Canadians: a group of biographical and critical essays. 1966.
Ethel Wilson. 1968.

PACKARD, VANCE (1914–)
American sociological writer and journalist; educated at Columbia University; reporter and columnist (1936–42); editor, *American Magazine* (1942–56); staff writer, *Collier's Magazine* (1956); lecturer, Columbia and New York universities

(1941–57); awarded honour for journalism; a contributor to various periodicals.

Bibliography
C.B.I.
Gale.

Works
How to pick a mate; guide to a happy marriage (with Clifford Rose Adams). 1946.
Animal IQ; the human side of animals. 1950.
The hidden persuaders. 1957.
The status seekers. 1959.
The waste makers. 1960.
The pyramid climbers. 1962.
The naked society. 1964.
Sexual wilderness. 1970.
Nation of strangers. 1972.

PACKER, *Lady* **JOY** (*née* **PETERSEN**) (1905–)
South African novelist and writer; born in Cape Town; educated at Cape Town University; journalist in Cape Town and London (1924–44); did propaganda work during the Second World War; a contributor to various periodicals; lives in South Africa.

Bibliography
Authors' and writers' who's who. 1971.
B.N.B.
Gale.
Who's who. 1973.

Novels
Valley of the vines. 1955.

Nor the moon by night (filmed 1958). 1957.
The high roof. 1959.
The glass barrier. 1961.
The man in the mews. 1964.
The blind spot. 1967.
Leopard in the fold. 1969.
Veronica. 1970.
Boomerang. 1972.

Other Works
Pack and follow (five autobiographies). 1945.
Grey mistress. 1949.
Apes and ivory. 1953.
Home from the sea. 1963.
The world is a proud place. 1966.

PADGETT, RON (†DANGERFIELD, †HARLAN, †TOM VEITCH) (1942–)

American poet; educated at Columbia College; worked as a garage mechanic and driver (–1962); poetry workshop instructor, St. Mark's-in-the-Bowery, New York (1968–); awarded several poetry prizes; represented in *Contemporary American poetry*, Penguin (1970); a contributor to *Paris Review*, *"C" Magazine*, etc.

Bibliography
C.B.I.
Contemporary poets.
Gale.

Poetry
In advance of the broken arm. 1964.
Bean spasms (with Ted Berrigan). 1967.
Tone arm. 1967.
Bun (with Tom Clark). 1968.
Great balls of fire. 1969.
The adventures of Mr. & Mrs. Jim and Ron (with James Dine). 1970.

PAGE, PATRICIA KATHLEEN (*Mrs.* WILLIAM IRWIN) (†JUDITH CAPE) (1916–)

English-born Canadian poet; educated in Alberta; co-editor of *Preview*; a contributor to various journals; represented in Ronald Hambleton's *Unit of five* (1944) as †Judith Cape and numerous other anthologies.

Bibliography
Canadiana.
C.B.I.
Contemporary poets.

Poetry
Ten as twenty. 1946.
The metal and the flower (Governor General's Award 1955). 1954.
Cry Ararat! 1968.

Novel
The sun and the moon. 1944.

PAINTER, GEORGE DUNCAN (1914–)

English biographer and incunabulist; educated at King Edward's School, Birmingham and Trinity College, Cambridge; Assistant Lecturer in Latin, Liverpool University (1937–8); Department of Printed Books, British Museum (1938–); Assistant Keeper in charge of fifteenth-century printed books (1954–); a contributor to the *Library*, *Book Collector*, *Gutenberg Jahrbuch*, etc.

Bibliography
B.N.B.
Who's who. 1973.

Works
André Gide, a critical biography. 1951.
The road to Sinodun, poems. 1951.
(André Gide) "Marshlands" *and* "Prometheus misbound" (trans.). 1953.
(Marcel Proust) "Letters to his mother" (trans.). 1956.
Marcel Proust, a biography, vol. I. 1959.
Marcel Proust, a biography, vol. II. 1965.
The "Vinland map" and the "Tartar relation" (with R. A. Skelton and T. E. Marston). 1965.
(André Maurois) "The Chelsea way or Marcel in England" (trans.). 1966.

PALANGYO, PETER K. (1939–)

Tanzanian novelist; educated as a biologist at St. Olaf College, Minnesota, the University of Minnesota and Makerere University College; taught in Tanzanian schools; now teaching at the State University of New York, Buffalo.

Bibliography
B.N.B.
Jahn and Dressler.
Zell and Silver.

Novel
Dying in the sun. 1969.

PALEY, GRACE (*née* **GOODSIDE**)
(1922–)
American novelist; educated at Hunter College
and New York University; taught at Columbia
and Syracuse universities; secretary of Greenwich
Village Peace Center; a contributor to *Atlantic*,
Esquire, *Accent*, etc.

Bibliography
C.B.I.
Gale.

Work
The little disturbances of man (stories). 1959.

PALMER, C. EVERARD (1930–)
Caribbean novelist; born in Jamaica; emigrated to
Canada (1964); educated at Lakehead University,
Canada; teaches in Red Rock, Ontario.

Bibliography
B.N.B.
C.B.I.

Novels
The cloud with the silver lining (for children).
1966.
Big Doc Bitterfoot (for children). 1968.
The sun salutes you. 1970.
The humming bird people. 1971.
The wooing of Beppo Tate. 1972.
A car called Boy (for children). 1973.

PARKES, FRANK KOBINA (1932–)
Ghanaian poet; educated at Adisadel College and
Inns of Court School of Law, London; editor of the
Eagle (1953–5); Ghana Radio producer (1955–9);
scriptwriter for film corporation; public relations
adviser, Ghana High Commission, London
(1963–6); a contributor to the *Sunday Mirror*, *Okyeame*, *New World Writing*, etc.

Bibliography
B.N.B.
Ghana national bibliography.

Poetry
Songs from the wilderness. 1965.
Figures. 1971.

PATON, ALAN STEWART (1903–)
South African novelist; born in Pietermaritzburg;
educated at Natal University; taught mathematics

and physics (1925–48); Hon. Commissioner,
Toc H T.B. settlement, Natal (1949–58); recipient
of various literary awards.

Bibliography
B.N.B.
Contemporary novelists.
Gale.

Novels
Meditation for a boy confirmed (stories). 1944.
Cry, the beloved country (filmed 1951). 1948.
Too late the phalarope. 1953.
The people wept. 1958.
Debbie go home (stories). 1961.
Tales from a troubled land (stories). 1961.

Other Works
South Africa today. 1953.
The land and people of South Africa. 1955.
South Africa in transition. 1956.
South Africa–her people. 1957.
Hope for South Africa. 1959.
Hofmeyr (biography). 1965.
Sponono (with Krishna Shah, a play, from stories
  in Tales from a troubled land). 1965.
The long view. 1968.
Instrument of thy peace. 1968.
Kontakion for you departed. 1969.

PATRICK, JOHN (1907–)
American playwright for stage and film; born in
Kentucky; educated at Glen, Columbia and Harvard universities; served in the army during the
Second World War (1942–4), N.B.C., San Francisco, radio writer (1933–6); freelance Hollywood
film scriptwriter (1936–8); recipient of several
awards; film scripts include *The President's lady*
(1953), *Three coins in the fountain* (1954), *The world
of Suzie Wong* (1960); some of his plays have been
produced but not published.

Bibliography
C.B.I.
Contemporary dramatists.

Plays
The willow and I (staged 1942). 1943.
The hasty heart (staged 1945). 1945.
The story of Mary Surratt (staged 1947). 1947.
The curious savage (staged 1950). 1951.
Lo and behold! (staged 1951). 1952.

The teahouse of the August moon (adapted from the novel by Vern Sneider, staged 1953, filmed 1956; revised musical version staged as Lovely ladies, kind gentlemen, 1970; Pulitzer Prize 1954). 1954.
Everybody loves opal (staged 1961). 1962.
Everybody's girl (staged 1967). 1968.
Scandal point (staged 1968). 1969.
Love is a time of day (staged 1969). 1970.
A barrel full of pennies (staged 1968). 1971.
Opal is a diamond (staged 1971). 1972.
Macbeth did it (staged 1972). 1972.
The dancing mice (staged 1972). 1972.
The savage dilemma (staged 1972). 1972.
Anybody out there? 1972.

PATRIDES, CONSTANTINOS APOSTOLOS (1930–)

American literary scholar; educated at Kenyon College and Oxford; served in the American Army (1952–4); Assistant Professor, California University, Berkeley (1959–64); Lecturer, later Reader, York University (1964–); resident in England since 1964; a contributor to many learned journals; his edited work is not listed below.

Bibliography
B.N.B.
Gale.

Works
Milton's "Lycidas"; the tradition and the poem. 1961.
The Phoenix and the ladder. 1964.
Milton and the Christian tradition. 1966.
Milton's epic poetry. 1967.
Approaches to "Paradise Lost". 1968.
The Cambridge Platonists. 1969.
The grand design of God. 1972.

PATTERSON, HORACE ORLANDO (1940–)

Jamaican novelist and sociologist; educated at the University of the West Indies, Kingston, Jamaica, and London School of Economics; after various academic posts in England and Jamaica, is now Professor of Sociology, Harvard, Mass. (1971–); a contributor to numerous periodicals.

Bibliography
B.N.B.
Contemporary novelists.

Novels
The children of Sisyphus. 1964.
An absence of ruins. 1967.
Die the long day. 1972.

Other Work
The sociology of slavery: an analysis of the origins, development and structure of Negro slave society in Jamaica. 1968.

PATTON, FRANCES (née GRAY) (1906–)

American novelist; educated at Duke University, North Carolina.

Bibliography
C.B.I.
Contemporary novelists.
Gale.

Novel
Good morning, Miss Dove. 1954.

Stories
The finer things of life. 1951.
A piece of luck. 1955.
Twenty-eight stories. 1969.

P'BITEK, OKOT (1931–)

Ugandan poet; educated at King's College, Budo, and at Bristol, Aberystwyth and Oxford universities; toured Britain with the Ugandan football team; on the staff of Makerere University College (1964–7); Director of Extramural Studies, University College, Nairobi (1968–); Director of Uganda's National Theatre, etc.; organised national arts festivals in Uganda and Kenya; currently writer-in-residence at the University of Iowa; a contributor to *Transition* and other journals; only his work in English is listed below.

Bibliography
B.N.B.
Contemporary poets.
Jahn and Dressler.
Zell and Silver.

Poetry
Song of Lawino. 1966.
Song of Ocol. 1970.
Song of a prisoner. 1971.

PEAKE, MERVYN (1911–68)

English poet, novelist, painter and illustrator; born in China; educated in China and England; the books he illustrated included *The hunting of the snark*, *Alice in Wonderland*, and *Treasure Island*; *Titus Groan*, *Mr. Pye* and *Rhyme of the flying bomb* were adapted as radio plays.

Bibliography
B.N.B.
Gale.
Who was who. 1961–70.

Novels
Captain Slaughterboard drops anchor (originally published as Captain Slaughterboard, 1939). 1945.
Titus Groan. 1946.
Ghormenghast. 1950.
Mr. Pye. 1953.
Titus alone. 1959.

Poetry
Ride a cock horse and other nursery rhymes. 1940.
Shapes and sounds. 1941.
Rhymes without reason (illustrated). 1944.
The glassblowers. 1950.
The rhyme of the flying bomb (illustrated). 1962.
A reverie of bone. 1967.

Other Works
The drawings of Mervyn Peake. 1945.
The craft of the lead pencil (illustrated). 1946.
Letters from a lost uncle (illustrated). 1948.
Figures of speech. 1954.
The wit to woo (play). 1957.

PEARCE, ANN PHILIPPA (*Mrs.* CHRISTIE) (1921–)

English children's novelist; educated at the Perse Girls' School, Cambridge, and Girton College, Cambridge; temporary civil servant (1942–5); B.B.C. scriptwriter and producer (1945–58); children's editor (1960–); children's book reviewer for periodicals and radio; editor of *People of the Past* (nos. 1–14) (1961–4).

Bibliography
B.N.B.
Gale.

For Children
Minnow on the Say. 1954.
Tom's midnight garden. 1958.

Still Jim and silent Jim. 1960.
Mrs. Cockle's cat. 1961.
A dog so small. 1962.
From inside Scotland Yard (with Sir H. Scott). 1963.
The strange sunflower. 1966.
The children of the house (with Brian Fairfax-Lucy). 1968.
The elm-tree lot. 1969.
The squirrel wife. 1971.
Stories from Hans Christian Andersen. 1972.
Beauty and the beast. 1972.
What the neighbours did, and other stories. 1973.

PEARSON, W. H. (1922–)

New Zealand novelist; born in Greymouth; educated at University of Otago, Dunedin, and King's College, London; served in the New Zealand Forces during the Second World War (1942–6); after the war taught in schools and university departments; Associate Professor of English, Auckland University (1970–); editor of Frank Sargerson's *Collected stories 1935–63* (1965).

Bibliography
B.N.B.
Contemporary novelists.

Novel
Coal flat. 1963.

Other Work
Henry Lawson among Maoris. 1968.

PERCY, WALKER (1916–)

American novelist, born in Birmingham, Alabama; studied medicine at North Carolina and Columbia universities; worked at Bellevue Hospital, New York (1942); retired from medical practice on contracting T.B.; full-time writer; has contributed philosophical, medical and literary articles to many journals.

Bibliography
C.B.I.
Gale.

Novels
The moviegoer. 1961.
The last gentleman. 1966.
Love in the ruins. 1971.

PETERS, LENRI LEOPOLD (1932–)
Gambian poet and surgeon; educated at Trinity
College, Cambridge, and University College
Hospital; F.R.C.S.; Surgical Registrar, North-
ampton General Hospital (1966–); lives in
London; represented in numerous anthologies; a
contributor to *Black Orpheus, Outposts, Trans-
atlantic Review*, etc.

Bibliography
B.N.B.
Contemporary poets.
Jahn and Dressler.

Novel
The second sound. 1965.

Poetry
Poems. Ibadan. 1964.
Satellites. 1967.

PETERSON, LEONARD BYRON
(1917–)
Canadian playwright, novelist and radio scriptwriter; born in Saskatchewan; educated at the
Northwestern University; served in the Canadian
Army in the Second World War; settled in Toronto
as a scriptwriter.

Bibliography
Canadiana.
C.B.I.

Novel
Chipmunk. 1949.

Plays
Look ahead. 1962.
The great hunger. 1967.

PETRY, ANN (*née* **LANE)** (1912–)
American novelist; born in Connecticut; educated
at the universities of Connecticut and Columbia;
pharmacist (1931–8); journalist (1938–44).

Bibliography
C.B.I.
Contemporary novelists.

Novels
The street. 1946.
Country place. 1947.
The narrows. 1953.
Miss Muriel and other stories. 1971.

For Children
The drugstore cat. 1949.
Harriet Tubman: conductor on the underground
railroad (English title, A girl called Moses).
1955.
Tituba of Salem Village. 1964.
Legends of the saints. 1970.

PICKARD, TOM (1946–)
English poet; co-founder of the Modern Tower
and the Ultima Thule bookshop, Newcastle; also
works as a publisher.

Bibliography
B.N.B.
Contemporary poets.

Novel
Guttersnipe. 1972.

Poetry
High on the walls. 1967.
New human unisphere. 1969.
An armpit of lice. 1970.
The order of chance. 1972.
Dancing under fire. 1973.

PIERCY, MARGE (*Mrs.* **SHAPIRO)**
American poet; educated at Michigan and Northwestern universities; full-time writer and gives
readings of her own poetry; a contributor to *Epoch,
Transatlantic Review*, etc.; represented in various
anthologies.

Bibliography
C.B.I.
Contemporary poets.
Gale.

Poetry
Breaking camp. 1968.
Hard loving. 1969.
Dance the eagle to sleep. 1970.
Small changes. 1973.
To be of use. 1973.

PINNER, DAVID (1940–)
English novelist, playwright and actor; unpublished plays include *The furies* (1972), *Potsdam
quartet* (1973) and *Cartoon* (1973); writes for radio,
television and film; many of his poems have been
published in *Poetry Review*.

Bibliography
B.N.B.
Contemporary dramatists.
Gale.

Novels
Ritual. 1967.
With my body. 1968.

Plays
Dickon (staged and produced on radio 1966). 1964.
Fanghorn (staged 1967). 1966.
The drums of snow (televised 1968). 1966.

PINTER, HAROLD (1930–   )
English playwright, actor and producer; acted as
†David Baron (1948–58); has written many unpublished film and radio scripts including *The servant* (1963); recipient of several awards.

Bibliography
B.N.B.
Contemporary dramatists.
John Russell Taylor. Harold Pinter. 1969.
Who's who. 1973.

Plays
The caretaker (staged 1950, filmed 1963). 1960.
The birthday party and other plays (staged 1960,
    filmed 1968). 1960.
The dumb waiter (with The caretaker; staged
    1957). 1961.
The room. 1961.
A night out (broadcast 1960, staged 1961). 1961.
Three plays: A slight ache, The dwarfs, and The
    collection. 1962.
The collection, and The lover (staged 1962). 1963.
The homecoming (staged 1965, filmed 1971).
    1965.
Tea party (televised 1965, staged 1968). 1965.
Early plays: A night out, Night school, and Revue
    sketches. 1968.
Landscape. 1968.
Landscape, and Silence. 1969.
Five screen plays (The servant, The pumpkin eater,
    The Quiller Memorandum, Accident, The
    go-between). 1971.
Old times (staged 1971). 1972.

Poetry
Poems. 1969.

Other Work
Mac (biography of Anew McMaster). 1968.

**PLATH, SYLVIA (†VICTORIA
LUCAS)** (1932–63)
American poet; born in Boston, Mass.; educated at
Smith College, U.S.A., and Newnham College,
Cambridge; married to the poet Ted Hughes (q.v.)
(1956); took her own life.

Bibliography
C.B.I.
Gale.
I. Melander. Sylvia Plath. 1971.
Charles Newman. The art of Sylvia Plath. 1970.

Novel
The bell jar (as †Victoria Lucas). 1963.

Poetry
The Colossus. 1960.
Ariel. 1965.
Uncollected poems. 1965.
Three women: a monologue for three voices. 1968.
Wreath for a bridal. 1970.
Crossing the water. 1971.
Million dollar month. 1971.
Winter trees. 1971.

PLUMB, *Professor* **JOHN HAROLD**
(1911–   )
English historian; educated at Leicester University
and Christ's College, Cambridge; Fellow of King's
College, Cambridge (1939–46); Fellow of Christ's,
Steward, Tutor, etc. (1946–   ); Professor of Modern English History (1966–   ); a contributor to
*Horizon, English Historical Review, New York
Times*, etc.; editor of *History and human society*
(1959–   ); editor of *Studies in social history* (1955)
and *Fontana History of Europe* series; a member of
several learned academies and recipient of
academic honours.

Bibliography
Authors' and writers' who's who. 1971.
B.N.B.
Gale.
Who's who. 1973.

Works
England in the eighteenth century. 1950.
G. M. Trevelyan. 1951.
West African explorers (with C. Howard). 1952.
Chatham. 1953.
Studies in social history (ed.). 1955.
The first four Georges. 1956.

Sir Robert Walpole: vol. I, The making of a states-
man. 1956.
Sir Robert Walpole: vol. II, The King's Minister.
1960.
The "Horizon" book of the Renaissance. 1961.
Men and places. 1962.
Crisis in the humanities. 1964.
The growth of political stability in England,
1675–1725. 1967.
The death of the past. 1969.
A first look at digging. 1973.

PODHERETZ, NORMAN (1930–)
American journalist and critic; educated at Col-
umbia and Cambridge universities and the Jewish
Theological Seminary; served in the U.S. Army
(1953–5); editor-in-chief, *Looking Glass Library*,
New York (1958–60); editor-in-chief, *Commentary*
(1960–); a contributor to *Commentary*, *New
Yorker*, *Esquire*, etc.

Bibliography
C.B.I.
Gale.

Works
Doings and undoings: the 50's and after in Ameri-
can writing. 1964.
Making it. 1968.

POIRIER, RICHARD (1925–)
American critic; educated at Yale, Harvard and
Cambridge universities; served in the U.S. Army
during the Second World War (1943–6); currently
chairman of the Department of English, Rutgers,
the State University, New Brunswick; editor of
the *Paris Review* (1963–); a contributor to many
journals; his edited work is not listed below.

Bibliography
C.B.I.
Gale.

Works
The comic sense of Henry James. 1960.
In defense of reading. 1962.
A world elsewhere. 1966.
Performing self. 1971.

POLANYI, *Professor* **MICHAEL** (1891–)
Hungarian-born scientist; awarded honorary
degrees from many British and American universities; educated in Budapest and Berlin; Pro-

fessor of Physical Chemistry, Manchester University (1933–48); Professor of Social Studies,
Manchester (1948–58); Senior Research Fellow,
Merton College, Oxford (1959–61); a member of
various British and foreign academies; a contributor to *Encounter*, *Twentieth Century*, *Der
Monat*, *Ethics*, etc.

Bibliography
Authors' and writers' who's who. 1971.
B.N.B.
N.C.B.E.L.
Who's who. 1973.

Works
Atomic reactions, 1932.
U.S.S.R.'s economics. 1936.
The contempt of freedom. 1940.
Patent reform. 1945.
The rights and duties of science. 1945.
Full employment and free trade. 1945.
Science, faith and society. 1946.
The logic of liberty. 1951.
Personal knowledge. 1958.
The study of man. 1959.
Beyond nihilism. 1960.
The tacit dimension. 1967.
Knowing and being. 1969.

POLLINI, FRANCIS (1930–)
American novelist; educated at Pennsylvania State
University; served in the U.S. Air Force (1952–7);
lives in Europe, working as a full-time writer.

Bibliography
C.B.I.
Gale.

Novels
Night. 1960.
Glover. 1965.
Excursion. 1966.
The crown. 1967.
Pretty maids all in a row. 1968.

Plays
Three plays (All mine, The row, Partners). 1967.

**POPE, DUDLEY BERNARD
EGERTON** (1925–)
English naval historian and novelist; served in the
Second World War (1941–3); naval correspondent,
Evening News (1944–57); deputy foreign editor

(1957–9); full-time writer (1959–   ); lived in Italy
(1959–63); sailed the Atlantic (1965).

Bibliography
Authors' and writers' who's who. 1971.
B.N.B.
Gale.
Who's who. 1973.

Novels
Ramage. 1965.
Ramage and the drum beat. 1967.
Ramage and the freebooters. 1969.
Governor Ramage, R.N. 1973.

Naval History
Flag 4: the battle of coastal forces in the Mediter-
    ranean. 1954.
The battle of the River Plate. 1956.
73 North. 1958.
England expects. 1959.
At 12 Mr. Byng was shot. 1962.
The black ship. 1963.
Guns. 1965.
The great gamble. 1972.

POPE-HENNESSY, JAMES (1916–74)
English biographer and writer, brother of John
Pope-Hennessy and son of Dame Una Pope-
Hennessy; educated at Downside and Balliol Col-
lege, Oxford; served in the army in the Second
World War (1940–5); literary editor of the *Spectator*
(1947–9).

Bibliography
B.N.B.
Who's who. 1973.

Works
London fabric (Hawthornden Prize 1940). 1939.
West Indian summer. 1943.
The Houses of Parliament. 1945.
America is an atmosphere. 1947.
Monckton Milnes, the years of promise. 1950.
Monckton Milnes, the flight of youth, 1851–1885.
    1952.
Aspects of Provence. 1952.
The baths of Absalom. 1954.
Lord Crewe: the likeness of a liberal. 1955.
Queen Victoria at Windsor and Balmoral. 1959.
Queen Mary. 1959.
Verandah. 1964.
Sins of the fathers. 1967.

Half-crown colony. 1969.
Anthony Trollope. 1971.

POPHAM, HUGH (1920–   )
English poet and novelist; educated at Repton and
Corpus Christi College, Cambridge; served in the
R.N.V.R. during the Second World War (1940–6);
taught in Barbados (1947–8); a contributor to
Blackwood's, Time and Tide, etc.; has written plays
for television and screen.

Bibliography
Authors' and writers' who's who. 1971.
B.N.B.
Gale.

Novels
Beyond the eagle's rage. 1951.
The sea beggars. 1961.
The shores of violence. 1963.
The house at Caine garden. 1966.

Poetry
Against the lightning. 1944.
The journey and the dream. 1945.
To the unborn—greetings. 1946.

Other Works
Sea flight (autobiography). 1954.
Cape of storms. 1957.
Monsters and marlinspikes (for children). 1958.
The fabulous voyage of the Pegasus. 1959.
Gentleman peasants. 1968.
The Somerset Light Infantry. 1968.
Into wind: a history of British naval flying. 1969.
The Dorset Regiment. 1970.

PORTER, HAL (1911–   )
Australian poet and short-story writer; born in
Melbourne; schoolmaster (1927–49); actor, producer, etc., Theatre Royal, Hobart (1951–2); Chief
Librarian in Victoria Libraries (1953–61); has
travelled round the world seven times; freelance
writer since 1961; recipient of several literary
awards; a contributor to *Vogue, London Magazine*,
etc.; represented in several anthologies; author of
television plays; his edited work is not listed
below.

Bibliography
Australian national bibliography.
Contemporary poets.

Janette Fince. A bibliography of Hal Porter, Adelaide. 1966.
Gale.

Novels
Short stories. 1943.
A handful of pennies. 1959.
The tilted cross. 1961.
A bachelor's children (stories). 1962.
The cars of Venice (stories). 1965.
Mr. Butterfly and other tales of new Japan. 1970.
Selected stories. 1971.
The right thing. 1971.

Poetry
Hexagon. 1957.
Elijah's ravens. 1968.
In an Australian graveyard. 1972.

Plays
The tower (in Three Australian plays). 1963.
The professor. 1966.
Eden House. 1969.
Parker. 1972.
The water rises. 1972.

Other Works
The watcher on the cast-iron balcony (autobiography). 1963.
Stars of Australian stage and screen. 1964.
The paper chase (autobiography). 1966.
The actors: an image of the new Japan (travel). 1968.
The history of Bairnsdale. 1972.

PORTER, PETER NEVILLE FREDERICK (1929–)
Australian poet; born in Brisbane; formerly a journalist, bookseller and advertising agent; has lived in England since 1951; now a full-time writer; represented in numerous anthologies; a contributor to *Ambit, Listener, London Magazine*, etc.

Bibliography
Australian national bibliography.
B.N.B.
Contemporary poets.

Poetry
Once bitten, twice bitten. 1961.
Penguin modern poets no. 2 (with K. Amis and D. Moraes). 1962.
Poems ancient and modern. 1964.
A Porter folio. 1969.

The last of England. 1970.
After Martial. 1971.
Preaching to the converted. 1972.

POTTER, DENNIS CHRISTOPHER GEORGE (1935–)
English playwright and journalist; educated at New College, Oxford; edited *Isis* (1958); B.B.C. television (1959–61); *Daily Herald* (1961–4); leader writer, the *Sun* (1964); television plays include *Where the Buffalo Roam, Beast with Two Backs*; a contributor to the *New Statesman, Punch, Sunday Times*, etc.

Bibliography
C.B.I.
Contemporary dramatists.
Who's who. 1973.

Plays
The Nigel Barton plays (Vote vote vote for Nigel Barton, staged 1968, and televised with, Stand up for Nigel Barton). 1968.
Son of man (television play). 1970.
Casanova (series). 1971.

Other Works
The glittering coffin. 1960.
The changing forest. 1962.

POTTS, PAUL HUGH PATRICK HOWARD (1911–)
Canadian poet; born in Berkshire; served in the Second World War; book reviewer, *Sunday Telegraph* (1964–); represented in various anthologies.

Bibliography
B.N.B.
Contemporary poets.

Poetry
Instead of a sonnet. 1944.

Other Works
Dante called you Beatrice (autobiography). 1960.
To keep a promise. 1970.

POWERS, JAMES EARL (1917–)
American novelist; educated at the Northwestern University, Chicago; worked at various jobs before he became a full-time writer; recipient of

many awards and literary honours; represented in numerous anthologies of short stories; a contributor to the *New Yorker, Nation, Collier's, Horizon*, etc.

Bibliography
C.B.I.
Contemporary novelists.
Gale.

Novels
Prince of darkness and other stories. 1947.
Presence of grace (stories). 1956.
Morte d'Urban. 1962.

PREBBLE, JOHN EDWARD CURTIS (†JOHN CURTIS) (1915–)
English novelist and author; educated in Canada and London; served in the army in the Second World War (1940–6); journalist (1934–60); author of several unpublished plays, scripts and television documentaries; a contributor to many journals.

Bibliography
Authors' and writers' who's who. 1971.
B.N.B.
Gale.
Who's who. 1973.

Novels
Where the sea breaks. 1944.
The edge of darkness (American title, Edge of night. 1948). 1947.
Age without pity. 1950.
The Mather story. 1954.
The brute streets. 1954.
Spanish stirrup. 1958.
My great-aunt, appearing day and other stories. 1958.
The buffalo soldiers. 1959.

History
Mongaso (with J. A. Jordan: biography). 1956.
The high girders. 1956.
Culloden. 1961.
The highland clearances. 1963.
Glencoe. 1966.
The Darien disaster. 1968.
The lion in the north. 1971.

PRESS, JOHN BRYANT (1920–)
English poet and critic; born in Norwich; educated at Corpus Christi College, Cambridge; served in the army in the Second World War (1940–5);

British Council officer (1946–); deputy representative, British Council, Paris (1966–); his edited work is not listed below.

Bibliography
B.N.B.
Contemporary poets.
Gale.
Who's who. 1973.

Poetry
Uncertainties. 1956.
Guy Fawkes night. 1959.
Rule and energy. 1963.
A map of modern English verse. 1969.
The lengthening shadows. 1971.

Other Works
The fire and the fountain. 1955.
The chequer'd shade. 1958.
Andrew Marvell. 1958.
Herrick. 1961.
Louis Macneice. 1964.

PRICE, EDWARD REYNOLDS
(1933–)
American novelist; educated at Duke University and Merton College, Oxford; assistant professor, Duke University (1958–); recipient of several awards.

Bibliography
C.B.I.
Contemporary novelists.
Gale.

Novels
A long and happy life. 1962.
Names and faces of heroes (stories). 1963.
A generous man. 1966.
Permanent errors (stories). 1970.
Things themselves (essays and scenes). 1972.

Poetry
Late warning: four poems. 1968.
Love and work. 1968.

PRINCE, FRANK TEMPLETON
(1912–)
South African-born poet; educated at Balliol College, Oxford; Visiting Fellow, Princeton (1935–6); Chatham House study groups department (1937–40); served in the Second World War

(1940–6); Professor of English, University of Southampton (1957–); Visiting Fellow, All Souls College, Oxford (1968–9); a contributor to the *Review of English Studies*.

Bibliography
B.N.B.
Contemporary poets.
N.C.B.E.L.
Who's who. 1973.

Poetry
Poems. 1938.
Soldiers bathing. 1954.
The stolen heart. 1957.
The doors of stone, poems 1938–62. 1963.
Memoirs in Oxford. 1970.

Criticism
The Italian element in Milton's verse. 1954.
In defence of English. 1959.
William Shakespeare: the poems. 1963.
The study of form and the renewal of poetry. 1965.

PRYCE-JONES, DAVID (1936–)
Welsh novelist and writer; son of the writer Alan Pryce-Jones; born in Vienna; educated at Eton and Magdalen College, Oxford; military service (1954–6); literary editor of *Time and Tide* (1961–2); *Spectator* drama critic (1963–4); Visiting Professor, University of Iowa (1964–5) and of the University of California (1970); his translated works are not listed below.

Bibliography
Authors' and writers' who's who. 1971.
B.N.B.
Gale.

Novels
Owls and satyrs. 1961.
The sands of summer. 1963.
Quondam. 1965.
The stranger's view. 1967.

Other Works
Graham Greene. 1963.
Next generation; travels in Israel. 1964.
The Hungarian revolution. 1969.

PURDY, ALFRED WELLINGTON (1918–)
Canadian poet; born in Ontario; served in the Air

Force in the Second World War; travelled widely; worked in many jobs (–1960); lives in southeastern Ontario; a contributor to *Fiddlehead*, *Tamarack Review*, *Canadian Forum*, etc.; represented in numerous anthologies.

Bibliography
Canadiana.
C.B.I.
Contemporary poets.

Poetry
The enchanted echo. 1944.
Pressed on sand. 1955.
Emu, remember. 1956.
The crafte so longe to lerne. 1959.
Poems for all the Annettes. 1962.
The blur in between. 1963.
The Cariboo horses (Governor General's Award 1966). 1965.
North summer: poems from Baffin Island. 1967.
Wild grape wine. 1968.
Fifteen winds. 1970.
Love in a burning building. 1970.
Storm warning: the new Canadian poets. 1971.
Selected poems. 1972.

PUZO, MARIO (1920–)
American novelist; educated at Columbia University; government official in New York and abroad for 20 years.

Bibliography
C.B.I.
Contemporary novelists.

Novels
The dark arena. 1955.
The fortunate pilgrim. 1965.
The godfather (filmed). 1969.

Other Works
The runaway summer of Davie Shaw (for children). 1966.
The godfather papers and other confessions. 1972.

PYNCHON, THOMAS (1937–)
American novelist; educated at Cornell University; served in the U.S. Navy for 2 years; after various jobs moved to Mexico to finish his first novel; a contributor to *Saturday Evening Post*.

Bibliography
C.B.I.
Contemporary novelists.
Gale.

Novels
V. (some chapters *The Noble Savage* and *New World Writing*). 1963.
The crying of lot 49 (sections *Esquire*). 1966.
Gravity's rainbow. 1973.

R

RABE, DAVID (1940–   )
American playwright; born in Iowa; educated at Villanova University, Pennsylvania; served in the U.S. Army for 2 years; consultant, Villanova University (1972–   ); recipient of many awards; *The orphan* produced (1973).

Bibliography
C.B.I.
Contemporary dramatists.

Plays
The basic training of Paulo Hummel, and Sticks and bones: two plays. 1972.

RAHV, PHILIP (1908–   )
American critic and scholar; Professor of English at Brandeis University; founding co-editor of the *Partisan Review*; edited the short novels of Henry James and *Modern occasions* (1966).

Bibliography
C.B.I.

Works
Image and idea. 1957.
The myth of the powerhouse. 1965.
Literature and the sixth sense. 1969.

RAINE, KATHLEEN JESSIE (*Mrs.* **MADGE)** (1908–   )
English poet; educated at Girton College, Cambridge; contributed to *New verse* in the 1930s; edited, with George Mills Harper, *Selected writings of Thomas Taylor the Platonist* (1969); her translations are not listed below.

Bibliography
B.N.B.

Contemporary poets.
N.C.B.E.L.
Who's who. 1973.

Poetry
Stone and flower. 1943.
Living in time. 1946.
The pythoness. 1949.
The year one. 1952.
Collected poems. 1956.
The hollow hill. 1965.
Six dreams. 1968.
Ninfa revisited. 1968.
Pergamon poets no. 4 (with Vernon Watkins). 1969.
The lost country. 1971.
On a deserted shore. 1972.

Criticism
William Blake. 1951.
Coleridge. 1953.
Poetry in relation to traditional wisdom. 1958.
Blake and England. 1960.
Defending ancient springs. 1967.
Blake and tradition (lectures delivered 1962). 1969.
William Blake. 1970.
A question of poetry. 1970.
Farewell happy fields: memories of childhood. 1973.

RAJAN, BALACHANDRA (1920–   )
Indian diplomat and scholar; born in Tourgoo, Burma; educated at the Presidency College, Madras, and Cambridge University; Fellow, Trinity College, Cambridge (1944–8); Director, Studies in English, Trinity College (1946–8); member, Indian Foreign Service (1948–   ); contributor to *Atlantic Monthly*, *Life and Letters*, *Listener*; edited *T. S. Eliot: a study by several hands*.

Bibliography
B.N.B.
C.B.I.
Indian national bibliography 1958–67.
National bibliography of Indian literature
1901–53.

Works
Paradise lost and the seventeenth century reader.
1947.
The novelist as thinker. 1948.
Modern American poetry. 1950.
Too long in the west. 1961.
W. B. Yeats. 1969.
Paradise lost: a tercentenary tribute. 1969.
Lofty rhyme: a study of Milton's major poetry.
1970.
The dark dancer (novel). n.d.

RAMANUJAN, ATTIPAT KRISHNASWAMI (1929–)

Indian poet and linguist; educated at Mysore,
Poona and Indiana universities; Fulbright Scholar
at Indiana University (1958–60); currently Professor of Dravidian Studies and Linguistics at the
University of Chicago; represented in various
anthologies; his translations from Tamil are not
listed below; a contributor to the *Illustrated Weekly
of India*, *London Magazine*, etc.

Bibliography
C.B.I.
Indian national bibliography 1958–67.
National bibliography of Indian literature
1901–53.

Poems
The striders. 1966.
The interior landscape. 1967.
Kuruntokai. 1969.
No flower in the navel. 1969.
Relations. 1971.
Speaking of Shiva. 1972.

RANDALL, DUDLEY (1914–)

Black American poet; born in Washington, D.C.;
educated at Wayne State and Michigan universities; Librarian (1958–); Librarian and poet-
in-residence, University of Detroit (1969–);
founder of the Broadside Press, Detroit; represented in various anthologies of Negro poetry; a
contributor to *Journal of Black Poetry*, *Peninsular
Poets*, etc.; his edited work is not listed below.

Bibliography
C.B.I.
Contemporary poetry.
Gale.

Poetry
Poem, counterpoem (with Margaret Danny).
1966.
Cities burning. 1968.
For Malcolm: poems on the life and death of
Malcolm X. 1969.
More to remember. 1971.
Love you, 2nd ed. 1972.

RANDALL, MARGARET (1936–)

Mexican poet of American birth; educated at the
University of New Mexico; travelled widely;
settled in Mexico (1961); editor of *El Corno
Emplumado* (1962–); recipient of several grants; a
contributor to *Evergreen Review*, *Poetry*, Chicago,
etc.

Bibliography
C.B.I.
Contemporary poets.

Poetry
Ecstasy is a member. 1961.
Poems of the glass. 1964.
Small sounds of the bass fiddle. 1964.
October. 1965.
25 stages of my spine. 1967.
Water I slip into at night. 1968.
Getting rid of blue plastic: selected poems. 1968.
So many rooms has a house but one roof. 1968.

Other Works
Los Hippies: expresión de una crisis. 1968.
Part of the solution; portrait of a revolutionary.
1973.

RANDHAWA, Dr. MOHINDER SINGH (1909–)

Indian scientist, writer and civil servant; born in
Ferozepore; educated in Punjab and Lahore; joined
the Indian Civil Service (1934); additional sec-
retary, Ministry of Food and Agriculture,
Government of India (1955–60); adviser, Natural
Resources Planning Committee (1961–4); special
secretary, Ministry of Food and Agriculture,
Government of India (1964–6).

Bibliography
C.B.I.

Indian national bibliography 1958–67.
National bibliography of Indian literature
  1901–53.

Works
Beautifying India. 1950.
Flowering trees in India. 1957.
Agriculture and animal husbandry in India.
  1958.
Farmers of India. 1959.
Basholi painting. 1959.
Kangra paintings of the Bhagavata Purana. 1960.
Beautiful trees and gardens. 1961.
Kangra paintings on love. 1962.
Kangra paintings of Gita Govinda. 1964.
Evolution of life. 1968.
Indian painting (with Professor J. K. Galbraith).
  1968.
The Kumaon Himalaya. 1971.
Kandra Ragamala paintings. 1973.
Travel in Western Himalayas. 1973.

**RAPHAEL, FREDERIC MICHAEL
(†MARK CAINE** *with Tom Maschler*)
(1931–　)
English novelist; born in Chicago, Illinois; educated at Charterhouse and St. John's College,
Cambridge; full-time novelist, critic and writer for
film, radio and television; recipient of various literary awards; a contributor to the *Sunday Times,
Time and Tide, New York Times,* etc.

Bibliography
Authors' and writers' who's who. 1971.
B.N.B.
Contemporary novelists.
Gale.

Novels
Obbligato. 1956.
The Earlsdon way. 1958.
The limits of love. 1960.
A wild surmise. 1962.
The graduate wife. 1962.
The trouble with England. 1962.
Lindmann. 1963.
Darling. 1965.
Orchestra and beginners. 1967.
Like men betrayed. 1970.
Who were you with last night? 1971.
April, June and November. 1972.
Richard's things. 1973.

Other Works (with Tom Maschler, as †*Mark Caine)*
The S-man: a grammar of success, 1961.
Two for the road (screen play). 1967.

RAU, SANTHA RAMA (*Mrs.*
FAUBIAN BOWERS) (1923–　)
Indian writer; educated at St. Paul's School for
Girls and Wellesley College, U.S.A.; a frequent
contributor to the *New York Times, Horizon,* etc.;
adapted for the stage E. M. Forster's *Passage to India*
(1962); lives in New York.

Bibliography
C.B.I.
Indian national bibliography 1958–67.
National bibliography of Indian literature
  1901–53.
Who's who. 1973.

Works
Home to India. 1945.
East of home. 1950.
This is India. 1953.
Remember the house. 1955.
View to the south-east. 1957.
My Russian journey. 1959.
Gifts of passage (autobiography). 1962.
The adventuress. 1971.

RAVEN, SIMON ARTHUR NOËL
(1927–　)
English novelist; educated at Charterhouse and
King's College, Cambridge; served in the army
(1953–7); his television plays include *Royal foundation* (1961), *The scapegoat* (1964) and drama-
tisations of Huxley, *Point counterpoint* (1968) and
Trollope, *The way we live now* (1969); a contributor
to the *Observer, Punch, Spectator,* etc.

Bibliography
B.N.B.
Contemporary novelists.
Who's who. 1973.

Novels
The feathers of death. 1959.
Brother Cain. 1959.
Doctors wear scarlet. 1960.
Close of play. 1962.
Alms in oblivion (contains, The rich pay late, 1964;
  Friends in low places, 1965; The sabre squadron,
  1966; Fielding Gray, 1967; The Judas boy, 1968;

Places where they sing, 1970; Sound the retreat, 1971; Come like shadows, 1972).

Other Works
The English gentleman. 1961.
Boys will be boys. 1963.
Royal foundation and other plays. 1966.

RAWORTH, THOMAS MOORE
(1928–)
English poet; born in London; educated at London College of Printing and Granada University, Spain; co-founder of the Goliard Press (1965); resident poet, Essex University (1969–70); represented in various anthologies; edited the *Penguin book of Latin American verse* (1971).

Bibliography
B.N.B.
Contemporary poets.

Novels
Betrayed. 1968.
A serial biography; part I. 1969.

Poetry
The relation ship. 1966.
Haiku (with John Esam and Anselm Hollo). 1968.
The big green day. 1968.
Selected poems. 1969.
Lion lion. 1970.
Moving. 1971.
Act: work. 1973.

RAYAPROL, MARTHANDAM SRINIVAS (1925–)
Indian poet; born in Secunderabad; educated at Madras, Benares and California; works as a civil engineer; represented in several anthologies; a contributor to *Illustrated Weekly of India*, etc., and to many journals.

Bibliography
C.B.I.
Indian national bibliography 1958–67.
National bibliography of Indian literature 1901–53.

Poetry
Bones and distances. 1969.
Married love. 1972.

†READ, MISS (DORA JESSIE SAINT, *née* READ SHAFE) (1913–)
English novelist; born in Surrey; educated at Homerton College, Cambridge; taught (1933–40); J.P. for Newbury, Berks.; author of school scripts for the B.B.C.; a contributor to *Punch*, *T.L.S.*, *Country Life*, etc.; her many books for young children are not listed below.

Bibliography
Authors' and writers' who's who. 1971.
B.N.B.
Gale.

Novels and autobiographical novels
Village school. 1955.
Village diary. 1957.
Storm in the village. 1958.
Hobby horse cottage. 1958.
Thrush Green. 1959.
Fresh from the country. 1960.
Winter in Thrush Green. 1961.
Miss Clare remembers. 1962.
Over the gate. 1964.
Chronicles of Fairacre (includes: Village school, Village diary, Storm in the village). 1964.
The market square. 1966.
The Howards of Caxley. 1967.
The Fairacre festival. 1969.
Emily Davis. 1971.
Tyler's row. 1972.
The Christmas mouse. 1973.

Other Work
Miss Read's country cooking, or To cut a cabbage leaf. 1969.

READ, PIERS PAUL (1941–)
English novelist; educated at Ampleforth and St. John's College, Cambridge; editorial staff of the *T.L.S.* (1965); a contributor to *The Times*, *T.L.S.*, *Queen*, etc.

Bibliography
B.N.B.

Novels
Games in heaven with Tussy Marks. 1966.
The Junkers. 1968.
Monk Dawson (Hawthornden Prize 1970; Somerset Maugham Award 1970). 1969.
The professor's daughter. 1971.

REANEY, JAMES CRERAR (1926–)
Canadian poet, playwright and scholar; educated
at the universities of Manitoba and Toronto; Professor of English at the University of Western
Ontario (1960–); editor of the little magazine
*Alphabet; a semi-annual devoted to the iconography of
the imaginatin* (1960–); a contributor to various
journals; represented in *The Oxford book of Canadian verse* and other anthologies.

Bibliography
Authors' and writers' who's who. 1971.
Canadiana.
C.B.I.
Contemporary dramatists.
Contemporary poets.

Poetry
The red heart and other poems (Governor Gen-
    eral's Award 1950). 1949.
A suit of nettles (Governor General's Award 1959).
    1958.
Twelve letters to a small town (Governor Gen-
    eral's Award 1963). 1962.
The dance of death at London, Ontario. 1963.
Poems. 1972.

Plays
The kildeer and other plays (contains The kildeer,
    The sun and the moon, One-man's masque).
    1962.
Colours in the dark (staged 1967). 1970.
Listen to the wind (staged 1965). 1972.

For Children
The boy with an R in his hand. 1965.
Let's make a carol; a play with music for children.
    1965
School plays (includes Names and nicknames,
    Ignoramus, Geography match, Apple butter).
    1973.

RECHY, JOHN FRANCISCO (1934–)
American novelist; born in El Paso, Texas; edu-
cated at New School of Social Research, New
York; served in the U.S. Army.

Bibliography
C.B.I.
Contemporary novelists.
Gale.

Novels
City of night. 1962.
Numbers. 1967.
This day's death. 1970.
Vampires. 1971.
The fourth angel. 1973.

RECKORD, BARRY (1928–)
Jamaican dramatist; educated at Oxford; lived in
London (1952–70), when he returned to Jamaica;
unpublished plays include *Don't gas the Blacks*
(1969), *A liberated woman* (1970) and *Give the gaffers
time to love you* (1973).

Bibliography
Anger and after.
B.N.B.
Contemporary dramatists.

Play
Skyvers (staged 1963, in Penguin New English
    dramatists no. 9). 1966.

Other Works
Does Fidel eat more than your father? Con-
    servations in Cuba. 1971.

REDGROVE, PETER WILLIAM
(1932–)
English poet; educated at Taunton School and
Queen's College, Cambridge; scientific journalist;
Visiting Poet, University of Buffalo, New York
(1961–2), Gregory Poetry Fellow, Leeds (1962–5);
Lecturer, Falmouth School of Art; a contributor to
*The Times, New Poems, T.L.S., Encounter, Poetry
Review*, etc.

Bibliography
B.N.B.
Contemporary poets.
Gale.
Who's who. 1973.

Poetry
The collector and other poems. 1960.
The nature of cold weather. 1961.
At the white monument. 1963.
The force and other poems. 1966.
The sermon. 1966.
The god trap. 1966.
Penguin modern poets no. 11 (with D. M. Black
    and D. M. Thomas). 1968.

Work in progress. 1969.
Love's journey; poems. 1971.
The mother, the daughter and the sighing bridge.
 1971.
Three pieces for voices. 1972.
Dr. Faust's sea-spiral spirit, and other poems. 1972.
Two poems. 1972.
The hermaphrodite album. 1973.

Novel
In the country of the skin. 1973.

REED, HENRY (1914–)
English poet and radio scriptwriter; born in Birmingham; educated at Birmingham University;
taught and wrote (1937–41); served in the army in
the Second World War (1941–2); Foreign Office
(1942–5); broadcaster, journalist and scriptwriter
(1945–   ); has translated three plays by Ugo Betti,
and Balzac, *Père Goriot*, etc.; represented in the
Faber book of modern verse, etc.

Bibliography
Authors' and writers' who's who. 1971.
B.N.B.
Contemporary poets.
N.C.B.E.L.
Who's who. 1973.

Poetry
A map of Verona. 1946.
Lessons of the war (some are included in A map of
 Verona). 1970.

Other Works
Moby Dick (radio version of Melville's novel).
 1947.
The novel since 1939. 1947.
Hilda Tablet and others (radio scripts). 1971.
Streets of Pompeii (radio scripts). 1971.

REED, ISHMAEL (1938–)
Black American novelist; born in Tennessee; educated at the University of Buffalo, New York;
vice-president of Yardbird Publishing Corporation (1971–   ).

Bibliography
C.B.I.
Contemporary novelists.

Novels
The free-lance pallbearers. 1967.

Yellow back radio broke-down. 1971.
Mumbo-jumbo. 1972.

Poetry
Catechism of D. Neo-American Woodoo Chuck.
 1970.
Conjure. Selected poems 1763–1970. 1972.
Chattanooga. 1973.
This one's on me. 1974.

REEMAN, DOUGLAS EDWARD
(†ALEXANDER KENT) (1924–)
English novelist; served in the Royal Navy during
the Second World War (1940–6); Metropolitan
Police (1946–50); children's welfare officer
(1950–60); scriptwriter for film and television; lecturer on eighteenth- and nineteenth-century naval
affairs; a contributor to *Books of the Month*, *Putnam's*
of New York, *Odham's Book Club*, etc.

Bibliography
Authors' and writers' who's who. 1971.
B.N.B.
Gale.

Novels
A prayer for the ship. 1958.
High water. 1959.
Send a gunboat. 1960.
Dive in the sun. 1961.
The hostile shore. 1962.
The last raider. 1963.
With blood and iron. 1964.
H.M.S. Saracen. 1965.
Path of the storm. 1966.
The deep silence. 1967.
The pride and the anguish. 1968.
To risks unknown. 1969.
The greatest enemy. 1970.
Rendezvous South Atlantic. 1971.
Go in and sink! 1973.

Novels as †Alexander Kent (The Bolitho series)
To glory we steer. 1968.
Form a line of battle. 1969.
Enemy in sight. 1970.
The flag captain. 1971.
Sloop of war. 1972.

Other Work
Against the sea. 1970.

REEVE, FRANKLIN DOLIER (1928–)
American novelist, poet and scholar; educated at

Columbia University; Lecturer, then Associate Professor, Columbia University, New York (1952–61); Associate Professor, later Professor of Russian, Wesleyan University, Middlestown, Conn. (1962–6); a contributor to anthologies, to the *New Yorker*, *Kenyon Review*, *Hudson Review*, etc.; broadcaster in the U.S. and the Soviet Union; his edited works and translations from the Russian are not listed below.

Bibliography
C.B.I.
Contemporary poets.
Gale.
L. of C.

Novels
The red machines. 1968.
Just over the border. 1969.
The brother. 1971.
White colors. 1973.

Poetry
The stone island. 1964.
Six poems. 1964.
In the silent stones. 1969.
The blue cat. 1973.

Other Works
Aleksandr Blok: between image and idea. 1962.
Robert Frost in Russia. 1964.
The Russian novel. 1966.
On some scientific concepts in Russian poetry at the turn of the century. 1966.
The Navajo Indians. 1973.
Miguel and his racehorse. 1973.

REEVES, JAMES (1909–   )
English poet, editor and broadcaster; educated at Stowe School and Cambridge; schoolmaster and training college lecturer (1932–52); now a full-time writer; his numerous edited works are not listed below.

Bibliography
B.N.B.
Contemporary poets.
Who's who. 1973.

Poetry
The imprisoned sea. 1949.
The password and other poems. 1952.
The talking skull. 1958.

Collected poems 1929–1959. 1960.
The questioning tiger. 1964.
Selected poems. 1967.
Subsong. 1969.
Selected poems. 1969.
Poems and paraphrases. 1972.

For Children
The wandering moon. 1950.
The blackbird in the lilac. 1952.
Man Friday. 1953.
English fables and fairy stories. 1954.
Pigeons and princesses. 1956.
Prefabulous animiles. 1957.
Mulbridge Manor. 1958.
Exploits of Don Quixote. 1959.
Titus in trouble. 1959.
Ragged robin. 1961.
The strange light. 1964.
Three tall tales. 1964.
The primrose and the winter witch. 1964.
Sailor Rumbelow and *Britannia*. 1965.
The road to a kingdom. 1965.
The story of Jack Timble. 1965.
The pillar-box thieves. 1965.
The secret shoemakers. 1966.
Rhyming Will. 1967.
The Trojan horse. 1968.
The angel and the donkey. 1969.
Heroes and monsters. 1969.
Mr. Horrox and the Gratch. 1969.
Snow white and Rose red (German folk tales). 1970.
Maedun the voyager. 1971.
How the moon began. 1971.
The path of gold. 1972.
The forbidden forest. 1973.
The complete poems for children. 1973.

Plays
Mulcaster Market. 1951.
The king who took sunshine. 1954.
A health to John Patch. 1957.

Other Works
The critical sense. 1956.
Teaching poetry. 1958.
A short history of English poetry. 1961.
Understanding poetry. 1965.
Commitment to poetry. 1969.
Inside poetry (with Martin Seymour-Smith). 1970.
How to write poems for children. 1971.

REID, *Professor* **JOHN COWIE** (1916–)
New Zealand critic and scholar; born in Auckland; educated at Sacred Heart College, and Auckland and Wisconsin universities; after various academic posts, Professor of English, Auckland University (1968–); a prominent member of literary, dramatic and broadcasting organisations; general editor, *New Zealand fiction* (1970–); a contributor to journals in New Zealand and overseas; his edited work is not listed below.

Bibliography
Gale.
N.Z. national bibliography.
Who's who in New Zealand. 10th edition. 1971.

Works
Secret years. 1945.
Creative writing in New Zealand. 1946.
The mind and art of Coventry Patmore. 1957.
Francis Thompson, man and poet. 1959.
The hidden world of Charles Dickens. 1962.
Thomas Hood. 1963.
Charles Dickens's Little Dorrit. 1967.
New Zealand non-fiction. 1968.
The literature of Australia and New Zealand (with G. A. Wilkes). 1970.
Bucks and bruises: Pierce Egan and Regency England. 1971.

REID, VICTOR STAFFORD (1913–)
Jamaican novelist; worked in advertising and journalism; travelled widely; chairman of a publishing and printing company in Jamaica; recipient of various literary fellowships.

Bibliography
B.N.B.
Contemporary novelists.

Novels
New day. 1949.
The leopard. 1958.

For Children
Sixty-five. 1960.
The young warriors. 1967.

REISCHAUER, EDWIN OLDFATHER (1910–)
American statesman and historian; born in Tokyo; educated at Harvard and in Paris, China and Japan; university posts in Far Eastern languages, finally professor (1946–); War Department during the Second World War (1942–6); U.S. Ambassador to Japan (1961–6); his edited works and his translations from the Japanese are not listed below.

Bibliography
C.B.I.
Gale.

Works
Japan, past and present. 1946.
The United States and Japan. 1950.
Wanted, an Asian policy. 1955.
Ennin's travels in T'ang China. 1955.
History of East Asian civilization: vol. I: East Asia, the great tradition (with J. K. Fairbank). 1960; vol. II: East Asia, the modern transformation (with J. K. Fairbank). 1965.
Beyond Vietnam, the United States and Asia. 1967.
Japan, the story of a nation. 1970.

REXROTH, KENNETH (1905–)
American poet and abstract painter; worked as a harvest hand, fruit picker, factory hand, etc.; held many one-man shows of his paintings; co-founder of the San Francisco Poetry Center; a conscientious objector during the Second World War; recipient of several awards for his poetry; editor of numerous anthologies of poetry; his translations of Chinese and Japanese poetry are not listed below.

Bibliography
C.B.I.
Contemporary dramatists.
Contemporary poets.
Gale.
L. of C.

Poetry
In what hour. 1940.
The phoenix and the tortoise. 1944.
The signature of all things. 1949.
The art of worldly wisdom. 1949.
The dragon and the unicorn. 1952.
In defence of the earth. 1958.
The homestead called Damascus. 1963.
Natural numbers, new and selected poems. 1963.
Penguin modern poets no. 9 (with D. Levertov and W. Carlos Williams). 1967.
The heart's garden, the garden's heart. 1967.
The spark in the tinder. 1968.
The collected longer poems. 1969.
Sky trees birds sea earth. 1970.

With eye and ear. 1970.
Thou shalt not kill. n.d.

Other Works
Beyond the mountain (verse plays). 1951.
Bird in the bush (essays). 1959.
Assays (essays). 1962.
An autobiographical novel. 1966.
Classics revisited. 1968.
The alternative society; essays from the other world. 1970.
American poetry in the twentieth century. 1971.

RHYS, KEIDRYCH (1915–   )
Welsh poet; journalist in London (1935–   ); served in the army during the Second World War (1939–45); Ministry of Information (1943–4); war correspondent (1944–5); founder of magazine *Wales* (1937); editor, *Poetry London* (1956–60); a contributor to the *New Statesman*, *T.L.S.*, etc.; represented in numerous anthologies; edited *Poems from the Forces* (1942), *More poems from the Forces* (1943) and *Modern Welsh poetry* (1944).

Bibliography
B.N.B.
Contemporary poets.
Who's who. 1973.

Poetry
The van pool and other poems. 1941.
Angry prayers. 1952.
The expatriates. 1964.

RICH, ADRIENNE CECILE (*Mrs.*
ALFRED CONRAD) (1929–   )
American poet; recipient of several literary awards; a contributor to *Poetry*, *Nation*, *New York Review of Books*, etc.; included in several anthologies.

Bibliography
C.B.I.
Contemporary poets.
Gale.
L. of C.

Poetry
A change of world. 1951.
The diamond cutters. 1955.
Snapshots of a daughter-in-law, poems 1954–1962. 1962.
Necessities of life. 1966.
Selected poems. 1967.
Leaflets; poems 1965–1968. 1969.

The will to change: poems. 1971.
Diving into the wreck: poems 1971–72. 1973.

RICHARDSON, JACK CARTER
(1935–   )
American playwright; educated at Columbia and Munich universities; served in the U.S. Army; unpublished plays include *Lorenzo* (1963) and *As happy as kings* (1968).

Bibliography
C.B.I.
Contemporary dramatists.
Gale.

Novels
The prison life of Harris Filmore. 1961.
Juan Feldman (in, Pardon me, sir, but is my eye hurting your elbow?). 1968.

Plays
The prodigal. 1960.
Gallows humor. 1961.
Xmas in Las Vegas (staged 1965). 1966.
Juan Feldman. 1968.

RICHLER, MORDECAI (1931–   )
Canadian-Jewish novelist; born in Montreal; educated at Sir George Williams University, Montreal; on the staff of the Canadian Broadcasting Corporation (1952–   ); writer-in-residence, Sir George Williams University (1968–9); settled in England; a contributor to the *Observer*, *Sunday Times*, *Guardian*, *New Statesman*, etc.; his short stories have been included in various anthologies.

Bibliography
Authors' and writers' who's who. 1971.
B.N.B.
Canadiana.
C.B.I.
Contemporary novelists.
Who's who. 1973.

Novels
The acrobats. 1954.
A choice of enemies. 1955.
Son of a smaller hero. 1957.
The apprenticeship of Duddy Kravitz. 1959.
The incomparable Atuk (American title, Stick your neck out). 1963.
Cocksure (Governor General's Award 1969). 1968.

St. Urbain's horseman. 1971.
A choice of enemies. 1973.

Other Works
Hunting tigers under glass (Governor General's
    Award 1969). 1969.
Canadian writing today. 1970.
The street (memoirs). 1972.

RICKS, CHRISTOPHER BRUCE
(1933–)
English literary scholar; educated at Balliol College, Oxford; served in the army (1951–3); Fellow
and Tutor, Worcester College, Oxford, later University Lecturer in English Literature; an editor of
Essays in Criticism; a contributor to the *Sunday
Times*, *New Statesman*, and learned journals; co-
editor, with Harry Carter, of Edward Rowe
Mores, *Dissertations upon English founders and foun-
deries* (1961); edited the collected poems of
Tennyson (1965) and other poets.

Bibliography
B.N.B.
Gale.

Works
Milton's grand style. 1963.
Tennyson. 1972.

RIDLER, ANNE BARBARA (*née*
BRADBY) (1912–)
English poet; born in Rugby; educated at King's
College, London; worked for Faber and Faber
(1935–40); married Vivian Ridler, Oxford University Printer (1938); recipient of several literary
awards; a contributor to the *Guardian*, *New Yorker*,
etc.; her edited work is not listed below.

Bibliography
Authors' and writers' who's who. 1971.
B.N.B.
Contemporary dramatists.
Contemporary poets.
Gale.
N.C.B.E.L.
Who's who. 1973.

Poetry
Poems. 1939.
A dream observed. 1941.
The nine bright shiners. 1943.
The golden bird. 1951.
A matter of life and death. 1959.

Selected poems. 1961.
Some time after. 1972.

Plays
Cain. 1943.
The shadow factory, a nativity play. 1946.
Henry Bly and other plays. 1950.
The trial of Thomas Cranmer (verse play). 1956.
Who is my neighbour? and How bitter the bread.
    1963.

Other Work
Olive Willis and Downe House. 1967.

RIESMAN, DAVID (1909–)
American critic and lawyer; educated at Harvard;
U.S. Supreme Court official (1933–6); after practising as a lawyer and holding various academic
posts, became Professor of Social Relations, Harvard (1958–); member of many learned and
other societies; recipient of several academic
honours; joint editor of *Culture and social character*
(1961).

Bibliography
C.B.I.
Gale.

Works
The lonely crowd (with others). 1950.
Faces in the crowd (with Nathan Glazer). 1952.
Thorsten Veblen: a critical interpretation. 1953.
Individualism reconsidered. 1954.
Constraint and variety in American education.
    1956.
Abundance for what? and other essays. 1964.
Conversations in Japan (with E. T. Riesman).
    1967.
The academic revolution (with C. Jencks). 1968.
Academic values and mass education. 1970.
Academic transformations (with Verne Stadt-
    man). 1973.

RIVE, RICHARD (1931–)
South African novelist and short-story writer;
born and brought up in Cape Town; educated at
the University of Cape Town; has taught in Cape
Town since 1949; edited anthologies of African
writing; toured Africa and Europe (1962).

Bibliography
C.B.I.
Gale.

Jahn and Dressler.
Zell and Silver.

Novels
African songs (short stories). 1963.
Emergency. 1964.

ROBERTS, DOROTHY (*Mrs.* A. R. LEISNER)

Canadian-born American poet; born in Fredericton, New Brunswick; educated in England and University of New Brunswick; in journalism until her marriage; has lived in Europe, and now in America; a contributor to *Canadian Forum, Fiddlehead, Queen's Quarterly, Dalhousie Review, Delta,* etc.; represented in several anthologies.

Bibliography
Canadiana.
C.B.I.
Contemporary poets.

Poetry
Dazzle. 1957.
In star and stalk. 1959.
Twice to flame. 1961.
Extended. 1967.

ROBINSON, *Rt. Reverend* JOHN ARTHUR THOMAS (1919–)

English theologian; educated at Marlborough College and Jesus and Trinity colleges, Cambridge; academic posts include Fellow and Tutor, Clare College, Cambridge (1951–9); Lecturer in Divinity (1954–9); Bishop Suffragan of Woolwich (1959–69); Assistant Bishop of Southwark (1969–); Lecturer in Divinity, Trinity College, Cambridge (1969–); a contributor to learned journals, mainly on New Testament subjects.

Bibliography
B.N.B.
Gale.
Who's who. 1973.

Works
In the end God. 1950.
The body. 1952.
Jesus and his coming. 1957.
Jesus Christ: history interpretation and faith (with others). 1957.
On being the church in the world. 1960.
Christ comes in. 1960.
Liturgy coming to life. 1960.

Twelve New Testament studies. 1962.
Honest to God. 1963.
Christian morals today. 1964.
The new reformation? 1965.
But that I can't believe! 1967.
Abortion. 1967.
Exploration into God. 1967.
Christian freedom in a permissive society. 1970.
The difference in being a Christian today. 1972.
The human face of God. 1973.

ROBINSON, ROLAND EDWARD (1912–)

Australian poet; born in Ireland; member of the Kirsova Ballet (1944–7); ballet critic of the Sydney *Morning Herald* (1956–66); editor of *Poetry Magazine*, Sydney; a contributor to the *Age*, Melbourne and *Meanjin*, etc.; represented in various anthologies.

Bibliography
Australian national bibliography.
C.B.I.
Contemporary poets.

Poetry
Beyond the grass-tree spears. 1944.
Deep well (contains: Language of the sand, Tumult of the swans, 1948). 1952.
Selected poems. 1972.

Story
Blackfeller—whitefeller. 1958.

Aboriginal Life and Myths
Legend and dreaming. 1952.
The feathered serpent. 1956.
The man who sold his dreaming. 1964.
Aborigine myths and legends. 1966.
The Australian aborigine in colour. 1968.
Wandjina. 1968.
Altjeringa and other aborigine poems. 1970.

ROCHE, PAUL (1928–)

English poet and translator; born in India; educated at the Gregorian University, Rome; instructor, Smith College, Northants, Massachusetts (1967–9); poet-in-residence, California Institute of the Arts (1972–); recipient of various poetry awards; a contributor to *Harper's Bazaar*, the *Listener, Poetry Review*, etc.; has translated Sophocles, Aeschylus, Sappho and Plautus.

Bibliography
Authors' and writers' who's who. 1971.
B.N.B.
Contemporary poets.
Gale.

Novels
O pale Galilean. 1954.
Vessel of dishonor. 1964.

Poetry
The rank obstinacy of things. 1962.
All things considered. 1966.
To tell the truth. 1967.

Other Work
The rat and the convent dove (fables). 1952.

RODGERS, WILLIAM ROBERT
(1909–)
Irish poet; born in Ulster; educated at Queen's
University, Belfast; clergyman in County Armagh
(1957–66); B.B.C. editor (1966–).

Bibliography
B.N.B.
N.C.B.E.L.

Poetry
Awake and other poems. 1940.
Europa and the bull. 1952.

Other Works
Ireland in colour. 1957.
Irish literary portraits. 1971.

ROETHKE, THEODORE (1908–63)
American poet; educated at Michigan State Uni-
versity and Harvard; taught at the University of
Washington (1947–63).

Bibliography
C.B.I.
Gale.

Poetry
Open house. 1941.
The lost son and other poems. 1948.
Praise to the end. 1951.
The waking (Pulitzer Prize 1954). 1953.
Words for the wind; collected verse. 1958.
I am! says the lamb. 1961.
The far field. 1964.
Collected poems. 1966.

Other Works
On the poet and his craft. 1965.
Selected letters. 1968.

ROSEN, MICHAEL (1946–)
English playwright; educated at Watford Grammar School, Middlesex Hospital Medical School
and Wadham College, Oxford; his first play,
Stewed figs, was produced in Durham (1968).

Bibliography
B.N.B.
Gale.

Play
Backbone (staged 1968). 1968.

ROSENBERG, HAROLD (1906–)
American art critic; educated as a lawyer; Office of
War Information (1943–6); Consultant to U.S.
Advertising Council (1946–), etc.; artist-
in-residence, Southern Illinois University; a con-
tributor of poems and art criticisms to *Poetry*, *New
Yorker*, *Vogue*, etc.; his edited and translated work
is not listed below.

Bibliography
C.B.I.
Gale.

Poetry
Trance above the streets. 1943.

Other Works
The tradition of the new. 1959.
Arshile Gorky: the man, the time, the idea. 1962.
Artworks and packages. 1969.
Act and the actor. 1971.
Barnett Newman: broken obelisk and other
  sculptures. 1971.
The re-definition of art: action art to pop the
  earthworks. 1972.
The anxious object: art today and its audience.
  1973.
De Kooning. 1973.
Discovering the present: three decades in art cul-
  ture. 1973.
Culture and politics. 1973.

ROSENTHAL, HAROLD DAVID
(1917–)
English music critic; educated at the City of
London School and University College, London;
taught English and history (1946–50); assistant

editor, later editor of *Opera* (1950–3); archivist of
the Royal Opera House, Covent Garden (1953–6);
chairman of the music section of the Critics' Circle
(1965–7); a contributor to the *Radio Times*,
Gramophone, *Grove's Dictionary of Music*, etc.;
edited *Opera Annuals* (1954–62) and *Mapleson
Memoirs* (1966).

Bibliography
Authors' and writers' who's who. 1971.
B.N.B.
Gale.
Who's who. 1973.

Works
Sopranos of today. 1956.
Two centuries of opera at Covent Garden. 1958.
A concise dictionary of opera (with John Warrack).
  1964.
The opera bedside book. 1965.
Great singers of today. 1966.
Opera at Covent Garden. 1967.

ROSS, ALAN (1922–)

English poet, publisher and journalist; educated at
Haileybury and St. John's College, Oxford; served
in the Royal Navy (1942–7); British Council
officer (1947–50); on the staff of the *Observer*
(1950–); cricket correspondent for M.C.C.
(1954–68); editor of the *London Magazine*
(1961–); founder of Alan Ross, publishers; his
edited and translated work is not listed below.

Bibliography
Authors' and writers' who's who. 1971.
B.N.B.
Contemporary poets.
R. N. Currey. Poets of the 1939–1945 war. 1960.
Gale.
N.C.B.E.L.
Who's who. 1973.

Novels
Summer thunder. 1941.
The onion man (for children). 1959.
Danger on Glass Island (for children). 1960.
Wreck of Moni (for children). 1965.
A castle in Sicily (for children). 1966.

Poetry
The derelict day. 1947.
Poetry 1945–50. 1951.
Something of the sea; poems 1942–52. 1954.
To whom it may concern; poems 1952–7. 1958.

African negatives. 1962.
North from Sicily; poems 1961–4. 1965.
Poems 1942–67. 1968.
Tropical ice. 1972.

On Cricket
Australia '55. 1955.
Cape summer. 1957.
Through the Caribbean. 1960.
Australia '63. 1963.
West Indies at Lord's. 1964.

Other Works
Time was away (Sicilian travel). 1948.
The forties. 1950.
The gulf of pleasure. 1951.
The bandit on the billiard table (republished as
  South to Sardinia. 1960). 1954.

ROSS, MAGGIE (*Mrs.* BARRY BURMANGE)

English novelist, critic and poet; educated at art
school in London; taught art before becoming a
full-time writer; a contributor of short stories,
poems and criticisms to numerous journals and to
B.B.C. radio and television.

Bibliography
B.N.B.

Novels
The gasteropod (James Tait Black Prize 1969).
  1968.
Totem. 1973.

ROSS, MALCOLM (1911–)

Canadian scholar; born in New Brunswick; educated at the universities of New Brunswick,
Toronto and Cornell; served on the Wartime
Information Board of the National Film Board
during the Second World War; Lecturer in English
at Manitoba University (1945–50); Queen's University (1950–62), becoming head of department;
Professor of English, Trinity College, Toronto
(1962–); his edited work is not listed below;
editor of *Queen's Quarterly* (1953–6).

Bibliography
Canadiana.
C.B.I.

Works
Milton's royalism. 1943.
Poetry and dogma. 1954.

ROSS, SINCLAIR (1908–)

Canadian novelist; born in Saskatchewan; worked for the Royal Bank of Canada in Winnipeg and Montreal for 43 years; a contributor to *Queen's Quarterly*, etc.; retired to Spain.

Bibliography
Canadiana.
C.B.I.
Contemporary novelists.

Novels
As for me and my house. 1941.
The well. 1958.
The lamp at noon and other stories. 1968.
Whir of gold. 1970.

ROTH, PHILIP MILTON (1933–)

American-Jewish novelist; educated at Bucknell and Chicago universities; writer-in-residence at Princeton and Pennsylvania universities; served in the U.S. Army (1955–6); awarded several literary prizes; a contributor to *Harper's*, *New Yorker*, *Esquire*, etc.

Bibliography
C.B.I.
Contemporary novelists.
Gale.

Novels
Goodbye, Columbus and five short stories. 1959.
Letting go (novella and stories). 1962.
When she was good. 1967.
Portnoy's complaint. 1969.
Our gang (starring Tricky and his friends). 1971.
Four. 1971.
The breast. 1973.
The great American novel. 1973.

ROTHENBERG, JEROME (1931–)

American poet; educated at the University of Michigan, Ann Arbor; served in the U.S. Army of Occupation in Germany; has travelled widely; editor of various little magazines; member of the Department of English, Mannes College of Music, New York; his edited and translated work is not listed below; a contributor to *Caterpillar*, *Poor, old, tired horse*, *El Corno Emplumado*, etc.; represented in numerous anthologies of *avant-garde* poetry.

Bibliography
C.B.I.

Contemporary poets.
Gale.

Poetry
White sun black sun. 1960.
The seven hells of the Jigoku Zashi. 1962.
Sightings I–IX. 1964.
The forty poems. 1966.
Between 1960–1963. 1967.
Conversations. 1968.
Poems 1964–67. 1968.
Sightings I–IX and Red easy a color. 1968.
Poland/1931. 1969.
The game of silence: selected poems, 1960–1970. 1970.

ROVERE, RICHARD HALWORTH (1915–)

American journalist; educated at Columbia University; associate editor, *New Madras* (1938–9); associate editor, *Nation* (1940–3); editor, *Common Sense* (1943–4); staff writer, *New Yorker* (1944–   ); U.S. correspondent of the *Spectator* (1954–62), etc.

Bibliography
C.B.I.

Works
Howe and Hummel: their time and scandalous history (alternative title, The magnificent shysters. 1948). 1947.
The General and the President (with A. M. Schlesinger, Jr.), revised as The MacArthur controversy and American foreign policy. 1951.
Affairs of state: the Eisenhower years. 1956.
Senator Joe McCarthy. 1959.
The American establishment. 1962.
The Goldwater caper. 1965.
Waist deep in the Big Muddy. 1968.

ROWBOTHAM, DAVID HAROLD (1924–)

Australian novelist, poet and critic; educated at Sydney and Queensland universities; served in the Royal Australian Air Force during the Second World War (1942–5); journalist (1952–5); Senior Tutor in English, Queensland University, Brisbane (1965–9); critic, later arts editor, *Courier Mail*, Brisbane (1955–   ); represented in various anthologies; a contributor to *Poetry Australia*, *Sydney Morning Herald*, etc.

Bibliography
B.N.B.
Contemporary poets.

Novels and Short Stories
Town and city (stories). 1956.
The man in the jungle. 1964.

Poetry
The makers of the ark. 1970.
Pen of feathers. 1972.

RUBADIRI, DAVID (1930–)
Malawi poet; educated at Makerere University
College and King's College, Cambridge; broadcaster for the B.B.C.; taught in Nyasaland; first
Malawi ambassador to the United States and the
U.N. (1964–5); returned to Africa (1965) to take up
a teaching post at Makerere University College;
edited, with David Cook, *Poems from East Africa*
(1971); his play *Come to tea* published in *New Africa*
(1965); represented in numerous anthologies of
poetry; a contributor to *Transition*, *East African
Journal*, etc.

Bibliography
B.N.B.
Contemporary poets.
Jahn and Dressler.
Zell and Silver.

Novel
No bride price. 1967.

**RUBENS, BERNICE RUTH (Mrs.
NASSAUER)** (1928–)
Welsh-Jewish novelist; born in Cardiff; educated at
the University of Wales, Cardiff; director of
documentary films since 1957; films include *Stress*
(awarded American Blue Ribbon 1968), *One of the
family*, *The spastic child*, *Call us by name*, *Dear Mum
and Dad*, and *Out of the mouths*.

Bibliography
Authors' and writers' who's who. 1971.
B.N.B.
Contemporary novelists.
Gale.

Novels
Set on edge. 1960.
Madame Sousatzka. 1962.
Mate in three. 1966.
The elected member (American title, Chosen
people; Booker Prize 1970). 1969.

Sunday best. 1971.
Go tell the lemming. 1973.

RUDKIN, JAMES DAVID (1936–)
English playwright; born into a strict evangelical
family that forbade the theatre; educated at St.
Catherine's College, Oxford; he began writing
stories in early childhood, and later composed
music; served in the army for 2 years; taught classics (1961–4); teaches music; his unpublished stage,
radio and television plays are not listed below.

Bibliography
Anger and after.
B.N.B.
Contemporary dramatists.

Plays, Libretti and Screenplays
Afore night comes (in Penguin New English
dramatists no. 7). 1963.
Moses and Aaron (libretto to Schoenberg opera).
1965.
Grace of Todd (music by Gordon Grosse). 1970.

RUHUMBIKA, GABRIEL (1938–)
Tanzanian novelist; educated at Makerere Uni-
versity College; at present Lecturer at University
College, Dar es Salaam; awarded D. ès L. by the
Sorbonne (1969)

Bibliography
B.N.B.
Jahn and Dressler.
Zell and Silver.

Novel
Village in Uhru. 1969.

RUTSALA, VERN (1934–)
American poet; member of the English faculty of
Lewis and Clark College, Portland, Oregon
(1961–); served in the U.S. Army (1956–8);
poetry editor of *December* (1959–62); a contributor
to *Paris Review*, *Nation*, etc.

Bibliography
Contemporary poets.
Gale.
L. of C.

Poetry
The window. 1964.
Small soups; a sequence. 1969.

RYLE, *Professor* **GILBERT** (1900–76)
English philosopher; educated at Brighton College and Queen's College, Oxford; Lecturer, later Censor, Christ Church (1925–); served in the Welsh Guards in the Second World War (1939–45); Waynflete Professor of Philosophy, Oxford (1945–68); editor of *Mind*; a contributor to *Mind*, the *Aristotelian Society Proceedings, Philosophy*, etc.

Bibliography
Authors' and writers' who's who. 1971.
B.N.B.
Who's who. 1973.

Works
The concept of mind. 1949.
Dilemmas. 1954.
Plato's progress. 1966.
Collected papers, vol. I Critical essays, vol. II Collected essays 1929–68. 1971.

S

SAHGAL, *Mrs.* **NAYANTARA PANDIT** (1927–)
Indian novelist; born in Allahabad; educated at Mussoorie and Wellesley, Massachusetts; lives in New Delhi; a contributor to Indian journals.

Bibliography
C.B.I.
Indian national bibliography 1958–67.
National bibliography of Indian literature 1901–53.

Novels
A time to be happy. 1958.
This time of morning. 1965.
Storm in Chandigarh. 1969.
The day in shadow. 1971.

Other Works
Prison and chocolate cake (autobiography). 1954.
From fear set free (autobiography). 1963.
Freedom movement in India (history). 1970.

ST. OMER, GARTH
West Indian novelist; born in St. Lucia; educated at the University of the West Indies, Kingston, Jamaica; lived in France and Ghana; settled in London.

Bibliography
B.N.B.
Contemporary novelists.

Novels
A room on the hill. 1968.
Shades of grey. 1968.
Nor any country. 1969.
J, Black Bam and the masquerades. 1972.

SALINGER, JEROME DAVID (1919–)
American novelist; served in the U.S. Army (1942–6) during the Second World War; a contributor to *Harper's, New Yorker, Saturday Evening Post*, etc.

Bibliography
C.B.I.
Contemporary novelists.
Gale.
Who's who. 1973.

Novels
The catcher in the rye. 1951.
Nine stories (English title, For Esme—with love and squalor). 1953.
Franny and Zooey. 1961.
Raise high the roof beam. 1963.

SALINGER, PIERRE EMILE GEORGE (1925–)
American journalist, state secretary and senator; educated at San Francisco University; reporter, etc., *San Francisco Chronicle* (1946–55); editor, *Collier's Magazine* (1955–6); served in the U.S. Navy (1943–6) during the Second World War; secretary

to Presidents Kennedy and Johnson and similar appointments (1957–64); senator from California (1964); other public appointments (1965–   ); co-editor of *A tribute to John F. Kennedy* (1964).

Bibliography
C.B.I.
Gale.
Who's who. 1973.

Works
With Kennedy. 1964.
On instructions of my government. 1971.

SALKEY, FELIX ANDREW ALEXANDER (1928–   )

Caribbean novelist; born in Panama; educated in Jamaica and London University; B.B.C. (1955–6); taught in London (1957–9); a contributor to B.B.C., numerous magazines, etc.; his edited work is not listed below.

Bibliography
Authors' and writers' who's who. 1971.
B.N.B.
Gale.
Jahn and Dressler.

Novels
A quality of violence. 1959.
Escape to an autumn pavement. 1960.
The late emancipation of Jerry Stover. 1968.
The adventures of Catullus Kelly. 1969.
Come home, Malcolm Heartland. 1972.
Anancy's score. 1973.

For Children
Hurricane. 1964.
Earthquake. 1965.
Drought. 1966.
The sharkhunters. 1966.
Riot. 1967.
Jonah Simpson. 1969.

Travel
Havana journal. 1971.
Georgetown journal. 1972.

SAMPSON, ANTHONY TERRELL SEWARD (1926–   )

English writer and journalist; educated at Westminster School and Christ Church, Oxford; served in the Royal Navy (1944–7); editor of *Drum Magazine* (1951–5); editorial staff of the *Observer*

(1955–66); editor of the *Observer Magazine* (1965–6); Associate Professor of the University of Vincennes, Paris (1968–   ).

Bibliography
Authors' and writers' who's who. 1971.
B.N.B.
Gale.
Who's who. 1973.

Works
Drum, a venture into the New Africa. 1956.
The treason cage. 1958.
Commonsense about Africa. 1960.
South Africa: two views of separate development (with S. Pienaar). 1960.
Anatomy of Britain. 1962.
Anatomy of Britain today. 1965.
Macmillan: a study in ambiguity. 1967.
The new Europeans. 1968.
The new anatomy of Britain. 1971.
Sovereign state. 1973.

SANDFORD, JEREMY (1930–   )

English writer and broadcaster; educated at Eton; first clarinet, R.A.F. band in Germany; critic for *Observer*, *Sunday Times*, *Evening Standard*, etc.; his unpublished plays include *Whelk and chromium*, *Until the end of the plums* and *Arlene*.

Bibliography
Authors' and writers' who's who. 1971.
B.N.B.
Contemporary dramatists.

Works
Cathy come home (televised). 1967.
Synthetic fun. 1967.
Edna the inebriate woman (televised). 1971.
Down and out in Britain. 1971.
In search of the magic mushroom. 1972.
Gypsies. 1973.

SANSOM, WILLIAM (1912–   )

English novelist; educated at Uppingham School; a contributor to many periodicals; worked variously in a bank, an advertising agency and as a film-script writer; gave his time to full-time writing (1945–   ).

Bibliography
Authors' and writers' who's who. 1971.
B.N.B.
Contemporary novelists.

Gale.
Who's who. 1973.

Novels
The body. 1949.
The face of innocence. 1951.
A bed of roses. 1954.
The loving eye. 1956.
The cautious heart. 1958.
The last hours of Sandra Lee. 1961.
Goodbye. 1966.
Hans Feet in love. 1971.

Short Stories
Fireman Flower. 1944.
Three. 1946.
Something terrible, something lovely. 1948.
South. 1948.
The equilibriad. 1948.
The passionate north. 1950.
A touch of the sun. 1952.
Lord love us. 1954.
A contest of ladies. 1957.
The stories of William Sansom. 1963.
The ulcerated milkman. 1966.
The vertical ladder and other stories. 1969.
The marmalade bird. 1973.

Other Works
Westminster at war. 1947.
Pleasures strange and simple (essays). 1953.
It was really Charlie's castle (for children). 1953.
The light that went out (for children). 1953.
The icicle and the sun. 1958.
The Bay of Naples. 1960.
Blue skies, brown studies. 1960.
Away to it all. 1964.
Grand Tour today. 1968.
Christmas. 1968.
The birth of a story. 1971.
Proust and his world. 1973.

SANTHI, S. (1934–)
Indian poet; born in Madras; educated at Loyola College, Madras University; civil servant in Indian government service (1960–); represented in *Modern Indian poetry in English* (1969).

Bibliography
Contemporary poets.
Indian national bibliography 1958–67.

Poetry
Lamplight in the sun. 1967.
Whispers near a Niagara. 1969.

SAROYAN, ARAM (1943–)
American poet; son of William Saroyan the novelist; educated at Chicago, New York and Columbia universities; publisher and editor of *Lines* (1964–5); a contributor to *Poetry*, etc.

Bibliography
C.B.I.
Contemporary poets.
Gale.

Poetry
Poems. 1963.
In. 1965.
Works. 1966.
Poems. 1967.
Aram Saroyan. 1968.
Pages. 1969.
Words and photographs. 1970.
The rest. 1971.
Poems. 1972.

Other Work
Cloth: an electric novel. 1971.

SASTHI, BRATA (1939–)
Indian writer; born and educated at Calcutta; now settled in London; a contributor to the *Guardian*, *New Statesman*, *Vogue*, *Cosmopolitan*, *Transatlantic Review*, etc.

Bibliography
B.N.B.
C.B.I.
Indian national bibliography 1958–67.
National bibliography of Indian literature 1901–53.

Works
My god died young (autobiography). n.d.
Confessions of an Indian woman eater. n.d.
She and he. n.d.

SAUNDERS, JAMES A. (1925–)
English playwright; educated at the University of Southampton; was a tutor for some years; full-time writer (1962–); has written many radio and television plays.

Bibliography
B.N.B.
Contemporary dramatists.
Who's who in the theatre. 1967.

Plays
Alas, poor Fred. 1960.
Barnstable (broadcast 1959, staged 1960). 1961.
Next time I'll sing to you. 1963.
A scent of flowers. 1965.
Double, double (staged 1962). 1965.
Neighbours and other plays (includes Ends and echoes, Barnstable, Committal, Return to a city, The pedagogue, A slight accident, Trio). 1968.
The Italian girl (adaptation of Iris Murdoch's novel). 1968.
The travails of Sancho Panza (adaptation from Don Quixote). 1970.
The borage pigeon affair (staged 1969). 1970.

SAUNDERS, THOMAS (1909–)
Canadian poet, born in Scotland; educated at University of Manitoba, Winnipeg; minister of the United Church of Canada; history editor, *Winnipeg Free Press* (1960–); represented in *Poetry 62* (1961).

Bibliography
B.N.B.
Canadiana.
Contemporary poets.

Poetry
Scrub oak. 1949.
Horizontal world. 1951.
Something of a young world is dying. 1958.
The devil and Cal McCabe. 1960.
Red river of the North. 1969.

SCANNELL, VERNON (1922–)
English poet and novelist; educated at Leeds University; served in the Gordon Highlanders during the Second World War (1941–5); amateur and professional boxer; freelance writer; a contributor to the *New Statesman, Encounter, Transatlantic Review*, etc.; represented in several anthologies.

Bibliography
B.N.B.
Contemporary poets.
Gale.

Novels
The fight. 1953.

The wound and the scar. 1953.
The big chance. 1960.
The shadowed place. 1961.
The face of the enemy. 1961.
The dividing night. 1962.
The big time. 1965.
The dangerous ones. 1970.

Poetry
Graves and resurrections. 1948.
A mortal pitch. 1957.
The masks of love. 1960.
A sense of danger. 1962.
Walking wounded. Poems 1962–65. 1968.
Epithets of war. 1969.
Mastering the craft. 1970.
Company of women. 1971.
Selected poems. 1971.

Other Works
Edward Thomas (criticism). 1962.
The dangerous ones (for children). 1970.
The tiger and the rose (autobiography). 1971.

SCARFE, FRANCIS HAROLD (1911–)
English poet, novelist and French scholar; educated at Durham University and Fitzwilliam House, Cambridge; served in the Second World War (1941–6); University Extension Lecturer, Oxford (1946–7); Senior Lecturer, Glasgow University (1947–59); director, British Institute, Paris (1959–65); Professor of French, University of London (1965–); O.B.E.; his translations from the French are not listed below.

Bibliography
Authors' and writers' who's who. 1971.
B.N.B.
Contemporary poets.
Who's who. 1973.

Novels
Promises. 1950.
Single blessedness. 1951.
Unfinished woman. 1954.

Poetry
Inscapes. 1940.
Forty poems and ballads. 1941.
Underworlds. 1950.
Our common days. 1972.

Criticism
Auden and after. 1942.

W. H. Auden. 1949.
The art of Paul Valéry. 1954.
La vie et l'œuvre de T. S. Eliot. 1964.
André Chénier; his life and work 1762–94. 1965.

SCHAFF, DAVID (1943–)

American poet; educated at Yale and Berkeley universities; Instructor in Art and History, University of California, Berkeley (1966–); a contributor to little magazines; editor of *Cassiopeia* and *Ephemeris* (1968–70).

Bibliography
C.B.I.
Gale.

Poetry
Tables. 1967.
The ladder. 1968.
The moon by day. 1971.

SCHEVILL, JAMES ERWIN (1920–)

American poet; born in Berkeley, California; educated at Harvard University; served in the U.S. Army (1942–6) during the Second World War; various academic posts; currently Professor of English at Brown University, Providence, Rhode Island (1969–); recipient of various awards and grants; represented in many anthologies; a contributor to the *New York Times*, *Saturday Review*, *New Yorker*, etc.; translated Corneille, *Le cid* (1961).

Bibliography
C.B.I.
Gale.
Who's who in America 1973–4.

Poetry
Tensions. 1947.
The American fantasies. 1951.
The right to greet. 1956.
Selected poems, 1945–1959. 1959.
Private dooms and public destinations: poems 1945–1962. 1962.
The Stalingrad elegies. 1964.
Release. 1968.
Violence and glory: poems 1962–1968. 1969.
The Buddhist car. 1971.

Plays
High sinners, low angels (musical). 1953.
The bloody tenet (poetic drama). 1957.
Voices of mass and capital. 1962.
The black president and other plays. 1965.
Lovecraft's follies. 1971.

Other Works
Sherwood Anderson: his life and works. 1951.
The roaring market and the silent tomb (biography). 1956.
Breakout: in search of new theatrical environments. 1972.

SCHISGAL, MURRAY JOSEPH (1926–)

American playwright; born in New York; educated at Brooklyn Law School and New School for Social Research, New York; served in the U.S. Navy (1944–6); jazz musician in the 1940s; practising lawyer (1953–5); taught English (1955–60); full-time writer (1960–); wrote the film scripts of *The tiger makes out* (1967) and a television play *The love song of Barney Kempenski* (1966).

Bibliography
C.B.I.
Contemporary dramatists.
Gale.

Plays
The typists, and The tiger (staged 1960). 1963.
Luv (staged 1963). 1963.
Fragments, Windows, and other plays (includes Reverberations, Memorial day, The old Jew). 1965.
Jimmy Shine (staged 1968, music by John Sebastian). 1969.
The Chinese, and Dr. Fish. 1970.

SCHLESINGER, ARTHUR MEIER, Jr. (1917–)

American historian, son of the historian Arthur Meier Schlesinger, Sr.; educated at Harvard University; offices of War Information and of Strategic Studies, Washington D.C. (1942–5); Professor of History, Harvard (1946–62); special assistant to President Kennedy and President Lyndon Johnson (1961–4); freelance writer (1964–); Albert Schweitzer Professor of Humanities, New York (1966–); member of many academic bodies, etc.; recipient of Pulitzer and other literary awards and academic honours; a contributor to learned and to popular journals; his edited work is not listed below.

Bibliography
C.B.I.
Gale.

Works
Orestes A. Brownson: a pilgrim's progress. 1939.
The age of Jackson. 1945.
The vital center; the politics of freedom. 1949.
The General and the President (with R. H.
   Rovere), revised as The MacArthur controversy
   and American foreign policy. 1951.
The age of Roosevelt. 3 vols. 1957–60: vol. I, The
   crisis of the old order. 1957; vol. II, The coming
   of the New Deal. 1959; vol. III, The politics of
   upheaval. 1960.
Kennedy or Nixon: does it make any difference?
   1960.
Paths of American thought (with Morton M.
   White). 1963.
The politics of hope (essays). 1963.
A thousand days: John F. Kennedy in the White
   House. 1965.
The bitter heritage: Vietnam and American demo-
   cracy. 1967.
Congress and the presidency (with Alfred de
   Grazier). 1967.
Violence: America in the sixties. 1968.
Crisis of confidence: ideas, power and violence in
   America. 1969.
The coming to power: critical presidential elec-
   tions in American history. 1972.
A history of the U.S. political parties. 1973.
The imperial presidency. 1973.

SCHULBERG, BUDD WILSON
(1914–)
American novelist and playwright; educated at
Dartmouth College, Hanover, New Hampshire;
served in the U.S. Navy during the Second World
War (1943–6); Hollywood screen writer (1936–9);
president, Schulberg Productions (1958–); recipient of various literary, screen and journalistic
awards; a contributor to *Esquire*, *Playboy*, etc.

Bibliography
C.B.I.
Contemporary novelists.
Gale.

Novels
What makes Sammy run? (produced as a musical
   1964). 1941.
The harder they fall. 1947.
The disenchanted. 1950.
Some faces in the crowd (stories, filmed 1958).
   1953.
Waterfront (filmed 1954). 1955.
Sanctuary V. 1970.

Poetry
A face in the crowd (screenplay). 1957.
Across the everglades (screenplay). 1958.
The disenchanted (from the novel). 1959.

Other Works
Loser and still champion: Muhammad Ali. 1972.
The four seasons of success. 1972.

SCHUYLER, JAMES MARCUS
(1923–)
American poet; born in Chicago; educated at
Bethany College, West Virginia; lived in Italy for
some years; works in the New York Museum of
Modern Art; represented in *New American poetry*
(1960).

Bibliography
C.B.I.
Contemporary poets.

Novels
Alfred and Guinevere. 1958.
A nest of ninnies (with John Ashbery). 1969.

Poetry
Salute. 1960.
May 24th or so. 1966.
Freely espousing. 1969.

Other Work
A picnic cantata (music by Paul Bowles). 1955.

SCOTT, FRANCIS REGINALD
(1899–)
Canadian poet and scholar; educated at Magdalen
College, Oxford, and McGill University; taught
(1919–23); called to the Quebec Bar (1927); after
various academic posts, Macdonald Professor of
Law (1955–67); Visiting Professor, French Canadian Studies Programme (1967–9); recipient of
numerous literary and academic awards; his edited
and translated work is not listed below.

Bibliography
B.N.B.
Contemporary poets.
Who's who. 1973.

Poetry
Overture. 1945.
Events and signals. 1954.
The eye of the needle; satires, sorties, sundries.
   1957.

Signature. 1964.
Selected poems. 1966.
Trouvailles; poems from prose. 1967.

Other Works
Make this your Canada; a review of C.C.F. history
and policy (with D. Lewis). 1943.
Cooperation or what? United States and the
British Commonwealth. 1944.
Civil liberties and Canadian federation. 1959.
Quebec states her case (with M. K. Oliver). 1964.

SCOTT, PAUL MARK (1920–78)
English novelist and critic; secretary to the Falcon
Press (1946–50); director of David Higham
Associates (1950–60); a contributor to *The Times*,
Country Life, etc.; adapted his novels for television.

Bibliography
Authors' and writers' who's who. 1971.
B.N.B.
Contemporary novelists.

Novels
Johnnie Sahib. 1951.
The alien sky. 1953.
A male child. 1956.
The mark of the warrior. 1958.
The Chinese love pavilion. 1960.
Birds of paradise. 1962.
The bender. 1963.
The corrida at San Feliu. 1964.
The jewel in the crown. 1966.
The day of the scorpion. 1968.
The towers of silence. 1971.

SCOTT, PETER DALE (†ADAM GREENE, †JOHN SPROSTON)
(1929–)
Canadian poet and writer; born in Montreal; educated at McGill University, Paris and Oxford; Lecturer in Political Science, McGill University
(1955–6); Canadian Foreign Service (1957–61);
Assistant Professor, University of California,
Berkeley (1961–); a contributor to *T.L.S.*
Encounter, Poetry, Tamarack Review, etc.

Bibliography
Canadiana.
C.B.I.
Gale.

Poetry
Poems. 1953.
Selected poems. 1968.

Other Works
Education at Berkeley (with others). 1966.
The politics of escalation in Vietnam (with others).
1966.
The war conspiracy. 1972.

SCOVELL, EDITH JOY (*Mrs.* ELTON)
(1907–)
English poet; born in Sheffield; educated at
Somerville College, Oxford; a contributor to the
Listener, New Statesman and Nation, T.L.S., etc.

Bibliography
Authors' and writers' who's who. 1971.
B.N.B.
Contemporary poets.
N.C.B.E.L.

Poetry
Shadows of chrysanthemums. 1944.
The midsummer meadow. 1946.
The river steamer. 1956.

SCULLY, JAMES (1937–)
American poet; educated at the University of
Connecticut; has travelled widely; Associate Professor of English, University of Connecticut
(1964–); represented in several anthologies;
editor of *Modern poets on modern poetry* (1966).

Bibliography
C.B.I.
Contemporary poets.
Gale.

Poetry
The marches. 1967.
Avenue of the Americas. 1971.

SEARLE, RONALD WILLIAM FORDHAM (†TIMOTHY SHY)
(1920–)
English artist, illustrator and writer; born in Cambridge; educated at the Cambridgeshire School of
Art; served in the Second World War (1939–46)
and was a prisoner of war in Japanese hands
(1942–5); cartoonist, successively to *Tribune, Sunday Express, News Chronicle, Punch* (1949–62);
joined the editorial board of *Punch* (1956); held
one-man shows throughout Europe (1947–); the

designer of many films; a contributor to *Punch*, *New Yorker*, *Holiday*, etc.

Bibliography
Authors' and writers' who's who. 1971.
B.N.B.
Gale.
Who's who. 1973.

Works
Forty drawings. 1946.
Le nouveau ballet anglais. 1947.
Hurrah for St. Trinian's! 1948.
The female approach. 1949.
Paris sketchbook (with Kaye Webb). 1950 and 1957.
Back to the slaughterhouse. 1951.
John Gilpin. 1952.
The terror of St. Trinian's (as †Timothy Shy with D. B. Wyndham Lewis). 1952.
Down with skool (with Geoffrey Willans). 1953.
Souls in torment. 1953.
Looking at London. 1953.
How to be topp (with Geoffrey Willans). 1954.
Modern types (with Geoffrey Gover). 1955.
Rake's progress. 1955.
Merry England, etc. 1956.
Whizz for atomms (with Geoffrey Willans). 1956.
The compleet Molesworth (with Geoffrey Willans). 1958.
The dog's ear book (with Geoffrey Willans). 1958.
The big city (with Alex Atkinson). 1958.
Back in the jug agane (with Geoffrey Willans). 1959.
The St. Trinian's story (with Kaye Webb). 1959.
U.S.A. for beginners (with Alex Atkinson). 1959.
Refugees 1960 (with Kaye Webb). 1960.
Russia for beginners (with Alex Atkinson). 1960.
Baron Munchausen. 1960.
The Penguin Ronald Searle. 1961.
Which way did he go? 1961.
A Christmas carol. 1961.
Escape from the Amazon! (with Alex Atkinson). 1964.
Searle in the sixties. 1964.
From frozen north to filthy lucre (with Groucho Marx and Jane Clapperton). 1964.
Those magnificent men in their flying machines (with A. Andrews and B. Richardson). 1965.
Pardong M'sieur. 1965.
Haven't we met before somewhere? (with Heinz Huber). 1966.
Searle's cats. 1967.
The square egg. 1968.

Take one toad. 1968.
Hello—where did all the people go? 1969.
Hommage à Toulouse-Lautrec. 1969.
Monte Carlo or bust! (with E. W. Hildick). 1969.
Secret sketchbook—the back streets of Hamburg. 1970.
The great fur opera (with Kildare Dobbs). 1970.
The addict: a terrible tale. 1971.
The subtle alchemist: a book of wine. 1973.

SELBOURNE, DAVID (1937–)
English playwright; educated at Manchester Grammar School and Balliol College, Oxford; Tutor in Politics, Ruskin College, Oxford.

Bibliography
B.N.B.
Contemporary dramatists.

Plays
The play of William Cooper and Edmund Dew-Nevett (staged 1968). 1968.
The two-backed beast (staged 1968). 1969.
Dorabella (staged 1969). 1970.
Samson, and Alison Mary Fagan (Samson staged 1970, Alison Mary Fagan staged 1972). 1971.
The damned (staged 1973). 1971.
Class plays (staged as Three class plays. 1972). 1973.

SELBY, HUBERT (1928–)
American journalist and novelist; served in the Marine Service (1944–6); in hospital with tuberculosis (1946–50); various jobs (1950–64); freelance copywriter for *National Enquirer* (1965–); a contributor to periodicals.

Bibliography
C.B.I.
Contemporary novelists.
Gale.

Novels
Last exit to Brooklyn. 1964.
The room. 1971.

SELORMEY, FRANCIS (1927–)
Ghanaian writer; born near Keta; educated at St. Augustine's College, Cape Coast, and in Germany; in charge of physical education at a training college in Hohoe, etc.; has written several film scripts.

Bibliography
B.N.B.
Ghana national bibliography.
Jahn and Dressler.

Novel
The narrow path. 1966.

SELVON, SAMUEL DICKSON
(1923–)
Trinidadian novelist; served with the Trinidad
R.N.V.R. during the Second World War (1940–5);
on the staff of the *Trinidad Guardian* (1946–50);
civil servant, Indian High Commission, London
(1950–3); full-time writer (1954–); awarded
various literary and authors' grants and fellowships; lives in London.

Bibliography
B.N.B.
Contemporary novelists.

Novels
A brighter sun. 1952.
An island is a world. 1955.
The lonely Londoners (paperback title, The lonely
    ones). 1956.
Ways of sunlight (stories). 1958.
Turn again, tiger. 1958.
I hear thunder. 1963.
The housing lark. 1965.
A drink of water. 1968.
The plains of Caroni. 1969.
Those who eat the Cascadura. 1972.

SERAILLIER, IAN LUCIEN (1912–)
English children's novelist and poet; educated at
Oxford; schoolmaster (1936–61).

Bibliography
B.N.B.
Contemporary novelists.
Gale.

For Children
They raced for treasure (simplified version as
    Treasure ahead. 1954). 1946.
Flight to adventure (simplified version as Moun-
    tain rescue. 1955). 1947.
Captain Bouncaboard and the pirates. 1949.
There's no escape. 1952.
The ballad of Kon Tiki. 1952.
Belinda and the swans. 1952.
Jungle adventure. 1953.

The adventure of Dick Varley. 1954.
Making good. 1955.
Guns in the wild. 1956.
The silver sword (educational version as Escape
    from Warsaw. 1963). 1956.
Katy at home. 1957.
Katy at school. 1959.
The Gorgon's head: the story of Perseus. 1961.
The way of danger: the story of Theseus. 1962.
The clashing rocks: the story of Jason. 1963.
The cave of death. 1965.
A fall from the sky. 1966.
Havelock the warrior. 1968.
The tale of three landlubbers. 1970.
The bishop and the devil. 1971.
The franklin's tale. 1972.

Poetry
Three new poets (with Roy McFadden and Alex
    Comfort). 1942.
The weaver birds. 1944.
Thomas and the sparrow. 1946.
The tale of the monster horse. 1950.
Everest climbed. 1955.
Poems and pictures. 1958.
Happily ever after: poems for children. 1963.
The challenge of the green knight. 1966.
Robin in the greenwood. 1967.
Robin and his merry men. 1969.
The ballad of St. Simeon. 1971.
Marko's wedding. 1972.

Other Works
Florina and the wild bird (joint translator from
    S. Chonz). 1952.
Wide horizon reading scheme (with R. Ridout). 4
    vols. 1953.
Beowulf the warrior (translation). 1954.
The ivory horn (adaptations of the Chansons de
    geste). 1960.
The midnight thief; a musical story (with Richard
    Rodney Bennett). 1963.
The enchanted island; stories from Shakespeare.
    1964.
Ahmet the woodseller; a musical story (with
    Gordon Crosse). 1965.
Chaucer and his world. 1967.
Heracles the strong. 1971.

SERUMAGA, ROBERT (1939–)
Ugandan playwright and actor; pioneer in starting
a Uganda National Theatre; educated in business
studies at Trinity College, Dublin; has acted in
London and Uganda; founder of Theatre Limited,

a professional acting company based on Uganda; his unpublished plays include *Elephants* produced by Theatre Limited (1969).

Bibliography
Jahn and Dressler.
Zell and Silver.

Novel
Return to the shadows. 1969.

Play
A play. 1968.

SEXTON, ANNE (*née* HARVEY)
(1928–   )
American poet; recipient of several poetry awards; American Academy of Arts and Letters travelling fellowship (1963–4), etc.; represented in various anthologies; a contributor to *Harper's*, *New Yorker*, *Saturday Review*, etc.

Bibliography
C.B.I.
Contemporary poets.
Gale.
L. of C.

Poetry
To Bedlam and part way back. 1960.
All my pretty ones. 1962.
Selected poems. 1964.
Live or die (Pulitzer Prize 1967). 1966.
Poems (with Thomas Kinsella and Douglas Livingstone). 1968.
Love poems. 1969.
Transformations. 1972.
The book of folly. 1973.

Other Work
Eggs of things (with Maxine W. Kumin). 1963.

SEYMOUR-SMITH, MARTIN (1928–   )
English poet and writer; educated at St. Edmund Hall, Oxford; served in the army (1946–8); tutor to Robert Graves's son in Majorca (1951–4); schoolmaster (1954–60); freelance writer (1960–   ); represented in various anthologies; a contributor to the *Spectator*, *New Statesman*, *Listener*, etc.; editor of *Shakespeare's sonnets* (1963), *Poems of Andrew Marvell* (1969), etc.

Bibliography
B.N.B.

Contemporary poets.
Gale.

Poetry
Poems (with others). 1952.
Fantasy pamphlet no. 9. 1953.
All devils fading. 1954.
Tea with Miss Stockport: 24 poems. 1963.
Reminiscences of Norma: poems 1963–70. 1971.

Other Works
Robert Graves. 1956.
Bluffer's guide to literature. 1965.
Fallen women: the prostitute in literature. 1969.
Poets through their letters. 1969.
Inside poetry (with James Reeves). 1970.
Lord Paramount of the turf. 1971.
Guide to modern world literature. 1973.

SHADBOLT, MAURICE FRANCIS RICHARD (1932–   )
New Zealand novelist; born and educated in Auckland; journalist and film scriptwriter (1952–7); full-time writer (1957–   ); lived in London and Spain (1957–60); recipient of several literary awards.

Bibliography
B.N.B.
Contemporary novelists.
Gale.

Novels
Among the cinders. 1965.
This summer's dolphin. 1969.
An ear of the dragon. 1971.
Strangers and journeys. 1972.

Stories
The New Zealanders: a sequence of stories. 1959.
Summer fires and winter country. 1963.
The presence of music: 3 novellas. 1967.

Other Works
New Zealand: gift of the sea (with B. Brake). 1963.
The Shell guide to New Zealand. 1968.
Isles of the South Pacific (with Olaf Ruben). 1968.

SHAFFER, ANTHONY (1926–   )
English novelist and playwright; twin brother of Peter Shaffer (q.v.); educated at St. Paul's School and Trinity College, Cambridge; barrister and journalist; his play *The savage parade* (1963) is

unpublished; film scripts include *Black comedy* (from his brother's play) and *Frenzy* (1972).

Bibliography
B.N.B.
Contemporary dramatists.

Novels with his brother (see below).

Play
Sleuth (filmed 1972). 1970.

SHAFFER, PETER LEVIN (†PETER ANTHONY) (1926–)
English playwright; educated at St. Paul's School and Trinity College, Cambridge; literary critic of *Truth* (1956–67); music critic of *Time and Tide* (1961–2); has written plays for radio and television; film scripts include *Lord of the flies* (1963), from William Golding's novel.

Bibliography
Authors' and writers' who's who. 1971.
B.N.B.
Contemporary dramatists.
John Russell Taylor. Peter Shaffer. 1974.
Who's who. 1973.

Novels
How doth the crocodile? (with Anthony Shaffer, as †Peter Anthony). 1951.
Woman in the wardrobe (with Anthony Shaffer, as †Peter Anthony). 1952.
Withered murder (with Anthony Shaffer). 1955.

Plays
Five finger exercise (staged 1958, filmed 1962). 1958.
The private ear (filmed as The pad, staged 1962 with The public eye, filmed as Follow me, 1972). 1962.
The royal hunt of the sun (staged 1964, filmed 1968). 1964.
Black comedy (staged 1965; published with White lies: two plays, 1967, and with The white liars). 1968.
White liars (staged with Black comedy. 1967). 1968.
The battle of shrivings. 1970.
Equus. 1973.

SHAHANE, *Dr.* **VASANT A.** (1923–)
Indian critic; born in Parbhani, Maharashtra; Ph.D. from Leeds; Visiting Professor in the University of Wisconsin, Wisconsin, U.S.A. (1967–8); Visiting Professor in the Wayne State University, Detroit, Michigan, U.S.A. (1970–1); currently Senior Professor of English and Principal, University College of Arts and Commerce, Osmania University; a contributor to Indian, British, American and European journals.

Bibliography
C.B.I.
Indian national bibliography 1958–67.
National bibliography of Indian literature 1901–53.

Works
E. M. Forster: a reassessment. 1962.
Perspectives on E. M. Forster's "A passage to India". 1968.
Khushwant Singh. 1972.
Rudyard Kipling, activist and artist. 1973.

SHAPCOTT, THOMAS WILLIAM (1935–)
Australian poet; educated at Queensland University; public accountant (1961–); a contributor to *Bulletin*, *Meanjin*, *Quadrant*, etc.; editor of *Australian poetry now* (1970).

Bibliography
Annals of Australian literature.
Australian national bibliography.

Poetry
Time on fire. 1961.
The mankind thing. 1964.
Sonnets. 1964.
A taste of salt water. 1967.
Inwards to the sun. 1969.
Fingers at air. 1970.
The seven deadly sins. 1970.

Other Work
Focus on Charles Blackman. 1967.

SHAPIRO, DAVID JOEL (1947–)
American poet and violinist; educated at Columbia University; a contributor to *Antioch Review*, *Minnesota Review*, etc.

Bibliography
C.B.I.
Contemporary poets.
Gale.
L. of C.

Poetry
January. 1965.
Neurotic styles. 1965.
Poems from Deal. 1969.
Man holding an acoustic panel and other poems.
    1971.
The page turner. 1973.

SHARMAN, GOPAL (1935–)
Indian poet; born in Calcutta; educated at the University of Lucknow; has travelled widely; Director of the Ramayana Theatre, Delhi; *Times* critic for the arts in India; a contributor to the *Illustrated Weekly of India*, etc.

Bibliography
C.B.I.
Contemporary poets.
Gale.
Indian national bibliography 1958–67.

Poetry
Full circle. 1969.

Other Work
Filigree in sound; form and content in Indian
    music. 1970.

SHARP, ALAN (1934–)
Scottish novelist; apprentice in local shipyards; private detective; teacher of English in Germany, etc.; served in the army (1952–4); author of television and radio plays.

Bibliography
B.N.B.
Gale.

Novels
A green tree in Gedde. 1965.
The wind shifts. 1967.
The hired hand. 1971.

SHAW, HELEN (1913–)
New Zealand poet; educated at Canterbury University, Christchurch, and University of New Zealand; taught until her marriage, and then turned to freelance writing; represented in several anthologies; a contributor to *Outposts*, *Fiddlehead*, etc.

Bibliography
B.N.B.
Contemporary poets.

Poetry
Out of dark. 1968.

Short Stories
The orange tree and other stories. 1957.
Lover from another time. 1973.

SHAW, ROBERT (1927–78)
English actor and novelist; was married to the actress Mary Ure (d. 1975); acted with the Shakespeare Memorial Theatre (1949–50 and 1953); Old Vic (1951–2); in numerous West End productions including *Tiger at the gates* and *The long and the short and the tall*; acted in numerous films including *The dam busters, A man for all seasons, Royal hunt of the sun*; has taken part in many television serials.

Bibliography
B.N.B.
Contemporary dramatists.
Contemporary novelists.
Gale.
Who's who. 1973.

Novels
The hiding place (The cure of souls, I). 1959.
The sun doctor (Hawthornden Prize 1962). 1961.
The flag (The cure of souls, II). 1965.
The man in the glass booth (The cure of souls, III)
    (dramatised and staged 1967). 1967.
A card from Morocco. 1969.

Plays
The man in the glass booth (from the novel). 1967.
Cato Street. 1970.

SHEPARD, SAM (1943–)
American playwright; worked at many jobs in New York; recipient of several awards; lives in London; film scripts include *Me and my brother* (1967) and *Ringaleerio* (1971); unpublished plays include *Cowboy* (1964), *Rocking chair* (1964) and *The tooth of crime* (1972).

Bibliography
C.B.I.
Contemporary dramatists.
Who's who in America. 1973–4.

Short Story
Hawk moon. 1972.

Plays

Five plays: Chicago, Icarus's mother, Red Cross, Fourteen hundred thousand, Melodrama play. 1967.

La turista (staged 1966). 1968.

Operation sidewinder (staged 1970). 1971.

The unseen hand and other plays (includes Forensic and the navigators, Back bog beast bait, Shaved splits, The holy ghostly, Rock garden). 1971.

Mad dog blues and other plays (includes Cowboy month, Cowboy #2). 1972.

Hawk moon. 1973.

SHERWIN, JUDITH JOHNSON
(1936–)

American poet and playwright; educated at Columbia University; promotion manager, Arrow Press (1961); housewife and full-time writer; recipient of many poetry awards; her plays, staged but unpublished, include *Belissa's love* (1959) and *En avant, Coco* (1962); a contributor to *Atlantic*, *Poetry*, *Sewanee Review*, etc.

Bibliography
C.B.I.
Gale.

Story
The life of riot. 1970.

Poetry
Uranium poems. 1969.
Impossible building. 1973.

SIGAL, CLANCY (1926–)

American novelist; educated at University of California, Los Angeles; served in the U.S. Army; full-time writer; settled in England (1957); regular contributor to the *New Statesman*, *Encounter*, *Time and Tide*.

Bibliography
C.B.I.
Contemporary novelists.
Gale.
Who's who in America. 1973–4.

Novels
Weekend in Dinlock. 1961.
Going away. 1962.

SILKIN, JON (1930–)

English poet; educated at Dulwich College and Leeds University; worked as a manual labourer (1950–6); taught English as a foreign language (1956–8); Gregory Poetry Fellow, Leeds University (1958–60); editor of the little magazine *Stand*; lecturer in writers' workshop, University of Iowa (1968–70); a contributor to *Encounter*, the *New Statesman*, *Time and Tide*, etc.; his translations and edited work are not listed below.

Bibliography
Authors' and writers' who's who. 1971.
B.N.B.
Contemporary poets.
Gale.
Who's who. 1973.

Poetry
The peaceable kingdom. 1954.
The two freedoms. 1958.
The re-ordering of the stones. 1961.
Nature with man. 1965.
Penguin modern poets no. 7 (with R. Murphy and N. Tarn). 1965.
Poems new and selected. 1966.
Amana grass. 1971.
Killhope wheel. 1971.
Air that pricks earth. 1973.

Criticism
Isaac Rosenberg, 1890–1918 (with M. de Sausmarez). 1959.
A critical study of poets of the First World War. 1971.
Out of battle: the poetry of the Great War. 1972.

SILLITOE, ALAN (1928–)

English novelist; born in Nottingham; left school at 14 and worked in various jobs; served in the R.A.F. (1946–9); recipient of several literary awards; literary adviser to W. H. Allen, publishers (1970–).

Bibliography
Authors' and writers' who's who. 1971.
B.N.B.
Contemporary novelists.
Gale.
Who's who. 1973.

Novels
Saturday night and Sunday morning (filmed 1960, staged 1964). 1958.

The loneliness of the long distance runner (Hawthornden Prize 1960, filmed 1962). 1959.
The general (filmed as Counterpoint, 1967). 1960.
Key to the door. 1961.
The ragman's daughter (short stories). 1963.
The death of William Posters. 1965.
A tree on fire. 1967.
Guzman, go home (short stories). 1968.
A start in life. 1970.
Travels in Nihilon. 1971.
Raw material. 1972.
Men, women and children. 1973.

Poetry
Without beer or bread. 1957.
The rats and other poems. 1960.
A falling out of love. 1964.
Shaman and other poems. 1968.
Love in the environs of Voronezh. 1968.

Plays
All citizens are soldiers (with Ruth Fainlight). 1969.
This foreign field. 1970.

Travel
Road to Volgograd. 1964.

For Children
The city adventures of Marmalade Jim. 1967.

SILVERBERG, ROBERT (†WALKER CHAPMAN, †WALTER DRUMMOND, †IVAR JORGENSON, †CALVIN M. KNOX, †DAVID OSBORNE, †ROBERT RANDALL (*with Randall Garrett*), **†LEE SEBASTIAN)**
American science fiction writer; educated at Columbia University; freelance writer; recipient of science fiction awards; only a selection of his writings is listed below.

Bibliography
C.B.I.
Gale.

Novels
Revolt on Alpha. C. 1955.
The thirteenth immortal. 1957.
Master of life and death. 1957.
The shrouded planet (as †Robert Randall). 1958.
Invaders from earth. 1958.
Starman's quest. 1958.

Invincible barriers (as †David Osborne). 1958.
Lest we forget thee (as †Calvin M. Knox). 1958.
Starhaven (as †Ivar Jorgenson). 1958.
Stepsons of Terra. 1958.
Aliens from space (as †David Osborne). 1958.
The plot against earth (as †Calvin M. Knox). 1959.
The dawning light (as †Robert Randall). 1959.
The planet killers. 1959.
Lost race of Mars. 1960.
Collision course. 1961.
The seed of earth. 1962.
Recalled to life. 1962.
Regan's planet. 1964.
To worlds beyond. 1965.
Conquerors from the darkness. 1965.
Planet of death. 1967.
The adventures of Nat Palmer. 1967.
Men against time. 1967.
The time hoppers. 1967.
The world of rain forest. 1967.
Hawksbill station. 1968.
Thorns. 1969.
The man in the maze. 1969.
The arrival of time. 1969.
The calibrated alligator. 1969.
To live again. 1969.
Three survived. 1969.
The cube root of uncertainty. 1970.
Nightwings. 1970.
Parsecs and parables (short stories). 1970.
Tower of glass. 1970.
A time of changes. 1971.
Dying inside. 1972.
The second trip. 1973.
Valley beyond time. 1973.
Earth's other shadow. 1973.

Other Works
Treasure beneath the sea. 1960.
First American into space. 1961.
Lost cities and vanished civilizations. 1962.
The fabulous Rockefellers. 1963.
Sunken history; the story of underwater archaeology. 1963.
Fifteen battles that changed the world. 1963.
Home of the red man; Indian North America before Columbus. 1963.
Empires in the dust. 1963.
The great doctors. 1964.
Akhnaten: the rebel pharaoh. 1964.
The man who found Nineveh: Austen Henry Layard. 1964.
Man before Adam. 1964.

Time of the great freeze. 1964.

The loneliest continent (as †Walker Chapman). 1964.

Socrates. 1965.

Scientists and scoundrels. 1965.

The mask of Akhnaten. 1965.

Men who mastered the atom. 1965.

The world of coral. 1965.

The old ones: Indians of the American South West. 1965.

The great wall of China. 1965.

Niels Böhr. 1965.

Forgotten by time. 1966.

Frontiers in archaeology. 1966.

Kublai Khan (as †Walker Chapman). 1966.

To the rack of Darius. 1966.

The long rampart. 1966.

Rivers (as †Lee Sebastian). 1966.

Bridges. 1966.

Earthmen and strangers. 1966.

Dawn of medicine. 1967.

The golden dream. 1967.

The morning of mankind. 1967.

The gate of worlds. 1967.

The light of the world: Edison and the power industry. 1967.

In search of El Dorado. 1968.

Stormy voyage: the story of Charles Wilkes. 1968.

The South Pole (as †Lee Sebastian). 1968.

Mound builders of Ancient America. 1968.

Four men who changed the universe. 1968.

The world of the ocean depths. 1968.

The challenge of climate. 1969.

How it was when time went away. 1969.

The auk, the dodo and the oryx. 1969.

Vanishing giants: the story of the Sequoias. 1969.

Wonders of ancient Chinese society. 1969.

Across a billion years. 1969.

Bruce of the Nile. 1969.

The world of space. 1969.

The seven wonders of the ancient world. 1970.

If I forget thee, O Jerusalem. 1970.

Mammoths, mastodons and man. 1970.

Worlds part 1992. 1970.

Clocks for the ages. 1971.

The pueblo revolt. 1971.

The world inside. 1971.

To the western shore. 1971.

John Muir, prophet among the glaciers. 1972.

The longest voyage. 1972.

The realm of Prester John. 1972.

The world within the tide pool. 1972.

SIMAK, CLIFFORD (DONALD)

(1904–)

American science fiction writer; educated at the University of Wisconsin; on the staff of the *Minneapolis Star and Tribune* (1939–); recipient of various science fiction awards.

Bibliography

C.B.I.

Gale.

Novels

Cosmic engineers. 1950.

Time and again. 1951.

City. 1952.

Ring around the sun. 1953.

Strangers in the universe. 1956.

Time is the simplest thing. 1961.

Aliens for neighbours. 1961.

They walked like men. 1962.

All the traps of earth. 1962.

Way station. 1963.

All flesh is grass. 1965.

Worlds without end. 1965.

Why call them back from heaven? 1966.

Best science fiction stories of Clifford Simak. 1967.

The werewolf principle. 1968.

The goblin reservation. 1969.

Out of their minds. 1970.

Destiny doll. 1971.

Prehistoric man. 1971.

A choice of gods. 1972.

Cemetery world. 1973.

Our children's children. 1973.

Other Works

The solar system. 1962.

Trilobite, dinosaur and man. 1965.

Wonder and glory: the story of the universe. 1970.

SIMON, MARVIN NEIL (1927–)

American playwright; educated at New York and Denver universities; served in the U.S. Air Force (1945–6); television plays include *Phil Silvers Show* (1948) and *Tallulah Bankhead Show* (1951); film scripts include *The out-of-towners* (1970); unpublished plays include *Sketches* (with Danny Simon, 1956).

Bibliography

C.B.I.

Contemporary dramatists.

Gale.

Plays
Adventures of Marco Polo (musical with William Friedburg). 1959.
Heidi (musical with William Friedburg). 1959.
Come blow your horn (with Danny Simon, staged 1961). 1963.
Barefoot in the park (staged as Nobody loves me, 1962; filmed 1967). 1964.
The odd couple (staged 1965). 1966.
Sweet charity (musical based on film, The nights of Cabiria) (also filmed 1968). 1966.
The star-spangled girl (staged 1966). 1967.
Plaza suite (staged 1968). 1969.
Promises, promises (musical based on the film The apartment, staged 1968). 1969.
Last of the red hot lovers (staged 1969, filmed 1972). 1970.
The gingerbread lady (staged 1970). 1971.
The prisoner of Second Avenue (staged 1971). 1972.
The comedy of Neil Simon. 1972.
The sunshine boys. 1973.

SIMPSON, LOUIS ASTON MARATZ

(1923–   )
Jamaican poet; educated at Columbia University; worked for Bobb-Merrill, publishers (1950–5); taught at Columbia University, New York (1955–9); Associate Professor of English, University of Berkeley, California (1959–   ); gives poetry readings in colleges and on the radio in England, Italy, and the U.S.A.; a contributor to the *New Yorker*, *New Statesman*, etc.

Bibliography
C.B.I.
Contemporary poets.
Gale.
L. of C.

Novel
Riverside drive. 1962.

Poetry
The arrivistes. 1949.
Good news of death. 1955.
A dream of governors. 1959.
At the end of the open road (Pulitzer Prize 1964). 1963.
Selected poems. 1965.
Adventures of the letter I. 1971.
North of Jamaica. 1972.

Other Works
James Hogg; a critical study. 1962.
An introduction to poetry. 1968.

SIMPSON, NORMAN FREDERICK

(1919–   )
English playwright; educated at London University; worked in a bank for 2 years; served in the Intelligence Corps during the war (1941–6); taught (1946–62); has written numerous television plays.

Bibliography
Anger and after.
B.N.B.
Contemporary dramatists.
Gale.

Plays
One way pendulum (staged 1959, screenplay 1964). 1960.
The form. 1961.
The hole, and other plays and sketches (includes A resounding tinkle, The form, Oh, gladly otherwise, One blast and Have done). 1964.
The Cresta run (staged 1965). 1966.
A resounding tinkle (staged 1956). 1968.
Some tall tinkles; television plays (We're due in Eastbourne in ten minutes, The best I can do by way of a gate-leg table is a hundred-weight of coal, At least it is a precaution against fire). 1968.
Was he anyone? (staged 1972). 1973.

SIMPSON, RONALD ALBERT

(1929–   )
Australian poet.

Bibliography
Annals of Australian literature.
Australian national bibliography.

Poetry
The walk along the beach. 1960.
This real Pompeii. 1964.

SINCLAIR, ANDREW ANNANDALE

(1935–   )
Scottish novelist and journalist; educated at Eton and at Trinity College, Cambridge; served in the army (1953–5); Fellow of Churchill College, Cambridge (1961–3); Fellow of the American Council of Learned Societies, New York (1964); Lecturer, University College, London (1965–7); film-maker and publisher since 1968; a contributor to *Atlantic Monthly*, *Observer*, *Guardian*, *Spectator*,

New Statesman; his translated work is not listed below.

Bibliography
Authors' and writers' who's who. 1971.
B.N.B.
Contemporary novelists.
Gale.
Who's who. 1973.

Novels
The breaking of Bumbo. 1959.
My friend Judas. 1959.
The project. 1960.
The Hallelujah bum (American title, The paradise bum). 1963.
The raker. 1966.
Gog. 1967.
Magog. 1972.

Screenplay
Under milk wood (from radio play by Dylan Thomas). 1972.

Play
Adventures in the skin trade (adaptation of Dylan Thomas). 1968.

Other Works
Prohibition, the era of excess. 1962.
The available man: the life behind the masks of Warren Gamaliel Harding. 1964.
The better half: the emancipation of the American woman (Somerset Maugham Award 1967). 1964.
A concise history of the United States. 1967.
The Greek anthology. 1967.
The last of the best; the aristocracy of Europe in the 20th century. 1969.
Guevara. 1970.

SINCLAIR, KEITH (1922–)

New Zealand poet and historian; educated at the University of Auckland; served in the New Zealand Naval Reserve (1944–6) during the Second World War; Lecturer, then Associate Professor, then Professor of History at the University of Auckland (1947–); edited J. E. Gorst, *The Maori King* (1959), etc.

Bibliography
B.N.B.
Contemporary poets.

Gale.
New Zealand national bibliography.

Poetry
Songs for a summer and other poems. 1952.
Strangers or beasts. 1954.
A time to embrace. 1963.
The fire wheel tree. 1973.

Other Works
The Maori land league. 1950.
Imperial federation: New Zealand 1880–1914. 1955.
The origins of the Maori wars. 1957.
A history of New Zealand. 1959.
Open account; the bank of New South Wales in New Zealand 1861–1961 (with William F. Mandle). 1961.
Distance looks our way. 1961.
William Ember Reeves, New Zealand Fabian. 1965.
The Liberal government 1891–1912. 1967.

SINCLAIR, LISTER SHEDDON (1921–)

Anglo-Canadian playwright and writer; born in Bombay; educated at St. Paul's School and universities of British Columbia and Toronto; mathematics lecturer at Toronto (1945–8); free-lance actor and writer before becoming a major contributor to the Canadian Broadcasting Corporation; appointed to the staff of the Toronto Conservatory of Music (1952); commissioned to write documentaries for the Ford Foundation (1953); his unpublished plays include *Socrates* (1947), *Encounter by moonlight* (1948) and *The empty frame* (1955); a contributor to many Canadian periodicals.

Bibliography
Canadiana.
C.B.I.

Play
A play on words and other radio plays. 1948.

Other Works
Leon Trotsky: a bibliography. 1972.
Sidelights on Robert Browning's "The ring and the book". 1972.

SINGH, JAGJIT (1912–)

Indian writer; born in Amritsar; educated at Lahore; Fellow of the Royal Statistical Society,

London; Member of the Indian Statistical Institute, Calcutta; received Unesco's Kalinga Prize for Science Popularisation.

Bibliography
C.B.I.
Indian national bibliography 1958–67.
National bibliography of Indian literature 1901–53.

Works
Statistical aids to railway operations. 1965.
Great ideas in information theory, language and cybernetics. 1967.
Modern cosmology. 1970.
Mathematical ideas. 1971.
Operations research. 1971.
Some eminent Indian scientists. n.d.
The story of our railways. n.d.

SINGH, KHUSHWANT (1915–)

Indian novelist and Sikh historian; educated in Delhi, Lahore and King's College, London; called to the Bar, Inner Temple; practised in High Court of Lahore (1939–47); press attaché, London and Ottawa (1947–51); Unesco (1954–6); Visiting Lecturer in Oxford and U.S. universities (1964–9); editor, *Illustrated Weekly of India* (1969–); his translated and edited work is not listed below; a contributor to the *New York Times*, *Observer*, *London Magazine*, etc.

Bibliography
B.N.B.
Contemporary novelists.
Gale.
Indian national bibliography. 1958–67.
National bibliography of Indian literature. 1901–53.
Who's who. 1973.

Novels
The mark of Vishnu and other stories. 1950.
Train to Pakistan (Indian title, Mano majira). 1955.
I shall not hear the nightingale. 1959.
Black jasmine. 1971.
The voice of God and other stories. n.d., reprinted 1971.
A bride for the Sahib and other stories. n.d.

Other Works
The Sikhs. 1952.
A note on G. V. Desani's "All about H. Hatterr", and "Hali" (with Peter Russell). 1952.
Jupji: the Sikh morning prayer. 1959.

The Sikhs today; their religion, history, culture, customs and way of life. 1959.
Fall of the kingdom of the Punjab. 1962.
A history of the Sikhs, 1469–1964. 2 vols. 1963 and 1966.
Ranjit Singh; Maharajah of the Punjab 1780–1839. 1963.
Shri Ram: a biography (with Arun Joshi). 1963.
Ghadar 1919: India's first armed revolution (with Satinda Singh). 1966.
Homage to Guru Gobind Singh (with Suneet Veer Singh). 1966.
Hymns of Nanak the guru. 1969.
Khushwant Singh's India. 1969.

SISSMAN, LOUIS EDWARD (1928–)

American poet; born in Detroit; educated at Harvard University; worked in publishing (1950–2); advertising (1953–); a contributor to *New Yorker*, *Atlantic Monthly*, etc.; editor, *Boston Magazine*.

Bibliography
C.B.I.
Gale.
Who's who in America. 1973–4.

Poetry
Dying: an introduction. 1968.
Scattered returns. 1969.
Pursuit of honor. 1971.

SKELTON, *Professor* ROBIN (1925–)

English poet; educated at Leeds University; Lecturer in English at Manchester, etc.; Associate Professor at Victoria University, British Columbia (1963–); a contributor to the *Critical Quarterly*, *Listener*, *London Magazine*, etc.; his edited work is not listed below.

Bibliography
Authors' and writers' who's who. 1971.
B.N.B.
Contemporary poets.
Gale.
Who's who. 1973.

Poetry
Patmos. 1955.
Third day lucky. 1958.
Two ballads of the muse. 1960.
Begging the dialect; poems and ballads. 1960.
The dark windows. 1962.
A valedictory poem. 1963.

An Irish gathering. 1964.
A ballad of Billy Barker. 1965.
Inscriptions. 1967.
The hold of our hands. 1968.
Because of this. 1968.
Selected poems 1947–67. 1968.
Answers. 1969.
An Irish album. 1969.
The hunting dark. 1971.
Remembering Synge; a poem in homage of the centenary of his birth. 1971.
A different mountain. 1971.
A private speech. 1971.
Three for herself. 1972.
Musebook. 1972.
Country songs. 1973.

Other Works
John Ruskin—the final years. 1955.
The poetic pattern. 1956.
Cavalier poets. 1960.
Poetry. 1963.
Georges Zuk. 1969.
The practice of poetry. 1971.
J. M. Synge and his world. 1971.
J. M. Synge. 1972.

SLAVITT, DAVID RYTMAN (†HENRY SUTTON) (1935–)

American poet and novelist; educated at Yale and Columbia universities; taught English at the Georgia Institute of Technology, Atlanta (1957–8); on the staff of *Newsweek*, New York (1958–65); a contributor to *Kenyon Review*, *New Republic*, etc.; has written a play *The cardinal sins*, and is represented in *The girl in the black raincoat*; has translated Virgil's *Eclogues* and *Georgics* (1971).

Bibliography
C.B.I.
Contemporary novelists.
Gale.

Novels
Rochelle, or virtue rewarded. 1967.
The exhibitionist (as †Henry Sutton). 1967.
Feel free. 1968.
The voyageur (as †Henry Sutton). 1969.
Vector (as †Henry Sutton). 1970.
Anagrams. 1970.

Poetry
Suits for the dead. 1961.
The carnivore. 1965.

Day sailing. 1969.
Child's play. 1972.
ABCD. 1972.

SMITH, BETTY (*Mrs.* JOE JONES) (1896–)

American novelist; educated at Michigan University and Yale Drama School; taught creative writing (1963–5); recipient of several literary awards.

Bibliography
C.B.I.

Novels
A tree grows in Brooklyn (as a musical play, with George Abbott, 1951). 1943.
Tomorrow will be better (English title, Streets of little promise). 1948.
Maggie—now. 1958.
Joy in the morning. 1963.

Plays
The boy Abe. 1944.
Lawyer Lincoln (with Chase Webb). n.d.

SMITH, EMMA (*Mrs.* R. L. STEWART-JONES) (1923–)

English novelist and children's writer.

Bibliography
B.N.B.
Contemporary novelists.
Who's who. 1973.

Novels
Maiden's trip (John Llewelyn Rhys Prize 1949). 1948.
The far cry (James Tait Black Prize 1950). 1949.

For Children
Emily: the story of a traveller. 1959.
Out of hand. 1963.
Emily's voyage. 1966.
No way of telling. 1972.

SMITH, IAIN CRICHTON (†SEAMUS MAC A'GHOBHAINN) (1928–)

Scottish poet and novelist; born in the Isle of Lewis; educated at Aberdeen University; served in the army (1950–2); taught (1952–5); a contributor to the *New Statesman*, *Listener*, *T.L.S.*, *Spectator*; represented in numerous anthologies; his works in Gaelic are not listed below.

Bibliography
B.N.B.
Contemporary novelists.
Contemporary poets.
Gale.

Novels
Consider the lilies (American title, The alien light.
    1969). 1968.
The last summer. 1969.
Survival without error. 1970.
My last duchess. 1971.
The black and the red. 1973.

Poetry
The long river. 1955.
Thistles and roses. 1961.
Deer on the high hills. 1962.
The law and the grace. 1965.
From bourgeois land. 1970.
Selected poems. 1970.
Love poems and elegies. 1972.
Penguin modern poets no. 21 (with G. Mackay
    Brown and N. MacCaig). 1972.

Other Works
The golden lyric (on Hugh MacDiarmid). 1967.
At Helensburgh. 1968.

SMITH, SYDNEY GOODSIR (1915–)
Scottish poet; born in New Zealand; educated at
Edinburgh and Oxford universities; British Council Officer (1945–); now a full-time writer, journalist and broadcaster; recipient of several poetry
prizes; represented in numerous anthologies; a
contributor to periodicals; his edited work is not
listed below.

Bibliography
B.N.B.
Contemporary poets.
N.C.B.E.L.

Poetry
Skail wind. 1941.
The wanderer and other poems. 1943.
The deevilis waltz. 1946.
Selected poems. 1947.
Under the eildon tree. 1948.
So late in the night. 1952.
Cokkils. 1953.
Omens. 1954.
Orpheus and Euridice. 1955.
Figs and thistles. 1959.

The vision of the prodigal son. 1960.
Kynd Kittock's land. 1965.
Fifteen poems and a play. 1969.
Collected poems. 1970.

Verse Play
The wallace. 1960.

Other Works
Carotid cornucopius. 1947.
A short introduction to Scottish literature. 1951.

SMITH, WILLIAM JAY (1918–)
American poet; educated at universities of
Washington, Columbia, Oxford, Florence; served
in the U.S. Navy during the Second World War
(1941–5); after various academic posts, lecturer and
poet-in-residence, Williams College (1959–);
member of various committees; on television programmes of poetry for children; represented in
many anthologies; a contributor to *Harper's*,
Poetry, Nation, Evergreen Review, etc.; his translations from French and Italian are not listed
below; edited Grainger's *Index to poetry*, 6th ed.
(1973).

Bibliography
C.B.I.
Contemporary poets.
Gale.
Who's who in America. 1973–4.

Poetry
Poems. 1947.
Celebration at dark. 1950.
Poems 1947–1957. 1957.
The tin can and other poems. 1966.
New and selected poems. 1970.

Poetry for Children
Laughing time. 1955.
Boy blue's book of beasts. 1957.
Puptents and pebbles. 1959.
Typewriter town. 1960.
What did I see? 1962.
Ho for a hat! 1963.
If I had a boat. 1966.
It rains—it shines. 1967.
Mr Smith and other nonsense. 1968.

Children's Novels
Little Dimity. 1963.
Big Gumbo. 1963.
Big and little. 1963.

Other Works
The spectra hoax. 1961.
Herrick. 1962.
Streaks of the tulip, selected criticism. 1972.

SMITHYMAN, WILLIAM KENDRICK (1922–)

New Zealand poet; born in Auckland; educated at Auckland University College; served in the Royal New Zealand Air Force during the Second World War; married Mary Stanley (q.v.); taught in primary school (1946–63); now Senior Tutor, Department of English, University of Auckland; Visiting Fellow in Commonwealth Literature, University of Leeds (1969); represented in various anthologies.

Bibliography
B.N.B.
Contemporary poets.
N.Z. national bibliography.

Poetry
Seven sonnets. 1946.
The blind mountain. 1951.
The gay trapeze. 1955.
Inheritance. 1962.
Flying to Palmerston. 1968.
Earthquake water. 1973.

Literary Criticism
A way of saying; a study of New Zealand poetry. 1965.

SNODGRASS, WILLIAM DE WITT (†S. S. GARDONS, †WILL McCONNELL, †KOZMA PRUTKOV) (1926–)

American poet; educated at the University of Iowa; served in the U.S. Army (1944–6); currently Professor of English and Speech, Syracuse University, New York (1968–); recipient of many awards; represented in numerous anthologies; a contributor to the *Hudson Review*, *New Yorker*, etc.; joint translator of C. Morgenstern, *Gallow songs* (1967).

Bibliography
C.B.I.
Contemporary poets.
Gale.

Poetry
Heart's needle (Pulitzer Prize 1960). 1959.
After experience . . . 1968.

SNYDER, GARY SHERMAN (1930–)

American poet of the underground; educated at University of California, Berkeley; one of the founders of the *Beat* movement; worked at various jobs and travelled widely; recipient of several travelling and literary awards; a contributor to *Janus*, *Evergreen Review*, *Nation*, *Poetry* and numerous other magazines; represented in numerous anthologies; his edited work and translations from the Japanese are not listed below.

Bibliography
C.B.I.
Contemporary poets.
Gale.

Poetry
Riprap. 1959.
Myths and texts. 1960.
The wooden fish: basic sutras and gaths of Rinzai Zen (with Kanetsuki). 1961.
The firing. 1964.
Nanao knows. 1964.
Across Lamarck Col (with others). 1964.
Hop, skip and jump. 1964.
Dear Mr. President (poster poem). 1965.
Riprap and cold mountain poems. 1965.
A range of poems (includes translations from the Japanese). 1966.
Six sections from mountains and rivers without end. 1967.
The back country. 1967.
Regarding wave. 1970.
Fudo trilogy. 1972.

Other Work
Earth house hold (essays). 1969.

SONTAG, SUSAN (1933–)

American novelist; educated at Chicago, Harvard, Oxford and the Sorbonne; editor with *Commentary* (1959); Lecturer in Philosophy at Columbia University; writer-in-residence, Rutgers University (1964–5); Guggenheim Fellow (1966); a contributor to *Nation*, *Commentary*, *New York Review of Books*, etc.

Bibliography
C.B.I.
Contemporary novelists.
Gale.

Novels
The benefactor. 1963.

Death kit. 1967.
Brother Karl. 1974.

Other Works
Against interpretation, and other essays. 1966.
Trip to Hanoi. 1969.
Styles of radical will (essays). 1969.
Duet for cannibals (screenplay). 1970.

SOUSTER, RAYMOND HOLMES (†RAYMOND HOLMES) (1921–)
Canadian novelist and poet; born in Toronto; educated at Toronto University and Humberside Collegiate Institute; accountant at the Canadian Imperial Bank of Commerce, Toronto (1939–); served in the Canadian Air Force during the Second World War (1941–5); a contributor to the anthology of modern Canadian poets *Unit of five* (1944); joint editor of the Contact Press with Dudek; his edited work is not listed below.

Bibliography
Authors' and writers' who's who. 1971.
Canadiana.
C.B.I.
Contemporary poets.
Gale.

Novel (as †Raymond Holmes)
The winter of time. 1949.

Poetry
When we are young. 1946.
Go to sleep, world. 1947.
City Hall Street. 1951.
Shake hands with the hangman. 1953.
A dream that is dying. 1954.
Walking death. 1955.
For what time slays. 1955.
Selected poems. 1956.
Selected poems 1955–1958. 1958.
Crêpe-hanger's carnival. 1958.
Place of meeting. 1962.
A local pride. 1962.
The colour of the times (Governor General's Award 1965). 1964.
Ten elephants on Yonge Street. 1965.
As is. 1967.
Lost and found. 1969.
So far so good. 1969.
The years. 1972.

SPARK, MURIEL SARAH (*née* CAMBERG)
Scottish novelist of German parentage; born in Edinburgh; educated at the James Gillespie School for Girls, Edinburgh; editor of the *Poetry Review* (1947–9); O.B.E. (1967); a contributor to the *Observer*, etc.; her edited work is not listed below.

Bibliography
Authors' and writers' who's who. 1971.
B.N.B.
Contemporary novelists.
Gale.
Patricia Stubbs. Muriel Spark. 1973.
Who's who. 1973.

Novels and Stories
The comforters. 1957.
Robinson. 1958.
The go-away bird and other stories. 1958.
Memento mori. 1958.
The ballad of Peckham Rye. 1960.
The bachelors. 1960.
Voices at play (radio stories and plays). 1961.
The prime of Miss Jean Brodie (staged 1966, filmed 1969). 1961.
The girls of slender means. 1963.
The Mandelbaum gate (James Tait Black Prize 1966). 1965.
Collected stories I. 1967.
The public image. 1968.
The driver's seat. 1970.
Not to disturb. 1971.
The hothouse by the East River. 1973.

Poetry
The fanfarlo and other verse. 1952.
Collected poems I. 1967.

Plays
The interview (in *Transatlantic Review*). 1960.
Doctors of philosophy (staged 1962). 1963.

Other Works
Child of light; a reassessment of Mary Shelley. 1951.
Emily Brontë; her life and work (with Derek Stanford). 1953.
John Masefield. 1953.
The very fine clock (for children). 1969.

SPEAR, CHARLES (1910–)
New Zealand poet and journalist; Lecturer in English, University of Canterbury, Christchurch;

represented in several anthologies; a contributor to *Landfall*.

Bibliography
B.N.B.
Contemporary poets.
N.Z. national bibliography.

Poetry
Twopence coloured. 1951.

SPEARS, HEATHER (*Mrs.* LEONARD GOLDBERG) (1934–)

Canadian poet and painter; born in Vancouver; educated at University of British Columbia and art schools in Vancouver and London; lives in Denmark; a contributor to *Prism International* and *Fiddlehead*; represented in the *Oxford book of Canadian verse* (1960).

Bibliography
Canadiana.
C.B.I.
Contemporary poets.

Poetry
Asylum poems. 1958.
The Danish portraits. 1967.

SPEIGHT, JOHNNY (1921–)

English playwright; born in the East End of London; served in the army during the Second World War (1939–45); has worked as factory hand and jazz musician; wrote the television script of the *Arthur Haynes Show* from 1956 until the latter's death; his many unpublished stage, television and screen plays are not listed below.

Bibliography
Anger and after.
B.N.B.
Contemporary dramatists.

Plays
If there weren't any blacks you'd have to invent them (televised 1965). 1965.
Till death us do part. 1973.

SPENCE, ELEANOR RACHEL (1928–)

Australian children's writer; born and educated in Sydney; librarian (1951–4).

Bibliography
Annals of Australian literature.
Australian national bibliography.
B.N.B.

For Children
Patterson's track. 1958.
Summer in between. 1959.
Lillipilly Hill. 1960.
The green laurel. 1963.
Australian books of the year. 1964.
The year of the currawong. 1965.
The Switherby pilgrims. 1967.
Jamberoo road. 1968.
Schoolmaster. 1969.
Cedar-cutter. 1971.
The nothing place. 1972.

SPENCER, BERNARD (1909–63)

English poet; born in India; educated at Marlborough and Corpus Christi, Oxford; taught for some years; worked in an advertising agency; joined the British Council (1941); posted to Greece, Egypt, Spain, Italy and Austria; gave travel talks on the B.B.C.; contributor to *New verse*, *Penguin new writing*, etc.; edited, with Lawrence Durrell and Nanos Valoris, translations from modern Greek.

Bibliography
B.N.B.
N.C.B.E.L.

Poetry
Aegean islands. 1946.
The twist in the plotting. 1960.
With luck lasting. 1963.
Collected poems. 1965.

SPENCER, ELIZABETH (*Mrs.* J. RUSHER) (1921–)

American novelist; educated at Vanderbilt University; recipient of various literary awards; a contributor to the *New Yorker*, *Texas Quarterly*, etc.

Bibliography
C.B.I.
Contemporary novelists.
Gale.

Novels
Fire in the morning. 1948.
This crooked way. 1952.

The voice at the back door. 1956.
The light in the piazza. 1960.
Knights and dragons. 1965.
No place for an angel. 1967.
Ship Island and other stories. 1968.
The snare. 1972.

SPILLANE, †MICKY (FRANK MORRISON) (1918–)

American detective novelist; started to study law at Kansas State College; served in the Second World War; wrote for television, comics, etc. (1935–7); became a Jehovah's Witness (1952); founded an independent film company (1969); a selection of his novels is listed below.

Bibliography
B.N.B.
C.B.I.
Gale.

Novels
I, the jury. 1947.
Vengeance is mine! 1950.
My gun is quick. 1950.
The big kill. 1951.
One lonely night. 1951.
The long wait. 1951.
Kiss me, deadly. 1952.
The deep. 1961.
The girl hunters. 1962.
Day of the guns. 1964.
The snake. 1964.
Bloody sunrise. 1965.
The death dealers. 1965.
The twisted thing. 1966.
The by-pass control. 1967.
The delta factor. 1967.
Me, hood. 1969.
"Survival zero!" 1970.
Tough guys. 1970.
Erection set. 1972.
The last copout. 1973.

SPURLING, JOHN (1936–)

English playwright; born in Kenya; educated at the Dragon School, Marlborough College and St. John's College, Oxford; national serviceman (1955–7); radio and book critic, *Spectator* (1966–70); television plays are *Hope* (1970), *Faith* (1971) and *The death of Captain Doughty* (1973); unpublished plays include *Char* (1959), *Peace in our time* (1972).

Bibliography
B.N.B.
Contemporary dramatists.

Plays
MacRune's Guevara. 1969.
In the heart of the British Museum (staged 1971). 1972.

Other Work
Samuel Beckett; a study of his plays (with John Fletcher). 1972.

STACEY, THOMAS CHARLES GERARD (1930–)

English novelist and writer on foreign affairs; educated at Eton; Hulton Press foreign correspondent (1952–4); *Daily Express* foreign correspondent (1959–60); *Sunday Times* (1960–5); travelled in Africa and made an anthropological study of the Bakonjo tribe; a contributor to *The Times*, *Daily Telegraph Magazine*, *New York Times*, etc.; his edited works are not listed below.

Bibliography
Authors' and writers' who's who. 1971.
B.N.B.
Contemporary novelists.
Gale.

Novels
The hostile sun (John Llewelyn Rhys Prize 1954). 1953.
The brothers M. 1960.

Other Works
Summons to Ruwenzori (autobiography). 1963.
Immigration and Enoch Powell. 1970.

STAFFORD, JEAN (*Mrs.* A. J. LIEBLING) (1915–)

American novelist; educated at Colorado and Heidelberg universities; taught; associated with *Southern Review*, Louisiana; awarded several literary prizes; a contributor to the *New Yorker*, *Vogue*, *Harper's Bazaar*, etc.; former wife of Robert Lowell (q.v.); represented in several volumes of short stories.

Bibliography
C.B.I.
Contemporary novelists.
Gale.

Novels and Short Stories
Boston adventure. 1944.
The mountain lion. 1947.
The catherine wheel. 1952.
Children are bored on Sunday (stories). 1953.
Bad characters (stories). 1964.
Collected stories (Pulitzer Prize 1970). 1969.
American coast. 1971.

For Children
Elphi, the cat with the high I.Q. 1962.

Other Work
A mother in history. 1966.

STAFFORD, WILLIAM EDGAR

(1914–)
American poet; born in Kansas; educated at the
universities of Kansas and Iowa; a conscientious
objector during the Second World War; currently
Professor of English Literature, Lewis and Clark
College, Portland, Oregon (1956–); recipient of
various awards; represented in numerous
anthologies; a contributor to *Harper's*, *New Yorker*,
Saturday Review, etc.

Bibliography
C.B.I.
Contemporary poets.

Poetry
West of your city. 1960.
Travelling through the dark. 1962.
Five American poets (with others). 1963.
Five poets of the Pacific Northwest (with others).
  1964.
The rescued year. 1966.
Eleven untitled poems. 1968.
Allegiances. 1970.
Someday, maybe. 1973.

Other Works
Down in my heart. 1947.
Friends to this ground. 1967.

STALLWORTHY, JON HOWIE

(1935–)
English poet; educated at Rugby and Magdalen
College, Oxford; worked at the Oxford Uni-
versity Press (1959–70); Newdigate Prize winner;
a contributor to the *London Magazine*, *Critical
Quarterly*, *Review of English Studies*, *T.L.S.*, etc.;
edited the P.E.N. anthology *New Poems* (1971) and
The Penguin book of love poetry (1973).

Bibliography
Authors' and writers' who's who. 1971.
B.N.B.
Contemporary poets.
Gale.

Poetry
The earthly paradise (pr. ptd.). 1958.
The astronomy of love. 1961.
Out of bounds. 1963.
The almond tree. 1967.
Root and branch. 1969.
Positives. 1969.

Critical Works
Between the lines; Yeats's poetry in the making.
  1963.
Vision and revision in Yeats's last poems. 1969.
Wilfrid Owen (Chatterton lecture). 1970.

STANFORD, DEREK (1918–)

English writer of literary criticism and poetry;
served in the army during the Second World War
(1940–5); lectured in literature and creative writing, City Literary Institute (1955–63); teacher of
art (1955–); a contributor to literary periodicals
in this country and abroad; his edited works are not
listed below.

Bibliography
B.N.B.
Contemporary poets.
Gale.

Poetry
A romantic miscellany (with John Bayliss). 1946.
Music for statues. 1948.

Critical Studies
The freedom of poetry; critical essays. 1948.
Christopher Fry; an appreciation. 1951.
Christopher Fry album. 1952.
Emily Brontë; her life and work (with Muriel
  Spark). 1953.
Dylan Thomas; a literary study. 1954.
Anne Brontë; her life and work (with Ada Har-
  rison). 1959.
Movements in English poetry 1900–1958. 1959.
John Betjeman; a study. 1961.
Muriel Spark; a biographical and critical study.
  1963.
Aubrey Beardsley's erotic universe. 1967.

STANLEY, MARY ISOBEL (*Mrs.* **WILLIAM KENDRICK SMITHYMAN)** (1919–)
New Zealand poet; born in Christchurch; educated at the University of Auckland; wife of William Kendrick Smithyman (q.v.); teaches; represented in several anthologies.

Bibliography
B.N.B.
Contemporary poets.
N.Z. national bibliography.

Poetry
Starveling year. 1953.

STARBUCK, GEORGE EDWIN (*né* **BEISWANGER)** (1931–)
American poet; educated at universities of California, Chicago and Harvard; served in the U.S. Army (1952–4); worked for Houghton Mifflin, publishers (1958–61); Fellow, American Academy, Rome (1961–3); librarian and lecturer, State University of New York, Buffalo (1963–4); Writers' Workshop, Iowa City (1964–); has contributed poems to *New Yorker, Harper's, Atlantic, New Republic,* etc.; recipient of several literary awards.

Bibliography
C.B.I.
Contemporary poets.
Gale.

Poetry
Bone thoughts. 1960.
White paper. 1966.

STEAD, CHRISTIAN KARLSON (1932–)
New Zealand poet and scholar; born in Auckland; educated at Auckland and Bristol universities; Professor of English, Auckland University (1969–); recipient of literary awards; represented in numerous anthologies; a contributor to *New Statesman,* etc.

Bibliography
Contemporary poets.
N.Z. national bibliography.

Novel
Smith's dream. 1971.

Poetry
Whether the will is free: poems 1954–62. 1964.
Crossing the bar. 1972.

Literary Criticism
The new poetic: Yeats to Eliot. 1964.

STEINER, *Professor* **GEORGE** (1929–)
English scholar and critic; educated in Paris, and at universities of Chicago, Harvard and Oxford; staff of *The Economist* (1952–6); Fellow, later Extraordinary Fellow, Churchill College, Cambridge (1961–); Fulbright Professor (1958–69); his edited work is not listed below.

Bibliography
B.N.B.
Who's who. 1973.

Works
Tolstoy or Dostoievsky. 1958.
The death of tragedy. 1960.
Anno domini (stories). 1964.
Language and silence. 1967.
Extraterritorial, essays on language. 1971.
In Bluebeard's castle (T. S. Eliot memorial lecture). 1971.

STEINER, GEORGE ALBERT (1912–)
American critic and historian; educated at the universities of Pennsylvania and Illinois; served in the Second World War (1943–6); Indiana University instructor, etc. (1937–9); currently Professor of Management Theory and director of Division of Research (1956–); consultant to various government agencies; recipient of several academic honours; managing editor of *California Management Review* (1957–62); his edited work is not listed below.

Bibliography
C.B.I.
Gale.

Works
Wartime industrial statistics (with David Novick). 1950.
Government's role in economic life. 1953.
National defence and Southern California. 1961.
Industrial project managing (with W. G. Ryan). 1968.
Top management planning. 1969.
Strategic factors in business success. 1969.
Business and society. 1970.

STERN, DANIEL (1928–)

American novelist and cellist; served in the U.S. Army (1946–7); played in the Indianapolis Symphony Orchestra (1948–9); freelance writer (1955–8); copywriter since then.

Bibliography
C.B.I.
Contemporary novelists.
Gale.

Novels
The girl with the glass heart. 1953.
The guests of fame. 1955.
Miss America. 1959.
Who shall live, who shall die. 1963.
Rose rabbi. 1971.

STEWART, DESMOND STIRLING (1924–)

English novelist and scholar; educated at Haileybury and Trinity College, Cambridge; Assistant Professor of English, Baghdad University (1948–56); Inspector of English in Beirut Islamic Schools (1956–8); lives in Cyprus; a contributor to the *Spectator*, *Encounter*, *Poetry*, etc.; one-time Middle East correspondent for the *Spectator*; his translated work is not listed below.

Bibliography
Authors' and writers' who's who. 1971.
B.N.B.
Gale.
Who's who. 1973.

Novels
Leopard in the grass. 1951.
Memoirs of Alcibiades. 1952.
The unsuitable Englishman. 1955.
A woman besieged. 1959.
The men of Friday. 1961.
The sequence of roles (a trilogy, The round mosaic, 1965; The pyramid inch, 1966; The Mamelukes, 1968).

Poetry
The besieged city. 1945.

Other Works
New Babylon, a portrait of Iraq (with J. Haylock). 1956.
Emma in blue (with G. Hamilton). 1957.
Young Egypt. 1958.
Turmoil in Beirut: a personal account. 1958.

The Arab world (with the editors of *Life*). 1962.
Turkey (with the editors of *Life*). 1965.
Cairo. 1965.
Early Islam (with the editors of *Life*). 1967.
Orphan with a hoop: Emil Bustani. 1967.
Great Cairo, mother of the world. 1968.
The Middle East: temple of Janus. 1971.
Pyramids and sphinx. 1972.
Ilbarana. 1972.

STEWART, HAROLD FREDERICK (1916–)

Australian poet; educated at Sydney Conservatorium of Music and Sydney University; represented in several anthologies of Australian poetry; a contributor to *Meanjin*, *Quadrant*, etc.; his translations from the Japanese are not listed below.

Bibliography
Australian national bibliography.
C.B.I.
Contemporary poets.

Poetry
Darkening ecliptic (with E. Malley). 1944.
Phoenix wings. 1948.
Orpheus and other poems. 1956.

STEWART, Lady MARY FLORENCE ELINOR (née RAINBOW) (1916–)

English novelist; born in Sunderland; educated at Durham University; served in the Second World War; taught at the Abbey School, Malvern (1940–1); Lecturer at Durham University (1941–55); full-time writer (since 1955); recipient of the British Crime Writers' Award (1960); has written radio plays and poetry.

Bibliography
Authors' and writers' who's who. 1971.
B.N.B.
Gale.
Who's who. 1973.

Novels
Madam, will you talk? 1954.
Wildfire at midnight. 1956.
Thunder on the right. 1957.
Nine coaches waiting. 1958.
My brother Michael. 1959.
The ivy tree. 1961.
The moonspinners (filmed 1964). 1962.
This rough magic. 1964.
Airs above the ground. 1965.

The Gabriel hounds. 1967.
The wind off the small isles. 1968.
The crystal cave. 1970.
The hollow hills. 1973.

For Children
The little broomstick. 1971.

STIRLING, MONICA

English novelist and biographer; lives in Paris.

Bibliography
B.N.B.

Novels and Short Stories
Lovers aren't company. 1949.
Dress rehearsal. 1951.
Adventurers please abstain (stories). 1952.
Ladies with a unicorn. 1953.
The boy in blue. 1955.
Some darling folly. 1956.
Journeys we shall never make (stories). 1957.
Sigh for a strange land. 1958.
Sniper in the heart. 1960.
The summer of a dormouse. 1967.

For Children
The little ballet dancer. 1952.

Biography
The fine and the wicked: the life and times of Ouida. 1957.
A pride of lions: a portrait of Napoleon's mother (American title, Madame Letizia). 1961.
The wild swan: the life and times of Hans Christian Andersen. 1965.

STOPPARD, TOM (1937–)

English playwright and novelist; born in Czechoslovakia; educated abroad; worked as a journalist on the *Western Daily Press*, Bristol (1954–8), Bristol *Evening World* (1958–60), and freelance (1960–3); has written numerous scripts for radio and television; his unpublished plays are not listed below.

Bibliography
B.M. catalogue.
C.B.I.
Contemporary dramatists.
Who's who. 1973.

Novels
Introduction (2 stories). 1964.
Lord Malquist and Mr. Moon. 1966.

Plays
Rosencrantz and Guildenstern are dead (staged 1967). 1967.
The real Inspector Hound (staged 1968). 1968.
Albert's bridge (radio production 1967) (also contains, If you're Glad I'll be Frank. 1964). 1968.
A walk on the water (televised 1963, revised as The preservation of George Riley, 1964; produced as Enter a free man, 1968). 1972.
After Magritte (staged 1970). 1972.
Jumpers (staged 1972). 1972.
Artists descending a staircase, and Where are they now? (staged 1970). 1973.

STOREY, DAVID MALCOLM (1933–)

English playwright and novelist; born in Yorkshire; educated at Queen Elizabeth Grammar School, Wakefield, and the Slade School of Art; worked as a bus conductor and teacher; professional Rugby League player (1952–6); recipient of several awards.

Bibliography
B.N.B.
Contemporary dramatists.
John Russell Taylor. David Storey. 1974.
Who's who. 1973.

Novels
This sporting life. 1960.
Flight into Camden (John Llewelyn Rhys Prize 1961; Somerset Maugham Award 1963). 1960.
Radcliffe. 1963.
Pasmore. 1972.
A temporary life. 1973.
Edward. 1973.

Plays
The restoration of Arnold Middleton. 1967.
In celebration. 1969.
The contractor. 1969.
Home. 1970.
The changing room. 1972.
The farm. 1973.
Cromwell. 1973.

STORY, JACK TREVOR (1917–)

English novelist; writes for film, radio, television, magazines, etc.

Bibliography
B.N.B.

Novels
The trouble with Harry (filmed 1955). 1949.
Protection for a lady. 1950.
Green to Pagan Street. 1952.
The money goes round and round. 1958.
Mix me a person (filmed 1962). 1959.
Man pinches bottom. 1962.
Live now, pay later (filmed 1962). 1963.
Something for nothing. 1963.
The urban district lover. 1964.
Company of bandits. 1965.
I sit in Hanger Lane. 1968.
Dishonourable member. 1969.
The blonde and the boodle. 1970.
The season of the skylark. 1970.
One last mad embrace. 1970.
Hitler needs you. 1971.
Little dog's day. 1971.
The wind in the snottygobble tree. 1972.
Letters to an intimate stranger. 1972.

STOW, JULIAN RANDOLPH (1935–)

Australian novelist; educated at the University of Western Australia; worked on mission for aborigines of Western Australia; assistant of government anthropologist, New Guinea; taught English intermittently at the universities of Adelaide, Western Australia, and Leeds; editor of *Australian Poetry* (1964); recipient of various awards.

Bibliography
B.N.B.
Contemporary novelists.
Gale.
Randolph Stow; a bibliography. Adelaide, Libraries Board of South Australia. 1968.
Who's who. 1973.

Novels
A haunted land. 1956.
The bystander. 1957.
To the islands. 1957.
Tourmaline. 1963.
The merry-go-round in the sea. 1965.

Poetry
Act one. 1957.
Outrider; poems 1956–1962. 1962.
A counterfeit silence: selected poems. 1969.

For Children
Midnite: the story of a wild colonial boy. 1967.

STRAND, MARK (1934–)

American poet; educated at Yale and Iowa State universities; after several university posts, Visiting Professor, University of Washington (1968–); recipient of several study awards; wrote film script of *I knew a girl*; editor of New American Library's *The contemporary poets* (1968); represented in anthologies; a contributor to the *New Yorker* and *New York Review of Books*.

Bibliography
C.B.I.
Gale.

Poetry
Sleeping with one eye open. 1964.
Reasons for moving. 1968.
Darker. 1970.
The Sargentville notebook. 1973.
The story of our lives. 1973.

STUART, DABNEY (1937–)

American poet; educated at Harvard; instructor in English, William and Mary College (1961–5); Instructor, later Assistant Professor of English, Washington and Lee University (1966–); recipient of Dylan Thomas Poetry Award; a contributor to the *New Yorker*, *Antioch Review*, etc.

Bibliography
C.B.I.
Contemporary poets.
Gale.
L. of C.

Poetry
The diving bells. 1966.
A particular place. 1969.

STYRON, WILLIAM (1925–)

American novelist; educated at Duke University; served in the U.S. Navy during the Second World War; recipient of various awards; a contributor to *Esquire*, *Harper's Bazaar*, etc.

Bibliography
C.B.I.
Contemporary novelists.
Gale.
Who's who in America. 1973–4.

Novels
Lie down in darkness. 1951.

The long march. 1956.
Set this house on fire. 1960.
The confessions of Nat Turner (Pulitzer Prize 1968). 1967.

Play
In the clap shack. 1972.

SUKENICK, RONALD (1932–)
American novelist and critic; educated at Cornell and Brandeis universities; currently writer-in-residence, University of California, Irvine (1970–).

Bibliography
C.B.I.
Gale.

Novels
Up. 1968.
The death of the novel, and other stories. 1969.
Out: a novel. 1973.

Other Work
Wallace Stevens: musing the obscure. 1967.

SULLY, KATHLEEN (1910–)
English novelist; educated at Taunton and St. Albans Art Colleges; has taught art and English, and done a variety of jobs from professional swimming to fashion modelling before becoming a full-time novelist; plays include *The waiting of Lester* (produced 1957).

Bibliography
B.N.B.
Gale.

Novels
Canal in moonlight (American title, Bikka Road). 1955.
Canaille. 1956.
Through the wall. 1957.
Merrily to the grave. 1958.
Burden of the seed. 1958.
A man talking to seagull. 1959.
Shade of Eden. 1960.
Skrine. 1960.
The undesired. 1961.
A man on the roof. 1961.
The fractured smile. 1965.
Not tonight. 1966.
Dear wolf. 1967.
Horizontal image. 1968.

A breeze on a lonely road. 1969.
A look at the tadpoles. 1970.

For Children
Small creatures. 1946.
Stoney Stream. 1946.

SUMMERS, HOLLIS SPURGEON, Jr. (†JIM HOLLIS) (1916–)
American novelist and poet; educated at State University of Iowa, etc.; taught English (1937–44); Professor of English, Georgetown College (1944–9); University of Kentucky (1949–59), Ohio University, Athens (1959–); recipient of literary and academic awards.

Bibliography
C.B.I.
Contemporary novelists.
Contemporary poets.
Gale.
L. of C.

Novels
City limit. 1948.
Brighten the corner. 1952.
Teach you a lesson (as †Jim Hollis, with James Rourke). 1955.
The weather of February. 1957.
The day after Sunday. 1968.
The garden. 1972.
Start from home. 1972.

Poetry
The walks near Athens. 1959.
Someone else (for children). 1962.
Seven occasions. 1965.
The peddler, and other domestic matters. 1967.
Sit opposite each other. 1970.

Other Works
Literature: an introduction (with Edgar Whar). 1960.
Note to myself (one act play). n.d.

SUTCH, WILLIAM BALL (1907–)
New Zealand economist and writer; born in England; educated in New Zealand and at Columbia University; advisory economist to the Ministry of Finance (1933–40); served in the Second World War; delegate to commonwealth and international conferences; chairman of various United Nations' bodies of economic and cultural organisations; his edited work is not listed below.

Bibliography
C.B.I.
N.Z. national bibliography.
Who's who in New Zealand. 1968.

Works
Price fixing in New Zealand. 1940.
Recent economic changes in New Zealand. 1940.
Poverty and progress in New Zealand. 1940.
The quest for security in New Zealand. 1941.
Local government in New Zealand. 1956.
The long depression 1865–95. 1957.
The importance of the arts today. 1958.
Education for industry. 1959.
Programme for growth. 1960.
Selling New Zealand exports. 1962.
The human factor. 1962.
Colony or nation? Economic crises in New Zealand from the 1860s to the 1960s. 1966.
Equal pay for New Zealand. 1971.
The industrial development of Palmerston North. 1971.
The responsible society in New Zealand. 1971.
Takeover New Zealand. 1972.
Women with a cause. 1973.

SUTCLIFF, ROSEMARY (1920–   )
English historical novelist.

Bibliography
Authors' and writers' who's who. 1971.
B.N.B.
Gale.
Who's who. 1973.

Historical Novels for Children and Adults
The chronicles of Robin Hood. 1950.
The Queen Elizabeth story. 1950.
The armourer's house. 1951.
Brother Dusty-feet. 1952.
Simon. 1953.
The eagle of the Ninth. 1954.
Outcast. 1955.
Lady in waiting. 1956.
The shield ring. 1956.
The silver branch. 1957.
Warrior scarlet. 1958.
Rider of the white horse. 1959.
The lantern bearers. 1959.
The bridge builders. 1960.
Knight's fee. 1960.
Beowulf: Dragonslayer. 1961.
Dawn wind. 1961.
Sword at sunset. 1963.

The hound of Ulster. 1963.
The mark of the horse lord. 1965.
The chief's daughter. 1967.
The high deeds of Finn McCool. 1967.
A circlet of oak leaves. 1968.
The flowers of Adonis. 1969.
The witch's brat. 1970.
Tristan and Iseult. 1971.
The Capricorn bracelet. 1973.

Non-fiction
Houses and history. 1960.
Rudyard Kipling. 1960.
Heroes and history. 1965.
A Saxon settler. 1966.

SUTHERLAND, EFUA THEODORA (*Mrs.* WILLIAM SUTHERLAND)
(1924–   )
Ghanaian playwright; educated at Saint Monica's School, Ghana, Homerton College, Cambridge, and the School of Oriental and African Studies, London; with her American husband, helped found a school in the Transvolta; founded a Ghana experimental theatre (1958–61) and the Ghana Drama Studio, Accra; Research Scholar in the Institute of African Studies, Ghana University (1963–   ).

Bibliography
B.N.B.
C.B.I.
Contemporary dramatists.
Jahn and Dressler.
Zell and Silver.

Plays
Foriwa. 1967.
Vulture! Vulture! and Tahinta; two rhythm plays. 1968.
Edufa. 1969.

Other Works
The roadmakers. 1961.
Playtime in Africa (for children). 1962.

SUTTON, DENYS (1917–   )
English art critic; educated at Uppingham School and Exeter College, Oxford; Foreign Office Research Dept. (1940–6); salesroom correspondent to the *Daily Telegraph*; art critic to *Country Life*; currently art critic to the *Financial Times*; editor of *Apollo* (1962–   ); a contributor to

art journals and magazines; his introductions are not listed below.

Bibliography
B.N.B.
Who's who. 1973.

Works
Watteau's Les charmes de la vie. 1946.
Matisse. 1946.
Picasso, blue and pink period. 1948.
American painting. 1948.
French drawings of the eighteenth century. 1949.
Flemish painting. 1950.
Artists in 17th century Rome (with Denis Mahon). 1955.
Bonnard. 1957.
Christie's since the war. 1959.
André Derain. 1959.
Nicholas de Staël. 1960.
Catalogue of French, Spanish and German schools in the Fitzwilliam Museum, Cambridge (with J. W. Goodison). 1960.
Gaspard Dughet. 1962.
Toulouse-Lautrec. 1962.
Titian. 1963.
Nocturne; the art of Whistler. 1964.
Painting in Florence and Siena (with St. John Gore). 1965.
Sergio de Castro. 1965.
Triumphant satyr. 1966.
Whistler; paintings, drawings, etchings and water-colours. 1966.
Diego Velasquez. 1967.
An Italian sketchbook by Richard Wilson, R.A. 1968.
Letters of Roger Fry. 1972.

SWADOS, HARVEY (1920–)

American novelist; educated at Michigan University; served in the U.S. Marines during the Second World War (1942–5); member of literature faculty, Sarah Lawrence College, Bronxville (1958–); recipient of various literary awards; edited several anthologies of stories; a contributor to *Nation*, *Saturday Evening Post*, *Esquire*, etc.; edited *Years of conscience: the muckrakers* (1962).

Bibliography
C.B.I.
Contemporary novelists.
Gale.

Novels and Short Stories
Out went the candle. 1955.
On the line (stories). 1957.
False coin. 1959.
Nights in the garden of Brooklyn. 1961.
The will. 1963.
A story for Teddy—and others. 1966.
Standing fast. 1970.
The mystery of the Spanish silvermine. 1971.

Essays
A radical's America. 1962.
A radical at large. 1968.
Standing up for the people; the life and work of Estes Kefauver. 1972.

SWANBERG, WILLIAM ANDREW
(1907–)
American biographer; educated at universities of Minnesota and New York; Dell Publishing Co. (1935–44); U.S. Office of War Information; full-time writer (1945–); a contributor to *Life*, *New Yorker* and many other magazines.

Bibliography
C.B.I.
Gale.

Works
Sickles the incredible. 1956.
First blood. 1957.
Jim Fisk. 1959.
Citizen Hearst. 1961.
Dreiser. 1965.
Pulitzer. 1972.
Luce and his empire. 1972.

SWARTHOUT, GLENDON FRED
(1918–)
American novelist and short-story writer; educated at the University of Michigan; served in the U.S. Army during the Second World War (1943–5); after holding various university posts (1946–63) became a full-time writer (1963); recipient of several literary awards; a contributor to *Collier's*, *Esquire*, *Saturday Evening Post*, etc.

Bibliography
C.B.I.
Contemporary novelists.
Gale.

Novels
Willow run. 1943.
They came to Cordura. 1958.
Where the boys are. 1960.
Welcome to Thebes. 1962.
The Cadillac cowboys. 1964.
The eagle and the iron cross. 1966.
Loveland. 1968.
Bless the beasts and children. 1970.
The tin Lizzie troop. 1972.

For Children (with Kathryn Swarthout)
The ghost and the magic saber. 1963.
Whichaway. 1966.
The button boat. 1969.
T. V. Thompson. 1972.

SWENSON, MAY (1919–)

American poet; educated at Utah State University; editor of *New Directions*; recipient of various literary awards and grants; represented in numerous anthologies in Europe and America; translated into Italian and German; a contributor to *Poetry*, *Nation*, *Saturday Review*, etc.

Bibliography
C.B.I.
Contemporary poets.
Gale.
L. of C.

Poetry
Another animal. 1954.
A cage of spines. 1958.
To mix with time, new and selected poems. 1963.
Poems to solve. 1966.
Half sun, half sleep. 1967.
Iconographs. 1970.
More poems to solve. 1970.

SYMONS, JULIAN GUSTAVE (1912–)

English novelist; younger brother of A. J. A. Symons; *Sunday Times* reviewer 1958–); chairman of the Crime Writers' Association (1958–9); edited his brother's works (1969); the author of several television plays; his edited work is not listed below.

Bibliography
Authors' and writers' who's who. 1971.
B.N.B.
Contemporary novelists.
Who's who. 1973.

Novels
Confusions about X. 1938.
The second man. 1944.
The immaterial murder case. 1945.
A man called Jones. 1947.
Bland beginning. 1949.
The thirty-first of February. 1950.
The broken penny. 1952.
The narrowing circle. 1954.
The paper chase. 1956.
The colour of murder (C.W.A. Critics' Award). 1957.
The gigantic shadow. 1958.
The progress of a crime (M.W.A. Edgar Allan Poe Award). 1960.
A reasonable doubt. 1960.
Murder! Murder! 1961.
The killing of Francis Lake. 1962.
The end of Solomon Grundy. 1964.
The Belting inheritance. 1965.
Francis Quarles investigates. 1965.
The man who killed himself. 1967.
The man whose dreams came true. 1968.
The man who lost his wife. 1970.
The players and the game. 1972.

Criticism and Biography
A. J. A. Symons. 1950.
Charles Dickens. 1951.
Thomas Carlyle. 1952.
Horatio Bottomley. 1955.
The General Strike. 1957.
The thirties. 1960.
The detective story in Britain. 1962.
Buller's campaign. 1963.
England's pride. 1965.
Critical occasions. 1966.
Crime and detection; an illustrated history from 1840. 1966.
Bloody murder: from the detective story to the crime novel, a history. 1972.
Notes from another country. 1972.

T

TARGET, GEORGE WILLIAM (1924–)
English novelist; served in the army during the
Second World War; worked in various jobs for
some years; production assistant for 4 years for
Cassell's, publishers; Visiting Instructor in Creative Writing at Colorado State University
(1964–); author of radio and television plays; a
contributor to various periodicals including *British
Weekly*.

Bibliography
C.B.I.
Gale.

Novels
The evangelists. 1958.
The teachers. 1960.
The missionaries. 1961.
Watch with me. 1961.
The shop stewards. 1962.
We, the crucifiers. 1964.
The Americans. 1964.
The scientists. 1966.
Under the Christian carpet. 1969.
Young lovers. 1970.

Other Works
Evangelism inc. 1968.
Confound their politicks. 1970.

TARN, NATHANIEL (1928)
English poet; born in Paris; educated at Clifton
College and the universities of Cambridge, the
Sorbonne and Chicago; an anthropologist
(1950–67); director of Cape–Goliard, publishers
(1967–9); Professor of English and Comparative
Literatures, universities of Buffalo, Princeton and
Rutgers (1969–70); translated the work of Pablo
Neruda, V. Segalen, etc.

Bibliography
Authors' and writers' who's who. 1971.
B.N.B.
Gale.

Poetry
Old savage/young city. 1964.
Penguin modern poets no. 7 (with R. Murphy and
J. Silkin). 1965.
Where Babylon ends. 1968.

The beautiful contradictions. 1969.
October (pr. ptd.). 1969.
A nowhere for Vallejo. 1971.
Choices (with October and A nowhere for
Vallejo). 1972.

TATE, JAMES VINCENT (1943–)
American poet; born in Kansas City; educated at
Kansas State College and University of Iowa;
Instructor in English, Iowa University (1966–7)
and University of California, Berkeley (1967–8);
poetry editor, *The Dickinson Review* (1967–); a
contributor to *New Yorker, Atlantic, Nation, Poetry*,
etc.; represented in numerous anthologies.

Bibliography
C.B.I.
Contemporary poets.
Gale.

Poetry
Cages. 1967.
The destination. 1967.
The lost pilot. 1967.
The notes of woe. 1967.
The torches. 1968.
Mystics in Chicago. 1968.
Camping in the valley. 1968.
Row with your hair. 1969.
Is there anything? 1969.
Shepherds of the mist. 1969.
The oblivion ha-ha. 1970.
Amnesia people. 1970.
Deaf girl playing. 1970.
Hints to pilgrims. 1971.
Absences. 1972.

TAYLOR, ELIZABETH (*née* **COLES**)
(1912–75)
English novelist; educated at the Abbey School,
Reading; a contributor to the *Cornhill, New Yorker*,
etc.

Bibliography
Authors' and writers' who's who. 1971.
B.N.B.
Gale.
Who's who. 1973.

Novels and Short Stories
At Mrs. Lippincote's. 1945.
Palladian. 1946.
A view of the harbour. 1949.
A wreath of roses. 1949.
A game of hide and seek. 1951.
The sleeping beauty. 1953.
Hester Lilly (stories). 1954.
Angel. 1957.
The blush (stories). 1958.
In a summer season. 1961.
The soul of kindness. 1964.
A dedicated man (stories). 1965.
Mossy Trotter (for children). 1967.
The wedding group. 1968.
The excursion to the source. 1970.
Mrs. Palfrey at the Claremont. 1971.
The devastating boys (short stories). 1972.

TAYLOR, JOHN RUSSELL (1935–)

English drama critic; educated at Jesus College, Cambridge; editorial assistant, *T.L.S.* (1960–2); film critic of *The Times* (1962–73); a contributor to the *Penrose Annual, Listener, London Magazine*, etc.

Bibliography
Authors' and writers' who's who. 1971.
B.N.B.
Gale.
Who's who. 1973.

Works
Joseph L. Mankiewicz. 1960.
Anger and after. 1962.
Anatomy of a television play. 1962.
Cinema eye, cinema ear. 1964.
Penguin dictionary of the theatre. 1966.
The art nouveau book in Britain. 1966.
The rise and fall of the well-made play. 1967.
Look back in anger; a casebook. 1968.
The art dealers (with Brian Brooke). 1969.
Harold Pinter. 1969.
The Hollywood musical. 1970.
The second wave: British drama in the seventies. 1971.

TAYLOR, PETER HILLSMAN (1917–)

American novelist; educated at Vanderbilt University, Southwestern College, Memphis, and Kenyon College, Ohio; served in the U.S. Army during the Second World War (1941–5); taught at various universities; Professor of English, University of Virginia, Charlottesville (1967–); recipient of various awards and fellowships.

Bibliography
C.B.I.
Contemporary novelists.
Gale.

Novels
A long fourth and other stories. 1948.
A woman of means. 1950.
The widows of Thornton (stories and a play). 1954.
Happy families are all alike (stories). 1959.
Miss Leonora when last seen (stories). 1963.
Collected stories. 1969.

Plays
Tennessee day in St. Louis. 1957.
A stand in the mountains. 1968.
Presences: seven dramatic pieces. 1973.

†TERSON, PETER (PETER PATTERSON) (1932–)

English playwright; educated at Newcastle and Bristol Training Colleges; served in the R.A.F. (1950–2); taught P.E. for 10 years; associated with The National Youth Theatre, etc.; recipient of several awards; unpublished plays include *I'm in charge of these ruins* (1966), *The ballad of the artificial mash* (1967), *Good lads at heart* (1971); television plays include *The last train through the Harecastle tunnel* (1969) and *Shakespeare—or bust* (1973).

Bibliography
B.N.B.
Contemporary dramatists.

Plays
A night to make the angels weep (staged 1964 and 1971, in New English dramatists 11). 1967.
The mighty reservoy (staged 1964 and 1967, in New English dramatists 14). 1970.
The apprentices (staged 1968). 1970.
The adventures of Gervase Beckett, or The man who changed places (staged 1969). 1970.
Zigger Zagger (staged 1967), and Mooney and his caravans (televised 1966, staged 1968). 1970.
Spring-heeled Jack (in Plays and players). 1970.
The samaritan (with Mike Butler, staged 1971, in Plays and players). 1971.
But Fred, Freud is dead (staged 1972, in Plays and players). 1972.

THAPAR, *Dr.* **ROMILA** (1931–)
Indian historian; born in Lucknow; educated at the
School of Oriental and African Studies; Reader in
History, Delhi University (1962); currently with
the Jawahar Lal University, Delhi.

Bibliography
C.B.I.
Indian national bibliography 1958–67.
National bibliography of Indian literature
   1901–53.

Works
Indian tales. 1961.
Ashoka and the decline of the Mauryas. n.d.
History of India. n.d.
Ancient India. n.d.
Medieval India. n.d.

THELWELL, NORMAN (1923–)
English humorous artist and writer; educated at
Liverpool College of Art; served in the army in the
Second World War (1942–7); teacher of illustration
and design at the Wolverhampton College of Art
(1950–7); a contributor to the *Sunday Express*,
Punch, etc.

Bibliography
B.N.B.
Gale.
Who's who. 1973.

Works Written and Illustrated by Thelwell
Angels on horseback and elsewhere. 1957.
Thelwell country. 1959.
A place of your own. 1960.
Thelwell in orbit. 1961.
A leg at each corner. 1962.
The Penguin Thelwell. 1963.
Top dog: Thelwell's complete canine com-
   pendium. 1964.
Thelwell's riding academy. 1965.
Ponies. 1966.
Compleat tangler. 1967.
Up the garden path. 1967.
Thelwell's book of leisure. 1968.
This desirable plot. 1970.
The effluent society. 1971.
Penelope. 1972.

THIELE, COLIN MILTON (1920–)
Australian poet and novelist; educated at the Uni-
versity of Adelaide; served in the Australian Air
Force during the Second World War (1942–5);

schoolmaster (1946–56); lecturer, etc., in English
(1957–65); Principal, Wattle Park Teachers' College (1965–); recipient of several literary awards
and fellowships; a contributor to many periodicals
and the radio; represented in many anthologies; his
edited works and unpublished radio dramas are not
listed below.

Bibliography
Australian national bibliography.
Gale.

Novels
The sun on the stubble. 1961.
Labourers in the vineyard. 1970.

Poetry
Progress to denial. 1945.
Splinters and shards. 1945.
The golden lightning. 1951.
Man in a landscape. 1960.
In charcoal and conte. 1966.
Selected verse 1940–1970. 1970.

For Children
The state of our state. 1952.
Gloop the gloomy Bunyip. 1962.
Storm boy. 1963.
February dragon. 1965.
The rim of the morning (stories). 1966.
Mrs. Munch and Puffing Billy. 1967.
Yellow-jacket Jock. 1969.
Blue fin. 1969.
Flash flood. 1970.
Flip flop and Tiger snake. 1970.

Other Works
Heyren of Hahnsdorf (biography). 1968.
Barossa Valley sketch-book. 1968.

THOMAS, AUDREY CALLAHAN
(*Mrs.* **THOMAS)** (1935–)
American-born Canadian poet; educated at the
University of British Columbia; lived in Ghana
(1964–6); a contributor to *Atlantic Monthly*.

Bibliography
Canadiana.
C.B.I.
Gale.

Short Story
Ten green bottles. 1967.

THOMAS, DONALD MICHAEL
(1935–)
Welsh poet; born in Cornwall; educated at New College, Oxford; Senior Lecturer at Hertford College of Education (1963–); a contributor to *Encounter*, the *London Magazine*, *New York Times*, etc.; represented in numerous anthologies.

Bibliography
Authors' and writers' who's who. 1971.
B.N.B.
Contemporary poets.

Poetry
Penguin modern poets no. 11 (with D. M. Black and P. Redgrove). 1968.
Two voices. 1968.
Logan stone. 1971.

THOMAS, GWYN (1913–)
Welsh novelist and playwright; educated at St. Edmund Hall, Oxford and Madrid University; university extension lecturer (1934–40); schoolmaster (1940–62); television broadcaster (1962–).

Bibliography
B.N.B.
Contemporary novelists.
Who's who. 1973.

Novels
The dark philosophers. 1946.
Where did I put my pity? 1946.
The alone to the alone (American title, Venus and the voters). 1947.
All things betray thee (American title, Leaves in the wind). 1949.
The world cannot hear you. 1951.
Now lead us home. 1952.
A frost on my frolic. 1953.
The stranger at my side. 1954.
Point of order. 1956.
Gazooka (stories). 1957.
The love man. 1958.
Ring delirium 123 (stories). 1959.
A hatful of humours. 1965.
Leaves in the wind. 1968.
The lust lobby (stories). 1971.

Plays
The keep. 1961.
Loud organs. 1962.
Jackie the jumper. 1962.

Autobiography
A few selected exits. 1968.

Humour
A Welsh eye. 1964.

THOMAS, *Professor* HUGH SWYNNERTON (1931–)
Welsh historian; educated at Sherborne and Queen's College, Cambridge; Foreign Office (1954–7); Secretary to the U.K. delegation to the U.N. Disarmament Sub-committee (1955–6); Professor of History, University of Reading (1966–); edited *The Establishment* (1959) and *Crisis in the Civil Service* (1968); a contributor to the *New Statesman*.

Bibliography
Authors' and writers' who's who. 1971.
B.N.B.
Gale.
Who's who. 1973.

Novels
The world's game. 1957.
The oxygen age. 1958.

Other Works
Disarmament: the way ahead. 1957.
The Spanish civil war (Somerset Maugham Award 1962). 1961.
The story of Sandhurst. 1961.
The Suez affair. 1967.
Cuba, or the pursuit of freedom. 1971.
Goya's "Third of May", 1808. 1972.
History of Wales, 1485–1600. 1972.
Europe: the radical challenge. 1973.
John Strachey. 1973.

THOMAS, RONALD STUART (1913–)
Welsh poet; educated at University of Wales and St. Michael's College, Llandaff; ordained priest (1937); vicar of Eglwysfach (1954–67); his edited work includes *A book of country verse* (1961) and a selection of George Herbert (1967).

Bibliography
B.N.B.
Contemporary poets.
N.C.B.E.L.
Who's who. 1973.

Poetry
Poems; stones of the field (pr. ptd.). 1947.

An acre of land. 1952.
The minister. 1953.
Song at the year's turning. 1955.
Poetry for supper. 1958.
Tares. 1961.
Bread of truth. 1963.
Pieta. 1966.
Not that he brought flowers. 1968.
H'm. 1972.
Young and old. 1972.

Criticism
Words and the poet. 1964.

THWAITE, ANTHONY SIMON
(1930–)
English poet; born in Chester; educated at Christ
Church, Oxford; Visiting Professor of English,
Tokyo University (1955–7); B.B.C. producer
(1957–62); literary editor, the *Listener* (1962–5);
Assistant Professor of English, Libya University;
literary editor of the *New Statesman* (1968–);
translator of *The Penguin book of Japanese verse*
(1964).

Bibliography
Authors' and writers' who's who. 1971.
Contemporary poets. 1970.
Gale.

Poetry
Poems. 1953.
Home truths. 1957.
The owl in the tree. 1963.
The stones of emptiness. 1967.
Penguin modern poets no. 18 (with A. Alvarez and
   R. Fuller). 1970.
Inscriptions. 1973.

Other Works
Contemporary English poetry. 1959.
Japan in colour. 1967.
The deserts of Hesperides (travel in Libya). 1969.

TILLER, TERENCE ROGER (1916–)
English poet; educated at Jesus College, Cambridge; Lecturer in English Literature at Fuad First
University, Cairo (1939–46); did cipher work for
G.H.Q., Middle East; B.B.C. editor and producer
(1946–); compiled *Chess treasury for the air* (1966);
his other edited work is not listed below.

Bibliography
B.N.B.

Contemporary poets.
N.C.B.E.L.

Poetry
Selected poems. 1941.
The inward animal. 1943.
Unarm, Eros. 1948.
Reading a medal. 1957.
Notes for a myth. 1968.

Verse Plays
The death of a friend. 1949.
Lilith. 1950.
The tower of hunger. 1952.

TILLOTSON, *Professor* GEOFFREY
(1905–69)
English scholar; husband of Kathleen Tillotson
(q.v.); educated at Balliol College, Oxford; Assistant Lecturer, later Reader in English Literature,
University College, London (1931–44); served
with the Ministry of Aircraft Production in the
Second World War (1940–4); Professor of English
Literature, Birkbeck College, London (1944–69);
Governor of the City Literary Institute, etc.; a contributor to learned journals; edited, with his wife,
over a period of years, the works of Pope and
Thackeray's *Vanity fair* (1963).

Bibliography
B.N.B.
Gale.
Who's who. 1969.

Works
On the poetry of Pope. 1938.
Pope's Rape of the lock. 1941.
Bibliography of Michael Drayton. 1941.
Essays in criticism and research. 1942.
Criticism and the nineteenth century. 1951.
Thackeray the novelist. 1954.
Newman. 1957.
Pope and human nature. 1958.
Augustan studies. 1961.
Mid-Victorian studies (with K. Tillotson). 1965.
The continuity of English poetry from Dryden to
   Wordsworth (lecture). 1967.
Thackeray (with D. Hawes). 1968.

TILLOTSON, *Professor* KATHLEEN
MARY (1906–)
English scholar; widow of the late Professor Geof-
frey Tillotson (q.v.); educated at The Mount
School and Somerville College, Oxford; Tutor at

Somerville and St. Hilda's Colleges, Oxford (1928–39); Lecturer, later Reader, at Bedford College, London University (1939–58); Hildred Carlile Professor of English, London (1965–   ); a contributor to many learned periodicals; has written the introduction to five Trollope novels and co-edited the works of Michael Drayton (1941), *Vanity fair* (1963) and *The letters of Charles Dickens* (1965); general editor of the Clarendon Dickens.

Bibliography
B.N.B.
Who's who. 1973.

Works
Novels of the eighteen-forties. 1954.
Matthew Arnold and Carlyle (Warton Lecture). 1957.
Dickens at work (with John Butt). 1957.
The tale and the teller (inaugural lecture). 1959.
Mid-Victorian studies (with G. Tillotson). 1965.

TITMUSS, *Professor* **RICHARD MORRIS** (1907–73)
English social historian; educated privately; industrial and commercial experience (1922–42); historian, Cabinet Office (1942–9); Professor of Social Administration, London School of Economics (1950–   ); Hon. LL.D., Edinburgh (1962) and other honorary degrees; a contributor to *The Times*, *New Statesman*, *Economic History Review*, etc.

Bibliography
Authors' and writers' who's who. 1971.
B.N.B.
Who's who. 1973.

Works
Poverty and population. 1938.
Our food problem (with F. Le Gros Clark). 1939.
Parents' revolt (with K. C. Titmuss). 1942.
Birth, poverty and wealth. 1943.
Problems of social policy (official war history). 1950.
The cost of the National Health Service (with B. Abel-Smith). 1956.
The social division of welfare. 1956.
Essays on the welfare state. 1958.
Law and opinion in England in the twentieth century (ed. M. Ginsberg). 1959.
Social policy and population growth in Mauritius (with B. Abel-Smith and T. Lynes). 1961.
Income distribution and social change. 1962.

The health services of Tanganyika (ed.). 1964.
Choice and the welfare state. 1967.
Commitment to welfare. 1968.
The gift relationship. 1971.

TOFFLER, ALVIN (1928–   )
American critic; educated at New York University; correspondent (1957–61); full-time writer (1961–   ); a contributor to *Life*, *Nation*, *New Republic*, *Saturday Review*, *The fictionists* (1972).

Bibliography
C.B.I.
Gale.

Works
The culture consumers. 1964.
Schoolhouse in the city. 1968.
Future shock. 1970.

TOMALIN, RUTH
Irish poet, novelist and writer; educated at King's College, London; worked as a journalist on various newspapers; a contributor to the *Observer*, *Country Life*, *Adelphi*, *Fortnightly*, etc.

Bibliography
B.N.B.
Gale.

Novels
All souls. 1952.
The garden house. 1964.
The spring house. 1968.
Away to the west. 1972.

Poetry
Threnody for dormice. 1947.
Deer's cry. 1952.

For Children
The daffodil bird. 1959.
The sea mice. 1962.

Other Works
The day of the rose (essays and portraits). 1947.
W. H. Hudson (biography). 1959.
Best country stories. 1969.

TOMELTY, JOSEPH
Irish playwright and actor.

Bibliography
B.M. catalogue.
B.N.B.

Plays
"Right again Barnum". 1950.
The apprentice. 1953.
Mug's money. 1953.
Is the priest at home? 1954.
All souls' night. 1955.
End house. 1962.

TOMLIN, ERIC WALTER FREDERICK (1913–)

English writer; educated at Brasenose College, Oxford; taught (1936–40); British Council (1941–71); postings abroad included Baghdad, Ankara, Tokyo and Paris; Visiting Professor, University of California (1961); Visiting Fellow, University College, Cambridge (1971–); a contributor to *Criterion*, *Scrutiny*, *T.L.S.*, etc.; his edited work is not listed below.

Bibliography
B.M. catalogue.
B.N.B.
Gale.
Who's who. 1973.

Works
Turkey the modern miracle. 1940.
Life in modern Turkey. 1946.
The approach to metaphysics. 1947.
Great philosophers: vol. I. The Western philosophers; an introduction. 1950; vol. II. The Eastern philosophers. 1953.
Simone Weil. 1954.
R. G. Collingwood. 1954.
Wyndham Lewis. 1955.
Living and knowing. 1955.
La vie et l'œuvre de Bertrand Russell. 1963.
Tokyo essays. 1967.
The last country. 1972.
Japan. 1973.
Man, time and new science. 1973.

TOMLINSON, ALFRED CHARLES (1927–)

English poet; born at Stoke-on-Trent; educated at Queen's College, Cambridge; Lecturer, Bristol University (1956–); Visiting Professor, New Mexico University, Albuquerque (1962–3).

Bibliography
B.N.B.
Gale.

Poetry
Relations and contraries. 1951.
The necklace. 1955.
Seeing is believing. 1958.
Versions from Tyutchev (translations with H. C. Gifford). 1960.
Castilian ilexes (translations of Antonio Machado, with H. C. Gifford). 1963.
A peopled landscape. 1963.
Poems; a selection (with Austin Clarke and Tony Connor). 1964.
American scenes. 1966.
The Matachines. 1968.
The poem as invitation. 1968.
Engraved on the skull of a cormorant. 1969.
Unaccompanied serpent. 1969.
Way of a world. 1969.
America West Southwest. 1969.
Penguin modern poets no. 14 (with A. Brownjohn and M. Hamburger). 1969.

TONKS, ROSEMARY

English novelist and poet; has lived in West Africa and India; reviews poetry for the B.B.C. European service; her poetry is represented in several anthologies; a contributor to the *Observer*, *New Statesman*, *Listener*, *T.I..S.*, etc.

Bibliography
B.N.B.
Contemporary poets.

Novels
Emir. 1963.
Opium fogs. 1963.
The bloater. 1968.
Business men as lovers. 1969.
The way out of Berkeley Square. 1970.
The halt during the chase. 1972.

Poetry
Notes on cafés and bedrooms. 1963.
Iliad of broken sentences. 1967.

For Children
On wooded wings; the adventures of Webster. 1948.
Wild sea goose. 1951.

TOWHARE, HONE

New Zealand Maori poet; born in Mangakin; a contributor to *Landfall*; represented in New Zealand anthologies.

Bibliography
Contemporary poets.
N.Z. national bibliography.

Poetry
No ordinary sun. 1964.
Come rain hail. 1970.
Sap-wood and milk. 1972.

TOWNSEND, JOHN ROWE (1922–)
English journalist and children's writer; on the
Guardian staff (1949–69); freelance writer
(1969–); a contributor to many journals and
papers; edited *Modern poetry in selection* (1971) and
*A sense of story; essays on contemporary writers for
children* (1971).

Bibliography
Authors' and writers' who's who. 1971.
B.N.B.

Novels for Children
Gumble's Yard. 1961.
Hell's edge. 1963.
Widdershins crescent. 1965.
The Hallensage sound. 1966.
Pirate's island. 1969.
The intruder. 1969.
Goodnight, Prof. Love. 1970.

Criticism
Written for children. 1965.

**†TREVOR, ELLESTON
(TREVOR DUDLEY-SMITH,
†ROGER FITZALAN, †CAESAR
SMITH, †ADAM HALL, †SIMON
RATTRAY, †WARWICK SCOTT,
†HOWARD NORTH)** (1920–)
English novelist; apprenticed as a racing driver;
served in the R.A.F. during the Second World War
(1939–45); full-time writer since 1945.

Bibliography
B.N.B.
Gale.
Who's who. 1973.

Adult Novels as †Elleston Trevor
Now try the morgue. 1948.
Chorus of echoes (filmed). 1950.

Tiger Street. 1951.
Redfern's miracle. 1951.
A blaze of roses. 1952.
The passion and the pity. 1953.
The big pick-up (filmed). 1955.
Squadron airborne. 1955.
The killing-ground. 1956.
Gale force (filmed). 1956.
The pillars of midnight (filmed). 1957.
The V.I.P. (filmed). 1959.
Silhouette. 1959.
The billboard madonna. 1960.
The mind of Max Duveen. 1960.
The burning shore. 1961.
The flight of the phoenix (filmed). 1964.
This seems chance. 1965.
The shoot. 1966.
The freebooters (filmed). 1967.
A place for the wicked. 1968.
Bury him among kings. 1970.
Toll plaza. 1972.

Children's Books as †Elleston Trevor
Over the wall. 1943.
By a silver stream. 1944.
Scamper Foot, the pine marten (reprinted as
  †Adam Hall). 1944.
Rippleswim the otter (reprinted as †Adam Hall).
  1945.
Double who double-crossed. 1945.
Wumpus (reprinted as †Adam Hall). 1945.
Deep wood (reprinted as †Adam Hall). 1945.
Heather Hill (reprinted as †Adam Hall). 1946.
Immortal error. 1946.
More about Wumpus (reprinted as †Adam Hall).
  1947.
Badger's beech (reprinted as †Adam Hall). 1948.
Island of the pines (reprinted as †Adam Hall).
  1948.
Secret travellers (reprinted as †Adam Hall). 1948.
Where's Wumpus? (reprinted as †Adam Hall).
  1948.
The wizard of the wood (reprinted as †Adam
  Hall). 1948.
Ant's castle (reprinted as †Adam Hall). 1949.
Badger's moon (reprinted as †Adam Hall). 1949.
Mole's castle. 1950.
Sweethallow Valley. 1951.
Challenge of the firebrand. 1951.
The secret arena. 1951.
Forbidden kingdom. 1959.
The crystal city. 1959.
Green glade. 1959.
Squirrel's island. 1963.

Novels as †Adam Hall
Volcanoes of San Domingo. 1964.
The Berlin memorandum (filmed as The Quiller memorandum). 1964.
The ninth directive. 1966.
The Striker portfolio. 1969.
The Warsaw document. 1971.
The Tango briefing. 1973.

Novels as †Warwick Scott
Image in the dust. 1951.
Domesday story. 1952.
Naked canvas. 1954.

Hugo Bishop Stories as †Simon Rattray
Knight sinister (reprinted as †Adam Hall). 1951.
Queen in danger (reprinted as †Adam Hall). 1952.
Bishop in check (reprinted as †Adam Hall). 1953.
Pawn in jeopardy (reprinted as †Adam Hall). 1954.
Rook's gambit (reprinted as †Adam Hall). 1955.
Dead silence. 1955.
Dead circuit. 1955.
Dead sequence. 1957.

Novels Under Other Names
Escape to fear (as †T. D. Smith). 1948.
Heatwave (as †T. D. Smith; filmed). 1957.
A blaze of arms (as †Roger Fitzalan). 1967.
Expressway (as †Howard North). 1973.

TREVOR, LUCY MERIOL (1919–)
English novelist; educated at the Perse Girls' School, Cambridge, and St. Hugh's College, Oxford; relief work in Italy (1946–7); now a full-time writer.

Bibliography
Authors' and writers' who's who. 1971.
B.N.B.
Gale.
Who's who. 1973.

Novels
The last of Britain. 1956.
The new people. 1957.
A narrow place. 1958.
Shadows and images. 1960.
The city and the world. 1970.
Holy images. 1971.

Poetry
Midsummer, midwinter. 1957.

Biography
Newman: the pillar of the cloud. 1962.
Newman: light in winter. 1962.
Apostle of Rome: a life of Philip Neri 1515–1595. 1966.
Pope John. 1967.
Prophets and guardian. 1969.
The Arnolds. 1973.

Children's Books
Forest and the kingdom. 1949.
Hunt the king, hide the fox. 1950.
Fires and the stars. 1951.
Sun faster, sun slower. 1955.
The other side of the moon. 1956.
Merlin's ring. 1957.
The treasure hunt. 1957.
Four odd ones. 1958.
Sparrow child. 1958.
The caravan war. 1963.
The rose round. 1963.
William's wild day out. 1963.
Lights in a dark town. 1964.
The midsummer maze. 1964.
The king of the castle. 1966.

†TREVOR, WILLIAM (WILLIAM TREVOR COX) (1928–)
Irish novelist; born in County Cork; educated at Trinity College, Dublin; taught history in County Armagh (1950–2); taught art at Rugby (1952–6); advertising copywriter (1960–); a contributor to the London Magazine, etc.

Bibliography
B.N.B.
Gale.
Who's who. 1973.

Novels
A standard of behaviour. 1958.
The old boys (Hawthornden Prize 1965, staged 1971). 1964.
The boarding-house. 1965.
The love department. 1966.
The day we got drunk on cake (short stories). 1967.
Mrs. Eckdorf in O'Neill's hotel. 1969.
Miss Gomez and the brethren. 1971.
The ballroom of romance. 1972.
Elizabeth alone. 1973.

Plays
Going home. 1972.
A night with Mrs. da Tanka. 1972.
Marriages. 1973.

TREVOR-ROPER, *Professor* **HUGH REDWALD** (1914–)
English historian; educated at Charterhouse and Christ Church, Oxford; Student of Christ Church (1946–57); Censor (1947–52); Regius Professor of Modern History, Oxford (1957–); edited *Essays in British history presented to Sir Keith Feiling* (1964) and *The age of expansion, Europe and the world 1559–1660* (1968); a contributor to the *Sunday Times, New York Times,* etc.

Bibliography
Authors' and writers' who's who. 1971.
B.N.B.
N.C.B.E.L.
Who's who. 1973.

Works
Archbishop Laud. 1940.
The last days of Hitler. 1947.
The gentry, 1540–1640. 1953.
Hitler's table talk (ed.). 1953.
The poems of Richard Corbett (ed. with J. A. W. Bennett). 1955.
Historical essays. 1957.
Jewish and other nationalism. 1962.
Hitler's war directives, 1939–45 (ed.). 1964.
The rise of Christian Europe. 1965.
George Buchanan and the ancient Scottish constitution. 1967.
Religion, the Reformation and social change. 1967.
The Philby affair. 1968.
The European witch-craze of the 16th and 17th centuries. 1969.
The Romantic movement and the study of history. 1969.
The past and the present; history and sociology. 1969.
The plunder of the arts in the 17th century. 1971.
Queen Elizabeth's historian; William Camden and the beginnings of English "civil history". 1972.

TREWIN, JOHN COURTENAY (1908–)
English dramatic critic; born in Cornwall; contributor to the *Observer* (1937–); literary editor (1943–8); dramatic critic (1948–53); radio critic, the *Listener* (1951–7), etc.; president of the Critics' Circle (1964–5); chairman, West Country Writers' Association (1964–); his edited work, not listed below, includes 38 volumes of *Plays of the Year* (Methuen).

Bibliography
Authors' and writers' who's who. 1971.
B.N.B.
Who's who. 1973.

Works
The Shakespeare Memorial Theatre. 1932.
The English theatre. 1948.
Up from the Lizard. 1948.
We'll hear a play. 1949.
London–Bodmin (with H. J. Willmott). 1950.
Stratford-upon-Avon. 1950.
The theatre since 1900. 1951.
The story of Bath. 1951.
Drama 1945–50. 1951.
Down to the lion. 1952.
Printer to the house (with E. M. King). 1952.
A play to-night. 1952.
The Stratford festival (with T. C. Kemp). 1953.
Dramatists of today. 1953.
Edith Evans. 1954.
Theatre programme (ed.). 1954.
Mr. Macready. 1955.
Sybil Thorndike. 1955.
Verse drama since 1800. 1956.
Paul Scofield. 1956.
The night has been unruly. 1957.
Alec Clunes. 1958.
The gay twenties: a decade of the theatre. 1958.
Benson and the Bensonians. 1960.
The turbulent thirties. 1960.
A sword for a prince. 1960.
John Neville. 1961.
The Birmingham Repertory Theatre. 1963.
Shakespeare on the English stage, 1900–1964. 1964.
Completion of Lamb's Tales. 1964.
Drama in Britain, 1951–64. 1965.
The drama bedside book (with H. F. Rubinstein). 1966.
Robert Donat. 1968.
The pomping folk. 1968.
Shakespeare's country. 1970.
Shakespeare's plays today (with Arthur Colby Sprague). 1970.
Peter Brook. 1971.
I call my name (verse pamphlet). 1971.
Portrait of Plymouth. 1973.

TRICKETT, MABEL RACHEL (1923–)
English novelist; born in Lathom, Lancs.; educated at Lady Margaret Hall, Oxford; Lecturer in English, Hull University (1946–54); Fellow and Tutor,

St. Hugh's College, Oxford (1954–73); Principal, St. Hugh's College (1973–   ); a contributor to *T.L.S.*, the *Review of English Studies, London Magazine, Cornhill*, etc.

Bibliography
Authors' and writers' who's who. 1971.
B.N.B.
Who's who. 1973.

Novels
The return home (John Llewelyn Rhys Prize 1953). 1952.
The course of love. 1954.
Point of honour. 1958.
A changing place. 1962.
The elders. 1966.
A visit to Timon. 1970.

Other Work
The honest muse (a study in Augustan verse). 1967.

TRYPANIS, CONSTANTINE ATHANASIUS (1909–   )

Greek poet and Greek scholar; educated at the universities of Athens, Berlin and Munich; Lecturer in Classics at Athens University (1939–47); Professor of Byzantine and Modern Greek, and Fellow of Exeter College, Oxford (1947–69); Professor of Classics, Chicago University (1969–   ); a contributor to the *T.L.S.*, *Encounter*, *New Yorker*, etc.; his edited work is not listed below; represented in the *Faber book of contemporary verse*, *Penguin book of Greek verse* (1971), etc.

Bibliography
B.N.B.
Contemporary poets.
Gale.
Who's who. 1973.

Poetry
Pegasus. 1955.
The stones of Troy. 1956.
The cocks of Hades. 1958.
Grooves in the wind (The stones of Troy, and The cocks of Hades). 1964.
Pompeian dog. 1965.
The elegies of a glass Adonis. 1966.

Other Works
The influence of Hesiod upon Homeric hymn of Hermes. 1939.

The influence of Hesiod upon Homeric hymn on Apollo. 1940.
Tartessos. 1945.
Eric Arthur Barber, 1888–1965. 1967.

TUCCI, NICCOLÒ (1908–   )

American novelist; born in Switzerland; educated in Florence; emigrated to U.S.A. (1938); started writing in German; wrote for *Politics Magazine* (1943–6); co-founder *Village Voice* (1954); a contributor to the *New Yorker, Harper's, Encounter*, etc.; and in Italian to *Corriere della Sera, Il Mondo*, etc.; recipient of several awards; his novels in Italian are *Il segreto* (1956), *Gli atlantidi* (1968), *Il muro del suo pianto* (1972) and *Guenther* (1973); his play *Posterity for sale* staged (1967).

Bibliography
C.B.I.
Contemporary novelists.

Novels in English
Before my time. 1962.
Unfinished funeral. 1964.
Love and death. 1973.
Those of the lost continent (self-translation of *Gli atlantidi*). n.d.

Other Works
Tico-Tico. 1950.
How to get away without murder. 1973.

TUOHY, FRANK (JOHN FRANCIS TUOHY) (1925–   )

English novelist; educated at Stowe School and King's College, Cambridge; Lecturer, Turku University, Finland (1947–8); Jagiellonian University, Krakow, Poland (1958–60).

Bibliography
B.N.B.
Gale.
Who's who. 1973.

Novels
The animal game. 1957.
The warm nights of January. 1960.
The admiral and the nuns (stories). 1962.
The ice saints (James Tait Black Prize 1965). 1964.
Fingers in the door and other stories. 1970.

Other Work
Portugal. 1970.

TURNBULL, ANDREW WINCHESTER (1921–70)

American biographer; educated at Princeton and Harvard universities; Instructor of Humanities, Massachusetts Institute of Technology (1954–8); full-time writer (1958–70); a contributor to the *New Yorker* and *Esquire*; edited the letters of Scott Fitzgerald (1963).

Bibliography
C.B.I.
Gale.

Biographies
Scott Fitzgerald. 1962.
Thomas Wolfe. 1969.

TURNBULL, GAEL LUNDIN (1928–)

Scottish poet; born in Edinburgh; educated in England, Canada and at Cambridge and Pennsylvania universities; M.C.P. and M.C.S.; in medical practice in Canada, England and the U.S.A.; a contributor to numerous little magazines.

Bibliography
Authors' and writers' who's who. 1971.
B.N.B.
Contemporary poets.

Poetry
Trio. Toronto. 1954.
To you I write. 1963.
A very particular hill. 1964.
Twenty words; twenty days. 1966.
Briefly. 1967.
A trampoline. 1952–64. 1968.
Shards. 1964–69. 1970.

TURNER, DAVID (1927–)

English playwright; born in Birmingham; educated at Birmingham University; taught for some years and started writing to supplement his salary; on winning a B.B.C. prize for a television play, *The train set*, he took up writing full time; a scriptwriter for *The Archers*, the radio serial; only one of his many plays, adaptations and television plays has been separately published.

Bibliography
Anger and after.
B.N.B.
Contemporary dramatists.

Plays
Semi-detached. 1962.
Way off beat (televised 1966, published in *Conflicting generations, five television plays*). 1968.

TURNER, GEORGE REGINALD (1916–)

Australian novelist; born in Melbourne; served in the Australian Forces during the Second World War (1939–45); Employment Officer (1945–).

Bibliography
Annals of Australian literature.
B.N.B.
Contemporary novelists.

Novels
Young man of talent (American title, Scobie). 1959.
A stranger and afraid. 1961.
The cupboard under the stairs. 1962.
A waste of shame. 1965.
The lame dog man. 1967.

TUTUOLA, AMOS (1920–)

Nigerian novelist; born in Abeokuta; served in the R.A.F. in Lagos (1943–6); Nigerian Broadcasting Company, Ibadan (1956–).

Bibliography
B.N.B.
H. R. Collins. Amos Tutuola, New York. 1969.
Contemporary novelists.
Jahn and Dressler.

Novels
The palm-wine drinkard and his dead palm-wine tapster in the dead's town. 1952.
My life in the bush of ghosts. 1954.
Simbi and the satyr of the dark jungle. 1955.
The brave African huntress. 1958.
The feather woman of the jungle. 1962.
Abaiyi and his inherited poverty. 1967.

TYLER, ANNE (1941–)

American novelist; educated at Duke and Columbia universities; Russian bibliographer at Duke University Library (1962–3); Assistant to the Librarian of the McGill Law Library, Montreal (1964–); a contributor to *Antioch Review*, *Southern Review*, etc.

Bibliography
C.B.I.

Contemporary novelists.
Gale.

Novels
If morning never comes. 1964.
The tin can tree. 1965.
A slipping down life. 1970.
The clock winder. 1972.
A help to the family. 1972.

TYNAN, KENNETH PEACOCK
(1927–)
English drama critic; educated at King Edward's
School, Birmingham, and Magdalen College,
Oxford; dramatic critic of the *Spectator* (1951),
Evening Standard (1952–3), *Daily Sketch* (1953–4),
Observer (1954–63), *New Yorker* (1958–60); film
critic of the *Observer* (1964–6); co-producer of

Soldiers new (1968); part author and deviser of *Oh,
Calcutta!* (1969); edited books on the National
Theatre productions of the *Recruiting officer* (1965)
and *Othello* (1966); literary manager, later consultant, of the National Theatre (1969–73).

Bibliography
B.N.B.
Gale.
Who's who. 1973.

Works
He that plays the king. 1950.
Persona grata (with Cecil Beaton). 1953.
Alec Guinness. 1954.
Bull fever. 1955.
The quest for Corbett. 1960.
Curtains. 1961.
Tynan right and left. 1967.

U

ULASI, ADAORO LILY
Nigerian novelist; daughter of an Ibo chief; educated in America; editor of the women's page of
the *Lagos Sunday Times* and *Daily Times*; a regular
contributor to these papers and broadcaster; has
travelled widely; now lives in Kent with her husband and children.

Bibliography
B.N.B.
Jahn and Dressler.
Zell and Silver.

Novels
Many thing you no understand. 1970.
Many thing begin for change. 1971.

UNSTEAD, ROBERT JOHN (1915–)
English writer of history for children; educated at
Goldsmith's College, London; schoolmaster
(1936–40); served in the R.A.F. during the Second
World War (1940–6); headmaster (1946–57);
chairman, Letchworth Primary Schools Committee (1960–4), etc.; general editor of Black's
Junior Reference series; a contributor to educational journals.

Bibliography
B.N.B.
Gale.
Who's who. 1973.

Works
Looking at history. 1953.
People in history. 1955.
Teaching history in the primary school. 1957.
Travel by road through the ages. 1958.
A history of houses. 1958.
Looking at ancient history. 1959.
Monasteries. 1961.
Black's children's encyclopaedia (co-author). 1961.
The medieval scene. 1962.
Crown and parliament. 1962.
Some kings and queens. 1962.
The rise of Great Britain. 1963.
A century of change. 1963.
Royal adventurers. 1964.
Early times. 1964.
Men and women in history. 1965.
Britain in the twentieth century. 1966.
The story of Britain. 1969.
Homes in Australia. 1970.
Castles. 1970.

Transport in Australia. 1970.
Pioneer homelife in Australia. 1971.
History of the English–speaking world. 1972.

UPDIKE, JOHN HOYER (1932–)
American novelist; educated at Harvard University; on the staff of the *New Yorker* (1955–7); a regular contributor to the *New Yorker* and *New Republic*; adapted the libretto of Mozart's *Magic flute* (1962) and Wagner's *The ring* (1964) for children.

Bibliography
Authors' and writers' who's who. 1971.
C.B.I.
Contemporary novelists.
Gale.
Spiller.
Who's who. 1973.

Novels and Short Stories
The poorhouse fair. 1959.
The same door (stories). 1959.
Rabbit, run (filmed 1969). 1960.
Pigeon feathers and other stories. 1962.
The centaur. 1963.
Olinger stories, a selection. 1964.
Of the farm. 1965.
The music school (stories). 1966.
Couples. 1968.
Bech: a book (stories). 1970.
Rabbit redux. 1971.
Museums and women (stories). 1972.

Poetry
The carpentered hen and other tame creatures (English title, Hoping for a hoopoe. 1959). 1958.
Telephone poles and other poems. 1963.
Midpoint and other poems. 1969.
Seventy poems. 1972.

For Children
A child's calendar. 1965.

Other Work
Assorted prose. 1965.

URE, PETER (1919–)
English scholar; educated at Liverpool University; Professor of English Literature, University of Newcastle upon Tyne (1960–); his edited work is not listed below.

Bibliography
B.N.B.
Gale.

Works
Towards a mythology; studies in the poetry of W. B. Yeats. 1946.
Shakespeare; the problem plays. 1961.
Yeats the playwright. 1963.
W. B. Yeats and the Shakespearean moment; a lecture. 1966.

URIS, LEON MARCUS (1924–)
American novelist; served in the U.S. Marines during the Second World War (1942–5); wrote several film scripts including *Exodus* (1960) and is a contributor to many journals.

Bibliography
C.B.I.
Contemporary novelists.
Gale.

Novels
Battle cry (filmed 1954). 1953.
The angry hills (filmed 1959). 1955.
Exodus (filmed 1960). 1958.
Mila 18. 1961.
Armageddon, a novel of Berlin. 1964.
Topaz (filmed 1968). 1967.
Q. B. Seven. 1970.

Other Works
Exodus revisited (American title, In the steps of Exodus). 1961.
The third temple (with Strike Zion by William Stevenson). 1967.

USTINOV, PETER ALEXANDER (1921–)
English actor, playwright and film director; educated at Westminster School; Rector of Dundee University (1968); goodwill ambassador for Unicef (1969); recipient of many awards.

Bibliography
B.N.B.
C.B.I.
Contemporary dramatists.
Gale.
N.C.B.E.L.
Who's who. 1973.
Geoffrey Williams, Peter Ustinov, Peter Owen, 1958.

Novels and Short Stories
Add a dash of pity (short stories). 1959.
The loser. 1961.
The frontiers of the sea (stories). 1966.
Krumnagel. 1971.

Plays
The house of regrets (staged 1942). 1943.
Beyond (staged 1942). 1944.
The Banbury nose (staged 1943). 1945.
Plays about people (including The tragedy of good
    intentions, staged 1945; Blow your own
    trumpet, staged 1943; The indifferent shepherd,
    staged 1948). 1950.
The love of four colonels (staged 1951). 1951.
The moment of truth (staged 1951). 1953.
Romanoff and Juliet (staged 1956; filmed 1961).
    1957.
Photo finish (staged 1962). 1962.
Five plays (Romanoff and Juliet, Moment of truth,
    Beyond, Love of four colonels, No sign of the
    dove). 1965.

The unknown soldier and his wife. 1968.
Halfway up the tree (staged 1967). 1970.

Other Works
Ustinov's diplomats (a book of photographs).
    1960.
We were only human (cartoons). 1961.
The wit of Ustinov. 1969.
Rectorial address, University of Dundee. 1969.

UZODINMA, EDMUND CHUKUEMEKA CHIEKE (1936–)

Nigerian novelist; born in Eastern Nigeria; educated at the University of Ibadan; currently teaching in Onitsha.

Bibliography
B.N.B.
Jahn and Dressler.

Novels
Brink of dawn. 1966.
Our dead speak. 1967.

V

VAIZEY, *Professor* JOHN (1929–)

English economic historian; educated at St.
Catherine's College, Cambridge; Fellow of St.
Catherine's College (1953–7); research director,
University of London (1960–2); Fellow of Wor-
cester College, Oxford (1962–); consultant to
Unesco, etc.; editorial board, Weidenfeld and
Nicolson, etc.; a contributor to *The Times, Spec-
tator, Encounter, Daily Herald,* etc.

Bibliography
B.N.B.
Gale.
Who's who. 1973.

Works
The trade unionist and full employment. 1950.
Costs of education. 1958.
Scenes from institutional life. 1959.
The brewing industry 1886–1951. 1960.
Guinness's brewery in the Irish economy
    1759–1886 (with P. Lynch). 1961.
The economics of education. 1962.

Britain in the sixties: education for tomorrow.
    1962.
The control of education. 1963.
Education in a class society. 1963.
Barometer man. 1966.
Economics of education (with E. A. G. Robinson).
    1966.
Education in the modern world. 1966.
Higher education in the stationary state. 1967.
The sleepless lunch. 1967.
Resources for education. 1968.
Industry and the intellectual. 1970.
The type to succeed. 1970.
Capitalism. 1970.
The political economy of education. 1972.
The economics of science and technology (with
    Keith Norris). 1973.

VANSITTART, PETER (1920–)

English novelist; born in Bedford; educated at
Haileybury and Worcester College, Oxford; full-
time writer since 1942; a contributor to the

Observer, London Magazine, Sunday Telegraph, The Times, etc.

Bibliography
Authors' and writers' who's who. 1971.
B.N.B.
Gale.

Novels
I am the world. 1942.
Enemies. 1947.
The overseer. 1948.
Broken canes. 1950.
A verdict of treason. 1952.
A little madness. 1953.
Orders of chivalry. 1958.
The game and the ground. 1958.
The tournament. 1959.
A sort of forgetting. 1960.
Carolina. 1961.
Sources of unrest. 1962.
The siege. 1962.
The friends of God. 1963.
The lost lands. 1964.
The story-teller. 1968.
Pastimes of a red summer. 1969.
Landlord. 1971.

Children's Books
The dark tower. 1965.
The shadow land. 1967.

Other Works
Green knights; black angels; the mosaic of history. 1969.
Dictators. 1973.
Worlds and underworlds. 1973.

†VAUGHN, RICHARD (ERNEST LEWIS THOMAS) (1904–)

Welsh novelist; served in the army (1942–6) during the Second World War; radio and television scriptwriter and journalist.

Bibliography
B.N.B.
Gale.

Novels
Mould in earth. 1951.
Who rideth so wild. 1952.
Son of Justin. 1955.
All through the night. 1957.
There is a river. 1961.

VIDAL, GORE (†EDGAR BOX) (1925–)

American novelist and playwright; educated at Phillips Exeter Academy; served in the U.S. Army (1943–6); many of his plays have been produced on Broadway; a contributor to *Nation, Encounter, New York Times,* etc.

Bibliography
C.B.I.
Contemporary novelists.
Gale.
Who's who. 1973.

Novels
Williwaw. 1946.
In a yellow wood. 1947.
The city and the pillar. 1948.
The season of comfort. 1949.
Dark green, bright red. 1950.
A search for a king. 1950.
The judgement of Paris. 1952.
Messiah. 1954.
A thirsty evil (stories). 1956.
Julian. 1964.
Washington D.C. 1967.
Myra Breckinridge (filmed 1969). 1968.
Two sisters: a novel in the form of a memoir. 1970.

Plays
Visit to a small planet and other television plays (filmed 1959). 1956.
The best man, a play about politics (filmed 1968). 1960.
On the march to the sea. 1962.
Three plays (Visit to a small planet, On the march to the sea, The best man). 1962.
Romulus, a new comedy (adapted from a play by Dürrenmatt). 1962.
Weekend. 1968.
An evening with Richard Nixon. 1972.

Plays as †Edgar Box
Death in the fifth position. 1952.
·Death before bedtime. 1953.
Death likes it hot. 1954.

Essays
Rocking the boat. 1962.
Reflections upon a sinking ship. 1969.
Homage to Daniel Shays (collected essays 1952–72). 1972.

VIERECK, PETER ROBERT EDWIN (1916–)

American poet and writer; educated at Harvard

and Christ Church, Oxford; served in the Second World War (1943–5); instructor at Harvard (1941–7); various academic posts include Professor of Modern European and Russian History (1955–65); and occupant of Mount Holyoke Alumnae Foundation Chair of Interpretive Studies (1965–); a contributor to numerous popular and learned journals.

Bibliography
C.B.I.
Contemporary poets.
Gale.
L. of C.

Poetry
Terror and decorum (Pulitzer Prize 1949). 1948.
Strike through the mask; new lyrical poems. 1950.
The first morning; new poems. 1952.
The persimmon tree. 1956.
The tree witch; a verse drama. 1961.
New and selected poems. 1967.

Other Works
Metapolitics; from the Romantics to Hitler (revised edition as Metapolitics, the roots of the Nazi mind, 1961). 1941.
Conservatism revisited; the revolt against revolt 1915–1949. 1949.
Shame and glory of the intellectuals. 1953.
Dream and responsibility; the tension between poetry and society. 1953.
The unadjusted man; a new hero for Americans. 1956.
Conservatism, from John Adams to Churchill. 1956.
Inner liberty; the stubborn grit in the machine. 1957.
Conservatism revisited, and the new conservatism; what went wrong? 1965.
Henault. 1969.
Sue's secondhand horse. 1973.

VIERTEL, PETER (1920–)
German-born American novelist and writer of film scripts; educated at University of California, Los Angeles; served in the U.S. Marines during the Second World War; lives in Switzerland; author of various film scripts, including that of *The old man and the sea* and *The sun also rises*.

Bibliography
C.B.I.
Gale.

Novels
The canyon. 1940.
Line of departure. 1947.
White hunter, black heart. 1953.
Love lies bleeding. 1964.
Bicycle on the beach. 1971.

Play
The survivors (with Irwin Shaw). 1948.

VOGT, ANTON (1914–)
New Zealand poet; Lecturer in English, Wellington Teachers' College; reviewer for Wellington radio; represented in several anthologies.

Bibliography
Contemporary poets.
N.Z. national bibliography.

Poetry
Anti and all that. 1940.
Poems for a war. 1943.
Love poems. 1952.
Poems unpleasant (with James K. Baxter and Louis Johnson). 1952.

VONNEGUT, KURT (1922–)
American science fiction novelist; educated at Cornell, Carnegie Institute of Technology and Chicago University; served in the U.S. Army during the Second World War (1942–5); journalist (1947–50); freelance writer from that time; Lecturer at University of Iowa Writers' Workshop (1965–); a contributor to *Saturday Evening Post*, *McCall's*, *Ladies' Home Journal*, etc.; his unpublished plays are not listed below.

Bibliography
C.B.I.
Contemporary novelists.
Gale.

Novels
Player piano. 1952.
Sirens of Titan. 1961.
Canary in a cathouse (stories). 1961.
Cat's cradle. 1963.
God bless you, Mr. Rosewater. 1965.
Mother night. 1966.
Welcome to the monkey house: a collection of short stories. 1968.
Slaughter-house five (filmed 1972). 1969.
Happy birthday, Wanda Jane. 1971.
Between time and Timbuktu. 1972.
Breakfast of champions. 1973.
The Vonnegut statement. 1973.

W

WADDINGTON, MIRIAM (†E. B. MERRIT) (1917–)

Canadian poet; born in Winnipeg; educated at the universities of Toronto and Philadelphia; Lecturer in English, York University; a contributor to the *Canadian Forum, Contemporary Poetry, Quarterly Review of Literature*, etc.; represented in numerous anthologies; a contributor to television; her translations from Yiddish are not listed below; edited the works of A. M. Klein (1973).

Bibliography
Canadiana.
C.B.I.
Contemporary poets.

Poetry
Green world. 1945.
The second silence. 1955.
The season's lovers. 1958.
Glass trumpet. 1966.
Say yes. 1969.
Dream telescope. 1970.
Driving home: poems new and selected. 1972.

Other Works
Call them Canadians. 1968.
Critical study of A. M. Klein. 1970.

WAGONER, DAVID RUSSELL (1926–)

American poet; educated at Pennsylvania State University and Indiana University; served in the U.S. Navy (1944–6); instructor, Pennsylvania State University (1950–4); Associate Professor, then Professor, University of Washington, Seattle (1954–); awarded a Guggenheim Fellowship (1956) and Ford Fellowship (1964); a contributor of poems to learned journals; editor of *Poetry Northwest* (1966), and *Straw from the fire: from the notebooks of Theodore Roethke 1943–63* (1970).

Bibliography
C.B.I.
Contemporary novelists.
Contemporary poets.

Novels
Dry sun, dry wind. 1953.
The man in the middle. 1954.

Money, money, money. 1955.
Rock. 1958.
The escape artist. 1965.
Baby, come on inside. 1968.
Where is my wandering boy tonight? 1970.

Poetry
A place to stand. 1958.
The nesting ground. 1963.
Staying alive. 1966.
New and selected poems. 1969.
Working against time: poems. 1970.
Riverbed. 1972.

WAIN, JOHN BARRINGTON (1925–)

English novelist; born in Stoke-on-Trent; educated at St. John's College, Oxford; Faraday Fellow, St. John's College, Oxford (1946–9); English Lecturer, Reading University (1949–55); Visiting Professor, Bristol University (1967) and Paris (1969); freelance writer since 1955; a contributor to the *Observer, New Yorker*, etc.; his edited work is not listed below.

Bibliography
Authors' and writers' who's who. 1971.
B.N.B.
Contemporary novelists.
Gale.
Who's who. 1973.

Novels
Hurry on down. 1953.
Living in the present. 1955.
The contenders. 1958.
A travelling woman. 1959.
Nuncle and other stories. 1960.
Strike the father dead. 1962.
The young visitors. 1965.
Death of the hind legs and other stories. 1966.
The smaller sky. 1967.
A winter in the hills. 1970.
The lifeguard (stories). 1971.

Poetry
A word carved on a sill. 1956.
Weep before God. 1961.
Wildtrack. 1965.
Letters to five artists. 1969.
The shape of Feng. 1972.

Criticism

Preliminary essays (Somerset Maugham Award 1958). 1957.
Gerard Manley Hopkins: an idiom of desperation. 1959.
Essays on literature and ideas. 1963.
The living world of Shakespeare. 1964.
Arnold Bennett. 1967.
A house for the truth. 1972.

Autobiography

Sprightly running. 1962.

WAKEFIELD, DAN (1932–)

American novelist; educated at Indiana and Columbia universities; journalist (1955–9); freelance writer (1959–); Visiting Lecturer, University of Illinois (1968–); recipient of several awards; a contributor to numerous magazines including *Atlantic, Esquire, Playboy*; his edited work is not listed below.

Bibliography

C.B.I.
Gale.

Novels

Island in the city: the world of Spanish Harlem. 1959.
Revolt in the south. 1961.
Between the lines. 1966.
Supernation at peace and war. 1968.
Going all the way. 1970.
Starting over. 1973.

WAKOSKI, DIANE (*Mrs.* SHERBELL) (1937–)

American poet; educated at the University of California, Berkeley; worked at British Book Center, New York (1960–3); taught in New York school (1963–); awarded the Robert Frost Fellowship in Poetry (1966); editor of *Dreamsheet* and *Software*; represented in various anthologies.

Bibliography

C.B.I.
Contemporary poets.
Gale.

Poetry

Coins and coffins. 1962.
Four young lady poets (with Rochelle Owens, Barbara Moraff, Carol Berge). 1962.
Discrepancies and apparitions. 1966.

George Washington poems. 1967.
Greed: parts 1 and 2. 1968.
The diamond merchants. 1968.
Inside the bloody factory. 1968.
Some poems for the Buddha's birthday. 1969.
The magellanic clouds. 1970.
Greed: parts 3 and 4. 1969; parts 5–7. 1971; parts 8, 9, 11. 1973.
The moon has a complicated geography. 1969.
The motorcycle betrayal poems. 1971.
Smudging. 1972.
Dancing on the grave of a son of a bitch. 1973.

WALCOTT, DEREK ALTON (1930–)

Caribbean poet and playwright; born in St. Lucia; educated at University of the West Indies, Jamaica; director, Little Caribbean Theatre Drama Workshop; artistic director, Trinidad Theatre Workshop (1959); a contributor to *Bim, Kyk-over-al, London Magazine*, etc.; represented in *Caribbean Voices* (1966), *New Voices of the Commonwealth* (1968), etc.; his plays *Ti-Jean and his Brothers* and *Malcochon* were staged at the Royal Court Theatre.

Bibliography

C.B.I.
Contemporary dramatists.
Contemporary poets.
Jahn and Dressler.

Poetry

Twenty-five poems. 1948.
Poems. 1953.
In a green night; poems 1948–1960. 1962.
Selected poems. 1964.
The castaway. 1965.
The gulf. 1969.
Another life. 1973.

Plays

Henrie Christophe; a chronicle. 1950.
Harry Dernier. 1951.
Ione; a play with music. 1954.
The sea at Dauphin. 1954.
The dream on Monkey Mountain and other plays (with Ti-Jean and his brothers, Malcochon, The sea at Dauphin). 1971.

WALKER, DAVID HARRY (1911–)

Scottish-born Canadian novelist; educated at Shrewsbury and Sandhurst; served in the Black Watch (1931–47); full-time writer since his retirement (1947); Canadian Commissioner (1965–).

Bibliography
B.N.B.
Canadiana.
Contemporary novelists.

Novels
The storm and silence. 1949.
Geordie (filmed 1955). 1950.
The pillar (Governor General's Award 1953). 1952.
Digby (Governor General's Award 1954). 1953.
Harry Black (filmed 1957). 1954.
Where the high winds blow. 1960.
Storms of our journey and other stories. 1963.
Winter of madness. 1964.
Mallabec. 1965.
Come back, Geordie. 1966.
Devil's plunge (American title, Cab–intersec). 1968.
The Lord's pink ocean. 1972.
Black Dougal. 1974.

For Children
Sandy was a soldier's boy. 1957.
Dragon Hill. 1962.
Pirate rock. 1969.
Big Ben. 1970.

WALKER, TED (1934–)
English poet; born at Lancing, Sussex; educated at St. John's College, Cambridge; taught French and Spanish in Chichester (1953–67); full-time author and broadcaster (1967–); the recipient of various awards; a contributor to the *Listener*, *Poetry Review*, *Sunday Times*, *New Yorker*, etc.; represented in numerous anthologies.

Bibliography
B.N.B.
Contemporary poets.
Gale.

Poetry
Those other growths. 1964.
Fox on a barn door. 1965.
The solitaries. 1967.
The night bathers. 1970.
Gloves to the hangman: poems 1969–72. 1973.

WALLACE, IRVING (1916–)
American novelist and short-story writer; free-lance writer from the age of 15; served in the U.S. Army (1942–6) in the Second World War; film script writer for Warner Brothers (1955–7); a contributor of short stories to numerous magazines.

Bibliography
C.B.I.
Gale.

Novels
The sins of Philip Fleming. 1954.
The square peg. 1957.
The Chapman report (filmed 1962). 1960.
The twenty-seventh wife. 1961.
The prize (filmed 1963). 1962.
The three sirens. 1963.
The man. 1964.
The Sunday gentlemen. 1965.
The plot. 1967.
The seven minutes. 1969.
The word. 1972.

Other Works
The fabulous originals. 1955.
The fabulous showman; the life and times of P. T. Barnum. 1959.
The writing of one novel. 1968.
The nympho and other maniacs: the lives, loves and the sexual adventures of some scandalous ladies. 1971.

WALLANT, EDWARD LEWIS (1926–62)
American novelist; educated at the New School for Social Research; served in the U.S. Navy (1944–6); graphic artist for advertising agencies (1950–62); recipient of several awards.

Bibliography
C.B.I.
Gale.

Novels
The human season. 1960.
The pawnbroker (filmed 1965). 1961.
The tenants of Moonbloom. 1963.
The children at the gate. 1964.

WALLER, Sir JOHN STANIER (1917–)
English author, poet and journalist; educated at Worcester College, Oxford; founder-editor of *Quarterly*, *Kingdom Come* (1939–41); served in the army (1940–6) during the Second World War; a contributor to numerous periodicals; edited the *Collected poems of Keith Douglas* (1951), etc.

Bibliography
B.N.B.
Who's who. 1973.

Poetry
The confessions of Peter Pan. 1941.
Fortunate Hamlet. 1941.
Spring legend. 1942.
The merry ghosts. 1946.
Crusade. 1946.
The kiss of stars. 1948.
Goldenhair and the two black hawks. 1971.

Humour
Shaggy dog. 1953.

WALTARI, MIKA (1908–)
Finnish writer; educated at Helsinki University;
editor of Finnish weekly magazine *Suomen
Kuvalehti* (1935–8); Finnish State Information
Bureau (1939–44); awarded literary prizes and
honours.

Bibliography
Authors' and writers' who's who. 1971.
B.N.B.
Gale.
Who's who. 1973.

Works
Sinuhe, the Egyptian (filmed as The Egyptian,
   1954). 1949.
Michael the Finn. 1950.
The sultan's renegade (paperback title, The wan-
   derer. 1961). 1951.
The dark angel. 1953.
A stranger came to the farm. 1953.
A nail merchant at nightfall. 1954.
Moonscape and other stories. 1955.
The Etruscan. 1957.
The tongue of fire. 1959.
The secret of the kingdom. 1961.
The tree of dreams and other stories. 1965.
The Roman. 1966.

WARNER, FRANCIS (1937–)
English poet; educated at Christ's Hospital and St.
Catherine's College, Cambridge; Lecturer, St.
Catherine's College (1959–65); Fellow and Tutor,
St. Peter's College, Oxford (1965–); founder of
the Samuel Beckett Theatre, Oxford (1967); edited
Studies in the arts; proceedings of the St. Peter's
College Literary Society (1969).

Bibliography
Authors' and writers' who's who. 1971.
B.N.B.
Contemporary poets.

Poetry
Perennia. 1962.
Early poems. 1964.
Experimental sonnets. 1967.
Madrigals. 1967.
The poetry of Francis Warner. 1970.

Other Works
Maquettes (play). 1970.
The absences of nationalism in the work of Samuel
   Beckett. 1970.

WARNER, OLIVER (1903–)
English naval historian; educated at Gonville and
Caius College, Cambridge; reader for Chatto and
Windus (1926–41); Admiralty Secretariat
(1941–7); British Council, director of publications
(1947–63).

Bibliography
Authors' and writers' who's who. 1971.
B.N.B.
Gale.
Who's who. 1973.

Works
A secret of the march. 1927.
Hero of the Restoration. 1936.
Uncle Lawrence. 1939.
Captains and kings. 1947.
An introduction to British marine painting. 1948.
Joseph Conrad. 1951.
The crown jewels. 1951.
Captain Marryat. 1953.
Introduction to centenary history of Chatto and
   Windus (with Margaret Meade-Featherstone-
   haugh). 1955.
Battle honours of the Royal Navy. 1956.
A portrait of Lord Nelson. 1958.
Trafalgar. 1959.
Emma Hamilton and Sir William. 1960.
The battle of the Nile. 1960.
Great seamen. 1961.
The glorious first of June. 1961.
Wilberforce. 1962.
A history of the inn-holders' company. 1962.
Great sea battles. 1963.
A history of the tin-plate workers' company. 1964.
English literature: a portrait gallery. 1964.
Uppark and its people (with Margaret Meade-
   Featherstonehaugh). 1964.
The sea and the sword: the Baltic 1630–1945. 1965.
Best sea stories (ed.). 1965.
Portsmouth and the Royal Navy. 1965.

Nelson's battles. 1965.
Cunningham of Hyndhope, Admiral of the Fleet.
  1967.
Marshal Mannerheim and the Finns. 1967.
The navy. 1968.
The life and letters of Lord Collingwood. 1968.
A journey to the northern capitals. 1968.
Admiral of the fleet; the life of Sir Charles Lambe.
  1969.
With Wolfe at Quebec. 1972.
Great battle fleets. 1973.

WATEN, JUDAH LEON (1911–)

Australian novelist; born in Russia; educated in
Perth and Melbourne; Australian civil servant for
many years; a reviewer for the *Sydney Morning
Herald* (1970–); translator of Harz Bergner,
Between sky and sea (1946).

Bibliography
Australian national bibliography.
B.M. catalogue.
Contemporary novelists.

Novels
Alien son (stories). 1952.
The unbending. 1954.
Shares in murder. 1957.
Time of conflict. 1961.
Distant land. 1964.
Season of youth. 1966.
So far no further. 1971.

Other Works
From Odessa to Odessa; the journey of an
  Australian winter. 1969.
The Depression years 1929–1939. 1971.

WATERHOUSE, KEITH SPENCER (†LEE GIBB, †HAROLD TROY)

(1929–)
English novelist; a journalist in Leeds and London;
film scripts include *Billy Liar*, *A kind of loving*, *Lock
up your daughters*; television and radio plays include
There is a happy land (1962), *The warmonger* (1970)
and series such as *Three's company* (1973).

Bibliography
C.B.I.
Contemporary dramatists.
Gale.
Who's who. 1973.

Novels
There is a happy land. 1957.
Billy Liar. 1959.
Jubb. 1963.
The bucket shop (American title, Everything
  must go west). 1968.

Plays (with Willis Hall)
Billy Liar (filmed 1962). 1960.
Norton. 1960.
Celebration. 1961.
All things bright and beautiful. 1963.
England, our England (a review). 1964.
Say who you are. 1965.
Whoops-a-daisy. 1968.
Children's day. 1969.
The card (musical). 1973.
Saturday, Sunday, Monday (adaptation from E. de
  Filippo). 1973.

Other Works
Café Royal (with Guy Deghy). 1956.
How to avoid matrimony (†Harold Troy with
  Guy Deghy). 1957.
Britain's voice abroad (with Paul Cave). 1957.
The future of television. 1958.
The Joneses; how to keep up with them (with Guy
  Deghy, as †Lee Gibb). 1959.

WATKINS, VERNON PHILLIPS

(1906–67)
Welsh poet; educated at Magdalene College, Cam-
bridge; served in the Second World War (1941–6);
worked in Lloyds Bank (1925–66); Visiting
Professor of Poetry, University of Washington,
Seattle (1967); edited Dylan Thomas, *Letters to
Vernon Watkins* (1957).

Bibliography
B.N.B.
Gale.
N.C.B.E.L.

Poetry
Ballad of the Mari Lwyd. 1941.
The lamp and the veil. 1945.
The lady with the unicorn. 1948.
Selected poems. 1948.
The North Sea (translations from Heine). 1951.
The death bell. 1954.
Cypress and acacia. 1959.
Affinities. 1962.
Selected poems 1930–1960. 1967.
Fidelities. 1968.

Uncollected poems. 1969.
Pergamon poets no. 4 (with Kathleen Raine). 1969.

WATSON, GEORGE (1927–)

Australian scholar; educated at Brisbane Boys' College, Queensland University and Trinity College, Oxford; information staff, Council of Europe (1952–7); Lecturer, then Fellow, of St. John's College, Cambridge (1959–); general editor, the *New Cambridge Bibliography of English Literature* (1969–); editor of *The Concise Cambridge Bibliography* (1958), etc.; his other edited work is not listed below; a contributor to the *Review of English Studies*, *T.L.S.*, *Encounter*, etc.

Bibliography
Authors' and writers' who's who. 1971.
B.N.B.
Gale.

Works
The unservile state. 1957.
The British constitution and Europe. 1958.
The literary critics. 1962.
The English mind (with Hugh Sykes Davies). 1964.
Coleridge the poet. 1966.
The English Petrarchans. 1967.
Is Socialism Left? 1967.
Literary English since Shakespeare. 1967.
The study of literature. 1969.
The literary thesis; a guide to research. 1970.
The English ideology. 1973.

WATSON, SHEILA (née DOHERTY) (1919–)

Canadian novelist; wife of Wilfred Watson (q.v.); educated at the universities of British Columbia and Toronto; taught in the Western foothills before her marriage; most of her output has been short stories contributed to the *Tamarack Review*, *Queen's Quarterly*, etc.

Bibliography
Canadiana.
C.B.I.

Novel
The double hook. 1959.

WATSON, WILFRED (1911–)

Anglo-Canadian poet; born in England and emigrated to Canada with his parents (1926); educated at Toronto University; served in the Second World War; Lecturer, later Professor of English, Alberta University (1951–); represented in various anthologies of Canadian verse; a contributor to *Fiddlehead*, etc.

Bibliography
Canadiana.
C.B.I.
Contemporary poets.

Poetry
Friday's child (Governor General's Award 1956). 1955.
Cockcrow and the gulls (religious verse drama). n.d.

Other Work
From cliché to archetype (with Marshall McLuhan). 1970.

WAUGH, AUBERON ALEXANDER (1939–)

English novelist and journalist; son of Evelyn Waugh; born in Somerset; educated at Downside and Christ Church, Oxford; served in the army (1958–9); journalist (1960–) with the *Daily Telegraph*, *I.P.C.*, *Spectator* and *Private Eye*; a contributor to *The Times*, *News of the World*, *Catholic Herald*, etc.; political correspondent of *Private Eye* (1970–).

Bibliography
Authors' and writers' who's who. 1971.
B.N.B.
Contemporary novelists.
N.C.B.E.L.

Novels
The foxglove saga. 1960.
Path of dalliance. 1963.
Who are the violets now? 1965.
Consider the lilies. 1968.
A bed of flowers. 1971.

Other Work
Biafra: Britain's shame (with Suzanne Croupe). 1969.

WEBB, CHARLES RICHARD (1939–)

American novelist; educated at Williams College.

Bibliography
C.B.I.
Gale.

Novels
The graduate (filmed 1969). 1964.
The products (filmed 1966). 1966.
Love, Roger. 1969.
The marriage of a young stockbroker (filmed 1971). 1970.
The last usher. 1971.

WEBB, PHYLLIS (1927–)

Canadian poet; educated at British Columbia and McGill universities; spent some time in England; on the staff of the English Department, British Columbia University, for 3 years; subsequently on the staff of the Canadian Broadcasting Corporation; her first group of poems, *Falling Glass*, was published in *Trio* (1954) with Eli Mandel and Gael Turnbull (qq.v.); represented in the *Oxford book of Canadian verse* (1960), etc.; a contributor to *Tamarack Review*, etc.

Bibliography
Canadiana.
C.B.I.
Contemporary poets.

Poetry
Even your right eye. 1956.
The sea is also a garden. 1962.
Naked poems. 1965.

WEIR, J. E. (1935–)

New Zealand poet; born in Nelson; ordained priest (1961); teacher at St. Bede's College, Christchurch; a contributor to the New Zealand *Listener*; represented in several anthologies.

Bibliography
Contemporary poets.
N.Z. national bibliography.

Poetry
The sudden sun. 1964.

Other Work
The poetry of James K. Baxter. 1971.

WEISS, THEODORE RUSSELL (1916–)

American poet and writer; educated at Columbia University; instructor in English at universities of Washington, North Carolina and Yale (1941–6); Associate Professor, then Professor, Bard College, Annandale-on-Hudson (1952–); Ford Fellowship (1953–4), etc.; a contributor to

anthologies and periodicals; edited *Selections from the note-books of Gerard Manley Hopkins* (1945).

Bibliography
C.B.I.
Contemporary poets.
Gale.
L. of C.

Poetry
The catch. 1951.
Outlanders. 1960.
Gunsight. 1962.
The medium. 1965.
The last day and the first. 1968.
World before us: poems 1950–1970. 1970.

Other Works
Food oils and their uses. 1970.
Breath of clowns and kings: a book on Shakespeare. 1971.

WELSH, ANNE (*née* FEETHAM) (1922–)

South African poet; born in Johannesburg; educated in Johannesburg, Roedean, University of Witwatersrand and Somerville College, Oxford; lecturer in economics at Witwatersrand University; a contributor to *New Coin*, *Contrast*, etc.; represented in *The Oxford book of South African verse* and other anthologies; editor of *Africa South of the Sahara* (1951).

Bibliography
Contemporary poets.

Poetry
Set in brightness. 1968.

WELTY, EUDORA (1909–)

American novelist; educated at the University of Wisconsin; honorary consultant in American letters, Library of Congress (1958–); recipient of various literary awards; a contributor to *Southern Review*, *Harper's Bazaar*, *Atlantic*, *New Yorker*, etc.

Bibliography
C.B.I.
Contemporary novelists.
Gale.
Spiller.

Novels and Short Stories
A curtain of green (stories). 1941.

The robber bridegroom (novella). 1942.
The wide net and other stories. 1943.
Delta wedding. 1946.
Short stories. 1949.
Golden apples (stories). 1949.
Select stories. 1953.
The Ponder heart. 1954.
The bride of Innisfallen and other stories. 1955.
The shoe bird (for children). 1964.
Thirteen stories. 1965.
Losing battles. 1970.
The optimist's daughter. 1972.

Other Works
Music from Spain. 1948.
Place in fiction. 1957.
Three papers on fiction. 1962.
One time one place. 1971.

WESKER, ARNOLD (1932–)
English playwright; after school served as a
furniture-maker's apprentice, carpenter's mate and
bookseller's assistant (1948–50); R.A.F. (1950–2);
plumber's mate, farm labourer, kitchen porter,
pastrycook, etc. (1952–8); director of Centre 42
(1961–70), when it dissolved.

Bibliography
B.N.B.
Contemporary dramatists.
Gale.
Glenda Leeming. Arnold Wesker. 1972.
Who's who. 1973.

Plays
Chicken soup with barley (staged 1958). 1959.
Roots (staged 1959). 1959.
I'm talking about Jerusalem (staged 1960). 1960.
The Wesker trilogy. 1960.
The kitchen (staged 1959, filmed 1961). 1961.
Chips with everything (staged 1962). 1962.
The four seasons (staged 1965). 1966.
Their very own and golden city (staged 1966).
  1966.
The friends (staged 1970). 1970.
The old ones (staged 1972). 1973.
The journalists. 1973.
The wedding feast. 1973.

Other Works
Fears of fragmentation (essays). 1970.
Six Sundays in January. 1971.
Labour and the arts: II or, what is to be done? n.d.

WEST, JESSAMYN (*Mrs.* **McPHERSON**)
(1907–)
American novelist and short-story writer; educated at the University of California and England;
taught at writers' conferences at various U.S. universities; recipient of various awards; a contributor
to *Harper's, Good Housekeeping, Reader's Digest,
New Yorker*, etc.; represented in various editions of
Best American short stories; edited *A Quaker reader*
(1961); her film scripts include *The friendly persuasion* (1956), *The big country* (1958) and *Stolen
hours* (1963).

Bibliography
C.B.I.
Contemporary novelists.
Gale.

Novels
The friendly persuasion (filmed 1956). 1945.
The witch diggers. 1951.
Cress Delahanty. 1953.
Love, death and the ladies' drill team (stories)
  (English title, Learn to say goodbye). 1955.
Love is not what you think. 1959.
South of the angels. 1960.
A matter of time. 1966.
Leafy Rivers. 1967.
Except for me and thee. 1969.
Crimson rambler of the world, farewell. 1970.

Play
A mirror for the sky. 1948.

Other Works
To see the dream. 1957.
How to look and feel ten years younger in ten days.
  1972.

WEST, MORRIS LANGLO
(**†MICHAEL EAST**) (1916–)
Australian novelist; educated at the University of
Melbourne; taught modern languages and
mathematics (1933–9); served in the Australian
Imperial Forces in the Second World War
(1939–43); managing director of Australasian
Radio Productions (1943–53); lives in New York.

Bibliography
Australian national bibliography.
B.N.B.
Contemporary novelists.
Gale.
Who's who. 1973.

Novels
Gallows on the sand. 1956.
Kundu. 1957.
Children of the sun. 1957.
The big story (American title, The crooked road; filmed 1964). 1957.
McCreary moves in. 1958.
Second victory (American title, Backlash). 1958.
The devil's advocate (James Tait Black Prize 1960). 1959.
The naked country. 1960.
Daughter of silence. 1961.
The shoes of the fisherman (filmed 1972). 1963.
The ambassador. 1965.
The tower of Babel. 1968.
Scandal in the assembly (with Robert Francis). 1970.
Summer of the red wolf. 1971.
The salamander. 1973.

Plays
Daughter of silence (based on the novel). 1962.
The heretic. 1970.

WEST, RAY B., Jr. (1908–)
American editor, poet and critic; educated at Utah and Iowa universities; after various university posts, Professor, San Francisco State College (1959–); editor of the *Western Review* (1936–59); advisory editor of *Contact* (1959–); a contributor to numerous journals and magazines; his edited work is not listed below.

Bibliography
C.B.I.
Contemporary novelists.
Gale.

Works
The short story in America. 1952.
Kingdom of the saints. 1957.
Katherine Anne Porter. 1963.
Writer in the room. 1968.
Reading the short story. 1969.

WEVILL, DAVID (1937–)
Canadian poet; born in Japan; lives in England; educated Caius College, Cambridge; taught for 2 years at Mandalay University; contributor to the *Listener*, *Observer*, *New Yorker*, etc.

Bibliography
B.N.B.

Contemporary poets.
Gale.

Poetry
Birth of shark. 1964.
A Christ of the ice floes. 1966.
Firebreak. 1971.

Other Work
Where the arrow falls. 1973.

WHALEN, PHILIP (1923–)
American poet; born in Portland, Oregon; served in the U.S. Army (1943–6) during the Second World War; a contributor to *Chicago Review*, *Evergreen Review*, etc.; represented in *New American Poetry 1945–60*, Grove (1960).

Bibliography
C.B.I.
Contemporary poetry.
Gale.

Poetry
Like I say. 1960.
Memoirs of an interglacial age. 1960.
Everyday: poems. 1965.
On Bear's Head: poems 1950–1967. 1969.
Scenes of life at the capital. 1971.
Imaginary speeches for a brazen head. 1972.

WHITBREAD, THOMAS BACON (1931–)
American poet and short-story writer; educated at Harvard University; instructor, then Assistant Professor of English, Texas University, Austin (1959–); a contributor to literary magazines; edited *Seven Contemporary Authors*, etc.

Bibliography
C.B.I.
Contemporary poets.
Gale.
L. of C.

Poetry
Four infinitives. 1964.

WHITE, ALAN (†JAMES FRASER)
English novelist; born in Yorkshire; his edited works are not listed below.

Bibliography
Authors' and writers' who's who. 1971.

B.N.B.
Gale.

Novels as Alan White
The long day's dying (filmed 1968). 1965.
The wheel. 1966.
The long night's walk. 1968.
The long drop. 1969.
The kibbutz. 1970.
The long watch. 1971.
The long midnight. 1972.
Climate of revolt. 1973.
The long fuse. 1973.

Novels as †James Fraser
Doctor and nurse. 1958.
The evergreen death. 1969.
Cock-pit of rose. 1969.
Deadly nightshade. 1970.

Other Work
Teach yourself home heating. 1965.

WHITE, JON MANCHIP (1924–)
Welsh novelist, poet, egyptologist, radio and television scriptwriter; educated at Cambridge University; served in the Second World War; Foreign Office (1952–6); settled in Gloucestershire (1958) to devote his time to writing; his many radio, television and film scripts have not been published; a contributor to the *Spectator, Financial Times, Listener*, etc.; his edited work is not listed below.

Bibliography
B.N.B.
Contemporary novelists.
Contemporary poets.
Gale.

Novels
Mark of dust (filmed as Mask of doubt, 1954). 1953.
The last race. 1953.
Build us a dam. 1955.
The girl from Indiana. 1956.
No home but heaven. 1957.
The mercenaries. 1958.
Hour of the rat. 1962.
The rose in the brandy glass. 1965.
Nightclimber. 1968.
The game of Troy. 1971.

Poetry
Dragon. 1943.

Salamander. 1946.
The rout of San Romano. 1952.
The mountain lion. 1971.

Other Works
Ancient Egypt. 1952.
Anthropology. 1952.
Cromwell. 1953.
Marshal of France. 1962.
Everyday life in Ancient Egypt. 1963.
Diego Velazquez; painter and courtier. 1969.
The land God made in anger; reflections on a journey through South West Africa. 1969.
Cortés and the downfall of the Aztec empire. 1971.

WHITE, TERENCE DE VERE (1912–)
Irish novelist and writer; educated at Trinity College, Dublin; practised as a solicitor (1933–61); Vice-Chairman, Irish National Library, etc.; Literary Editor, *Irish Times* (1961–); a contributor to the *Sunday Times, Observer, Horizon*, etc.; edited *A leaf from the yellow book* (1958).

Bibliography
Authors' and writers' who's who. 1971.
B.N.B.
Who's who. 1973.

Novels
An affair with the moon. 1959.
Prenez garde. 1961.
The remainder man. 1963.
Lucifer falling. 1965.
Tara. 1967.
The Lambert mile. 1969.
The March hare. 1970.
Mr. Stephen. 1971.
The distance and the dark. 1973.

Other Works
The road of excess (biography of Isaac Butt). 1945.
Kevin O'Higgins. 1949.
The story of the Royal Dublin Society. 1955.
A fretful midge. 1957.
The parents of Oscar Wilde. 1967.
Leinster. 1968.
Ireland. 1968.
The Anglo-Irish. 1972.

WHITE, THEODORE HAROLD (1915–)
American journalist and writer on modern affairs; educated at Harvard University; Far East correspondent, *Time Magazine* (1939–45); chief

European correspondent, the *Reporter* (1945–6); Columbia Broadcasting System consultant (1961–4); freelance writer (1956–); recipient of many literary awards; a contributor to *Life*, *Time*, *Saturday Review*, *Collier's*, etc.; edited the *Stillwell papers* (1948).

Bibliography
C.B.I.
Gale.

Works
Thunder out of China (with Annalee Jacoby). 1946.
Fire in the ashes; Europe in mid century. 1953.
The mountain road. 1958.
The view from the fortieth floor. 1960.
The making of the president—1960. 1961.
The making of the president—1964. 1965.
Caesar at the Rubicon; a play about politics. 1968.

WHITEHORN, KATHARINE ELIZABETH (*Mrs.* GAVIN LYALL) (1928–)

English journalist; educated at Roedean and Newnham College, Cambridge; publisher's reader (1950–3); on the staff of *Picture Post*, *Woman's Own*, *Spectator* (1956–61); *Observer* columnist (1960–); member of various advisory committees.

Bibliography
B.N.B.
Who's who. 1973.

Works
Cooking in a bedsitter. 1960.
Roundabout. 1961.
Only on Sundays. 1966.
Whitehorn's social survival. 1968.
Observations. 1970.
How to survive in hospital. 1972.

WHITING, JOHN ROBERT (1915–63)

English playwright and actor; trained at R.A.D.A.; served in the Second World War.

Bibliography
Anger and after.
B.M. catalogue.
B.N.B.

Plays
Marching song. 1954.
The plays of John Whiting (Saint's day, staged

1952; A penny for a song, staged 1951; Marching song, staged 1954, filmed 1971). 1957.
The devils (adapted from Aldous Huxley, The devils of Loudun, filmed 1971). 1961.
Saint's day. 1963.
Collected plays; 2 vols. (edited R. Hayman). 1969.

Other Works (Posthumous)
On theatre. 1966.
The art of the dramatist. 1970.

WHITTEMORE, EDWARD REED, Jr. (1919–)

American poet; educated at Yale and Princeton universities; editor of *Furioso* (1939–53), of *Carleton Miscellany* (1960–4); served in the U.S. Army during the Second World War (1941–5); Professor in English, Carleton College, Minnesota (1947–); consultant in poetry, Library of Congress (1964–5).

Bibliography
C.B.I.
Contemporary poets.
Gale.
L. of C.

Poetry
Heroes and heroines. 1946.
An American takes a walk. 1956.
The self-made man and other poems. 1959.
The boy from Iowa. 1962.
The fascination of the abomination (includes stories and essays). 1963.
Poems, new and selected. 1967.
Fifty poems fifty. 1970.

Other Work
Little magazines. 1963.

WHYTE, WILLIAM HOLLINGSWORTH (1917–)

American sociologist; educated at Princeton University; served in the U.S. Marines during the Second World War (1941–5); assistant managing editor, *Fortune Magazine* (1953–8); now a full-time writer; a contributor to *Harper's*, *Encounter*, *Life*; edited and contributed to *The exploding metropolis*(1958).

Bibliography
C.B.I.
Gale.

Works
Is anybody listening? 1952.
The organization man. 1956.
Securing open space for urban America: con-
　servation easements. 1959.
Last landscape. 1968.

WICKRAMASINGHE, NALIN CHANDRA (1939–)

Ceylonese poet, mathematician and astronomer;
educated at the University of Ceylon and Trinity
College, Cambridge; Fellow of Jesus College,
Cambridge (1963–).

Bibliography
B.N.B.
Contemporary poets.

Poetry
Poems. 1958.

Other Work
Light scattering functions for small particles. 1973.

WIENERS, JOHN JOSEPH (1934–)

American poet; born in Boston, Mass.; educated at
State University of New York in Buffalo;
magazine salesman; founder and editor of *Measure*
(1957–); recipient of poetry awards; has written
and had produced two plays; a contributor to
Nation, Evergreen Review, etc.; represented in
numerous anthologies.

Bibliography
C.B.I.
Contemporary poets.
Gale.

Poetry
Ace of pentacles. 1964.
Gardenias. 1966.
Pressed wafer. 1968.
Selected poems. 1968.
The Hotel Wentley poems. 1968.
Nerves. 1971.
Selected poems. 1972.

WIKKRAMASINGHE, LAKDASA NIMALASIRI (1941–)

Ceylonese poet; born in Kandy; teaches English in
a village school; lives in Kandy; only his poetry
written in English is listed below.

Bibliography
C.B.I.
Contemporary poets.

Poetry
Lustre poems. 1965.
15 poems. 1970.

WILBUR, RICHARD PURDY (1921–)

American poet and writer; educated at Amherst
College and Harvard University; served in the
U.S. Army during the Second World War
(1943–5); Junior Fellow, then Associate Professor
in English, Harvard University (1947–57); Professor, Wesleyan University, Middletown, Conn.
(1957–); recipient of numerous literary awards
and prizes for translation; his edited work and
translations are not listed below.

Bibliography
C.B.I.
Contemporary poets.
Gale.
L. of C.
Spiller.

Poetry
Beautiful changes and other poems. 1947.
Ceremony and other poems. 1950.
Things of this world (Pulitzer Prize 1957). 1956.
Poems 1943–1956. 1957.
Advice to a prophet and other poems. 1961.
The poems of Richard Wilbur. 1963.
Walking to sleep; new poems and translations.
　1969.
Digging for China. 1970.
Opposites. 1973.

Other Works
Candide (comic opera based on Voltaire's work).
　1957.
Emily Dickinson; three views (with Louise Bogan
　and Archibald MacLeish). 1960.
Loudmouse (for children). 1963.

WILES, JOHN (1924–)

South African novelist; educated at the University
of Cape Town; theatre director in South Africa;
B.B.C. television (1957–); served in the army
(1941–6) during the Second World War; has written several stage and television plays.

Bibliography
B.N.B.
Gale.

Novels
The moon to play with (John Llewelyn Rhys Prize 1955). 1954.
The try-out. 1955.
Scene of the meeting. 1956.
The asphalt playground (with R. P. Menday). 1958.
The everlasting childhood (with R. P. Menday). 1959.
The march of the innocents. 1964.
A short walk abroad. 1969.
Grand trunk road. 1972.

Play
Leap to life (with Alan Garrard). 1957.

WILKINSON, ANNE (*née* GIBBONS) (1910–61)

Canadian poet; born in Toronto; educated in America and Europe; founding editor of and contributor to the *Tamarack Review*.

Bibliography
Canadiana.
C.B.I.

Poetry
Counterpoint to sleep. 1951.
The hangman ties the holly. 1951.

Other Works
Lions in the way (family history). 1956.
Swann and Daphne (for children). 1960.

WILLIAMS, DENIS

Guyanan novelist; educated at the Camberwell School of Art; taught at the Central School of Art; lectured on African art in Khartoum and the University of Makerere, etc.; returned to Guyana (1968) and settled on his farm on the Mazaruni River; now a full-time writer.

Bibliography
B.N.B.

Novel
The third temptation. 1968.

Other Work
Icon and image. 1973.

WILLIAMS, ERIC (1911–)

Caribbean statesman and historian of the West Indies; born in Trinidad; educated at St. Catherine's College, Oxford; Assistant Professor, later Associate, then full Professor of Social and Political Science, Harvard University, Washington D.C. (1938–); after a distinguished political career, Prime Minister of Trinidad and Tobago (1961–); Pro-chancellor, University of the West Indies; a contributor to learned journals.

Bibliography
B.N.B.
Who's who. 1973.

Works
The negro in the Caribbean. 1942.
The economic future of the Caribbean (joint author). 1943.
Capitalism and slavery. 1944.
Education in the British West Indies. 1950.
History of the people of Trinidad and Tobago. 1962.
Documents of West Indian history, vol. I, 1492–1655. 1963.
Inward hunger: the education of a prime minister. 1969.
From Columbus to Castro: the history of the Caribbean 1492–1969. 1970.

WILLIAMS, ERIC ERNEST (1911–)

English writer; interior designer at John Lewis Partnership (1932–40); served in the Second World War (1939–46) and escaped from German prison camp (1943); book buyer, John Lewis (1946–9); freelance writer (1950–); set out on a 20-year slowest expedition round the world (1959); edited *Great escape stories* (1958).

Bibliography
Authors' and writers' who's who. 1971.
B.N.B.
Gale.
Who's who. 1973.

Works
Goon in the block. 1945.
The wooden horse (filmed 1950). 1949.
The tunnel. 1951.
The escapers. 1953.
Complete and free. 1957.
Dragoman Pass. 1959.
The borders of barbarism. 1961.

More escapers in war and peace. 1968.
Great air battles. 1971.

WILLIAMS, HEATHCOTE (1941–)
English novelist and playwright; associate editor, *Transatlantic Review*; founding editor of *Suck*, Amsterdam; recipient of various awards.

Bibliography
B.N.B.
Contemporary dramatists.
Gale.

Novels
The speakers (a documentary novel). 1964.

Plays
Local stigmatic (in Traverse plays, staged 1965). 1966.
AC/DC (staged 1970). 1972.

WILLIAMS, HUGH ANTHONY GLANMOR (1904–69)
British actor and playwright jointly with his wife Margaret; educated at Haileybury and the Imperial Service College, Switzerland; Liverpool Repertory Company (1923–6); toured Australia (1927–9); played many leading roles on the London stage; served in the army during the Second World War (1939–45); acted in many films.

Bibliography
B.N.B.
Gale.
Who was who. 1961–70.

Plays with his wife, Margaret, née Vynor
Plaintiff in a pretty hat (staged 1956). 1957.
The happy man (staged as Father's match, 1957). 1958.
The grass is greener (staged 1958, filmed 1960). 1960.
Double yolk (contains By accident, and With interest). 1960.
The irregular verb to love (staged 1959). 1966.
Past imperfect. 1966.
Let's all go down the Strand (staged 1967). 1969.
The flip side. 1969.

WILLIAMS, JOHN EDWARD (1922–)
American poet and novelist; educated at Denver and Missouri universities; served in the U.S. Army during the Second World War; university instructor, etc., universities of Missouri and Denver

(1950–64); Professor of English at Denver (1964–); has travelled widely; a contributor to literary journals; editor of *Twentieth Century Literature* (1954–6), *English Renaissance Poetry* (1963), etc.

Bibliography
C.B.I.
Gale.

Novels
Nothing but the night. 1948.
Butcher's crossing. 1960.
Stoner. 1965.

Poetry
The broken landscape. 1949.

WILLIAMS, JONATHAN CHAMBERLAIN (1929–)
American poet; educated at Princeton University, Black Mountain College; served in the U.S. Army (1952–4); publisher of Jargon Books (1951–); President of the Nantala Foundation (1960–); recipient of a Guggenheim Fellowship, and of a grant for editing Jargon Books (1960); a contributor to *Evergreen Review*, *Vogue*, *Contact*, *Art International*, etc.; represented in beat and other anthologies.

Bibliography
C.B.I.
Gale.

Poetry
Red/Gray. 1951.
Four stoppages. 1953.
The empire finals at Verona. 1959.
Amen/huzza/selah. 1960.
In England's green. 1962.
Emblems for the little dells, and nooks and corners of Paradise. 1962.
Lullabies twisters gibbers drags. 1963.
Elegies and celebrations. 1963.
Lines about hills above lakes. 1964.
Jammin' the Greek scene. 1964.
Ear in Bartram's tree: selected poems 1957–1967. 1969.
Imaginary postcards. 1973.

Other Works
Mahler. 1969.
Clarence John Laughlin: an aperture monograph. 1973.

WILLIAMS, PIETER DANIEL de WET
(1929–   )
South African poet; born in Transvaal; educated at Witwatersrand and Stellenbosch universities; travelled, studied and taught in Europe (1954–6); Vice-principal of a Cape Town High School (1965–   ).

Bibliography
Contemporary poets.

Poetry
Eden and after. 1969.

WILLIAMS, RAYMOND HENRY
(1921–   )
Welsh novelist and literary critic; born in Abergavenny; educated at Trinity College, Cambridge; served in the army in the Second World War (1941–5); staff tutor to the Oxford University Delegacy for Extra-mural Studies (1946–61); Fellow of Jesus College, Cambridge (1961–7); University Reader (1967–   ); has written several television plays; Editor of the *New Thinker's Library* (1961–   ); edited *Politics and letters* (1946–7), *May Day manifesto* (1968), and the *Pelican book of English prose* vol. 2 (1970).

Bibliography
B.N.B.
Contemporary novelists.
Gale.
Who's who. 1973.

Novels
Border country. 1960.
Second generation. 1964.
The volunteers. 1972.

Other Works
Reading and criticism. 1950.
Drama from Ibsen to Eliot. 1952.
Preface to film (with Michael Orram). 1954.
Drama in performance. 1954.
Culture and society 1780–1950. 1958.
The long revolution. 1961.
Communications and community. 1961.
The existing alternatives in communications. 1962.
Modern tragedy. 1966.
Drama from Ibsen to Brecht. 1968.
The English novel from Dickens to Lawrence. 1970.
Orwell. 1971.

A letter from the country. 1971.
The country and the city. 1973.

WILLIAMS, TENNESSEE (*né* THOMAS LANIER WILLIAMS) (1914–   )
American playwright; educated at the universities of Missouri, Washington and Iowa; held numerous jobs including that of teleoperator, theatre usher and waiter; awarded numerous literary prizes; his unpublished plays are not listed below; unpublished film scripts include *Senso* (1949), *The fugitive kind* (1960) and *Boom* (1968).

Bibliography
C.B.I.
Contemporary dramatists.
Contemporary novelists.
Gale.
Spiller.
Who's who. 1973.

Novels and Short Stories
One arm, and other stories. 1948.
The Roman spring of Mrs. Stone (filmed 1961). 1950.
Hard candy (stories). 1954.
Three plays of a summer game (stories). 1960.
The knightly quest. A novella and four short stories. 1967.

Plays
Battle of angels (produced 1940). 1945.
The glass menagerie (staged 1944, filmed 1950). 1945.
27 waggons full of cotton and other one-act plays. 1946.
You touched me! (with Donald Windham, produced 1946). 1947.
A streetcar named Desire (Pulitzer Prize 1948, filmed 1951). 1947.
American blues (5 one-act plays). 1948.
Summer and smoke (filmed 1962). 1948.
I rise in flames, cried the phoenix (produced 1959). 1951.
The rose tattoo (staged 1950, filmed 1955). 1951.
Camino Real. 1953.
Cat on a hot tin roof (Pulitzer Prize 1955, filmed 1955). 1955.
Baby doll (film script). 1956.
Four plays. 1956.
Suddenly last summer (staged 1957, filmed 1959). 1958.
Garden district (Something unspoken, and Suddenly last summer). 1958.

A perfect analysis given by a parrot. 1958.
Orpheus descending (revision of Battle of angels, produced 1957, filmed as The fugitive kind. 1960). 1959.
Sweet bird of youth (filmed 1962). 1959.
Period of adjustment (produced 1959, filmed 1962). 1960.
The night of the iguana (produced 1961, filmed 1963). 1962.
The milk train doesn't stop here anymore (produced 1963, filmed 1968). 1964.
The eccentricities of a nightingale. 1965.
Lord Byron's love letter. 1965.
Slapstick tragedy (2 plays, The mutilated, and The Gnädiges Fräulein). 1965.
Kingdom on earth. 1968.
The two-character play (produced 1967). 1969.
Dragon country: a book of plays (with In the bar of a Tokyo hotel, produced 1969). 1970.
The theatre of T.W. vols. 1, 2 and 3. 1971.
Small craft warnings. 1972.

Poetry
In the winter of cities. 1956.

WILLINGHAM, CALDER BAYNARD, Jr. (1922–)
American novelist and playwright; educated at the University of Virginia; his film scripts include *End as a man, Paths of glory* and *The Vikings*; his plays include *Another darling*.

Bibliography
C.B.I.
Contemporary novelists.
Gale.

Novels
End as a man (produced on stage and screen). 1947.
Geraldine Bradshaw. 1950.
Reach to the stars. 1951.
The gates of Hell (stories). 1951.
Natural child. 1952.
To eat a peach. 1955.
Eternal fire. 1963.
Providence Island. 1969.
Rambling rose. 1972.

WILLIS, EDWARD HENRY, *Baron Willis* (TED WILLIS) (1918–)
English playwright; son of a London bus driver; left school at 15 and worked at various casual jobs before turning to freelance journalism; served in the Second World War; after the war J. B. Priestley

guaranteed him a sum of money to support himself for a year so that he could establish himself as a playwright; his film scripts include *Bitter Harvest*; television scripts include *Dixon of Dock Green* series (1953–76), *Big city, Days of vengeance* serial; he has written numerous scripts for War Office films and Ministry of Information documentaries; created life peer (1963).

Bibliography
B.M. catalogue.
B.N.B.
Gale.
Who's who. 1973.

Novel
†Dixon of Dock Green: My life by George Dixon (with Charles Hatton). 1960.

Plays
God bless the guv'nor. 1945.
The lady purrs. 1950.
George comes home. 1955.
Doctor in the house (with Gordon Ostlere). 1957.
Woman in a dressing gown, and other television plays (Woman in a dressing gown filmed 1958). 1959.
Hot summer night (filmed as Flame in the streets, staged 1957). 1959.
Brothers in law (with Henry Cecil). 1959.
The eyes of youth (adapted from novel by Rosemary Timperley, A dread of burning). 1960.
The days of vengeance. 1961.
The little goldmine. 1962.
No trees in the street. n.d.

Autobiography
Whatever happened to Tom Mix? 1970.

For Children
Devil's churchyard. 1957.
Seven gates to nowhere. 1958.
The adventures of Black Beauty. 1973.

WILLY, MARGARET ELIZABETH (1919–)
English poet; born in London; educated at Goldsmiths' College, London University; copywriter for publishers and book wholesalers (1936–42); lecturer, British Council and Goldsmiths' College (1950–); served in the Women's Land Army (1942–6) in the Second World War; editor of the *Journal of English Association* (1954–); her edited work is not listed below; a contributor to the

Birmingham Post, Observer, Books and Bookmen, T.L.S., etc.; represented in many anthologies.

Bibliography
Authors' and writers' who's who. 1971.
B.N.B.
Contemporary poets.
Gale.

Poetry
The invisible sun. 1946.
Every star a tongue. 1951.

Other Works
Life was their cry (critical biographies). 1950.
The South Hams (topography). 1955.
Three metaphysical poets (criticism). 1961.
The English diarists: Pepys and Evelyn. 1963.
Three women diarists. 1964.
Wuthering Heights (criticism). 1966.
Browning's Men and women (criticism). 1968.
The metaphysical poets. 1971.

WILSON, ANGUS FRANK JOHNSTONE (1913–)

English novelist; born in South Africa; educated at Westminster School and Merton College, Oxford; Foreign Service (1942–6); British Museum Reading Room (1949–55); Lecturer and Visiting Professor in universities in England and the United States (1959–); Professor of English, University of East Anglia since (1966); Chairman, National Book League (1971–4); member of various committees of the arts, etc.; his play, *The mulberry bush*, produced (1955); television plays are *After the show* (1959), *The stranger* (1960), *The invasion* (1963).

Bibliography
B.N.B.
Contemporary novelists.
Gale.
K. W. Gransden. Angus Wilson. 1969.
N.C.B.E.L.
Who's who. 1973.

Novels and Short Stories
The wrong set (stories). 1949.
Such darling dods (stories). 1950.
Hemlock and after. 1952.
Anglo-Saxon attitudes. 1956.
A bit off the map (stories). 1957.
The middle age of Mrs.Eliot (James Tait Black Prize 1959). 1958.
The old men at the zoo. 1961.
Late call. 1964.

No laughing matter. 1967.
As if by magic. 1973.

Other Works
Emile Zola. 1950.
For whom the cloche tolls. 1953.
The wild garden. 1963.
The world of Charles Dickens. 1970.
England (with Edwin Smith and Olive Cook). 1971.

WILSON, COLIN HENRY (1931–)

English writer; born in Leicester; did various jobs in Leicester, Paris and London (1948–54); national service with the R.A.F. (1949–50); Visiting Professor, University of Seattle, etc. (1966–9); a contributor to the *London Magazine, Encounter, Reynolds News, Sunday Times, Sunday Telegraph*, etc.

Bibliography
Authors' and writers' who's who. 1971.
B.N.B.
Gale.
Who's who. 1973.

Novels
Ritual in the dark. 1960.
Adrift in Soho. 1961.
The man without a shadow (paperback title, The sex diary of Gerard Sorme). 1963.
Necessary doubt. 1964.
The mind parasites. 1966.
The glass cage. 1966.
The philosopher's stone. 1968.
The god of the labyrinth. 1970.
The killer. 1970.
The black room. 1970.

Other Works
The outsider. 1956.
Religion and the rebel. 1957.
The age of defeat. 1959.
An encyclopaedia of murder (with Patricia Pitman). 1961.
The strength to dream. 1962.
The origins of the sexual impulse. 1963.
The world of violence. 1963.
Rasputin and the fall of the Romanovs. 1964.
The brandy of the damned (musical essays) (paperback title, C. W. on music). 1964.
Beyond the outsider. 1965.
Eagle and earwig. 1965.
Introduction to the new existentialism. 1966.
Sex and the intelligent teenager. 1966.

Strindberg (play). 1968.
Bernard Shaw: a reassessment. 1969.
Voyage to a beginning. 1969.
A casebook of murder. 1969.
Poetry and mysticism. 1970.
Lingard. 1970.
The strange genius of David Lindsay (jointly). 1970.
The occult. 1971.
New pathways in psychology. 1972.
Order of assassins. 1972.

WILSON, ETHEL (née BRYANT) (1890–)

Canadian novelist; born in South Africa; spent her early childhood in England; orphaned (1898) and went to live with relations in Vancouver; taught until her marriage (1920); a contributor to the *New Statesman* and many Canadian and American magazines.

Bibliography
Canadiana.
C.B.I.
Contemporary novelists.

Novels and Short Stories
Hetty Dorval. 1947.
The innocent traveller. 1949.
Equations of love (with Tuesday and Wednesday, and Lilly's story). 1952.
Swamp angel. 1954.
Love and salt water. 1956.
Mrs. Golighty and other stories. 1961.

Other Work
O Canada; an American's notes on Canadian culture. 1968.

WILSON, GUTHRIE EDWARD MELVILLE (†JOHN PAOLOTTI)

New Zealand novelist; educated at University College, Wellington; taught classics in New Zealand and Australia; a contributor to *Argosy* and the Australian and New Zealand broadcasting services.

Bibliography
Authors' and writers' who's who. 1971.
B.N.B.
N.Z. national bibliography.

Novels
Brave company. 1951.

Julien Ware. 1952.
The feared and the fearless. 1954.
Sweet white wine. 1956.
Strip Jack naked. 1957.
Dear Miranda. 1959.
The incorruptibles. 1960.
The return of the snow-white Puritan (as †John Paolotti). 1963.

WILSON, MITCHELL (†EMMETT HOGARTH) (1913–)

American novelist; educated at New York and Columbia universities; tutor in physics at Columbia University, later research physicist (1938–54); freelance writer since that date; a contributor to the *Observer*, *Nation*, etc.

Bibliography
C.B.I.
Contemporary novelists.
Gale.

Novels
The goose is cooked (with Abraham Polansky, as †Emmett Hogarth). 1940.
Footsteps behind her. 1941.
Stalk the hunter. 1943.
None so blind. 1945.
The panic stricken. 1946.
The Kimballs. 1947.
Live with lightning. 1949.
My brother, my enemy. 1952.
The lovers. 1954.
Meeting at a far meridian. 1961.
The huntress. 1966.
Passion to know. 1972.

Other Works
American science and invention. 1954.
The human body. 1959.
The body in action (edition of *The human body, for children*). 1962.
Energy (with the editors of *Life*). 1963.
See-saws and cosmic rays: a first view of physics. 1967.

WILSON, PATRICK SEYMOUR (1926–)

New Zealand poet; educated at Victoria University of Wellington and Trinity College of Music, London; lives in London; Senior Lecturer in Education, Goldsmiths' College (1968–); represented in various anthologies; a contributor to *Landfall*.

Bibliography
Contemporary poets.
Gale.
N.Z. national bibliography.

Poetry
The bright sea. 1951.
Staying at Ballisodare. 1960.

For Children
Tauranga adventure. 1963.

WILSON, SANDY (1924–)
English composer, lyric writer and playwright;
educated at Oriel College, Oxford; wrote lyrics
and words for many post-war musicals including
Valmouth (1959), Danny la Rue's *Charlie's aunt*
(1969).

Bibliography
B.N.B.
Who's who. 1973.

Works
This is Sylvia (illus. by the author). 1954.
The boy friend (illus. by the author, filmed 1971).
  1955.
Who's who for beginners. 1957.
Prince what shall I do? 1961.
The poodle from Rome. 1962.

WILSON, SLOAN (1920–)
American novelist; educated at Harvard Uni-
versity; served in the U.S. Coastguard during the
Second World War; journalist (1946–8); Assistant
Professor of English, Buffalo University (1952–5);
Assistant Director, White House conference on
education (1956); a contributor to *New Yorker*,
Harper's, *Life*, etc.

Bibliography
C.B.I.
Contemporary novelists.
Gale.

Novels
Voyage to somewhere. 1947.
The man in the grey flannel suit. 1955.
A summer place. 1958.
A sense of values. 1960.
Georgie Winthrop. 1963.
Janus Island. 1967.
All the best people. 1970.

Other Work
Away from it all. 1969.

WISDOM, *Professor* **ARTHUR JOHN
TERENCE DIBBEN** (1904–)
English philosopher; educated at Fitzwilliam
House, Cambridge; Lecturer in Moral Sciences,
later Fellow, Trinity College, Cambridge
(1934–68); Professor of Philosophy, Oregon University (1968–); a contributor to the *Proceedings
of the Aristotelian Society*, *Mind*, etc.

Bibliography
B.N.B.
Who's who. 1973.

Works
Other minds. 1952.
Philosophy and psycho-analysis. 1952.
Paradox and discovery. 1966.

WISEMAN, ADELE (1928–)
Canadian-Jewish novelist; born in Winnipeg; educated at the University of Manitoba; worked in the
Jewish Girls' Hospital, Stepney (1955–); recipient of several awards.

Bibliography
Canadiana.
C.B.I.
Contemporary novelists.

Novel
The sacrifice (Governor General's Award 1957).
  1956.

Other Work
Old markets, new world. 1964.

WOLFE, THOMAS KENNERLY, Jr.
(TOM WOLFE) (1931–)
American journalist; educated at Yale University;
reporter on *Springfield Union* (1956–9), *Washington
Post* (1959–62), *New York Magazine* (1962–); a
contributor to *Esquire*, *Harper's Bazaar*, etc.

Bibliography
C.B.I.
Gale.

Works
The kandy-kolored tangerine-flake streamline
  baby (essays). 1965.
Electric kool-aid acid test. 1968.

The mid-Atlantic man. 1968.
Radical chic and mau mauing the flake catchers.
  1970.
The regent stuff. 1973.

WOLFF, GEOFFREY ANSELL (1937–)
American novelist; born in Los Angeles; educated
at Princeton University and Churchill College,
Cambridge; Lecturer at Istanbul University
(1961–3); book editor, *Washington Post* (1964–9);
Lecturer in Baltimore and Washington (1965–9);
book editor, *Newsweek* (1969–); recipient of
Woodrow Wilson Fellowship (1961–2 and
1963–4) and Fulbright Scholar (1963–4); founder
of the literary magazine *Golden Horn* (1962); a contributor to *The Times, New Republic, Mademoiselle*,
etc.

Bibliography
C.B.I.
Gale.

Novels
Bad debts (original title, Worldly goods). 1969.
Lodos. 1974.
The sight see. 1974.

WOOD, CHARLES (1933–)
English dramatist; educated at Birmingham College of Art; served in the 17th/21st Lancers
(1950–5); works as a stage designer; recipient of
several awards; plays published in *New English
Dramatists* are *Cockade* (produced 1963) and *Fill up
the stage with happy hours* (staged 1966); his film
scripts include *The knack* (1965), *Help!* (1965), *The
charge of the Light Brigade* (1968) and *Fellini Satyricon*
(1969); radio and television plays include *Drums
along the Avon* (1961), *Prisoner and escort* (1962) and
A bit of vision (1972); only his separately published
plays are listed below.

Bibliography
B.N.B.
Contemporary dramatists.

Plays
Dingo. 1969.
H, being monologues at front of burning cities.
  1970.
Veterans. 1972.

WOODCOCK, GEORGE (1912–)
Canadian poet and writer; born in Winnipeg; spent
his childhood and early youth in England; returned

to Canada (1950); Lecturer in English, University
of British Columbia; editor of *Canadian Literature*;
became a full-time writer (1961); a contributor to
*Encounter, New Statesman, Tamarack Review, His-
tory Today*, etc.; his verse plays have been broadcast
on the Canadian radio; edited the letters of Charles
Lamb (1950).

Bibliography
Authors' and writers' who's who. 1971.
B.N.B.
Contemporary poets.
Gale.

Poetry
The white island. 1940.
The centre cannot hold verse. 1943.
Imagine the South. 1947.
Selected poems. 1967.

Other Works
New life to the land. 1942.
Anarchy and chaos. 1944.
William Godwin. 1946.
The incomparable Aphra. 1948.
The writer and politics. 1948.
The paradox of Oscar Wilde. 1950.
The anarchist prince, Peter Kropotkin. 1950.
Ravens and prophets (travel). 1956.
Pierre-Joseph Proudhon. 1956.
To the city of the dead (travel). 1957.
Incas and other men (travel). 1959.
Anarchism. 1962.
Faces of India (travel). 1964.
The Greeks in India. 1966.
Asia, gods and cities (travel). 1966.
The crystal spirit; a study of George Orwell
  (Governor General's Award 1967). 1966.
Kerala. 1967.
The Doukhobors. 1968.
Henry Walter Bates. 1969.

**WOODHOUSE, Hon. CHRISTOPHER
MONTAGUE** (1917–)
English writer and civil servant; son of 3rd Baron
Terrington; educated at Winchester, New College,
Oxford, and Grays Inn; served in the Second
World War (1939–43); Foreign Service in Athens
and Tehran and London (1945–52); Parliamentary
Secretary, Ministry of Aviation and Joint Under-
secretary, Home Office (1961–4), etc.; Fellow,
Trinity College, Cambridge (1950); a contributor
to journals and frequent broadcaster.

Bibliography
B.N.B.
Who's who. 1973.

Works
Apple of discord. 1948.
One omen. 1950.
Dostoievsky. 1951.
The Greek war of independence. 1952.
Britain and the Middle East. 1959.
British foreign policy since the Second World War.
    1961.
Rhodes (with J. G. Lockhart). 1963.
The new concert of nations. 1964.
The battle of Navarino. 1965.
Post-war Britain. 1966.
The story of modern Greece. 1968.
The Philhellenes. 1969.
The modern environment of classical studies.
    1970.
Capodistria: the founder of Greek independence.
    1973.

WOUK, HERMAN (1915–)
American novelist; educated at Columbia University; served in the U.S. Navy (1942–6) during the Second World War; gagman for radio comedians, scriptwriter, etc. (1934–41); freelance writer (1946–); Visiting Professor of English, Yeshiva University (1952–).

Bibliography
C.B.I.
Contemporary novelists.
Gale.
Who's who. 1973.

Novels
Aurora dawn, or The history of Andrew Peale.
    1947.
The city boy (filmed 1951). 1948.
The Caine mutiny (Pulitzer Prize 1952; produced
    as a play, filmed and published 1954). 1951.
Marjorie Morningstar (filmed 1958). 1955.
Youngblood Hawke (filmed 1963). 1962.
Don't stop the carnival. 1965.
Lomokome papers. 1968.
The winds of war. 1971.

Plays
The traitor. 1949.
The Caine mutiny court martial (from the novel).
    1954.
Nature's way (produced 1957). 1958.

Other Work
This is my god. 1959.

WREFORD, JAMES (WATSON, JAMES WREFORD) (1915–)
Scottish poet; born in north China; educated at Edinburgh University; taught at McMaster University and worked as government geographer in Ottawa (1939–44); returned to Edinburgh; his poetry appeared in *Unit of Five*, an anthology of modern Canadian poets; edited, with Ronald Miller, *Geographical essays in memory of Alan G. Ogilvie* (1959).

Bibliography
B.N.B.
C.B.I.

Poetry
Of time and the lover (Governor General's Award
    1951). 1950.

WRIGHT, JAMES ARLINGTON
(1927–)
American poet; educated at Kenyon College and the University of Seattle; currently English Instructor at Hunter College, New York; recipient of several fellowships and awards; a contributor to the *New Yorker*, *Hudson Review*, *Poetry*, Chicago, etc.; represented in numerous anthologies; his verse translations are Theodor Storm, *The rider on the white horse* (1964), *20 poems of Georg Trakl* (1963), *20 poems of Cesar Vallejo* (1964) and, with Robert Bly, *20 poems of Pablo Neruda* (1968).

Bibliography
C.B.I.
Contemporary poets.

Poetry
The green wall. 1957.
Saint Judas. 1959.
The branch will not break. 1963.
Shall we gather at the river. 1968.
Salt mines and such. 1971.

WRIGHT, JUDITH (Mrs. JUDITH ARUNDELL McKINNEY) (1915–)
Australian poet; educated at the University of Sydney; worked as a secretary (1938–46); part-time lecturer in Australian literature; awarded various academic honours by Queensland and New England universities, etc.; represented in

numerous anthologies; her edited works are not listed below.

Bibliography
Australian national bibliography.
Contemporary poets.
Gale.
Who's who. 1973.

Novels
The generations of men. 1959.
The nature of love (stories). 1966.

Poetry
The moving image. 1946.
Woman to man. 1949.
The gateway. 1953.
The two fires. 1956.
Birds. 1962.
Five senses. 1963.
Selected poems. 1963.
City sunrise. 1964.
The other half. 1966.
Collected poems 1942–1970. 1971.

For Children
Kings of the dingoes. 1959.
The day the mountains played. 1963.
Range the mountains high. 1963.
The river to the road. 1966.

Other Works
Charles Harpur (biography). 1963.
Country towns. 1964.
Preoccupations in Australian poetry. 1965.

WYMARK, OLWEN MARGARET
American playwright; widow of the actor Patrick Wymark; lives in London; unpublished plays include *No talking* (1970), *Speak now* (1971), *Tales from Whitechapel* (1972).

Bibliography
B.N.B.
Contemporary dramatists.

Plays
Three plays (Lunchtime concert, The inhabitants, Coda). 1967.
The gymnasium and other plays (The gymnasium, staged 1967; Technicians, staged 1969; Stay where you are, staged 1969; Neither here nor there, staged 1971; Jack the giant killer, staged 1972). 1972.

†WYNDHAM, JOHN (JOHN BENYON HARRIS) (1903–69)
English science fiction writer; educated at Bedales School; worked in farming, advertising and other occupations; a contributor to American pulp magazines during the twenties, thirties and forties.

Bibliography
B.N.B.
C.B.I.

Novels
The day of the Triffids (filmed 1962). 1951.
The Kraken wakes (American title, Out of the deeps). 1953.
The Chrysalids. 1955.
Re-birth. 1955.
The Midwich cuckoos (filmed as The village of the damned. 1960). 1957.
Outward urge (with Lucas Parkes). 1959.
Trouble with lichen. 1960.
Chocky. 1968.

Short Stories
Jizzle. 1954.
The seeds of time. 1956.
Consider her ways. 1961.

Y

YAFFE, JAMES (1927–)

American novelist; educated at Yale University; served in the U.S. Navy (1945–6); a contributor to *Atlantic Monthly*, *Saturday Review*, *Ellery Queen's Mystery Magazine*, etc.; author of various television plays.

Bibliography
C.B.I.
Contemporary novelists.
Gale.

Novels
Poor cousin Evelyn (stories). 1951.
The good-for-nothing. 1954.
Angry Uncle Dan. 1955.
What's the big hurry? 1956.
Nothing but the night. 1959.
Mister Margolies. 1962.
Nobody does you any favours. 1966.
The voyage of the *Franz Joseph*. 1970.

Plays
The deadly game. 1961.
Ivory tower. 1969.

Other Works
The American Jews. 1968.
Justice is for people: the story of a community court (English title, So sue me). 1972.

YATES, RICHARD (1926–)

American novelist; worked in advertising (1947–59); served in the U.S. Army (1944–6) during the Second World War; taught creative writing (1959–62); a contributor to *Esquire*, *Atlantic Monthly*, etc.; wrote the screenplay of William Styron's *Lie down in darkness* (1962); edited *Stories for the sixties* (1963).

Bibliography
C.B.I.
Contemporary novelists.
Gale.

Novels
Revolutionary road. 1961.
Eleven kinds of loneliness (stories). 1962.
A special providence. 1969.

YERBY, FRANK GARVIN (1916–)

American novelist; educated at Fisk and Chicago universities; instructor in English (1939–41); laboratory technician, etc. (1941–5); full-time writer since 1945; lives in Madrid; a contributor to *Collier's*, *Harper's*, etc.

Bibliography
C.B.I.
Contemporary novelists.
Gale.

Novels
The foxes of Harrow. 1946.
The vixens. 1947.
The golden hawk. 1948.
Pride's castle. 1949.
Floodtide. 1950.
The woman called Fancy. 1951.
The Saracen blade. 1952.
The devil's laughter. 1953.
Benton's Row. 1954.
Bride of liberty. 1954.
The treasure of Pleasant Valley. 1955.
Captain rebel. 1956.
Fairoaks. 1956.
The serpent and the staff. 1958.
Jarrett's jade. 1959.
Gillian. 1960.
The Garfield honour. 1961.
Griffin's way. 1962.
The old gods laugh. 1964.
An odour of sanctity. 1965.
Goat song: a novel of Ancient Greece. 1968.
Judas, my brother. 1968.
Speak now. 1969.
The man from Dahomey. 1971.
The girl from Storyville. 1972.

YOUNG, CHARLES KENNETH (1916–)

English biographer and journalist; educated at Leeds University; served in the Second World War (1939–45); B.B.C. (1948); journalist (1949–60); editor, *Yorkshire Post* (1960–4); broadcaster and editor of television series, the *Bookman*; political and literary adviser, Beaverbrook newspapers (1965–); edited the diaries of Sir Robert Bruce Lockhart, vol. I (1973).

Bibliography
B.N.B.
Who's who. 1973.

Works
D. H. Lawrence. 1952.
John Dryden. 1954.
Ford Madox Ford. 1956.
A. J. Balfour; authorised biography. 1963.
The press and the universities. 1964.
Churchill and Beaverbrook; a study in friendship and politics. 1966.
Rhodesia and independence; a study in British colonial policy. 1967.
Sir Compton Mackenzie; an essay. 1967.
Music's great days in the spas and watering-places. 1968.
The Greek passion: a study in people and politics. 1969.
Sir Alec Douglas-Home. 1970.
Chapel. 1972.
H. G. Wells, an essay. 1973.

YOUNG, DOUGLAS CUTHBERT COLQUHOUN (1913–)

Scottish poet; educated at the University of St. Andrews and New College, Oxford; Senior Lecturer in Greek, St. Andrews (1947–); Visiting Professor, Minnesota University (1963–4); Professor of Greek, University of North Carolina (1970–); his edited work is not listed below.

Bibliography
B.N.B.
Contemporary poets.
Gale.

Poetry
Auntran blads. 1944.
A braird o thristles. 1948.
Chasing an Ancient Greek, selected poems. 1950.
The puddocks (Scots verse translation of Aristophanes). 1958.
The burdies (Scots verse translation of Aristophanes) (pr. ptd.). 1959.

Other Works
Edinburgh in the age of Sir Walter Scott. 1965.
Edinburgh in the age of reason. 1967.
St. Andrews: town and gown, royal and ancient. 1969.
Scotland. 1971.

YOUNG, WAYLAND HILTON (*2nd Baron* KENNET) (1923–)

English political writer; educated at Stowe School and Trinity College, Cambridge; served in the Royal Navy in the Second World War (1942–5); Foreign Office (1946–51); Parliamentary Secretary, Ministry of Housing and Local Government (1966–70); editor of *Disarmament and Arms Control* (1962–5); a contributor to *Encounter, Observer, Guardian, Tribune,* etc.

Bibliography
Authors' and writers' who's who. 1971.
B.N.B.
Who's who. 1973.

Works
The Italian left. 1949.
The deadweight. 1952.
Now or never. 1953.
Old London churches (with Elizabeth Young). 1956.
The Montesi scandal. 1957.
Still alive tomorrow. 1958.
Strategy for survival. 1959.
The socialist imagination (with Elizabeth Young). 1960.
Disarmament: Finnegan's choice (with Elizabeth Young). 1961.
The Profumo affair. 1963.
Bombs and votes. 1964.
Eros denied. 1965.
Thirty-four articles. 1965.
Existing mechanisms of arms control (ed.). 1965.
Controlling our environment. 1970.
Preservation (as Wayland Kennet). 1972.

Z

ZAKARIA, *Dr.* **RAFIQ** (1920–)
Indian writer and journalist; born in Sopara, Thana District, Maharashtra; educated at Bombay and London universities and Lincoln's Inn; chairman of the Maulana Azad Educational Trust and founder of the Maulana Azad College of Arts, Science and Commerce, Aurangabad; India's representative to the General Assembly of the United Nations (1965); Chancellor of the Jamia Urdu of Aligarh (1973); Minister in Government of Maharashtra (1964).

Bibliography
C.B.I.
Indian national bibliography 1958–67.
National bibliography of Indian literature 1901–53.

Works
A study of Nehru. n.d.
Razia—Queen of India (historical biography). n.d.
Rise of Muslims in Indian politics. n.d.

ZINDEL, PAUL (1936–)
American novelist and playwright; taught chemistry (1960–9); recipient of various awards; unpublished plays include *Dimensions of peacocks* (1959), *A dream of swallows* (1962) and *The secret affairs of Mildrid Wild* (1972); film *Up the sandbox* (1973).

Bibliography
C.B.I.
Contemporary dramatists.

Novels
The pigman. 1968.
My darling, my hamburger. 1969.
I never loved your mind. 1970.

Plays
The effects of gamma rays on man-in-the-moon marigolds (staged 1965, filmed 1972). 1971.
And Miss Reardon drinks a little (staged 1967). 1972.

ZINSSER, WILLIAM KNOWLTON (1922–)
American humorist and social critic; educated at Princeton University; served in the U.S. Air Force during the Second World War (1943–5); *New York Herald Tribune* (1946–59); freelance writer (1959–); television commentator (1964–5); a contributor to *Look, Life Magazine*, etc.

Bibliography
C.B.I.
Gale.

Works
Any old place with you. 1957.
Seen any good movies lately? (English title, Seen any good films lately?). 1958.
Search and research. 1961.
The city dwellers. 1962.
Five boyhoods (co-author). 1962.
Weekend guests. 1963.
The haircurl papers. 1964.
Pop goes to America. 1966.
The paradise bit. 1967.
The lunacy boom. 1970.

ZUKOFSKY, LOUIS (1904–)
American poet and writer; born in New York; educated at Columbia University; Associate Professor of English, Polytechnic Institute of Brooklyn (1947–); edited Catullus (1969).

Bibliography
C.B.I.
Contemporary poets.
Gale.
L. of C.

Poetry
Some time. 1956.
All: it was. 1961.
The collected short poems (1923–1958). 1965.
All: the collected short poems 1956–1964. 1966.
Ferdinand (with It was). 1968.
Little. 1970.
A twenty-four. 1972.
Arise, arise. 1973.

Other Works
A test of poetry. 1948.
Bottom: on Shakespeare (music by Celia Zukofsky). 2 vols. 1963.
Propositions: the collected critical essays. 1967.
Autobiography. 1970.

Select list of
literary prizes and awards,
with their winners, 1940–73

THE BOOKER PRIZE FOR FICTION (Founded 1968)
Given for a novel in English published in the United Kingdom.

1969. P. H. Newby: Something to answer for (q.v.).
1970. Bernice Rubens: The elected member (q.v.).
1971. V. S. Naipaul: In a free state (q.v.).
1972. John Berger: G (q.v.).
1973. J. G. Farrell: The siege of Krishnapur (q.v.).

GOVERNOR GENERAL'S AWARD (Founded 1936)
In 1959 the original categories were revised into prizes for drama and poetry; fiction and drama; non-fiction. Only the English-language winners in the first categories are listed below.

Fiction
1940. Franklin D. McDowell: The Champlain road.
1941. Ringuet: Thirty acres.
1942. Alan Sullivan: Three came to Ville Marie.
1943. Herbert Sallans: Little man.
1944. Thomas H. Randall: The pied piper of Dipper Creek.
1945. Gwethalyn Graham: Earth and high.
1946. Hugh MacLennan: Two solitudes (q.v.).
1947. Winifred Bambrick: Continental revue.
1948. Gabrielle Roy: The tin flute.
1949. Hugh MacLennan: The precipice (q.v.).
1950. Philip Child: Mr. Ames against time.
1951. Germaine Guèvrement: The outlander.
1952. Morley Callaghan: The lived and the lost.
1953. David Walker: The pillar (q.v.).
1954. David Walker: Digby (q.v.).
1955. Igor Gouzenko: The fall of Titan.
1956. Lionel Shapiro: The sixth of June.
1957. Adele Wiseman: The sacrifice (q.v.).
1958. Gabrielle Roy: Street of riches.

1959. Colin McDougall: Executive.
1960. Hugh MacLennan: The watch that ends the night (q.v.).
1961. Brian Moore: The luck of Ginger Coffey (q.v.).
1962. Malcolm Lowry: Hear us O Lord.
1963. Kildare Dobbs: Running to paradise.
1964. Hugh Garner: Hugh Garner's best stories (q.v.).
1965. Douglas Lepan: The deserter (q.v.).
1966. No English award.
1967. Margaret Laurence: A jest of God (q.v.).
George Woodcock: The crystal spirit (q.v.).
1968. Eli Mandel: An idiot joy (q.v.).
Alden Nowlan: Bread, wine and salt (q.v.).
1969. Alice Munro: Dance of the happy shades (q.v.).
Mordecai Richler: Cocksure, and Hunting tigers under glass (q.v.).

Poetry

1940.	Arthur S. Bourinot: Under the sun.
1941.	E. J. Pratt: Brebeuf and his brethren.
1942.	Anne Marriott: Calling adventures.
1943.	Earle Birney: David and other poems.
1944.	A. J. M. Smith: News of the Phoenix.
1945.	Dorothy Livesay: Day and night.
1946.	Earle Birney: Now is time.
1947.	Robert Finch: Poems.
1948.	Dorothy Livesay: Poems for people.
1949.	A. M. Klein: The rocking chair and other poems (q.v.).
1950.	James Reaney: The red heart and other poems (q.v.).
1951.	James Wreford: Of time and the lover (q.v.).
1952.	Charles Bruce: The Mulgrave road.
1953.	E. J. Pratt: The last spike.
1954.	Douglas Lepan: The net and the sword (q.v.).
1955.	P. K. Page: The metal and the flower (q.v.).
1956.	Wilfred Watson: Friday's child (q.v.).
1957.	R. A. D. Ford: A window on the north (q.v.).
1958.	Jay Macpherson: The boatman (q.v.).
1959.	James Reaney: A suit of nettles (q.v.).
1960.	Irving Layton: A red carpet for the sun (q.v.).
1961.	Margaret Avison: Winter sun (q.v.).
1962.	Robert Finch: Acis in Oxford.
1963.	James Reaney: Twelve letters to a small town; the kill deer and other plays (q.v.).
1964.	No English award.
1965.	Raymond Souster: The colour of the times (q.v.).
1966.	Alfred Purdy: The Cariboo horses (q.v.).
1967.	Margaret Atwood: The circle game (q.v.).

THE HAWTHORNDEN PRIZE (Founded 1919)

Given for a work of imaginative literature to an English writer under 41 years of age. This can include biography.

1940.	James Pope-Hennessy: London fabric (q.v.).
1941.	Graham Greene: The power and the glory.
1942.	John Llewelyn Rhys: England is my village.
1943.	Sidney Keyes: The cruel solstice, and The iron laurel (q.v.).
1944.	Martyn Skinner: Letters to Malaya.
1945–57.	No awards.
1958.	Dom Moraes: A beginning (q.v.).
1959.	Emyr Owen Humphreys: A toy epic (q.v.)..
1960.	Alan Sillitoe: The loneliness of the long distance runner (q.v.).
1961.	Ted Hughes: Lupercal (q.v.).
1962.	Robert Shaw: The sun doctor (q.v.).
1963.	No award.
1964.	V. S. Naipaul: Mr. Stone and the knight's companion (q.v.).
1965.	William Trevor: The old boys (q.v.).
1966.	No award.
1967.	Michael Frayn: The Russian interpreter (q.v.).
1968.	Michael Levey: Early Renaissance (q.v.).
1969.	No award.
1970.	Geoffrey Hill: King Log (q.v.). Piers Paul Read: Monk Dawson (q.v.).

JAMES TAIT BLACK MEMORIAL PRIZE FOR FICTION (Founded 1918)

Given for the best novel in English published in the preceding year. There is also a James Tait Black Prize for biography (not listed below).

1940.	Aldous Huxley: After many a summer.
1941.	Charles Morgan: The voyage.
1942.	Joyce Cary: A house of children.
1943.	Arthur Waley: Translation of Monkey by Wu Ch'eng-en.
1944.	Mary Lavin: Tales from Bective Bridge (q.v.).
1945.	Forrest Reid: Young Tom.
1946.	L. A. G. Strong: Travellers.
1947.	Oliver Onions: Poor man's tapestry.
1948.	L. P. Hartley: Eustace and Hilda.
1949.	Graham Greene: The heart of the matter.
1950.	Emma Smith: The far cry (q.v.).
1951.	Robert Henriques: Through the valley.
1952.	W. C. Chapman-Mortimer: Father Goose.
1953.	Evelyn Waugh: Men at arms.
1954.	Margaret Kennedy: Troy chimneys.
1955.	C. P. Snow: The new men, and The masters.

1956.	Ivy Compton-Burnett: Mother and son.	1966.	Muriel Spark: The Mandelbaum gate (q.v.).
1957.	Rose Macaulay: The towers of Trebizond.	1967.	Christine Brooke-Rose: Such (q.v.).
1958.	Anthony Powell: At Lady Molly's.		Aidan Higgins: Langrishe, go down (q.v.).
1959.	Angus Wilson: The middle age of Mrs. Eliot (q.v.).	1968.	Margaret Drabble: Jerusalem the golden (q.v.).
1960.	Morris West: The devil's advocate (q.v.).	1969.	Maggie Ross: The gasteropod (q.v.).
1961.	Rex Warner: Imperial Caesar.	1970.	Elizabeth Bowen: Eva Trout.
1962.	Jennifer Dawson: The ha-ha (q.v.).	1971.	Lily Powell: The bird of paradise.
1963.	Ronald Hardy: Act of destruction (q.v.).	1972.	Nadine Gordimer: A guest of honour (q.v.).
1964.	Gerda Charles: A slanting light (q.v.).		
1965.	Frank Tuohy: The ice saints (q.v.).	1973.	John Berger: G (q.v.).

JOHN LLEWELYN RHYS MEMORIAL PRIZE (Founded 1940)

Given for a "memorable work" by a British or Commonwealth writer under 30 years of age.

1942.	Michael Richey: Sunk by a mine.	1959.	Dan Jacobson: A long way from London (q.v.).
1943.	Morwenna Donelly: Beauty from ashes.		
1944.	Alun Lewis: The last inspection (q.v.).	1960.	David Caute: At fever pitch (q.v.).
1945.	James Aldridge: The sea eagle (q.v.).	1961.	David Storey: Flight into Camden (q.v.).
1946.	Oriel Malet: My bird sings.	1962.	Robert Rhodes James: An introduction to the House of Commons (q.v.).
1947.	Anne-Marie Walters: Moondrop to Gascony.		Edward Lucie-Smith: A tropical childhood and other poems (q.v.).
1948.	Richard Mason: The wind cannot read (q.v.).	1963.	Peter Marshall: Two lives.
1949.	Emma Smith: Maiden's trip (q.v.).	1964.	Nell Dunn: Up the junction (q.v.).
1950.	Kenneth Allsop: Adventure lit their star (q.v.).	1965.	Julian Mitchell: The white father (q.v.).
		1966.	Margaret Drabble: The millstone (q.v.).
1951.	E. J. Howard: The beautiful visit (q.v.).	1967.	Anthony Masters: The Seahorse (q.v.).
1952.	No award.	1968.	Angela Carter: The magic toyshop (q.v.).
1953.	Rachel Trickett: The return home (q.v.).	1969.	Melvyn Bragg: Without a city wall (q.v.).
1954.	Tom Stacey: The hostile sun (q.v.).	1970.	Angus Calder: The people's war: Britain 1939–45 (q.v.).
1955.	John Wiles: The moon to play with (q.v.).		
1956.	John Hearne: Voices under the window (q.v.).	1971.	Shiva Naipaul: Fireflies.
		1972.	Susan Hill: The albatross (q.v.).
1957.	Ruskin Bond: The room on the roof (q.v.).	1973.	Peter Smalley: Warm gun.
1958.	V. S. Naipaul: The mystic masseur (q.v.).		

PULITZER PRIZES (Founded 1917)

There are six prizes for a published work by an American author of drama, fiction, poetry, history, biography and one for a book not covered by the preceding categories.

Pulitzer Prize for Drama

1940.	William Saroyan: The time of your life.	1947.	No award.
1941.	Robert E. Sherwood: There shall be no light.	1948.	Tennessee Williams: A streetcar named Desire (q.v.).
1942.	No award.	1949.	Arthur Miller: Death of a salesman (q.v.).
1943.	Thornton Wilder: The skin of our teeth.	1950.	Richard Rodgers, Oscar Hammerstein II and Joshua Logan: South Pacific.
1944.	No award.		
1945.	Mary Chase: Harvey.	1951.	No award.
1946.	Russel Crouse and Howard Lindsay: State of the union.	1952.	Joseph Kramm: The shrike (q.v.).
		1953.	William Inge: Picnic (q.v.).

1954. John Patrick: The teahouse of the August moon (q.v.).
1955. Tennessee Williams: Cat on a hot tin roof (q.v.).
1956. Albert Jackett and Frances Goodrich: Diary of Anne Frank.
1957. Eugene O'Neill: Long day's journey into night.
1958. Ketti Frings: Look homeward, angel.
1959. Archibald MacLeish: J.B.
1960. Jerome Weidman and George Abbott: Fiorelli! (music by Jerry Bock).
1961. Tad Mosel: All the way home (q.v.).

1962. Frank Loesser and Abe Burrows: How to succeed in business without really trying.
1963. No award.
1964. No award.
1965. Frank D. Gilroy: The subject was roses (q.v.).
1966. No award.
1967. Edward Albee: A delicate balance (q.v.).
1968. No award.
1969. Howard Sackler: The great white hope.
1970. Charles Gordone: No place to be somebody.

Pulitzer Prize for Fiction

1940. John Steinbeck: The grapes of wrath.
1941. No award.
1942. Ellen Glasgow: In this our life.
1943. Upton Sinclair: Dragon's teeth.
1944. Martin Flavin: Journey in the dark.
1945. John Hersey: A bell for Adano (q.v.).
1946. No award.
1947. Robert Penn Warren: All the king's men.
1948. James A. Michener: Tales of the South Pacific (q.v.).
1949. James Gould Cozzens: Guard of honor.
1950. A. B. Guthrie, Jr.: The way west (q.v.).
1951. Conrad Richter: The town.
1952. Herman Wouk: The Caine mutiny (q.v.).
1953. Ernest Hemingway: The old man and the sea.
1954. No award.
1955. William Faulkner: A fable.
1956. MacKinlay Kantor: Andersonville.
1957. No award.

1958. James Agee: A death in the family.
1959. Robert Lewis Taylor: The travels of Jaimie McPheeters.
1960. Allen Drury: Advise and consent (q.v.).
1961. Harper Lee: To kill a mockingbird (q.v.).
1962. Edwin O'Connor: The edge of sadness (q.v.).
1963. William Faulkner: The Reivers.
1964. No award.
1965. Shirley Ann Grau: The keepers of the house (q.v.).
1966. Katherine Anne Porter: The collected stories of Katherine Anne Porter.
1967. Bernard Malamud: The fixer (q.v.).
1968. William Styron: The confessions of Nat Turner (q.v.).
1969. N. Scott Momaday: House made of dawn (q.v.).
1970. Jean Stafford: Collected stories (q.v.).

Pulitzer Prize for Poetry

1940. Mark van Doren: Collected poems.
1941. Leonard Bacon: Sunderland capture.
1942. William Rose Benet: The dust which is God.
1943. Robert Frost: A witness tree.
1944. Stephen Vincent Benet: Western star.
1945. Karl Shapiro: V-letter and other poems.
1946. No award.
1947. Robert Lowell: Lord Weary's castle (q.v.).
1948. W. H. Auden: The age of anxiety.
1949. Peter Viereck: Terror and decorum (q.v.).
1950. Gwendolyn Brooks: Annie Allen (q.v.).
1951. Carl Sandburg: Complete poems.

1952. Marianne Moore: Collected poems.
1953. Archibald MacLeish: Collected poems 1917–1952.
1954. Theodore Roethke: The waking (q.v.).
1955. Wallace Stevens: Collected poems.
1956. Elizabeth Bishop: Poems—north and south (q.v.).
1957. Richard Wilbur: Things of this world (q.v.).
1958. Robert Penn Warren: Promises: Poems 1954–1956.
1959. Stanley Kunitz: Selected poems: 1918–1958.

1960. W. D. Snodgrass: Heart's needle (q.v.).
1961. Phyllis McGinley: Times three: selected verse from three decades.
1962. Alan Dugan: Poems (q.v.).
1963. William Carlos Williams: Pictures from Breughel.
1964. Louis Simpson: At the end of the open road (q.v.).

1965. John Berryman: 77 dream songs (q.v.).
1966. Richard Eberhart: Selected poems 1930–1965.
1967. Anne Sexton: Live or die (q.v.).
1968. Anthony Hecht: The hard hours (q.v.).
1969. George Oppen: Of being numerous.
1970. Richard Howard: Untitled subjects: poems (q.v.).

SOMERSET MAUGHAM AWARD (Founded 1946)

Founded by Somerset Maugham to encourage young writers to travel. It is given to a promising author residing in Britain and under 35 years of age for a published work in the field of poetry, fiction, criticism, biography, history, philosophy, belles-lettres, or travel.

1947. A. L. Barker: Innocents (q.v.).
1948. P. H. Newby: A journey to the interior (q.v.).
1949. Hamish Henderson: Elegies for the dead in Cyrenaica.
1950. Nigel Kneale: Tomato Cain and other stories.
1951. Roland Camberton: Scamp.
1952. Francis King: The dividing stream (q.v.).
1953. Emyr Humphreys: Hear and forgive (q.v.).
1954. Doris Lessing: Five short novels (q.v.).
1955. Kingsley Amis: Lucky Jim (q.v.).
1956. Elizabeth Jennings: A way of looking (q.v.).
1957. George Lamming: In the castle of my skin (q.v.).
1958. John Wain: Preliminary essays (q.v.).
1959. Thom Gunn: The sense of movement (q.v.).

1960. Ted Hughes: The hawk in the rain (q.v.).
1961. V. S. Naipaul: Miguel Street (q.v.).
1962. Hugh Thomas: The Spanish civil war (q.v.).
1963. David Storey: Flight into Camden (q.v.).
1964. Dan Jacobson: Time of arrival (q.v.).
1965. Peter Everett: Negatives.
1966. Michael Frayn: The tin men (q.v.).
      Julian Mitchell: The white father (q.v.).
1967. B. S. Johnson: Trawl (q.v.).
      Andrew Sinclair: The better half (q.v.).
1968. Paul Bailey: At the Jerusalem.
      Seamus Heaney: Death of a naturalist (q.v.).
1969. Angela Carter: Several perceptions (q.v.).
1970. Jane Gaskell: A sweet, sweet summer (q.v.).
      Piers Paul Read: Monk Dawson (q.v.).

Select list of critical and literary journals and little magazines

SOURCE: *Ulrich's International Periodicals Directory*, 14th ed. 2 vols. New York, Bowker. 1971–2

AFRICAN

African Literature Today: a journal of explanatory criticism. Association of African literature in English bulletin (1968)
Annual..

Okyeame (1961)
A Ghanaian literary magazine issued half-yearly.

Transition (1961)
A Ghanaian magazine issued every 2 months.

Zuka: a journal of East African creative writing (1967)
A Ghanaian journal in English and Swahili.

AMERICAN

Ajax (1916)
An international monthly of poetry, literature and criticism.

American poetry: the voice of the American Poets Fellowship Society (1963)
Quarterly.

Arlington Quarterly: a journal of literature, comment and opinion (1967)

Atlantic Monthly (1968)

Brown Paper: an occasional magazine of poetry (1966)

California Review (1967)
Irregular.

Chelsea: a magazine of poetry, plays, stories and translations (1958)

Chicago Review (1946)
Quarterly.

Consumption: a magazine of the living arts (1967)

Contemporary Literature (1960)
Quarterly, formerly *Wisconsin Studies in Contemporary Literature*.

Evergreen Review (1957)
Monthly.

Field: contemporary poetry and poetics (1970)
Twice yearly.

Fragments: a literary magazine, Seattle, Department of English (1957)

Freelance: a magazine of poetry and prose (1952)
Fortnightly.

Gambit (1968)
Quarterly.

Harper's (1850)
Quarterly.

Kenyon Review (1939)
Quarterly.

Left
Monthly, formerly *Focus*.

Little Magazine (1966)
Biennial, formerly *Quest*.

Massachusetts Review (1962)
Quarterly.

Michigan Quarterly Review (1962)

Minnesota Review (1960)
Quarterly.

Motive (1941)
Monthly.

Nation (1865)
Monthly.

New England Review (1969)
Fortnightly.

New Yorker (1925)
Weekly.

Notes on Contemporary Literature (1971)
Quarterly.

Paper (1965)
Fortnightly, underground magazine.

Perspective (1947)
3 or 4 times a year.

Poetry, Chicago (1912)
Monthly.

Rat (1968)
Fortnightly underground magazine of the Women's Liberation Movement.

Seventies (1958)
Irregular, a magazine of poetry and opinion, formerly *Sixties*.

Virginia Quarterly Review (1925)
A national journal of literature and discussion.

Yale Review (1911)
Quarterly.

AUSTRALIAN

Crosscurrents: recent Australian poetry (1968)
Quarterly.

Meanjin Quarterly (1940)
Issued from Melbourne University.

Poetry Australia (1964)
Every 2 months.

Twentieth Century (1947)
A quarterly review.

BRITISH

Agenda (1959)
A poetry quarterly.

Akros (1965)
A poetry quarterly.

Ambit (1959)
A quarterly of poems, short stories, drawings and criticism.

Approach magazine (1965)
A quarterly edited from St. Peter's College, Oxford.

Blackwood's (1817)
A quarterly of short stories.

Breakthru, international poetry magazine (1961)
Three times a year.

Carcanet (1961)
Three times a year.

Critical Quarterly (1959)

Critical Survey (1962)
Issued twice a year by the University of Manchester.

English (1935)
Quarterly journal of the English Association.

English Literature, Criticism, Teaching (1906)
Quarterly of the English Association.

Envoi (1957)
A poetry magazine, twice a year.

Essays in Criticism
Quarterly journal of literary criticism.

Format (1966)
A poetry quarterly.

Imprint (1967)
A half-yearly poetry magazine.

Journal of Commonwealth Literature (1966)
Half-yearly, published by the University of Leeds.

London Magazine (1954)
Monthly literary miscellany.

New Departures: an international review of literature and the lively arts (1959)
Half-yearly, published and edited by Michael Horovitz.

The New Statesman (1913)
Weekly.

Oz (1967)
A monthly of the underground.

Poetry Review (1909)
The quarterly journal of the Poetry Society.

Priapus (1962)
A poetry journal, issued 3 times a year.

Private Eye (1961)
Fortnightly, a magazine of wit and humour.

SELECT LIST OF CRITICAL AND LITERARY JOURNALS

Punch (1841)
Weekly, of wit and humour.

Quill Magazine (1963)
A quarterly of letters and poems.

Review: a magazine of poetry and criticism
Quarterly.

Rumpus (1968)
A poetry magazine issued 2 or 3 times a year by
University College, Swansea.

Scrip (1962)
A poetry quarterly.

Tagus (1970)
A poetry magazine superseding *Wen Three*.

T.L.S.: The Times Literary Supplement (1902)
A weekly of book reviews.

Transatlantic Review (1959)

Workshop: a magazine of new poetry (1967)

CANADIAN

Alphabet (absorbed the *Waterloo Review* 1961)
edited by James Reaney, devoted to the iconography of the imagination.

Ariel: a Review of English Literature (1960)

Canadian Forum (1920)

Canadian Literature/Littérature Canadienne (1959)
A quarterly of criticism and review.

Dalhousie Review (1921)
A quarterly of literature and opinion.

Fiddlehead (1945)
Literary quarterly.

Hudson Review (1948)
Quarterly.

Queen's Quarterly (1893)
Issued from Kingston, Ontario.

Tamarack Review (1956)
Quarterly.

CARIBBEAN

Bim
A literary magazine issued from Barbados every 2
years.

Caribbean Quarterly (1949)
Issued by the University of the West Indies.

Expression (1966)
A magazine of creative writing from the Caribbean, issued in Guyana.

Kyk-over-al

INDIAN

Indian Writing Today (1967)
Quarterly.

Mira (1933)
Monthly.

Miscellany (formerly *Writers' Workshop Miscellany*)
Every 2 months.

Transition (1967)
Quarterly.

NEW ZEALAND

Arena: a literary magazine (1943)
Quarterly.

Landfall (1947)
Quarterly.

Geographical – chronological index to authors

COMPILED JENNY DRUMMOND

AMERICA

351

AUSTRALIA

1911 Mudie, Ian
1911 Porter, Hal
1911 Waten, Judah
1912 Johnston, George
1912 Robinson, Roland (b. Ireland)
1913 Greenwood, Gordon
1914 Cowan, Peter
1915 Auchterlounie, Dorothy (b. England)
1915 Campbell, David
1915 Clark, Manning
1915 Manifold, John
1915 Wright, Judith
1916 Brickhill, Paul
1916 Stewart, Harold
1916 Turner, George
1916 West, Morris
1917 Cato, Nancy
1917 Cleary, Jon
1917 Iggulden, J. M.

1917 McAuley, James
1918 Aldridge, James
1919 Boyd, Robin
1920 Dobson, Rosemary
1920 Thiele, Colin
1921 Braddon, Russell
1921 Harris, Max
1921 Horne, Donald
1921 Lambert, Eric (b. England)
1921 Lawler, Ray
1921 Macdonald, Nan
1922 Barry, Clive
1922 Dutton, Geoffrey
1923 Glaskin, G. M.
1923 Keesing, Nancy
1924 Rowbotham, David
1925 Astley, Thea
1925 Buckley, Vincent
1927 Osborne, Charles
1927 Watson, George

1928 Beaver, Bruce
1928 Brissenden, R. F.
1928 Harrower, Elizabeth
1928 Spence, Eleanor
1929 Cook, Ken
1929 Gaskin, Catherine (b. Ireland)
1929 Mathew, Ray
1929 Porter, Peter
1929 Simpson, R. A.
1931 Hazzard, Shirley
1931 Oakley, B. K.
1935 Hall, Rodney (b. England)
1935 Keneally, Thomas
1935 Shapcott, Thomas
1935 Stow, Randolph
1938 Murray, L. A.
1939 Baxter, John
1939 Greer, Germaine

BARBADOS

1893 Collymore, Frank
1924 Drayton, Geoffrey

1927 Lamming, George
1930 Braithwaite, Edward

1934 Clarke, Austin C.
1934 Kizerman, Rudolph

CAMEROON

1936 Dipoko, Mbella Sonne

CANADA

1871 Carr, Emily
1885 Costain, T. B.
1890 Wilson, Ethel
1899 Scott, F. R.
1901 Hutchison, Bruce
1902 Daniells, Roy
1902 O'Hagan, Howard
1907 McCourt, Edward
1907 MacLennan, Hugh
1908 Buckler, Ernest
1908 Klinck, Carl
1908 Ross, Sinclair
1909 Klein, A. M.
1909 Saunders, Thomas
1910 Wilkinson, Anne
1911 McLuhan, Marshall
1911 Potts, Paul
1911 Ross, Malcolm

1911 Walker, David (b. Scotland)
1911 Watson, Wilfred
1912 Frye, Northrup
1912 Layton, Peter
1912 Marlyn, John (b. Hungary)
1912 Woodcock, George
1913 Allen, Ralph
1913 Davies, Robertson
1913 Garner, Hugh
1913 Johnston, George
1914 Cornish, John
1914 Lepan, Douglas
1914 Mitchell, W. O.
1915 Ford, R. A. D.
1916 Bissell, C. T.
1916 Page, P. K. (b.

England)
1917 Cogswell, Fred
1917 Hambleton, Ronald (b. England)
1917 Pacey, Desmond (b. New Zealand)
1917 Peterson, Len
1917 Waddington, Miriam
1918 Avison, Margaret
1918 Purdy, A. W.
1919 Nicol, Eric
1919 Watson, Sheila
1920 Berton, Pierre
1920 Hailey, Arthur (b. England)
1920 Miller, Peter
1921 Moore, Brian (b. Ireland)

354

CHINA

CYPRUS

DENMARK

ENGLAND

1936	Dunn, Nell	1939	Harwood, Lee	1947	Glyn, Caroline
1936	Gilbert, Martin	1939	Hunter, Jim	1947	Hare, David
1936	†Gray, Simon	1939	Waugh, Auberon	n.d.	†Charles, Gerda
1936	Halliwell, David	1940	Carter, Angela	n.d.	Dawson, Jennifer
1936	Rudkin, David	1940	Lennon, John	n.d.	Erskine-Lindop,
1936	Spurling, John	1940	Pinner, David		Audrey
1937	Fuller, John	1941	Crossley-Holland,	n.d.	Figes, Eva (b.
1937	McGough, Roger		Kevin		Germany)
1937	Selbourne, David	1941	†Ellis, Royston	n.d.	Garland, Patrick
1937	Stoppard, Tom	1941	Gaskell, Jane	n.d.	Harling, Robert
1937	Warner, Francis	1941	Read, P.P.	n.d.	Lejeune, C. A.
1938	Benedictus, David	1941	Williams, Heathcote	n.d.	Masters, Anthony
1938	Horovitz, Frances	1942	Bingham, Charlotte	n.d.	Norton, Mary
1939	Ayckbourn, Alan	1942	Hill, Susan	n.d.	Pearce, Philippa
1939	Bragg, Melvyn	1943	Bold, Alan	n.d.	Ross, Maggie
1939	Delaney, Shelagh	1946	Hampton, Christopher	n.d.	Stirling, Monica
1939	Drabble, Margaret	1946	Pickard, Tom	n.d.	Tonks, Rosemary
1939	Frost, David	1946	Rosen, Michael	n.d.	White, Alan

FINLAND

1908	Waltari, Mika	1934	Hollo, Anselm

GAMBIA

1932	Peters, Lenri

GHANA

1909	Nkrumah, Kwame	1935	Awoonor, Kofi	n.d.	Brew, Kwesi
1924	Sutherland, Efua	1938	Armah, Ayi Kwei	n.d.	De Graft, John
1927	Selormey, Francis	1942	Aidoo, Ama Ata	n.d.	Duodo, Cameron
1932	Konadu, Asare	n.d.	Abruquah, Joseph	n.d.	Okai, John
1932	Parkes, F.K.	n.d.	Asare, Bediakoi		

GREECE

1909	Trypanis, Constantine	1926	Cicellis, Kay

GUYANA

1909	Mittelholzer, Edgar	1925	Carew, Jan	1930	Nicole, Christopher
1912	Braithwaite, E.R.	1925	Goveia, Elsa	1934	Dathorne, Ronald
1921	Harris, Wilson	1927	Carter, Martin	n.d.	Williams, Denis

HUNGARY

1891	Polanyi, Michael	1912	Mikes, George

INDIA

IRELAND

ISRAEL

JAMAICA

JAPAN

KENYA

1909 Desani, G. V.	1930 Ogot, Grace	1938 Ngugi, James

LIBERIA

n.d.   Dempster, Ronald

MALAWI

1930 Rubadiri, David	n.d. Kayira, Legson

NEW ZEALAND

1897 Alley, Rewi	1920 Alexander, Colin James	1926 McEldowney, Dennis
1907 Sutch, W. B.	(b. England)	1926 Wilson, Pat
1908 Ashton, Warner	1920 De Mauny, Erik (b.	1928 Doyle, C. (b. England)
1910 Dowling, Basil	England)	1929 Hilliard, Noel
1910 Spear, Charles	1922 Duggan, Maurice	1930 Leeming, Owen
1913 Davin, Dan	1922 Pearson, Bill	1932 Shadbold, Maurice
1913 France, Ruth	1922 Sinclair, Keith	1932 Stead, C. K.
1913 Shaw, Helen	1922 Smithyman, Kendrick	1934 Adcock, Fleur
1914 Joseph, M. K. (b.	1924 Ballantyne, David	1935 Crump, Barry
England)	1924 Brathwaite, E. F.	1935 Weir, J. E.
1914 Vogt, Anton	1924 Frame, Janet	1936 Billing, Graham
1916 Cole, J. R.	1924 Johnson, Louis	1936 Cowley, C. J.
1916 Reid, J. C.	1925 Campbell, Alistair	1937 O'Sullivan, Vincent
1917 Gilbert, Ruth	1925 Cross, Ian	n.d. Audley, E. H.
1919 Alpers, Antony	1925 Middleton, O. E.	n.d. Towhare, Hone
1919 Dallas, Ruth	1925 Oliver, W. H.	n.d. Wilson, Guthrie
1919 Stanley, Mary Isobel	1926 Baxter, James K.	

NIGERIA

1918 Aluko, Timothy	1928 Nzekwu, Onuora	1936 Uzodinma, Edmund
1920 Tutuola, Amos	1929 Munonye, John	1938 Egbuna, Obi
1921 Ekwensi, Cyprian	1930 Achebe, Chinua	1943 Omotoso, Kole
1921 Okara, Gabriel	1932 Okigbo, Christopher	n.d. Nwapa, Flora
1924 Henshaw, James	1934 Amadi, Elechi	n.d. Ulasi, Adaoro
1926 Dawes, Neville	1935 Clark, Pepper	

PAKISTAN

1910 Ali, Ahmed	1934 Mehta, Ved Parkash	1935 Ghose, Zulifikar

PANAMA

1928   Salkey, Andrew

PHILIPPINES

1920 Demetillo, Ricardo D.	1921 Angeles, Carlos	1925 Moreno, Virginia

RHODESIA

1908 Brettell, Noel (b. England)	1912 Griffiths, Reginald 1940 Montgomery, Stuart	1948 Mazani, Eric

ST. LUCIA

1930 Walcott, Derek	n.d. St. Omer, Garth

SCOTLAND

1905 Dent, Alan	1915 Smith, Sydney (b. New Zealand)	1929 Longrigg, Roger
1906 Highet, Gilbert		1931 Calder, Nigel
1907 McInnes, Helen	1915 Wreford, James	1932 Macbeth, George
1910 Cameron (*Prof.*) James	1918 Graham, W. S.	1934 Sharp, Alan
1910 MacCaig, Norman	1920 Morgan, Edwin George	1935 Sinclair, Andrew
1911 Cameron, James		1938 Hamilton, Ian
1911 McLean, Fitzroy	1922 Boyle, Andrew	1938 Jackson, Alan
1912 Home, W. D.	1922 Maclean, Alistair	1941 Black, David
1912 Jenkins, Robin	1925 Finlay, I. H.	1942 Calder, Angus
1913 Forsyth, James	1925 Fraser, George	1944 MacKay, Shena
1913 MacKinnon, Donald	1927 Laing, R. D.	n.d. †Niall, Ian
1913 Young, Douglas	1928 Smith, Iain	n.d. Spark, Muriel
1914 Maxwell, Gavin	1928 Turnbull, G. L.	

SIERRA LEONE

1924 †Nicol, Abioseh	n.d. Easmon, Raymond Sarif

SOUTH AFRICA

1903 Paton, Alan	1922 Welsh, Anne	1929 Williams, Pieter
1905 Packer, Joy	1923 Gordimer, Nadine	1931 Rive, Richard
1910 Krige, Uys	1923 La Guma, Alex	1932 Burmeister, Jon
1912 Prince, F. T.	1923 MacNab, Roy	1932 Fugard, Athol
1913 Cope, Jack	1923 Modisane, Bloke	1932 Livingstone, Douglas
1916 Delius, Anthony	1924 Brutus, Dennis	1936 Nkosi, Lewis
1918 Butler, Guy	1924 Hutchinson, Alfred	1937 Head, Bessie
1919 Abrahams, Peter	1924 Wiles, John	1939 Driver, C. J.
1919 Lessing, Doris	1926 Clouts, Sydney	n.d. Heywood, Terence
1919 Mphahlele, Ezekiel	1929 Jacobson, Dan	n.d. Jabavu, Noni

SRI LANKA (CEYLON)

1939 Wickramasinghe, N.C.

1941 Wikkramasinghe, Lakdasa

TANZANIA

1938 Ruhumbika, Gabriel

1939 Palangyo, P.K.

TRINIDAD

1911 Williams, Eric
1923 Selvon, Sam

1925 Lushington, Claude
1932 Anthony, Michael

1932 Naipaul, V.S.
1944 Hodge, Merle

UGANDA

1931 P'Bitek, Okot

1939 Lo Liyong, Taban

1939 Serumaga, Robert

WALES

1904 †Vaughn, Richard
1906 Watkins, Vernon
1913 Thomas, Gwyn
1913 Thomas, R.S.
1914 Daniel, Glyn
1915 Lewis, Alun
1915 Rhys, Keidrych
1918 Mortimer, Penelope
1919 Humphreys, Emyr

1921 Williams, Raymond
1922 Anglesey, *Marquess of* (George Paget)
1922 Jones, Mervyn
1923 Abse, Dannie
1924 Owen, Alun
1924 White, J.M.
1928 Rubens, Bernice
1929 Ferris, Paul

1931 Conran, Anthony (b. India)
1931 Thomas, Hugh
1935 Thomas, D.M.
1936 Pryce-Jones, David
1945 Evans, Paul
n.d. Guest, Harry

ZAMBIA

1928 Mulikita, F.M.

Alphabetical title–author index

A

A&B&C&: an alphabet: Lochead, Douglas

ABC of plain words: Gowers, Ernest

ABC of show business: Mankowitz, Wolf

ABCD: Slavitt, David

ABCs of space: Asimov, Isaac

ABCs of the ocean: Asimov, Isaac

AC/DC: Williams, Heathcote

A.J. Balfour; authorised biography: Young, Kenneth

A.J.A. Symons: Symons, Julian

APO-33: a metabolic regulator: Burroughs, W.S.

A for Andromeda: Hoyle, Fred

A to Z of soccer, The: Hall, Willis

A to Z of television, The: Hall, Willis

Aaron's field: Bridson, D.G.

Abaiyi and his inherited poverty: Tutuola, Amos

Abélard and Héloïse: Duncan, Ronald

Abode of love, The: Menen, Aubrey

Aborigine myths and legends: Robinson, Roland

Abortion: Robinson, J.A.T.

Abortion: an historical romance, The: Brautigan, Richard

About time: Kavanagh, Patrick

Above ground: Ludwig, Jack

Above suspicion: McInnes, Helen

Abraham's knife: Garrett, George

Absence of ruins, An: Patterson, Orlando

Absences: Tate, James

Absences of nationalism in the work of Samuel Beckett, The: Warner, Francis

Absent lover: Delderfield, R.F.

Absolute beginners: MacInnes, Colin

Absorbing fire, The: Kenyon, Frank Wilson

Absurd person singular: Ayckbourn, Alan

Abuliafia song: Meltzer, David

Abundance for what? and other essays: Riesman, David

Aby Warburg, an intellectual biography: Gombrich, E.

Academic revolution, The: Riesman, David (with C. Jencks)

Academic transformations: Riesman, David (with Verne Stadtman)

Academic values and mass education: Riesman, David

Academic year: Enright, D.J.

Accident: Janeway, Elizabeth

Accident: Pinter, Harold

Accident on route 37: Janeway, Elizabeth

Accidental man, An: Murdoch, Iris

Ace of pentacles: Wieners, John

Achievement of James Dickey: Lieberman, Laurence J.

Achievement of Randall Darrell, The: Hoffman, Frederick J.

Achievement of Robert

Lowell: a comprehensive selection of his poems, with a critical introduction by William J. Marty, The: Lowell, Robert

Achilles his armour: Green, Peter

Acre of land, An: Thomas, R.S.

Acrobat admits: Grossman, Alfred

Acrobats: Horovitz, Israel

Acrobats, The: Richler, Mordecai

Across a billion years: Silverberg, Robert

Across Lamarck Col: Snyder, Gary

Across the everglades: Schulberg, Budd

Across the sea of stars: Clarke, Arthur C.

Act and the actor: Rosenberg, Harold

Act of destruction: Hardy, R.H.

Act one: Stow, Randolph

Act; work: Raworth, Tom

Action at sea: Johnston, George

Action cookbook: Deighton, Len

Actors; an image of the new Japan, The: Porter, Hal

Actress: Mitchell, Yvonne

Adam and his works: collected stories: Goodman, Paul

Adam's woman: Baxter, John

Adaptable man, The: Frame, Janet

Adastral bodies: Boothroyd, Basil

Add a dash of pity: Ustinov, Peter

C

E

F

G

I

K

Killer, The: Wilson, Colin

Killer dies twice, The: Banks, Lynne Reid

Killer's choice: (†Ed McBain) Hunter, Evan

Killer's payoff: (†Ed McBain) Hunter, Evan

Killer's wedge: (†Ed McBain) Hunter, Evan

Killhope wheel: Silkin, Jon

Killing everybody: Harris, Mark

Killing of Francis Lake, The: Symons, Julian

Killing of sister George, The: Marcus, Frank

Killing time: Berger, Thomas

Killing-ground, The: †Trevor, Elleston

Kimballs, The: Wilson, Mitchell

Kind eagle, The: Carter, Martin

Kind of act of, The: Creeley, Robert

Kind of homecoming, A: Braithwaite, E. A.

Kind of loving, A: Barstow, Stan

Kind of loving, A (film script): Hall, Willis (with Keith Waterhouse)

Kinds of affection: Miles, Josephine

King Arthur and the knights of the round table: Fraser, Antonia

King Creole: (†Peter Grange) Nicole, Christopher

King Dido: Baron, Alexander

King Edward the Seventh: Magnus-Allcroft, Philip

King Horn: Crossley-Holland, Kevin

King Log: Hill, Geoffrey

King of a rainy country, The: Brophy, Brigid

King of Hackney Marshes and other stories, The: Glanville, Brian

King of hearts: Kerr, Jean (with Eleanor Brooke)

King of the castle, The: Trevor, Meriol

King of the mountain: Garrett, George

King who saved himself from being saved, The: Ciardi, John

King who took sunshine, The: Reeves, James

King with the golden eyes, The: Bond, Edward

Kingdom of the saints: West, Ray B., Jr.

Kingdom of the sun, The: Asimov, Isaac

Kingdom on earth: Williams, Tennessee

King-makers: Bhagat, O. P.

King's daughter: Gaskell, Jane

Kings of the dingoes: Wright, Judith

King's ransom: (†Ed McBain) Hunter, Evan

Kingsley Martin: Jones, Mervyn

Kinship: Hunter, Jim

Kinsman and foreman: Aluko, Timothy

Kipling's place in the history of ideas: Annan, Noel

Kiss kiss: Dahl, Roald

Kiss me, deadly: †Spillane, Micky

Kiss of stars, The: Waller, John

Kiss'd the girls and made them cry: Hale, John

Kitchen, The: Wesker, Arnold

Kitchener – a portrait of an imperialist: Magnus-Allcroft, Philip

Kite, The: Mitchell, W. O.

Kite that won the revolution, The: Asimov, Isaac

Klee Wyck: Carr, Emily

Klondike fever: Berton, Pierre

Knack, The: Jellicoe, Ann

Knack, The (film script): Wood, Charles

Knight sinister: (†Simon Rattray; †Adam Hall) †Trevor, Elleston

Knightly quest; a novella and four short stories, The: Williams, Tennessee

Knights and dragons: Spencer, Elizabeth

Knight's fee: Sutcliff, Rosemary

Knock upon silence: Kizer, Carolyn

Knots: Laing, R. D.

Knots: Meltzer, David

Know about football: Glanville, Brian

Knowing and being: Polanyi, Michael

Ko, or A season on earth: Koch, Kenneth

Kon in the springtime: Connor, Tony

Konek landing: Figes, Eva

Konfessions of an Elizabethan fan dancer: Nichol, B. P.

Kontakion for you departed: Paton, Alan

Kraj Majales: Ginsberg, Allen

Kraken wakes, The: †Wyndham, John

Krumnagel: Ustinov, Peter

Kublai Khan: (†Walker Chapman) Silverberg, Robert

Kumaon Himalaya, The: Randhawa, M. S.

Kundu: West, Morris

Kurrirrurriri: Cobbing, Bob

Kuruntokai: Ramanujan, A. K.

Kynd Kittock's land: Smith, Sydney

L

Laboratory, The: Campton, David

Labour and the arts II; or, what is to be done?: Wesker, Arnold

Labour case, The: Jenkins, Roy

Labourers in the vineyard: Thiele, Colin

Lytton Strachey; the unknown years: Holroyd, Michael

Lytton Strachey; the years of achievement: Holroyd, Michael

M

Mac: Pinter, Harold

MacArthur controversy and American foreign policy, The: Rovere, Richard (with Arthur M. Schlesinger, Jr.)

Macbeth did it: Patrick, John

Machineries of joy, The: Bradbury, Ray

Mackenzie's grave: Chadwick, Owen

Mackerel plaza, The: De Vries, Peter

Mackintosh man, The (*film*) *see under* Bagley, Desmond

Macmillan; a study in ambiguity: Sampson, Anthony

MacRune's Guevara: Spurling, John

Maculan's daughter: Gainham, Sarah

Mad dog blues and other plays: Shepard, Sam

Mad Jack's gnomes and Visitors to Shakespeare: Macbeth, George

Mad Macmullochs, The: Mittelholzer, Edgar

Madam, will you talk?: Stewart, Mary

Madame Letizia: Stirling, Monica

Madame Sousatzka: Rubens, Bernice

Madame Tussaud: Cottrell, Leonard

Made to measure: Delderfield, R.F.

Madheart: Jones, Leroi

Madness is the second stroke: Nandy, Pritish

Madrigal: Gardner, John

Madrigals: Warner, Francis

Maedun the voyager: Reeves, James

Magellanic clouds, The: Wakoski, Diane

Maggie Cassidy: Kerouac, Jack

Maggie—now: Smith, Betty

Magic barrel, The: Malamud, Bernard

Magic bed-knob, The: Norton, Mary

Magic finger, The: Dahl, Roald

Magic Flute, The: Crozier, Eric

Magic in the blood: Henshaw, James

Magic lantern of Marcel Proust, The: Moss, Howard

Magic of Shirley Jackson, The: Jackson, Shirley (ed. Stanley Edgar Hyman)

Magic papers and other poems: Feldman, Irving

Magic perambulator, The: Brooks, Jeremy

Magic toyshop, The: Carter, Angela

Magic will; stories and essays of a decade, The: Gold, Herbert

Magician, The: Massingham, Harold

Magnificent century, The: Costain, T.B.

Magnificent defeat, The: Buechner, Frederick

Magnificent shysters, The: Rovere, Richard

Magog: Sinclair, Andrew

Magus, The: Fowles, John

Mahler: Williams, Jonathan

Maiden's trip: Smith, Emma

Maidstone: Mailer, Norman

Main experiment, The: Hodder-Williams, Christopher

Majollika and company: Mankowitz, Wolf

Major adjectives in English poetry: from Wyatt to Auden: Miles, Josephine

Make me a murderer: Butler, Gwendoline

Make me an offer: Mankowitz, Wolf

Make this your Canada; a review of C.C.F. history and policy: Scott, F.R. (with D. Lewis)

Makers of the ark, The: Rowbotham, David

Makeshift rocket, The: †Anderson, Poul

Making do: Goodman, Paul

Making good: Seraillier, Ian

Making good again: Dathorne, Ronald

Making it: Podheretz, Norman

Making moral decisions: MacKinnon, Donald (with others)

Making of a moon, The: Clarke, Arthur C.

Making of a quagmire, The: Halberstam, David

Making of Moo, The: Dennis, Nigel

Making of the nation, The: Berton, Pierre

Making of the president—1960, The: White, Theodore H.

Making of the president—1964, The: White, Theodore H.

Malayan trilogy: Burgess, Anthony

Malaysia in focus: McKie, Ronald

Malcochon: Walcott, Derek

Malcolm: Albee, Edward

Malcolm: Nkosi, Lewis

Malcolm's mooney land: Graham, W.S.

Male child, A: Scott, Paul

Male response, The: Aldiss, Brian

Mallabec: Walker, David

Malleson at Melbourne: (†William Godfrey) †Christopher, John

Mamelukes, The: Stewart,

N

O

P

Q

S

T

U

V

W

515

X

Y

Carlos

Year from Monday: new lectures and writings, A: Cage, John

Year in San Fernando, The: Ansen, Alan

Year in time, A: Mitchell, Yvonne

Year of battle, A: Moorhead, Alan

Year of Salamis, 480–479 B.C., The: Green, Peter

Year of the angry rabbit, The: Braddon, Russell

Year of the comet, The: †Christopher, John

Year of the currawong, The: Spence, Eleanor

Year of the fog, The: Nichol, B.P.

Year of the lion, The: Hanley, Gerald

Year one, The: Raine, Kathleen

Year round, The: Clark, Leonard

Years, The: Souster, Raymond

Years as catches, first poems 1939–46, The: Duncan, Robert

Yeats: Bloom, Harold

Yeats: the man and the masks: Ellmann, Richard

Yeats the playwright: Ure, Peter

Yellow aeroplane, The: Mayne, William

Yellow back radio broke-down: Reed, Ishmael

Yellow drum (*musical*): Elmslie, Kenward

Yellow flowers in the antipodean room: Frame, Janet

Yellow room: love poems: Hall, Donald

Yellow sweater and other stories, The: Garner, Hugh

Yellow-jacket Jock: Thiele, Colin

Yes from No-man's-land: Kops, Bernard

Yes, m'Lord: Home, W.D.

Yesod: Meltzer, David

Yesterday's folly: Black, Hermina

Yo Banfa: Alley, Rewi

You and your wife: †Cannan, Denis

You can't be serious: Boothroyd, Basil

You can't come back: Beaver, Bruce

You can't get there from here: Hood, Hugh

You can't see round corners: Cleary, Jon

You did it, you feel sorry: Canaway, W.H.

You know I can't hear you when the water's running: Anderson, R.W.

You know who: Ciardi, John

You only live twice (*film script*): Dahl, Roald

You only live twice: Fleming, Ian

You read to me, I'll read to you: Ciardi, John

You touched me!: Williams, Tennessee (with Donald Windham)

You want the right frame of reference: †Cooper, William

You'll never guess: Jellicoe, Ann

Young and old: Thomas, R.S.

Young doctors, The (*film*) *see under* Hailey, Arthur

Young Egypt: Stewart, Desmond

Young lovers, The (*film script*): Garrett, George

Young lovers: Target, G.W.

Young man Luther: a study in psychoanalysis and history: Erikson, Erik

Young man of talent: Turner, George

Young May moon, The: Newby, P.H.

Young people: †Cooper, William

Young traveller in South Africa: Delius, Anthony

Young traveller in space, The: Clarke, Arthur C.

Young visitors, The: Wain, John

Young warriors, The: Reid, V.S.

Youngblood Hawke: Wouk, Herman

Your guide map to North West Scotland: Lyall, Gavin

Your hand in mine: Cornish, Samuel

Your Sunday paper: Hoggart, Richard

Your turn to curtsy, my turn to bow: Goldman, William

Your wedding guide: Bingham, Madeleine

You're a big boy now: Benedictus, David

Yours: Callow, Philip

Youth: change and challenge: Erikson, Erik

Yucatan adventure: Clark, Leonard

Yukon and northwest territories, The: McCourt, Edward

Z

ZBC of Ezra Pound, A: Brooke-Rose, Christine

Zebra-striped hearse, The: Millar, Kenneth

Zee & Co.: O'Brien, Edna

Zen there was murder: Keating, H.R.F.

Zero hour: Millar, Ronald

Zhorani: (†Karl Maras) Bulmer, Kenneth

Zigger Zagger: †Terson, Peter

Zinzin road, The: Knebel, Fletcher

Zionist idea: Heller, Joseph

Zohana: Drayton, Geoffrey